A Complex Culture of the British Columbia Plateau

This volume provides a detailed examination of traditional resource exploitation in two British Columbia native communities located near Lillooet to explain how and why complex hunter/gatherer societies develop. The authors explore the relation between resource characteristics and hunter/gatherer adaptations and examine the use of fish, animal, and plant species, documenting their availability and the techniques used in their gathering, processing, and storing. The book also shows how critical practices, such as raiding, potlatching, and stewardship of resources, can be explained from a cultural ecological point of view.

An important contribution to the study of hunting and gathering cultures in the Northwest, this book is the most detailed examination of the subsistence base of a particular hunting and gathering group to date. Its exploration of the reasons why complex hunting and gathering societies emerge, as well as the ecological relationships between cultures and resources, will make an important contribution to the study of cultural ecology and contemporary archaeology.

BRIAN HAYDEN is a professor in the Department of Archaeology at Simon Fraser University.

EDITED BY
BRIAN HAYDEN

A Complex Culture of the British Columbia Plateau

Traditional *Stl'átl'imx* Resource Use

UBC Press / Vancouver

ISBN 0-7748-0405-X

Canadian Cataloguing in Publication Data

Main entry under title:

A Complex culture of the British Columbia plateau

Includes bibliographical references and index.
ISBN 0-7748-0405-X

1. Lillooet Indians. 2. Shuswap Indians.
3. Indians of North America – British Columbia –
Fountain. 4. Indians of North America – British
Columbia – Pavilion. I. Hayden, Brian, 1946-

E99.L4C65 1992   971.1'3100497'9   C92-091233-8

This book has been published with the help of a grant
from the Social Science Federation of Canada, using
funds provided by the Social Sciences and Humanities
Research Council of Canada.

This book has been financially assisted by
the Province of British Columbia through
the British Columbia Heritage Trust and
BC Lottery Fund.

Publication of this book was also made possible
by ongoing support from The Canada Council,
the Province of British Columbia Cultural
Services Branch, and the Department of
Communications of the Government of Canada.

UBC Press
University of British Columbia
6344 Memorial Rd
Vancouver, BC V6T 1Z2
(604) 822-3259
Fax: (604) 822-6083

Contents

Figures, Plates, and Tables

FIGURES

Chapter 1

Chapter 2

Chapter 3

Chapter 4

Chapter 6

PLATES

TABLES

Preface and Acknowledgments

The present volume on the traditional resources of the Lillooet and Shuswap native communities of Fountain and Pavilion draws on many sources of research. Basic data collection for some of this research began decades before this book was conceived. However, it was the archaeological work at Keatley Creek, situated between the modern communities of Fountain and Pavilion, which provided the impetus for the collaboration between researchers resulting in the present work. In carrying out excavations at Keatley Creek, it became evident that in order to understand the full nature of the prehistoric society and how it was structured, it was necessary to understand what the resource base of the prehistoric inhabitants of Keatley Creek was and how this resource base affected important aspects of the inhabitants' lives. I was aware that considerable background work had already been undertaken in the area by researchers such as Nancy Turner (botany), Randy Bouchard and Dorothy Kennedy (fishing and hunting), and Steve Romanoff (fishing and hunting), yet much of their work was unpublished and not strictly oriented to obtaining a complete perspective on the full resource base. In order to fill in critical information pertaining to these resources, I initiated an ethnoarchaeological program of research on resource use and procurement in the Keatley Creek area. This project was clearly related to, but separate from, the excavation program at Keatley Creek. In 1986 and 1987, the ethnoarchaeological program was undertaken in collaboration with Diana Alexander, Aubrey Cannon, Nancy Turner, and Rob Tyhurst. Funding for this research was generously provided by the federal Multiculturalism Directorate and by the BC Heritage Trust, with the Fountain Band providing funds for conducting data gathering in localities of specific interest to it.

In carrying out this research, it became apparent that previously completed but unpublished work on the fishing locations of the Fountain Band was very similar in orientation to the goals of the ethnoarchaeological project that we were undertaking. This research had been written up by Randy Bouchard and Dorothy Kennedy specifically for the Fountain Band in 1986. For the purposes of modelling pre-contact subsistence, I engaged Bouchard and Kennedy to supplement their original study with additional data and interviews. The result is their chapter on fishing.

Similarly, Michael Kew had carried out considerable research on salmon abundance and fishing along the Fraser River. This research addressed a very different aspect of fish resources than did the other authors and provided a very important perspective. Because his research was still unpublished and fit in so well with the overall goals of the project, I decided to approach Kew to determine if he would collaborate with the other authors in producing a comprehensive volume on resource use. Finally, because this volume, in essence, constituted a definitive compilation of what was known of traditional resources in the Lillooet area, it would have been a serious omission not to include Steven Romanoff's work. Romanoff's work on fishing and hunting was completed in the 1960s and had already been published in the regional journal, *Northwest Anthropological Research Notes*. These articles are so important to the full understanding of Lillooet resources and society that reprinting them in this volume for a wider audience seemed essential. Rick Sprague, the editor of *NARN*, graciously assented to the reprinting of these articles.

The serendipitous conjunction of all of the above research endeavours has led to the present volume, which the collaborators have taken great satisfaction in producing. On behalf of them all I would like to express extreme gratitude to the members of both band communities who have shared their knowledge and understanding with us and who have helped create this record of their past and present lives. I am also extremely grateful to the chiefs and councillors for their support, and to the other funding agencies which have supported our endeavours. I am particularly grateful to Desmond Peters, Sr., who shared so generously his knowledge of traditional ways, and Roger Adolph, who has had the foresight to sponsor and support research on traditional resource use. The late Sam Mitchell was also a major figure in much of the work represented in this volume. Many many others have also shared their knowledge for the benefit of their own communities as well as for the understanding of traditional ways by non-Indians. Over the many decades during which the research in this book was undertaken, these people have included Lawrence and Maggie Adolph, the late William Adolph, Trevor Chandler, Bill

Edwards, the late Paul Hickson, the late Slim Jackson, the late Charlie Mack of Mount Currie, the late Susan Mitchell, Edith O'Donaghey, Louie Phillips of Lytton, the late Madeline Sampson, Mrs. A. Zabatel, Tommy Napoleon, Jim Nason, Wilfred Ned, Bucky Ned, Charlie Billy, Chris Bob, Doris and Emily Lulua (from the Chilcotin), and Annie York of Spuzzum. Dr. J. Powell of the University of British Columbia kindly permitted contributors to use some of the information he obtained from the late Solomon Peters of Shalalth. I would like to thank all of these people; without their help, and the help of many others acknowledged in the individual articles, this project would not have been possible and much knowledge would have been lost forever.

Numerous other experts who study fish and wildlife in British Columbia have also assisted our endeavours by generously providing information, opinions, and discussions on topics of great interest for this study. William Ricker (formerly with the Department of Fisheries and Oceans), Jim Woody (Pacific Salmon Commission), Neil Shubert, Sandy Argue, Robin Harrison, Al MacDonald, Kaarina McGivney (all of the Department of Fisheries and Oceans), Duncan Stacey (a fisheries consultant), Dave Low (Senior Wildlife Biologist for the BC Ministry of the Environment, Kamloops), Randall Peterman (Simon Fraser University), Carl Walters (University of British Columbia), and Grant Keddie (Royal BC Museum) have all contributed invaluable information to this project. I would also like to thank Bruce Winterhalder for his comments and suggestions on an early draft, Chris Hildred (Simon Fraser University) for photographic and helicopter support, Jaclynne Campbell (Simon Fraser University) for illustrations, and Anita Mahoney (Simon Fraser University) for processing much of this manuscript.

Similarly, without the help of various funding agencies, this work would not have been possible. On behalf of the collaborators involved in this research, I would like to thank the Federal Multiculturalism Directorate, the Canada Council, the Social Sciences and Humanities Research Council of Canada, the Canadian Ethnology Service of the National Museum of Man, the British Columbia Heritage Trust, the BC Provincial Secretary Ministry, the BC Education Ministry, the Fountain Band, and the Simon Fraser University Special Research Project Fund for their generous financial support for original research. The Social Sciences Federation of Canada and the Simon Fraser University Publications Committee provided welcome financial support for publication.

BRIAN HAYDEN

A Complex Culture of the British Columbia Plateau

CHAPTER ONE

Introduction: Ecology and Culture
Brian Hayden

The Middle Fraser Canyon of British Columbia is a fascinating place for the study of cultural ecology. It is a rich place to compare ideas about culture. It is a captivating place to work.

From a scientific perspective, the Middle Fraser Canyon has several advantages. The arid and mountainous environment provides relatively few resources in abundance compared to areas such as the Coast. The subsistence economy is simple, with few staples; these include salmon, trout, deer, saskatoon berries, choke cherries, spring beauty corms, and lily bulbs. It is, therefore, comparatively easy to describe the most important subsistence resources and to create uncomplicated models for their exploitation and cultural-ecological relationships.

The Middle Fraser Canyon also has the advantage of having sharply demarcated environmental zones with clear boundaries. Grasslands stop abruptly at the edge of river terraces, and montane forests begin on mountain slopes just as abruptly; at higher elevations, alpine meadows begin where the treeline stops. These sharply demarcated zones, too, make it relatively easy to define, describe, and model subsistence-related behaviour. Given this situation and a minimal amount of environmental change over the last 4,500 years, together with the continuity of culture that characterizes the area, it is possible to assume some constancy in the nature of the resource base during late prehistoric occupations and to archaeologically test some of the ethnographically derived models of culture and environment.

This area also has the advantage of having been written about by good, late nineteenth-century ethnographers, such as James Teit and George Dawson, who recorded important aspects of traditional indigenous cultures. They documented an unusually complex culture for hunter/gatherers in which private ownership of key resources, wealth, hereditary élites, intense trading, slavery, polygyny, seasonal sedentism, and high population densities occurred. The Middle Fraser region was spared severe Euro-Canadian impacts until 1858, and, thus, these early ethnographies hold the prospect of providing valuable data on relatively unaffected traditional cultures. More recently, archaeological investigations and the detailed ethnographic studies presented in this volume have supplied a wealth of information on aboriginal cultures of the area that are difficult to rival. By combining the early and the more recent data, it is possible to create reliable descriptions of the subsistence ecology and compare this information to models of cultural adaptations. The area is also ideally suited for archaeological investigations, with clearly identifiable villages, structures, and living floors together with well preserved faunal and botanical remains.

Finally, the Middle Fraser Canyon is of interest to ethnologists and archaeologists because there exist contrasting models of the fundamental nature of Plateau culture, entailing contrasting expectations. On the one hand, as Cannon notes in Chapter 10, Ray (1939), Lane (1953), Jorgensen (1980), and others view Plateau cultures as essentially egalitarian and peaceful, with elements of social inequality, potlatching, and warfare being late introductions from coastal societies. On the other hand, Cannon (Chapter 10), Pokotylo et al. (1987), Chance and Chance (1982:428), Shiner (1961:164), Cressman (1960:37) and others assume that the Plateau was neither homogeneous nor uniformly egalitarian in the past, but that at least some centres were characterized by pronounced socioeconomic stratification and warfare. The Middle Fraser Canyon around Lillooet is a focus of these contentious claims. The entire subject of the nature and conditions associated with early forms of socioeconomic inequality is itself of considerable theoretical interest to a broad spectrum of anthropologists and archaeologists. The specific factors related to the emergence of inequality are topics of ongoing research in many parts of the world. With all the advantages of the Middle Fraser Canyon study area, we can at least hope that a better understanding of the nature and origins of socioeconomic inequality might emerge from a detailed investigation of culture and ecology in this region.

In order to be able to address these issues, as well as to provide data for examining other relationships between culture and ecology, what is required above all is a detailed description of the important aspects of resource use by traditional cultures in the region. Good ethnographic descriptions of the nature of these traditional communities are also required. The principal aim of this volume is, therefore, to provide the requisite detailed descriptions of traditional resource use and cultural behavior needed for addressing broader questions of culture-ecology relationships.

In order to help situate the importance of these observations in theoretical contexts, Romanoff (Chapter 9), Cannon (Chapter 10), and myself (Chapter 11), use the observations presented in this volume to examine a number of important cultural ecological issues, notably, competitive feasting systems, warfare, slavery, and the emergence of socioeconomic inequality.

PERTINENT CULTURAL ECOLOGICAL ISSUES

What are the most important areas in which a strong relationship between ecology and culture might be suspected for hunter/gatherers? There are many. Certainly, population density and demography, degrees of mobility (Shott 1986; Parry and Kelly 1987; Johnson 1987), residential versus logistical mobility (Binford 1980; Chatters 1987), foraging versus collecting strategies (ibid.), patterns of dispersal and aggregation (Lee and Devore 1968), task group sizes (Freeman 1968), adherence or deviation from cost-benefit priorization of resource use (Winterhalder and Smith 1981), critical dietary concerns (lipids, minerals, vitamins – Speth and Spielmann 1983; Reidhead 1979), and reasons for abandoning settlements are all important topics that most researchers, given specific technological constraints, have concluded are heavily influenced by ecological factors. With adequate observations on the ecology and technology of groups in our study area, detailed and rewarding analyses could be carried out on all of these topics.

However, for the purposes of the present volume, the question of relationships between social organization and ecological factors possesses more exciting theoretical potential. This topic is broader and less well investigated (or at least there is less consensus) than those already mentioned. Because of the underdeveloped state of inquiry into some aspects of ecological effects on social organization, a good deal of the following discussion will be programmatic or exploratory as opposed to definitive. Nevertheless, as Chapters 9 and 10 (by Romanoff and Cannon, respectively) illustrate, there are clearly opportunities for generating and testing important insights in this domain, notably concerning resource ownership, hunting specialization, warfare, and slavery.

The social topics that I specifically would like to deal with in this and in the concluding chapter are closely interrelated. These include: (1) the ecological conditions conducive to the development of ownership of both resources and valued personal property (I use the term 'ownership' loosely as a convenient way to refer to any restriction of access to an item or resource within a community); (2) the ecological (including economic) conditions under which socioeconomic inequality emerges and is maintained; and (3) the ecological conditions favouring the development of residentially based corporate groups.

My previous research on these questions has involved both some cross-cultural comparative studies and detailed documentation and analysis of a specific area: the Middle Fraser Canyon around Lillooet. This volume presents the basic ecological documentation for the investigation. At this point in the investigation of the three social-ecological topics, it is possible to identify many pertinent questions, concepts, and observations needed to evaluate models of social-ecological relationships; it is possible to formulate provisional models; it is possible to identify some probable relationships; and it is even possible to state some relatively certain conclusions. Establishing the basic background considerations and relevant variables is the goal of this chapter. These concepts should serve to highlight the importance of various types of observations in the chapters that follow.

I will also provide a general description of the study area and its history of research in this chapter. In the concluding chapter, I will show how many of the observations of preceding chapters can be integrated into a model of social-ecological relationships for the study area, especially when broader patterns from prehistory and other cultures are taken into account. Definitive conclusions for all aspects of the three basic questions outlined above may not be attainable at this point, but we will at least have advanced understanding of the problems significantly and placed the inquiry on the firm footing required to make further progress.

THE ECOLOGICAL APPROACH

From the outset, it should be recognized that culture encompasses very different kinds of phenomena, which are expressed in different ways and with different kinds of consequences. For instance, culture includes economic and subsistence behaviour with tangible consequences for individual well-being; culture includes social relationships on many levels, ranging from casual acquaintances to work environments to kinship and marriage; culture includes psychological activities such as the creation of idealized models and justifications for one's behaviour or thoughts; culture includes symbolic communication and stored information; culture includes emotional expressions involving the self and others; and culture includes mental illnesses, aspects of the subconscious, delusions, preconceptions, and fringe belief systems.

With this vast panoply of interrelated behaviour and thought, what aspects are to be considered central to understanding change in culture? To a great extent, the answer depends on how culture is defined and what is viewed as the most important aspect of culture by the researcher. Social and cognitive archaeologists often stress the centrality of values, rules, and language (Hodder 1985). They therefore place these variables in primary positions, or at least at levels of importance equal to economic and subsistence variables. Within the culture-as-cognition framework, selection mechanisms that create ordered changes and the details concerning how these selection mechanisms operate are often poorly dealt with. Some cognitive and post-processual studies have emphasized the role of the decisionmaking individual in cultural change. This accounts well for the creation of variability but does not aid in understanding how or why directional changes, such as increasing specialization or inequality, come about.

Ecological and mainstream archaeological perspectives tend to share important assumptions that differentiate them from social and cognitive approaches to cultural change. Ecology and archaeology both deal primarily with the results of actual behaviour rather than with rules, values, or emic models of how the world does or should work. Most ecologists view behaviour as the most important aspect of any organism. Behaviour determines whether an individual lives or dies, succeeds or fails, reproduces or dead-ends. Specific behaviours can be justified on many ideological grounds using wide varieties of belief systems; one does not have to be Semitic to abstain from pork, or Buddhist to be vegetarian, or Puritan or capitalist to engage in commerce. What is important for the ecological study of culture is that no matter what the values or justification, behaviour leading to such phenomena as socioeconomic inequality or private ownership is manifested. Similarly, archaeology deals primarily with the results of behaviour not with how individuals emically may have justified such behaviour. Both archaeology and ecology tend to deal with a simplified version of culture in which the most time and energy consuming activities, together with some more episodic behaviors that affect survival (e.g., warfare), are accorded the greatest importance.

Both mainstream archaeology and ecology view broad changes in survival-related behaviour over time as the most interesting explanatory problems, although they also deal with other types of problems. Wherever cultural behaviour is related to survival and constrained by time and energy, ecological assumptions seem like useful starting points for understanding that behaviour (Smith 1979; Winterhalder 1980, 1986). From the archaeological and ecological viewpoint, many social anthropologists might be criticized for becoming so engrossed in the details of the colourful fabric of culture that they fail to perceive the fundamental dynamics or structure of culture; they concentrate on pointillist dots of colour rather than on the images; they see the trees but not the forest.

In addition, ecology employs an explicit selection mechanism capable of structuring and constraining behaviour: natural selection. Not only has the importance of this mechanism been demonstrated in the natural sciences, but it can also be applied to cultural behaviour, although not necessarily in the sociobiological or evolutionary ecological sense. Simply put, natural selection in biology is a means for eliminating or maintaining new genetic variations under specified environmental conditions. Either the genetic variation works in a given environment or it does not. If it does not work it is eliminated. Both genes and learned culture are basically ways of coding information, although one is biologically based and the other is culturally based and more flexible. In terms of *learned* behaviour, new cultural variations are constantly being generated, just as new genetic variations are constantly being generated. As with biological natural selection, what determines whether new learned behavioural variations remain part of a culture is whether they work or do not work under given conditions. If they do not work they are eliminated. This can be viewed as a type of culturally based natural selection but should not be confused with biologically based natural selection.

One other principle needs to be added to understand the ecological perspective. Some behaviour, such as which hand one uses to hold a fork or specific leisure activities, may not entail significant consequences that affect most individuals' success or well-being. These behaviours are not as affected by natural selection because they involve relatively minor amounts of time and energy or are not appreciably different in effect from alternate behaviours. Because these behaviours are less responsive to natural selection (although they may be selected for or against over the long term), they can be expected to emerge and disappear in relatively non-directional or random fashion, characteristically lasting only for brief periods.

The *behaviours most subject to the effects of natural selection should thus be those that involve significant time and energy as well as behaviours that are critical for survival.* Moreover, as long as environment and technology do not change, these behaviours can be expected to persist over long periods of time or to exhibit directional changes in concert with changes in key environmental or resource variables. From these considerations, it is possible to conclude that cultural behaviours (1) involving significant time and energy (or which are critical for survival) and (2) that persist over long periods of time or demonstrate strong directional changes should be the most amenable to explanation using ecological models. This does not automatically exclude other, less important, types of behaviour from being explained through the use of the ecological paradigm, but it provides a promising starting point for examining culture-ecology relationships.

Using these criteria, the social aspects of central concern in the present chapter (access to resources, socioeconomic inequality, investment in large communal structures, warfare) should be among the most explainable cultural behaviours from the perspective of ecological models. From a comparative as well as a case-study viewpoint, behaviour in all of these domains exhibits considerable persistence or directional change in concert with changes in technology and resource characteristics. I have previously charted some of these relationships (Hayden 1981) for generalized and complex hunter/gatherers – terms that will be defined shortly.

To summarize some of the more germane diachronic conclusions concerning resources and culture from prehistoric research, it can be stated with relative confidence that for almost 2,000,000 years, until the late Upper Paleolithic, population levels of hunter/gatherers were very low. From this it can be inferred that the resources available, given the technology of the time, were quite limited. Mobility seems to have been relatively high and of the residential type. There is no evidence for storage (Soffer 1989), and this implies that little or no seasonal food surpluses were generated. Valued personal items are either totally absent or, toward the end of this initial period, quite rare. This indicates either that individual ownership of items was not recognized, or that status display (and, by extension, significant inequality) did not exist, or both. Nor is there evidence for the construction of large communal residential structures requiring major investments of labour. This implies that there were no strongly bonded residential corporate groups as defined by Hayden and Cannon (1982).

This pattern characterizes the Lower, Middle, and early Upper Paleolithic throughout several major glacial and interglacial periods. Significant changes begin to occur in both the technology and the nature of the societies in select areas only during the late Upper Paleolithic. These changes become even more pronounced in optimally situated areas in the Old World Mesolithic and New World Archaic. In these cases, there are substantial increases in population density, which must be predicated on an increased and more stable extraction of resources. Given prior climatic changes without such increases in population density, it would seem that changes in technology rather than climate were largely responsible for increased resource extraction. Important technological changes certainly did occur at these times and involved improved procurement, processing, and extractive abilities. Technological improvements may have also involved the development of sophisticated storage technologies.

In terms of procurement and processing, the Late Upper Paleolithic and Mesolithic/Archaic witness the first systematic use of fish and the development of fishing technology, the first use of grinding stones to process seeds, the first mortars and pestles, the first use of boiling (revealed by fire-cracked rock), the first use of the bow and arrow, the first firing of landscapes to enhance food productivity, and the possible first use of complex basketry, snares and traps, transport aids (sleds and canoes), and dogs. Faunal remains display a considerable increase in dietary variety during this period, adding further to the resources available. As Soffer (1989) has demonstrated, storage pits also first occur at this time. Storage technology is not simply dependant upon the ability to dig a pit, but it is also dependant on proper preparation of foods for storage, including the ability to dry them and keep them away from animals. Successful long-term storage in bulk requires considerable experience and expenditure of effort. Meat or large fish in particular require fine filleting, the construction of shelters for drying and smoking, and additional protection of the material to be stored. None of these features can be said to be apparent in the archaeological record to any significant degree prior to about 25,000-15,000 years ago.

From the viewpoint of non-ecological paradigms, these changes would not necessarily be very noteworthy. One might expect increases in population densities to occur as a result of technological improvements but little else. Yet in other subsystems of culture, dramatic changes sometimes occurred as well. In select resource areas with very high resource extraction potentials, the new procurement and storage technology became associated with the first semi-sedentary settlements, with the first evidence of socioeconomic inequalities (as revealed by differential grave goods as well as the proliferation of status display items), with the first cemeteries (argued by some to indicate the presence of corporate groups – Chapman 1981; Pardoe 1988) as well as with the first megaliths (Scarre 1984:329), with the first large communal structures, some of which required considerable labour inputs and have even been termed monumental (Klima 1962; Gladkih et al. 1984), and with the first evidence for owned resources (storage) and owned personal valuables. Given the long preceding period, wherein none of these features occurred, the changes are nothing less than remarkable. These kinds of procurement, storage, and social features also characterize the communities in the present case study.

What is important at this point is the very strong general patterning that emerges where there are low resource levels and no indication of hierarchical social features versus the periods of much higher resources (and populations) associated with prestige display items, socioeconomic inequality, ownership, and the first indications of corporate groups. I will refer to the first type of communities, without complex social features or technology, as 'generalized hunter/gatherers' and the second, more socially complex communities, as 'complex hunter/gatherers.'

Thus, there is considerable support from prehistory for the expectations derived from ecological principles that the major social phenomena that I will focus on are, in fact, strongly related to some aspect of resources and technology. They persist over long periods of time and exhibit directional change in concert with technological and resource changes. Precisely which ecological resource factors play critical roles is not entirely clear at this point, but several factors will be evaluated in the conclusions. The next question is to determine whether the synchronic ethnographic data also support a general relationship between resources and social complexity.

Without entering into an exhaustive analysis of ethnographic groups, an unusually high correspondence can be detected between areas of low resource density and generalized hunter/gatherers on the one hand and areas of very abundant resources and complex hunter/gatherers on the other hand. Certainly, at the extremes, the examples are precisely what are expected. In desert areas of Australia, South Africa, and North America, hunter/gatherers, such as the Aranda, Western Desert groups, Bushman, Hadza, and Shoshoni, display the same typical generalized hunter/gatherer characteristics as those inferred for the early prehistoric period mentioned above. Hunter/gatherers living in resource poor Arctic and Subarctic environments also exhibit the same characteristics.

In contrast, virtually all the examples of complex hunter/gatherers come from extremely rich and productive resource areas. These include the Northwest Coast Indians, some Northwest Plateau communities, the Point Barrow whaling and storage-based communities (Sheehan 1985), the Calusa of Florida (Widmer 1988), the Ainu, and perhaps to a more limited extent the groups in southeast Australia that dug canals for eel harvesting (Lourandos 1980; Williams 1987). Thus, the ethnographic data also appear to conform to the basic expectations of a strong relationship between resources and the basic social characteristics of concern.

In addition to supporting the notion that we are at least pursuing a potentially useful, and perhaps fundamental, avenue of inquiry,

ethnological studies provide the additional advantage of being able
to specify in clear terms the nature of social-ecological relationships.
Research among hunter/gatherers over the last score years has greatly
advanced understanding of this relationship and provides some of
the more important principles that will be used subsequently for
examining the Mid Fraser study area. Unfortunately, almost all detailed
research has been carried out with generalized hunter/gatherers such
as the !Kung. The present study should help to extend the substan-
tive and theoretical results of the work on generalized hunter/gatherers
to complex hunter/gatherers.

GENERALIZED HUNTER/GATHERERS

The following summary is based on the research of Strehlow (1965),
Lee (1972a,b), Harris (1971), Ford (1972, 1977), Yengoyan (1976), Cashdan
(1980), Bettinger (1980), Gould (1982), Hennigh (1983), Kaplan et al.
(1984), Kaplan and Hill (1985a,b), Smith (1981), Minc (1986), Winterhalder (1986), Wiessner (1977, 1981), Silberbauer (1981:178-9), as well
as some of my own work. Resource characteristics of *complex* hunter/
gatherers are dealt with in Chapter 11.

The resource characteristics that appear to typify *generalized*
hunter/gatherers throughout the world as well as throughout prehistory are the limited abundance of extractable resources, the substantial and often unpredictable fluctuations in resource levels, and the
vulnerability to overexploitation of at least some critical resources. The
low population densities that characterize these groups (generally
0.001-0.1 people per square kilometre – Bettinger 1980:192) are important indicators of the at least periodically limited nature of the resources
on which these groups depend.

There are four important consequences for the present study of
these resource conditions. Sharing, alliances, and fluid group membership with high mobility all become very adaptive, if not essential,
for survival because of the limited, fluctuating, and vulnerable nature
of generalized hunter/gatherer resources. On the other hand, economically based competition is destructive of resources and should be
proscribed as a behaviour.

Sharing

Because extractable resources are limited and to some degree unpredictable in location or capture success, the chances of any one given
individual or family consistently procuring enough food on a daily
or even weekly basis are fairly low. Even the best hunters often return

without meat. In fact, success rates of bow and arrow hunting for individual Hadza hunters indicate that only about one in ten hunts result in the attainment of meat. Plant foods are more reliable, but even nuts, berries, and fruits are notoriously variable, which is certainly the case around Lillooet. Some patches would fail to produce in certain years, and trips to these patches may yield few results for a day's work. In short, on a daily and even longer basis, the risk of hunger is something that must be reckoned with among generalized hunter/gatherers.

They appear to deal with these situations by pooling both risks and gains. This means sharing almost all food that is brought back to camp with whomever wants or needs a share. Generalized reciprocity prevails. In essence, this behaviour constitutes a type of hunting and gathering insurance system. For it to work, sharing becomes socially obligatory, and no personal ownership of resources is tolerated (Winterhalder 1986; Hayden 1981). Obligatory sharing is often also extended to personal effects.

Mobility

One other consequence of the limited levels of extractable resources is that it is necessary to travel considerable distances in foraging and hunting. The group must relocate periodically to assure that foragers who leave and return to camp by day will encounter undepleted ranges. Under these conditions, the smallest groups are the most economical (Lee 1972a,b). However, in order to ensure a constant and reliable flow of food, it is necessary to have other families with which to share. As a result, generalized hunter/gatherer communities typically contain five to ten active hunters or about twenty-five to fifty people in all.

Alliances

Besides the short-term fluctuations in food gathering success, there are also much less frequent, but much more severe and longlasting, downturns in resource availability. In fact, resources can be predicted to fail almost completely one or more times in the lifetime of most individuals. Under these conditions, the within-group sharing ethic that keeps a community alive in most circumstances no longer is of great use. Faced with continued prolonged failure, there are only two options: to move to an area not as severely affected or to die. In order to move to other areas occupied by bands in less dire straits, it would be necessary to either drive those bands out forcibly or to be on very good terms with them. The use of force on the part of a half-starved population would be extremely risky but might be a last resort. It appears that most generalized hunter/gatherers chose the other option; they attempted to create and to maintain a widespread network of alliances with surrounding and distant groups. The aim of these alliances was to ensure friendly receptions in times of resource crises. These alliances were established by arranged intergroup marriages, by co-participation in rituals, by establishing fictive kinship or other special relationships, by the exchange of gifts, and by frequent visiting. For the alliance system to work, it was essential to have relatively open boundaries between participating communities and frequent exchange of personnel (e.g., Suttles 1987). This fluidity and movement of people also helped deal with more temporary and localized resource fluctuations. Sharing, alliances, and mobility are three of the most important adaptive features of generalized hunter/gatherers wherever they occur in the world.

Competition

The fourth distinctive feature of generalized hunter/gatherers is a proscription on economically competitive behaviour. Under conditions of obligatory sharing, there are no incentives to exert oneself in economic competition. However, equally important is the fact that limited extractable resources are often vulnerable to depletion through over-exploitation. Any competition based on the use of such vulnerable resources will have disastrous, self-destructive effects for the community. Unbridled competition between humans over desirable animals has repeatedly driven species to, or over, the brink of extinction in historical times, as the cases of aurochs, bison, whales, moas, and countless other species demonstrate. Among generalized hunter/gatherers, the egocentric aggrandizive behaviour and attitudes that engender the competitive and selfish use of resources, that is, that threaten the resource base on which others in the community depend, are systematically eliminated. They are eliminated through a wide variety of control mechanisms, including ignoring individual claims to exclusive use of resources, ridicule, ritual proscriptions, public denouncements, fights, expulsions, and even executions. Thus, obligatory sharing of everything, even personal property, ensures not only that temporary fluctuations in resource availabilities are evened out within the community, but also that economically based aggrandizive behaviour cannot become established. It ensures that no one can own wild resources to which everyone in a community would want to have access during times of stress.

In sum, sharing, alliances, mobility, and economic egalitarianism constitute the foundation stones for successful adaptation on the part of generalized hunter/gatherers given the limited, fluctuating, and vulnerable characteristics of their resources. These relationships constitute important principles for the inquiry which follows. These cultural ecological principles explain why the occurrence of prestige items requiring considerable effort and time to manufacture are rare or totally absent wherever resources are limited, fluctuating, and vulnerable, whether prehistorically or ethnographically. Not only are the egocentric, aggrandizive attitudes which these items imply systematically eliminated, but the obligatory sharing of all possessions in these societies makes it futile to invest in personal objects of value. As I have witnessed in Australia, others can and will simply appropriate attractive or desirable objects for their own temporary pleasure and then pass them on to even more distantly related individuals.

OPERATIONAL VARIABLES

The principles outlined above constitute important clues for understanding the social developments that I will focus on, because they indicate what general types of factors may be most relevant in explaining the emergence of economically based inequality and private resource ownership. I have also argued that some of these same factors should provide insights into the emergence of residential corporate groups (Hayden and Cannon 1982).

The principles that structure generalized hunter/gatherer societies provide a framework of concepts that appear to be promising for the understanding of the major social differences between generalized and complex hunter/gatherers; however, the exact definitions of these concepts are still somewhat imprecise. 'Resources' have many characteristics, such as size, nutritional values, reproductive and growth rates, processing requirements, density, distribution, accessibility, availability, and many more. All these characteristics can vary over time and space in complex fashions. At this point, it is difficult to determine exactly which characteristics may play the most critical roles in affecting social variables such as restrictions on access to resources. However, from work carried out by other cultural ecologists (Dyson-Hudson and Smith 1978; Beckerman 1983; Kaplan et al. 1984; Kaplan and Hill 1985a,b; Smith 1979, 1981; Winterhalder 1980, 1986), some of the more likely candidates can be identified (Table 1).

Foremost among the specific variables to be considered are those related to *absolute abundance* and *fluctuations over time* of staple resources. Because of the dominant role of salmon in the study area,

TABLE 1

Resource variables of potential relevance for understanding
social characteristics of generalized and complex hunter/gatherers

---

Absolute abundance
Diversity and evenness
Density
Patchiness
Vulnerability to overexploitation
Fluctuation over time: seasonal or short-term fluctuations (<3 yrs)
    long-term, more drastic fluctuations (10-100+ yrs)
Travel time to procurement areas
Procurement time
Processing time
Processing time constraints
Processing labour requirements
Caloric return
Other dietary values
Storage potential
Labour required for long-term storage
Potential duration of storage
Potential scheduling conflicts for simultaneously exploiting two or
    more resources
Technology available

---

considerable care has been taken to examine their overall abundance
(Chapter 4) as well as seasonal and yearly fluctuations (Chapters 4-6).
While it is important to document absolute abundance in order to
understand the nature and limits of the resource base, the effective
access to the resource via technology and procurement sites is equally
important. This determines the actual amount of a resource that families can obtain. Physical access, technology, and harvested amounts
of fish are dealt with by Romanoff and by Kennedy and Bouchard
(Chapters 5 and 6). Quantitative data for these same variables are more
difficult to obtain for hunted animals and gathered plant resources.
Nevertheless, approximate or relative densities have been obtained
for the most important species. Turner provides estimates of harvested
amounts of plants in Chapter 8, and Alexander establishes the limits
of mammal exploitation in Chapter 2.

Fluctuations in resource levels have been singled out as being relatively important for understanding generalized hunter/gatherer adaptations. Certainly, *seasonal and short-term*, year-to-year cycles of
fluctuations in abundance are relatively easy to observe and describe

even today. These have important consequences in terms of storage strategies as well as in terms of other strategies for coping with predictable periods of scarcity. As Romanoff documents in Chapter 9, these fluctuations can be unexpectedly complex in nature and consequences. However, there are also much *longer term,* unpredictable, and *drastic fluctuations* which may only occur a few times during a lifetime but which can severely affect survival. It is much more difficult to obtain information on these fluctuations because of their irregular occurrence over long intervals, especially under traditional conditions before records were kept. We are often forced to rely on anecdotal and oral history accounts pertaining to indefinite periods of the past. In most cases, these constitute all the information that is or will be available, and their occasional mention in the following chapters is of special significance.

Other variables that have played considerable importance in the development and testing of resource use models such as optimal foraging and linear programming models, include considerations of *travel time, procurement time, processing time,* and *caloric return* from specific resources. While hourly estimates are not provided in most of the papers in this volume, relative estimates are often provided in terms of the number of days spent collecting or processing given amounts of resources (Chapter 8), travel distances and approximate times, the processing or cooking times for both fish and plants, and the amount harvested. Estimates of travel times can also be made from the specific maps provided by both Tyhurst and Turner (Chapters 7 and 8).

In some of the initial models of corporate group formation it was suggested that *labour for processing* major staples, such as salmon and, possibly, root foods, might play important roles in shaping social adaptations. This can be particularly important where *processing time constraints* are tight, as with salmon. Thus, in reading the following accounts, special attention should be paid to labour requirements. Future research plans include the use and refinement of data on resource procurement to generate a quantitative model of resource use based on cost-benefit and abundance rankings. Optimal settlement sizes and locations can also be modelled with this data. However, these are not the goals of the present volume.

Dietary values are characteristics of resources that are also important. While most studies tend to assume that calories were the limiting factors in traditional survival, Reidhead (1979) has demonstrated that minerals, such as calcium, and vitamins can be equally important. Speth and Spielmann (1983) as well as myself have similarly argued for the importance of lipids in traditional diets. In the study area, some resources, such as berries, may not be important so much for their caloric contributions to the diet as for their vitamin contributions, especially when dried and preserved for winter consumption. The detailed documentation of the nutritional value of traditional resources, however, is a vast undertaking and is beyond the scope of the present work. Moreover, nutritional research can be undertaken at any time in the future, whereas the basic information that we have concentrated on is rapidly disappearing with the economic and demographic transformations of recent decades.

The *diversity and evenness* of food species has also figured prominently in describing subsistence economies and in explaining their characteristics. Measures of richness are relatively easily calculated for both prehistoric and ethnographic observations. However, it may be more meaningful to examine staple richness (species that contribute more than 10 per cent to the total diet) as opposed to total richness (all species used as food). Evenness is more difficult to quantify on the basis of the data presented in this volume; however, it should be possible to generate relative or even approximate evenness values. This, too, is an undertaking for subsequent analysis.

Vulnerability to overexploitation was singled out as an important variable for understanding generalized hunter/gatherer adaptations earlier in this chapter. Vulnerability can be measured simply in terms of the number of offspring produced per adult and the number of years required to reach sexual maturity. Salmon, for instance, lay an average of 4,500 (but up to 7,000) eggs at sexual maturity (Rounsefell and Kelez 1935:10) and are, therefore, relatively resilient to overexploitation. Mountain sheep, on the other hand, produce only one individual per year, and their numbers can easily be decimated. Except for trees and shrubs which are not destroyed by the harvesting of their usable fruits, plants exhibit a similar range of characteristics. Ecologists refer to those species which have relatively short lifespans and copious offspring as *r*-selected species; those which have relatively long lifespans and few offspring are *K*-selected. *K*-selected species are much easier to overexploit than *r*-selected species.

Resources can also vary in terms of *density* and *patchiness*, both of which affect travel and search times. Resources that are sparsely distributed require increased search times. At the extreme, more energy may be spent looking for very sparse resources than is obtained from their procurement. Patchiness is the degree of clumping together of resources, generally plant resources. Travelling to one large clump is easier and more efficient than making the rounds of several smaller clumps. Many of the resources in the study area are coarse-grained patches, occurring in large clumps (e.g., spring beauty, salmon); others may be more fine-grained (e.g., various berries). Absolute values for such resource measures are difficult to obtain, but, once again, the present data provide good relative estimates of most of these parameters.

Storage potential is a characteristic that is frequently overlooked in creating ecological models; however, in the study area, this is a vitally important attribute of staple resources, as is the amount of *labour required for effective storage* and the *potential duration of stored foods*. A number of authors (Testart 1982; Soffer 1989) have even argued that storage is responsible for the emergence of complex hunter/gatherers.

Scheduling conflicts due to peak availability of some resources in zones far removed from each other are also important considerations in understanding resource use. Thus, considerable effort has been devoted to documenting species availability by zone in the following chapters. *Technology* and *seasonal movements*, too, constitute essential elements of resource use, and these topics are described in as much detail as possible.

These, then, are the principal variables of interest that I will use in my initial examination of the relationship between key social aspects of culture and ecology as well as in subsequent models of resource use. Some of the original research presented in this volume was gathered before the development of presently used models of optimal foraging and similar approaches. Thus, the form in which the data are presented does not always correspond to the precise formulation of variables and concepts listed above. Nevertheless, relevant information pertaining to most of these variables, or at least general approximations, can be elicited from descriptions in the individual chapters. In most cases, the research presented here represents years of original investigation that, in aggregate, is difficult to duplicate for other hunting/gathering cultures in North America or elsewhere. It is a tribute to the earlier research of Kennedy, Bouchard, Romanoff, and Turner that so much of their work is still relevant and useful for contemporary research problems. It is a rare opportunity to be able to bring together the expertise of such researchers, as well as the talents of Alexander, Tyhurst, and Cannon, in one collaborative presentation.

STUDY AREA

My own involvement in research on the Middle Fraser Canyon began in 1982 when I learned of unusually large prehistoric housepits located in the vicinity of Lillooet. Because I had previously been involved in attempting to understand very large residential structures in Ontario (Hayden 1977), my interest was aroused by these large housepits, and I subsequently began a research program to explain the occurrence of these remarkable structures. The specific focus of this problem soon led to considerations of resources, socioeconomic inequality, and resource ownership. It seemed that all of these factors might be intimately related.

My prehistoric investigations focused on the largest prehistoric village with the largest housepits in the Lillooet region: the Keatley Creek site located about midway between Fountain and Pavilion at the montane edge of the Fraser River Terrace. In order to understand why the Keatley Creek site and a number of other villages of the region were so large, and in order to explore the possible relationships between resources of the region and the development of large residential corporate groups, it was clearly necessary to document the resources that would have been available and used in the past. Initial inquiries indicated that no resource model could be complete without considering the major salmon fishery five miles downriver at the confluence with the Bridge River (Six Mile, or 'The Fountain' – so named in the first instance because of its distance from 'Mile o' on the Cariboo Goldrush Trail beginning at Lillooet and in the second instance because of the constriction in the river and the fall in river level at that point). The impact of trading in surplus fish from this site extended throughout the Plateau and even to the Coast.

Thus, in initially setting the limits of a study area that would be specifically relevant to the prehistoric economy of the Keatley Creek site, the traditional exploitation ranges of both the Pavilion and Fountain Indian bands were considered immediately appropriate as well as the most important fishing resources further downstream (Figure 1). The prospect of undertaking a thorough inventory of resources, their use-description, resulting settlement pattern, and study of other ethnoarchaeological aspects of relevance to the problems I wished to address was enormously daunting given the range of expertise and skills required. Botanical, zoological, piscatory, linguistic, ethnographic, ecological, and archaeological training were all essential skills. As it turned out, the choice of Keatley Creek as the focus of prehistoric ecological relationships was particularly serendipitous, because some of the most intensive ethno-environmental research by some of the most skilled researchers in western Canada had occurred precisely in the Fountain, Pavilion, and Lillooet areas. Much of this data remained unpublished and needed to be supplemented for environmental zones not intensively studied up until 1982. However, clearly, the foundations for a solid ecological study of the area surrounding Keatley Creek had already been laid. Roger Adolph, Chief of the Fountain Band, and Desmond Peters, Councilor for Cultural Affairs of the Pavilion Band, were also keenly interested in

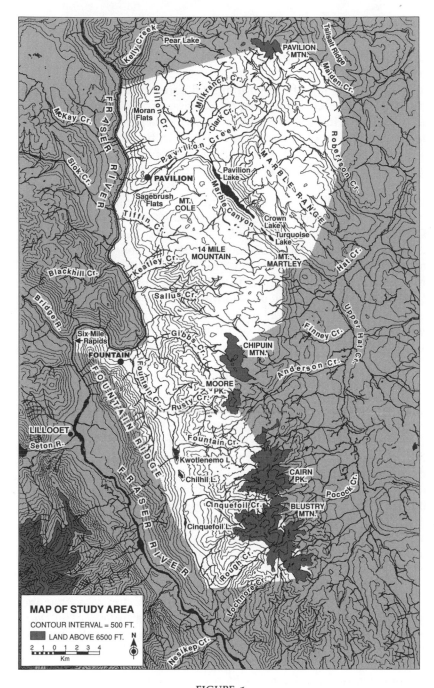

FIGURE 1
Map of the core study area

documenting the traditional resources used by members of their communities.

Details of the specific environmental zones of the study area are presented by Alexander in Chapter 2. Here, I will only briefly situate the study area in its wider context, describe its general features, and relate the history of change and research in the area.

The Middle Fraser Canyon is on the periphery of the culture and geographic area which I will refer to as the Northwestern Plateau. This plateau has two basic subdivisions: the British Columbia Interior Plateau, consisting of tablelands and low mountains between the coastal mountains and the Rocky Mountains (Holland 1964); and the Columbia Plateau, consisting of a Tertiary lava plateau also lying between the coastal mountains and the Rocky Mountains but in the states of Washington, Idaho, and Oregon. The northern boundary of the Northwest Plateau occurs in the area of the great bend in the Fraser River at the northern limit of Shuswap territory (Figure 2), while the southern boundary merges south of the Columbia and Snake rivers into the Great Basin. Ray (1939) and others consider native cultures within this area to be distinctive, and it is commonly called the Plateau culture area.

Geographically, whether the Lillooet region should be considered within the Northwestern Plateau is debatable, since high alpine mountains surround it on all sides. Nevertheless, culturally, there is no question that the Indian communities belong to the Plateau culture area. Geographic position and climate has an important effect not only on the types of resources that occur in the area (Chapter 2) but also on the preservation of resources. The Coast Mountain Range rises precipitously from the western boundary of the study area and serves as a barrier to moisture arriving from the prevailing east-flowing air off the Pacific Ocean. At lower elevations, the resultant hot, dry, semiarid Lillooet environment is ideal for drying fish and other foods. The distance upstream from the ocean also ensures that the fat content of salmon in this area is neither too high for optimal drying and storage nor too low for balanced nutrition and taste.

Elevations in the Lillooet region range from 198 m (650 ft) at the mouth of Texas Creek to 2,332 m (7,650 ft) on Cairn Peak. The Mid-Fraser River is more rugged than any other region of the Interior Plateau. Ryder (1978:56) summarizes the physical geology:

> In the Lillooet area, the Fraser River follows a deep, winding trench that is flanked by high mountain ranges. The floor of the trench consists of extensive benchlands of unconsolidated Quaternary sediments standing above a deeply incised river channel. These present-day land-

forms are late-Pleistocene glacial features that have been modified by Holocene fluvial processes and mass wasting. The Fraser Valley itself, however, is chiefly the product of millions of years of fluvial erosion along a geological fracture zone.

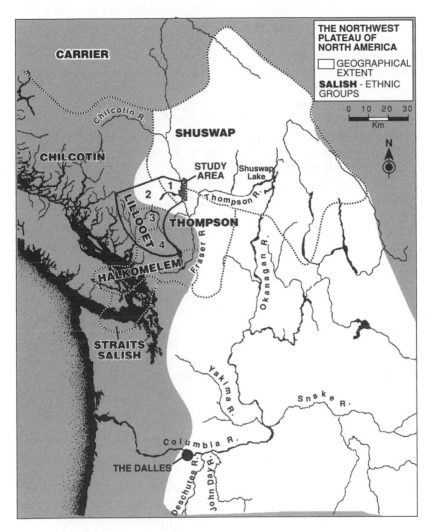

FIGURE 2

Northwest Plateau showing linguistic divisions in the British Columbia Interior of the Plateau, the divisions of Lillooet, and coastal groups referred to in this volume. Within the Lillooet area, 1=Fraser River Band, 2=Lake Band, 3=Pemberton Band, 4=Lillooet River Band.

The benchlands she refers to are river terraces that vary in elevation above the riverbed. The width of the valley varies from one segment of the river to another. Near the town of Lillooet, and for about 8 km downstream, the valley is several kilometers wide and the terraces are broad and relatively low. Stream banks are gravelly with little bedrock showing. Upstream, starting at the Six Mile fishery, the valley is much more constricted and begins an 'S' curve through a rocky gorge, with frequent jetties of bedrock extending into the river. Above Fountain flats, the valley again begins to broaden and straighten out. The terraces are higher than those around Lillooet, but river edges are still predominantly gravel except for the rock outcrops near Sallus Creek and an extremely steepsided, narrow gorge immediately upstream from Keatley Creek. Beyond Pavilion, the valley once again narrows into a rocky gorge and road access ceases. At the back edges of the river terraces, the mountains on either side of the river are covered in coniferous forests, which give way at higher elevations to cool alpine meadows. Areas of open grassland and lakes sometimes occur at middle altitudes. The much more extensive lakes southwest of the town of Lillooet (Seton and Anderson lakes) empty into the Fraser River via Seton River and, formerly, were major salmon spawning and harvesting zones. Food resources were obtained from virtually all environmental zones of the area, although some zones were clearly much more important than others. The climate is continental, with temperatures reaching extremes in both summer and winter, although milder coastal air masses sometimes intrude into the region during winter months.

Culturally, there are two linguistic groups that share the study area today: the Lillooet and the Shuswap. Both are members of the Interior Salish language family. The orthographic system used to transcribe these languages in this volume is presented in Appendix 1. The major ethnographies for each group (Teit 1906, 1909) are primarily synthetic cultural descriptions that omit most distinctions between the bands within each area. The distinction between the 'Lower Lillooet' and the 'Upper Lillooet' is particularly important. The Lower Lillooet inhabited a fundamentally coastal type of environment on the upper reaches of Harrison Lake, Lillooet Lake, and the Lillooet River. Resources were much more diverse and availability was much more evenly spaced throughout the year. The Upper Lillooet occupied the much drier, more seasonal, and ecologically more simplified environment of the Lillooet region along both banks of the Fraser River, Seton Lake, and Anderson Lake. The Lillooet term for these people is *Stl'átl'imx*, a term that is being used with increasing frequency. Kennedy and Bouchard (1978) specifically deal with this group in their earlier ethnographic summary as well as in their chapter for this volume.

Oral traditions recorded at the turn of the century indicate that in early times the Lillooet may have only occupied the west side of the Fraser River (Teit 1906:200, 253). Through intermarriage, the Fountain Band on the east side of the river became a mixture of Shuswap and Lillooet-speaking families. This process continued in more recent times. Thus, in 1909, the Pavilion Band was predominantly Shuswap-speaking; since then it has become predominantly Lillooet-speaking (Teit 1909:46L; Kennedy and Bouchard 1978:35; Desmond Peters, personal communication).

CHANGES

Other major changes that need to be considered in any attempt to create models of pre-Euro-Canadian resources based on ethnographic information include major demographic and economic effects. From archaeological and ethnographic evidence, it is clear that longstanding significant exchange occurred throughout the region and between regions for several thousand years. When Simon Fraser travelled past Lillooet in 1808, Indian communities had already been obtaining European trade goods for some time, presumably from intermediaries on the Coast. Traditional demography and culture does not seem to have been significantly affected by this early indirect trade, although some enhancement of competition, conflict, and the power of high ranking traders might be expected due to the desirability of industrial goods. Such changes have been documented for other Interior groups farther to the north (Bishop 1983, 1987 – compare also Fitzhugh 1985:37). Some people suggest that European diseases, such as smallpox, may have spread to many parts of the province by the 1780s (Duff 1964:38-9), and Hunn (1990:27-8) documents epidemics on the neighbouring Columbia Plateau from 1770 to 1853. Boyd (1985) and Campbell (1989) raise the possibility of the even earlier spread of European diseases. However, by 1808, when Simon Fraser travelled through the Interior, disease does not appear to have been of major concern or note. Fraser makes little or no mention of the topic, whereas all of his descriptions of indigenous life appear to reflect relatively healthy, vigorous communities not significantly debilitated by disease or population loss. Simon Fraser noted over 1,000 people fishing near Lillooet. Subsequently, the Northwest Company (amalgamated with the Hudson's Bay Company in 1821) sent traders from their Kamloops Post (established in 1810) to obtain thousands of fish every year at the Lillooet fisheries (Chapter 6). No permanent trading post was estabblished at Lillooet, however, and thus there was no apparent modification of indigenous cultures from resident Euro-Canadians during this period. Nevertheless, the high volume of fish and industrial items exchanged around Lillooet from 1821 to 1858 may indicate relatively indiscriminate access to industrial goods on the part of all native families and a consequent reduction in the power of high ranking members of surrounding Indian communities. Similar developments took place on the Coast.

The period of relatively indirect effects of Euro-Canadian contact was suddenly and dramatically disrupted in 1858 by the discovery of gold in the immediate vicinity of Lillooet and other areas farther in the Interior. Lillooet became the major staging ground for continued Interior exploration and blossomed into a major boom town. In addition to the local impacts on native communities from a rampant cash economy, competition with miners over fish and game, alcohol, evangelism, and firearms, changes may also have begun by the 1870s in the supply of spring (chinook) salmon. This is indicated by the fact that at least some Lillooet families caught considerably more spring salmon than sockeye in the early part of this century or before, whereas now spring salmon constitute only a very minor part of the catch and most of the spring salmon fishing sites are unused (Chapters 5 and 6). There are several possible explanations for these reported changes. First, spring salmon may have only been available in quantity to owners of particularly well-situated fishing rocks, and the principal informants for Chapters 5 and 6 may have had access to these rocks. If this was so, the total number of spring salmon taken need not have been great (perhaps 10,000-20,000), and springs may not have been easy to capture further upstream where there are fewer rock jetties. The lesser importance of salmon in recent decades might be explained in terms of decreasing criticalness of fats from natural foods (due to the availability of commercially rich foods), scheduling conflicts engendered by wage labour (see Chapter 5), or reduced availability (due to overexploitation or stream degradation).

A second possibility for the decreased reliance on spring salmon may be that the reports of large numbers of spring salmon being caught refer to early twentieth-century decades when sockeye salmon were either overexploited at the mouth of the Fraser River or were prevented from successfully negotiating the Hell's Gate area due to slides (discussed below). Because of the lesser desirability of springs for commercial canning or the greater ability of springs to negotiate river blockages, springs may have been overrepresented during these decades (Figure 3). This scenario is perhaps the least likely given the explicit statements of Sam Mitchell about the catches of spring salmon

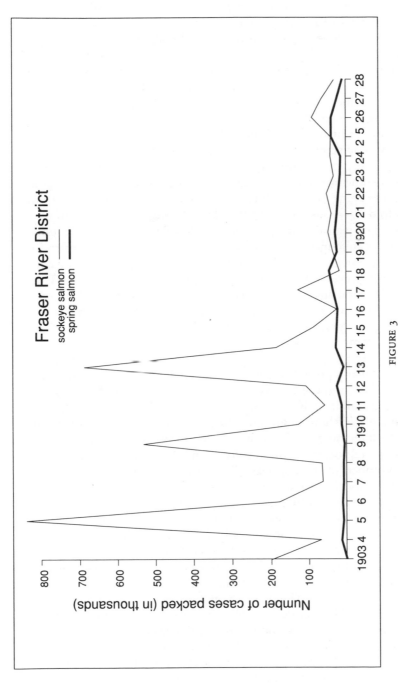

FIGURE 3

Number of cases of sockeye and spring salmon packed in the Fraser River

District between 1903 and 1928 (Cobb 1930:580-3)

before the Hell's Gate slide (Chapter 5), although large commercial catches downstream may have reduced the quantity of sockeye available in the Lillooet region even before the slide.

A third possibility that may account for the greater perceived importance of spring salmon in earlier periods is that the numbers of spring salmon may have declined dramatically before the turn of the century due to exploitation by commercial fishermen and canneries beginning in 1866 (Rounsefell and Kelez 1938:697). Consumption by urban and industrial populations living around the Gulf of Georgia may have had significant effects on the numbers of spring salmon due to their likely use by Aboriginals for trade with Euro-Canadians as well as fishing by the settlers. Rathburn (1899:258, 280) describes spring salmon as being first in quality and as standing 'most in favor for the fresh trade' (see also Rounsefell and Kelez 1938:795). Unfortunately, there are no statistics on spring salmon until the 1900s. Urban populations began to increase greatly in the 1860s, and, with the introduction of ice storage and mild brine curing, far more spring salmon could be caught, preserved, and used in the growing coastal centres. These industrial populations were clearly responsible, via either direct hunting or trade-induced hunting, for the extirpation of elk in the Gulf of Georgia region in order to feed the early settlers (R. Bouchard, personal communication 1990). The last elk in the Richmond area was killed in the 1870s. Starvation of Indians along the Harrison-Lillooet trail was also reported in the *Victoria Gazette* (14 April) in 1859, and may be related to the overexploitation of fauna by gold rush miners using the trail in 1858. Salmon traps were set up everywhere along the shallow offshore migration routes to the Fraser River beginning in these same decades. Traps accounted for almost 40 per cent of the total regional sockeye salmon catch from 1873 to 1934 as well as 'enormous numbers of other species' (Rounsefell and Kelez 1938:714-16). The traps were so effective in capturing salmon that regulations were introduced in 1897 limiting trap leads to 2,500 feet in order to prevent a complete blockade of entire salmon migration routes (ibid.).

By 1898, sockeye salmon stocks began to be significantly depleted, particularly in low cycle years (Ricker 1987). By 1902, the situation was so serious for Interior bands that there were attempts to close the commercial fishery entirely. Rather than closure, the federal regulation of the fishery emerged. The overexploitation of sockeye salmon stocks, and, presumably, the spring salmon stocks with them, must have greatly increased the risk and frequency of famines in the Lillooet area during the decades around the turn of the century. The issue of the subsistence importance of spring salmon is an important one. However, at this juncture in our research, only a preliminary assessment is possible. Certainly throughout the twentieth century, spring salmon have never been considered the most desirable commercial species for canning, and before the Hell's Gate slide in 1913, spring salmon catches and escapement estimates were generally a small fraction of the sockeye estimates. This seems to indicate that spring salmon have never been very numerous, and that even when protected by fishing regulations their numbers failed to rival those of sockeye. The implications are that only some families in earlier times had good access to spring salmon fishing locations and, therefore, caught unusually high proportions of spring to sockeye salmon, while the majority of families that did not own spring salmon fishing sites predominantly caught sockeye salmon at the public fisheries. This is the view endorsed by Romanoff in Chapter 5 and appears to be the most likely scenario at this point. However, clearly, other factors need to be invoked in order to explain the contemporary lack of interest in, and procurement of, spring salmon. As alluded to at the beginning of this discussion, these factors may be related to commercial nutrition (versus traditional foods), wage labour conflicts, and/or degraded spawning areas. Spring salmon spawn primarily in main stem rivers and streams rather than in lakes. In the late nineteenth century, gold rush placer mining created havoc with stream and river beds throughout the Interior for many decades, especially in the Lillooet region. Subsequently, dams such as the Carpenter Dam (constructed in 1948) on the upper reaches of the Bridge River near Lillooet eliminated major portions of prime spring salmon spawning streams. Thus, abundance and availability of spring salmon may have been severely affected starting in the 1860s. However, the issue is more complex, since reduced availability does not account for changes in attitudes toward spring salmon. The contemporary expressed preference for sockeye salmon as the best preserving fish and trading fish (DP, RA) seems to indicate a major shift in the value of spring salmon not related to their availability. This implies changes in nutritional values, such as the critical importance of fats in the past, as perhaps the most important factor; however, more than one of these factors may be responsible for the decline in the use of the spring salmon.

Following the massive influx of prospectors, miners, and support populations, the federal government created the Indian Reserve system during the 1860s and 1870s. It assigned land around the major Indian winter villages and the most important fishing locations to the Indian reserves, designating the rest of lands traditionally used by natives as Crown property. Some parcels that consisted of good natural or irrigable grassland for raising cattle, including the major ranches of Hat Creek and Pavilion Mountain, were pre-empted for private individuals to develop.

By the end of the nineteenth century, Indian populations in the Lillooet region seem to have decreased by half, if the early population observations of Simon Fraser are compared to the census figures of Teit in the 1890s. Certainly the groups observed by Fraser may have been inflated by visitors; however, this was probably balanced out by the use of alternate fishing localities by band members. If the effects of disease and economic disruption during early years of direct contact in other parts of North America are any indication, a population reduction of 50 per cent does not seem unrealistic. This must have had some effects on traditional rights to resources and associated restrictions on their use, but there are no hard data to document such changes.

Extensive interior logging, mining, and the building of roads and railroads during the first two decades of the twentieth century continued to adversely affect the salmon resources on which the Fraser Lillooet and Shuswap depended. The most catastrophic of these impacts was the dumping of tunnel tailings at Hell's Gate into the Fraser River, followed by a slide in 1913 which effectively prevented salmon from migrating farther upstream for several years (Mitchell 1925; Ricker 1987, 1989). Babcock (1919:54-7) records four million sockeye arriving in Quesnel Lake in 1909. In 1913, only 550,000 arrived, while in 1917 a mere 28,000 reached the lake. In the decades since the Great Depression, wage economies, regulated fishing, and industrial impacts have continuously eroded the importance of traditional subsistence practices, beliefs, and language. Nevertheless, fishing and hunting still continue to play important roles in native subsistence and culture in the area. It is remarkable that a considerable amount of traditional knowledge that seems to refer to the pre-gold rush era was preserved up until the 1970s when it was recorded by Romanoff, Bouchard, and Kennedy.

To return briefly to the prehistoric situation, whether the prehistoric occupants of the Keatley Creek site had full access to the traditional area encompassed by both the Fountain and Pavilion bands, or whether this area was shared with, or divided up between, the occupants of other large sites near the present locations of these two bands is difficult to determine. Whatever the case, for heuristic purposes it is possible to designate the traditional ranges of the Fountain and Pavilion bands as the 'core study area' (i.e., the area to which residents of Keatley Creek might have had direct access), and the broader Lillooet area from Texas Creek to Kelly Creek along both sides of the Fraser River, including Seton Lake and Bridge River, as the 'extended study area' (Figure 1). Defined in this way, the core study area runs from the Fraser River to the Alpine meadows on the top of the Clear Range and Fountain Ridge and then partway toward Hat Creek. It includes Pavilion Mountain, Mount Cole, Chipuin Mountain, Moore Peak, Cairn Peak, Blustery Mountain, Pavilion Creek Valley, Marble Canyon, Fountain Creek Valley, and Pavilion and Fountain lakes.The resulting core study area encompasses approximately 530 square kilometres (205 square miles) and extends from a point opposite Texas Creek to Kelly Creek on the east bank of the Fraser River. I estimate the population at the Keatley Creek site alone to have been as large as 500 at its peak, and the combined populations of the contemporaneous Fountain site, Bell site, and Pavilion site must have at least equalled that figure, yielding, with reasonable confidence, a peak prehistoric population of over 1,000 or a density of two people or more per square kilometre.

A second, independent means of estimating prehistoric population supports this conclusion. Teit (1906:199) estimates the population of the expanded study area (including Lillooet and Bridge River bands) to have been about 500 at the turn of the century. The expanded study area is approximately three times that of the core study area, using Teit's (ibid.) estimate of band ranges. This constitutes a population density of only 0.3 people per square kilometre. However, given Teit's estimates of a 60 per cent reduction in population due to introduced small pox epidemics in 1858 (ibid.), the population density in proto-Historic times must have been about one person per square kilometre. Archaeological evidence for even larger villages and denser populations about 1,000 years ago make estimates of one to two people per square kilometre quite reasonable.

HISTORY OF INVESTIGATION

Simon Fraser, in 1808 (Lamb 1960), was the first person to leave a written record of the Lillooet region. However, he was simply travelling through the area and his observations are brief. No further published observations of substance were recorded until legal proceedings were initiated in the 1860s due to mistreatment of native people, destruction of their resources, and retaliatory stealing. Judge Begbie (1861) was particularly noteworthy for his observations and decisions concerning native people. The archives of the Hudson's Bay post at Kamloops contain some insightful observations, especially on the availability of salmon around Lillooet, the absolute amounts and types procured during the pre-gold rush period, and the frequency of fish failures. However, these have not been analyzed in detail as yet.

The first major ethnographic studies in the area took place in the

1890s when James Teit carried out his systematic ethnographies of the
Thompson, Lillooet, Shuswap, and Chilcotin Indians (1898, 1900, 1906,
1909, 1912). He himself was married to a Thompson Indian woman
from Spence's Bridge, and his observations are invaluable sources of
information on traditional lifestyles remembered from the pre-gold
rush period. Franz Boas edited Teit's manuscripts, and they reflect the
editor's biases in organization, subject matter, and theoretical orientation. Even earlier, beginning in the 1870s, the geologist George
Dawson travelled extensively throughout the Interior and was an
observant ethnographer and naturalist. He recorded numerous careful observations on Interior Indians, including the Lillooet (Dawson
1892). Charles Hill-Tout (1905) added to this turn-of-the-century literature with an ethnographic sketch of the Lillooet based on data from
a man who was both Halkomelem and Lillooet. Babcock (1904, 1914)
provided important observations on the effects of commercial fishing
on the Interior Indians. Farrand (1900) published an account of Lillooet
basketry.

For almost fifty years little more was added to this data base,
although Ricker (1987, 1989) has recently documented the effects of
the Hell's Gate slide on pink and sockeye salmon on the middle and
upper Fraser River. Ray (1939) included the Lillooet and surrounding
groups in his analysis of Plateau culture traits.

Interest in the Lillooet region appears to have revived in the 1950s
when Michael Ames (1956) examined economic change at Fountain
as part of his BA degree. Melina Nastich (1954) recorded extensive
information on traditional socioeconomic ranking and warfare from
the Shalalth area, and Phair (1959) wrote a history of Lillooet which
was never published. Lane (1953) also wrote a dissertation on the cultural relations between the Chilcotin and neighbouring groups,
including the Shuswap.

Beginning in the late 1960s and extending into the 1970s, a broad
range of much more specialized investigations was initiated. June
Ryder (1978) investigated the Quaternary geology of the area, and Rolf
Mathewes (1978) began climatic and botanical research. Steven
Romanoff (1971, 1972) undertook his studies of fishing and hunting,
focusing on older individuals in the Fountain Band. Nancy Turner
(1974, 1987) of the Botany Unit of the Royal British Columbian Museum
began her ethnobotanical researches in the Lillooet area, which have
continued up until the present. Dorothy Kennedy and Randy
Bouchard began ethnographic and linguistic research with both the
lower and upper Lillooet (Bouchard and Kennedy 1977; Kennedy and
Bouchard 1975, 1978, in press). And Arnoud Stryd (1973, 1978; Stryd
and Baker 1968; Stryd and Hills 1972) began archaeological investiga-

tions that centred on the Fountain area and, in particular, the Bell site. Blake (1974) and Rittberg (1976) also contributed to these investigations. Farther downstream at Nesikep Creek, David Sanger (1970) conducted excavations of middle and late prehistoric components as part of his doctoral degree and also studied a series of burials at Texas Creek (1968), while the archaeology of Lytton had been investigated by Smith (1900), with techniques appropriate for the beginning of the century.

Throughout the 1970s and into the 1980s, the Lillooet area continued to draw the interest of a variety of specialists. Van Eijk (1985) conducted doctoral research on the Lillooet language. Nancy Turner continued her ethnobotanical work (1988a, b, 1989; Turner et al. 1987). David Pokotylo (1978, 1981; Pokotylo and Froese 1983; Pokotylo et al. 1983) conducted extensive surveys and excavations in the Hat Creek drainage and the Clear Range. Miriam King, Rolf Mathewes, and Richard Hebda (Mathewes 1985; Mathewes and King 1989; Hebda 1979, 1982) analyzed pollen cores from the area and reconstructed climatic conditions since deglaciation. June Ryder and Michael Church (1986) conducted studies of the river terraces in the Lillooet area and are continuing their investigations of major slide events. Nic Mortimer also undertook some geological hardrock mapping which has not been published. I began excavations at the Keatley Creek site in 1986, and Diana Alexander and Rob Tyhurst began ethnoarchaeological work in the area the same year.

In compiling the material for this volume, a wide variety of older members of the native communities around Lillooet were consulted. In conformity with the standard usage that has been adopted by the principal researchers in the area, information obtained from these individuals is indicated by the use of their initials in parentheses after specific statements. Full names and short biographies for all individuals referred to in this way are provided at the end of this chapter (Appendix 2).

VOLUME ORGANIZATION

This volume is organized according to major topics and types of resources. Chapter 2, by Diana Alexander, sets out the resource use zones employed in the analysis of the study area; each zone is described in physical, biological, and climatic terms. Chapter 3, also by Alexander, is a major synthesis of resource use and seasonal mobility, focusing on group compositions and locations at various times of the year. She also documents the types of activities that took place in each environmental use zone and the archaeological remains that might be expected from those activities.

Salmon is the single most important resource of the area, and the next three chapters deal in increasingly specific terms with this resource. Chapter 4, by Mike Kew, estimates the total numbers and weights of salmon that would have passed through the entire Fraser River drainage and, specifically, the Lillooet region, under optimal conditions and during various phases of cyclical variations. It also examines the evolution of fishing technology in the Fraser drainage. Chapter 5, by Steven Romanoff, further documents important aspects of technology and the general principles of fish accessibility and use in the Lillooet region. Of critical importance for the present volume, Chapter 5 documents three types of culturally determined access to fishing sites, ranging from nearly open access to privately owned fishing sites. Chapter 6, by Dorothy Kennedy and Randy Bouchard, offers the most specific treatment of salmon and carefully documents specific salmon fishing sites, their characteristics, family consumption, and episodic shortages of salmon. It provides a still more detailed overview of all the variations in fishing technology employed by the Lillooet.

Chapter 7, by Rob Tyhurst, extends and completes the inventory of fishing sites for the core study area and raises important issues about other possible prehistoric fish exploitation sites in the core study area. The bulk of Chapter 7, however, examines resource exploitation and ownership in the Alpine and Montane Parkland zones, providing specific site locations as well as general criteria used for selecting camping and extraction sites.

Chapter 8, by Nancy Turner, offers a detailed presentation of plant resources, their distribution, use, harvesting characteristics, yields per family, and relative importance.

The next two chapters, by Steven Romanoff and Aubrey Cannon, respectively, employ the cultural ecological perspective to explain the unusual importance of specialized hunters for the Lillooet (Chapter 9) and to explain the patterns and intensity of warfare and slavery throughout the Interior (Chapter 10). The discussion of the role of meat, of the specialized hunter, and of 'potlatching' in Lillooet traditional culture is particularly important for the questions of social-ecological relationships that I will deal with in Chapter 11. This last chapter demonstrates how the information presented in the preceding chapters can be synthesized with other comparative data to generate a provisional model for the emergence of socioeconomic inequality, private ownership of resources, and large residential corporate groups.

APPENDICES

1: Orthographic Key to Transcriptions of Stl'átl'imx Terms

The practical writing system for the *Stl'átl'imx* terms appearing in the present report is explained below. This description is adapted from a manuscript prepared in 1970 by Randy Bouchard and revised in 1973, entitled 'How to Write the Lillooet Language (Fraser River Dialect).'

In the listing that follows, the symbols of Bouchard's writing system are followed by their phonemic equivalents in the version of the International Phonetic Alphabet used by many linguists.

1 The following symbols represent *Stl'átl'imx* sounds which are approximately similar to those sounds represented by the same symbols in English:

   h /h/   k /k/   l /l/   m /m/   n /n/   p /p/
   s /š/   t /t/   ts /č/   w /w/   y /y/   z /z/

2 **lh** /ɬ/   Similar to the 'thl' sound in English 'athlete.'

3 **tl'** /ƛ̓/   A strongly-exploded *Stl'átl'imx* 't' and 'lh,' pronounced together as one sound.

4 **x** /x/   A 'friction' sound made with the tongue in the same position as it is for the *Stl'átl'imx* 'k.'

5 **g** /ɣ/   A voiced 'friction' sound that is similar to *Stl'átl'imx* 'k.'

6 **7** /ʔ/   A 'glottal stop' or 'catch in the throat.'

7 **a** /a/ ([a] [æ])   Sounds which vary from the first vowel sound of English 'father' to the vowel sound of English 'bat.'

8 **e** /ə/ ([ʌ] [ə] [ɨ] [ʊ])   Sounds which vary from the vowel sound of English 'but' to the vowel sound of English 'earth' to the vowel sound of English 'put.'

9 **i** /i/ ([i] [I] [e] [ei])   Sounds which vary from the vowel sound of English 'beat' to the vowel sound of English 'bit' to the vowel sound of English 'bait.'

10 **o** /ɔ/   [ɔ]   Similar to the vowel sound of British English 'cot.'

11 **u** /u/ ([u] [o])   Sounds which vary from the vowel sound of English 'boot' to the vowel sound of English 'boat.'

12 An apostrophe ' beside the symbol indicates *Stl'átl'imx* sounds which are 'strongly exploded' (glottalized), as in:

   k' /k̓/   ḵ' /q̓/   kw' /k̓ʷ/   ḵw' /q̓ʷ/   p' /p̓/   tl' /ƛ̓/   ts' /č̓/

13 An apostrophe ' above the symbol indicates *Stl'átl'imx* sounds which are 'weakly exploded' (glottalized resonants), as in:

   ǵ /ɣ̓/   ǵw /ɣ̓ʷ/   ḡ /ʕ̓/   ḡ /ʕ̓ʷ/   í /l̓/   ḿ /m̓/   ń /n̓/   ẃ /w̓/   ý /y̓/   ź /z̓/

14 Underlining (_) indicates *Stl'átl'imx* sounds which are produced relative-

ly 'further back in the mouth' (uvular or pharyngeal), as in:

g /ʕ/　ġ /ʕ̓/　gw /ʕʷ/　ġ /ʕ̓ʷ/　ḳ /q/　ḳ' /q̓/　ḳw /qʷ/　ḳw' /q̓ʷ/　x /x̣/　x̣w /x̣ʷ/

15 A 'w' beside the symbol indicates *Stl'átl'imx* sounds which are produced with 'rounded lips' (labialized), as in:

gw /γʷ/　g̣ʷ /γ̓ʷ/　gw /ʕʷ/　ġ /ʕ̓ʷ/　kw /kʷ/　kw' /k̓ʷ/　ḳw /qʷ/　ḳw' /q̓ʷ/　xw /xʷ/　x̣w /x̣ʷ/

16 Stress is marked (´) over the vowel that is pronounced the loudest in all *Stl'átl'imx* terms containing two vowels or more.

17 A hyphen (-) is used to separate potentially ambiguous sequences of practical phonemes.

18 With the above-mentioned exception (#17), this practical writing system follows standard English punctuation practices.

2: Biographic Summary of Informants

LA

Lawrence Adolph is Roger Adolph's father and an elder from the Fountain Band. His knowledge is based largely on first-hand experience in the area.

MA

Maggie Adolph is Roger Adolph's mother and an elder from the Fountain Band. Her knowledge is based largely on first-hand experience in the area.

RA

Roger Adolph is currently chief of the Fountain Band. He has a keen interest in the traditional life of his people. He bases his information primarily on discussions with the elders from the band, especially Sam Mitchell.

WA

William Adolph was born in 1893 and died in 1978. He lived primarily around Fountain and alongside the Fraser River near the BC Railway bridge. He was an ardent reader and gained immense pleasure from revolutionary publications. In later life, WA lived much of the time alone, tending his vegetable garden and his small home situated above his fishery.

CB

Charlie Billy is an elder from the Fountain Band. He provided information on the use of Chipuin Mountain-Moore Peak during a three-day horse back trip to the area. His knowledge is based largely on first-hand experience.

KB

Chris Bob is an elder from the Fountain Band. His accounts of traditional practices are largely based on his own experiences.

BE

Bill (Francis) Edwards was born in 1922 and, like his father, has spent his entire life at Pavilion. His grandfather spent part of his life at Mount Currie. Since boyhood BE has taken part in hunting and fishing activities and has a good knowledge of traditional resources, including plant resources, based on his own experience and stories related by family members. In recent years, BE has played an active role in church activities throughout the Lillooet area in his capacity as a Catholic deacon.

SJ

Slim Jackson was born in 1903 and died in 1979. He spent his early life in the Lillooet area before moving to Mount Currie in 1920. SJ was a quiet man who had a strong interest in his people's history. He acted as an ethnographic and linguistic consultant to Bouchard and Kennedy in the 1970s. Historic accounts and ethnographic data that SJ provided have been published in Bouchard and Kennedy (1977) and Kennedy and Bouchard (1978).

DL

Doris Lulua is in her fifties and has spent her entire life in the vicinity of Eagle Lake and the Potato Mountains in the Chilcotin. She is one of the few Indians in the area who continues to travel to the mountains to hunt deer and collect roots. Her information is based largely on her own experience and stories told to her by her immediate family.

EL

Emily Lulua is Doris's aunt and is in her eighties. Emily does not speak English, so Doris was used as an interpreter in interviews with Emily. Emily continues to practise some of the traditional subsistence practices and was involved in others in her youth. She bases her information on her own experience and stories she heard from elders when she was younger.

SM

Sam Mitchell was born in 1894 and died in 1985. He was the major Native contributor to this volume. He was from Fountain, and was extremely knowledgeable about all aspects of traditional *Stl'átl'imx* culture, including plant names and uses. In 1974, he took Nancy Turner up to Pavilion Mountain, where he showed her the traditional 'Indian potato' harvesting grounds, how to dig Indian potatoes, harvest lodgepole pine inner bark, and dig and prepare balsamroot. From 1971-4 Turner spent many hours with him, as did Randy Bouchard, Dorothy Kennedy, Steve Romanoff, and Jan van Eijk (linguist), recording information on traditional resources and life. Mitchell was not an owner of a fishing rock nor did he hold the role of a specialized hunter. Despite SM's busy life, which included many years as a chief of the Fountain Band, he always found time to assist outside researchers and his own people with their questions about *Stl'átl'imx* culture and language. SM was extremely knowledgeable and generously shared his knowledge with everyone. He delighted in telling historical anecdotes. SM continued hunting and fishing around Lillooet until he was well into his eighties. The exceptional quality of the wind-dried salmon produced by Sam and his wife, Susan, was renowned throughout British Columbia and Washington State. Among the many publications in which SM's contributions have played a major role are:

Bouchard and Kennedy (1977); Kennedy and Bouchard (1978); Romanoff (1985, 1990); and Turner (1974, 1987, 1988, 1989). SM was also a major source for both Van Eijk's linguistic work and Bouchard's.

SUM

Susan Mitchell, wife of Sam Mitchell, was born in 1898 and spent her early life at Leon Creek and Bridge River before marrying SM and moving to Fountain. She died in 1988. SUM was renowned for her buckskin work and for her traditionally-prepared foods.

BN

Bucky (Les) Ned is a member of the Pavilion Band, as was his father and grandfather. He provided some information on the use of Mount Cole based on his trips to the area with his father in the early 1960s, while he was still a child.

JN

Jim Nason is a Bonaparte Band member in his sixties, who lives on Hat Creek and has hunted extensively in Marble Canyon, on Pavilion Mountain, and on Bald Mountain.

WN

Wilfred Ned is an elder from the Fountain Band. His knowledge of traditional practices is based on stories related to him by his parents and his own experiences in the area.

EO

Edith O'Donaghey was born in 1921 and presently lives in Lillooet. She was born and raised at Shalalth. As a girl and young woman she actively participated in harvesting and preparation of traditional foods and still eats them today whenever possible. She took part in several family expeditions to Mission Ridge above Shalalth to harvest berries and roots and had close contact with her grandparents, who taught her many things about traditional resources. For her relatively young age, she has an exceptional knowledge of plant names and traditional foods and medicines.

DP

Desmond Peters, Sr. was born in 1933. Although originally from Shalalth, Desmond has lived at Pavilion since the early 1950s and was chief of the Pavilion Band for ten years. He has made many hunting and fishing trips throughout the area traditionally used by the Pavilion Band. He made many trips in the fifties and sixties with elders from the band, whom he actively questioned about traditional practices. He also wrote notes based on his discussions with them. As a younger brother of EO, he was too young to take part in family trips to Mission Ridge but did take an active role in hunting and fishing throughout the region and has maintained a deep interest in traditional resources through his life.

MLR

Martina LaRochelle of Lillooet was born about 1902 and died in 1974. She accompanied SM, Jan van Eijk, and Nancy Turner on several field trips. Jan van

Eijk worked with her extensively on Lillooet linguistics while Turner worked with her on ethnobotanical materials.

MS

Madeline Sampson from the Bridge River reserve was born in 1920 and died in 1980. She was active in the gathering and preparation of traditional Lillooet foods.

REFERENCES

Ames, Michael. 1956. 'Fountain in a Modern Economy.' Unpublished BA thesis, Department of Economics, Political Science, and Sociology, University of British Columbia

Babcock, J.P. 1903. 'Report of the Fisheries Commissioner for British Columbia for the Year 1902.' Annual Reports of the Department of Fisheries, Ottawa

–. 1903. 'Report of the Fisheries Commissioner for British Columbia for the Year 1903.' Annual Reports of the Department of Fisheries, Ottawa

–. 1914. 'Statement to the Royal Commission on Indian Affairs for British Columbia, at a conference with representatives of the Dominion and Provincial Fisheries Departments, 5 April 1914.' In Transcript of Cowichan Agency Evidence, Provincial Archives of British Columbia, Add mss. 1056

–. 1919. 'Statement by John Babcock.' British Columbia Report of the Commissioner of Fisheries for the Year Ending December 31st, 1918. Victoria

Beckerman, Stephen. 1983. 'Optimal foraging group size for a human population: The case of Bari fishing.' American Zoologist 23:283-90

Begbie, M. 1861. 'Journey into the interior of British Columbia.' Journal, Royal Geographical Society 31:237-48

Bettinger, Robert. 1980. 'Explanatory/predictive models of hunter-gatherer adaptation.' In Michael Schiffer (ed.), Advances in Archaeological Method and Theory 3:189-255. New York: Academic Press

Binford, Lewis. 1980. 'Willow smoke and dogs' tails: Hunter-gatherer settlement systems and archaeological site formation.' American Antiquity 45:4-20

–. 1983. 'Limiting access to limited goods: The origins of stratification in Interior British Columbia.' In Elizabeth Tooker (ed.), The Development of Political Organization in Native North America. Pp. 148-61. Washington, DC: American Ethnological Society

Bishop, Charles. 1987. 'Coast-interior exchange: The origins of stratification in northwestern North America.' Arctic Anthropology 24:72-83

Blake, T. Michael. 1974. 'Ollie site (EeRk 9) final report.' Report on file with the Archaeological Sites Advisory Board of British Columbia

Bouchard, Randy and Dorothy Kennedy (eds.). 1977. 'Lillooet stories.' Sound Heritage 6(1):1-78

Boyd, Robert. 1985. 'The Introduction of Infectious Diseases among the Indians of the Pacific Northwest, 1774-1874.' Unpublished PhD dissertation, Department of Anthropology, University of Washington

Campbell, Sarah. 1989. 'Post Columbian Culture History in the Northern Columbia Plateau: AD 1500-1900.' Unpublished PhD dissertation, Anthropology Department, University of Washington

Cashdan, Elizabeth. 1980. 'Eligalitarianism among hunters and gatherers.' *American Anthropologist* 82:116-20

Chance, David and Jennifer Chance. 1982. 'Kettle Falls: 1971 and 1974.' Anthropological Research Manuscripts Series, No. 69, University of Idaho, Laboratory of Anthropology

Chapman, Robert. 1981. 'The emergence of formal disposal areas and the "problem" of megalithic tombs in prehistoric Europe.' In Robert Chapman, Ian Kinnes, and Klavs Randsborg (eds.), *The Archaeology of Death.* Pp. 71-81. Cambridge: Cambridge University Press

Chatters, James. 1987. 'Hunter-gatherer adaptations and assemblage structure.' *Journal of Anthropological Archaeology* 6:336-75

Cobb, John. 1930. 'Pacific salmon fisheries.' Bureau of Fisheries Document No. 1092. Washington, DC: U.S. Department of Commerce

Cressman, L.S. 1960. 'Cultural sequences at the Dalles, Oregon.' *Transactions, American Philosophical Society* 50(10):1-108

Dawson, George. 1892. 'Notes on the Shuswap people of British Columbia.' *Proceedings and Transactions of the Royal Society of Canada for the Year 1891* 9(2):3-44

Duff, Wilson. 1964. *The Indian History of British Columbia. The Impact of the Whiteman.* Victoria: BC Provincial Museum

Dyson-Husdon, Rada and Eric Smith. 1978. 'Human territoriality: An ecological reassessment.' *American Anthropologist* 80:21-41

Farrand, L. 1900. 'Basketry designs of the Salish Indians.' *American Museum of Natural History, Memoirs 2, Anthropology* 1:391-8

Fitzhugh, William. 1985. 'Early contacts north of Newfoundland before AD 1600: A review.' In W. Fitzhugh (ed.), *Cultures in Contact.* Pp. 23-44. Washington, DC: Smithsonian Institution Press

Ford, Richard. 1972. 'Barter, gift, or violence.' *Anthropology Papers* 46:21-45. Museum of Anthropology, University of Michigan

–. 1977. 'Evolutionary ecology and the evolution of human ecosystems: A case study from the midwestern USA.' In James Hill (ed.), *Explanation of Prehistoric Change.* Albuquerque: University of New Mexico Press

Freeman, Leslie G. Jr. 1968. 'A theoretical framework for interpreting archaeological materials.' In Richard Lee and Irven Devore (eds.), *Man the Hunter.* Pp. 262-7. Chicago: Aldine Press

Gladkih, Mikhail, N. Kornietz, and Olga Soffer. 1984. 'Mammoth-bone dwellings on the Russian Plain.' *Scientific American* 251(5):164-75

Gould, R. Richard. 1982. 'To have and have not: The ecology of sharing among hunter-gatherers.' In N. Williams and E. Hunn (eds.), *Resource Managers:*

North American and Australian Hunter-gatherers. Pp. 69-92. Canberra: Australian Institute of Aboriginal Studies

Harris, Marvin. 1971. *Culture, Man and Nature.* New York: Crowell

Hayden, Brian. 1981. 'Research and development in the stone age: Technological transitions among hunter-gatherers.' *Current Anthropology* 22:519-48

– and Aubrey Cannon. 1982. 'The corporate group as an archaeological unit.' *Journal of Anthropological Archaeology* 1:132-58

– and Rob Gargett. 1990. 'Big man, big heart? A Mesoamerican view of the emergence of complex society.' *Ancient Mesoamerica* 1:3-20

Hebda, Richard. 1979. 'Pollen analysis of Finney Lake sediments, Hat Creek Valley, BC.' Report to Hat Creek Archaeological Project, Anthropology/Sociology Department, University of British Columbia

–. 1982. 'Postglacial history of grasslands of southern British Columbia and adjacent regions.' In A. Nicholson, A. McLean, and T. Baker (eds.), *Grassland Ecology and Classification Symposium Proceedings.* Pp. 157-94. Ministry of Forests, Victoria, BC: Queen's Printer

Hennigh, Lawrence. 1983. 'North Alaskan Eskimo alliance structure.' *Arctic Anthropology* 20:23-32

Hill-Tout, Charles. 1905. 'Report on the ethnology of the StlatlumH of British Columbia.' *Journal, Anthropoligical Institute of Great Britain and Ireland* 35:126-218

Hodder, Ian. 1985. 'Postprocessual archaeology.' In M. Schiffer (ed.), *Advances in Archaeological Method and Theory.* Vol. 8. Pp. 1-26. New York: Academic Press

Holland, S. 1964. 'Landforms of British Columbia: A physiographic outline.' *British Columbia Department of Mines and Petroleum Resources.* Bulletin 48

Hunn, Eugene. 1990. *Nch'i-Wana, 'The Big River': Mid-Columbia Indians and their Land.* Seattle: University of Washington Press

Johnson, Jay. 1987. 'Introduction.' In J. Johnson and C. Morrow (eds.), *The Organization of Core Technology,* Pp. 1-12. Boulder: Westview Press

Jorgensen, Joseph. 1980. *Western Indians: Comparative Environments, Languages, and Cultures of 172 Western American Indian Tribes.* San Francisco: W.H. Freeman

Kaplan, Hillard and Kim Hill. 1985a. 'Hunting ability and reproductive success among male Ache foragers: Preliminary results.' *Current Anthropology* 26:131-3

–. 1985b. 'Food sharing among Ache foragers: Tests of explanatory hypotheses.' *Current Anthropology* 26:223-46

Kaplan, H., K. Hill, K. Hawkes, and A. Hurtado. 1984. 'Food sharing among Ache hunter-gatherers of eastern Paraguay.' *Current Anthropology* 25:113-15

Kennedy, Dorothy and Randy Bouchard. 1975. 'Utilization of fish by the Mount Currie Lillooet Indian people of British Columbia.' Unpublished ms. BC Indian Language Project, Victoria

–. 1978. 'Fraser River Lillooet: An ethnographic summary.' In Arnoud Stryd and S. Lawhead (eds.), *Reports of the Lillooet Archaeological Project, No. 1. Introduction and Setting*. National Museum of Man, Mercury Series, Archaeological Survey of Canada, Paper No. 73. Pp. 22-55

–. In press. 'The Lillooet.' In Deward Walker (ed.), *Handbook of North American Indians: The Plateau*. Washington, DC: Smithsonian Institute

Klima, Bohuslav. 1962. 'The first ground-plan of an Upper Paleolithic loess settlement in middle Europe and its meaning.' In R. Braidwood and G. Willey (eds.), *Courses Toward Urban Life*. Pp. 193-210. Chicago: Aldine Press

Lamb, W. Kaye (ed.). 1960. *The Letters and Journals of Simon Fraser 1806-1808*. Toronto: MacMillan

Lane, R. 1953. 'Cultural Relations of the Chilcotin of West Central British Columbia.' Unpublished PhD dissertation, University of Washington

Lee, Richard. 1972a. '!Kung spatial organization: An ecological and historical perspective.' *Human Ecology* 1:125-47

–. 1972b. 'Work effort, group structure and land use in contemporary hunter-gatherers.' In Peter Ucko, R. Tringham, and G. Dimbleby (eds.), *Man, Settlement and Urbanism*. Pp. 177-85. London: Duckworth

– and Irven Devore. 1968b. 'Problems in the study of hunters and gatherers.' In Richard Lee and Irven Devore (eds.), *Man the Hunter*. Pp. 3-12. New York: Aldine

Lourandos, Harry. 1980. 'Change or stability? Hydraulics, hunter-gatherers and population in temperate Australia.' *World Archaeology* 2:245-64

Mathewes, Rolf. 1978. 'The environment and biotic resources of the Lillooet area.' In A. Stryd and S. Lawhead (eds.), *Reports of the Lillooet Archaeological Project. No. 1. Introduction and Setting*. National Museum of Man, Mercury Series, No. 73. Pp. 68-99

–. 1985. 'Paleobotanical evidence for climatic change in southern British Columbia during the late-glacial and Holocene times.' In C.R. Harrington (ed.), 'Climatic change in Canada 5: Critical periods in the Quaternary climatic history of northern North America'. *Syllogeus* 55:344-96

– and Miriam King. 1989. 'Holocene vegetation, climate and lake level changes in the Interior Douglas fir biogeoclimatic zone, British Columbia.' *Canadian Journal of Earth Sciences* 26:1811-25

Minc, Leah. 1986. 'Scarcity and survival: The role of oral tradition in mediating subsistence crises.' *Journal of Anthropological Archaeology* 5:39-113

Mitchell, D.S. 1925. 'A Story of the Fraser River's Great Sockeye Runs and their Loss.' Unpublished ms. on file with the Pacific Salmon Commission and BC Archives and Records Service (Ms. 1/B/M69)

Nastich, Milena. 1954. 'The Lillooet: An Account of the Basis of Individual Status.' Unpublished MA thesis, Department of Economics, Political Science and Sociology, University of British Columbia

Pardoe, Colin. 1988. 'The cemetery as symbol. The distribution of prehistoric Aboriginal burial grounds in southeastern Australia.' *Archaeology in*

Oceania 23:1-16

Parry, William and Robert Kelly. 1987. 'Expedient core technology.' In Jay Johnson and Carol Morrow (eds.), *The Organization of Core Technology.* Pp. 285-304. Boulder: Westview Press

Phair, A.W. 1959. 'The history of Lillooet.' British Columbia Archives and Records Service, Add ms. 275

Pokotylo, David. 1978. 'Lithic Technology and Settlement Patterns in Upper Hat Creek Valley, BC.' Unpublished PhD dissertation, Department of Anthropology and Sociology, University of British Columbia

– and Patricia Froese. 1983. 'Archaeological evidence for prehistoric root gathering on the Southern Interior Plateau of British Columbia: A case study from the Upper Hat Creek Valley.' *Canadian Journal of Archaeology* 7:127-57

–, Sheila Greaves, and Linda Burnard. 1983. 'Archaeological reconnaissance in the Clear Range, BC.' Paper presented at the sixteenth annual meeting of the Canadian Archaeological Association, Halifax, Nova Scotia

–, Marian Binkley, and Joanne Curtin. 1987. 'The Cache Creek burial site (EERh 1), British Columbia.' *British Columbia Provincial Museum Contributions to Human History.* No. 1

Rathburn, Richard. 1899. 'A Review of the Fisheries in the Contiguous Waters of the State of Washington and British Columbia.' Report of the U.S. Fish Commission for 1899

Ray, Verne. 1939. 'Cultural Relationships in the Plateau of North-western America.' *Publications of the Frederick Webb Hodge Anniversary Publication Fund* 3. Los Angeles: Southwest Museum

Reidhead, Van A. 1979. 'Linear programming models in archaeology.' *Annual Review of Anthropology* 8:543-78

Ricker, W.E. 1987. 'Effects of the fishery and of obstacles to migration on the abundance of Fraser River sockeye salmon (oncorhynchus nerka).' *Canadian Technical Report of Fisheries and Aquatic Sciences.* No. 1522. Department of Fisheries and Oceans, Fisheries Research Branch, Pacific Biological Station, Nanaimo, BC

–. 1989. 'History and present state of the odd-year pink salmon runs of the Fraser River region.' *Canadian Technical Report of Fisheries and Aquatic Sciences* No. 1702. Department of Fisheries and Oceans, Fisheries Research Branch, Pacific Biological Station, Nanaimo, BC

Romanoff, Steven. 1971. 'Fraser Lillooet Salmon Fishing.' Unpublished BA thesis, Division of History and the Social Sciences, Reed College, Portland

–. 1972. 'The Lillooet Hunter.' Unpublished ms.

Rounsefell, George and George Kelez. 1935. 'Abundance and seasonal occurrence of the salmon in the Puget Sound region and the development of the fishery.' U.S. Department of Commerce, Bureau of Fisheries, Special Report. Washington, DC

–. 1938. 'The salmon and salmon fisheries of Swiftsure Bank, Puget Sound, and the Fraser River.' *Bulletin, U.S. Bureau of Fisheries* 48:693-823

Ryder, June. 1978. 'Geomorphology and late Qaternary history of the Lillooet area.' In A. Stryd and S. Lawhead (eds.), *Reports of the Lillooet Archaeological Project, No. 1. Introduction and Setting.* National Museum of Man, Mercury Series, Archaeological Survey of Canada, Paper No. 73, 56-67

– and Michael Church. 1986. 'The Lillooet terraces of the Fraser River: A palaeoenvironmental enquiry.' *Canadian Journal of Earth Sciences* 23:869-84

Sanger, David. 1968. 'The Texas Creek burial site assemblage, British Columbia.' *National Museum of Canada, Anthropology Papers* 17

–. 1970. 'The archaeology of the Lochnore-Nesikep locality, BC.' *Syesis* 3(Supplement 1)

Scarre, Christopher. 1984. 'A survey of the French Neolithic.' In C. Scarre (ed.), *Ancient France.* Pp. 223-70. Edinburgh: Edinburgh University Press

Sheehan, Glenn. 1985. 'Whaling as an organizing focus in northwestern Alaska Eskimo societies.' In Doug Price and James Brown (eds.), *Prehistoric Hunter-gatherers.* Pp. 123-54. Orlando, FL: Academic Press

Shiner, J. 1961. 'The McNary Reservoir: A study in Plateau archaeology.' *Bureau of American Ethnology, Bulletin* 179

Shott, Michael. 1986. 'Technological organization and settlement mobility: An ethnographic examination.' *Journal of Anthropoligical Research* 42:15-51

Silberbauer, George. 1981. Hunter and habitat in the central Kalahari Desert. Cambridge: Cambridge University Press

Smith, Eric. 1979. 'Human adaptation and energetic efficiency.' *Human Ecology* 7:53-74

–. 1981. 'The application of optimal foraging theory to the analysis of hunter-gatherer group size.' In B. Winterhalder and E. Smith (eds.), *Hunter-gatherer Foraging Strategies.* Pp. 36-65. Chicago: University of Chicago Press

Smith, Harlan. 1900. 'The archaeology of Lytton.' *Memoirs, American Museum of Natural History, Jesup North Pacific Expedition* 2(6):401-42

Soffer, Olga. 1989. 'Storage, sedentism and the Eurasian Palaeolithic record.' *Antiquity* 63:719-32

Speth, John and Katherine Spielmann. 1983. 'Energy source, protein metabolism, and hunter-gatherer subsistence strategies.' *Journal of Anthropological Archaeology* 2:1-31

Spielman, Katherine. 1986. 'Interdependence among egalitarian societies.' *Journal of Anthropological Archaeology* 5:279-312

Strehlow, T.G.H. 1965. 'Culture, social structure, and environment in Aboriginal Central Australia.' In Ronald Berndt and Catherine Berndt (eds.), *Aboriginal Man in Australia.* Pp. 121-45. Sydney: Angus and Robertson

Stryd, Arnoud. 1973. 'The Later Prehistory of the Lillooet Area, British Columbia.' Unpublished PhD dissertation, Department of Archaeology, University of Calgary

–. 1978. 'An introduction to the Lillooet Archaeological Project.' In A. Stryd and S. Lawhead (eds.), *Reports of the Lillooet Archaeological Project, No. 1. Introduction and Setting.* National Museum of Man, Mercury Series 73:1-21

– and J. Baker. 1968. 'Salvage excavations at Lillooet, British Columbia.' *Syesis* 1:47-56

– and L. Hills. 1972. 'An archaeological site survey of the Lillooet-Big Bar area, British Columbia.' *Syesis* 5:191-209

Suttles, Wayne. 1987. 'Affinal ties, subsistence, and prestige among the Coast Salish.' In *Coast Salish Essays.* Vancouver: Talonbooks; and Seattle: University of Washington Press

Teit, James. 1898. 'Two traditions of the Lillooet.' *Traditions of the Thompson River Indians of British Columbia.* American Folklore Society

–. 1900. 'The Thompson Indians of British Columbia.' *Memoirs, American Museum of Natural History, Jesup North Pacific Expedition* 1(4):163-392

–. 1906. 'The Lillooet Indians.' *Memoirs, American Museum of Natural History* 2(5):193-300

–. 1909. 'The Shuswap Indians.' *Memoirs, American Museum of Natural History* 4:443-758

–. 1912. 'Traditions of the Lillooet Indians of British Columbia.' *Journal of American Folklore* 25:287-358

Testart, Alain. 1982. 'The significance of food storage among hunter-gatherers.' *Current Anthropology* 23:523-37

Turner, Nancy. 1974. 'Plant taxonomies and ethnobotany of three contemporary Indian groups of the Pacific Northwest: Haida, Bella Coola and Lillooet.' *Syesis* 7 (Supplement 1)

–. 1987. 'General plant categories in Thompson and Lillooet, two Interior Salish languages of British Columbia.' *Journal of Ethnobiology* 7:55-82

–. 1988a. 'Ethnobotany of coniferous trees in Thompson and Lillooet Interior Salish of British Columbia.' *Economic Botany* 42(2):177-94

–. 1988b. ' "The importance of a rose": Evaluating cultural significance of plants in Thompson and Lillooet Interior Salish.' *American Anthropologist* 90(2):272-90

–. 1989. ' "All berries have relations": Medieval folk plant categories in Thompson and Lillooet Interior Salish.' *Journal of Ethnobiology* 9(1):60-110

Turner, Nancy J., Randy Bouchard, Dorothy Kennedy, and Jan Van Eijk. 1987. 'Ethnobotany of the Lillooet Indians of British Columbia. Unpublished ms, Royal British Columbia Museum, Victoria, BC

Van Eijk, J. 1985. 'The Lillooet Language.' Unpublished PhD dissertation, University of Amsterdam, Netherlands

Widmer, Randolph. 1988. *The Evolution of the Calusa: A Nonagricultural Chiefdom on the Southwest Florida Coast.* Tuscaloosa: University of Alabama Press

Wiessner, Pauline. 1977. 'Hxaro: A Regional System of Reciprocity for Reducing Risk among the !Kung San.' Unpublished PhD dissertation, Department of Anthropology, University of Michigan, Ann Arbor

–. 1981. 'Measuring the impact of social ties on nutritional status among the

!Kung San.' *Social Science Information* 20:641-78

Williams, Elizabeth. 1987. 'Complex hunter-gatherers: A view from Australia.' *Antiquity* 61:310-21

Winterhalder, Bruce. 1980. 'Environmental analysis in human evolution and adaptation research.' *Human Ecology* 8:135-70

–. 1986. 'Diet choice, risk, and food sharing in a stochastic environment.' *Journal of Anthropological Archaeology* 5:369-92

– and Eric Alden Smith (eds.). 1981. *Hunter-gatherer Foraging Strategies.* Chicago: University of Chicago Press

Yengoyan, Aram. 1976. 'Structure, event and ecology in Aboriginal Australia.' In Nicolas Peterson (ed.), *Tribes and Boundaries in Australia.* Pp. 121-32. Canberra: Australian Institute of Aboriginal Studies, Social Anthropology Series No. 10

CHAPTER TWO

Environmental Units

Diana Alexander

The environmental classification scheme used in this volume is designed for application to the entire Interior Plateau and divides the region into units that are internally uniform in terms of culturally important resources. Within the study area, differences in climate, soils, vegetation, and fauna vary significantly with changes in elevation. These differences have been summarized in a biogeoclimatic classification system developed by Krajina (1965, 1969) and modified and refined by Mitchell and Green (1981). This system recognizes climate as the overall controlling environmental parameter, with temperature and precipitation patterns defining the basic unit – the zone. This system was adopted as the primary means of defining the environmental units used in this study, although some of these zones have been grouped together or divided into two units to more accurately reflect environmental differences perceived by native informants. Therefore, the study area has been divided into seven environmental units: (1) Alpine, (2) Montane Parkland, (3) Montane Forests, (4) Intermediate Grasslands, (5) Intermediate Lakes, (6) River Terraces, and (7) River Valleys (Figure 1). This scheme is derived from an earlier version devised for the study area (see Tyhurst, Chapter 7).

Each of the following descriptions of the environmental units includes a brief overview of the climate, physical geography, and seasonal abundance of important traditional food items. Species with little or no economic importance, such as insects, amphibians, reptiles, or many of the smaller species of birds, fish and mammals, are largely excluded from the discussion. Only common names of mammals, birds, fish, and plants are given in the text. The equivalent Latin names are listed in Appendices 1, 2, 3, and 4.

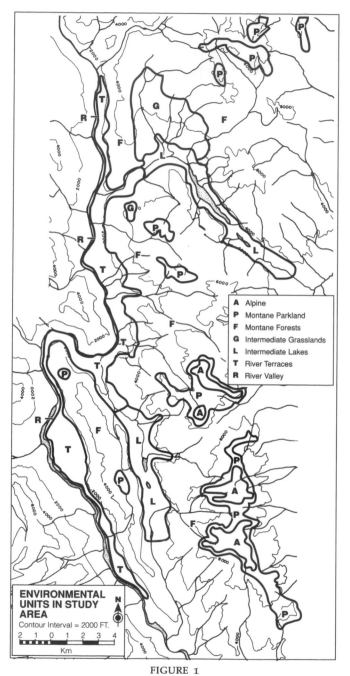

A	Alpine
P	Montane Parkland
F	Montane Forests
G	Intermediate Grasslands
L	Intermediate Lakes
T	River Terraces
R	River Valley

ENVIRONMENTAL
UNITS IN STUDY
AREA

Contour Interval = 2000 FT.

2 1 0 1 2 3 4

Km

FIGURE 1
Environmental units in the study area

ALPINE

The Alpine unit is the same as the Alpine Tundra biogeoclimatic zone (Mitchell and Green 1981). It occurs on mountain tops with rounded summits and gently sloping undissected uplands (Plate 2.1), usually at elevations above 1,980 m (6,500 ft) (Figure 2). In the Mid-Fraser River area, Alpine environments are found on Blustry Mountain, Cairn Peak, Moore Peak, and Chipuin Mountain (Figure 1; and Chapter 1, Figure 1). Small open areas also exist atop Mount Cole, Pavilion Mountain, Fountain Ridge, and at the headwaters of Sallus Creek, but, given that the treeline is rarely more than 200 m away, these areas are classified as Montane Parkland.

PLATE 2.1
The Alpine environment on Cairn Peak (part of Bald Mountain)

Severe winters, heavy snowfalls, and a short growing season are typical of the Alpine unit, with the mean monthly temperature below freezing for seven to eleven months of the year (Beil et al. 1976:51). Strong winds, especially at higher elevations, make the effective temperatures even colder and most (72-74 per cent) of the annual precipitation falls as snow. The cold climate, together with the low moisture and rugged terrain, hinders soil formation processes in the Alpine. Exposed bedrock and rock 'pavements' are common at the higher elevations, where frost action is accelerated and the wind prevents the

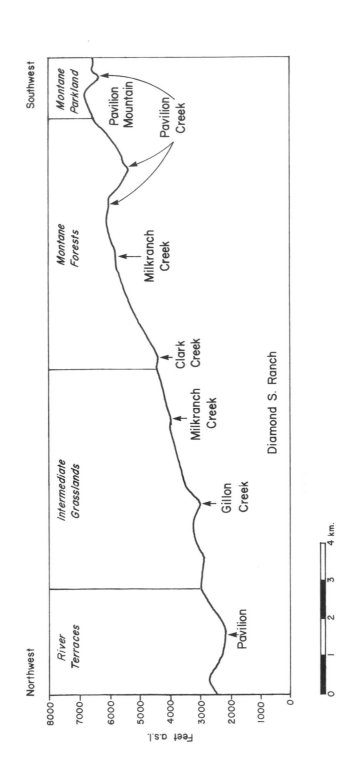

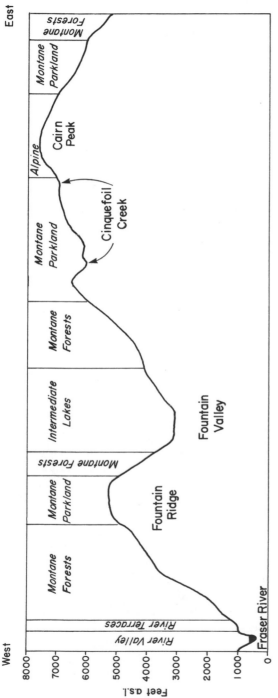

FIGURE 2

Cross-section of study area showing environmental units in northern half (top) and in southern half (bottom)

accumulation of insulating snow. During the summer months, the weather is generally sunny and warm during the day with a mean July temperature of 7-11°C (45-52°F) (Table 1). However, the evenings are generally cold, and frost, even snow, may occur any day of the year.

The Alpine unit is characterized by a predominance of low shrubs, grasses, and sedge species. Alpine meadows, with a rich and varied herbaceous flora, occur on flat or gently sloping topography where snow packs last longer and provide moister conditions than is the case in other areas. Although the unit is essentially treeless, krummholz (stunted) forms of a number of subalpine species do occur (Mitchell and Green 1981), including whitebark pine, subalpine fir, lodgepole pine, and Engelmann spruce.

Mammal species that were utilized by the Shuswap and Lillooet and are currently found in the Alpine include: deer, grizzly bear, black bear, wolf, coyote, wolverine, and long-tailed weasel (Cowan and Guiguet 1965). According to Cowan and Guiguet, yellow-bellied marmot do not occur in the study area; however, in 1988 I witnessed large colonies of yellow-bellied marmot living along subalpine roads on Pavilion Mountain. This animal may also have lived in other mountainous localities, though it is currently absent from Cairn Peak and Blustry Mountain (Tyhurst, Chapter 7). If the marmot were present in these subalpine localities in the past, they could also have occurred and been hunted in the Alpine. Because of the deep winter snows, the above mammal species are usually found in the Alpine only during the summer and early fall.

Although many of the bird species eaten by the Lillooet and Shuswap could have potentially used Alpine localities in the study area, only the white-tailed ptarmigan is known to occur in any abundance. Ptarmigan are not mentioned by name in the ethnographic literature, but I assume they are one of the 'grouse' hunted in the area (Teit 1900:249, 1906:227, 1909:782). Over twenty species of swans, geese, and ducks (see Appendix 2) are listed as either breeding in or migrating through the study area (Robbins et al. 1966:38-60). However, suitable wetland habitats are either very small or are lacking in the Alpine localities, and it is likely that very few, if any, of these birds were seen in this environmental unit. No lakes or streams in these Alpine localities support fish or shellfish populations.

The most important food plants found in this unit are spring beauty corms, avalanche lily bulbs, and dwarf mountain blueberry. Other significant Alpine plants traditionally used in the study area are listed in Table 2. The whitebark pine located in this environmental unit are too small to produce cones large enough for harvesting. Spring beauty appear as soon as the snows begin to melt in April and some are ready for harvesting as early as mid-May, although they are at their peak in early June. The avalanche lily is ready for gathering in July and August, while the dwarf mountain blueberries are ripe in August. The harvesting times of other plants are listed in Table 3.

In general, Alpine environments are extremely complex, with the topography, micro-climate, and vegetation changing significantly over short distances. Each mountain top is like an island, and these environmental parameters vary considerably from mountain to mountain.

Precontact Ungulate Populations in the Study Area

Ungulate species and population densities fluctuated on the Interior Plateau before and after the arrival of Euro-Canadians. According to oral traditions, deer were very numerous along the lower Thompson River until 1780, when they were supplanted by large populations of elk and bighorn sheep and smaller populations of mountain goat (Teit 1900:230). By 1850 the elk had disappeared, and mountain goat and bighorn sheep were scarce and restricted to the Spences Bridge area, while deer populations had increased. Teit supports this claim of larger elk populations with observations on scattered elk antlers in the higher mountains and plateaus of the Nicola and Thompson Rivers (1900:230). Similarly, elk were once abundant in the Shuswap territory, especially on the open hillsides around Kamloops (Smith 1900:401), but had become scarce as early as 1840 and were extinct in Shuswap territory by about 1860 (Teit 1909:513).

Teit attributes the decline in elk populations to the introduction of guns (1909:513); however, some of the changes in the ungulate populations appear to predate widespread use of guns in the area, and some species, such as deer, increased despite their use. An alternative explanation attributes the population shifts to minor changes in vegetation. The population of deer and moose, primarily browsers, fluctuated inversely with that of the grazers – elk, bighorn sheep, and mountain goats. The earlier population shifts may be correlated with a cool spell from AD 1800 to 1250, which would have promoted tree and shrub growth at the expense of grasslands (Lepofsky 1987:18) and grazing herds. After 1860, most natural grasslands were used for farming and ranching, effectively reducing the grazers' habitat. Similarly, Dave Low (Senior Wildlife Biologist, Ministry of the Environment, Kamloops: personal communication) proposes an increase in elk and bighorn sheep populations and a corresponding decline in deer between AD 1400 and 900 and again between 600 and 400 based on known changes in vegetation.

Deer and bighorn sheep are currently the most abundant ungulates

TABLE 1

Environmental summary according to environmental units

Environmental unit	Biogeoclimatic zone(s)	Elevation (m)	Temperature (°C)					Frost free days
			Mean annual	Jan. mean	July mean	Absolute maximum	Absolute minimum	
Alpine	Alpine Tundra	above 1980	-4 to -1	-18 to -7	7 to 11	21 to 28	-45 to -33	<25
Montane Parkland	Englemann Spruce-Subalpine Fir: parkland subzone	2,135-1,525	-2 to 2*	-18 to -7	9 to 14*	24 to 34*	-56 to -34.5	15-75*
Montane Forests	Englemann Spruce-Subalpine Fir, Interior Douglas-fir	1,980-610	1 to 9	-18 to -3	12 to 21	32 to 43	-56 to -32	50-200
Intermediate Grasslands	Interior Douglas-fir	1,370-915	4 to 9	-12 to -3	17 to 21	36 to 43	-46 to -32	75-200
Intermediate Lakes	Interior Douglas-fir	1,070-610	4 to 9	-12 to -3	17 to 21	36 to 43	-46 to -32	75-200
River Terraces	Ponderosa Pine-Bunchgrass	610-305	6 to 10	-8 to -3	18 to 22	38 to 44	-41 to -21	100-200
River Valley	Ponderosa Pine-Bunchgrass	below 610	6 to 10	-8 to -3	18 to 22	38 to 44	-41 to -21	100-200

Precipitation (cm)

Annual total	Annual snowfall	Snowfall as % of annual total	Driest month	Wettest month	Location	Environmental description
70-280	531-1,955	72-74	2.3-12.2	7.6-36.2	Blustry Mtn., Cairn Peak, Moore Peak, Chipuin Mtn.	alpine meadows; Krummholz trees
55-231*	353-1,486*	43-72	1.5-6.6	6.4-25.4	as above, plus: Pavilion Mtn., Mount Cole, Fountain Ridge, Sallus Creek Headwaters	parkland meadow; Krummholz trees; open forest: subalpine fir, Engelmann spruce, lodgepole pine, whitebark pine
36-183	76-1,016	21-72	1.3-6.6	5.1-25.4	all continuous canopy forests	closed forests: as above or Douglas-fir, lodgepole pine aspen, white pine, cottonwood, Rocky Mtn. maple
36-56	76-178	21-35	1.3-2.8	5.1-8.9	grasslands above and north of Pavilion, Sagebrush flats	grassland meadows surrounded by Douglas-fir forest
36-56	76-178	21-35	1.3-2.8	5.1-8.9	Upper Pavilion and Fountain Creek valleys	grassland meadows and Douglas-fir forest at edge of lakes and streams
19-36	50-152	19-42	0.7-1.5	2.9-5.1	Fraser River terraces >60m above river	grasslands; treeless sagebrush; open forest: ponderosa pine, deciduous trees along water courses
19-36	50-152	19-42	0.7-1.5	2.9-5.1	lands within 60m (vertical) of bank of Fraser River	as above

NOTES: *Figure estimated from lower half of range for Alpine Tundra and upper portion of range for Englemann-Spruce-Subalpine Fir zone. Figures for the Alpine Tundra and ESSF zone should be viewed only as rough approximations, as very little data is available on these zones. Information in figure derived from Mathewes (1978) and Turner (Chapter 8).

TABLE 2
Major traditional plant resources used in study area according to environmental unit

Alpine

Food plants	Non-food plants*
spring beauty: corms	pinegrass: plant
avalanche lily: corms	common horsetail: stem
tiger lily: bulbs	- - - - - - - - - - - - - - - - -
nodding onion: bulbs	Indian hellebore: root
balsamroot: roots, shoots	cow-parsnip: root
cow-parsnip: stems	Indian celery: leaves, seeds
Indian celery: leaves	yarrow: leaves, roots
fireweed: shoots	Pacific anemone: leaves, stems
dwarf mtn. blueberry: berries	

Montane Parkland: meadows

Food plants	Non-food plants
spring beauty**: corms	pinegrass: plant
avalanche lily: corms	common horsetail: stem
tiger lily: bulbs	- - - - - - - - - - - - - - - - -
balsamroot: roots, shoots	Indian hellebore: root
cow-parsnip: stems	cow-parsnip: root
Indian celery: leaves	Indian celery: leaves, seeds
fireweed: shoots	yarrow: leaves, root
dwarf mtn. blueberry: berries	Pacific anemone: leaves, stems
wild strawberry: berries	kinnikinnick: leaves
kinnikinnick: berries	wild strawberry: berries, plants
nodding onion: bulbs	

Montane Parkland: forest margins

Food plants	Non-food plants
black lichen: plant	subalpine fir: branches, pitch
whitebark pine: seeds	Engelmann spruce: roots, bark,
lodgepole pine: inner bark	wood
false Solomon's seal: shoots,	lodgepole pine: wood, pitch, bark
berries, rhizomes	pinegrass: plant
cow-parsnip: stems	black lichen: plant
kinnikinnick: berries	common horsetail: stem
soapberry: berries	- - - - - - - - - - - - - - - - -
dwarf mtn. blueberry: berries	common juniper: berries
black huckleberry: berries	*Indian hellebore*: roots

swamp gooseberry: berries wild
strawberry: berries
wild rose: hips
white-stemmed gooseberry:
   berries
blackcap: berries, shoots
thimbleberry: berries, shoots
oval-leaved blueberry: berries
wild raspberry: berries, shoots
fireweed: shoots

cow-parsnip: roots
yarrow: leaves, roots
black twinberry: stems
false box: branches
kinnikinnick: leaves
baneberry: plant
Pacific anemone: leaves, stems
wild rose: flowers, stems
swamp gooseberry: branches
blackcap: shoots
soapberry: berries
strawberry: berries, plants

Montane Forests: high elevation only

Food plants	Non-food plants
black lichen: plant	black lichen: plant
whitebark pine: seeds	*subalpine fir*: branches, pitch
tiger lily: bulbs	*Engelmann spruce*: roots,
dwarf mtn. blueberry: berries	bark, wood
black huckleberry: berries	- - - - - - - - - - - - - - - - -
oval-leaved blueberry: berries	Indian hellebore: root
swamp gooseberry: berries	*devil's club*: stems, roots
wild raspberry: berries, shoots	*black twinberry*: stems
thimbleberry: berries, shoots	*false box*: branches
	labrador tea: leaves
	swamp gooseberry: branches

Montane Forests: all elevations

Food plants	Non-food plants
lodgepole pine: inner bark	*lodgepole pine*: wood, pitch, bark
nodding onion: bulbs	*white pine*: bark
balsamroot: shoots, roots	*pinegrass*: plant
false Solomon's-seal: shoots,	Rocky Mtn. juniper: wood,
berries, rhizomes	berries, branches
cow-parsnip: stems	*Douglas-fir*: wood, boughs, pitch
Indian celery: leaves	Rocky Mtn. maple: wood,
fireweed: shoots	inner bark
soapberry: berries	Sitka alder: bark
kinnikinnick: berries	bitter cherry: bark
wild strawberry: berries	aspen: wood, bark powder
bitter cherry: berries	common horsetail: stem

(continued on next page)

TABLE 2 (continued)

wild rose: hips	– – – – – – – – – – – – – – – –
blackcap: berries, shoots	common juniper: berries
white-stemmed gooseberry:	*cow-parsnip*: roots
berries	Indian celery: leaves, seeds
	yarrow: leaves, roots
	kinnikinnick: leaves
	baneberry: plant
	Pacific anemone: leaves, stems
	wild rose: flowers, stems
	blackcap: shoots
	soapberry: berries
	wild strawberry: berries, plant

Montane Forests: low elevation only

Food plants	Non-food plants
Oregon-grape: berries	*red cedar*: roots, bark, branches,
saskatoon: berries	wood
choke cherry: berries	Rocky Mtn. juniper: wood,
	branches, berries
	Douglas-fir: wood, branches, pitch
	Rocky Mtn. maple: wood,
	inner bark
	Oregon-grape: inner bark
	mock-orange: wood, bark,
	flowers, leaves
	saskatoon: wood, branches
	Sitka willow: branches
	Pacific willow: wood, bark
	stinging nettle: stem fibres,
	plants
	– – – – – – – – – – – – – – – – –
	waxberry: berries

Intermediate Grasslands: watercourses

Food plants	Non-food plants
cottonwood: inner bark	paper birch: bark, wood, withes
false Solomon's-seal: shoots,	Rocky Mtn. maple: wood, bark
berries, rhizomes	Sitka alder: bark
cow-parsnip: stems	red-osier dogwood: branches
red-osier dogwood: berries, seeds	saskatoon: wood, branches
white-stemmed gooseberry:	bitter cherry: bark

berries
swamp gooseberry: berries
bitter cherry: berries
wild rose: hips
wild raspberry: berries, shoots
thimbleberry: berries, shoots
soapberry: berries
saskatoon: berries
blackcap: berries, shoots
Oregon-grape: berries

cottonwood: wood, bark,
  branches, buds
aspen: wood, bark powder
Sitka willow: branches, bark
Oregon-grape: inner bark
stinging nettle: stem fibres,
  plants
Pacific willow: wood, bark
common horsetail: stems
Rocky Mtn. juniper: wood,
  branches, pitch
Douglas-fir: wood, branches,
  pitch
pinegrass: plant

- - - - - - - - - - - - - - - - - -

black twinberry: stems
baneberry: plant
wild rose: flowers, stems
common juniper: berries
cow-parsnip: roots
waxberry: berries
Pacific anemone: leaves, stems

Intermediate Grasslands: meadows

Food plants	Non-food plants
nodding onion: bulbs	pinegrass: plant
balsamroot: shoots, roots	- - - - - - - - - - - - - - - - - -
spring beauty: corms	yarrow: leaves, roots
fireweed: shoots	kinnikinnick: leaves
wild strawberry: berries	wild strawberry: berries, plant
kinnikinnick: berries	

Intermediate Lakes: valley slopes

Food plants	Non-food plants
Ponderosa pine: seeds	*Rocky Mtn. juniper*: wood, berries, branches
nodding onion: bulbs	red cedar: roots, bark, branches, wood
mariposa lily: bulbs	Ponderosa pine: gum, needles, wood
balsamroot: shoots, roots	Douglas-fir: wood, branches,
desert parsley: roots	
false Solomon's-seal: shoots, berries, rhizomes	

(continued on next page)

TABLE 2 (continued)

fireweed: shoots	pitch
Oregon-grape: berries	bunchgrass: plant
soapberry: berries	pinegrass: plant
kinnikinnick: berries	big sagebrush: inner bark,
saskatoon: berries	branches
wild strawberry: berries	Oregon-grape: inner bark
choke cherry: berries	saskatoon: wood, branches
wild rose: hips	- - - - - - - - - - - - - - - - -
wild raspberry: berries, shoots	wild rose: flowers, stem
blackcap: berries, shoots	common juniper: berries
thimbleberry: berries, shoots	desert parsley: roots
Indian celery: leaves	yarrow: leaves, roots
	waxberry: berries
	kinnikinick: berries
	Pacific anemone: leaves, stems
	wild strawberry: berries, plant
	blackcap: shoots
	Indian celery: leaves, seeds

Intermediate Lakes: valley bottoms

Food plants	Non-food plants
cottonwood: inner bark	*cottonwood*: wood, bark, buds,
cottonwood mushrooms: plants	branches, resin, roots
red-osier dogwood: berries, seeds	aspen: wood, bark powder
white-stemmed gooseberry: berries	*Sitka willow*: branches, bark
swamp gooseberry: berries	*Pacific willow*: wood, bark
water parsnip: roots	rope willow: branches, bark
silverweed: roots	*Rocky Mtn. maple*: wood,
	bark
	Sitka alder: bark
	paper birch: bark, wood, withes
	red-osier dogwood: branches
	branchless horsetail: stems
	common horsetail: stems
	tule: stems
	reed canary grass: stems
	cattail: leaves, fluff
	stinging nettle: stem fibres,
	plants
	- - - - - - - - - - - - - - - - -
	wild mint: stems, leaves

River Valley: grasslands
River Terraces: grasslands

Food plants	Non-food plants
mariposa lily: bulbs	*big sagebrush*: inner bark,
desert parsley: roots	branches
prickly-pear cactus: stems	*bunchgrass*: plant
	- - - - - - - - - - - - - - - - -
	yarrow: leaves, roots
	desert parsley: roots

River Valley: water courses
River Terraces: water courses and forest margins

Food plants	Non-food plants
Ponderosa pine: seeds	Ponderosa pine: gum, needles,
cottonwood: inner bark	wood
cottonwood mushrooms: plants	cottonwood: wood, bark,
nodding onion: bulbs	branches, roots, resin, buds
mariposa lily: bulbs	aspen: wood, bark powder
desert parsley: roots	Sitka willow: branches
balsamroot: shoots, roots	Pacific willow: wood, bark
prickly-pear cactus: stems	*Rope willow*: branches, bark
Indian celery: leaves	Rocky Mtn. juniper: wood
cow-parsnip: stems	berries, boughs
fireweed: shoots	Rocky Mtn. maple: wood, inner
false Solomon's-seal: shoots,	bark
berries, rhizomes	Sitka alder: bark
Oregon-grape: berries	*paper birch*: bark, wood, withes
kinnikinnick: berries	bunchgrass: plant
saskatoon: berries	*Indian hemp*: stem
black hawthorn: berries	big sagebrush: inner bark,
choke cherry: berries	branches
wild rose: hips	*mock-orange*: wood, bark, flower,
soapberry: berries	leaves
wild strawberry: berries	*saskatoon*: berries
red-osier dogwood: berries, seeds	*black hawthorn*: wood, thorns
white-stemmed gooseberry:	*oceanspray*: wood

(continued on next page)

TABLE 2 (continued)

berries	cattail: leaves, fluff
swamp gooseberry: berries	tule: stems
bitter cherry: berries	branchless horsetail: stem
wild raspberry: berries, shoots	common horsetail: stems
blackcap: berries, shoots	Oregon-grape: inner bark
thimbleberry: berries, shoots	*red-osier dogwood*: branches
	stinging nettle: stem fibres, plants
	bitter cherry: berries
	- - - - - - - - - - - - - - - - - -
	wild rose: flowers, stems
	desert parsley: roots
	Indian celery: leaves, seeds
	yarrow: leaves roots
	kinnikinnick: leaves
	Pacific anemone: leaves, stems
	wild tobacco: leaves
	common juniper: berries
	waxberry: berries
	cow-parsnip: roots
	baneberry: plant
	blackcap: shoots
	swamp gooseberry: branches
	wild mint: stems, leaves
	soapberry: berries
	strawberry: berries, plant

NOTES: These lists are based on work by Turner (Chapter 8). Only plants of very high, high, or moderate significance are included in these lists.

*Non-food plants above dotted line were used in technology, i.e., in constructing tools, baskets, mats, structures, traps, canoes, fires, or pits. Plants below dotted line were used medicinally or to make a beverage.

**Italics indicate that this is the environment in which the species is most abundant, based on Turner's comments and the author's own observations.

in the study area, with 100 deer and 50 sheep present under normal winter snowfalls (Low, personal communication). In milder winters the deer move out of the area to more remote high elevation ranges and the population can drop to 75, while isolated severe winters can drive deer from the surrounding mountains and elevate the local population to a high of 600 (ibid.). The less mobile sheep population can increase to 175 in mild conditions and decline to 25 in harsh weather. A series of bad winters (which may occur every eighteen to twenty

TABLE 3

Harvesting time of major traditional food plants*

Alpine

	Mar.	Apr.	May	Jun.	Jul.	Aug.	Sep.	Oct.	Nov.–Feb.
Balsamroot shts.		xxXXXXXXXXxx							
Nodding onion		xxxXXXXXXXxxxxxxxxxxxxxx							
Cow-parsnip stms.		xxXXXXXXXXXxxx							
Balsamroot rts.		xxxxXXXXxxxxx			xxXXXXXxx				
Indian celery lvs.		..xxXXXXXXxx..							
Spring beauty crms.		..xxXXXXXXxxxxxxXXXxxxxx....							
Fireweed shts.		..xxXXXxx..							
Avalanche lily				xxxxxxXXXXXXxxx					
Tiger lily				xxxxxxXXXXXXXxxxxxx					
Dwf. mt. blueberry						xxXXXXxxx			

(continued on next page)

TABLE 3 (continued)

Montane Parkland – meadows

	Mar.	Apr.	May	Jun.	Jul.	Aug.	Sep.	Oct.	Nov.-Feb.
Balsamroot shts.		xxXXXXXXXxx							
Nodding onion		xxXXXXXXXxxxxxxxxxxxxx							
Cow-parsnip stms.		xxXXXXXXXXxxx							
Balsamroot rts.		xxxxXXXXxxxxx		xxXXXXXxx					
Indian celery lvs.		..xxXXXXXXxx..							
Spring beauty crms.		..xxXXXXXXxxxxxxXXXxxxxx....							
Firewood shts.		..xxXXXxx..							
Wild strawberries		xxxxxxxx							
Avalanche lily		xxxxxXXXXXXxx							
Tiger lily		xxxxxxXXXXXXXxxx xx							
Dwf. mt. blueberry		xxXXXXxxx							
Kinnikinnick fr.	....	...xxxxxxxxxxxxxxxxx............							

Montane Parkland – forest margins

	Mar.	Apr.	May	Jun.	Jul.	Aug.	Sep.	Oct.	Nov.-Feb.
F. Solomon's-seal		xxXXXXXxxxx							
L. pine inner bk.	xxxxXXXXXxxx								
Cow-parsnip stms.			xxXXXXXXXXxxx						
Fireweed shts.			..xxXXXXXXxx..						
Black lichen	............xxxxxxXXXXxxxxxxxxxxxxxxxxxxxxxxxxxxxxxxxxx.............								
Wild strawberries				xxxxxxxx					
Soapberry				xxxXXXXxxx					
Wild raspberry					xxxxxx				
Swamp gooseberry					..xxxx..				
Wild gooseberry					xxXXXxx				
Blackcap fr.					xXXXx				
Thimbleberry fr.					xxXXxx				
Oval-lvd. blueberry					xxxXXXXXxx				
Black huckleberry					xxxXXXXXxx				
Dwf. mt. blueberry						xxxXXXXxxx			
Wild rose fr.	..					xxxxxxxxxx............			
Kinnikinnick fr.	...					..xxxxxxxxxxxxx............			
Whiteb. pine sds.							xxXXXXXXXXxxx.........		

(continued on next page)

TABLE 3 (continued)

Montane Forests – high elevations

	Mar.	Apr.	May	Jun.	Jul.	Aug.	Sep.	Oct.	Nov.-Feb.
Black lichen	....	..xxxxxx	XXXXXxx	xxxxxxx	xxxxxxx	xxxxxxx	xxxxxxxx	xxxxxx..	....
Wild raspberry					xxxxxx				
Swamp gooseberry					.xxxx..				
Tiger lily				xxxxxxX	XXXXXXXx	xxxxx			
Thimbleberry fr.					xxXXxx				
Oval-lvd. blueberry					xxxXXX	XXxx			
Black huckleberry					xxxXXX	XXxx			
Dwf. mt. blueberry						xxxXXX	Xxxx		
Whiteb. pine sds.						xxXXXX	XXXXXxxx	......	

Montane Forests – low elevations

	Mar.	Apr.	May	Jun.	Jul.	Aug.	Sep.	Oct.	Nov.-Feb.
Saskatoon fr.				xxXXXX	Xx....				
Oregon-grape fr.					xxXXX	xxxxx			
Choke cherry fr.					xxXX	XXxx			

Montane Forests – all elevations

	Mar.	Apr.	May	Jun.	Jul.	Aug.	Sep.	Oct.	Nov.–Feb.
Nodding onion		xxXXXXxxx							
Indian celery lvs.		..xxXXXXXXxx..							
Balsamroot shts.		xxXXXXXXxx							
L. pine inner bk.		xxxxXXXXxxx							
F. Solomon's-seal			xxxXXXXXxxxx						
Balsamroot rts.			xxxXXXXxxxx			xxXXXXxx			
Cow-parsnip stms.			xxXXXXXXXxxx						
Fireweed shts.			..xxXXXXXXxx..						
Wild strawberries				xxxxxxx					
Soapberry				xxxXXXXxxx					
Wild gooseberry					xxXXXxx				
Blackcap fr.					xXXXx				
Bitter cherry fr.						xxxx			
Wild rose fr.	.:					xxxxxxxxxxx.........			
Kinnikinnick	.:					..xxxxxxxxxxxxxxxxx........			

(continued on next page)

TABLE 3 (continued)

Intermediate Grasslands – watercourses

	Mar.	Apr.	May	Jun.	Jul.	Aug.	Sep.	Oct.	Nov.-Feb.
F. Solomon's-seal	xxXXXXXxxxx								
Cottonwood in. bk.		..xXXXXx....							
Cow-parsnip stms.		xxXXXXXXxxx							
Saskatoon fr.				xxXXXXXXx....					
Soapberry				xxxXXXXxx					
Blackcap fr.					xXXXx				
Thimbleberry fr.					xxXXxx				
Wild raspberry					xxxxxx				
Swamp gooseberry					..xxxx..				
Wild gooseberry					xxxXXXxx				
Oregon-grape fr.					xxXXXxxxxx				
Bitter cherry fr.						xxxxx			
Wild rose fr.	..					xxxxxxxxxxxx..........			

Intermediate Grasslands – meadows

	Mar.	Apr.	May	Jun.	Jul.	Aug.	Sep.	Oct.	Nov.–Feb.
Balsamroot shts.	xxXXXXXXxx								
Nodding onion	xxXXXXxxx								
Balsamroot rts.		xxxxXXXXxxxxx							
Fireweed shts.		..xxXXXxx..							
Spring beauty crms.		..xxXXXxxxxxxxxxXXXxxxx...							
Wild strawberries				xxxxxxx					
Kinnikinnick fr.	....				...xxxxxxxxxxxxxxxxxxxxx...			

(continued on next page)

TABLE 3 (continued)

Intermediate Lakes – valley slopes

	Mar.	Apr.	May	Jun.	Jul.	Aug.	Sep.	Oct.	Nov.–Feb.
F. Solomon's-seal	xxXXXXXxxxx								
Mariposa lily	xxxXXXXXXXXXXXxxxxxxx								
Nodding onion		xxXXXxxx							
Balsamroot shts.		xxXXXXXXXXxx							
Indian celery lvs.		..xxXXXXXxx..							
Desert parsley rts.		..xxXXXXXxxxxx...							
Blackcap shoots			.xxx.						
Balsamroot rts.		xxxXXXXxxxxx				xxXXXXXxx			
Fireweed shts.			..xxXXXxx..						
Saskatoon fr.				xxXXXXXXx...					
Soapberry				xxxXXXXxx					
Blackcap fr.					xXXXx				
Wild raspberry					xxxxxx				
Thimbleberry fr.					xxXXxx				
Pond. pine seeds					xxxxxxxx				
Oregon-grape fr.					xxXXXxxxxxx				
Choke cherry fr.					xxXXXXxx				
Wild rose fr.	...					xxxxxxxxxx...			
Kinnikinnick fr.	...					...xxxxxxxxxxxxxxxx			

Intermediate Lakes – watercourses

	Mar.	Apr.	May	Jun.	Jul.	Aug.	Sep.	Oct.	Nov.–Feb.
Cottonwood in. bk.									
Silverweed		..xXXXXx....							
Water-parsnip		...xxxXXXXXxx..............				..xxXXXXx........			
Swamp gooseberry		..xxxXXXXxxxx....							
Red-os. dogwood fr.					..xxxx...				
Wild gooseberry					...xxxxxxx....				
Cottonwd. mushroom					xxxXXXxx		xxxXXXXXxxx		

(continued on next page)

TABLE 3 (continued)

River Terraces – forest margins and watercourses

River Valley

	Mar.	Apr.	May	Jun.	Jul.	Aug.	Sep.	Oct.	Nov.–Feb.
F. Solomon's-seal	xxXXXXXxxxx								
Mariposa lily	xxxxXXXXXXXXXXXxxxxxxx								
Nodding onion		xxXXXXxxx							
Balsamroot shts.		xxXXXXXXxx							
Prickly-pr. cactus	. . . . . . xx XXXXXXX xxxxxxxxxxxxxxxxxxxxxxxxx								
Desert parsley rts.		. . . xxXXXXXxxxxx							
Indian celery lvs.		. . xxXXXXXXxx . .							
Cow-parsnip stms.		xxXXXXXXxxx							
Blackcap shts.			. . xxx . .						
Balsamroot rts.		xxxxXXXXxxxxx				xxXXXXxx			
Fireweed shts.			. .xxXXXxx. .						
Saskatoon fr.				xxXXXXXXx					
Soapberry					xxXXXXXxxx				
Thimbleberry fr.					xxXXxx				
Pond. pine seeds					xxxxxxxx				
Black hawthorn fr.					xxxxxxx				
Wild gooseberry					xxxXXXxx				
Red-os. dogwood fr.					. . . xxxxxxx . . .				
Oregon-grape fr.					xxXXXxxxxxx				

Blackcap fr.

Bitter cherry fr.

Choke cherry fr.

Wild rose fr.   : :

Kinnikinnick fr.   : :

Cottonwd. mushroom

| xXXXx
| xxxx
| xxxXXXXxx
| xxxxxxxxxx . . . .
| . . xxxxxxxxxxxxxxxxxxxxx . . . .
| xxxXXXXXxxx

River Terraces – open

	Mar.	Apr.	May	Jun.	Jul.	Aug.	Sep.	Oct.	Nov.-Feb.

Mariposa lily   xxxxXXXXXXXXXxxxxxx

Prickly-pr. cactus   . . . . xx XXXXXXXxxxxxxxxxxxxxxxxxxxxxxxxxxx . . . .

Desert parsley rts.   . . . xxXXXXXxxxxx . . .

NOTES: These lists are based on work by Turner (Chapter 8). Only plants of very high, high, or moderate significance are included in these lists.

*The symbols used to denote harvesting times are as follows:

. . . .   Harvesting is casual or infrequent; probably does not have a major impact on movement patterns or resource users

xxxx   Harvesting is more intensive; may influence movement patterns of resource users to some extent

XXXX   Harvesting is intensive; probably does influence movement patterns of resource users

years) may eliminate the bighorn sheep herds and reduce deer to a population as low as twenty-five in the study area. The archaeological record is probably not sensitive enough to detect these short-term fluctuations in ungulate populations, which may explain why deer are always more abundant than are bighorn sheep in the local faunal assemblages (Langemann 1987: Tables 30b,c). Interestingly, deer and bighorn sheep are also the only ungulates to appear in any abundance in archaeological assemblages (Langemann 1987:162-90; Kusmer 1987), suggesting that they have been the dominant ungulate species in the study area for at least the last 4,000 years.

Bighorn sheep and deer generally move into the mountains between May and October, looking for better food, and then return to the valleys in the winter to avoid the deep snow. Consequently, in the summer, 90-95 per cent of the deer are found in the Montane Parkland, while during the winter, they congregate in groups of three to thirty in the Intermediate Grasslands above Pavilion and in some lower elevation draws (Low, personal communication). In February and March, a few deer may frequent the River Terraces, but the highest concentrations are found along the north side of Pavilion Valley in high draws with mature Douglas-fir and deciduous trees (ibid.).

Bighorn sheep have been reintroduced in the study area near Pavilion Creek, and, during the summer of 1988, I saw at least forty from this herd (females with young) frequenting the slopes of the Fraser River Valley. The males generally remain in the more open portions of the Montane Forests (Low, personal communication). Few open high-altitude environments in the Pavilion area are available to them for what would typically be their summer range, possibly explaining their presence in wintering grounds during the summer (Cowan and Guiguet 1965:395). This evidence suggests that any pre-contact populations of bighorn sheep in the Pavilion area may also have spent summers on their wintering grounds. On the other hand, bighorn sheep appear to mostly forage at the edge of cultivated and irrigated pastures and fields, and their foraging pattern may have been altered by agricultural practices. In the Fountain area, any bighorn sheep would have had access to large Alpine environments for summer range and may have followed a different seasonal pattern.

Elk are not currently found in the study area (Cowan and Guiguet 1965:357-62), but they were abundant in other surrounding areas in the past (see above) and a herd of seventy-five now frequent the adjoining Hat Creek Valley (Low, personal communication). Therefore, a few elk may have been present in the Mid-Fraser area at one time. However, suitable habitat, especially for winter foraging, is uncommon along the Fraser River (Environment Canada n.d.), and it is unlikely that the study area ever had the capability to support large populations of elk.

Mountain goats are uncommon in the Mid-Fraser River and are largely restricted to the west side of the Fraser River (Cowan and Guiguet 1965:388-93). They require wintering areas at or above the treeline, with rocky terrain and south or west facing slopes where snow conditions are not too severe (Cowan and Guiguet 1965:388-93). Most high elevation localities in the study area are not rugged enough for mountain goats. Consequently, they are currently restricted to Fountain Ridge (Tyhurst, Chapter 7) and the cliffs above Pavilion Lake, where Low (personal communication) estimates that six to ten goats may occasionally be found. Given the habitat restrictions and current low numbers, it seems unlikely that large populations of mountain goat used the study area in the past and, if present at all, were restricted to the more rugged areas near Fountain Ridge and Pavilion Lake.

Moose were absent from the Interior Plateau prior to 1920 (Cowan and Guiguet 1965:378), and a sharp decline in the deer population in 1916-18 (Low, personal communication) may have allowed for their expansion. Even now moose are uncommon in the study area due to lack of suitable habitat (ibid), and they were probably absent during the last 4,000 years.

Caribou once occupied the southern parts of the Shuswap territory (Teit 1909:513) and the extreme northeast corner of the Lillooet territory (Teit 1906:225), where they no longer exist, raising the possibility that they were once present in the study area. However, caribou inhabit alpine environments (Cowan and Guiguet 1965:381-5), which are restricted in the study area except for the Cairn Peak-Blustry Mountain locality, and even this locality could only have supported a very small caribou population. Moreover, caribou is the only ungulate not present in local archaeological assemblages (Langemann 1987; Kusmer 1987). Given the lack of habitat and archaeological evidence, caribou were probably as absent in the recent past as they are today.

In summary, deer, bighorn sheep, mountain goats, and moose are the only ungulate species currently using the study area. Prior to 1920, moose were absent while elk and caribou may have been present prehistorically. However, given the available environmental and archaeological information, it seems unlikely that large numbers of elk or mountain goat ever existed in the study area or that caribou have been present in the recent past. Unlike mountain goats, who stay above treeline all year, deer, bighorn sheep, and elk avoided montane environments during the heavy winter snows. Therefore, few, if any, ungulates were available for capture in the Alpine except in the summer. In general, the Alpine areas in the study area are considered to have moderate limitations on the production of ungulates, except for Moore Peak, which has slight limitations (Environment Canada n.d.).

MONTANE PARKLAND

The Montane Parkland unit is equivalent to the Parkland subzone of the Engelmann Spruce-Subalpine Fir zone (Mitchell and Green 1981). This transitional subzone between the alpine meadows and the sub-alpine forests is characterized by a mosaic of parkland meadows, krummholz tree clumps, and very open stands of subalpine tree species (Plate 2.2). Trees only occur in the Parkland where the snow cover is particularly heavy, providing an increase in the moisture supply during the growing season (Beil et al. 1976:52). Tree species found in this unit include whitebark pine, Engelmann spruce, sub-alpine fir, and lodgepole pine.

In the study area, Montane Parkland may be found below the Alpine on Blustry Mountain, Cairn Peak, Moore Peak, Chipuin Mountain, on top of Mount Cole, Pavilion Mountain, Fountain Ridge, and at the headwaters of Sallus Creek (Figure 1; Chapter 1, Figure 1). Elevations in these Parkland localities range from about 1,525 to 2,135 m (5,000 to 7,000 ft) (Figure 2). For the purpose of this study, the Montane Park-land includes all open meadows within 200 m of the treeline and forest-ed areas within 50 m of the treeline. Although somewhat milder, the climate of this unit is very similar to that of the Alpine unit (Table 1), with severe winters, heavy snowfalls, and generally warm but un-predictable weather during the summer. The most notable difference is the reduction in the winds due to the shelter provided by the trees and surrounding slopes.

Mammals present in both the Alpine and Montane Parkland include: deer, bighorn sheep, mountain goat, grizzly bear, black bear, and yellow-bellied marmot, which were hunted for food and skins, and wolf, coy-ote, wolverine, and long-tailed weasel, which were captured solely for their pelts. In addition to the Alpine species, the following animals were also utilized by the Shuswap and Lillooet and may be found in the Montane Parkland: (1) food species: snowshoe hair, porcupine, red squirrel, and northern flying squirrel, (2) non-food species: cougar, lynx, bobcat, red fox, marten, mink, fisher, and short-tailed weasel. The Mon-tane Parkland is especially important as summer range for deer, who typically use the fringes of open grassy areas, particularly those which offer nearby escape terrain in the form of bluffs and broken slopes. As discussed in the Alpine section on ungulates, bighorn sheep and elk may once have been present in low numbers.

PLATE 2.2

A traditional basecamp (in the midground where the treeline begins) in a valley of the Montane Parkland on Pavilion Mountain. Note the flowering spring beauty creating a white carpet on the grass in the midground. Montane Forest covers the hills in the background.

Although most of the smaller animals and mountain goats winter in the Montane Parkland, the following mammals move to lower elevations to avoid the winter snows: deer, bighorn sheep, elk (in the past), black bear, grizzly bear, wolf, coyote, wolverine, cougar, bobcat, lynx, and marten. The most abundant food species were probably deer, snowshoe hare, and squirrels. In general, these animals are more abundant in the Parkland than in the Alpine due to the shelter and cover provided by the Parkland trees and the lusher grasses and shrubs used as food. Few bears are found in the study area since it is marginal bear habitat (Low, personal communication).

As with the Alpine unit, there are no lakes or streams in the Montane Parkland that can support fish or shellfish populations or more than the occasional wetland bird (see Appendix 2 for a list of swan, geese, ducks, and other wetland birds). Ruffed grouse occur in the unit year round, blue grouse are present in the winter, and spruce grouse are present all year but are scarce (Mathewes 1978:90-1; Robbins et al. 1966:84).

Most of the food plants found in the Alpine also occur in the more open portions of the Montane Parkland (Table 2) but generally in greater numbers due to the greater moisture and milder climatic conditions. Some species infrequently found in the Alpine but relatively common in the Montane Parkland include tiger lily, nodding onion, balsamroot, cow-parsnip, and Indian celery. Other important food plants are found in the open forests at the edge of the meadows, including the nutlets from the whitebark pine, soapberries, and a variety of other plants with berries. Food plants found in the Montane Parkland are suitable for harvesting between mid-May and early November (Table 3). Each Montane Parkland locality in the study area is unique in terms of the quantity and variety of plant and animal species present.

MONTANE FORESTS

The Montane Forests unit includes all continuous canopy forests in both the Engelmann Spruce-Subalpine Fir (ESSF) and the Interior Douglas Fir (IDF) zones (Mitchell and Green 1981). The Montane Forests are located below the Montane Parkland at elevations ranging from approximately 1980 to 610 m (6,500 to 2,000 ft) (Figure 2). More than half of the study area is covered by Montane Forests (Figure 1).

The most frequently occurring tree species in the higher ESSF zone are subalpine fir, Engelmann spruce, and lodgepole pine, with whitebark pine occurring on sunny, dry slopes. At middle elevations, ranging from 915 to 1,220 m (3,000 to 4,000 ft), the ESSF zone gives way to the IDF zone, with Douglas-fir as the dominant climax species. Other common tree species in the IDF zone include lodgepole pine, ponderosa pine, western white pine, and grand fir. In wetter areas, the following deciduous species are common: aspen, cottonwood, Douglas maple, paper birch and scrub birch (Mitchell and Green 1981). Western red cedar and Rocky Mountain juniper, important tree species traditionally used in native technology, are found in low frequencies at lower elevations, with the red cedar seemingly restricted to the Fountain Creek Valley (Turner, Chapter 8). The generally well-developed herb layer of the Montane Forests is dominated by pinegrass, with bunchgrass more common at lower elevations.

The Montane Forests are warmer and drier than the Montane Parkland unit. The range of temperature and precipitation levels (Table 1) for the forests is large, since this environment is found at elevations as much as 1,370 m (4,500 ft) apart. In general, precipitation decreases and temperature increases as the elevation drops, resulting in less snow and a longer growing season. The mean monthly temperature is below 0°C for as much as six months at higher elevations and as little as two months at lower elevations (Beil et al. 1976:51-3). The summers are generally warm and dry, with the mean July temperature ranging from 12 to 21°C (54 to 70°F) (Mathewes 1978:74).

All of the mammal species noted as occurring in the Montane Parkland are also present in the Montane Forests, with the exception of the mountain goat. In fact, with the exception of mountain goats, all of the species listed in Table 4 may occur in all of the low and mid-elevation environmental units, with the abundance of any particular species varying according to habitat and season. For example, deer use all habitats and can potentially be found in low numbers in any habitat at any time of the year, but their preference for forest margins and parklands makes them most abundant in these habitats. Within these habitats, their numbers are highest at upper elevations in summer and lower elevations in winter. In the following descriptions of the Montane Forests and other low and mid-elevation environments, discussions are limited to the most abundant *food* species in any particular habitat.

The highest frequencies of squirrels, porcupine, beaver, and moose in the Montane Forests can be expected in the more heavily forested sections, with beaver and moose concentrated in wetlands. The highest frequencies of snowshoe hare, yellow-bellied marmot, deer, bear, and elk (in the past) are found at the forest margins. The deer, moose, and elk (in the past) congregate at higher elevations in summer and lower elevations in the winter. Bear are at higher elevations in the early summer and late fall, travelling to lower elevations during late summer

TABLE 4
Mammal species traditionally utilized

Mammals hunted for food and skins

Mammals which move seasonally

Species	Preferred habitat			
	1	2	3	4
Deer		X		
Bighorn sheep	X			
Mountain goat	X			
Moose*			X	X
Elk*		X		
Black bear	X	X	X	
Grizzly bear	X	X	X	

Sedentary Mammals

Species	Preferred habitat			
	1	2	3	4
Snowshoe hare		X	X	
Yellow-bellied marmot	X	X		
Beaver			X	X
Porcupine			X	
Red squirrel			X	
Northern flying squirrel			X	

Mammals hunted primarily for skins (rarely eaten)

Mammals which move seasonally

Species	Preferred habitat			
	1	2	3	4
Cougar		X	X	
Lynx		X	X	
Bobcat*		X	X	
Wolf	X	X	X	
Coyote	X	X	X	
Red fox	X	X	X	
Wolverine			X	
Marten			X	

Sedentary mammals

Species	Preferred habitat			
	1	2	3	4
Mink				X
Muskrat				X
Fisher			X	
Long-t. weasel	X	X	X	X
Short-t. weasel	X	X	X	X

Preferred habitat: (1) meadows
(2) parkland, forest margins
(3) forests
(4) wetlands

NOTES: *Moose are present in the study area now but are probably recent migrants, while elk are absent now but were possibly present in the past (see this chapter for explanation). Bobcat may have recently spread into the study area (Banfield 1974:354).

and early fall. The bear populations are not high in the study area, with generally only one male for each stream drainage.

This habitat is generally unsuitable for wetland birds (see Appendix 2 for list of bird species present) due to a scarcity of wetlands. Ruffed grouse are common in all seasons and at all elevations, while spruce grouse may be found occasionally at higher elevations and blue grouse only in spring, summer, and fall (Mathewes 1978:90-1). Grouse prefer forest margins and are rare in closed canopy forests. No lakes or streams in the Montane Forests contain fish or shellfish.

Some of the most important food plants found in the Montane Forests are black lichen and the inner bark of lodgepole pine (Table 2). The more open forests and forest edges contain a wide variety of plants with berries, including soapberry, wild strawberry, blackcap, and white-stemmed gooseberry. Higher elevations also have black huckleberry, oval-leaved blueberry, wild raspberry, and thimbleberry, with oregon-grape, choke cherry, and saskatoon at lower elevations. Other important food plants found in the Montane Forests include tiger lily, false Solomon's-seal, cow-parsnip, Indian celery, and fireweed. Wild onions are abundant in the open forests. Many of the shoots and roots of the above listed plants were harvested between late March and June, while most berries were ripe between June and August (Table 3).

An old burn on the western slope of Fountain Ridge is dominated by saskatoon berries in the shrub stratum (Mathewes 1978:77-8), suggesting that burns would have been an important micro-environment to native populations. Other plants traditionally used by local Indians are found in this burn, including: choke cherry, bitter cherry, strawberry, Rocky Mountain juniper, wild rose, Rocky Mountain maple, mock-orange, yarrow, and Pacific anemone. Ungulates, such as deer, are also attracted to these old burns before the climax forest reestablishes itself.

INTERMEDIATE GRASSLANDS

The Intermediate Grasslands unit is found within the Interior Douglas Fir zone at elevations between 915 and 1,370 m (3,000 and 4,500 ft) (Figure 2). It consists of open grasslands, which are now used primarily for pasture or the growing of hay (Plate 2.3). The terrain is generally flat or gently sloping toward the stream valleys, with steep rolling slopes at the edges near the mountains. In the study area, such environments may be found on the flats north and above Pavilion and on Sagebrush Flats (Figure 1; Chapter 1, Figure 1). Another Intermediate Grassland environment exists to the east of the study area in the Hat Creek Valley.

These localities existed as mostly open grasslands prior to the introduction of farming and ranching in the area (DP). Since then the open land has been increased a little (DP) and new species of grasses have been introduced by Euro-Canadians (Mathewes 1978:77). Streams are typically enclosed in deciduous or mixed forests with dense underbrush. Deciduous species common to the stream courses and meadow edges include: aspen, cottonwood, Douglas maple, paper birch, and scrub birch. In general, the winters are cool and snowy and the summers warm and dry, with temperature and precipitation levels equivalent to those found at the lower elevations in the Montane Forest unit (Table 1).

Most of the mammals using the Intermediate Grasslands would have been concentrated at the forest margins and along the stream courses (Table 4). Food species that would have been relatively abundant, especially along the streams and forest margins, include: snowshoe hare, beaver, squirrels, bears, deer, and elk (in the past). The terrain is probably not rugged enough to sustain many yellow-bellied marmots or bighorn sheep. Animals that move into higher elevations during the summer, such as deer, bighorn sheep, and elk, were probably most abundant in the Grasslands in the spring and late fall as they moved between the Montane Parkland and the River Terraces. Deer often prefer to spend winters near the borders of Montane Forests and Intermediate Grasslands.

No fish or shellfish are present in this unit and wetland birds

PLATE 2.3

This Intermediate Grassland environment at Gillon Creek, Pavilion, was once used for the procurement of spring beauty, according to the late Sam Mitchell. The creek runs through the line of trees in the midground of this photograph. Wild gooseberry, wild raspberry, cow-parsnip, wild strawberry, aspen, alder, wild rose, yarrow, Pacific anemone, and stinging nettle can be found along the creek edges.

(Appendix 2) are infrequent due to a scarcity of suitable habitat. Ruffed grouse are common all year round and blue grouse are present in the spring, summer, and fall. Sharp-tailed grouse are no longer present but have been identified in an archaeological assemblage (Langemann 1987:134-41), suggesting that they may have been present in the past.

The forested areas along the watercourses would have provided a good environment for some of the food plants that prefer damper conditions, such as false Solomon's-seal, cow-parsnip, and red-osier dogwood (Table 2). A variety of plants with berries would also have been present, though perhaps not in large quantities. Some of the most important food resources in the surrounding meadows would probably have been spring beauty, balsamroot, nodding onion, fireweed, and strawberry. Spring beauty and balsamroot are now very abundant and their roots and corms would have been primarily harvested in late May-early June and possibly again in August (Table 3). The berry plants would have been primarily available in June, July, and early

August, while the shoots and stems of balsamroot, false Solomon's-seal, and cow-parsnip were ready between March and May.

The Intermediate Lakes environmental units include land adjacent to all the mid-altitude (less than 1,070 m or 3,500 ft) lakes and the adjacent reaches of their outlet and inlet streams (Plate 2.4). These lands are within the Interior Douglas Fir zone and include some of the more open portions of this zone. Within the study area, this environmental unit can be found along the upper reaches of Pavilion Creek and Fountain Creek valleys. Both valleys are narrow and steep-sided, with forested slopes (Figure 1; Chapter 1, Figure 1).

PLATE 2.4

Intermediate Lakes environment surrounding Cinquefoil Lake in Fountain Valley. The lake is named for the common silverweed (cinquefoil), a plant with edible roots; however, a preliminary survey of the lakeshore by N. Turner revealed no indication of the plant which has probably been severly reduced in recent years by cattle. Visible in the foreground is a dense patch of cattail, important for mat-making. Also present are tule, mint, saskatoons, wild gooseberries, blackcaps, wild raspberries, kinnikinnick, and soapberries. In mid-July, these berries were not ripe at the lake, but were fully ripe or past ripening at lower elevations along the Fraser River.

The largest lakes in the area are Pavilion and Kwotlenemo (Fountain), which, though artificially enlarged, have lengths of only 5.7 km and 0.4 km, respectively. The water levels in the lakes and rivers fluctuate both seasonally and yearly, with the highest levels occurring during the spring run-off, generally in May (DP). The magnitude of this spring freshet is dependent on the size of the winter snow pack at higher elevations. Yearly and long range oscillations in precipitation are the result of variations in this snow pack. Lake levels have dropped noticeably over the last fifty years, which local informants attribute to smaller snow packs as well as to the demands of increased agriculture and irrigation.

Cool winters and warm, dry summers are typical in this environment, with temperature and precipitation figures similar to those of the Intermediate Grasslands and lower Montane Forests (Table 1). The dominant tree species in this area is Douglas-fir. Many deciduous trees also flourish in the moist conditions along the lakes and streams, with the most common species including cottonwood, aspen, maple, and alder.

These areas have only moderate restrictions on deer, which are relatively abundant in this area in the spring, late fall, and winter. Bighorn sheep and elk may have been present in small numbers in the past. Bears, snowshoe hare, yellow-bellied marmot, porcupine, and squirrels were probably all relatively common in the drier environments. Species preferring a wetland habitat, such as beaver, mink, and muskrat, are also relatively common.

The lakes contain large numbers of trout, which spawn in the inlet and outlet streams in the latter half of May (DP). It seems unlikely that the trout reached most of these lakes on their own, since all of the outlet streams, except Cinquefoil, have a steep precipice between them and the Fraser River. Since the local Indians maintain that trout were present in some of these lakes prior to Euro-Canadian contact, the Indians probably stocked the lakes themselves, a practice discussed by Teit (1900:348). As far as I can determine, except for Dolly Varden and squawfish in Cinquefoil Lake, and possibly squawfish at the head of Fountain Creek (Kennedy and Bouchard, Chapter 6), there are no shellfish nor any fish species other than trout in these lakes.

Grouse are relatively common in this environmental unit. Ruffed grouse are found all year, blue grouse are present in the spring, summer, and fall, and sharp-tailed grouse may have been present in the past. Wetland birds are more numerous here than anywhere else in the study area, but even these lakes generally do not support large populations of wetland birds nor do they attract many migrating waterfowl. The largest lake, Pavilion, has severe limitations for waterfowl

due to adverse topography, deep water, and reduced marsh edge
(Mathewes 1978:85). Other lakes have slightly better conditions. For
example, Mathewes reports seeing approximately seventy-five ducks,
mostly Barrow's Goldeneye, on Chilhil Lake in mid-May (1978:85).

The Intermediate Lakes unit provides the best wetland environment
in the study area. Some important wetland plant food species would
be most abundant in these localities, such as cottonwood mushrooms,
water parsnip, silverweed, and gooseberries (Table 2). Cattails, tule,
reed canary grass, and willows, important to the material technology,
were also most abundant in this environment. The drier and more
open slopes above the lakes were important locations for collecting
soapberry, saskatoon, nodding onion, balsamroot, blackcap, and
oregon-grape, the berries being especially abundant in old burns.
Many of the shoots and roots of food plants would have been available for harvest between March and May, the berries between June and
July, the cattails and tule in August, and the mushrooms in October
(Table 3).

RIVER TERRACES

The River Terraces unit includes all terraces along the Fraser River
Valley at elevations between ca. 300 and 600 m (1,000 and 2,000 ft)
(Figure 2). In the study area, these terraces are in the Ponderosa Pine-
Bunchgrass zone (Green and Mitchell 1981) and below the Montane
Forests unit (Plate 2.5). By definition, the River Terraces unit does not
include lands between the bank of the Fraser River and elevations 60
m (200 ft) above the river (Figure 1). The terraces in this unit are gent-
ly sloping, long, broad, and well-defined.

This zone is the driest in the province and contains the hottest
summer temperatures (Table 1). The mean monthly temperature is below freezing only two to four months of the year (Beil et al. 1976:54).
Ponderosa pine is the dominant tree species in this zone. Open, parkland stands of ponderosa pine are found on the lower slopes and drier
valley bottoms. Wetter and more shaded locations, at the edge of
streams and rivers, may also contain Douglas-fir, cottonwood, aspen,
and birch. On finer soils, trees are often absent, and the predominant
vegetation consists of bluebunch wheat grass, antelopebush, and, in
more heavily grazed areas, sagebrush (Beil et al. 1976:54).

This dry zone does not support significant numbers of deer, primarily because of the thin vegetative cover, though there is some
limited winter, spring, and early summer use of the area (DP). A herd
of bighorn sheep currently spends the year in the lower portion of
the Pavilion Creek Valley and along the margin of the Fraser River

PLATE 2.5

River Terrace (Fountain Flats) and River Valley environments at the mouth of Fountain Creek. The ravine containing Fountain Creek is at the bottom of the photograph. Note the steep sides of the terrace edges and mountains along the Fraser River. Montane Forest covers the slopes in the background.

Valley. They appear to forage mostly at the edge of cultivated and irrigated pastures and fields, raising the question of whether the bighorn sheep could have survived in this locality without human intervention. However, wild grasses were more abundant in the area prior to heavy grazing pressure on the lands by cattle and horses since the late 1800s (Tisdale 1947; Brayshaw 1970; Anderson 1973), and, prehistorically, they could have subsisted by moving into Montane Parkland habitats during the summer. In general, bighorn sheep, like deer (Tyhurst, Chapter 7), may have been more seasonally plentiful at lower elevations in the past. Elk, with similar dietary preferences, may also have been present during the winter.

Given the hot, dry climate of this unit and the scarcity of streams and springs, it seems unlikely that moose or beaver were ever common on the River Terraces. Bears, snowshoe hare, yellow-bellied marmot, and squirrels are relatively common, and porcupine are expected to be in their highest densities in the open pine forests at the edge of the terraces. Trout occur in low numbers at the lower ends of Pavilion and Fountain creeks. None of the other creeks in the area can support fish populations due to winter freeze-up and/or low summer-fall flow. No other fish species or shellfish are known to occur in this unit. Ruffed grouse occur all year in the wetter stream valleys, blue grouse are present in the spring and summer, and sharp-tailed grouse may have been present in the past. No suitable habitats for wetland birds are available in the unit.

For the most part, the River Terraces are covered with grasses and sagebrush. This environment supports few food plants except for Mariposa lily, cactus, and desert parsley (Table 2). However, a variety of food plants is available at the edge of the forests and in the wet stream valleys that dissect the terraces, with balsamroot and saskatoon being the most important. Many of the shoots, roots, and leaves collected from the River Terraces are available in the spring between March and May. During the summer (June-August) most of the berries ripen, and in October the mushrooms are ready for harvesting (Table 3).

RIVER VALLEY

The River Valley unit consists of a narrow stretch of land along the bank of the Fraser River, and, by definition, the unit is restricted to lands less than 60 m (200 ft) above the river (Figures 1-2). In the study area, the Fraser River Valley is very steep and rugged with little level ground (Plate 2.5). Only near Lillooet does the valley broaden and produce low terraces in the River Valley unit. Like the River Terraces unit, this unit is within the Ponderosa Pine-Bunchgrass biogeoclimatic zone, and, thus, the vegetation and climate are the same (Table 1). The climate is dry, windy, cold in the winter, and hot in the summer. The dominant vegetation is sagebrush and grasses with scattered ponderosa pine. Deciduous trees and brush are present in the wetter stream valleys and where springs emerge along the river bank.

Some of the large mammals, such as bears, deer, bighorn sheep, and elk (in the past), use the river as a travel corridor and a source of drinking water, as evidenced by the many game trails. Bears are most likely to be found in this unit in the summer and early fall when the salmon spawn, while ungulates are most likely to be found in the winter and spring. Smaller mammals, such as snowshoe hare, yellow-bellied marmot, porcupine, and squirrels, occur may be expected in low numbers in the wetter, treed localities. Ruffed grouse are common in these wetter localities all year, blue grouse are present in the spring and summer, and sharp-tailed grouse may have been present in the past. D. Low (personal communication) estimates that as many as 800 grouse may be found in the entire study area.

Most plant species found on the River Terraces are also found in the River Valley (Table 2), although few places along the river have the moist conditions needed to support the vegetation typically found along the creeks in the River Terraces unit. Notable exceptions are found at the mouth of major creeks such as Pavilion, Fountain, and Sallus (Chapter 1, Figure 1).

Freshwater mussels do not appear to be abundant in the study area, although Turner (personal communication) reports significant beds in Seton Lake. Three species may be present in the Fraser River: *Margaritifera falcata*, *Anodonta kennerlyi*, and *Anodonta nuttalliona* (Langemann 1987:121-7). Although sometimes abundant at archaeological sites near Kamloops (Smith 1900:408), mussel shells occur only in low numbers at River Terrace sites in the study area (Langemann 1987:121-7). This evidence suggest that mussels are either rare or hard to gather because of the steep, narrow valley walls typical of most of the study area.

The primary resource of this unit is salmon, which pass up the Fraser River between May and September on their way to spawning grounds further north. Four species of salmon use the river: sockeye, spring, pink, and coho (Table 5). The most abundant species is sockeye, which runs between early June and September, and is at its peak in July and August. Their population fluctuates in four-year cycles, with as much as a hundred-fold difference between the highest and lowest years (Kew, Chapter 4). Large portions of this run may be diverted to Seton Creek if low water levels block the runs at Six Mile Falls (ibid). Spring, the largest species, run from April to August, with the main run in July and August. Pink spawn between August and October (in two-year cycles) but do not now generally go above the falls at Six Mile (Kew, Chapter 4; Kennedy and Bouchard, Chapter 6). Their numbers have dropped dramatically since 1915, with the Seton watershed runs dropping from about 200,000 to 60,000 (Mathewes 1978:97). Coho are the least abundant and run in August and September. More detailed historic accounts of the timing, abundance, and fluctuations in these runs are provided in Chapters 4 and 6.

Other fish species that are present in the river and may have been caught by the Aboriginal people are: sturgeon, steelhead, largescale sucker, Dolly Varden, northern squawfish, peamouth chub, burbot, and perhaps white sucker, longnose sucker, and bridgelip sucker (Table 5).

TABLE 5

Availability of fish species in the Fraser River

Species	Jan.	Feb.	Mar.	Apr.	May	Jun.	Jul.	Aug.	Sep.	Oct.	Nov.	Dec.
Sockeye*						xxxxxx	xxxXX	XXXXX	xxxxxx			
Spring				xxxxxx	xx	xxxxxx	XXXXX	XXXXX				
Coho								xxx	xxxxxx			
Pink**									XXXXX	XXXXX		
Steelhead	xxxxxx	xxxxxx	xxxxxx	xxxxxx	....	......	......	......	......	......	......	xxxxxx
Dolly Varden	......	......	......	......	......	......	......	.xxx	xxxxxx	xxxxxx	xxx..	......
Sturgeon	......	......	xxxxxx	xxxxxx	xxxxxx	......	......	......	......	......	......	......
Burbot	......	xxxxxx	......	......	......	......	......	......	......	......	......	......
Northern Squawfish	......	......	......	......	xxxxxx	xxx..	......	......	......	......	......	......
Sucker: Largescale	......	......	......	xxxxxx	xxxxxx	xxxxxx	......	......	......	......	......	......
Sucker: White	......	......	......	......	xxxxxx	xxx..	......	......	......	......	......	......
Sucker: Longnose	......	......	......	xxxxxx	xxxxxx	xxxxxx	......	......	......	......	......	......
Sucker: Bridgelip	......	......	......	......	xxxxxx	......	......	......	......	......	......	......
Peamouth Chub	......	......	......	......	xxxxxx	xxx..	......	......	......	......	......	......
Rocky Mtn. Whitefish	......	......	......	......	......	......	......	......	......	......	xxxxxx	......
Sculpin	......	..xxx	xxxxxx	xxxxxx	xxxxxx	xxxxxx	......	......	......	......	......	......
Cutthroat Trout	......	xxxxxx	xxxxxx	xxxxxx	xxxxxx	......	......	......	......	......	......	......

SOURCE: Based on Carl et al. (1959), Kew (Chapter 4), Kennedy and Bouchard (Chapter 6), DP

NOTES: *4-year cycle of dominance; **2-year cycle of dominance

Symbols denoting availability of fish species are: X major spawning run; x spawning; ...... present

APPENDICES

1: Scientific Names of Mammals Mentioned in the Text

Nomenclature for these animals follows Cowan and Guiguet (1965) and Banfield (1974).

bear, black (*Ursus americanus*)
bear, grizzly (*Ursus arctos horribilis*)
beaver (*Castor canadensis leucodontus*)
bobcat (*Lynx rufus fasciatus*)
caribou (*Rangifer tarandus montanus*)
chipmunk (*Eutamias amoenus*)
cougar (*Felis concolor*)
coyote (*Canis latrans lestes*)
deer, mule (*Odocoileus hemionus hemionus*)
elk (*Cervus canadensis nelsoni*)
fisher (*Martes pennanti columbiana*)
lynx (*Lynx canadensis canadensis*)
marten (*Martes americana*)
marmot, hoary (*Marmota caligata*)
marmot, yellow-bellied (*Marmota flaviventris avara*)
mink (*Mustela vision energumenos*)
moose (*Alces alces andersoni*)
mountain goat (*Oreamnos americanus*)
muskrat (*Ondatra zibethica*)
packrat (*Neotoma cinerea occidentalis*)
pika (*Ochotona princeps*)
porcupine (*Erethizon dorsatum nigrescens*)
red fox (*Vulpes fulva*)
sheep, bighorn (*Ovis canadensis*)
skunk (*Mephitis mephitis hudsonica*)
snowshoe hare (*Lepus americanus pallidus*)
squirrel, northern flying (*Glaucomys sabrinus*)
squirrel, red (*Tamiasciurus husonicus*)
weasel, long-tailed (*Mustela frenata*)
weasel, short-tailed (*Mustela erminea richardsoni*)
wolf (*Canis lupus*)
wolverine (*Gulo luscus luscus*)
yellow badger (*Taxidea taxus taxus*)

2: Scientific Names of Birds Mentioned in the Text

The scientific and common names listed below follow Robbins, Bruun, and

Zim (1966) and Godfrey (1966). A list of birds which breed in the study area is provided by Mathewes (1978). This list includes hawks, falcons, and many small birds, such as the passiformes, not discussed in this paper or listed below.

Swans
whistling swan (*Olor columbianus*)
trumpeter swan (*Olor buccinator*)
Geese
Canada goose (*Branta canadensis*)
snow goose (*Chen hyperborea*)
Ducks
mallard (*Anas platyrhynchos*)
pintail (*Anas acuta*)
gadwall (*Anas strepera*)
American widgeon (*Mareca americana*)
shoveler (*Spatula clypeata*)
blue-winged teal (*Anas discors*)
cinnamon teal (*Anas cyanoptera*)
green-winged teal (*Anas carolinensis*)
redhead (*Aythya americana*)
canvasback (*Aythya valisineria*)
ring-necked (*Aythya collaris*)
greater scaup (*Aythya marila*)
lesser scaup (*Aythya affinis*)
common goldeneye (*Bucephala clangula*)
Barrow's goldeneye (*Bucephala islandical*)
bufflehead (*Bucephala albeola*)
harlequin (*Histrionicus histrionicus*)
white-tailed scoter (*Melanitta deglandi*)
ruddy duck (*Oxyura jamaicensis*)
Other Wetland Birds
common loon (*Gavia immer*)
western grebe (*Aechmophorus occidentalis*)
red-necked grebe (*Podiceps grisegena*)
horned grebe (*Podiceps auritus*)
eared grebe (*Podiceps caspicus*)
pied-billed grebe (*Podilymbus podiceps*)
least grebe (*Podiceps dominicus*)
common merganser (*Mergus merganser*)
red-breasted merganser (*Mergus serrator*)
hooded merganser (*Lophodytes cucullatus*)
Grouse
blue grouse (*Dendragapus obscurus*)

spruce grouse (*Canachites canadensis*)
ruffed grouse (*Bonasa umbellus*)
sharp-tailed grouse (*Pedioecetes phasianellus*)
Eagles
golden eagle (*Aquila chrysaetos*)
bald eagle (*Haliaeetus leucocephalus*)
Owls
screech owl (*Otus asio*)
great horned owl (*Bubo virginianus*)
short-eared owl (*Asio flammeus*)
snowy owl (*Nyctea scandiaca*)
great gray owl (*Strix nebulosa*)
boreal owl (*Aegolius funereus*)
saw-whet owl (*Aegolius acadicus*)
pygmy owl (*Glaucidium gnoma*)
Other Birds
willow ptarmigan (*Lagopus lagopus*)
white-tailed ptarmigan (*Lagopus leucurus*)
red-shafted flicker (*Colaptes cafer*)
pileated woodpecker (*Dryocopus pileatus*)
sandhill crane (*Grus canadensis*)
great blue heron (*Ardea herodias*)
mourning dove (*Zenaidura macroura*)
robin (*Turdus migratorius*)
varied thrush (*Ixoreus naevius*)
magpie, black-billed (*Pica Pica*)

3: Scientific Names of Fish Mentioned in the Text

The taxonomy used below is based on Carl et al. (1959).

burbot (*Lota lota*)
Dolly Varden (*Salvelinus malma*)
mountain whitefish (*Prosopium williamsoni*)
northern squawfish (*Ptychocheillus oregonensis*)
peamouth club (*Mylocheilus caurinus*)
salmon, coho (*Oncorhynchus kisutch*)
salmon, pink (*Oncorhynchus gorbuscha*)
salmon, spring (*Oncorhynchus tschawytscha*)
salmon, sockeye (*Oncorhynchus nerka*)
sculpin, Aleutian (*Cottus aleuticus*)
sculpin, prickly (*Cottus asper*)
sucker, bridgelip (*Catostomus columbianus*)

sucker, largescale (*Catostomus macrocheilus*)
sucker, longnose (*Catostomus catostomus*)
sucker, northern mountain (*Catostomus platyrhynchus*)
sucker, white (*Catostomus commersoni*)
steelhead (see trout, rainbow)
sturgeon (*Acipenser transmontanus*)
trout, cutthroat (*Salmo clarki clarki*)
trout, rainbow (*Salmo gairdneri*)

4: Scientific Names of Plants Mentioned in Text

The scientific and common names listed below are derived from Turner (Chapter 8).

alder, Sitka (*Alnus sinuata*)
anemone, Pacific (*Anemone multifida*)
aspen, trembling (*Populus tremuloides*)
avalanche lily, yellow (see lily, yellow avalanche)
balsam poplar (see cottonwood)
balsamroot (*Balsamorhiza sagittata*)
baneberry (*Actaea rubra*)
birch, paper (*Betula papyrifera*)
bitterroot (*Lewisia rediviva*)
black tree lichen (*Bryoria fremontii*)
blackcap (*Rubus leucodermis*)
blueberry, dwarf mountain (*Vaccinium, caespitosum*)
blueberry, oval-leaved (*Vaccinium ovalifolium*)
bluebunch wheat grass (see grass, bluebunch wheat)
bulrush, round-stem (see tule)
bunchgrass (see grass, bluebunch wheat)
cactus, prickly-pear (*Opuntia fragilis, O. polyacantha*)
cascara (*Rhamnus purshiana*)
cattail, common (*Typha latifolia*)
cedar, red (see cedar, western red)
cedar, yellow (*Chamaecyparis nootkatensis*)
cedar, western red (*Thuja plicata*)
cherry, bitter (*Prunus emarginata*)
cherry, choke (*Prunus virginiana*)
chocolate lily (see lily, chocolate)
chocolate-tips (*Lomatium dissectum*)
choke cherry (see cherry, choke)
cottonwood, or balsam poplar (*Populus balsamifera*)
cottonwood mushroom (*Tricholoma populinum*)

cow-parsnip (*Heracleum lanatum*)
crabapple, Pacific (*Malus fusca*)
desert parsley (*Lomatium macrocarpum*)
devil's-club (*Oplopanax horridus*)
Douglas-fir (see fir, Douglas-)
elderberry, red (*Sambucus racemosa*)
false box (*Paxistima myrsinites*)
false onion (*Triteleia grandiflora* ?)
false Solomon's-seal (*Smilacina racemosa*)
field wormwood (see wormwood, field)
fir, balsam (see fir, subalpine)
fir, Douglas- (*Pseudotsuga menziesii*)
fir, subalpine (*Abies lasiocarpa*)
fireweed (*Epilobium angustifolium*)
gooseberry, white-stemmed (*Ribes inerme*)
gooseberry, swamp (*Ribes lacustre*)
grass, bluebunch wheat (*Agropyron spicatum*)
grass, bunch- (see grass, bluebunch wheat)
grass, giant wild rye (*Elvmus cinereus*)
grass, reed canary (*Phalaris arundinacea*)
grass, pine (*Calamagrostis rubescens*)
hawthorn, black (*Crataegus douglasii*)
hazelnut (*Corylus cornuta*)
hellebore, Indian (see Indian hellebore)
hemlock, mountain (*Tsuga mertensiana*)
hemlock, western (*Tsuga heterophylla*)
highbush cranberry (*Viburnum edule*)
hog-fennel (see desert parsley)
horsetail, branchless (*Equisetum hyemale*)
horsetail, common (*Equisetum arvense*)
huckleberry, black mountain (*Vaccinium membranaceum*)
huckleberry, red (*Vaccinium parvifolium*)
Indian celery (*Lomatium nudicaule*)
Indian hellebore (*Veratrum viride*)
Indian potato (see spring beauty)
Indian rhubarb (see cow-parsnip)
Indian-hemp (*Apocynum cannabinum*)
'ironwood' (see oceanspray)
juniper, common (*Juniperus communis*)
juniper, Rocky Mountain (*Juniperus scopulorum*)
kinnikinnick (*Arctostaphylos uva-ursi*)
Labrador-tea (*Ledum groenlandicum*)
lichen, black tree (see black tree lichen)

lily, chocolate (*Fritillaria lanceolata*)
lily, desert (see lily, mariposa)
lily, mariposa (*Calochortus macrocarpus*)
lily, tiger (*Lilium columbianum*)
lily, yellow avalanche (*Erythronium grandifloru*)
maple, Rocky Mountain (*Acer glabrum* var. *douglasii*)
mariposa lily (see lily, mariposa)
mint, wild (*Mentha arvensis*)
mock-orange (*Philadelphus lewisii*)
mosses, general (espec. 'long' types) (*Bryophytes*)
mushroom, cottonwood (see cottonwood mushroom)
mushroom, slimey top (unidentified)
nettle, stinging (see stinging nettle)
oceanspray (*Holodiscus discolor*)
onion, nodding wild (*Allium cernuum*)
Oregon-grape, tall (*Mahonia aquifolium*)
pine, lodgepole (*Pinus contorta*)
pine, ponderosa (*Pinus ponderosa*)
pine, white (*Pinus monticola*)
pine, whitebark (*Pinus albicaulis*)
pine, yellow (see pine, ponderosa)
pinegrass (see grass, pine-)
plantain, broad-leaved (*Plantago major*)
potato, Indian or mountain (see spring beauty)
raspberry, wild (*Rubus idaeus*)
red-osier dogwood (*Cornus sericea*)
'red willow' (see red-osier dogwood)
roses, wild (*Rosa nutkana, R. acicularis, R. woodsii*)
saskatoon berry (*Amelanchier alnifolia*)
sagebrush, big (*Artemisia tridentata*)
silverberry (*Elaeagnus commutata*)
silverweed (*Potentilla anserina spp. anserina*)
soapberry (*Shepherdia canadensis*)
spring beauty (*Claytonia lanceolata*)
spring sunflower (see balsamroot)
spruce, Engelmann (*Picea engelmannii*)
stinging nettle (*Urtica dioica*)
strawberries, wild (*Fragaria vesca, F. virginiana*)
thimbleberry (*Rubus parviflorus*)
'timbergrass' (see pinegrass)
tobacco, wild (*Nicotiana attenuata*)
twinberry, black (*Lonicera involucrata*)
tule (*Scirpus acutus,* syn. *S. lacustris*)

water-parsnip (*Sium suave*)
waxberry (*Symphoricarpos albus*)
willows, general (*Salix* spp.)
willow, Pacific (*Salix lasiandra*)
willow, 'rope' (see sandbar willow)
willow, sandbar (*Salix exigua*)
willow, Sitka (*Salix sitchensis*)
wormwood, field (*Artemisia campestris*)
wormwood, northern (*Artemisia frigida*)
yarrow (*Achillea millefolium*)
yew, western (*Taxus brevifolia*)

REFERENCES

Anderson, T.W. 1973. 'Historical evidence of land use in a pollen profile from Osoyoos Lake, British Columbia.' Geological Survey of Canada, Report of Activities, Part A. Pp. 178-9. *Geological Survey of Canada, Paper 73-1*. Ottawa, Ontario

Banfield, A.W.F. 1974. *The Mammals of Canada*. National Museum of Natural Science, National Museum of Canada. Toronto: University of Toronto Press

Beil, Charles E., Roy L. Taylor, and Geraldine A. Guppy. 1976. 'The biogeo-climatic zones of British Columbia.' *Davidsonia* 7(4):44-55

Brayshaw, T.C. 1970. 'The dry forests of southern British Columbia.' *Syesis* 3:17-43

Carl, G.C., W.A. Clemens, and C.C. Lindsay. 1959. *The Fresh-Water Fishes of British Columbia*. Handbook of the BC Provincial Museum, No. 5, Victoria

Cowan, I. McT. and C.J. Guiguet. 1965. *The Mammals of British Columbia*. BC Provincial Museum Handbook, No. 11. Victoria: Queen's Printer

Environment Canada. n.d. *Map of Land Capability for Wildlife: Ungulates*. Ash-croft 921, Ministry of the Environment, Ottawa

Godfrey, W.E. 1966. *The Birds of Canada*. Bulletin of the National Museum of Canada, No. 203, Ottawa

Kennedy, D.I.D. and Randy Bouchard. 1978. 'Fraser River Lillooet: An ethno-graphic summary.' In A.N. Stryd and S. Lawhead (eds.), *Reports of the Lillooet Archaeological Project, No. 1: Introduction and Setting*. Pp. 22-55. Paper of the Archaeological Survey of Canada, No. 73, Mercury Series. National Museum of Man, Ottawa

Krajina, V.J. 1965. 'Biogeoclimatic zones and classifications of British Columbia.' *Ecology of Western North America* 1:1-17. University of British Columbia, Botany Department, Vancouver

-. 1969. 'Ecology of forest trees in British Columbia.' *Ecology of Western North America* 2(1). University of British Columbia, Botany Department, Vancouver

Kusmer, Karla D. 1987. 'The Fraser River investigations into corporate group archaeology project: Zooarchaeological analysis.' Unpublished ms. in possession of the author

Langemann, E.G. 1987. 'Zooarchaeology of the Lillooet Region, British Columbia.' Unpublished MA thesis, Department of Archaeology, Simon Fraser University, Burnaby, BC

Lepofsky, Dana. 1987. 'Fraser River investigations into corporate group archaeology: Report on floral analysis.' Unpublished ms. in possession of author

Mathewes, Rolf W. 1978. 'The Environment and Biotic Resources of the Lillooet Area.' In A.H. Stryd and S. Lawhead (eds.), *Reports of the Lillooet Archaeological Project, No. 1: Introduction and Setting*. Pp. 68-99. Paper of the Archaeological Survey of Canada, No. 73, Mercury Series. National Museum of Man, Ottawa

Mitchell, W.R. and R.E. Green. 1981. *Identification and Interpretation of Ecosystems of the Western Kamloops Forest Region*. Province of British Columbia, Ministry of Forests, Victoria

Robbins, Chandler S., Bertel Bruun, and Herbert S. Zim. 1966. *Birds of North America: A Guide to Field Identification*. New York: Golden Press

Smith, H.I. 1900. 'Archaeology of the Thompson River region, British Columbia.' *Memoir, American Museum of Natural History, Jesup North Pacific Expedition* 2(1):401-42

Teit, J. 1900. 'The Thompson Indians of British Columbia.' *Memoir, American Museum of Natural History, Jesup North Pacific Expedition* 1(4):163-392

–. 1906. 'The Lillooet Indians.' *Memoir, American Museum of Natural History, Jesup North Pacific Expedition* 2(5):193-300

–. 1909. 'The Shuswap.' *Memoir, American Museum of Natural History, Jesup North Pacific Expedition* 2(7):447-789

Tisdale, E.W. 1947. 'The grasslands of the Southern Interior of British Columbia.' *Ecology* 28:346-83

A Reconstruction of Prehistoric Land Use in the Mid-Fraser River Area Based on Ethnographic Data

Diana Alexander

INTRODUCTION

This chapter synthesizes ethnographic information on native subsistence and settlement patterns in the Mid-Fraser River area in order to reconstruct native land use practices as they existed prior to contact with Euro-Canadians in the early 1800s. It consolidates information from a large and varied collection of ethnohistoric, ethnographic, and ethnoarchaeological reports, including early ethnographies by Teit, my own work, and material presented in this book by Turner, Romanoff, Tyhurst, and Kennedy and Bouchard. Using this reconstruction, predictions are made for the content and distribution of archaeological sites in the study area.

The primary objective of this research is to provide archaeologists with the ethnographic information they need to interpret prehistoric cultures on the Interior Plateau. The ethnoarchaeological reconstruction may also be used as a model for hunter-gatherer subsistence and settlement in environmentally similar regions where the ethnographic record is less complete.

Most Interior Plateau ethnographies do not describe the practices of individual bands (or villages) but give general accounts for the larger ethno-linguistic groupings. Since both the Lillooet and Shuswap have used the study area in the past, this ethnographic research includes the examination of both groups. Reports on the Lillooet and Shuswap are numerous, but the record of their traditional subsistence and settlement patterns remains incomplete. To further augment the existing data base, the ethnographies of two other neighbouring groups on the Interior Plateau are examined – the Thompson and the Athapaskan-speaking Chilcotin (Chapter 1, Figure 2). These latter two groups occupy environments similar to those found in the study area, and they have adapted to and traditionally used their environment in a manner similar to the Lillooet and Shuswap. In addition, the Thompson, Lillooet, and Shuswap all belong to the Interior Salish language family.

In terms of current theoretical models of hunter-gatherers, the Lillooet and Shuswap were traditionally 'logistical collectors' (Binford 1980). They had semi-sedentary villages (see Appendix for a definition of site types) where large amounts of food were stored and they maintained a variety of specialized basecamps from which salmon, deer, or plants were procured and processed for storage. Assuming that tools were discarded primarily at the location where they were most intensively used (Hayden 1987; Binford 1980:12), I predict that specialized tool assemblages should be found at basecamps and resource procurement locations. On the other hand, winter villages may contain a greater diversity of cultural material due to gearing up activities and tool storage (Binford 1980:18).

The 'mobility strategy' or the type and frequency of moves made by a group of people also affected site form, contents, and location. For example, a study on the neighbouring Columbia Plateau (Chatters 1987) illustrated how mobility frequency determined the duration and repetition of site use and, thus, the ability to clearly recognize features in an archaeological context.

The Fountain and Pavilion bands occupied a territory of about 530 square kilometres and had a combined pre-contact population of more than 500 people (see Alpine Section). Little if any mobility occurred during the winter. In other seasons the village population split up into family groups that made two or more trips to the Montane Parkland, one or more to the Lakes to fish trout and to gather plants, and one or more to the River Valley to catch salmon, totalling at least four residential move a year over a travel distance of about 100 kilometres/year. Most travel was confined to 'logistical' foraging trips from the villages and basecamps by individuals or same-sex task groups. This pattern is at the low end of residential mobility for hunter-gatherers, and my predictions about site content are based partially on the known influences of low residential mobility and the frequency of features such as tools and faunal remains.

ETHNOARCHAEOLOGICAL RECONSTRUCTION

The ethnographic reconstruction of land use in the study area and the derivative predictions for archaeological patterning are presented according to the environmental units outlined in Chapter 2 (Table 1, Figures 1-2). While the general ethnographic and archaeological patterns of resource use and group movements outlined below are often applicable to the entire Interior Plateau culture area, the timing of events and the importance and availability of individual plant and animal species vary with latitude. Critical environmental factors that influenced traditional land use patterns include increasingly colder weather, heavier snow falls, and smaller and later salmon runs on a gradual cline from south to north. Since the main focus of this book is on the Mid-Fraser River area, the detailed descriptions that follow refer only to this area unless otherwise stated.

ALPINE

Ethnographic Summary

Until recently, very little was known about traditional native use of alpine environments. The inaccessibility of mountain top environ ments has prevented most ethnographers from actually visiting these locations. In addition, many of the ethnographers working in the area have focussed on an analysis of the important salmon fisheries along the Fraser River and have, therefore, underemphasized or overlooked the significance of hunting and plant gathering in the mountains (cf. Teit 1900, 1906, 1909a; Dawson 1892; Bouchard and Kennedy 1977; Kennedy and Bouchard 1978; Romanoff 1985; Lane 1953; Boas 1891). Most of the available information on the use of montane resources comes from recent studies by myself and other authors included in this book (Alexander et al., 1985; Alexander 1986, 1987; Tyhurst, Chapter 7; Turner, Chapter 8, 1978; Romanoff, Chapter 9). These studies have shown that montane environments were an important element in the seasonal round of subsistence activities for the Shuswap and Lillooet. Salmon was the major source of protein and calories, but, when salmon runs were unproductive, the Indians were more dependent than ever upon the deer, roots, and berries found in the mountains.

The Alpine (Chapter 2, Figures 1-2, Plate 2.1) was used primarily for the hunting of deer and the collection of food plants in early summer and fall. The snow began melting at higher elevations generally in April (Table 1). However, it was not until mid to late May that some of the Alpine food plants were harvestable (Chapter 2: Tables 2 and 3; Turner, Chapter 8), the weather warm enough, and the ground dry enough to make travelling to, and hunting on, the mountain tops a feasible undertaking. In mid-May small family groups began making short (i.e., several days to one to two weeks) trips into the mountains, hunting and plant gathering as they followed the deer and ripening plants up the slope (DP; Tyhurst, Chapter 7). However, at

TABLE 1
Monthly calendar

South   North

Moon	Thompson (below Lytton) (Teit 1900:238-9)	Thompson (Spences Bridge to Ashcroft) (Teit 1900:237-8)	Lillooet (Fountain to Anderson Lk) (Teit 1906:223-4)	Shuswap (Dawson 1892:40)	Shuswap (on Fraser R. north of Pavilion) (Teit 1909a:517-8)	Chilcotin (Lane 1953:219)
1 (Nov.)	Deer rut	Deer rut, hunt	Gets cold Enter winter houses	Return from hunt	Deer rut Some enter winter houses	Go in underground house
2 (Dec.)	Some enter winter houses	Gets cold Most enter winter houses	Winter solstice	Remain at home	First real cold	Ice
3 (Jan.)	All enter winter houses	Bucks shed antlers, does lean	Coldest weather, ice on rivers	Midwinter	Suns turns	Eagle
4 (Feb.)	Chinook winds Some camp out in lodges	Chinook winds, snow goes Plants sprouts Many leave winter houses	Leave winter houses		Chinook winds, snow goes	Snow hard
5 (Mar.)	Last cold All in winter houses	Grass grows All leave winter houses	Warm weather, chinook winds Grass grows Some fish & hunt		Snow leaves low ground Few spring roots dug Many leave winter houses	Snow goes away

Month						
6 (Apr.)	Fish with bag-nets All leave winter houses	Trees leaf, water increases Trap lake fish, trout with dip nets	Trees and bushes leaf	Grass	Grass grows fast Snow leaves highground Dig roots	Ice coming down
7 (May)	Short Hunts	Dig roots	Small fish First salmon Strawberries ripe	Root digging	Fish at lakes	Red mouth fish
8 (June)	Pick berries	Service-berries begin to ripen Deer drop young	Service & most other berries ripen	Strawberry	Service-berries ripen	
9 (July)	Start salmon fishing	All berries ripen Summer solstice Some hunt	Pick berries Warmest	Berry	Salmon arrive	Spring salmon
10 (Aug.)	Fish and cure salmon	Sockeye salmon, first run	A lot of salmon corne Fish	Salmon	Fish salmon all month	Sockeye salmon
11 (Sep.)	Prepare fish oil	Cohoes run Salmon runs get poor	Prepare salmon oil	Salmon get bad	Cache fish Leave rivers to hunt	Pink salmon
12 (Oct.)	Hunt large game Trap	Hunt Trap Bucks begin to run	Hunt Trap game	Deer travel	Hunt in mountains Trap game in mountains	Wind

(continued on next page)

NOTE TO TABLE 1: The seasonal cycle of subsistence is reflected in the names and 'principal characteristics' of the 'moons' or months as described by native informants. The above table summarizes the main environmental cues and subsistence activities which were used by the Chilcotin, Shuswap, Lillooet, and Thompson to signify the moons. The exact timing of these natural and cultural events would vary each year depending on climatic conditions. Strong similarities exist between all the calendars, with variations reflecting differences in the timing of events due to increased latitude and the accompanying colder climates as well as smaller and later salmon spawning runs.

According to Teit, the Shuswap, Lillooet, and Thompson all began their year sometime in November (1900:237, 1906:223, 1909a:518), although the natural event which signalled the beginning of the year varied. Some Chilcotin also maintained that the year started with the first snows, which generally occurred in November (Lane 1953:219-20). Consequently, I have also chosen November to begin my description of the seasonal cycle.

Pavilion many families went trout fishing from mid-May to the beginning of June and would not have used the mountains at this time (DP).

In June and early July many of the plants were in their prime (Chapter 2, Table 3), and short trips to the Alpine areas to harvest them and to hunt deer were more frequent. Sometimes one to three women travelled to the Alpine without their families for a day or two to gather plants (Turner, Chapter 8). Men also travelled without their families to hunt deer (DP). Although daytrips were sometimes staged from the village (Figure 1), all other Alpine excursions were from basecamps in the Montane Parkland. Late July and early August were primarily devoted to salmon fishing (Table 1) and the mountains were largely abandoned until the end of the salmon runs in mid-August or early September (DP; BE).

Deer hunting was most intense immediately following the salmon fishing (Romanoff, Chapter 9) when almost all families moved up to the mountains and camped in large groups for up to one or two weeks (Tyhurst, Chapter 7; Turner, Chapter 8; DP; BE; WN; RA). These gatherings were similar to larger events in the Chilcotin where 100 to 200 people gathered in late July in the Potato Mountains (Alexander et al., 1985:65). Except for dwarf mountain blueberries, the food plants were past their prime (Chapter 2, Table 3). Spring beauty plants cannot be collected with a traditional digging stick unless the plant is visible above the ground (DL). Since these plants would have died back by August, they could only be located by searching caches of marmots and other rodents (BE; WN; Turner, Chapter 8).

In late August and September, the primary Alpine activity was acquisition of deer that were at their best, that is, fattest and with the best hides (Boas 1891:636; Romanoff, Chapter 9). It is assumed that Alpine hunts for most other ungulates would have occurred at the same time as those for deer. On the other hand, hunts for mountain

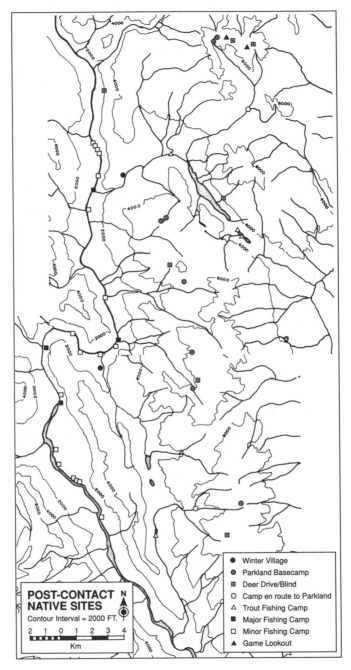

FIGURE 1

Post-contact native sites in the study area

goat could have taken place later in the season after the deer, bighorn sheep, and elk (in the past) had moved down to their wintering grounds. Marmots were also in their prime in August and September. The basecamps for these Alpine activities were generally in the Montane Parkland. The intensity and duration of any hunt was probably dependent on the number of salmon caught prior to the hunt. Hunting by men (alone or in small groups) could have continued into October and early November (Table 1; Tyhurst, Chapter 7), though the game began to move down to lower elevation by October (Lane 1981:405).

In November, the Alpine was abandoned as the weather got colder and stormier (Table 1). Teit mentions the hunting of deer and elk in the mountains during the winter snows (1900:248), however, snow would have driven these animals to lower elevations and these references would not seem to apply to the Alpine environmental unit.

Ethnoarchaeological Reconstruction

A variety of site types were created in the Alpine by native activities. They included burial sites, short-term transit camps, and resource procurement locations such as plant-gathering sites, small or medium-sized mammal kill sites, ungulate kill and/or butchering sites, ungulate hunting blinds and drives with associated kill and/or butchering sites, and game lookouts (see Appendix 1 for definition of site types).

Native informants maintain that no one camped overnight in the Alpine (DP, DL). The Alpine is frequently cold and windy even during the day in mid-summer and temperatures below or near freezing are common on summer nights (Chapter 2, Table 1). These informants point out that the lack of trees in the Alpine means that there is little or no shelter from the winds and no wood for the fires needed to provide warmth and a means of cooking food. In most locations, water is also scarce, especially in drier and/or warmer years when snow packs and their runoff disappear early. Given the lack or scarcity of shelter, firewood, and water in the Alpine, even short-term (one to two nights) campsites were probably extremely rare in the prehistoric past. Ethnographic accounts do, however, describe daytime forays into the Alpine from the Parkland basecamps. Subsistence activities during these forays consisted primarily of plant gathering by women and hunting and butchering by men.

Plant Gathering

Women, alone or in small groups, used the Alpine during the day to gather plant foods (DL; DP; see also Dawson 1892:19). They were sometimes assisted by older children (DL; Turner, Chapter 8), while men occasionally helped pick berries (Turner, Chapter 8). Young children (i.e., less than nine years old: KB) were generally left at the lower elevation camps (DL; DP; WN; Turner, Chapter 8), probably because they could not help significantly in the work and would have slowed travel during the arduous trip to the mountain. The men, women, and older children (occasionally dogs assisted), using tump-lines, carried the food and gear in large baskets and bags (Teit 1900:256, 1906:230, 1909a:532).

The species of plants collected depended on the season and the availability of species on any particular mountain top. In general, the Blustry Mountain-Cairn Peak locality seems to have been a better place for plant gathering than was the Chipuin Mountain-Moore Peak locality (Chapter 1, Figure 1; Tyhurst, Chapter 7). Although occurring in high densities in some spots, the overall abundance of food plants in the study area localities is not as great as that found at other culturally important Alpine locations, such as Potato Mountain in the Chilcotin (Alexander et al., 1985) and 'Many Roots' near Bridge River (Teit 1906:256, 237; Turner, Chapter 8). Nevertheless, each family collected large quantities of plants for immediate consumption and storage (e.g., 5-20 kg of avalanche lily, 10-25 or more kg of spring beauty, 'large quantities' of balsamroot) (Turner, Chapter 8). Densities probably remained relatively stable given the harvesting techniques. The plant foods were not shared outside the immediate family (WN). However, contemporary practices in the Chilcotin include the exchange of plant foods for salmon between two related families (DL).

Traditionally, baskets and bone or wood digging sticks with bone, antler, horn, or wood handles were the only tools used to gather roots (Teit 1909a:514; Dawson 1892:19). When gathering dwarf mountain blueberries, baskets, bark trays, and wooden combs or scoops were used (Teit 1906:216, 1909a:497,515, 1909b:781; Dawson 1892:21). The production of these tools was labour-intensive, therefore they were probably highly curated. Given their high reuse value, any damaged baskets or digging sticks were probably taken to the basecamp for repair rather than being discarded in the Alpine. One exception might have been broken wooden shafts of the digging sticks, which could have been abandoned in the Alpine and replaced with wood found at the basecamp. Digging sticks and all other tools and weapons were made and repaired by men (Teit 1900:295; Lane 1981:403; Turner, Chapter 8). Given the curation of most of these tools and their perishable nature, little, if any, evidence of plant-gathering activities is expected to be found in prehistoric Alpine sites. Broken or lost knives used to cut shoots, leaves, and stems (Turner, Chapter 8) may be the only evidence of plant gathering to survive, and such remains would be highly dispersed and isolated.

Few if any plant storage pits should be expected in the Alpine. Most plants require some processing prior to storage (Turner, Chapter 8) and this time-consuming cooking and drying of the plants is reported to have occurred at the Montane Parkland basecamp or at the winter village (DL; Tyhurst, Chapter 7; Turner, Chapter 8). The women and older children may have made small campfires from dried brush, but they would probably contain little cultural material and would be hard to locate.

Hunting

Men used the Alpine for hunting. Deer, the most common prey (DP; WN; BE; RA), were killed with bows and arrows (Teit 1900:241, 244, 249, 1906:226, 1909a:523; Dawson 1892:17). In the past, dogs were sometimes used to run down deer (Boas 1891:636-7; Teit 1900:244, 248, 1909a:523), especially if a man was hunting alone or with only one or two others (cf. Teit 1900:244, 248, 1909a:523). My informants (DP; WN) maintain that dogs frightened the game and were never used in hunting. This disparity may reflect a change in the breed of dog commonly owned (Teit 1900:246; a parallel situation occurred in Australia, see Hayden 1975) or the abandonment of appropriate dog training skills. Snares could only have been used in forested environments.

Lone hunters could ambush deer at salt licks, at drinking holes, or on rocky promontories where the deer go to escape the flies and mosquitoes (Teit 1900:245, 1906:226; DP). Deer were, however, killed wherever they were encountered in the mountains, and, consequently, kill site locations could occur anywhere in the Alpine. These activities would leave few durable remains other than arrow points broken or lost during the hunt and knives and/or flakes used in butchering.

Communal Hunting

Men often hunted alone, but parties of three to seven men were not uncommon (DP; BE; WN). These communal hunts were most frequent in the fall (when large groups of people were gathered in the Montane Parkland), but they may have taken place in any season, though perhaps in different locations.

Traditionally, two types of hunting leader existed. The first, a 'hunting steward,' regulated hunting in a specific location and apparently inherited his position (Romanoff, Chapter 9, n.4). Those who wanted to hunt in this location were led by the steward and shown where they could hunt. The second type was a 'professional trained hunter,' who was not necessarily associated with a specific location and did not inherit his position (ibid.). This hunter received special spiritual, technical, and physical training that involved learning the habits of deer, shooting a bow and arrow, and running down game. He often organized hunts, directed the hunts to some degree, killed the deer, and perhaps bled and cut the animal. Romanoff argues that these trained hunters were from high-ranking families and their skills garnered them greater prestige and wealth through gift-giving and acquisition of many (up to eight) wives. Certainly, hunting was considered 'the most honourable occupation' (Teit 1900:295). An individual could be both a steward and a trained hunter, but there may have been only one or two trained hunters in each village (Romanoff n.d.:41).

The allotment of deer meat and skins acquired in a hunt seems to have varied. In some cases, the skins were divided equally among all the hunters (Teit 1906:256, 1900:295). When many deer were captured, the best hunters got the greater part of the skins (Teit 1909a:573) and perhaps an additional share of fat (Teit 1900:295). If only one deer was shot the leader or the man who shot the deer took the hide and the leader divided all or most of the meat equally or according to need among the others (Teit 1900:248, 294-5, 1906:256, 1909a:573; Romanoff, Chapter 9; Tyhurst, Chapter 7; WN; DP; BE). If a friend was invited to hunt, he was given the skin (Dawson 1892:14). A lone hunter almost always gave a large part of his meat to neighbours but no one had a right to demand it from him (Teit 1900:295, 1909a:573).

Hunting Drives and Blinds

Hunting parties in the Alpine and other environments often captured deer by drives. Although as few as two men could manage a drive (Teit 1909a:675), three or four men were more common (WN), while occasionally five to ten men worked together (Romanoff n.d.:40). Larger hunting parties may have been more common before the large declines in the native population in the 1860s. In general, the more people involved, the greater the chances of a successful hunt. With more people a larger area could be covered and more deer enclosed within the ring of people, with less chance of the deer doubling back and escaping between them. When few men were available, women and boys assisted with the drives (Teit 1900:246).

The nature of the drives differed according to the local topography. Teit discusses a method used by the Thompson: 'On mountains culminating in small, round open tops, bands of deer and sheep were encircled by a numerous band of hunters from below, and were gradually driven up to the top, where surrounding hunters closed in and shot them' (Teit 1909a:521).

A similar technique was used on Mount Cole (Chapter 1, Figure 1), where three or four men drove the deer up a treed valley into an open area in the Montane Parkland, at which time the deer were shot by any one of the hunters as they were spotted (DP). Alternatively, deer could be driven downhill by three or four men placed one above the other in a line, with the deer killed as spotted (WN). On the slopes above Pavilion Lake, deer were also driven into a big gully where they could not escape (DP). Normally, the hunters used vocal and hand signals to inform each other of their location or a successful kill (Teit 1900:287).

A different technique was used where the terrain funnelled the deer toward a narrow passage at the top of a slope (Plate 3.1). Here the animals were driven by as many as six men up the valley to the narrow passage where they were shot by one or two hunters (often older, less agile men) hidden in a natural depression or behind a man-made blind (DP; BE; KB). Teit also describes driving deer downslope to a blind (1900:248-9). In the mountains, these blinds are constructed of loosely piled rocks. Two inspected on Blustry Mountain consisted of a semi-circular stone wall about two feet high and three feet across and another one, standing on Pavilion Mountain, was described as a straight wall about two feet high and ten feet long (DP) (Figure 1; Chapter 1, Figure 1). These blinds should be expected at high points overlooking game trails, particularly where the terrain funnels the animals up a broad valley into a narrow pass.

Since the waiting hunter often had to remain at the blind for long periods of time, it is expected that low densities of cultural debris should be found, including food and hunting gear (especially points and knives). Some minor resharpening and repair of hunting gear may have also occurred there, though it is assumed that the hunter would have come prepared for the hunt and that most such work would have taken place earlier at the basecamp. In general, hunters were expected to avoid noisy activities or fires that would alert game to their presence.

Cultural Remains at Kill and Butchering Sites

No faunal remains or other evidence of butchering should be found at blinds or other frequently used kill sites. Pokotylo and Hanks (1985:7) have shown that Mountain Dene hunters will try to eliminate all signs of a kill (even lithics) from a hunting blind, maintaining that the scent

PLATE 3.1

An area used as a deer funnel drive on the slope of Blustry (or Bald)
Mountain. In this photograph, the Montane Forest cover gives way to Alpine and Montane Parkland environments on the top of Blustry Mountain. A hunting blind is located at the crest of the slope, indicated by an
arrow; another blind is located to the right on a small knoll (arrow).

of blood will scare away animals in future hunts. Only a few small retouch flakes and a biface fragment were found near the blinds on Blustry Mountain.

Artefact densities should also be low at single event kill sites. On the other hand, since these sites would not be reused, it is more likely that some faunal remains and hearths might be found. For example, in one Shuswap story a hunter killed four bighorn sheep, cut them up on the spot, then built a fire and ate some of the meat (Teit 1909a:714).

Few faunal remains should be expected at Alpine butchering sites. Most of the deer processing probably took place at the Montane Parkland basecamps where the hides and dried meat were prepared (DP; BE). Any preliminary butchering to aid transport that might have taken place at or near the kill site did not seem to involve the removal and discarding of bones (Teit 1900:248, 1906:227; Tyhurst, Chapter 7). The transport of whole animals (DP; BE) was probably more common after horses became plentiful in the mid-1800s (Teit 1909a:533), but if the snow and ground cover were suitable it was also possible to drag the animal to camp on the skin (ibid.:533). Otherwise, the meat had to be carried on the hunter's back (ibid.). Finally, faunal remains left on the surface would be largely destroyed by scavengers and weathering, since there is little soil (and this is generally acidic).

Hearths may have been a common feature at butchering sites. Hunters, especially when travelling alone, carried little food (i.e., dried saskatoons or salmon) or no food (Teit 1900:244-5, 1906:227; Romanoff, Chapter 9; DP; BE) and would sometimes eat part of the kill (Teit 1900:347). Organ meats, especially the liver and heart, were the parts most commonly cooked at the butchering site (DP; BN), resulting in low expectations for calcined bone remains at such sites. Hunters in search of game may also have built small campfires for warmth, but they would be very difficult to locate in an archaeological survey given their small size, low artefact densities, and the traditional absence of any rocks used in their construction (DL).

Higher concentrations of cultural debris may be expected at butchering sites near locations, such as salt licks, routinely checked by lone hunters. The highest densities may be expected at butchering sites associated with, but not at, the hunting blinds that were maintained in the same location from generation to generation (DP).

Another type of site that might be found in the Alpine is a game look-out. On high points of land overlooking trails and open slopes frequented by deer, a hunter would sometimes wait for signs of the deer below (DP; BE). When one was spotted, the hunter used hand signals to inform hunters below that a deer was approaching (DP). The look-out sites can be expected to contain hunting and, possibly, butchering gear. Given that the wait may have been long, it is also possible that a hearth and food remains may occur at such sites, however, the cultural remains should be few and difficult to locate.

Bighorn sheep, mountain goats, and (formerly) elk were also hunted in the mountains with bows and arrows (Teit 1909a:249, 1909a:523). Dogs were also used to capture elk (Teit 1909a:523), and bighorn sheep were caught in drives (Teit 1909a:521). Although elk were driven over cliffs by the neighbouring Thompson (Teit 1900:248), there is no mention of such practices among the Shuswap and Lillooet (Teit 1906:226). However, as discussed in Chapter 2, mountain goat and elk were probably uncommon in the study area. Moreover, mountain goats, 'although numerous in many places, were not much hunted' by the Shuswap (Teit 1909a:523), nor did they usually eat goat meat except when other meat was scarce (ibid.:513). The remains of elk and mountain goat should be uncommon in the archaeological record. However, if the local bighorn sheep were using the Alpine for summer range, their remains could be relatively numerous at Alpine sites. Although the location of any mountain sheep (or mountain goat) kill and/or butchering sites may differ from those of deer, who prefer less rugged habitat, the form and frequency of artefacts, faunal remains, and features at such sites should be similar. Storage pits for meat are unlikely to occur in the Alpine. Meat was rarely stored in cache pits and the time-consuming drying required prior to storage was performed at the basecamp (see Montane Parkland Section).

Precontact Indian and Ungulate Populations

It is difficult to accurately estimate the number of ungulates that could have been taken each year in the Fountain-Pavilion territory. In Chapter 2, evidence is given that suggests local populations of deer may have ranged from 25 to 600 and sheep from 0 to 175, while the elk in Hat Creek Valley varied between 0 and 75. The lower numbers probably occurred every 18 to 20 years, when severe winters reduced populations by as much as 50 to 75 per cent. Low (personal communication) suggests that only 20-22 per cent of these ungulates could be killed on a sustained basis, though deer populations could be reduced by as much as 75 per cent and re-establish themselves in four years (partly through migration from surrounding areas). Low also estimates that cougars take two deer for every one hunted and that the situation would have been similar prehistorically. This evidence suggests that hunters in the study area could take about 7 per cent of the ungulates every year, that is two to forty-two deer and zero to twelve sheep.

In 1906, Teit (1909a:465) estimated that the population at Pavilion consisted of only sixty-eight people, while the total for the Fountain, Bridge River, and Lillooet bands was 500. Based on informant testimony he was also able to make an estimate of band populations in 1850, prior to major population declines resulting from smallpox epidemics and the disruption of the economy by a large influx of gold miners. Assuming that the Fountain Band comprised one-third of the people in the combined figures for the three bands, its 1850 population would have been approximately 335. The 1850 population figure for the Pavilion Band was estimated at only 150. Interestingly, these 1850 figures approximate the 1977 census, which gives populations of 385 for Fountain and 142 for Pavilion (Duff 1969:30-1). Overall, this information suggests a combined population of about 500 for Fountain and Pavilion in 1850. If anything, the precontact population was higher, prior to the introduction of Euro-Canadian diseases, which may have appeared as early as the 1780s (ibid.:38-9).

Based on the above estimates, the population of 500 or more people from the Fountain and Pavilion bands could have harvested two to fifty-four sheep and deer (eleven under normal winter conditions) each year on a sustained basis. This low ratio of ungulates to people helps explain why buckskin seemed to be a rare commodity (Romanoff, Chapter 9) and why a large dressed buckskin cost the equivalent of 300 dried salmon (Teit 1900:260-2). The value of the hides also helps to explain why a higher status was given to hunters than to fishermen (Teit 1900:325). In exceptional years, where the ungulate population was high and hunting conditions were good, more animals were probably taken. When heavy snows restricted the mobility of deer and sheep, hunters could catch them in large numbers.

To acquire large quantities of meat for a potlatch, a group of men would hunt for several months (Romanoff, Chapter 9). In one account, a hunter who travelled to Clinton was able to kill 100 deer by going ahead of his followers, killing, bleeding, and gutting the animals, and then telling the others where to find the deer the next day for drying (ibid.). The marked difference between the size of this large kill and Low's estimates suggests that either Low's figures are too conservative (although he makes allowances for large in-migrations in harsh years) or the numbers in the story were exaggerated – or both. In the historic period, each hunter may have claimed two deer during a trip (DP), with the size of a hunt limited by the fact that a man could only carry two dried bucks at a time (Romanoff n.d.:45). If each hunter in the study area claimed two deer per year, under normal conditions, Low's estimates again seem conservative. However, even if I double or triple his estimates, there is still a low ratio of ungulates to people.

These low estimates for ungulate kills reinforces both the expectations for low densities of faunal remains at the Alpine sites and the repeated use of blind sites.

Hunting of Other Prey

Bears were also hunted in the Alpine, for food and skins, with bows and arrows, and dogs (Teit 1906:226-7, 1900:249). It is unlikely that deadfalls were used in the Alpine where there is little soil deposition. Since the bears were after many of the same resources as the Indians, unpredictable and infrequent encounters probably occurred in the mountains. In general, bears were not abundant in the area, with perhaps only one or two in each drainage (Low, personal communication). Bears would have been in their prime (i.e., best fur and fattest) in the fall, and they were most likely hunted then. Kill and/or butchering sites for bears were probably single event sites and randomly scattered throughout the Alpine.

Alpine populations of coyote, wolf, wolverine, marmot, and short-tailed weasel may have been captured for their pelts (Chapter 2, Table 4; Teit 1906:227). Only marmot were commonly eaten, while coyote were eaten during famine (Teit 1906:225, 1909a:648). All these mammals were either trapped or snared (Teit 1906:227, 1909a:523), but the marmot could also be chased (Teit 1909a:523) and shot with a bow and arrow.

Except for marmots, few of these small mammals appear to have been hunted in the Alpine (cf. Teit 1909a:554, 578). In general, the few resulting kill and butchering sites are expected to reveal low artefact densities and poor bone preservation. On the other hand, marmot colonies were highly visible and may have been visited each year, resulting in sites with higher artefact densities but few faunal remains, since the marmot skeletons were probably taken back to the basecamp where the meat was prepared.

Birds were not a dietary staple (Kennedy and Bouchard 1978:41) and little mention is made of bird species hunted by the Shuswap and Lillooet. Of the few food species that may occur in the Alpine, only ptarmigan are common (Teit 1906:227, 1909a:506, 649). Like grouse, ptarmigan were probably snared or chased with bow and arrow with perishable bone or wood points (Teit 1900:248, 1909a:519, 523, 781-2) and few archaeological traces of these activities are expected.

Montane Burials

Since people were generally buried close to the winter village (Dawson

1892:10; Teit 1909a:592), burials should be uncommon in montane environments. However, those who were poor and/or died in distant places were sometimes buried where they died (Teit 1900:330). The Lillooet, Shuswap, and Thompson commonly marked graves with a pile or circle of rocks (Teit 1900:328, 1906:269, 1909a:592) similar to the low mound of rocks marking a grave on Blustry Mountain. Given the general lack of soil development in the Alpine, it seems likely that most burials in this environmental unit would take the same form.

Summary

Any seasonal indicators should suggest prehistoric use of the Alpine between early May and late November. In any given year, the intensity of the fall hunt would also have varied according to the success of the salmon fishing. The most intensive use would have occurred after the main salmon runs in late August and early September, when the largest ungulate drives occurred and the greatest number of people was present. Therefore, a large proportion of the prehistoric sites in the Alpine are probably the result of this early fall occupation. The intensity of use depended largely upon the available resources. Therefore, the Mount Chipuin-Moore Peak locality, where the hunting and plant harvests were better, was probably used more frequently and by larger groups of people than was the Blustry Mountain-Cairn Peak locality.

Although frequently used, the Alpine is expected to contain only small, scattered, and largely hard to locate archaeological sites. Only the stone hunting blinds and burial cairns would be highly visible. The most common sites are expected to be small kill and, possibly, butchering sites, with only a few discarded or lost tools. Butchering sites near the hunting blinds or marmot colonies, where repeated kills were made, may be more visible due to greater densities of material. No large hearths, roasting ovens, food caches, shelters, or drying racks are expected.

MONTANE PARKLAND

Ethnographic Summary

To exploit resources found in the mountains, basecamps were established in the Montane Parkland (Chapter 2, Figures 1-2, Plate 2.2). Beginning in mid-May, a few families began moving to these basecamps (Figure 1), while other families gathered at the lakes to catch trout that spawned in the latter half of May (DP; MA). Small task groups of men or women also used the basecamps for short stays during the spring.

Since many different Parkland localities were utilized at this time (DP; BE; CB; WN), and some families were fishing, few people were probably camped at any one montane locality at any one time.

Spring beauty, seemingly the most abundant and reliable high elevation root in the study area, reached its peak bloom in mid-June (based on observations made on Pavilion Mountain in 1986) and was best collected just before or after blooming. Other important food plants were also available in the mountains in early June, including nodding onion, cow-parsnip, and Indian celery (Chapter 2, Table 3). The inner bark of lodgepole pine was also probably collected with bark strippers and sap scrapers made of bone (Lane 1981:403; Teit 1900:233).

With increasingly abundant plant foods and fatter deer in the mountains, short montane trips of several days to one or two weeks became more common in June and July. These trips were generally made by single families or groups of one to three men or women (DP; BE; CB). Where the Parkland locality was close to the village, day trips were sometimes made with the village as a basecamp (DP.; WN; Turner, Chapter 8). Boys in training often camped alone in the mountains for up to two months in good weather (Teit 1900:318).

The mountains were largely abandoned between mid-July and mid-August while everyone camped on the Fraser River for the salmon fishery. Immediately following the fishing, however, most families moved collectively to the Parkland basecamps for one or two weeks (DP; BE; RA; WN). Deer were in their prime in the fall and the collection of food plants in the mountains was generally of secondary importance in relation to the efforts spent in the capture and processing of deer.

In mid-August, it was still possible to collect some roots, such as avalanche lily, spring beauty, and tiger lily, though they were best harvested earlier in the month (Chapter 2, Table 3). Since some plants, like spring beauty, would not have been visible above ground, they were collected from rodent caches (Turner, Chapter 8; DP; BE; WN;). Many berries were also available (Chapter 2, Table 3), and, on Mission Ridge, they were the most important plant resource in the Parkland (Turner, Chapter 8). However, berry plants were not abundant in the montane portions of the study area and were an unreliable resource, since their numbers varied considerably depending on the weather (ibid.).

In September, the seeds of the whitebark pine were plentiful in the Parkland and were collected in abundance by women and, more recently, by men on hunting trips. The women camped in the Parkland for days while gathering the seeds, collected after cutting down the trees (Dawson 1892:22). Black lichen was also harvested at this time

(Turner, Chapter 8).

Hunting continued until early November, when the mountains were abandoned because of cold and stormy weather. These hunts were generally undertaken by single men or male hunting groups of up to ten men (Tyhurst, Chapter 7; DP; BE; WN; Romanoff n.d.:40) and could last anywhere from a few days to several months (Romanoff, Chapter 9; DP). Although seemingly an uncommon practice, some Thompson hunting parties travelled to more remote areas and were absent for up to seven months (Teit 1900:239). Women were probably more common on these fall hunts in the past, when plant collection and hide preparation were more important to the economy.

These hunts were primarily for deer, but other food species were also captured in the Parkland, including: bighorn sheep, mountain goat, bears, marmot, snowshoe hare, porcupine, and squirrels (Chapter 2, Table 4). The Parkland animals most commonly trapped for their furs were marten, mink, fisher, fox, and lynx (ibid.: Teit 1909a:518). Trapping increased after contact and the introduction of the fur trade, making it difficult to ascertain the importance of small mammals in the prehistoric economy. However, all the ethnographic evidence seems to suggest that small mammals ranked far below the importance of salmon and ungulates in the traditional diet. Since the pelts of these animals were in their prime in the fall, it is assumed that any trapping in the Parkland would have occurred between early September and early November.

Ethnoarchaeological Reconstruction

As with the Alpine, most of the information available on the use of the Montane Parkland comes from recent ethnographic research. The following account of the use of Parkland localities is based largely on my own research in the area (generally conducted with Tyhurst). I have visited the following localities with native informants: Pavilion Mountain (with DP; BE), Mount Cole (DP; BN), the headwaters of Sallus Creek (DP), Cairn Peak-Blustry Mountain (CB), and Chipuin Mountain-Moore Peak (DP; RA; Chapter 2: Figure 1). Information on resource abundance, distance from the winter village, and the number of camp-sites is based on my observations and informants' comments. In general, information on male hunting parties is much more detailed than that on family trips, since the use of montane plant resources has declined and few women have travelled to the mountains in the last fifty years.

Types of sites that occur in this zone include basecamps, transit camps (both long-term and short-term), and resource procurement locations such as look-outs, hunting drives, hunting blinds, hunting fences, kill and/or butchering sites, and plant gathering sites (see Appendix for definition of site types).

Basecamps

The size and composition of the groups using the Parkland basecamps and the duration of their stay seems to have varied according to five factors: (1) distance of the locality from the winter village, (2) the general abundance of plant and animal resources at the locality, (3) the seasonal variations in resource abundance, (4) the number of available campsites, and (5) the danger of attack from other ethno-linguistic groups.

Travelling and camping in larger groupings helped to minimize the danger of attack by 'strangers' in the mountains, who might be after the same resources. It was not unusual for small parties or single hunters to be attacked or disappear while hunting and gathering in the mountains (Teit 1906:237, 240, 244). People camping in localities with relatively abundant resources at the border between two or more ethno-linguistic groups seem to have been especially prone to attacks (ibid.). Therefore, group size at these localities would tend towards the upper limits known to occur in the study area, that is, four or more families.

In the recent past, distance from the winter village seems to have influenced both the duration of the stay and the size of the group. Threat of attack by strangers would tend to encourage larger groups at camps more distant from the village. Parkland localities closer to the village were apparently safe enough for travel by single women (DP), with day trips limited to localities within a return trip distance of twelve to fourteen miles or seven hours (WN; BE). Since comparatively less time and energy was expended to get to the closer localities, day trips or short stays of two or three days were likely to be fruitful (DP; WN). On the other hand, more resources would have to be collected and longer stays would be necessary to make the more distant trips profitable. The use of localities close to the village and containing few resources was generally limited to individuals from the local band (village) (DP; BN). In one exception, the Bonaparte Band sometimes hunted deer on Mount Cole (Chapter 1, Figure 1) in exchange for the Pavilion Band hunting moose on Bonaparte land (DP).

Upper limits were placed on group size by the abundance of resources and the number of suitable campsites. In some localities (e.g., Sallus Creek headwaters), not enough plants and/or animals were present at any one time to ensure that everyone in a large group could get enough resources to make the energy and time expended on travelling to the montane worthwhile (DP; WN). In other localities (e.g., Mount Cole), there were not enough good campsites to accommodate large groups (DP) (Chapter 1, Figure 1).

The duration of a stay at a resource locality was determined in large part by the relative ease of acquiring the desired resource. On hunting trips, the group often stayed at the Parkland camp until they caught a deer (DP). Presumably, a group of women would stay until they had gathered enough plants to make the trip worthwhile. If more than one family was present, it seems likely that they would stay until they had enough deer and/or plants for each family. Weather probably also played a role in the duration of the stay, with longer stays occurring in good weather.

One important factor to remember is that the location of the main winter village changed over time (e.g., from Keatley and Gibbs creeks to Pavilion and Fountain creeks) and, therefore, the distance from any Parkland locality to the main village also changed. Moreover, some families had winter dwellings away from the main village (Teit 1909a:457) so that the distance from their winter house to any Parkland locality differed from that for other band members. These differences may have affected the relative prehistoric importance of any one locality.

In all Parkland localities, trips by individuals, small same-sex task groups, and groups of one to three nuclear families could occur almost anytime between mid-May and early November. However, these trips would probably be more frequent when resources were most abundant. Groups of women would be more common when plants were abundant (mid-May to early June and mid-August to early September) and groups of men more common when deer were at their peak and plants past harvesting (late September to early November). These task groups were often comprised of family members, for example, sisters or brothers; fathers and sons or mothers and daughters; aunt and niece or uncle and nephew; grandmother and granddaughters or grandfather and grandsons (BN; DP; Turner, Chapter 8).

Larger Parkland gatherings of four or more nuclear families occurred once a year. At Pavilion Mountain, Chipuin Mountain-Moore Peak, and Cairn Peak-Blustry Mountain these larger gatherings took place in the early fall (late August to early September) following the main sockeye run (DP; BE; WN; RA; Turner, Chapter 8). As many as four or five families gathered on Blustry Mountain-Cairn Peak (WN), while three to four families camped at Pavilion Mountain (DP). In many cases, the families were not only from the local band but from other bands from the same ethno-linguistic group (Turner, Chapter 8; DP).

Some resource-rich localities in the Mid-Fraser River area attracted larger groups. For example, six to twelve families camped on Mission Mountain (Turner, Chapter 8), while the 'Many Roots' area north of Bridge River attracted people from as many as six bands (Teit 1906:237,256). At Potato Mountain in the Chilcotin, as many as 200 people gathered in July (Alexander et al. 1985) and at a similar Nez Perce camp on the Columbia Plateau, 400-500 people gathered in late May to early June (Ames and Marshall 1980:33). This evidence suggests that precontact gatherings in the study area may have been larger than those seen historically; but based on my knowledge of local Parkland campsites and resources, I estimate the upper limit to have been less than 100 and probably close to 50 people.

The larger Parkland gatherings had an important social component, with games, contests, races, story-telling, and resource exchange (DL; WN; DP; Turner, Chapter 8). Gambling was also a common activity for women and men. For example, women are known to have bet one day's collection of plants on the result of a game (DL; Turner, Chapter 8). In general, these aggregations were seen as happy, friendly, and sociable occasions where food was plentiful and the weather mild.

The camps were set up on flat, dry land, close to water, and at the edge of the forest (Turner, Chapter 8; Tyhurst, Chapter 7; DL; DP). The trees provided shelter from the wind and rain, and firewood for the roasting pits and hearths. They could also be used as a wind break for the meat drying racks so that the smoke from the smudge fire could linger and keep the flies away (DL). Where feasible, the camps were set on the lee side of the trees, with the open meadows in front of the trees being used for general camp activities (DL).

Each family that travelled to the Montane Parkland took its own supplies and maintained a separate campsite and hearth (BE; Turner, Chapter 8). In the Chilcotin, a family reused the same campsite each year (DL), and at large gatherings in Botanie Valley, each band had 'its separate and recognized camping-ground' (Teit 1900:294). However, the families that gathered at each locality would vary from year to year and season to season (Lane 1981:407). These practices were probably commonly followed in the study area. The campsites were usually within 5 to 100 metres of each other so that people could socialize and share food (DP; DL; Turner, Chapter 8). The actual distance depended on the availability of flat land, but the families were usually camped within sight or sound of each other (DP; Lane 1981:407). Other clusters of families may have camped on the mountain at the same time (Lane 1981:407).

In some cases, large groups (four to five families) would move their entire camp during a long stay in the mountains (WN). This practice may have been undertaken to ensure adequate feed for the horses, though depletion of other resources, such as firewood and food plants, may also have stimulated such moves.

The women were generally responsible for setting up and maintaining the basecamp, including gathering and collecting firewood, cooking, and erecting the lodges. In addition, they had to gather and process any plant foods and dry and process the meat and hides (Teit 1900:295-6; Turner, Chapter 8; WN; DP; BE). They were assisted in some of the simpler tasks by any children who may have come along on the trip (DL). Men also sometimes assisted in putting up lodges and tanning hides (Teit 1900:295). As mentioned previously, the young children and the elderly and infirm did not generally make the arduous trip to the mountains. I assume that they remained at the winter village or at a low elevation summer camp, depending on the season.

The men would also offer casual assistance to the women but spent most of their time hunting, cutting trees, constructing racks and other structures, or maintaining tools (Teit 1900:295; Turner, Chapter 8). One man often stayed behind to make firewood for the women (BE). When a large group of men (e.g., four to five individuals) travelled together, one man might be 'selected' to maintain camp while the others hunted. (BE recounted to me how he was unwillingly singled out for this chore.) Otherwise, the men shared camp duties such as cooking, gathering firewood and water (KB), building shelters, and drying meat.

Archaeological Expectations at Basecamps

Many different activities took place at the Parkland basecamps, resulting in the construction of a variety of features and structures, including hearths, drying racks, roasting ovens, storage pits, shelters, sweathouses, menstrual lodges, and tanning frames. Basecamps should be the largest, most common, and most conspicuous prehistoric sites in the Montane Parkland. Due to the scarcity of suitable camping locations, basecamps were reused many times over the year, sometimes by family groups and other times by same-sex hunting or plant-gathering parties. Therefore, basecamps should contain: (1) floral and faunal material suggesting an occupation from mid-May to early November, (2) tools and organic remains indicative of the acquisition and processing of a wide variety of plant and animal species, and (3) features indicative of both large and small group size. However, since the largest and one of the longest gatherings took place after the salmon runs, the assemblages (at least in the resource-rich localities) should be dominated by material from these large, multi-family gatherings.

The archaeological assemblage should be diverse, with tool kits associated with cooking, eating, hunting, butchering, plant gathering, plant processing, hide preparation, tool manufacture and maintenance, and the construction of shelters, drying racks, and pits. Given the importance of gambling and games at the larger, more important Parkland basecamps, gaming artefacts, such as dice of marked beaver or marmot teeth (Teit 1906:248), are expected to be more common at these basecamps than at other Montane sites.

Observations on contemporary use of Montane Parkland basecamps in the Chilcotin suggest that the caching of tools may have been a common practice in the past. In the Potato Mountains, DL cached a cooking pot and an iron digging stick under a tree at the edge of her campsite. I also observed many other historic camps where pots and pans in good condition were abandoned in the trees bordering the camps. These items were cached for a planned return trip despite the fact that there were horses to bring them down the mountain. If this was a common practice in the past, caches of prehistoric tools may also be expected at the margins of prehistoric campsites. Similarly, the frames of sweathouses, drying racks, shelters, and other structures were probably left at the basecamp for future use.

Bone preservation should vary considerably from one Parkland basecamp to another. Considerable amounts of bone were probably discarded at the basecamp sites, since some, if not all, of the final butchering and drying of meat in the Montane occurred at these sites. Unfortunately, the soils are generally acidic and the climatic conditions vary dramatically between seasons, thus promoting rapid decay. Moreover, some of the bones removed from the carcass by the Lillooet were thrown into the water or burnt so that the dogs would not defile them (Teit 1900:346, 1906:281, 1909a:603; Boas 1891:644), thus diminishing their chances of preservation. Similarly, bear skulls were placed on top of tall poles (Teit 1909a:603; 1909b:789). Nevertheless, where soils accumulated rapidly, bone preservation might be good (though never excellent).

Most of the activity areas should be in the open areas in front of the trees, but some activities, such as meat drying, may be expected just within the forest margins. The basecamps would have initially consisted of a cluster of small camps, each with its own fire, shelter, drying racks, refuse areas, and other features and activity areas. Continual reuse of these sites and the superposition of individual sites would ultimately result in what appears to be a few large sites with varying densities of artefacts and features (see O'Connell 1987).

Cooking and Drying Foods

Historically, dried salmon and other foods were brought along to minimize cooking at the basecamp (DP; BE; Turner, Chapter 8). This practice also ensured a varied diet and an essential food supply until some of the Parkland foods could be caught or gathered, or in case a hunt was unproductive. This practice undoubtedly had prehistoric analogs, and archaeological sites in the Montane Parkland may contain some remains of foods that did not naturally occur in this environment.

At the basecamps, a number of different techniques were used to cook fish, meat, and plants for immediate consumption. The food could be boiled or steamed in baskets using heated stones, (Teit 1900:200, 236, 1906:215, 223, 280, 1909a:489, 496; Boas 1891:637), roasted in front of a fire, cooked in the ashes of a fire, or roasted and steamed in underground ovens (Teit 1900:236, 1909a:633, 683; Turner, Chapter 8). Archaeological evidence for cooking may include boiling stones, roasting pits, and hearths with postholes from cooking racks.

In recent times, a group of four or five families would need three or four pack horses to bring all the newly acquired food resources down from the mountain (WN). Before the introduction of the horse, it would have been difficult to bring down large quantities of plants or meat without drying them first. With drying, the resources had less weight, took up less space, preserved better, and could be transported without damage (Turner, Chapter 8).

Meat Preparation

Teit lists five means of drying meat (and fish): 'by the sun's rays; by wind, in the shade; by smoke in the lodges; by heat from the fire; by hot air, in a sweat-house or in houses constructed like a sweat-house but larger' (1909a:517; see also Teit 1900:234). Drying in the sun or wind would require the construction of a drying rack and, possibly, a fire to accelerate drying and reduce flies (DL; DP; Boas 1891:635). All of these techniques were probably used in the Parkland localities in the study area.

Large sweathouse-like structures were also occasionally used to dry meat (Teit 1909:517) and may have been used in the mountains where higher precipitation made air-drying of meat more difficult. Since these structures were built solely for meat-drying, they were probably located at the basecamp. Butchering tools may be associated with such structures. While in the mountains, local informants prefer to dry the meat on a pole or sticks over, or in front of, a fire or on a drying rack

(Turner, Chapter 8; DP; BE). In some cases, the meat was only partially dried in the mountains and the task was completed at the village (Tyhurst, Chapter 7). Meat dried by these techniques lasted six months (Romanoff, Chapter 9) to two years in storage (DP). At prehistoric Parkland sites, the complexity and abundance of meat-drying structures and associated artefacts is expected to be influenced by some of the same factors that dictated the duration of the stay at the sites and the size and composition of groups using these sites. The greater the distance between the locality and the winter village, the greater the abundance of animal resources in the area; and the greater the number of available campsites, the more elaborate the drying technology was likely to be.

The choice of drying technique probably depended on the presence of sweathouses and lodges, the planned length of stay, the weather, and the amount of meat to be dried. Although drying racks were constructed on Pavilion Mountain, DP did not think they were used on Mount Cole, where hunting trips were generally shorter and less productive (making the time and energy involved in constructing a drying rack less rewarding). In other words, the more meat and the longer the stay, the more likely that a drying rack or perhaps other drying facilities would be built. In cold, wet weather, the option would have been either to build a shelter or to take the meat to the village for drying. The closer the locality was to the village, the more likely a trip with undried meat would seem feasible.

Archaeological evidence of meat-drying racks may be difficult to find in the Parkland. To dry the meat by sun and wind, it was cut into thin strips and placed on a frame of poles five feet high (Teit 1900:234). Based on personal observations of the construction of drying racks in the Chilcotin Parkland, it would seem that live trees were often substituted for the upright poles, reducing the number of postholes. The tree roots would also obfuscate any structural evidence.

Marrow and fat were also collected and stored. The bones could be broken with a small cobble and a smooth flat stone or a small hammer and a large flat stone hollowed a little in the centre (Teit 1909a:675). The marrow was then melted down and stored in a deer, elk, or caribou bladder (Teit 1900:234; 1909a:517). The fat from large game, such as deer, elk, and bear, was cut off and stored in deerskin sacks or strips were melted down into a bark, wood, or stone dish in front of a fire and stored (Teit 1900:234). Fat prepared in the fall was less likely to go rancid over the winter (Romanoff, Chapter 9), another reason for concentrating hunting efforts in the fall. Much of the marrow preparation probably took place at the Parkland basecamps in order to avoid carrying the bones down the mountain. Hammers, anvils, and broken bones should, therefore, be common. Some hide preparation may also have been needed to make deerskin sacks to hold the fat.

Plant Preparation

A variety of techniques were used to dry plant foods. At least two or three days of dry, sunny weather were needed to air dry whole berries on woven mats (Teit 1900:235-6, 1909b:780, 1909a:516; Turner, Chapter 8). Alternatively, the berries were boiled in bark baskets with boiling stones, then made into cakes, which were dried in the sun on mats, leaves, grass or pine-needles (ibid.). Boiling stones are the only indicators of these activities likely to be preserved archaeologically.

Whitebark pine seeds could be removed from their cones after roasting in an open fire (Turner, Chapter 8). Other plants, especially those collected in large quantities, were cooked in underground ovens prior to storage or transport (DL; Turner, Chapter 8). For example, tree lichen was often cleaned, leached in water, and then cooked before transport (Turner, Chapter 8). Most groups living on the Interior Plateau also had access to a number of economically important plants, whose roots provided a significant part of the diet. In the study area, the two most common and heavily exploited of these plants were spring beauty and balsamroot (DP; DL; EL).

To prevent spoilage, many roots had to be processed soon after collection by cooking or partially cooking then drying for preservation (DL; EL). With a few of the roots, such as spring beauty and Mariposa lily, pre-cooking was not always necessary and the roots could be dried by hanging them in strings or spreading them on mats (Teit 1909a:516-17). The Lower Lillooet usually ate the spring beauty immediately and rarely stored any for winter (Bouchard and Kennedy 1977:75). However, the Chilcotin commonly pit-cooked the spring beauty and stored large quantities (DL; EL). It is possible that the relative quantities of the plants determined how spring beauty (and other plants) were prepared, that is, if few plants were available, they were eaten immediately, if moderate quantities were collected, they were air-dried, and if large volumes were collected in a single trip, they were roasted in pits, then dried for storage (Dawson 1892:9).

Drying eased transport and storage, while preparatory roasting also improved the nutritional value of some of the plants (e.g., wild onion, balsamroot, and yellow avalanche lily) by making their carbohydrate content easier to digest (Turner 1987:11). Although the availability of metal pots ultimately resulted in an abandonment of roasting pits, this technique was used within the lifetime of my Chilcotin informants

(DL; EL). As a result, I was able to collect detailed information on the construction and function of Chilcotin roasting pits.

According to my informants, rocks were either heated in a fire close to the roasting pit and then manoeuvred into the pit with long sticks, or a fire was lit in the pit and rocks placed on top (DL; EL). After the fire died down, a layer of leaves was placed above the rocks to provide moisture and to prevent the roots from scorching. The roots were piled onto this layer of leaves, and covered with another layer of leaves. Earth, or another layer of heated rocks and earth, was added to the top of the pit. Invariably, holes were left in the roasting pit, made by piling the contents around one or more sticks. When these sticks were removed, water was poured down the holes and steam was produced. The holes were then sealed until the roots were cooked or the next addition of water was required.

Other detailed accounts of roasting pit construction are provided for the Chilcotin (Ray 1942:137-8), Lillooet (Ray 1942:137-8; Bouchard and Kennedy 1977:72), Shuswap (Teit 1909a:516; Ray 1942:137-8; Boas 1891:637), and Thompson (Ray 1942:137-8; Teit 1900:236; Dawson 1892:20). All groups used the same basic construction techniques as those described, but some variation was noted in rock content, type of insulating vegetation, and use of strings and baskets to hold the roots during cooking.

Much time and effort was expended in preparing a roasting pit. After gathering the food plants, the women could spend two or three days gathering the insulating vegetation, while the men may have cut down a tree for firewood (Dawson 1892:20). Rocks also had to be gathered. After digging the hole with wooden spades, maintaining a fire for a few hours, arranging the various layers for vegetation and soil, and perhaps building subsequent fires on top, the cooking could take several days (ibid.). Men were not allowed to participate in the actual cooking (Boas 1891:637; Dawson 1892:19; Teit 1900:349). As many as seven days may have been needed to prepare a roast, from the gathering of the plant foods to their consumption, although many other activities would also take place during this time. To minimize individual effort, each pit may have been used by more than one family.

The type of plant being roasted affected the length of cooking time, the quantity of rock in the pit, and the overall size of the pit. Teit noted that roots 'remain in the oven – according to the kind being cooked – from twelve to twenty-four hours' (1900:236). According to Chilcotin informants, balsamroot required at least two days to cook, nodding onions and lilies required one day, while spring beauty needed only a couple of hours (EL; DL). Other accounts confirm that balsamroot

needed two or three days (ibid.; Dawson 1892:20), while black lichen
needed to cook overnight (Bouchard and Kennedy 1977:72), and a mixture of camas and lichen needed one day (Dawson 1892:20). The longer
the required cooking time, the more heated rocks were needed to keep
the oven hot and to cook the plants. Balsamroot needed a thickness
of more than 30 cm (12 in.) of rock, mountain potatoes required as
little as 10 cm (4 in.), and the requirements for lilies and onions was
somewhere in between (DL; EL). Of course, the volume of rock in the
pit reduced the volume of space left for the insulating vegetation and
foods. In other words, a larger pit was needed to cook a given volume
of balsamroot than a similar volume of spring beauty.

Two other factors may have affected roasting pit size. First, the depth
and texture of the soil matrix could have affected pit size, with smaller
pits being excavated in more rocky and/or hard pack soils to minimize
the work effort. Second, the size of the social group that used the
pit may have influenced pit size, with larger groups requiring more
food and, therefore, larger pits.

The minimum size of a roasting pit was estimated at 90 cm (3 ft.)
across (DL; EL). The effort of digging the pit, collecting the firewood,
rocks, and insulating vegetation, and heating the rocks would have
been extremely wasteful of time and energy unless a relatively large
quantity of plants could be cooked. A pit smaller than 90 cm probably could not hold the volume of rocks, vegetation, and foods necessary to make the entire process worthwhile. The upper limits on size
were determined by how many roots were cooked in the pit (DL; EL).
For example, a 3 m (10 ft.) wide roasting pit was used to cook 880 litres
of camas and 2 or 3 bunches of black lichen (Dawson 1892:20).

Estimates of pit depth given by Ray (1942:137-8), range from 30 cm
(12 in.) for the Chilcotin to 50 cm (18 in.) for the Lillooet and Thompson.
These estimates seem low in light of eye-witness accounts of roasting
pits used by the Thompson that record depths of 60 cm (24 in.)
(Dawson 1892:20) and 80 cm (30 in.) (Teit 1900:236). Some ethnographers
also mention meat and fish being cooked in the pits (Hill-Tout 1907:102;
Teit 1909a:683; Turner et al. 1980:148; Steedman 1930:478; Ray 1942:137).
However, given the infrequency with which this practice was mentioned in the ethnographic accounts, it was not a common event.

Roasting pits were usually located away from dwellings but close
to a stream (Turner et al. 1980:11) and often in the vicinity of the root
digging grounds (Dawson 1892:9). Roasting pits should occur at the
Montane Parkland basecamps where the processing of Alpine and
Parkland plants took place. The large depressions left by abandoned
roasting pits makes them easy to spot in a surface survey. Since roasting pit construction and use produced a lot of debris, such as fire-

cracked rock, charcoal, and insulating vegetation, they would most logically be located at the margins of the site, away from the main traffic areas.

The number of roasting pits at any locality probably varied according to the abundance of local resources, the typical size of groups using the site, and the length of their stay. For example, DP thought that roasting pits would have been constructed infrequently, if at all, on Mount Cole, where plant resources were not abundant and most trips were made by small groups for a few days. Related factors included the distance from the winter village, the abundance of campsites in the area, and the danger of attack by strangers.

Food Storage

The Lillooet and Shuswap used two types of caches for storing food – the underground cache pit (Teit 1906:215, 1909a:495) and the elevated wooden cache (Teit 1909a:495; Hill-Tout 1978a:58, 1978b:110, 1907:108). Both types of caches were also constructed by the Thompson and Chilcotin (Teit 1900:198-9, 1909b:776). The following ethnographic evidence indicates that cache pits, and possibly elevated caches, were used in the Montane Parkland.

Although expedient elevated caches were sometimes built in trees (Teit 1900:198), most elevated caches had platforms constructed on four posts (DP; Teit 1909a:495). These posts supported a large wooden box five or six feet above the ground (Teit 1900:199; Boas 1891:635). The Upper Lillooet and Shuswap constructed the box out of poles, roofed it with bark (Teit 1909a:495; 1906:215), and provided access with a ladder or notched log (1909a:495). An 8 x 8 ft. elevated cache could store 'a couple hundred fish' (DP). Archaeological evidence for elevated caches would probably be limited to postholes, a few wood-working tools, and, possibly, some bone remains and bark wrappings from the stored food. However, Teit also mentions 'utensils' being stored in the caches (1900:198), suggesting that a variety of other artefacts might also be present.

Scaffolds built 'near their houses' (Teit 1900:199) and at the 'regular camps' (Teit 1909a:495) were also used for storage (Plate 3.2). They were not used for food storage but, rather, to keep cumbersome articles, such as utensils, skins, ropes, and saddles, away from the dogs (Teit 1900:199; 1909a:495). Like the elevated caches, they were built on poles about five feet above the ground (1909a:199), suggesting that, in an archaeological context, the two structures could be easily confused.

The Shuswap and Lillooet used cache pits (Teit 1906:215; 1900:495) to store food at food procurement sites, such as those found in the

Parkland, as well as near the winter villages and fishing sites on the River Terraces. These 'Indian cellars' were generally smaller than roasting pits (DL; EL) with widths ranging from .9 to 1.8 m (3-6 ft.) and depths from 1.2 to 1.8 m (4-6 ft.) (Teit 1900:198; 1909b:776; DL; EL; Dawson 1892:9; Hill-Tout 1907:108).

PLATE 3.2
Bark-covered dwelling lodge and 'cache' near Kamloops, BC

Teit provides a detailed description of the cache pits' roof construction, in which the pit was covered by small, closely aligned poles, then pine needles and earth. A door was generally left in the centre but fish cellars made in the side of a bank had a side door (Teit 1900:199). Dawson offers a similar description of cache pits with a bark and earth covering (1892:9) and Hill-Tout with a pole or board and earth or sand covering (1978a:58).

Within the cache pits, berries and roots were placed in baskets wrapped in birch bark (Teit 1900:199), while dried fish were wrapped in birch bark to prevent moisture damage and mould (DP; Teit 1900:234; Hill-Tout 1978a:58). The pits were also sometimes lined in birch bark and/or grass (DL; Teit 1900:234). In fish caches, grass and pine needles discouraged mice, while juniper berries (*Juniperus communis*) kept insects away (Romanoff, Chapter 5).

The Lillooet had two kinds of underground caches. One type contained 'all the surplus food not required during the winter,' including roots and berries, and was left undisturbed 'until spring' (Teit 1906:223). The second kind of cache was 'situated near the house, and made with less care' (Teit 1906:223). 'From them provisions were taken as required during the winter' (Teit 1906:223). The Shuswap, Thompson, and Chilcotin had similiar caches (Teit 1906:215, 1909a:495, 1909b:776) at or near their winter dwellings and fishing sites (Lane 1981:406; Kennedy and Bouchard, Chapter 6; Dawson 1892:9; Hill-Tout 1907:108; Kennedy and Bouchard 1978:43).

The Chilcotin also used cache pits for the temporary storage of food at Montane procurement sites with abundant resources (DL; EL). For example, in the Montane Parkland sections of the Potato Mountains, more spring beauty were collected than could be carried in a single trip, and the dried roots were stored in cache pits until they could be taken to the winter camp (EL). The pits were also occasionally used to keep the undried roots fresh for processing while the diggers were in the mountains (EL). With the introduction of the horse (c. 1870, according to Teit 1909a:783), the use of cache pits in the mountains declined, since a horse could carry all of the collected roots to the winter camp in a single trip (EL). A similar pattern is assumed for the Mid-Fraser River area, although there are no specific ethnographic accounts of such.

The Thompson and, by implication, the other Salish groups used pits solely for storing 'berries, fish, etc' (Teit 1900:198), which were 'kept fresher in them than in any other kind of cache' (Teit 1909a:495; see also Hill-Tout 1978b:151-2). The Chilcotin also stored fish and roots in caches (DL). Teit (1900:234) adds that the Lower Thompson used the elevated caches to store fish all winter and that only the fish left over in the spring were stored in the cellars until the following spring. The Lillooet may have shared this latter practice before contact but abandoned it (see Kennedy and Bouchard 1978:43) when lowering salmon runs and/or supplements of Euro-Canadian foods no longer allowed or necessitated the use of cache pits. The reduction of intergroup raiding after contact may also have led to a decline in the use of the more easily concealed cache pits. This evidence suggests that cache pits were traditionally used to store plant foods and salmon while the elevated caches were primarily used as alternate fish storage locations.

No ethnographic account mentions meat being stored in cache pits. Instead, meat appears to have been primarily stored in the house rafters (Teit 1900:234; Hill-Tout 1907:101) or in elevated caches (Kennedy and Bouchard 1978:43). The ethnographic accounts offer no reason why meat would not be stored in the cache pits, though perhaps meat does not preserve well in pits.

Hill-Tout maintains that elevated caches were usually found 'only where the ground is rocky, or of such a nature as makes excavations difficult or impossible' (1978a:58). Teit also indicates that cache pits were associated with a dry climate and sandy soil, while elevated caches were more common in more timbered areas (1909a:495). It is probably for these environmental reasons that the Lower Lillooet, Lower Thompson, and Upper Shuswap preferred elevated caches while the Upper Lillooet, Upper Thompson, and Southern Shuswap preferred cache pits (Teit 1906:215, 1909a:495; Hill-Tout 1907:108).

Elevated caches and cache pits were probably constructed at some prehistoric Parkland sites. Cache pits were favoured when large quantities of plant foods had to be stored, while elevated caches were probably constructed when more meat was acquired than could be transported in one trip. Exceptions might have been made for very short term storage.

Given the generally rocky, shallow soil in the Parkland and the abundance of timber for construction, one might expect a preference for elevated caches. On the other hand, in more distant and/or productive localities, cache pits would likely be preferred because the stored food could be better hidden from 'strangers.' The distance and productivity would have also increased the need for storage facilities at these localities. Factors which could have influenced cache pit size are much the same as those suggested for roasting pits: (1) soil matrix, (2) size of the social group using the pit, (3) the kind of foods stored in the pit, and (4) the length of storage time, whether seasonal or long term.

Shelters

The Montane Parkland trees provided shelter, and, even at present, the Lillooet and Shuswap sometimes shun the use of tents in favour of sleeping in dense groves of subalpine fir. These groves provided shelter from the wind, kept out most of the rain and snow, and, with a fire, were warm and secure (DL; DP). A large spruce tree could also be used in a similiar fashion (DP). On trips where the weather was warm and dry and/or where a shorter stay was planned, these trees were probably the most common shelter.

Since these shelters were naturally occurring, they would not leave any structural evidence that could be identified archaeologically. Their former existence may be indicated by the presence of a campfire and other cultural debris in a restricted area, but it is also a strong possibility that tree growth in the area would largely mask artefact and feature patterning.

Temporary bark and brush shelters could also be constructed with little effort. Thompson 'brush-houses' generally consisted of a square or conical framework of light poles covered with spruce or fir branches. Square shelters were more common where spruce, balsam fir, or black-pine were abundant and long wide strips of their bark could be used as covering (Teit 1900:196-7). Similiar structures were also used by the Lillooet (Teit 1906:215) and Shuswap (Teit 1909a:494-5), whose shelters are described as 'very varied and quite irregular' (Dawson 1892:8). They were constructed by hunting parties in the winter or early spring and used only once (Teit 1900:196), suggesting their primary use was as temporary shelters in the cold weather. Presumably, the trees provided sufficient shelter in milder conditions. These shelters would also probably be hard to detect archaeologically, since the poles were probably not substantial enough to leave posthole impressions and the short occupation would not produce a clearly delimited distribution of cultural material.

Dwelling Lodges

Teit also described a variety of differently shaped and sized structures that he called 'summer lodges' or 'mat lodges' (1900:195-7, 1909a:493-4, 1906:215), though some Lillooet and Shuswap families also lived in these structures in the winter (1906:213, 1909a:493). He referred to the same structures as 'hunting lodges' when they were used at a hunting camp (1900:196; 1909a:494; 1906:215). For simplicity, I will refer to all of these structures as dwelling lodges.

All the dwelling lodges described by Teit had a framework of poles tied together with willow withes but otherwise varied according to: (1) shape, that is, square, rectangular, oblong, or circular, (2) size, that is, large or small, and (3) roof covering, that is, mats, bark, poles, or branches (Plates 3.2 and 3.3). The preferred shape, size, and roof covering, in turn, varied according to season, environment, and danger of attack by strangers.

Circular lodges were preferred, especially at lower elevations (Plate 3.2; Teit 1909a:493). However, square or rectangular lodges were more common in forested environments because the abundant bark was generally used for roofing, and the strips of bark were hard to fit on a circular lodge (ibid.) (Plate 3.2). A square or rectangular shape was also built at 'fishing-resorts near lakes or rivers, where large numbers of people congregated for a short time, and to accommodate people at feasts and potlatches' (Teit 1909a:493, see also 1900:196, 1909a:696; Hill-Tout 1907:59).

The Lillooet and Shuswap typically used mats to cover their dwelling lodges (Teit 1906:215, 1909a:493-4). These mats, measuring 5 by 12 ft (Teit 1900:195), were usually made of tule, but grass and rush were

PLATE 3.3
A square, earth-banked dwelling lodge used during winter and covered
with mats (photographed by Harlan I. Smith in 1898, seventeen miles
from Spence's Bridge)

also used (Teit 1909a:493). However, in forested areas, the lodges were
covered with black pine, spruce, cottonwood, or cedar bark (Teit
1900:196, 1909a:493) (Plate 3.2). Dwelling lodges used while hunting
or trapping were sometimes covered with poles running up and down,
brush, sticks, or fir branches (1900:196, 1909a:494-5). Although some
of the Thompson bands used hides on their lodges (Teit 1900:196),
the Shuswap did not use hides because they were too valuable and
because bark and mats were plentiful (Teit 1909a:494).

Circular lodges used as winter dwellings were covered with two or
three layers of mats with bark around the bottom as a foundation for
a layer of earth 15 to 50 cm high (Teit 1906:213, 1909a:493). Lodges built
near deer fences were also sometimes 'covered with earth to a height
of about one metre' (Plate 3.3; Teit 1909a:494). Earth banking was probably reserved for structures that were used frequently and/or for long
periods of time to provide better insulation against the cold tempera-

tures occurring in the late fall and winter.

A few lodges were made with 'logs laid one on top of the other as in a log-cabin, and chinked with moss or grass' (Teit 1906:215). In frequently used hunting areas, like those near deer fences, the log walls were only about one metre high and were merely used at the bottom of other, more common, square or rectangular lodges (Teit 1906:215, 1909a:494). Hunting lodges in 'places where the party was liable to attack by an enemy' had log walls four or five feet high, sometimes covered with earth (Teit 1909a:494).

In summary, the type of covering on the dwelling lodges varied according to environmental location, season of use, and the threat of attack. These variations in building materials would probably be difficult to detect in the archaeological record due to their perishable nature. Where no organics remained, the building materials might be inferred from the environmental setting and the outline of cultural debris deposited within the walls. Earth coverings should be indicated by a small raised rim.

Teit provides illustrations and lengthy descriptions of the techniques used to construct dwelling lodges (1900:195-7, 1906:215, 1909a:493). These accounts indicate that prehistoric dwelling lodges should exhibit a central hearth or hearths with symmetrical arrangements of postholes. Square lodges were typically 10 to 12 ft. across and large ones were up to 50 or 60 ft. long, while circular lodges often measured 15 to 20 ft. in diameter and were 12 ft. high (Teit 1900:195-6; see also Hill-Tout 1907:59).

Bedding typically consisted of bear, goat, sheep, or deer skins spread over a mattress of boughs, but if skins were not available, goat hair blankets (Teit 1906:210, 215, 260, 1909a:496), grass mats (Teit 1900:199), or rush mats (Teit 1906:215) were occasionally used. The floor of the lodge was covered in small fir branches (Teit 1900:196).

Permanent 'hunting-lodges' were occasionally constructed 'in the sheltered valleys in the mountains, close to good hunting-ground' (Teit 1900:196) or at 'places much frequented' (Teit 1906:215) and 'especially on the lower grounds' (Teit 1909a:494). They were used primarily in the fall and spring (Teit 1900:196; Dawson 1892:8). 'Trapping-lodges,' constructed in the same manner, were 'generally built near the deer fences' (Teit 1909a:494). These comments imply that the dwelling lodges were most common at lower elevation hunting localities and only used at the more desirable and frequently used Parkland localities.

Thus, Parkland dwelling lodges should generally be square or rectangular, with bark, pole, stick, or brush coverings. Earth covering on lower walls may also be expected, and log walls may have occurred in resource-rich areas, distant from the winter village (where attacks were feared). A few of the Parkland sites in the study area may have attracted groups large enough to warrant construction of the large square or rectangular lodges.

Sweathouses

The Lillooet, Shuswap, Thompson, and Chilcotin all built the same type of sweathouse (Teit 1900:198, 370, 1909a:495, 1909b:776, 1906:215, 285; Dawson 1892:9; Plate 3.4). The small dome-shaped structure had a frame of bent saplings (typically willow) covered with bark, blankets, or earth and accommodated up to four people (Teit 1900:198). Sweat-houses were constructed at localities that were used for long stays and/or frequently revisited (Teit 1900:198, 346, 1906:215, 1909a:495, 776). They were always built near water (Teit 1900:198) 'so that on issuing therefrom the bather may at once plunge into cold water' (Dawson 1892:9). Men's sweathouses were built some distance away from the village (Teit 1906:267; see also Dawson 1892:8) with some men, includ-ing shamans, building their own private sweathouses (Teit 1900:354, 1906:282). Women also built and used their own sweathouses (Teit 1906:267), and each boy constructed a sweathouse at puberty, in some wild and lonely part of the mountains (Boas 1891:645; Teit 1900:319, 1906:266-7, 1909a:588-9). Therefore, sweathouses were probably com-mon at Montane Parkland basecamps, especially those used for long stays.

All sweathouses were designed for reuse and, therefore, these struc-tures should produce relatively clear archaeological remains in the form of postholes from the frame, soil discolouration and organic debris from the flooring, a small hole inside to contain the hot rocks, and charcoal and rocks from the fires used to heat the rocks outside the sweathouse. The more permanent structures with earthen roofs would probably also leave a raised circular rim.

Structures for Women

Three types of lodges were built solely for use by women. The girl's puberty lodge was a small conical structure of fir branches sometimes covered with bark or mats (Teit 1900:198, 1906:215, 262, 265, 296, 1909a:495, 587; Hill-Tout 1978b:112). A girl was required to stay in her lodge all day for anywhere from four months to four years after her first menses, though the lodge was rebuilt or moved at least once a month (Teit 1900:265, 312, 317, 1906:264-5, 1909a:587; Hill-Tout 1978b:112). The woman's menstrual lodge, possibly accommodating several

PLATE 3.4
Traditional native sweathouse near Kamloops, BC

women, was also typically a conical shelter, though in winter a minia-
ture pithouse was sometimes built (Teit 1900:198, 326-7, 1906:215,
1909a:495). A woman used the lodge for four days during her menses
(Teit 1906:296). A woman's birthing lodge may have been similar to
the two other lodges (Teit 1906:261) but was built close to the woman's
dwelling lodge or pithouse (Hill-Tout as cited in Teit 1906:295) rather
than outside the village or camp. It was used by the mother and child
for one to three months following a woman's first birthing but for only
four to twenty days following subsequent births (Teit 1906:295).

Although perhaps similar in form, the content of the woman's
shelters should be different from that of the temporary summer
shelters used by both men and women. Any associated tools should
be those used in woman's activities, such as making mats, baskets,
thread, and garments (Teit 1900:314, 1906:264, 1909a:587), while food
restrictions suggest that the remains of large game, especially deer,
should be absent (Teit 1900:317, 326; Boas 1891:642; Ray 1939). A girl's
puberty lodge might also have a large hole in the centre (Teit 1900:198,
312; Hill-Tout 1978b:112) and, possibly, the remains of her bone comb,
scratcher, drinking tube, or whistle (Boas 1891:642; Teit 1900:312-3,
1906:264, 1909a:580).

Except for the more permanent women's menstrual lodges found near the winter village, all the structures seem to have been simple brush or bark shelters primarily designed for use by one woman. Most lodges were built on the outskirts of the main encampment. Their short-term use and isolation might make these structures hard to locate in an archaeological context. Puberty and menstrual lodges should be expected near the Montane Parkland basecamps, but, since heavily pregnant women probably avoided the arduous mountain trip, birthing lodges are unlikely to occur.

Hide Preparation

The Lillooet, Thompson, Chilcotin, and Shuswap all used the same tools and methods to prepare hides (Teit 1900:184, 1906:204, 1909a:476, 1909b:764). Deer and elk hides were the most important, but bear, wolf, coyote, lynx, fox, marmot, hare, and marten were also used. Deer and other ungulates were skinned and the hides were partly cleaned immediately after the kill (WN; DP). The hides were further cleaned at the basecamp, and, if the hides were not to be used as blankets or robes, the hair was removed 'at the hunting-camp, while they were still fresh' (Teit 1909a:477). These activities would have produced considerable debris and would have required a large area away from camp and, therefore, produced a special activity area (Albright 1984:52).

According to Teit, the hides 'were then dried and folded up until winter, which was the time for skin-dressing' (1909a:477). In cold weather the skins were dressed inside the house (Teit 1900:185), while in warmer weather they were dressed just outside the house (Teit 1909a:717). WN also states that 'hide tanning' was done only at the village. However, informants from the Chilcotin (DL) and Pavilion (BE; DP) said that hide tanning also took place at the Parkland basecamps. It seems likely that hide tanning in the mountains, like meat drying, was more common before the horse made it easier to transport unprocessed resources to the village and made short stays in the mountains more feasible. The two methods of preparing hides were clearly summarized by Teit and are not included in this report (1909a:184-6; see also Teit 1900:185, 1906:203, 205, 1909b:764; Boas 1891:636; Albright 1984:54-5).

Apart from the stone and, possibly, bone tools used to scrape the skins, little evidence from hide preparation is expected in the archaeological record. A few smudge pits might be located, but, for the most part, hide smoking appears to be a recent introduction to the study area (Teit 1906:215, 1909a:477). The frames and poles used when scraping and stretching the skins would not preserve well, and no post holes were created by these structures. Small fires were sometimes used to dry the skins, but it would be difficult to discern a hide-drying function for any given hearth.

The Parkland basecamps should contain some hide-working tools. Preliminary hide preparation was undertaken in the mountains, though the final dressing of the hides seems to have occurred more commonly at the winter village. When many deer were killed in a hunt, the effort needed to cut and dry all the meat probably allowed the women very little time to work hides in the mountains. Since the deer skulls would have been difficult to transport down the mountain, the remains of skulls, from which the brains were removed for tanning, may be relatively common at the Parkland basecamps. In general, evidence of these activities should be found at the edge of the village or camp.

Deer Fences

Teit (1900:246, 1906:226, 1909a:521) reports that the Thompson, Upper Lillooet, and Shuswap all used deer fences. None of my Indian or Euro-Canadian informants have ever seen or heard of deer fences being used in the area, suggesting that their use was abandoned soon after contact. Perhaps fence construction ended with the widespread use of guns and horses about 1840 (Teit 1909a:540), which provided a more successful and less labour-intensive method of catching deer. The use of bow and arrow was definitely discontinued by 1868 (Teit 1909a:544). The only account of deer fence design and use is provided by Teit:

> A favourite method of procuring deer was by means of deer fences. These were formerly very numerous, and their remains may still be seen in several parts of the mountains . . .
>
> Some of these fences were built in order to catch deer in the summertime, but most of them were intended for capturing deer from the later part of September to the beginning or middle of December, since they were placed in those parts of the mountains which the deer frequent at that time of the year. They were generally built in little valleys or defiles between mountains, and especially in those which were favourite places of deer crossing from one mountain to another, or at spots where large numbers of deer generally passed on their way down from the higher mountains to their wintering grounds.
>
> At these places a fence was roughly constructed. It was seldom over four feet or four feet and a half in height, and consisted of poles, limbs of trees, etc., placed close enough together to hinder the deer from

passing through. Sometimes these fences were from half a mile or more in length. At intervals of every eighty or a hundred yards a gate or opening was left wide enough to allow a deer to easily pass through. In the middle of each opening a shallow hole was scooped out, and a snare made of bark string was placed in it. (Teit 1900:245-6)

The snare was attached to a long spring pole so that when the deer stepped into the snare it triggered the pole and the deer was suspended in the air or lifted off the ground by its leg (ibid.). 'This method of hunting was very successful if the snares were kept dry' (ibid.). 'In wooded districts, where trails followed by the deer in their fall migration crossed small creeks,' spears with stone points were used instead of snares (Teit 1909a:521). These spears, set in the bank, pierced the deer as it jumped across the creek. The fences were sometimes built co-operatively by a group of families camped nearby (Lane 1981:407), but the animals trapped by a party were owned by the men who built the traps or snares (Teit 1906:256).

At Spences Bridge, the hunting of deer at crossing places usually occurred during the November rut and 'at a later date when the deer came down from the higher mountains to their winter grounds in the lower hills' (Teit 1900:245). Some Shuswap bands also used fences or corrals to capture deer as they crossed a lake during their fall migration (Teit 1909a:521-3), but, in the study area, the deer did not typically cross the lakes in their migration and it is doubtful that this technique was used.

Based on ethnographic accounts, it appears that the fences were not built in open areas, though the evidence is inferential. Fences half a mile long would be difficult to construct in a treeless environment, especially fences high enough to pen a deer. Moreover, the fences were generally located in valleys between mountains which were invariably totally or partly forested. Other ungulates, especially elk and sheep, may also have been captured with the use of these fences. The size of the hunting party would probably have varied in a fashion similar to that noted for the hunting drives, that is, generally three to seven men with women and children filling in where necessary.

The deer fences would probably not be well preserved in the archaeological record. The structures were made with perishable material and, from the description, were not necessarily set into the ground, so few postholes would be created. Since the fences were sometimes burnt on the death of the owner, charcoal concentrations might indicate their presence, though it would probably be difficult to distinguish this evidence from a natural forest fire.

Scattered along the length of the deer fence one would expect to find wood-working tools used in the construction of the fence and snares, and hunting and butchering tools from the deer kills. The remains of 'hunting lodges' (see previous sections) might also be found near frequently used fences. The faunal remains from deer (and possibly other ungulates) might be expected to occur near but not at the fence. Much of this evidence would be difficult to locate in a surface survey due to the trees, poor preservation, and heavy litter mat. Nevertheless, it should be possible to speculate on the location of the deer fences, based on topography and existing game trails, and to undertake sub-surface archaeological testing in these areas.

Other Hunting Sites

As in the Alpine, a variety of mammal kill and/or butchering sites can be expected in the Montane Parkland. The type of sites (e.g., game look-outs, single event kill and/or butchering sites, and multiple kill and/or butchering sites – see Appendix) and the associated material remains would be much the same in both environments (see sections on Alpine hunting sites). Any significant differences are noted below.

In contrast to the open Alpine, the more forested portions of the Parkland allowed lone hunters to use snares along frequently used trails. Hunting drives could have been conducted by larger hunting parties using snares in more forested environments as well as blinds in more open areas. Butchering sites from kills at deer fences should be distant from the kill sites for the same reasons as those at blinds should be distant from kill sites. Only preliminary butchering seems to have taken place at the kill sites and most bony parts of the animals were taken to the basecamps. Unlike those in the Alpine, the kill sites along the fences may contain evidence of wood-working tools used to construct the fence and snares. Other than the stone blinds, most Montane Parkland hunting sites would be hard to detect, though the more permanent and frequently used sites would produce denser lithic scatters.

In the Montane Parkland, bears could be caught with spring traps and deadfalls as well as with bows and arrows and dogs (Teit 1900:249, 1906:226-7, 1909a:522). Pits from the deadfalls may be detected in an archaeological survey, though it is unclear where one should expect to find them. Kill and/or butchering sites for bears were probably single event sites randomly scattered throughout the Parkland.

A large variety of small mammals was hunted in the Montane Parkland. Of those animals trapped largely for their fur, the most commonly captured were lynx, fox, marten, mink, and fisher (Chapter 2, Table 4; Teit 1909a:518). Cougar, wolf, coyote, wolverine, lynx, and bobcat were trapped less frequently (Teit 1906:227) and coyote, lynx, and others were eaten only during famines (Teit 1906:225). Parkland mammals that were hunted for food as well as hides (or quills) included: marmot, snowshoe hare, porcupine, and squirrels (Teit 1909a:649; Chapter 2, Table 4). Hunting for these fur-bearing animals would peak in the fall when the pelts were best.

Most of these animals were either snared or trapped (Teit 1906:227, 1909a:523) and, in some cases (as with marmot, snowshoe hare, and squirrels), they could also be chased and shot with a bow and arrow. The form, content, and distribution of the resulting kill and butchering sites would be the same as those noted for Alpine sites.

Birds that may have been found in the local Parkland environments and that were known to be hunted by the Shuswap and Lillooet include: swans, geese, ducks, grouse, red-shafted flicker, red-headed woodpecker, owls, and eagles, with the latter four being hunted for their feathers (Teit 1906:277, 225, 1909a:513, 649, 478, 509). Birds were not a staple in the diet (Kennedy and Bouchard 1978:41), and it is doubtful that any of these birds were taken in large numbers in the Parkland. The nature of any associated sites would be the same as those in the Alpine.

Ownership of Resources

Having discussed the importance of the Montane resources and the technology used to acquire them, it is now possible to address the issue of ownership. Each band had its habitual hunting and trapping grounds near its home, but these grounds were considered the common property of the entire tribe and access was given to members of other bands and tribes who were blood-related (Teit 1900:293, 1906:256, 1909a:572; Boas 1891:638). This evidence initially appears to contradict Dawson's statement that 'all the Shuswap formerly had hereditary hunting grounds, each family having its own peculiar hunting place or places' (1892:14; see also Boas 1891:638). However, I think Dawson was actually referring to the former system of hunting stewards. We know that hunting at specific locations was regulated by individual hunting stewards who inherited their position and whose family habitually used these locations. However, they did not 'own' the land and they allowed others access to their area. Those caught hunting without permission were merely required to share the meat with the steward (Dawson 1892:14).

The band was defined as those people associated with a given village (Teit 1909a:457), and the band's territory would include all lands regulated by its members. Again, there is no evidence to suggest that access was denied to others outside the band, unless they were 'strangers,' that is, unrelated. In fact, in some especially resource-rich areas, members of different bands would hunt together or one after another without arousing any animosity (Teit 1900:293, 1906:256). However, strangers caught trapping, hunting, or plant gathering within the tribal territory of another group were driven off or killed (Teit 1900:293, 1906:227). Therefore, the lands may be seen as the common property of the tribe, while specific locations were still 'regulated,' though not 'owned,' by individual families. The regulation of hunting in a specific location would prevent the over-depletion of resources in that area, while habitual use by a specific family would keep a band's members dispersed throughout the territory.

A deer fence was owned by the individual who built or maintained it and was inherited by the next of kin, who could keep it, give it to another relative, or sell it to someone outside the family (Teit 1900:293-4, 1909a:573). In some cases, the fence was burned and a new one erected in the same place by the heir (Teit 1900:328). If it was abandoned for a number of years, anyone could erect a new one and snare deer in that place (Teit 1909a:573), though members of one sub-division of a tribe were not allowed to build fences in the territory of another sub-division (Teit 1900:293). The number of fences was regulated, since the 'erection of another fence in the same pass, in proximity to the first, would materially affect chances of capturing deer by it' (ibid.:294). Deer blinds, on the other hand, do not appear to have been owned. This difference may be explained by the fact that deer fences, sometimes miles long, took a long time to construct and had to be regularly repaired, while blinds were small, quickly constructed, and easily maintained.

Trails, berry-picking areas, and root-digging grounds were common tribal property (Teit 1900:294, 1906:256, 1909a:573). Use of the largest and most important berry-picking areas was regulated by a chief (Teit 1906:256, 282, 1909a:573; Boas 1891:637), based on the advice of young men ('Teit 1909a:573) or an experienced old woman who watched the ripening of the fruit (Dawson 1892:21; Teit 1900:294). When the berries were ripe, the women picked and cured them in one spot before moving to the next (Teit 1909a:573). This monitoring practice may have only applied to berry patches 'in the villages and on the lower parts of the mountains' (Teit 1906:256).

Starting in 1800, some Salish bands, including Pavilion, adopted some social practices from the coastal tribes that resulted in changes in the ownership practices discussed above. With the creation of clans and an hereditary nobility, hunting territories, root-digging grounds, berrying resorts, and Montane basecamps became the common property of the nobility of the band (Teit 1909a:575-6, 581-2). 'In a great many places, however, the more distant hunting-grounds and root-digging and berrying places were looked upon as tribal property; and the nobility of the bands either did not claim them, or, being unable to enforce their claims, had decided to leave them as common property' (Teit 1909a:583). Trapping grounds were divided among the crest groups of nobility of each band, who collected 'rents' (e.g., skins, dried fish, oil) from any common people and strangers using the area and drove away or fined anyone trapping without permission (ibid.). Berries were divided after a communal picking, with the chief receiving the greatest portion (Boas 1891:638). These changes were not accepted by all bands.

The adoption of these new social practices was probably stimulated by trade with Euro-Canadians. With the fur trade, many coastal peoples realized they could profit heavily by acting as middle-men between the fur traders and the fur-rich interior peoples (Duff 1969:58). Increased commerce and subsequent intermarriage between the two sides led to some interior bands adopting the social system and ceremonies of their more powerful neighbours. With the rising importance of trade and the intervention of Euro-Canadians, warfare declined and prestige was increasingly sought through potlatching rather than warfare (ibid.). In the prehistoric past, Interior peoples may have adopted (and later abandoned) these coastal practices, when economic conditions stimulated intense trade.

Summary

Montane Parkland localities with more resources, at a greater distance from the winter village, and with many potential campsites were used by more people and for longer stays. Consequently, these localities (e.g., Blustry Mountain, Pavilion Mountain, Figure 1; Chapter 7, Figure 5) should have more sites with higher artefact densities. These conditions also created a greater demand for temporary storage and processing facilities in addition to more elaborate and numerous shelters. The circular depressions produced by cache pits and roasting ovens would probably be the most easily recognized evidence of any structures or features. Although not as numerous or as conspicuous, depressions produced by smudge pits, sweathouses, earth-banked lodges, and girls' puberty lodges may also be evident at the surface. Since most activities in the Montane Parkland occurred at the basecamps, they should be the largest, most obvious, and most numerous archaeological sites in this environment (Figure 1; Chapter 7, Figure 5).

Stone hunting blinds and burial cairns would be uncommon but easy to spot in the more open areas. On the other hand, isolated kill and/or butchering sites for ungulates, bears, small mammals, or birds would be numerous but would lack large features or high densities of artefacts to indicate their presence. Butchering sites near blinds, deer fences, salt licks, and other localities where ungulates were frequently encountered would contain higher artefact densities and might be more easily identified, though the trees and ground cover in the forested areas would conceal most lithic scatters and features. As in the Alpine, plant collecting sites in the Montane Parkland would leave few, if any, archaeological remains. Although the processing and storage of the plant foods typically occurred at basecamps, a few isolated roasting pits and cache pits should also be expected outside the basecamps.

In summary, it should be much easier to locate prehistoric sites in the more productive and heavily used Parkland localities, such as Pavilion Mountain and Blustry Mountain-Cairn Peak. The sites would be larger and contain more numerous and more permanent features that could be readily identified during survey. At less important localities, such as Mount Cole, these structures were probably either missing or more temporary, and the resulting low density sites would be hard to locate with the heavy ground cover.

MONTANE FORESTS

Ethnographic Summary

Ethnographic accounts of traditional native use of this environmental unit are few and very sketchy. The forested valleys are primarily seen as corridors to the rich Alpine and Montane Parkland environments, and the only known Forest campsites are located in clearings along the transit routes (DP; BE; RA) (Figure 1). Presumably, the generally low resource densities discouraged anything but casual use of the Forests (Chapter 2, Figures 1-2; Plates 2.2, 2.5). Not surprisingly, the most frequented portions appear to have been open woods near forest margins and open areas along streams and trails where the variety and abundance of plant and animal species was greatest (Chapter 2: Table 4).

The lower elevation Forests were probably used most frequently between early November and late April, when most people were living in the winter village, close to the treeline (see the River Terraces section). Deer wintered in these areas and, although lean and tough in late winter and spring, they were hunted from the winter village whenever weather permitted (DP), especially if the stored foods were running low. Other ungulates, such as sheep and elk (in the past), might also have been hunted nearby, and small game animals, especially snowshoe hare, would have also have been available at the forest margins where the brush was abundant. Most of these resources were eaten fresh as an alternative, or supplement, to the dried foods stored in, or near, the houses.

In early spring, these lower elevation Forests provided the first fresh plant resources of the season. In late March and April, food plants, such as onions, Indian celery, and balsamroot shoots, were harvested in the open areas of the Douglas-fir forests (Chapter 2, Tables 2 and 3) while families still lived at, or near, the winter village. The wood and boughs from Douglas-fir and Rocky Mountain juniper were also obtained at this time (Turner, Chapter 8). In moister areas along streams, it was possible to find shoots from false Solomon's-seal, cow-parsnip, and fireweed, roots from water parsnip and silverweed, bitter cherry bark and red cedar roots for basketry, and rope willow and Rocky Mountain maple for cordage (Turner, Chapter 8). Small mammals, grouse, and ungulates were also available, though still in poor condition.

As people left the winter villages in April, they began to move to higher elevations to exploit some of the higher Montane Forests, especially those bordering the Intermediate Grasslands and Lakes, where they established basecamps. Between late April and mid-May, Forest resources such as lodgepole pine inner bark, black lichen, and Indian celery leaves were exploited at mid-elevations (Chapter 2, Table 3; Turner, Chapter 8). Deer and other ungulates also began moving to higher elevations at this time and were relatively abundant in mid-elevation Forests. Grouse and small game provided another dietary supplement (Chapter 2, Table 4).

In late May and June, women gathered spruce roots for basketry in the high elevation Montane Forests (Chapter 2, Table 3; Turner, Chapter 8). Later in June and July, many women returned to the lowland Forests to gather the ripening fruits, especially soapberries and saskatoons (Turner, Chapter 8). Historically, families based their berry-picking activities at the villages (ibid.), but it is unclear if this was the precontact practice. The whitebark pine seeds, another important forest resource, were collected in large quantities in September (ibid.). High elevation resources were presumably gathered either on the way between the Montane Parkland and the River Terraces or while at the Parkland basecamps.

Hunting, especially for deer, occurred in the Forests in the fall as the men followed the animals down the mountains from the Parkland to lower elevations. All animals, small and large, were in their prime at this time of year and were eagerly sought. Both plant and animal resources were more abundant in areas which had been burned (DP), resulting in more frequent use of these niches and encouraging the practice of selective burning to promote plant growth. The route followed by the animals, and therefore the best for hunting, probably changed to make the best use of the open land.

In the study area, the only remembered source of basalt (the primary rock used in tool-making) was in the Montane Forests at the headwaters of Maiden Creek. Local informants maintain that the exact location was kept secret because of the rock's importance as a trade item and as a raw material in stone tool manufacture (DP; BE; RA). It is unclear whether this resource was collected while hunting nearby on Pavilion Mountain (embedded procurement) or whether separate trips were made to acquire the basalt resulting in specialized procurement campsites. It is also possible that people from the study area travelled to the 'mountains north of Lytton' to get the native copper that occurred there (Smith 1899:133; see also Boas 1891:637).

Ethnoarchaeological Reconstruction

Based on existing ethnographic and environmental information, I predict a low density of archaeological sites within the Montane Forests unit. These sites should include: single use kill and/or butchering sites, multiple use hunting sites at deer fences, plant gathering sites, and short- and long-term transit camps along streams (Appendix).

The majority of sites in the Forests are expected to be resource procurement sites used by task groups based in other environments. The lowland Forest resources were probably most commonly exploited from the winter houses, mid-elevation Forests from basecamps at the Lakes or in the Grasslands, and high elevation Forests from the Parkland basecamps. A few small basecamps might have existed in clearings in the higher elevation Forests where groups of men, with or without their families, camped while hunting deer in the fall. Transit camps used by many different groups, varying in size and composition, were located in the Forests along the routes to the Montane.

Since most sites in the Forests were probably used only by small task groups during day trips from a basecamp, features should be limited to hearths and the insubstantial remains of temporary shelters. Associated artefacts should reflect hunting and plant-gathering activities, while tools and features from food processing should be absent. In a few sites, along the trail to the Parkland, artefact densities could be moderately high, since the sites were reused every year by many different groups. Deer fences (described in the Montane Parkland section) could also have been located in some forested areas. The kill and/or butchering sites associated with such sites would have higher artefact densities than would the latter. These localities and other important hunting sites may also be expected to contain the remains of dwelling lodges, smudge pits, meat drying racks, and elevated caches. The dwelling lodges should generally be small, square structures with bark, pole, or branch coverings and perhaps earth and logs on the lower parts of the walls (Plate 3.3).

Small scattered kill and butchering sites, with few artefacts and low visibility, are expected throughout the area. Since beaver were available in this environment, the bone and antler harpoons used to hunt these animals (Teit 1906:226, 1909a:523) would be one tool form that may be present in these assemblages but absent from the Parkland and Alpine assemblages. Look-out sites would probably be rare, given the general lack of good overviews in this forested environment. The only deer drive identified in the Montane Forest is located on the rocky slopes above Pavilion Lake, where three or four men could trap and kill deer within a rocky gully (DP) (Figure 1).

INTERMEDIATE GRASSLANDS

Ethnographic Summary

The Intermediate Grasslands (Plate 2.3; Chapter 2: Figures 1-2) include some of the first agricultural lands to have been claimed and farmed by Euro-Canadians. As a consequence, the Indians were prohibited from using these lands soon after contact, and recent attempts to collect information on traditional land use practices were largely unsuccessful. Much of the following ethnographic reconstruction must be extrapolated from environmental data and practices recorded for adjoining environmental units.

Two of the most important food plants, spring beauty (corms) and balsamroot (roots, shoots, and leaves) are very abundant in the Grasslands and are at their prime between late April and mid-May (Chapter 2, Tables 2 and 3). Balsamroot is, in fact, more abundant and more accessible in the Grasslands than in the Parkland and was more commonly gathered at these lower elevations (DP). Fireweed shoots and nodding onion are also present. Along the streams which cross the Grasslands, species preferring moister conditions, such as cow-parsnip and false Solomon's-seal, are common (Chapter 2, Table 3). If families harvested these plants in April and May, the area was used after the winter villages were vacated and before moving to the Montane Parkland or to the trout-fishing streams at the Intermediate Lakes. In the

Chilcotin, large traditional gatherings took on the form of native 'rodeos' after contact (Alexander et al., 1985). Spring use is also suggested by the historic use of lands on the Diamond S Ranch for an Indian Rodeo in the 1930s and 1940s during the Victoria Day weekend (24 May) (DP).

In Botanie Valley, a Grassland locality near Lytton, very large aggregations of families (over 1,000 people) occurred in May and June (Teit 1900:294, 374; Boas 1898:9), when the root crops (e.g., spring beauty, avalanche lily, chocolate tips) were at their peak (Teit 1900:294; Dawson 1892:20). These families came from many local bands and at least three ethno-linguistic groups – Thompson, Lillooet, and Shuswap (Teit 1909a:536-7; Turner, Chapter 8). It is possible that some families from Fountain were included in these gatherings. This evidence suggests the possibility that large groups of people also gathered in the Grasslands above Pavilion, though not in the numbers made possible by the exceptionally rich resources of Botanie Valley. Later, in June, July, and August, the Grasslands may have been visited by women collecting berries in the area (Chapter 2, Table 3).

In the neighbouring Upper Hat Creek Valley, the Grasslands were the hunting grounds of the Spences Bridge Band (Upper Thompson) (Teit 1900:170). Wintering deer are not as common in the Grasslands of the study area as they are in Hat Creek Valley (Environment Canada, n.d.), but deer often concentrate between November and May in forests surrounding the local Grasslands (Low, personal communication). Thus, the margins of the local Grasslands were probably seen as important hunting areas in these months. Although some deer remained in Grasslands all year, hunting activity would have been most productive in early spring and late fall as the deer migrated through the Grasslands on their way to and from higher elevations. The same is true of other ungulates.

Grouse and small mammals could also have been hunted all year in the Grasslands, though any animal hunted for furs (Chapter 2, Table 4) would most likely have been taken in the fall. Men hunting on their own, or with a few other men, could have made day trips from the winter village to capture these species.

The most commonly used trails between Pavilion Valley and Pavilion Mountain passed through the Grasslands, using the route subsequently followed during the Caribou Gold Rush (DP; BE). Similarly, the route to Mount Cole passed through the Grasslands on Sagebrush Flats (Chapter 1, Figure 1).

Ethnoarchaeological Reconstruction

Site types expected in this environment include basecamps, transit camps, plant-gathering locations, kill and/or butchering sites, and, possibly, deer fences (Appendix). Given the weak ethnographic data on the seasonal use of the Grasslands, the reconstruction of prehistoric use of the area is not as detailed as it is for other environments. In the early spring (April-May), when deer, balsamroot, and spring beauty were abundant, the Grasslands may have been a selected destination, with at least small family groups establishing basecamps for a few days to a week. Since the Grasslands were not far from the winter villages, women could have collected berries during day trips to the area in June and July and men could have hunted deer during the winter. Late fall basecamps may also have occurred there, as the hunters followed the deer down out of the mountains. Since some of the major trails between the River Terraces and the Montane Parkland cut through the Grasslands, it seems likely that short-term transit camps (about one to three days) were made by families and same-sex hunting and gathering groups travelling between these two environments. These short-term camps would have occurred between mid-May and November.

The short-term transit camps should contain evidence of basic camp activities such as cooking and the construction of temporary shelters. Basecamps used in the spring and fall to collect plants and to hunt deer may contain evidence of roasting pits, storage pits for plants, storage platforms, and hide-smoking pits. Given the short stays and close proximity to the winter village, where unprocessed resources could be stored, these features are not expected to be abundant. Sweathouses and women's seclusion lodges may also have been constructed at these camps. Artefact assemblages should include tools used in cooking, construction, plant and animal procurement, plant processing, hide preparation, and meat drying. In general, the Grasslands are expected to contain a low density of small sites with few features, though a few larger sites may occur in preferred camping locations as a result of frequent reuse by small groups.

A remote possibility exists that the Grasslands were used by some families as a wintering place. A few housepits exist in Hat Creek Valley, and elders from Pavilion claim to have seen housepits in the Grasslands above Pavilion (DP) (though none could be found during a survey of the area). Given the long hauling distance from Fraser River fishing stations, it is unlikely that a major village was located in the Grasslands. I cannot, however, discount the possibility that one or two families may have chosen to build their winter lodges or housepits at this distant locality.

INTERMEDIATE LAKES

Ethnographic Summary

Trout were the most important food resource found in the Intermediate Lakes unit (Plate 2.4; Chapter 2, Figures 1-2). They were common all year in the lakes, but the largest quantities were caught in spring as they spawned in small streams leading into and out of the lakes (Table 1; DP). Spawning usually occurred in the latter half of May, although cold weather could cause a delay (DP). The following is an account of historic fishing practices at the outlet to Pavilion Lake, provided by DP.

Groups of up to fifty people (comprised of five or six families) would camp near the fishing site and work together to catch the trout, using stone weirs, basket traps, and bag nets. Two or three weirs were constructed on Pavilion Creek, using loose boulders to make a wall two to three feet high. A small opening in the centre of the wall allowed the fish to pass into a basket trap placed behind the opening. Fish were then driven down the stream to the weir, where they were trapped. The basket trap was made of red willow or red osier dogwood, which grew abundantly along the stream (see also Teit 1906:228; Dawson 1892:16-7; Kennedy and Bouchard, Chapter 6). The weirs had to be rebuilt each year after they were washed out by the spring floods. Bag nets were also used to scoop the fish out of the pools, although this appears to be a postcontact practice. The trout weirs and traps were not owned (see also Teit 1909a:572).

People stayed at the camp as long as the trout continued to spawn in large number (usually about two weeks), catching sixty to seventy fish per day. The eldest person distributed the trout among those present (Romanoff, Chapter 9). The fish were dried and smoked for winter on numerous A-frame racks set over fires. After drying in this manner, the fish lasted about one year.

Not all families took advantage of the spawning runs. With the spring beauty and other important plant foods reaching their peak in late May and early June, some families concentrated their efforts on gathering plants and hunting in the Grasslands and Montane Parkland. It seems unlikely that the trout population was large enough to provide a reasonable return if all the band members participated in the fishing.

Fishing continued into June, but as the month progressed, it was abandoned by most families in favour of hunting and plant gathering in the mountains (DP). On the other hand, some families from Pavilion travelled from Pavilion Lake to Loon Lake on Bonaparte Band lands to catch more trout (Chapter 1: Figure 1). People from Fountain also went to Loon Lake for two weeks and, in exchange, allowed Bonaparte people to fish at Six Mile in August and September (Romanoff 1985:146; Kennedy and Bouchard, Chapter 6). The importance of trout in the diet is indicated by the fact that lakes were sometimes stocked through the transport of live fish (Teit 1900:348, 333).

While the majority of men and women at camp were fishing, some men hunted deer that passed closeby on game trails as they moved from the valleys to the mountains (DP). The deer were not at their prime at this time but were not as lean and tough as they had been a month or two earlier, before the warm weather had stimulated new plant growth. The Thompson also participated in short hunts (Table 1) and the Chilcotin 'men would hunt cooperatively along game trails while the women continued fishing' (Lane 1981:406). The few flocks of migratory wetland birds which passed through the study area were also at the Lakes at this time and were hunted as the opportunity arose.

Between late April and mid-May, a variety of plants were available for harvesting in this environmental unit. On the valley bottom, it was possible to collect the inner bark of cottonwood, silverweed, and cow-parsnip, while on the drier slopes there were false Solomon's-seal, mariposa lily, nodding onion, balsamroot shoots and leaves, Indian celery leaves, desert parsley, and blackcap shoots (Chapter 2, Tables 2 and 3; Turner, Chapter 8). The women may have collected these plants while waiting for the runs to begin at the fishing sites.

Women returned to the area in June and early July to collect berries on the surrounding slopes (Turner, Chapter 8). Saskatoons, soapberry, and blackcaps were especially abundant, though only saskatoons were available in large quantities every year (ibid.; Dawson 1892:21). The quantity of berries available in any given year varied considerably, with the hot, dry conditions in the study area sometimes causing them to dry up before they reached maturity, thus producing a poor crop. The Lakes environments may have been especially important at these times, since the creeks and lakes promote somewhat milder and moister conditions. Fires, either natural or deliberately set, also encouraged the growth of berry plants along the valley slopes (DP; Turner et al., 1980; Turner 1987:4; Turner, Chapter 8). Controlled burning was probably practised in this area to increase berry crops as well as to improve the root harvest (Teit 1900:230).

The Lakes were probably also visited by the women briefly in August to collect not only cattails and tule for mat-making (Turner, Chapter 8), but Oregon-grape, choke cherries, wild gooseberries, and balsamroot (Chapter 2, Table 3). In September and October, silverweed and cottonwood mushrooms could be harvested at the Lakes (WN; Turner, Chapter 8). These resources were largely absent from other environmental units. Fishing was a fall activity in more southern areas (Teit 1900:154), and some trout fishing may have been undertaken in the study area at this time, possibly in conjunction with plant-gathering activities.

Ice fishing was a common subsistence activity in the winter, with Cinquefoil, Fountain, and Pavilion lakes designated as good localities (WN; DP; Chapter 1: Figure 1; Kennedy and Bouchard, Chapter 6). Ice fishing was probably best in early December and March when the ice was not so thick (cf. Lane 1981:406). Historic accounts describe winter fishing by single men during day trips from winter villages such as Pavilion (DP; Lane 1981:406; Table 1). Women also used a hook and line to ice fish, sometimes building a small fir bough shelter for themselves over the hole (Kennedy and Bouchard, Chapter 6).

During the late fall and winter, deer were also hunted during day trips to the Lakes (DP), where a few of them overwintered. Small mammals (Chapter 2, Table 4) and grouse were available near the Lakes all year and were probably hunted on a casual basis while individuals were in the area getting other resources. Ethnographic accounts suggest that small animals may also have been sought during day trips from the winter village (DP; WN). These fresh foods provided variety to a winter diet of dried foods and became crucial to survival if these dried supplies ran out.

Ochre was available on the slopes above Pavilion Lake (DP) (one of three major sources in the Interior Plateau recorded by Dawson (1892:17) and may have been collected during any of the trips to the Lakes. At least two panels of pictographs are located in the area (DP). These paintings were sometimes assigned a mythological origin (Teit 1900:239, 1906:275, 1909a:598), but others were made by boys and girls during their puberty rituals or by men to record their dreams (Teit 1900:317, 321, 1906:265, 275, 282, 1909a:590).

Ethnoarchaeological Reconstruction

This environment should contain the following site types: basecamps, transit camps, and resource procurement locations such as plant-gathering sites, lookouts, kill and/or butchering sites, and, conceivably, hunting drives and fences (Appendix). The most conspicuous sites at the Intermediate Lakes should be the spring basecamps associated with trout fishing, and, to a lesser degree, hunting and plant gathering. These sites should be located on the banks of streams near the inlets and outlets of the lakes.

Structural features at the fishing camps would include hearths, fish drying racks, weirs, temporary shelters, sweathouses, and women's seclusion lodges. Dwelling lodges, predominantly those consisting of small circular mat lodges (described in the Montane Parkland section), may also have been constructed at the sites, since the sites were used for a relatively long period of time each year and the weather could often be inclement. Meat-drying racks, hide-stretching frames, and smudge pits may also have been constructed to process deer. On the other hand, these features should be uncommon, since deer do not seem to have been caught in large numbers at this time of year and their hides were not in prime condition. Cache pits for temporary storage of trout and plants may have been located near the basecamps.

The basecamps may also have been briefly occupied in other seasons while hunting, fishing, or gathering plants, though other small camps may have been established on the lakeshore for these activities. These smaller camps were probably not occupied for more than a few days and, in many cases, may have only been used during the day for trips originating from the winter village. Few features, other than hearths and postholes from temporary shelters, should be expected from these occupations. Some of the cultural debris from ice fishing would probably have ended up in the lake, since much of the cultural activity took place on the ice. Game look-out sites may be expected on the slopes overlooking the valley, and isolated ungulate kill and/or butchering sites can be expected throughout the valleys. Hunting activities in the fall and winter may also have produced small hunting camps used by one to three men, with higher densities of artefacts occurring near frequently used kill sites.

RIVER TERRACES

Ethnographic Summary

Wintering sites were located almost exclusively on the River Terraces (Chapter 2, Figures 1-2, Plate 2.5). They were typically situated along the principal rivers, in valleys with a warm southern exposure and sheltered from the cold down-river winds (Dawson 1892:8). Dry, sandy, or gravelly soils and easy access to water were also important considerations when selecting a village site (Dawson 1892:8; Teit 1900:192). These villages were generally close to the fishing stations, though, with contact, many such locations were abandoned in favour of those with good agricultural land (Teit 1900:179) or better access to trade with Euro-Canadians. In the study area, villages were located near the tree-line adjoining a tributary stream of the Fraser River (Figure 1). In the

Pavilion and Fountain Creek valleys, settlements were also located in the creek valley itself (Chapter 1, Figure 1).

Prehistoric Thompson villages often contained only one and rarely more than three or four pithouses (ibid.:192), while their historic villages consisted of only three or four families (ibid.:174-5). Lillooet villages and houses were larger in size. In 1860 'there were nine large underground lodges at the Fountain, and two others near by, on the same side of the river' (Teit 1906:199). Other villages in the Lillooet area contained between eight and ten pithouses, though a few scattered pithouse and dwelling lodges also existed (ibid.).

Villages were three or four miles apart on average, though the next village could be as many as ten miles away or just across the Fraser River (Teit 1900:171-4, 1906:196-9, 1909a:451-2). Prior to population decreases associated with Euro-Canadian contact, 'the smoke of Indian camp-fires was always in view' (Teit 1900:175) while travelling on the Thompson River.

Although most band members lived in the main village during the winter, some families opted to live a few miles away in smaller villages. A family might live apart because they could not get along with other people (Teit 1909a:687), felt they were being mistreated (Teit 1909a:709), or had twins who had to remain apart from the community for four years (Boas 1891:644; Teit 1900:311, 1906:263, 1909a:587). The location of the small villages changed frequently and band membership was quite fluid, except for a core of closely related families that consistently resided at or near the main village (Teit 1900:325, 1909a:457). Not all families lived in pithouses, but they were the preferred winter dwelling because they were well insulated against the cold (Teit 1900:195). Ethnographic information on the use and construction of pithouses would take a great deal of space to summarize and will be undertaken in detail as part of the analysis of excavations at Keatley Creek. Published accounts are provided by: Teit (1900:192-5, 1906:212-14, 1909a:492-3), Boas (1891:633-5), Dawson (1892:7), and Laforet and York (1981).

Wars with distant bands and feuds between individuals and families were common (perhaps more frequent after contact) among all Interior Plateau cultures (Cannon, Chapter 10). Consequently, men always carried weapons (Teit 1906:270) and fortresses were built near some villages (Boas 1891:638). Weapons included antler or stone clubs; stone spears; knives and tomahawks; bone daggers; bows and arrows; as well as tunics, armour, and shields of wood and hide (Teit 1900:263-6, 1906:234, 1909a:538). The fortresses consisted of a 2-3 m high log wall or stockade around a large house or group of houses (Teit 1906:235-6, 1909a:539-40). The shape varied, but all had underground passages for a quick escape (ibid.). None have been found archaeologically, but Simon Fraser saw a palisaded village at Lillooet in 1808 (Lamb 1960:120-1).

The River Terraces were primarily used during the winter months. Timing of the move to the winter dwellings was dependent upon the weather, with the move delayed in warmer years and advanced in colder years. November, which, typically, brought the first snows, was the month when most people moved back to their winter camps or villages to begin living in their semi-permanent winter dwellings (Table 1).

In the Chilcotin, people hunted and fished near the village while the winter dwellings 'were being prepared' (Lane 1981:405), and the same was probably true for the Lillooet and Shuswap. Hunting was the dominant activity at this time as the deer, sheep, and (formerly) elk moved out of the mountains to their wintering ground. All animals had prime stores of fat and thick fur. Deer were especially easy prey since, during their rut in the first two weeks of November (Cowan and Guiguet 1975:372), they gathered in large numbers and responded readily to hunting calls (DP). Sometimes all the men went out hunting while the women and children stayed at the village (Teit 1906:242-3).

December was largely spent inside the winter dwellings, living on stored foods, especially salmon. In this month the weather became very cold and ice formed on the lakes (Table 1). The cold, stormy weather largely prevented hunting, except for hares and grouse that could be found near the winter dwellings. In milder weather, the winter dwelling was used as a basecamp from which the men could go ice fishing on nearby Intermediate Lakes (DP) or hunting deer (and other ungulates) in their wintering places in the Forests or around the Intermediate Lakes and Grasslands. Historically, men commonly conducted these hunts on their own in December (DP; BE). Traditionally, hunters used dogs and snowshoes in these pursuits (Teit 1900:248). Dancing, feasts, simple social gatherings, games, and story-telling were also common during the winter (Teit 1900:296-7, 309-10, 350, 367, 385, 1906:249, 284, 1909a:574, 610, 617). The men also spent part of the winter manufacturing spears, daggers, and other weapons for warfare (Teit 1906:239), while the women dressed hides (WN; Teit 1900:185, 1909a:477, 722-3).

The coldest month was January and almost all outdoor activities stopped. Hunting was rarely undertaken and ice fishing yielded 'poor returns' (cf. Lane 1981:406). The ungulates were lean (Table 1) and generally provided a poor return for the effort expended in hunting them. During the lean months, snowshoe hare and grouse could provide an important supplement to the winter diet and were available close to the village.

The weather began to warm in February and the plants began to sprout. In more southerly areas, where the Chinook winds warmed the air and melted the snow, some of the people opted to temporarily move out of the winter dwellings into dwelling lodges (Table 1). In general, people seemed to have been anxious to move out of the pit-houses as soon as possible but delayed their move until February or the beginning of March according to 'the severity of the winter' (Teit 1900:194). Travel was generally easier this time of year, with the snow melting in the southerly areas and crusted snow forming in more northerly areas (Lane 1981:406). As a result, game was easier to run down and kill, though it was scarce and in poor condition (Lane 1981:406). Plants that were available year round on the Terraces, such as cactus and kinnikinnick, could be gathered if food was short.

Late February was the beginning of a critical period, when stored food may have become low or exhausted (Lane 1981:406; Teit 1909a:703, 713, 718, 724). If the warm weather was late in arriving or the snowfalls became wet and heavy, the people could not hunt or fish and starvation was a possibility (Lane 1981:406). On occasion, food shortages may have been remedied by raiding other groups in the early spring (Teit 1906:243; Cannon, Chapter 10). This critical period extended into early March (Lane 1981:406). It was during this month that the last of the extremely cold weather could have forced everyone back into their winter dwellings (Table 1).

By the end of the March, the weather was much warmer, the grass began to grow, the snow left the lower elevations, and most families had moved out of their winter dwellings (Table 1). In April, as the trees began to leaf, the last of the people moved into their summer dwellings (Table 1) and began to exploit the diverse, but not plentiful, food resources now becoming available. Some travelled to the Lakes for ice fishing, others hunted the more accessible ungulates or gathered the new roots and plants available at lower elevations (Lane 1981:406; Teit 1909a:703-4, 718).

Many plants could be harvested on the Terraces near the winter village. In the sagebrush clearings and open woods, onion, mariposa lily, desert parsley, Indian celery, and balsamroot were available, while false Solomon's-seal, cow-parsnip, and fireweed were found in moister localities along streams (Chapter 2, Tables 2 and 3; Turner, Chapter 8). Other plants, used in the material technology, could also be collected now, including mock orange, saskatoon, ocean spray, and juniper for bows and arrows; birch and cottonwood bark for vessels; bitter cherry for hafting; and rope willow and Rocky Mountain maple bark for cordage (Turner, Chapter 8).

People returned to the terraces in June. The ripening of the berries, especially saskatoons (the most common berry on the Interior Plateau), was the event most commonly used to signify the month (Table 1). The upper edge of the Terraces, near the treeline, was one of the most important locations for gathering saskatoons and soapberries (DP), and their harvesting and drying continued into July (Lane 1981:406). Gathering wild onions was also an important activity in early July (Dawson 1892:20). Some men spent a lot of time at the river fishing for spring salmon in June, even though the daily catches were small (Romanoff 1985:142).

It is difficult to ascertain where families traditionally camped while picking berries on the River Terraces. Historically, the women picked berries with relatives, using the winter village as a basecamp (DP; WN). In the past, the Lillooet sometimes occupied their pithouses during the summer (Kennedy and Bouchard 1978:37), but it is unclear whether or not this correlates with berry picking. Teit mentions that, at least among the Shuswap and Thompson, people gathered to dance for the mid-summer solstice 'at their summer gathering-places' (Teit 1906:284, 1909a:604). A similar dance at Spences Bridge lasted several days and involved a large group of people feasting and dancing on a flat above the river that was prepared with clay (Teit 1900:351, 1906:268). Unfortunately, he does not specify where these places were located in the study area, though his statement implies that they were distinct from the winter village. He may well be referring to localities at or near the fishing basecamps on the river or basecamps in the Grasslands, Lakes, or Parkland.

The winter village was probably revisited frequently throughout the warmer months to store food and supplies. It could also have served as a residence for the elderly, and perhaps the children and infirm, while the others were in the mountains (Teit 1909a:709-10). Since all bands in the study area, especially those in control of Six Mile Falls, usually had a large, dependable source of salmon, they may have been more sedentary than were other Lillooet and Shuswap groups (see Teit 1909a:513) and must have spent more time at the village in the spring, summer, and fall.

Burials

Nearly all burial areas were located close to the winter village, on a prominent point of land in the main river valley (Teit 1900:330, 1909a:592; Dawson 1892:10). The body was tied up in a sitting position and placed within a shallow circular hole dug in loose, sandy soil (Teit 1900:328, 1906:269; Boas 1891:643). Graves could be marked with a small pile of boulders, a conical pole hut, carved or painted figures, or with poles bearing some of the person's belongings, including tools, weapons, ornaments, and dogs (Teit 1900:328, 1906:269, 1909a:592; Dawson 1892:9). Slaves captured in war (women, boys, and girls) were sometimes killed and buried in the grave (Teit 1906:270, 1909a:592; Boas 1891:643). As many as 100 burials may have occurred in one location (Dawson 1892:9).

People who were poor or died in distant places were sometimes buried where they died and only covered with sticks, branches, bark, or stones (Teit 1900:330, 1906:270). In most cases family members either took the body immediately to the burial ground (sometimes after cremation) or temporarily buried the body at the death site before interring it in a burial area one or two years later (ibid.; Teit 1909a:592, 548, 554; Boas 1891:643). Wealthy individuals were sometimes dug up and reburied at a feast (Teit 1900:331, 1909a:593).

If two or more deaths occurred while away from the regular burial grounds, or in winter when the ground was frozen, the bodies were placed around the hearth inside the dwelling lodge, which was then abandoned and usually burned (Teit 1900:331, 1906:270). 'In after years, when other relatives died, they were often buried at the same place; and thus a burial ground came to be where the lodge had been' (Teit 1906:270). Pithouses were also burnt after two or more deaths (Teit 1906:273).

Ethnoarchaeological Reconstruction

Site types expected to occur in this environment include: burials, winter villages, transit camps (primarily short-term), and resource procurement locations such as plant gathering sites, hunting drives, kill and/or butchering sites (Appendix). Winter villages would be the largest and most conspicuous sites on the River Terraces. Most hunting and plant-gathering activities in this environment were staged from the village, so few if any basecamps are expected. Most resource procurement sites would have been used by same-sex task groups rather than by family groups and would rarely have been occupied for more than one day. Plant gathering sites are very difficult to detect (see Alpine), and it is doubtful that any plant processing or storage occurred at sites so close to the village. Although roasting pits and plant storage pits are not expected at the procurement sites, cache pits for storing dried salmon may be expected along the edge of the lowest terrace close to the fishing stations.

Given the wide range of activities that took place at the winter village, the long occupation, and the storage of resources from many environments, these sites should contain the most diverse tool and faunal assemblages. Evidence of gaming (e.g., beaver or marmot teeth dice) and dancing (e.g., beads) should occur sporadically.

Hunting activities are likely to produce a number of different archaeological sites, including game look-outs and kill and/or butch-ering sites. Most of these sites should be small, with low densities of artefacts, but any localities where ungulates were frequently encountered may contain higher densities due to reuse of the site on a yearly basis. At one location above Moran Flats, deer were driven along an open slope to a hidden hunter (DP). Given the open terrain, this form of hunting may not have been possible without horses, and most deer hunted on the dry, open Terraces were probably caught at waterholes and salt licks.

Village sites should be found along the Fraser River at intervals of between one and ten miles, with isolated houses scattered between the main villages. Pithouses should be the most common dwellings at the villages but above-ground lodges designed for winter or sum-mer use may also occur. A few large, square lodges may also have been built for special occasions when large groups of people gathered. Sweathouses, women's seclusion lodges, drying racks, elevated storage boxes, storage pits, and smudge pits should be common, although not all would be easily recognized archaeologically. Burial sites should be common on prominent hills near the winter villages.

RIVER VALLEY

Ethnographic Summary

The River Valley (Chapter 2, Figures 1-2, Plate 2.5) was used primarily for salmon fishing. The first spawning salmon appeared in the rivers in April (Table 1; Chapter 2, Table 5; Kennedy and Bouchard, Chapter 6) and some people would make short trips to the fishing stations (Figure 1) to catch these early spring salmon and other fish species. These early salmon runs were small and erratic, resulting in low yields (DP; WN). Therefore, only a few people engaged in this activity and only for short periods of time, for example, a few days to one week (DP; Romanoff, Chapter 5). It is possible that the amount of time spent at the spring fishing sites was greater before the reduction in the importance of this run in the early 1900s (Kennedy and Bouchard, Chapter 6). A second spring run was caught late in May (DP) and June (Kennedy and Bouchard, Chapter 6).

The salmon that were caught in the spring were generally eaten fresh (not dried for storage (DP)) and were not shared with others outside the family (WN). Salmon were caught throughout the summer, but those caught earlier than August (usually springs) were considered difficult to dry and were often eaten fresh (BE; Turner, Chapter 8; Romanoff 1985:134; Kennedy and Bouchard, Chapter 6). July was the warmest month and the largest salmon runs began then (Table 1). Late July and early August were devoted almost entirely to catching salmon, primarily sockeye. Coho also ran at this time but were rarely caught (Kennedy and Bouchard, Chapter 6), presumably because of their low numbers. Spring salmon ran in deeper water than sockeye in July and August (Kennedy and Bouchard, Chapter 6) and, being further from the shore, were also infrequently caught.

In the historic period, one month was a common stay during the July-August run (Turner, Chapter 8), though some families and individuals stayed only one or two weeks (WN; BE). In general, they camped at the site as long as the runs were good or as long as it took to catch and dry enough fish for winter (WN). The September salmon runs were usually poor, and the families generally moved away from the fishing basecamps in August after preparing salmon oil and storing dried salmon (Table 1).

When fishing slackened in the Chilcotin, 'men made snowshoes and other equipment for winter while women wove baskets from the roots collected earlier' (Lane 1981:406). The same activities may have occurred while people waited at fishing stations in the study area. They may also have collected Indian hemp along the Fraser River in August and September (Chapter 2, Table 3; Kennedy and Bouchard, Chapter 6) prior to making the dried hemp into twine and nets in September and October (Romanoff, Chapter 5; Teit 1900:191, 1909a:491). Jade or nephrite used in tool manufacture may also have been sought in the gravel banks and bars of the river (Dawson 1892:18-9; Smith 1900:407). With the long and lengthy gatherings at the fishing basecamps, many people also engaged in social activities such as visiting, dancing, gambling, and arranging marriage alliances (Romanoff, Chapter 5).

At this time of year, everyone usually had a wealth of dried fish and goods and could find people at their fishing stations if they wanted to trade. Most of this trading occurred at large, important fishing sites such as those at the mouth of the Nicola Valley (Teit 1900:167, 1909a:616) and at Fountain or Six Mile (Chapter 1, Figure 1; Teit 1900:259, 1906:231-2, 1909a:536). At these sites, large groups of people from many neighbouring and distant tribes would meet to exchange luxury items for salmon, especially if fish runs were poor in their own area that year (Teit 1900:259). For example, large groups of Lower Lillooet, Shuswap, and Thompson gathered in August and September to trade

(Teit 1906:231), and Simon Fraser saw about 1,000 Indians at the same site in mid-July of 1808 (Lamb 1960:120-1). Included among the less perishable trade items were dentalium, copper sheets, tubes and bracelets, bone and antler beads, steatite for pipes, horn spoons, red ochre, and abalone shells (Teit 1900:258-62, 1906:231-3, 1909a:535-7, 1909b:783; Boas 1891:637).

The success of the catch during this run largely determined the ability of the local people to survive the winter. Fresh foods acquired during the winter months no doubt provided a welcome break from a diet dominated by dried salmon, but they provided only a very small portion of the essential calories and nutrients. In the past, if runs were poor in July and August, the fall runs of pinks in September and October would assume more importance. Pinks may have been called famine food (Kennedy and Bouchard 1978:39) because of their importance in such circumstances. Hunting and plant gathering also probably intensified when the runs were poor (Romanoff, Chapter 9). Cannon (Chapter 10) suggests raiding and warfare as yet another means to mitigate economic shortfalls.

Kennedy and Bouchard (Chapter 6) provide a brief account of other Fraser River fish that were caught in small numbers (Chapter 2, Table 5). Dolly Varden were available year round (DP), while squawfish and sucker were available in the spring. Burbot, whose liver was highly prized, were also caught. Sculpin and peamouth chub were caught by children as a game, while sturgeon were sometimes netted while fishing for salmon.

The River Valley was also used for hunting, especially in the winter when some ungulates took refuge there. Winter hunts were only undertaken if the weather was mild or food supplies low. Men usually conducted these hunts alone or in small groups, using the winter village as a basecamp. Hunting was easier later in the winter (February) when the snow melted (Table 1) and game, though scarce and in poor condition, was easier to run down and kill. Although the River Valley was generally poor in food plants (Chapter 2, Tables 2 and 3), the more productive areas were probably exploited in late March and April while most people were still living in the winter village.

Romanoff and Kennedy and Bouchard thoroughly discuss fishing technology in their articles in this book (Chapters 5 and 6). To avoid repetition, the following account of fishing practices in the study area only covers relevant information not found in these articles.

Although the Fraser River was usually too muddy for their use, spears and harpoons were sometimes used to catch salmon. In addition to the bone and wood harpoon heads described by Kennedy and Bouchard (Chapter 6), stone spearheads were also used (DP; WN).

These stone heads, sometimes made from old spearheads found on the ground, were not as effective as were the bone harpoons (WN; see also Teit 1906:228).

Salmon drying racks were built on the river close to the fishing rock. These structures were up to 15 x 25 ft. and consisted of a fir pole frame supported on four uprights or tripods (Romanoff, Chapter 5). In the Chilcotin the spanners were always peeled and curated while the upright poles and crossbars were left unpeeled (Alexander et al., 1985:116). Standing trees (ibid.) and the river banks (Boas 1891:635) were substituted for pole supports where possible. Each family had its own drying rack and camp (DP; BE; Kennedy and Bouchard, Chapter 6) that was generally built close to the fishing rock. The family built its own shelter using ponderosa pine needles for a mattress (Turner, Chapter 8). In some cases the drying rack was used as a shelter and living area (Romanoff, Chapter 5). Roasting pits, shared by three or four families, were also constructed to cook salmon (Romanoff n.d.:40).

While it was possible for a man to catch 300 salmon in a day (BE), a woman could only process a maximum of 50 to 60 fish in a day (Romanoff, Chapter 5), and, unless there were many women to process the salmon, a large catch would be wasted. Although many men had only one wife, two to four wives were common and some had seven or eight (Teit 1900:326, 1906:269, 1909a:592). Women slaves captured in warfare often became wives of the warriors (Teit 1900:269, 1906:243, 1909a:540) and could have also helped process the fish. The large yearly catches of salmon (400 sockeye and 500-600 spring) reported for individual families by Romanoff (Chapter 5) may pertain to large families with up to eight wives. Romanoff estimates that this many salmon could feed twenty-four people (1985:142). These fish were kept in caches at the village or near the river for up to two years (DP; Romanoff, Chapter 5) (see Montane Parkland Section for discussion of storage facilities).

Ownership of Fishing Resources

Fishing platforms were primarily associated with spring salmon fishing sites. They took three days to build and had to be dismantled after fishing to prevent them from being washed away in the spring (Romanoff, Chapter 5). Given the effort required to build and maintain these structures, it is not surprising to discover that they were the property of the individuals who built them (Teit 1900:294; Romanoff, Chapter 5). Maintenance and rights to use the platform and associated camp were preferentially passed on from father to eldest son, though a daughter or other family member could inherit the site in the absence of a son (Teit 1906:255). This fishing 'steward' was much like the hunting steward who regulated rather than restricted use of the fishing site. He was, however, the most frequent user of the site and maintained his own drying rack and net at the site (Romanoff, Chapter 5).

These sites were probably regulated more closely than others since there were a limited number and each was only useable part of the year (Romanoff, Chapter 5, n.d.:9). Large sites with many fishing rocks and little need for scaffolds, such as Six Mile, were seen as public sites where people from many different bands could freely fish (Romanoff, Chapter 5). However, all sites, whether individually or publicly owned, were identified as belonging to a particular band or village (Teit 1909a:572) with ownership presumably based on the continued use of that site by a member of the band.

Fishing sites were most commonly shared with related families. For example, Fountain and Pavilion bands commonly shared fishing stations, as did Pavilion and Bonaparte bands, but Fountain and Bonaparte bands rarely shared because the members were not usually related (DP). Since a man could only use a dip net for about thirty minutes at a stretch before tiring (DP) and a woman could only process a limited number of fish each day, sharing made the most efficient use of the site. By sharing with people from other bands, members of a band could also gain access to important trout fishing sites outside their territory (Romanoff, Chapter 5; DP).

Ethnoarchaeological Reconstruction

Only two types of sites are expected to occur in the River Valley zone: fishing basecamps and hunting and/or butchering sites (Appendix). Given the long-term and continued reuse of the few available fishing sites, high artefact densities should be expected. Moreover, there should be evidence of cache pits and elevated caches for salmon storage, roasting pits and hearths for cooking, and fish drying racks. Exotic artefacts should also occur at the fishing sites, especially the larger sites where trading was more prevalent. Evidence of small, mat dwelling lodges may be expected, as well as large, square or rectangular lodges at the larger sites.

In the Fraser Canyon study area, much of the fishing activity occurred on land that was flooded in the spring, and many artefacts will have been lost to erosion. Large benches just above floodline, more commonly found near Lillooet, are more likely to contain intact fishing assemblages. Artefacts from the hunting activities would be thinly scattered throughout the valley. Small kill and/or butchering sites with low artefact densities should be most common. However, camps located near important trails leading from the Terraces to River Valley might have been regularly reused and therefore contain higher artefact densities.

CONCLUSIONS

Seasonal Round of Subsistence Activities

The following is a brief summary of the seasonal round of subsistence activities, aggregations, and dispersions mentioned in the preceding sections (Figure 2).

The year began for the Lillooet and Shuswap in November when most families moved back to their winter houses on the River Terraces. While the houses were being prepared for the winter, men hunted and fished at lower elevations. December, January, and February were largely spent indoors living on stored foods, primarily salmon. To supplement the dried foods during these months, men continued to hunt deer and other animals on the River Terraces, in the River Valley, in the Montane Forests, and around the Intermediate Lakes and Grasslands. Ice fishing for trout was also undertaken at the Lakes, weather permitting. Late February and early March was a critical period of the year when stored food may have become low or exhausted. Game was poor and hard to catch, and the plants were not yet ready to harvest.

By late March the weather had usually warmed to the point where most families had moved out of their winter houses and into summer dwelling lodges. In late March and April, families dispersed throughout the area gathering plants and hunting at lower elevations in the Montane Forests, on the River Terraces, in the Intermediate Grasslands, and around the Intermediate Lakes. A few individuals then, and throughout the summer, would also catch salmon in the River Valley.

In mid-May some families moved to trout fishing stations by the Lakes to take advantage of the spawning season, while others moved to the Intermediate Grasslands and Montane Parkland. At the fishing stations, families caught and dried large quantities of trout and a few deer. Plants and migrating waterfowl were also acquired when available. Families scattered in the Grasslands and in the many Parkland localities concentrated on collecting roots and hunting for deer. In late May some families may also have travelled outside the study area to catch trout at Loon Lake or to gather roots in Botanie Valley. Montane hunting and plant gathering by isolated families or same-sex task groups continued sporadically throughout the summer.

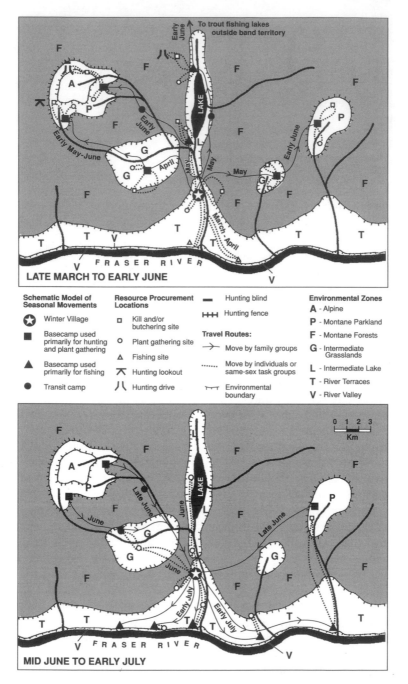

FIGURE 2
Schematic representation of seasonal movements in the study area

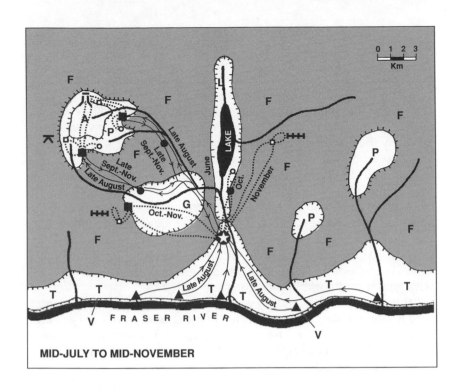

MID-JULY TO MID-NOVEMBER

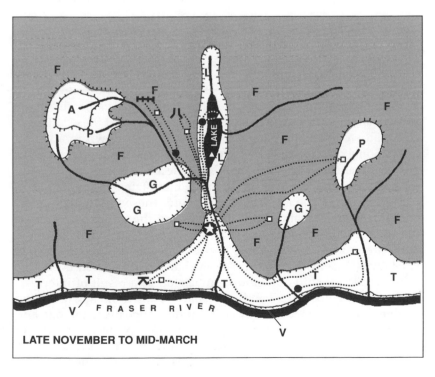

LATE NOVEMBER TO MID-MARCH

In June and July most women collected large quantities of berries, especially saskatoons. They were most abundant on the River Terraces and around the Intermediate Lakes but other berries could be collected slightly later in the Grasslands and Parkland. The winter village was generally used as a base for these activities. Fishing for spring salmon was also a popular activity at this time of year.

From mid-July to mid-August the vast majority of people lived at the salmon fishing stations along the Fraser River. Trading with people from other bands and ethno-linguistic groups was common at these sites in August and September. Immediately following the salmon fishing, most families gathered together at the Parkland basecamps. Deer hunting was the primary activity at these sites although some plants were also collected. These gatherings were important social events, with games and gambling as common activities.

Between September and November, the men spent much of their time hunting, following the deer as they migrated from the Parkland to lower elevations. In the precontact period, women may have travelled with men or stayed in the winter basecamp to exploit lower elevation plant foods.

VARIABILITY IN THE
ETHNOARCHAEOLOGICAL PATTERNING

This ethnographic summary of the Shuswap and Lillooet describes the land use pattern commonly followed by most people. Lane points out how this pattern might vary between families and from year to year. 'Band location, individual need and interest, weather, interpersonal relations, and a variety of other things could alter these patterns. In a mild winter, some people might never settle down in a winter camp. Some men lingered in preferred activities. An inveterate gambler might remain long at fishing sites, while another man might prefer the solitude to be found hunting in the mountains' (Lane 1981:406).

Fortunately for the archaeological record, these individual preferences were the exception, not the rule, and the group pattern was the one that dominated. In general, small scale fluctuations from the norm are unlikely to be visible in the archaeological record, which is relatively insensitive to short-term changes or isolated events.

While historic shifts in band membership as a result of intermarriage with neighbouring bands may have resulted in changes to the predominant language used by each band, change in technology and subsistence patterns are expected to be minor. In these, as in other band societies, the high rate of exchange and intermarriage between neighbouring bands means that all bands in an area generally have access to the same information concerning technology and subsistence practices. This factor, together with the environmental similarities, undoubtedly explains the marked similarity in archaeological materials throughout the Interior Plateau. Therefore, any changes in local band composition probably had only minor effects on local settlement and subsistence patterns.

Archaeologists should be aware that seasonal, yearly, and long-range variation in, and predictability of, the climate, fauna, and vegetation assuredly occurred and must have altered parts of the land use pattern presented here. Nevertheless, paleobotanical evidence indicates a relatively stable climate in southern British Columbia over the last 4,500 years (Mathewes 1985). The small-scale environmental changes which have occurred during this period, such as short-lived 'ice-ages', are not expected to have significantly changed the boundaries of the bioclimatic zones discussed above. Even the Alpine Tundra, though fragile, appears to have been very stable. Evidence from similiar biogeoclimatic zones in Colorado, for example, suggests that the present alpine treeline was established at least several thousand years ago (Ives and Hansen-Bristow 1983:151). However, any application of the ethnoarchaeological reconstruction to prehistoric sites predating 4,500 BP must be made with caution.

Topography must also be considered. The entire Interior Plateau was ice-free and the present drainage system was established by at least 9,500 BP (Fulton 1971:17). Since then, the topography has undergone a number of changes (Ryder 1971). The most significant change was an increasing entrenchment of the river channels. The rate of downcutting in the Mid-Fraser River area is uncertain. Ryder and Church (1986) estimate a rate of 15 to 30 m (50 to 100 ft.) every thousand years. A more conservative estimate can be derived from a date of 5,635 ± 190 BP (GX408) from the Nesikep Creek site (EdRk 8) located just 65 m (210 ft.) above the Fraser River (Sanger 1970). This information provides a rate of downcutting of about 12 m (39 ft.) every 1,000 years. A third estimate is based on a date of 2,840 ± 70 BP (SFU 643) from a cultural horizon at EeRl 195 only 9.5 m (31 ft.) above the Fraser River. In this final case, the downcutting rate is only 3 m (10 ft.) every 1,000 years. This evidence suggests that the rate of downcutting may have slowed with time. On the basis of a conservation rate of 12 m per 1,000 years, I estimate that over the last 4,500 years the river has downcut less than 60 m (200 ft.) and, except for some areas near Lillooet, the general shape of the Fraser River Valley has changed very little. However, changes to the topography must have affected some of the prehistoric land use patterns. Downcutting of the river would have changed the width and shoreline geomorphology of the rivers and influenced the location of fishing stations, associated villages, and campsites.

Cultural adaptations in the area have been relatively stable during the last 3,500 years. Throughout this period, salmon was the main dietary staple, large ungulates and montane resources were exploited, and pithouses were used as winter dwellings (Richards and Rousseau 1987). On the other hand, Kew (Chapter 4) points out that there are many factors which could have significantly altered prehistoric salmon populations. It is highly likely that prehistoric Indian populations in the study area witnessed changes in the species of salmon present in the river, in the size and cyclical dominance patterns of these salmon, and in the time and duration of the salmon runs.

Given the strong dependence of native populations on salmon as a food source, these changes in the salmon runs must have either restricted or allowed for an expansion in the size of the local population, villages, and social groups. Hayden (Hayden et al. 1986, 1987) is currently examining the relationship between village size, housepits size, and social complexity in the Mid-Fraser River area. Site distribution, technology, and reliance on other resources may also have been affected by changes in the salmon runs. For example, some fishing stations are only suitable for catching one species of salmon and would not be used if that species declined in numbers. Similarly, the need to use wooden fishing platforms is also influenced by the abundance of certain species of salmon. In other words, although the general subsistence and settlement patterns have changed little over the last 3,500 years, some short-term local variations should be expected.

The ethnographic data presented in this chapter clearly show that the traditional subsistence and settlement practices in the study area were predictable and patterned. Variability within the general pattern may have existed due to individual preferences, but most band members followed the same schedule of resource use. Adherence to this schedule allowed each band member to: (1) take advantage of seasonal peaks in the abundance of important local resources, (2) participate in large intra-band and inter-band gatherings which provided pleasurable and socially important activities such as gambling, games, dancing, and story-telling, and (3) participate in large inter-band and inter-tribal gatherings which included similiar social activities, and, more importantly, promoted the formation of alliances as well as the trade and exchange of resources, status goods, and information from other areas. Plans for warfare, marriages (Romanoff, Chapter 9), and competitive feasting would also have taken place at their large gatherings.

In the study area, large predictable aggregations of band members could be expected at the main winter village between late November and early March, at the trout spawning streams in the latter half of May, at the large salmon fishing stations in July and early August, and at the resource-rich mountain localities, such as Pavilion Mountain and Cairn Peak-Blustry Mountain, in late August and early September. Families from other neighbouring bands could be expected at the fall mountain camps, while families from neighbouring and more distant bands could be expected at the summer fishing stations. The large mountain gatherings helped promote peaceful relationships between neighbouring bands (sometimes from different ethnolinguistic groups) and provided relaxing and sociable events. The large gatherings at the fishing stations were dominated by trade and exchange and, although generally friendly, were not infrequently scenes of conflict (cf. Dawson 1892:27-8). Raids could also be expected or planned at this time (ibid.).

The patterning seen in the ethnographic record and a knowledge of site formation processes enables investigators to make meaningful predictions about the archaeological patterning of late prehistoric sites. By comparing the late prehistoric patterns to those from earlier time periods, it should be possible to determine how changes in the environment, technology, and even social structure may have produced the observed early prehistoric patterns.

APPENDIX

Definition of Site Types

Winter village: A semi-permanent winter residence with housepits or, less commonly, dwelling lodges. Typically located on the River Terraces, though occasionally found in other environments close to the River Terraces. These sites may contain only one housepit or more than 100, but, except for Keatley Creek and the Bell site, all the villages in the study area contain fewer than twelve housepits.

Basecamp: A temporary residential camp used by families or task groups. Basecamps were established in close proximity to one or more important resource localities which task groups exploited by travelling to the locality, procuring the resource, and returning to the basecamp for final processing of the resource. Bascamps may be found: (1) in the River Valley near salmon fishing rocks, (2) by the Intermediate Lakes near trout fishing streams, and (3) in the Intermediate Grasslands and Montane Parkland near plant-gathering and hunting grounds.

Resource Procurement Location: A place where a resource was gathered or captured. These locations include plant-gathering sites, hunting blinds, hunting fences, hunting drive sites, game look-outs, and kill and/or butchering sites. The kill and/or butchering sites are further divided into four subtypes depending on whether they were used once or multiple times, and whether they were used to capture ungulates or small to medium-sized animals.

Transit camp: Temporary camps used by individuals, task groups, or families while travelling between basecamps or between a basecamp (or village) and a resource procurement location. Transit camps used only briefly during the day are referred to as short-term, while those used over one or two nights are referred to as long-term.

Burial: A location used only for burying the dead. Burials were most commonly located on the River Terraces.

Note: This terminology is similiar to that used by Binford. A winter village is equivalent to his 'residential base,' basecamp to 'field camp,' and resource procurement location to 'location' and 'station' (1980:9-12).

ACKNOWLEDGMENTS

This study would not have been possible without the help and support of the Fountain and Pavilion Indian bands. I would like to thank the following people for generously sharing their knowledge of traditional practices with me: at Pavilion - Desmond Peters Sr., Bill Edwards, Mama Edwards, Harriet MacDonald, and Bucky Ned, and, at Fountain - Roger Adolph, Lawrence Adolph, Maggie Adolph, Chris Bob, Charlie Billy, and Wilfred Ned.

I also want to thank J.E. and John Termuende for permitting me to camp on the Diamond S. Ranch and Tony and Trudy Takacs for generously allowing me to camp for two months behind their home at the Pavilion General Store. The help and friendship of the Takacs family was greatly appreciated.

I also wish to thank Robert Tyhurst. In 1986, Rob worked with me for three weeks during my two month survey of the Pavilion area and was co-director of the Bald Mountain study. The following year we worked together for two months, surveying and testing sites, and conducting ethnographic interviews at Pavilion and Fountain. I greatly appreciated both his insights and his enthusiasm.

Funding for these studies came from three sources. In 1986, an ethnoarchaeological study of Pavilion was funded by the British Columbia Heritage Trust through their Student Employment Program. The same year, the Fountain Indian Band provided money to do a similar study of Bald Mountain (Cairn Peak and Blustry Mountain). In 1987, further ethnoarchaeological work in the Pavilion-Fountain area was supported by the Secretary of State, Multiculturalism Directorate, Ethnic Studies Program. The Heritage Trust also provided funding for testing of some of the archaeological sites found during this survey. I would like to thank these agencies for their support.

The awards from the Heritage Trust and Multiculturalism Canada were made to Dr. Brian Hayden (Department of Archaeology, SFU), who supervised my work in the area. His support, encouragement, and advice were invaluable. I also wish to thank Dr. R.G. Matson (Department of Anthropology and Sociology, UBC) for stimulating my initial interest in Interior Plateau cultures and supporting and guiding my earlier research in the Chilcotin.

REFERENCES

Albright, Sylvia L. 1984. *Tahltan Ethnoarchaeology*. Occasional Publication of the Department of Archaeology No. 15, Simon Fraser University, Burnaby, BC

Alexander, Diana. 1986. 'Ts'kw'aylaxw ethnoarchaeology: A preliminary survey.' Report prepared for the Heritage Conservation Branch of British Columbia (Permit No. 1986-26), the BC Heritage Trust, and the Pavilion Indian Band

–. 1987. 'A preliminary inventory and assessment of archaeological resources on Bald Mountain, Southwestern British Columbia.' Report prepared for the Heritage Conservation Branch of British Columbia (Permit No. 1986-26) and the Fountain Indian Band

Alexander, Diana, Robert Tyhurst, R.G. Matson, and Linda Burnard. 1985. 'A preliminary ethnoarchaeological investigation of the Potato Mountain Range and the Eagle Lake Area.' Report prepared for the Heritage Conservation Branch of British Columbia (Permit No. 1984-14), the Canadian Ethnic Studies Program, and the Nemiah Valley Indian Band Council

Ames, Kenneth and Alan Marshall. 1980. 'Villages, demography and subsistence intensification on the southern Columbia Plateau.' *North American Archaeologist* 2(1):25-52

Banfield, A.W.F. 1974. *The Mammals of Canada*. National Museum of Natural Science, National Museums of Canada. Toronto: University of Toronto Press

Binford, L.R. 1980. 'Willow smoke and dogs' tails: Hunter-gatherer settlement systems and archaeological site formation.' *American Antiquity* 15(1):4-20

Boas, F. 1891. 'The Shuswap: Second general report on the Indians of British Columbia.' *Report of the Sixth Meeting of the British Association for the Advancement of Science, 1890*, Newcastle-upon-Tyne. Part 4, pp. 632-47

–. 1898. 'Operations of the Expedition in 1897.' *Memoirs, American Museum of Natural History, Jesup North Pacific Expedition* 2(1):7-11

Bouchard, Randy and Dorothy I.D. Kennedy (eds.). 1977. 'Lillooet stories.' *Sound Heritage* 6(1):1-78

Carl, G.C., W.A. Clemens, and C.C. Lindsey. 1959. *The Fresh-Water Fishes of British Columbia*. BC Provincial Museum Handbook, No. 5. Victoria: Queen's Printer

Chatters, James C. 1987. 'Hunter-gatherer adaptations and assemblage structure.' *Journal of Anthropological Archaeology* 6:336-75

Cowan, I. McT. and C.J. Guiguet. 1975. *The Mammals of British Columbia*. BC Provincial Museum Handbook, No. 11. Victoria: Queen's Printer

Dawson, George W. 1892. 'Notes on the Shuswap People of British Columbia.' *Proceedings and Transactions of the Royal Society of Canada* 9(2):3-44

Duff, Wilson. 1969. 'The Indian history of British Columbia.' Vol. 1. 'The impact of the White Man.' In *Anthropology in British Columbia*. Provincial Museum Memoir No. 5, Victoria, BC

Ellis, C. and Jonathan Lathrop. 1989. *Eastern Paleoindian Lithic Resource Use*. Boulder: Westview Press

Environment Canada. n.d. *Map of Land Capability for Wildlife: Ungulates, Ashcroft 921*. Ministry of the Environment, Ottawa

Fulton, R.J. 1971. 'Radiocarbon chronology of southern British Columbia.' *Geological Society of Canada*, Paper 71-37

Godfrey, W.E. 1966. *The Birds of Canada*. National Museum of Canada, Bulletin No. 203, Ottawa

Hayden, Brian. 1975. 'Dingoes: Pets or producers?' *Mankind* 10:11-15

–. 1987. 'Past to present uses of stone tools and their effects on assemblage characteristics in the Maya highlands.' In B. Hayden (ed.), *Lithic Studies Among the Contemporary Highland Maya*. Pp. 160-234. Tucson: University of Arizona Press

Hayden, Brian, Diana Alexander, Karla Kusmer, Dana Lepofsky, Dale Martin, Mike Rousseau, and Pierre Friele. 1986. 'Report on the 1986 excavations at Keatley Creek.' Report prepared for the Social Sciences and Humanities Research Council of Canada and the Heritage Conservation Branch of British Columbia

Hayden, Brian, J. Breffitt, P. Friele, R. Gargett, M. Greene, W.K. Hutchings, D. Jolly, I. Kuijt, K. Kusmer, D. Lepofsky, B. Muir, M. Rousseau, and D. Martin. 1987. 'Report on the 1987 excavations at Keatley Creek.' Report prepared for the Social Sciences and Humanities Research Council of Canada and the Heritage Conservation Branch of British Columbia

Hill-Tout, C. 1907. 'The far west: The home of the Salish and Dene.' In *British North America*, Vol. 1. London: Archibald Constable

–. 1978a. *The Salish People, Volume 1: The Thompson and Okanagan*, Ralph Maud (ed.). Vancouver: Talonbooks

–. 1978b. *The Salish People, Volume 2: The Lillooet*, Ralph Maud (ed.). Vancouver: Talonbooks

Ives, Jack D. and K.J. Hansen-Bristow. 1983. 'Stability and instability of natural and modified upper timberline landscapes in the Colorado Rocky Mountains, USA.' *Mountain Research and Development* 3(2):149-55

Kennedy, D.I.D. and Randy Bouchard. 1978. 'Fraser River Lillooet: An ethnographic summary.' In A.N. Stryd and S. Lawhead (eds.), *Reports of the Lillooet*

Archaeological Project, Number 1: Introduction and Setting. Pp. 22-55. Paper of the Archaeological Survey of Canada, No. 73, Mercury Series. National Museum of Man, Ottawa

Laforet, Andrea and Annie York. 1981. 'Notes on the Thompson winter dwelling.' In D. Abbott (ed.), *The World is as Sharp as a Knife: An Anthology in Honour of Wilson Duff.* Pp. 115-22. BC Provincial Museum, Victoria

Lamb, W. Kaye. 1960. *The Letters and Journals of Simon Fraser 1806-1808.* Toronto: MacMillan

Lane, R. 1953. 'Cultural Relations of the Chilcotin of West Central British Columbia.' Unpublished PHD dissertation, University of Washington, Seattle

–. 1981. 'Chilcotin.' In J. Helm (ed.), *Subarctic.* Pp. 402-12. Handbook of North American Indians, Vol. 6. Smithsonian Institution, Washington, DC

Mathewes, Rolf W. 1978. 'The environment and biotic resources of the Lillooet area.' In A. Stryd and S. Lawhead (eds.), *Reports of the Lillooet Archaeological Project, No. 1: Introduction and Setting.* Pp. 68-99. Paper of the Archaeological Survey of Canada, No. 73, Mercury Series. National Museum of Man, Ottawa

–. 1985. 'Paleobotanical evidence for climatic change in southern British Columbia during late-glacial and holocene time.' *Syllogeus* 55:344-96

O'Connell, James F. 1987. 'Alyawara site structure and its archaeological implications.' *American Antiquity* 52:74-108

Parry, William and Robert Kelly. 1987. 'Expedient core technology.' In J. Johnson and C. Morrow (eds.), *The Organization of Core Technology.* Pp. 285-301. Boulder: Westview Press

Pokotylo, David L. and Christopher C. Hanks. 1985. 'Mountain Dene ethnoarchaeology: Some preliminary perspectives.' Paper presented at the Fiftieth Annual Meeting of the Society for American Archaeology, Denver, Colorado

Ray, V.F. 1939. 'Cultural relationships in the Plateau of north-western America.' *The Southwest.* Publications of the Frederick Webb Hodge Anniversary Publication Fund, Vol. 3. Los Angeles

–. 1942. 'Culture element distributions, XXII: Plateau.' *University of California, Anthropological Records* 8(2):99-257

Reidhead, V.A. 1979. 'Linear programming models in archaeology.' *Annual Review of Anthropology* 8:543-78

Richards, Thomas H. and Mike K. Rousseau. 1987. *Late Prehistoric Cultural Horizons on the Canadian Plateau.* Department of Archaeology, Simon Fraser University, Occasional Paper Series, No. 16, Burnaby, BC

Robbins, Chandler S., Bertel Bruun, and Herbert S. Zim. 1966. *Birds of North America: A Guide to Field Identification.* New York: Golden Press

Romanoff, Steven. n.d. 'The Lillooet hunter.' Unpublished ms. in possession of author

–. 1985. 'Fraser Lillooet salmon fishing.' *Northwest Anthropological Research Notes* 19(2):119-60

Ryder, J.M. 1971. 'The stratigraphy and morphology of para-glacial alluvial fans in South-Central British Columbia.' *Canadian Journal of Earth Sciences* 8:279-98

Ryder, J.M. and M. Church. 1986. 'The Lillooet terraces of the Fraser River: A palaeoenvironmental enquiry.' *Canadian Journal of Earth Sciences* 23(6):869-84

Sanger, D. 1970. 'The archaeology of the Lochnore-Nesikep locality British Columbia.' *Syesis* 3(1)

Smith, H.I. 1899. 'Archaeology of Lytton, British Columbia.' *Memoir, American Museum of National History, Jesup North Pacific Expedition* 8(3):129-61

–. 1900. 'Archaeology of the Thompson River region, British Columbia.' *Memoir, American Museum of Natural History, Jesup North Pacific Expedition* 2(1):401-42

Steedman, E.V. 1930. 'Ethnobotany of the Thompson Indians of British Columbia.' *Annual Report of the Bureau of American Ethnology* 46:443-552

Teit, J. 1900. 'The Thompson Indians of British Columbia.' *Memoir, American Museum of Natural History, Jesup North Pacific Expedition* 1(4):163-392

–. 1906. 'The Lillooet Indians.' *Memoir, American Museum of Natural History, Jesup North Pacific Expedition* 2(5):193-300

–. 1909a. 'The Shuswap.' *Memoir, American Museum of Natural History, Jesup North Pacific Expedition* 2(7):447-789

–. 1909b. 'Notes on the Chilcotin Indians.' *Memoir, American Museum of Natural History, Jesup North Pacific Expedition* 2(7):759-89

Turner, Nancy J. 1978. *Food Plants of British Columbia Indians, Part 2: Interior Peoples*. Provincial Museum Handbook, No. 36. Victoria, BC

–. 1987. 'Ethnobotany of the Lillooet Indians of British Columbia.' Unpublished ms. in possession of the author

Turner, N.J., Randy Bouchard, and D.I.D. Kennedy. 1980. 'Ethnobotany of the Okanagan-Colville Indians of British Columbia and Washington.' *Occasional Papers of the British Columbia Provincial Museum*, No. 21, Victoria, BC

Winterhalder, Bruce and Eric Alden Smith. 1981. *Hunter-gatherer Foraging Strategies: Ethnographic and Archaeological Analysis*. Chicago: University of Chicago Press

Salmon Availability, Technology, and Cultural Adaptation in the Fraser River Watershed

Michael Kew

Existence of a close connection between salmon and aboriginal cultures of the Northwest is not a new observation. Indian oral literature asserts it, and every ethnographer and archaeologist to study Fraser River people has been similarly impressed by the place of salmon in Indian life. Then why another paper on an old theme? Salmon are not simply salmon. The five species of Pacific salmon differ in size, behaviour, occurrence within the same stream system, and in their accessibility and value to humans. Surprising differences of behaviour occur between different populations of the same species. The thrust of this paper is to make ethnologists and archaeologists aware of the gains to be made in the tasks of reconstructing cultural systems and understanding their functioning through studying in more detail the ecological systems in which humans live. Salmon, as part of the environment of humans, are not a simple constant. We can only know the parts they played in human history by knowing in full detail what they were like in different places and times. The full story of salmon and humans has not been told.

The aim of this volume is to assemble as much information as possible on resource use in the Lillooet area and so to strengthen our understanding of historic and prehistoric social and cultural developments in that pivotal region. Given the central role of salmon in the life of these people (discussed in Chapter 3; see also Chisholm et al. 1983; Lovell et al. 1986), it is crucial to be able to know as much as possible about abundance of salmon, especially the scope and nature of fluctuations in supply and the variables of human knowledge which create salmon products for human use.

This chapter approaches the subject from a perspective of the whole Fraser River watershed and thus goes beyond the local area. Such a wider view is essential for assessing the role of salmon. The interdependencies of human populations and their cultural systems are immediately apparent when one considers Fraser River salmon. All of the indigenous fishers were, and are today, users of the same resource since salmon pass through the entire watershed. The fishing of any one culture has some degree of potential effect upon every other culture. Fishing and processing technologies can be expected to have evolved and spread within the area. The products of one area of the River were exchanged with occupants of others.

This wider perspective facilitates inferences about interior prehistoric and protohistoric cultural developments that might otherwise be missed. Since this chapter is about salmon, it pertains directly to the River Valley zone of resource utilization as defined by Alexander in Chapter 2.

In this paper I have been guided by the following questions: What is the nature of the occurrence of salmon in the Fraser River system? What are the natural physical circumstances of that system? How do these relate to the varied uses made of salmon by indigenous people within that watershed?

Data collection for this paper began in a graduate seminar a decade ago, in which a group of students set out to learn as much as possible about resources and their relationships to Indian cultures of the Fraser River watershed. I have revised and extended the work I began then on salmon in order to make more accessible the information and to provide an example of insights to be gained from close consideration of the important natural resources of a region.[1]

GENERAL CHARACTERISTICS OF FRASER RIVER SALMON

The Fraser River has been historically, and still remains, one of the greatest producers of salmon in the world (Northcote and Larkin 1988). Five species of Pacific salmon are present in the Fraser: chinook or spring (*Oncorhynchus tshawytscha*), coho (*O. kisutch*), chum (*O. keta*), pink (*O. gorbuscha*), and sockeye (*O. nerka*). All begin life in fresh water, journey to the sea where they disperse and achieve rapid growth, and then return, at ages from two to seven or eight years, to spawn in their natal streams and then die (for summations of life histories and other data see: Aro and Shepard 1967; Carl, Clemens, and Lindsey 1967; Foerster 1968; Hart 1973; Scott and Crossman 1968). Since there is a high rate of return to the natal stream, each localized spawning population constitutes a distinct breeding population or race, which will be called here a *run*.

Each run returns to the Fraser in concentrated numbers at unique but regular and predictable times and proceeds upstream at distinctive rates. Arrivals of runs in the lower Fraser, and continuing upstream migrations, are timed so that optimal water and temperature conditions occur for spawning.

It is important, in comprehending the significance of salmon, to remember that they are anadromous fishes. Their territory is not bounded by the banks of a river system. To one degree or another their territory is a river plus some portion of the whole north Pacific Ocean. Salmon grow rapidly in the ocean, feeding over a vast range on a variety of small organisms and other fishes. They then transport this energy back to the mouth of the river, where some species, including sockeye but not chinook, cease feeding and use up their stored energies in the processes of sexual maturation and upstream migration. They are natural collectors of energy in locations relatively inaccessible to human predators, and they transport this stored energy to the river. Salmon concentrate energy in time and space. That is why they are so beneficial to humans.

Another notable characteristic of salmon is their substantial rate of reproduction. Females bear between 1,500 and 5,000 eggs (Hart 1973:109ff.), and salmon populations respond in a compensatory way to mortalities occurring in various phases of their life cycles. High rates of mortality in one phase will result in lower, compensatory rates in a later phase, and vice versa (see Foerster 1968:52f.; and Neave 1966a,b). These reproductive and survival features are characteristic of a class of organisms which reproduce only once or a few times during life but do so in large numbers. Hayden (1981) has argued that use of forms with these high reproductive potentials has been crucial to complex evolutionary adaptations by many human hunter-gatherers, a point I will return to below.

The reproductive characteristics of salmon are important for two reasons. First, they are major enabling factors in the oft-remarked capacity of salmon populations to fluctuate markedly over time. It is a natural condition of salmon runs to experience failures from such cataclysms as land slides, flooding, drought, and the like, yet to be able to recover in a few cycles. They are resilient populations. Second, human predation, be it more or less regular and not overwhelming, has no adverse long-term effect upon the sizes of the runs (with one possible qualification, mentioned below). In fact, some biologists argue that controlled commercial fishing with modern industrial technology (and this would hold for aboriginal fishing as well) has the effect of actually increasing production of adult salmon bound for their natal streams. Ideally, modern commercial fishing removes adult salmon surplus to numbers necessary for maximum productivity (Foerster 1968:54). For this reason, we can be reasonably sure that fishing by downstream tribes, assuming relatively consistent application of technology and demand from one salmon cycle to the next, would have had no long-term negative effect on availability of salmon in upstream areas.

It is also this characteristic which compels me to disagree with Hewes's reconstruction (Hewes 1947:237; 1973:145), which envisages a 'hypothetical pre-human abundance of salmon' greater than the salmon population subject to aboriginal predation. The modest portion of the total salmon population which Hewes estimates to have been taken by Indians in pre-contact times (less than 15 per cent, Hewes 1973:145) would not have come close to sustainable harvest levels proposed by biologists and maintained by commercial fisheries. These proposals are quite variable, but catches of over 50 per cent have been maintained (see, for example, Foerster 1968:54-62; Neave 1962:6f.). There is no basis to be found in anthropological or biological data for a view which casts aboriginal inhabitants in the role of reducers of, or threats to, the salmon resource. More appropriate, however, is Hewes's admonition that biologists have neglected the place of Indians in biological systems before white contact. Humans have been part of 'nature' in North America since the first hunters set foot on the continent some twenty thousand or more years ago. The Indian salmon fishery stands as a prime example of high utilization and dependence by humans over a long period of time with no depletion of the resource.

It should not be the conclusion, however, that salmon resources have been constant in any watershed over this period. To the contrary. It is clear that temperature, turbidity, velocity, and a host of other conditions affect the suitability of stream systems for salmon. These conditions are not constant in the long run and in the Northwest must have continuously changed as deglaciation occurred. Just as salmon are not uniformly distributed within the Fraser watershed, by species or numbers, so is their wider distribution varied. What we know as the historic pattern is but the last in a changing succession of patterns as glaciers have receded within watersheds and over the coast as a whole.[2] Reconstruction of human history in the area will be immensely informed by a fuller understanding of salmon history.

MODEL OF SALMON AVAILABILITY

In the early years of the twentieth century, the commercial value of salmon spurred attention of fisheries officers to collecting information on escapement to spawning grounds. Subsequent biological studies supported by governments concerned with redressing the negative effects on the resource of accidental and deliberate stream obstruction has added to the wealth of data on salmon. Although mysteries of their life cycles and behaviour remain unsolved, enough is known to lay out the main features of distribution and escapement for all sectors of the Fraser River system (a comprehensive introduction to the literature and to the general biology of one region, the Lower Fraser, is given in Northcote 1974). This section presents a model of the Fraser River salmon abundance intended to provide for students of human history a means of assessing the sizes and variations of salmon resources likely to have been available in major parts of the river system before industrial development by Euro-Canadians.

DISTRIBUTION

Salmon species do not occur uniformly throughout the Fraser system. Probably the most widespread is the largest, chinook, with an average weight of 6.8 kg (15 lb.) in the Fraser River (Milne 1964:1, 18). They are found in some numbers in all accessible watersheds of the system, spawning in the very headwaters of the main river (see Aro and Shepard 1967:266).

Sockeye, with an average weight in the Fraser of 2.7 kg (6.0 lb.) (Killick and Clemens 1963:55), are nearly as widely distributed, although their spawning grounds are close to lakes where the young spend their first year, and the large runs are associated with the large lakes of the interior plateau.

Coho spawn in tributaries of the lower Fraser, including tiny streams, many of which have been extinguished by settlement and agricultural development. They ascend to the upper Lillooet River, and, passing through the Fraser River canyon, they ascend to the North Thompson and tributaries of Shuswap Lake. While they did not ascend the Fraser above the Thompson a few decades ago, a small number now reach the Quesnel River, and it is possible their numbers were significant before the Hell's Gate slide in 1913. The average weight of Fraser River coho is about 4.1 kg (9 lb.) (Milne 1964:36).

Pink salmon, the smallest of the five species, have an average weight of 1.9 kg, just over four pounds (Neave 1966a:73). Pinks ascend many small tributaries of the lower Fraser, but their main spawning ground is now in the Fraser River itself, below Hope. Upriver runs were formerly much greater in size than those below the canyon. They were extinguished for a while by the Hell's Gate slide but have now recolonized the Seton and Nicola Rivers. There is also evidence of a small number of pinks even further upstream.

Chum salmon, with an average weight of 5.4 kg (11.7 lb.) (Neave

1966b:82), have the most restricted distribution, spawning no further
up the system than the main Fraser below Hope and in the Harrison
River. Therefore, in the study area above Bridge River, only chinook,
sockeye, pink, and a few coho occur.

NUMBERS

While the territories of salmon species are well established and fairly
straightforward, estimating their numbers is more difficult. For populations in their spawning locations – defined as the *escapement* of a
run – there is a body of data which allows fair estimates for many runs
in the historic period and strong inferences for earlier times. Means
have also been developed in the last four decades for identifying individual runs of salmon in the sea and lower reaches of the river systems
(Henry 1961). These have been applied especially to sockeye and pink
stocks, enabling more accurate estimates of the commercial fishery
catch of specific runs. These catch estimates, supplemented by counts
and estimates of escapements, provide a reasonable picture of the total
production or abundance of most major runs (see Appendix 1). But
the abundance of those years in which there has been a regular and
heavy commercial catch, beyond the size of the aboriginal catch, will
be greater than the abundance of years in which there is a smaller,
regular fishery. With continuing reduced catch levels, escapements
will initially increase but only to a 'saturation' level, beyond which
abundance will decrease.

Matters are further complicated by the fact that two species of
salmon exhibit natural cyclical fluctuations in population, which
require any descriptive model of availability to encompass at least four
years. Among sockeye runs which ascend beyond the Fraser River
canyon to reach spawning areas, there is a pattern of quadrennial
dominance. One year out of four will have a large number of fish,
the next year will be sharply reduced, and the remaining two, smaller
still. The same order of a high, a moderate, and two low years is
repeated in a continuing sequence. The differences between low and
high years varies but has occurred in ratios as great as several thousand to one (see, for example, Killick and Clemens 1963:4).

Fraser River pink salmon runs show a still greater natural fluctuation in numbers. The pink salmon appear as adults in runs of several
millions in size but only every other (odd-numbered) year. Scarcely
any appear in the Fraser in intervening years. It is worth noting that
a similar two-year cycle is exhibited by pink salmon on the north coast
and Queen Charlotte Islands, some being dominant in even years;
while in some streams, such as the Bella Coola, runs occur in both

even and odd years (see Aro and Shepard 1967:295-6). The dominant sockeye year on the Fraser is also an odd-numbered year, so that the pink salmon, where they occur, augment the numbers of salmon in the first and third years of the four. The significance of these regular fluctuations varies, of course, according to location. Today, pink variation makes no difference to availability of salmon above Seton River, while the effect of sockeye cycles there is extreme.

One explanation offered for quadrennial dominance in upper Fraser sockeye is depensatory mortality of sockeye caused by freshwater predators, especially rainbow trout, which feed on sockeye eggs, fry, and fingerlings which are lake residents in their first year (Ward and Larkin 1964). Depensatory mortality is that which occurs when a greater percentage of a population dies when it is small in number than when it is larger in number – the percentage of mortality is inversely related to population size (Ricker 1962:182). From examination of fur traders' records from the early nineteenth century and from Department of Fisheries records, biologists have concluded that quadrennial dominance existed coincidentally throughout the Upper Fraser runs at the time of contact and has persisted among most runs up to the present era (Ward and Larkin 1964). However, it is also apparent that dominance does shift, and some analysts advise caution in assuming a regular coincident pattern of dominance in the early nineteenth century (see Walters and Staley 1987). Ricker has reviewed the issue of pink salmon cycles and offers eight hypotheses or possible factors contributing to the marked pattern of dominance as evident on the Fraser. These are also conditions of depensatory mortality and include predation by other fish in fresh water and the sea, cannibalistic predation, and fishing (human predation). Ricker favours a view that these cyclic fluctuations are multi-causal (1962:191-2). These same causes might well contribute to the quadrennial dominance pattern of upper Fraser sockeye.

Ricker (1962:190-1) also gives credence to the possibility that human fishing activity may be critical, making this statement: 'the effects of fishing seem potentially capable of explaining most of the observed characteristics of dominance. Nevertheless the fact is that in many places dominance was well developed before commercial fishing started.' This early dominance is evident for the Fraser – both for pinks and sockeye. The cyclical dominance of sockeye appears to have been present in the Stuart Lake runs from the earliest days of the fur trade, that is, when Indians were the only fishers (Jackson 1953:23; Ward and Larkin 1964). Indian fishing may have played a part in establishing these dominance patterns. It is evident that the pattern of Indian fishing, which consisted of taking sufficient fish for immediate need and that of the forthcoming year, was one of striving for a regular, absolute amount of fish in proportion to the human population rather than for a fixed proportion of the run. In other words, it would be predation of an inherently depensatory kind. This point is made by Walters and Staley (1987:383). While this predation might have had little consequence where aboriginal fishing took a small toll, as may have been the case for pink salmon on the Fraser River (the runs Ricker was discussing), it would be greater for upriver sockeye runs, which were fished by all groups. Should one of those sockeye runs have been decimated in one season by a landslide, for example, then human predation might well have been one of the several factors contributing to dominance of one remaining strong year of the run.[3] In fact, the major landslide reported by Ryder and Church (1986) at Texas Creek within the last 3-4,000 years may have played such a major role in initiating a cycle of dominance. The history of such land shifts is clearly of more than passing interest for prehistorians, a point noted by Sanger (1973:197-9) with reference to the Columbia River.

While the patterns of salmon escapement as we know them on the Fraser and, consequently, the model of availability in aboriginal times must incorporate known facts of cyclical dominance in sockeye and pinks, ethnologists and archaeologists seeking to understand the nature of the resource over long spans of time should not take the known pattern to be fixed. Sockeye dominance for at least one run on the Fraser has shifted. All of the upper Fraser runs, where they showed the dominance pattern, were apparently coincident in the 1901 cycle year in the early nineteenth century (Ward and Larkin 1964). This included the Adams River run, which was decimated by the effects of the Hell's Gate slide of 1913 and a flush dam for log drives on the Adams River. In 1922, a successful spawning occurred in the year following the old year of dominance, and the Adams River run has since grown and re-established dominance albeit in a new cycle (Thompson 1945:65f). In streams other than the Fraser, pinks have also exhibited shifts in their dominant years, and in some streams they show little or no dominance (Ricker 1962:167).

In the long-term view, it is not fixed numbers and ratios that will aid ethnologists and archaeologists to reconstruct conditions but knowledge of possibilities and of factors creating variations in conditions. Cyclical dominance of sockeye and pinks is a condition which exists and may have considerable antiquity, but we know that patterns of dominance shift and that they may disappear. Change is thus a 'normal' condition.

Quadrennial dominance of sockeye is not widespread (like dominance in pinks) and may be restricted to the upper Fraser system. Foerster (1968) does not find such patterns in streams other than the Fraser. The condition may be related to the fact that up-river Fraser runs consist predominantly of four-year-old fish (Aro and Shepard 1967:239), while in other systems the ages of spawners are spread over two or more years. In Rivers Inlet and Smith Inlet sockeye, the numbers of four and five-year-old adults are about equal (ibid.:242); and in Skeena River sockeye, mainly Babine Lake fish, they are similar (Foerster 1968:356). Restriction of spawning age to the same year is, of course, a condition which would magnify the effect of depensatory mortality. Pink salmon are highly restricted to two-year-old adults and exhibit the most marked dominance patterns (see Neave 1962). The greater richness of Babine Lake salmon resources, remarked upon by early fur traders and contrasted with salmon runs of the Nechako tributaries, is clearly related to the relative lack of dominance in the Babine runs. Here again, however, there is some evidence for a five-year cycle of salmon fluctuation in the historic period (Ricker 1966:61).

It has become increasingly apparent that there are, in addition to such regular cycles, other variations in salmon population which are irregular and unpredictable – at least in a practical, short-term sense. Some of the failures of runs can be linked to drought, winter flooding, and consequent scouring of spawn from streambeds, landslides, and other freshwater conditions. Marine survival rates are highly variable as well. For example, for some pink runs the rates of survival are reported to vary by a magnitude of six times (Manzer and Shepard 1962:113f.). Conditions affecting marine survival are much more difficult to study but certainly include temperature and ocean currents. While this model strives to present the usual or normal occurrence of salmon over a four-year period, it must be understood that the 'normal' is just that – a norm that in fact was subject to variations – occasionally of dramatic proportions.

The model presented here derives from information originating in this century, but I have made some changes, increasing estimates of sizes of runs which have been substantially reduced by industrial accident and development and placing some quadrennially dominant sockeye in the same sequence they were in at time of contact (see Appendix 1 for more detail). With these changes, the model is presented as a description of the presence of salmon in the Fraser River at time of contact, circa 1800. It is a conservative model; that is, if and where it errs it does so by underestimating sizes of runs.

The model can be stated in numbers of fish or in total weight, which gives a more accurate picture of significance as food since species vary considerably in size. An even more accurate picture, in terms of food, could be created by correcting for loss of weight and food value as the fish ascend the river system. This would take account of an important feature of Pacific salmon considered as food. Since many of these fish cease feeding as they enter fresh water, they literally consume their own bodies as they move up-stream and through the spawning cycle. As a general rule, the further from the sea a salmon is, the less fat and protein it carries. The loss is considerable. Total caloric value of a sockeye, measured at the river mouth, will be reduced to nearly one-half when it reaches the Upper Stuart spawning grounds, one thousand kilometres from the sea. After their enriched gonads have been expended in spawning and the fish die on these upper streams, they will have lost over 90 per cent of their fat and one-half to two-thirds of their protein (Idler and Clemens 1959; reviewed in Foerster 1968:74-6). Fish in the Lillooet area still retain high proportions of their food value. This feature, in combination with their accessibility at the rapids and the prevalence of ideal conditions for drying and storage, combine to make the area highly suited to production of dried salmon (see Romanoff, Chapter 5).

Table 1 provides a summary of the availability, that is, presence of salmon, in the main sections of the Fraser River over a four-year period. The four-year period, to repeat, is necessary because of the quadrennial dominance pattern of sockeye and the resultant repetition of a four-year cycle. The dominant year of 1901 falls in four-year intervals as: . . . 1893, 1897, 1901, 1905 . . . and so on. And it is in that cycle that the dominant year occurred at the beginning of the nineteenth century (see Appendix 1). Table 2 shows the availability of salmon expressed in weight for sections of the mainstem river, and Table 3 shows the numbers of fish, by species, and their combined weights for five major tributary systems.

TABLE 1

Model of salmon availability in thousands of fish
(using estimated abundance TABLE F)

Section of Fraser	Species	Cycle Years			
		1901	**1902**	**1903**	**1904**
Mouth of river	Sockeye	60,000	10,000	10,000	13,000
	Chinook	2,000	2,000	2,000	2,000
	Coho	2,000	2,000	2,000	2,000
	Pink	24,000	—	24,000	—
	Chum	4,000	4,000	4,000	4,000
Above Pitt R.	Sockeye	59,700	9,500	9,450	12,415
	Chinook	1,992	1,992	1,992	1,992
	Coho	(1,603)	(1,603)	(1,603)	(1,603)

	Pink	<24,000	—	<24,000	—
	Chum	<2,392	<2,392	<2,392	<2,392
Above Chilliwack R.	Sockeye	59,400	9,200	8,900	12,155
	Chinook	1,988	1,988	1,988	1,988
	Coho	(1,206)	(1,206)	(1,206)	(1,206)
	Pink	<24,000	—	<24,000	—
	Chum	2,392	2,392	2,392	2,392
Above Harrison R.	Sockeye	58,200	8,000	7,700	10,725
	Chinook	1,450	1,450	1,450	1,450
	Coho	558	558	558	558
	Pink	<24,000	—	<24,000	—
	Chum	64	64	64	64
Above Hope	Sockeye	58,200	8,000	7,700	10,725
	Chinook	1,448	1,448	1,448	1,448
	Coho	524	524	524	524
	Pink	16,800	—	16,800	—
	Chum	—	—	—	—
Above Thompson R.	Sockeye	23,760	5,300	7,300	10,465
	Chinook	828	828	828	828
	Coho	54	54	54	54
	Pink	4,560	—	4,560	—
	Chum	—	—	—	—
Above Bridge R.	Sockeye	23,580	5,050	7,100	10,075
	Chinook	808	808	808	808
	Coho	6	6	6	6
	Pink	—	—	—	—
	Chum	—	—	—	—
Above Chilcotin R.	Sockeye	21,180	3,550	2,500	1,300
	Chinook	658	658	658	658
	Coho	6	6	6	6
	Pink	—	—	—	—
	Chum	—	—	—	—
Above Quesnel R.	Sockeye	12,780	3,300	2,250	1,235
	Chinook	546	546	546	546
	Coho	—	—	—	—
	Pink	—	—	—	—
	Chum	—	—	—	—
Above Nechako R.	Sockeye	180	200	200	130
	Chinook	320	320	320	320
	Coho	—	—	—	—

(continued on next page)

TABLE 1 (continued)

Section of Fraser	Species	Cycle Years			
		1901	1902	1903	1904
	Pink	—	—	—	—
	Chum	—	—	—	—
Above Bowron R.	Sockeye	—	—	—	—
	Chinook	216	216	216	216
	Coho	—	—	—	—
	Pink	—	—	—	—
	Chum	—	—	—	—

SOURCE: See Appendix 1

TABLE 2
Model of salmon availability in weight of fish

Section of Fraser	Weight of fish (in 1000s of kg) by cycle year			
	1901	1902	1903	1904
Mouth of river	251,000	70,400	116,000	78,500
Above Pitt R.	239,825	58,685	104,150	66,555
Above Chilliwack R.	237,360	56,220	101,010	64,198
Above Harrison R.	215,233	34,093	78,883	41,451
Above Hope	201,055	33,595	64,705	40,952
Above Thompson R.	78,668	20,162	34,226	34,107
Above Bridge R.	69,194	19,163	24,698	32,731
Above Chilcotin R.	61,685	14,084	11,249	8,009
Above Quesnel R.	38,219	12,623	9,788	7,047
Above Nechako R.	2,662	2,716	2,716	2,527
Above Bowron R.	1,469	1,469	1,469	1,469

SOURCE: See Appendix 1
NOTE: Weights used are averages of adults in sea or river mouth: sockeye – 2.7 kg (6 lb.) (Killick and Clemens 1963:55); chinook – 6.8 kg (15 lb.) (Milne 1964:1,18); coho – 4.1 kg (9 lb.) (Milne 1964:36) pink – 1.9 kg (4 lb.) (Neave 1966a:73); chum – 5.4 kg (12 lb.) (Neave 1966b:82)

To summarize salmon abundance for the Lillooet study area, above Bridge River, there would have been at least 23,580,000 sockeye passing through in peak years, with at least 5,050,000 in low years. A minimum of 808,000 chinook would have passed through annually. There is some archaeological evidence suggesting that pink runs may have

TABLE 3

Numbers of salmon by species and combined weights
by major Fraser River tributaries
(Fish in 1000s, weight in 1000s of kg)

Tributary	Species	Cycle years			
		1901	1902	1903	1904
	Numbers of:				
Harrison R.	Sockeye	1,200	1,200	1,200	1,430
	Chinook	538	538	538	538
	Coho	648	648	648	648
	Pink	<5,280	—	<5,280	—
	Chum	2,328	2,328	2,328	2,328
	Weight	<32,158	22,126	<32,158	22,747
	Numbers of:				
Thompson R.	Sockeye	34,440	2,700	400	260
	Chinook	618	618	618	618
	Coho	456	456	456	456
	Pink	12,000	—	12,000	—
	Chum	—	—	—	—
	Weight	121,860	13,362	29,952	6,774
	Numbers of:				
Chilcotin R.	Sockeye	2,400	1,500	4,600	8,875
	Chinook	150	150	150	150
	Coho	—	—	—	—
	Pink	—	—	—	—
	Weight	7,500	6,070	13,440	24,983
	Numbers of:				
Quesnel R.	Sockeye	8,400	250	250	65
	Chinook	112	112	112	112
	Coho	6	6	6	6
	Weight	23,466	1,461	1,461	962
	Numbers of:				
Nechako R.	Sockeye	12,600	3,100	2,050	1,105
	Chinook	132	132	132	132
	Weight	34,918	9,268	6,433	3,881

SOURCE: See Appendix 1

existed in this part of the system about 1,000 years ago (Berry 1991),
and, of course, the numbers of chinook may well have been much

Michael Kew

higher than this model shows. Romanoff's data in Chapter 5 suggest heavy utilization of chinook, and, being the largest of the salmon, this species may have initially suffered the heaviest from the selective effect of the gill net fishery in the last hundred years. In any case, the total weight of salmon present in the study area, conservatively estimated, would have ranged from 19,163,000 kg in low years to 69,194,000 kg in peak years.

TIME AND DURATION OF RUNS

In addition to numbers, account should be taken of the duration of time in which salmon are available. Table 4 summarizes for major sec-

TABLE 4
Duration of salmon presence in portions of Fraser River mainstem

Sector of river	Species	Months
		Jan. Feb. Mar. Apr. May Jun. Jul. Aug. Sep. Oct. Nov. Dec.
Mouth to Hope	Sockeye	. . *** **** **** **** **** **** *** .
	Chinook	. * **** **** **** **** **** **** **** *** . .
	Coho	** . . . . ** **** **** **** **** ***
	Pink	. *** **** *** . . .
	Chum	. . . *** **** **** ***
Hope to Lytton	Sockeye	. . * **** **** **** * . .
	Chinook	. *** **** **** **** . .
	Coho	. . * **** **** *** . .
	Pink	. **** ** .
Lytton to Bridge R.	Sockeye	. . **** **** *** .
	Chinook	. . *** **** **** . .
	Coho	. . ** *** . .
	Pink	. **** ** .
Bridge R. to Quesnel	Sockeye	. . **** **** *** .
	Chinook	. . ** **** **** . .
Quesnel to Nechako	Sockeye	. . *** **** *** .
	Chinook	. . ** **** . .
Above Nechako	Sockeye	. . * ***** * . .
	Chinook	. . * *** . .

SOURCE: Aro and Shepard (1974), Northcote (1967)
    * heavy runs
    . light runs

tors of the system the time of year in which adults of different species of salmon are present. Again, it is apparent that downstream locations provide advantages. Upper tributaries have much shorter seasons of salmon presence than do lower tributaries or sections of the river. About 80 per cent of the Stuart Lake sockeye runs will pass a given point in their migration routes within two weeks. That constitutes the major duration of the salmon fishing season for some Carrier. The farther downstream, the more runs must pass a given river location, and, since run timing varies, the fishing seasons there are longer than they are upstream. Stalo tribes along the lower Fraser could fish salmon most of the year. Tribes having access to both river and sea could add to the time in which river runs were available by catching salmon in all months of the year in the sea. I will return to methods of sea fishing, but it should be noted that the very widespread technique of trolling with baited hooks (used by coastal tribes) is effective only for salmon in the sea (where they are feeding) and only for chinook and coho salmon. Sockeye, pinks, and chums feed primarily on small organisms, and, although they occasionally take lures, especially artificial lures which have been applied recently in the troll fishery (Scott and Crossman 1973:152, 157, 171), there is no evidence that Indian fishers were successful, with their heavy baited hooks, in taking species other than chinook and coho.

While runs destined for tributaries far inland generally move quickly into and through the river, sockeye runs to Adams River, in the Thompson River system, may stay in the vicinity of the Fraser River mouth for up to two weeks before entering the river and proceeding in concentrated numbers to their destination (Killick 1955:59). Similarly, sockeye runs to tributaries below the Fraser canyon display a delaying action off the Fraser River mouth and in its lower reaches, principally in Stalo territory (Verhoeven and Davidoff 1962). They enter the lower Fraser and remain there in large schools for varying periods of time, some runs staying for a month or more. Consequently, concentrations of fish are built up in the lower river at certain times. Pinks also delay off the Fraser mouth, congregating there before moving upstream (Gilhousen 1962:109), and there is evidence of a similar delay by chums (Neave 1966b:82). Somewhat analogous behaviour is exhibited by certain runs of sockeye far upstream as well. The Stellako and Chilco runs arrive in the vicinity of their spawning grounds as early as three weeks ahead of time, remaining in schools in deeper parts of the spawning stream or in lakes above or below spawning locations before moving onto the spawning grounds themselves (Killick 1955:57-8).

As noted above, extraordinary and unpredictable disasters may alter the normal patterns of availability, but, again, it should be pointed out that such factors affect upstream areas more severely than those close to the sea in a large river system such as the Fraser. Flood conditions and landslides present barriers or delaying conditions whose probability of occurrence is greater for those fish which travel further – a sheer matter of greater hazard for greater length of river migration. To this must be added, however, the fact that the tolerance of delay in migration is reduced for fish which must travel further upstream. As they proceed they deplete energy stocks and have a lower margin of reserves. The upper Fraser River runs (with the exception, perhaps, of the Chilco and Stellako sockeye just noted) cannot as readily tolerate delays as can those destined for the lower parts of the system (see Talbot 1950:38f).

What conclusions can be drawn about availability of salmon on the Fraser watershed? To recapitulate in point form:

(1) In salmon runs, varying natural conditions in fresh and ocean water may engender large and unpredictable short-term fluctuations in numbers.

(2) The marked ability of salmon to respond with compensatory effect to mortality enables them to withstand natural disasters of a temporary nature as well as heavy human predation.

(3) The numbers of salmon available in the river system diminish dramatically as one proceeds upstream, and the marked reductions above each tributary emphasize the strategic value of stream confluences as residential locations.

(4) Variance of availability within the four-year cycle is marked. Along the lower part of the river it is due to dominance of sockeye and pinks. In upper tributaries, where sockeye constitute a higher proportion of salmon, their dominance cycle imparts extreme variance from year to year.

(5) Seasonal duration of presence of salmon in any part of the main river system, and in the major tributaries, decreases as distance from the sea increases.

(6) Weight of fish and food value decrease as distance from the sea increases.

(7) Natural hazards to salmon (and their effects) increase as distance from the sea increases.

(8) The total weight of salmon present in the study area, conservatively estimated, would have ranged from 19,163,000 kg in low years to 69,194,000 kg in peak years.

SALMON AVAILABILITY AND HUMAN POPULATIONS

Salmon are rich resources for all predators. Sea lions and seals congregate around the mouth of the Fraser during salmon runs, and seals follow the fish as far as Hope and Harrison Lake. Inland, bears congregate on spawning grounds to feed, trout and waterfowl gorge on salmon eggs and on emerging fry and sea-bound fingerlings. At the peak of the food chain, human hunters and fishermen tapped a wide spectrum of these interdependent resources, taking fellow non-human predators as well as common prey (see Monks 1987 for a coastal example of such multiple predation). There can be no doubt of human dependence upon salmon as well as upon other animal resources in the Northwest. The relative density of aboriginal populations of the Northwest Coast culture area is a simple confirmation of those relationships.

The plainly evident dependence of Northwest Coast peoples on marine proteins has been confirmed by the recent analyses of bone collagen by Chisholm and associates (Chisholm et al., 1983), and subsequent tests of human skeletal material from NLaka'pamux (Thompson), Lillooet, and Shuswap portions of the Fraser watershed confirm a lower but still high dependence upon protein probably derived from salmon. The proportions of ocean-derived protein indicated in the skeletal remains range around 90 per cent for the Coast, (Chisholm et al. 1983:397). Lillooet samples were still over 60 per cent (Lovell, Chisholm et al. 1986:102). This has provided firm, supplementary, empirical confirmation of the ethnographic data that tell us of the central importance of salmon in the diets of Plateau people.

Were numbers of humans directly dependent upon abundance of salmon? Without resorting to any numerical tests, Table 3 discloses a telling feature about one Fraser River watershed, the Quesnel. While it has a large number of salmon in the dominant sockeye year, the other years are extremely low in total salmon available – the lowest of the major tributaries shown. While most other tributaries had substantial Indian villages in the historic period, there is no indication of any large recent Shuswap occupation of the Quesnel River watershed. The energy potential of the salmon resource for that system alone, being governed by the low cycle years, is slim indeed and is consistent with an apparently low human population.

Sneed carried out a preliminary test for the Fraser watershed, showing a correlation between the carrying capacity of salmon streams and relative sizes of aboriginal populations (Sneed 1971). For a different region of the Northwest, Donald and Mitchell demonstrated a close correspondence between relative sizes of Southern Kwakiutl tribal populations, tribal political rank, and the rank order of total salmon escapements in tribal territories (Donald and Mitchell 1990).

None of these studies, however, have claimed a simple dependent link between salmon and human populations, and it would be entirely misleading to conclude that these studies establish a necessary dependency of human population sizes upon salmon alone or that salmon were the only critical resource. There certainly were smaller human and salmon populations in the upper reaches of the Fraser system and larger numbers of people and salmon near the mouth of the river, but both features are part of a wider pattern of varied richness of all biotic forms in the whole watershed. The up-river regions have higher altitudes, shallower soils, reduced growing seasons, and so on. That populations of human hunter-gatherers are consistent with a general variance in richness of the biomass should not be surprising but is a fundamental baseline for understanding social and cultural adaptations in particular areas.

Opening any of the numerous ethnographies of the area also reveals human dependence on other important resources – deer, elk, freshwater fishes, and a wide range of plant products. In such diversified subsistence economies with limited storage capacities, all resources may be critical at some time, and so the relative value is difficult to determine and might only be evaluated securely with empirical data on utilization by a village group over a number of years. Such information is not available.

Additionally, it is important to remember that the presence of a resource does not inevitably translate into an abundance of human food. Fish, including salmon, must be caught, processed for eating, preserved for later times if they are in immediate surplus, and distributed to those who can benefit from them. This is to say that there are cultural factors to be taken into account when humans are part of an ecological system. The complexity of cultural factors in respect to salmon is forcefully outlined for the Lillooet by Romanoff (Chapter 5), who records, among other features, that although they relish fat salmon for fresh consumption they find them difficult to preserve by drying and, for that, prefer thinner fish. Thus, abundance and high caloric content of fish does not equate directly and simply with greater usability. Similar close study of other fishing groups of the Fraser would undoubtedly reveal other difficulties and preferences bearing on utilization of salmon and other resources.

The importance of local cultural variations and their potential consequences for food production and population size within what appears to be similar natural settings is convincingly illustrated by Langdon in his discussion of Haida and Tlingit adaptation to the Prince of Wales archipelago. Social organization, technology of fishing, and other cultural factors are shown to differ between the two groups and to be of such significance for exploiting the same region that they could account for difference in population size (Langdon 1979).

But if salmon are not the linchpin that holds the whole of Northwest Indian culture together, there surely is sufficient strength of association to urge continued attention to the role of salmon. And other migratory species also warrant attention. Hunting-fishing economies are ideally equipped to take advantage of the natural energy-concentrating systems represented by migratory animal and fish populations. Salmon are probably the pre-eminent family of such animals in the North Pacific to which consideration must be given in reconstructing culture history, however, to them should be added other anadromous fishes, such as eulachon, lamprey, and sturgeon; herring and surf smelts, which concentrate in inshore waters to spawn; such mammals as porpoise, harbour seals, sea-lions, and bears (which feed upon migratory and spawning fish); pelagic animals like whales and fur seals; and, finally, a long list of waterfowl, which move to the area either to nest or to winter.

Two different, variable qualities of these resources can be distinguished: (1) whether the form is r-selected (reproduces only once or a few times but in great numbers) or K-selected (reproduces repeatedly but in small numbers); and (2) whether the form is localized or migratory. Table 5 lists, with these distinctions, the main food resources used within the area under discussion. Hayden (1981) has drawn attention to the significance of r-selected forms, and their role in human cultural evolution, particularly the rapid transitions from Paleolithic to Mesolithic (Eurasia) and Paleo-Indian to Archaic (Americas), suggesting that increased utilization of r-selected forms, being 'comparatively inexhaustible and highly productive' (528), allowed and fostered the complex processes of cultural specialization and population growth which are associated with those transitions. Localized r-selected forms, particularly plants which may be domesticated, offer the greatest possibilities for intensification through cultural evolution. But the migratory r-selected forms are not far behind in their possibilities. This is because of their energy-concentrating potential, as noted above, and their capacity to withstand predation. They are analogous to plant domesticates in their potential return, offering, in the case of salmon, relative ease of access, immediate return for specialization of effort, and expansion of production to levels that were only achieved at the beginning of the twentieth century. It is specialization of use of these resources that underlies the complexity of Northwest Coast societies (see Matson 1983, 1985 for discussion of the salmon resource and and its relationship to the emergence of ranked societies and sedentary residence). Thus, there are numerous compelling reasons for examining closely the relationship between salmon resources and cultural forms throughout British Columbia.

It is to the matter of the evolution of technology for fishing salmon that I now turn. This constitutes a case of technological evolution which illustrates, for a restricted area, the model put forth by Hayden (1981).

AVAILABILITY, ACCESSIBILITY, AND FISHING TECHNOLOGY

Availability of salmon – the number of fish presenting themselves in a given territory – is an important measure. But availability is only half the equation. Accessibility of salmon must also be considered.

TABLE 5
Food resources available to Mainland Halkomelem

	Migratory	Sedentary
r-selected (short life, reproducing a few times in large numbers)	(a) salmon eulachon surf smelt herring	(b) plant foods
Intermediate	(c) sturgeon geese ducks	(d) shellfish rockfish flatfish ling-cod partridge
K-selected (long life, reproducing repeatedly, in small numbers)	(e) sea lions murres	(f) harbour seal porpoise deer elk bear mountain goat

NOTE: These distinctions in forms of resources may assist in distinguishing important local variations in resources in any given region. A few minutes reflection will point out significant variations. For example, in compiling a similar table for *Nuu-Chah-Nulth* (Nootka), one would subtract eulachon from cell (a), sturgeon from cell (c), mountain goat from cell (f); but add sea otter to cell (f), and whales and fur seals to cell (e).

This is a variable condition, independent of mere presence and mediated by at least two classes of factors: natural conditions of the environment in which the fish live and cultural conditions of knowledge and technology which humans apply to obtain salmon.

Among natural conditions which affect accessibility are: first, features of the water – its volume, speed, turbulence, and turbidity; and second, patterns of salmon activity – swimming and schooling behaviour, modes and times of feeding, and the like. Reduced volumes of water in shallow and constricted channels concentrate fish. Speed of currents opposing migration slow the rate of travel of salmon and induce them to seek paths where lighter currents are met. Turbidity of water reduces a fish's visibility and capacity to avoid traps as it reduces a predator's ability to see fish. All of these conditions combine to determine, in different locations, the variable accessibility of fish. The particular nature of these variables for the Lillooet study area are provided in Romanoff (Chapter 5), Kennedy and Bouchard (Chapter 6), and Tyhurst (Chapter 7).

Viewing the Fraser system as a whole, there is, roughly speaking, a gradient of natural accessibility from the sea to uppermost tributaries. Salmon are least accessible in the open sea; accessibility increases as they enter the channels through the large archipelagos in Georgia Strait; it increases again as they enter the Fraser River, although here turbidity conceals and reduces accessibility as well. As they ascend to the turbulent canyon and then to smaller tributaries, accessibility again increases. After spawning, Pacific salmon die and wash ashore, becoming then virtually a free resource available, in the end, to gulls and maggots. But where they are least accessible they are most nutritious and valuable as food, and where they are most accessible they are of least value.

There is, between humans and the salmon resource, a gulf of varying difficulty of access. Evolution of knowledge and technology have combined to create cultural systems which reduce this gulf in varying degrees. Is there any regularity behind such processes of evolution? Data available for aboriginal Fraser River cultures offer some suggestive clues. In a subsistence system in which the maximum return has not been reached, there is, as it were, a possible margin of increase. Humans may achieve and experience greater returns by innovations that apply old technology in new areas, by invention and application of new technology, and by discovery of new knowledge about natural systems and animal behaviour. I suggest that technology and knowledge will tend to evolve, becoming more complex, elaborate, and changing where such elaboration and change pays off, that is, where it offers greater returns. This will tend to be where value of a resource or availability is high and where access is difficult. Changes of technology and knowledge in such circumstances will be incremental, because innovations which provide better returns will be favoured. Thus, we should expect technology of salmon fishing on the Fraser to be more complex where availability is high and accessibility is low, that is, near the sea. A review of salmon fishing on the Fraser system bears out this simple proposition. Furthermore, it reveals a plausible sequence for the evolution of aboriginal salmon fishing technology.

Ignoring, for the present, the total array of fishing devices utilized throughout the watershed and concentrating upon major salmon fishing devices, that is, those reported as the major instruments used to tap the main Fraser River runs, there are four devices used in, and directly associated with, four distinct natural zones.

Islands Zone

The San Juan and Gulf Islands region is not part of the Fraser River in a conventional sense, but it is a region through which the bulk of the Fraser salmon runs pass, especially sockeye and pinks, in regular predictable migrations en route to the river. This is a marine environment; the sea is relatively clear and is subject to regular tidal currents. Fish movement is restricted only by their migratory urges, which tend to follow regular patterns from year to year. Here, in Straits Salish territory, the main salmon fishing device was the reef net, without doubt the most complicated and highly specialized aboriginal fishing apparatus in the whole area. It was essentially a trap consisting of a large net suspended horizontally a few feet below the surface of the sea between two large canoes (this account follows Suttles 1951:152f.). The canoes and the net itself were held in position with main and side lines fastened to anchors made of huge boulder clusters set anew each season. The net was set in owned locations and simulated a path for the fish over a reef or through kelp beds (see Stewart 1977 for illustrations of all the fishing devices discussed here). It required a crew of six to twelve plus ancillary helpers who came out from shore to remove the catch. It could only be operated on a flood tide when conditions of light and wind allowed the crew leader to see a school of fish enter the trap, at which point he gave an order for its closure. Reef nets were effective mainly for sockeye and pinks, taking scarcely any of the other species, but, of these, coho and chinook were taken in the sea by trolling.

Lower Fraser River Zone

The next region or zone is the Lower Fraser itself, from its mouth to Yale, where the canyon begins. This is the territory of Halkomelem-speaking people. Subject to tidal influence for some distance, the river is broad, deep, with a moderate current, and laden with silt. Salmon travel dispersed through the stream in schools which sometimes concentrate in certain reaches, resting or waiting for the change of tide before moving on.

Throughout this region trawl nets were used (see Appendix 2 for an early ethnographic description of these nets and the other salmon fishing devices in upstream zones). Two types of these large bag-like nets are reported, one being attached to poles held by men in two canoes which were propelled slowly downstream to extend the net behind. The other type had floats and sinkers and was similarly pulled by lines held in two canoes. Pulled with the current but slightly faster, with the mouth open in the path of upstream migrating salmon, the nets were closed and lifted when fish were felt in them (Duff 1952:68-9; Suttles 1955:21-2). Such devices could not be used in rapids but worked well in moderate currents with turbid water preventing fish from seeing them. It is worth noting that, among Halkomelem, these nets were made with three different-sized meshes for salmon, eulachon, and sturgeon, respectively.

Canyon Zone

This zone, occupied by *NLaka'pamux*, Lillooet, and Shuswap, extends from Yale to Soda Creek and includes the tumultuous Fraser Canyon and the long series of rapids and canyons ending at Soda Creek. Navigation was impractical throughout this area except for crossings and short distances in swift current between rapids. Salmon take advantage of eddies and slack water wherever it is found, thus conserving energy (Brett 1965). They move close to the precipitous banks of the river over the greater part of this section, and here dip nets prevailed for fishing (see Chapters 5 and 6 for full descriptions). These are like huge landing nets, wielded by one person either in a scooping motion, sweeping downstream with the current or, as was preferred, held immersed in an eddy or back-current with the net mouth opening downstream. This requires less effort but can be done only where conditions of turbulence close to shore are suitable – constricted canyons and protruding points of rock are ideal and occur frequently in the Lillooet study area. The great turbidity of the Fraser increases the effectiveness of dipnets and they were used in daylight hours. Teit reports that in the clear waters of the Thompson River dip nets were used only at night (Teit 1900:251).

There were two types of these nets, one with the mesh fastened directly to a hoop in a fixed position; the other, and more productive form, had the net fastened to horn rings which slid on the hoop. The latter type was held open with a line extending up the handle. Simultaneously dropping this line and pulling the net up closed its mouth like a purse. Dip nets were operated from natural stands, such as rock ledges or protruding boulders, or from board or log stagings set over the river.

Upper Fraser Zone

Above Soda Creek Canyon, near the northern margin of Shuswap territory, the characteristics of the Fraser change again. Its speed is reduced as it becomes a broad, fast-flowing, navigable river bounded by alternate steep banks of gravel and gently sloping flats or bars of silt and gravel. Natural stations suitable for dip nets are infrequent.

The Carrier of this region in the early historic period applied versions of the widespread lattice-work weir and trap. These consisted of a lattice fence set against piles, the fence projecting diagonally downstream from the shore. Cylindrical lattice traps were set at openings in the fence on the upstream side. These devices obstructed only a small inshore portion of the total width of the river. Essential conditions for successful operation were the turbidity of the water (in clear streams salmon easily dodge around such obstructions) plus the tendency for salmon to avoid heavier currents toward the centre of the river. Fur traders at Fort Alexandria described these traps as capable of yielding up to 400 sockeye per night (HBC 1827: Sept. 6) when the runs were heavy and also reported one to have caught a seven foot sturgeon (HBC 1824, Jul. 24), so we may be sure they were large and substantially built.

In the major salmon-supporting tributaries of the upper Fraser a variety of fishing devices were used. In streams such as the Thompson and Chilcotin, which were too large for full weirs, dip nets and harpoons prevailed. Full weirs were constructed in moderate sized streams, where this was possible, including the Stuart River for chinook and sockeye, and the Nautley, taking sockeye from the Stellako and Nadina runs.

It is worth noting at this point that Fraser River Indians continue to depend upon salmon for subsistence. Despite government-imposed restrictions on their fishing and annual commercial catches in recent decades of over 13 million fish, Indians still catch an average of over half a million fish per year (Schubert 1986:5). Although some changes in technology have occurred, dip nets continue to be used in parts of the canyon region (a review of contemporary Indian fishing methods is given in Schubert 1986:1-3). A notable feature is the disappearance of traps and weirs, prohibited by the Department of Fisheries in the early decades of this century.

EVOLUTION OF FISHING TECHNOLOGY

The aboriginal fishing devices dominant in the four zones outlined above are separable into two different evolutionary sequences. In the first three of these zones, where nets dominate, the fixed dip net is technically the simplest and, I suggest, the parent device, being utilized in the canyon areas of the river where natural barriers exist to make salmon unusually accessible to humans. But the most effective dip net used in the area is the improved, technically more complex, collapsing dip net – surely derived from the fixed net. The trawl net, in its mechanics, is remarkably similar, suggesting its derivation from the collapsing dip net. Both are bag nets pulled downstream in the path of upward moving salmon, and both can be closed or pursed around entrapped fish. The trawl is an enlarged and more complex version of a dip net, enabling successful operation in slower water where fish are more dispersed.

The reef net existed only among Straits Salish people. It is not obviously derived from a trawl, but, as it shares some features, the best explanation of the reef net's origin seems to be its evolution from a trawl. Suttles obtained a description of a device he called a 'weir net.' These were used by Lushootseed-speaking Swinomish in the Swinomish Slough in northern Puget Sound. The weir net consisted of a trawl net operated from two canoes anchored at the open apex of a 'V'-shaped stake fence, with the tide running into the 'v.' The trawl net caught the migrating salmon as they emerged from the fence which guided them through the muddy tidal waters. These net sites, like those for reef nets, were privately owned (Suttles n.d.). Such devices were clearly intermediate between the two developed forms and illustrate the way in which trawls could have been developed into reef nets.

There are a series of similarities of form and function between these nets: both reef and trawl nets are operated from two canoes; both intercept migrating salmon. Like the dip net in an eddy, the reef net is anchored against currents with which the fish are swimming, and, both other nets, the reef net is closed by the fishermen around the captive fish. The reef net differs from both other forms, and from a trawl operated as a trap, in that it can be, indeed must be, operated in daylight and in clear water, for the crew leader must be able to see the salmon enter the net before giving the order for its closure. The reef net is an adaptation allowing a river device to be operated in the clear water of the sea.

From examination of the salmon resource, its characteristics, and the natural conditions of the sea and stream, it is clear that, aside from their spawning grounds (where they are in least desirable condition), salmon are most accessible in the canyon, including the Lillooet study area, less accessible downstream, and least accessible in the sea. I suggest that the progressively more complex sequence of technology, from dip net to trawl net to reef net, represents stages of increasingly specialized adaptation, and that the adaptive mechanism was an increment in productivity at each stage as each device made available more valuable fish, in greater numbers, over a longer period of time, and in a wider area. Each device, by overcoming barriers of accessibility, would have opened up increased production by more fishing units.

It is worth considering as closely as possible the nature of changes to productivity which would have ensued. It has been suggested that a major limiting factor in salmon utilization in the Northwest was the ability to process and preserve fish rather than the ability to catch them (Suttles 1968:63-4; Romanoff Chapter 5). To the extent that this is true, advantages of improved catch technology and incentives to adopt them would be reduced. If one is easily catching all the fish which one can preserve, why strive for more?

The answer is not simply more fish by one operator or production unit of fisher/butcher/dryer but the opportunity for more production units to be at work and for a longer season. Adoption of trawl nets by people fishing with dip nets at the lower feasible dip net stations would have allowed an expansion of fishing territories and made immediate access to the main salmon runs available to all residents along the lower river. In fact, in the early historic period this portion of the Fraser was used by people from far-off villages as well, including Halkomelem from Vancouver Island (Duff 1952:25). Again, invention of the reef net would have provided Straits Salish direct access to Fraser River pinks and sockeye. The sequence of changes in catch technology suggested here would have expanded the *territory* within which local groups could operate highly productive fisheries on the main Fraser salmon runs. It would also have brought significant increments in total time available for processing salmon.

Dispersed local groups in the Lower Fraser valley and in Georgia

Strait and Juan de Fuca Strait would *always* have had access to local salmon runs in small and medium-sized streams – runs of short duration and mainly occurring in the late fall. Access to the great Fraser runs would have extended their salmon fishing season into the summer. It would have facilitated a greater total production of salmon and supported a larger human population.

A similar principle of adaptation of fishing technology to natural conditions is revealed by the difference between Interior Salish and Carrier salmon fishing. In Carrier territory, salmon numbers and nutritional value were lower than in neighbouring Interior Salish territory, yet Carrier traps were much more technologically complex devices than were Salish dip nets. Given the differences in stream flow and river topography, the more complex traps offered an advantage over dip nets, but they were not derived from those nets. Carrier weirs and traps, as applied in the Fraser River, should probably be seen as a separate evolutionary development, derived from the weir and trap complex so widespread in the Western Sub-Arctic, Plateau, and Northwest Coast culture areas. Carrier traps were specialized applications of a short fence combined with a trap, a partial river obstruction that could not block fish migration but, given high turbidity and hard current, enabled the resource to be fished. Stepping out of the Fraser watershed for a moment to consider the highly specialized salmon traps operated by Gitksan and *Wet'suwet'en* (Western Carrier) in Hagwilget (Skeena River) and Moricetown canyons (Bulkley River), I suggest that they also represent specialization in a different form of the ubiquitous weir/trap.

Figure 1 summarizes these suggested separate lines of technological evolution of salmon fishing devices. I should hasten to point out that these sequences are not intended to show the total distribution of these devices nor to make a claim about the place of invention or development from one form to another. More study and data are needed to attempt a complete reconstruction. Nevertheless, the geographic distribution of these forms is more or less consistent with the widely accepted age/area hypothesis that older forms will have wider distribution.

Lattice-work fences and traps and fixed dip nets are relatively simple devices and are widespread in both North America and Northern Europe and Asia. They have a more or less continuous distribution in Northwest America and can safely be viewed as ancient forms. Berringer's helpful survey of Northwest Coast fishing devices indicates the uniqueness of the complex Upper Skeena lattice-work traps operated in canyon locations (1982:101f.) – they clearly were local specializations. The partial weir/traps used by Carrier on the upper

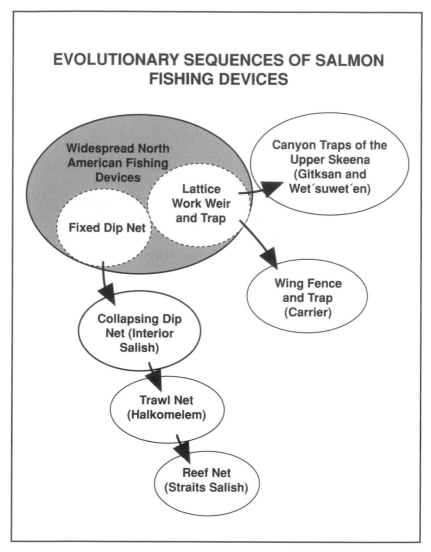

FIGURE 1
Proposed evolutionary sequence of salmon fishing devices

Fraser are not widespread, although the Koyukuk and Kutchin on the
Yukon River system used devices which must have been similar in
similar river conditions (see Clark 1974:152; Nelson 1973:57). To what
extent the two distant occurrences may be related is not clear. They
might well be independent developments. On this point, a thorough

review of Athapascan fishing technology might reveal additional series of technological evolutions.

Returning to the Salish groups on the Fraser, the collapsing dip net tied to sliding rings was used by the *NLaka'pamux*, Shuswap, Lillooet, and Upper Stalo on the Fraser. Groups on the Columbia and Klamath rivers, where fixed dip nets in a variety of forms were used, also made a pursing dip net, the action apparently being achieved by a line which gathered the mesh together (Berringer 1982:119-20; Hewes 1947:82). The type set on sliding rings appears to be restricted to the Fraser River Salish and to represent a local development from the older, widespread, and simpler fixed dip net. Trawl nets, which I suggest are derivatives of dip nets, have a wider distribution, being used by Haida, Tsimshian, Haisla, Bella Coola, Nootka, Makah, all the Coast Salish (Twana excepted), Quilleute, Quinalt, Lower Chinook, and the groups on the Klamath (Berringer 1982:249-51). This is a much wider distribution than that of collapsing dip nets, a fact which at first glance does not support my suggested evolutionary sequence.

But association of greater age with wider distribution cannot be taken as invariable and conclusive. In this instance, considering the diffusion of specialized fishing gear, the factor of natural river conditions, that is, accessibility, must be considered. Pursing dip nets, indeed any dip nets used to take salmon in open streams, work well only in conditions of extreme turbulence with such natural barriers as rapids or canyons. In small streams they can be replaced by a variety of traps, but in large, rapid, and turbid streams ordinary traps are inadequate and dip nets excel. This is to say that pursing dip nets are specialized devices with limited applicability. Trawl nets, on the other hand, can be operated in the lower reaches of streams in moderate currents where the water is sufficiently turbid. They are applicable in a much wider range of places in salmon streams, and their rapid diffusion, after invention, along a coastline with numerous tidal river mouths, would be expected. Precisely where their place of origin might be is another matter, but the pattern of distribution is not inconsistent with Coast Salish origin.

Finally, the reef net has the most limited distribution of the four major devices being considered – being known, the world over, only among Straits Salish. Although it, too, requires special conditions for successful operation, not being a device suitable to all parts of the sea coast, its distribution and the suggested evolution from trawl nets mark its probable late arrival on the scene.

Returning to the Lillooet study area, we can be confident that dip nets would have been used there for several thousand years. Just when the innovation of the sliding dip net would have been introduced is

less clear, but there is no reason to doubt that it, too, is of considerable antiquity.

CONCLUSION

A major part of this chapter has presented a model of salmon availability within the Fraser River watershed. There is a wealth of data on
salmon, and their utility for reconstructing the history and understanding the nature of Indian cultures is clear. As Suttles (1968:60) suggested twenty years ago, archaeologists and ethnologists have much to
gain from colleagues' work in the natural sciences.

While this model of salmon availability is presented with a seeming fixity and accuracy about it, these features ought to be taken cau-
tiously. The value of biological data for those concerned with human
cultures does not reside so much in the specificity of descriptive detail,
whether it be numbers of animals, pounds of flesh, or calories per
gram, but in the understanding which they provide of processes and
relationships within ecological systems.

It is helpful to know the actual numbers of salmon passing Hell's
Gate and numbers passing beyond the mouth of the Bridge River and
what their differences were. But it is more helpful to know the general features of salmon distribution and variation, to know that they
will be reduced above each tributary and that unpredictable and substantial variations in numbers are normal. Likewise, it helps to know
the particular facts about quadrennial dominance of Fraser sockeye
and what this has meant in the historic period in terms of numbers
of salmon available from year to year. It is much more important to
know the conditions which create that dominance, to be cognizant
of the fact that it may change, and that it is not a fixed and immutable
feature of a fixed and immutable natural world.

A second part of this chapter has been an application of this model
in the form of an inquiry into cultural evolution and its relationship
to natural resources. Examination of the primary salmon fishing
devices within the Fraser River watershed and their probable sequence
of development reveals associations with the natural conditions of the
salmon resource and the stream itself. The technology is fitted to the
natural conditions; and the sequence of evolution, which is one of
increasing mechanical complexity, reveals the greatest complexity in
that part of the river system where the potential for intensification of
production is greatest.

Comparative studies of cultures in the Northwest cannot fail to be
strengthened by casting those comparisons against the frameworks,
which biological data provide, of the nature and variations in salmon

resources in different major river systems and climatological zones. Particular case studies, too, such as those of the large prehistoric villages and complex societies at Keatly Creek and Bridge River, will greatly benefit from detailed studies of salmon in their vicinities. And, of course, data are there or will be forthcoming not only for salmon but for other fish, invertebrates, mammals, birds, and plants – as the remaining chapters in this volume amply attest.

APPENDICES

1: Constructing a Model of Fraser River Salmon Distribution

Method

My objective in this part of the study is to construct for the Fraser River system a profile of the amounts of salmon and the times they were available for use by aboriginal peoples. It is an attempt to reconstruct the extent of the salmon resource for the whole system at the time of white contact. Two parts of this goal are relatively easily achieved. Distribution of salmon runs within the river system and the times at which they enter the system and when they spawn are given in the records of fisheries officers and studies by biologists.

When it comes to defining the sizes of the many runs, that is, the numbers of fish in each, the task becomes more difficult. This derives from the fact that salmon are not a fixed resource. In the final analysis, of course, no elements in this universe, none of the objects and species which humans use, are fixed in their amounts and forms. Although some things change so little or so slowly that they can be treated as fixed, many life forms with which humans interact cannot be so treated. This is specially so of salmon. Modern biological knowledge provides a most convincing confirmation of the implicit message of native Indian mythology that salmon and humans are locked in interdependent, complementary relationships. The sizes of salmon runs today are shaped by the nature of our fisheries and our treatment of salmon environments. So, too, the sizes of salmon runs in 1800 were what they were not in spite of humans or independent of humans but because of humans and how they fished and interacted with the fish. There is no pristine time in recent millennia when salmon existed apart from humans within the Fraser River system.

It is a misapprehension of nature that induces some students of human history to suppose that salmon resources of the Northwest were at a maximum in the remote past before Europeans came along. It was this misunderstanding which led Hewes to postulate that the maximum population of salmon existed before Indian fishing began. The overwhelming evidence of the resilience of salmon to predation requires the conclusion that Indian fishing increased the abundance of adult salmon and that these could be taken, and were taken, by the aboriginal fishery with no diminution of the resource. The commercial fishery in its early years and over the long term has maintained catches well beyond the sizes of escapement – that is, it has taken consistently more than half of the number of fish returning to the river. By what measure, then, can the size of the resource available to Indian culture of 1800 be assessed?

There is certainly no written record of the proto-historic abundance of salmon nor of Indian catches at that time. Estimates have been made of annual individual consumption of salmon and, by multiplying them by estimates of human population, crude estimates of total salmon catch have been generated (see Hewes 1947:212f.). But these are of limited value for reconstructing history because of the uncertainty of aboriginal population sizes and the lack of firm information on aboriginal diet. Recent research measuring the ratio of marine derived stable carbon isotopes in human bone promises a precise means for determining relative dependence of humans upon marine as opposed to terrestrial sources of protein (Lovell, Chisholm, et al. 1986:99-106). This work reveals a high dependence of individuals from the NLaka'pamux, Lillooet, and Shuswap areas on marine protein, presumably derived from salmon. But again, it does not yet allow us to determine what the total catch might have been nor, more to the point in this context, the availability or abundance of the resource.

Department of Fisheries data on commercial and Indian catches during the last hundred years are available and can be added to estimates of escapement of salmon to spawning grounds to produce estimates of total salmon abundance. But such estimates for recent decades, when there have been reductions of salmon due to over-fishing and environmental degradation, do not represent the period of aboriginal use. On the other hand, figures for the earlier years of commercial production might well overstate sustainable abundance, for those peak years were times of unbridled exploitation, when the relatively new and uncontrolled commercial fishery was carried beyond sustainable levels. What best represents the case in 1800? The most useful answer, perhaps, is given in non-quantitative terms by saying that the Fraser salmon resource was flexible, and capable of expansion by regular, well-distributed human predation, far beyond the levels at which it was then being used.

But since my aim is to provide a more tangible assessment that might show the relative amounts of salmon available in different parts of the watershed, it will help to be able to attach a reasonable quantitative estimate. My solution is to examine levels of escapement by species and to calculate their relative distribution through the main parts of the watershed. Some adjustments have been made for known historic changes in stream conditions in order to have the distributions approximate more closely conditions with a time horizon of 1800. Assuming this distribution to be more or less constant, one may then estimate total escapement of each species to the Fraser River and their distribution to spawning grounds within the watershed in order to provide a profile of the annual presence (abundance) of salmon. I have engaged in some guessing about changes and made adjustments as described below. Other changes could be made if one wished to approximate conditions and consequences of natural disaster in one part of the watershed upon the total system or if one wished to see the likely distribution, given a different estimate of the total resource size. The construction of this model may be summarized in the following steps.

Step 1: Data on escapement were used to create an annual percentage distribution of the presence of each species in the various parts of the watershed. These data are given in tables A, B, C, D, and E, which were constructed in the following way: Table A presents a summary of *chinook* distribution. It was constructed from Department of Fisheries and Oceans records of escapement (Farwell et al. 1987:14-34), using averages for the years 1981-5. Although these data run from 1951 to 1985, the later years appear to be more accurate. In earlier years there were many cases of 'no record' for small spawning streams. Many streams used by chinook have undoubtedly suffered from environmental degradation. In the absence of detailed assessments of the consequences for each stream affected, I have chosen not to amend the percentage distribution – with two exceptions. I have doubled the percentage escapement to the Quesnel and Nechako River systems and adjusted the other escapements proportionally. The Quesnel River and such Fraser tributaries as the Cottonwood, Swift, and Antler suffered severe disruption from nineteenth-century placer mining, and the Nechako suffered from marked reduction of flow due to construction of the Kenney Dam in the 1950s.

Table B shows *coho* distribution and was obtained from the same source (Farwell et al. 1987:56-83), using the average escapements for 1981-5. No attempt was made to change these relative distributions, although some stream degradation has also affected coho. Of particular note has been degradation and even elimination, mainly through agricultural development, of many small tributary streams below Hope (see Northcote and Larkin 1988:5).

Table C shows *pink* distribution. These fish were severely affected by the 1913 Hell's Gate slide, which eliminated pink runs above that point. They have re-colonized upstream locations since completion of fishways, although the upper runs have not yet returned to their former capacity (see Vernon 1962, and Ricker 1989, for reviews of these runs). Pink runs above Hell's Gate were in the range of 'several tens of millions' and the relative sizes of upper and lower runs has been estimated at a ratio of more than three to one (Ricker 1987:20 and Ricker 1989:2-3). In recognition of these changes, I have increased substantially over present ratios the proportions of the up-river runs and decreased proportionately the downstream runs. The proportions derived from 1981-5 escapement data (Farwell et al. 1987:85-96) are shown in brackets. It should be noted that pinks, two years old at maturity, run in alternate, odd-numbered years in the Fraser, so that this distribution is for those years only; in even years there are virtually no pinks present.

Table D provides the distribution of *chum* as derived from the 1981-5 average escapement figures (Farwell 1987:35-53). This species, like coho, has suffered from losses of small spawning streams below Hope, but the pattern of distribution in the system as a whole has probably not altered substantially.

Table E presents *sockeye* distribution data. Because of quadrennial dominance of sockeye it is necessary to take account of their distribution over a four-year period. Fortunately, an average of cycle year escapements for the main runs has been calculated for the years 1951-62 (Aro and Shepard 1967:302). This has provided the base for my calculations of sockeye distribution.

TABLE A
Percentage distribution of chinook in Fraser system

Section of Fraser mainstem	Per cent	Tributaries	Per cent
Mouth of Fraser River	100.0		
		Pitt River	.4
Above Pitt River	99.6		
		Chilliwack, etc.	.2
Above Chilliwack River	99.4		
		Harrison system	26.9
Above Harrison River	72.5		
		Minor tributaries	.1
Above Hope	72.4		
		Minor tributaries	.1
		Thompson system	30.9
Above Thompson River	41.4		
		Seton, Bridge, etc.	1.0
Above Bridge River	40.4		
		Chilcotin, etc.	7.5
Above Chilcotin River	32.9		
		Quesnel River	5.6
Above Quesnel River	27.3		
		Westroad River	3.6
		Other minor	1.1
		Nechako River system	6.6
Above Nechako River	16.0		
		McGregor, Bowron, etc.	5.2
Above Bowron River	10.8		
		Upper Fraser	10.8
		Total	100.0

SOURCE: See Appendix 1

TABLE B
Percentage distribution of coho in Fraser system

Section of Fraser mainstem	Per cent	Tributaries	Per cent
Mouth of Fraser River	100.0		
		Tributaries below Harrison River	39.7
		Harrison River system	32.4
Above Harrison River	27.9	Minor tributaries	1.7
Above Hope	26.2	Minor tributaries	.7
		Thompson system	22.8
Above Thompson River	2.7	Seton, Bridge, etc.	2.4
Above Bridge River	.3		
Above Chilcotin River	.3	Quesnel River	.3
Above Quesnel River	0		

SOURCE: See Appendix 1

TABLE C
Percentage distribution of pinks in Fraser system
(odd years only)

Section of Fraser mainstem	Per cent	Tributaries		Per cent
Mouth of Fraser River	100.0	Mainstem and all tributaries below Hope		
		– early runs	(69.5)	22.0
		– late runs		8.0
Above Hope	(22.5) 70.0	Minor tributaries	(1.3)	1.0
		Thompson system	(12.0)	
		– Nicola		20.0
		– Upper Thompson		30.0
Above Thompson River	(9.2) 19.0	Seton, Bridge, etc.	(9.2)	19.0
Above Bridge River	present	Churn Creek		present
		Quesnel River		
Above Quesnel River	0			

SOURCE: See Appendix 1
NOTE: Percentages in brackets derived from Farwell et al. (1987:85-6)

TABLE D
Percentage distribution of chum in Fraser system

Section of Fraser mainstem	Per cent	Tributaries	Per cent
Mouth of Fraser River	100.0		
		Tributaries below Harrison River	40.2
		Harrison River system	58.2
Above Harrison River	1.6		
Above Hope	0	(occasional)	

SOURCE: See Appendix 1

TABLE E
Percentage distribution of sockeye in Fraser system
for main tributaries and cycle years (in 1000s of fish)

Tributary	Percentage of annual total by cycle year			
	/01	/02	/03	/04
Pitt River	.5	5.0	5.5	4.5
Cultus/Chilliwack	.5	3.0	5.5	2.0
Harrison/Lillooet	2.0	12.0	12.0	11.0
Thompson River	57.4	27.0	4.0	2.0
Bridge/Seton	.3	2.5	2.0	3.0
Chilcotin	4.0	15.0	46.0	67.5
Quesnel	14.0	2.5	2.5	.5
Nechako	21.0	31.0	20.5	8.5
Bowron	.3	2.0	2.0	1.5
Totals:	100.0	100.0	100.0	100.0

However, these escapement figures do not actually show relative proportions of sockeye escapement for the early historic period. The cycles of quadrennial dominances are not coincident, as they seem to have been at that early time (see Ricker 1966:60). I have altered the Aro and Shepard figures by: (1) placing the Thompson returns so the dominant year falls in the 1901 sequence; (2) increasing the size of the dominant year escapement in the Quesnel system to the average of the last three cycle years as given in more recent returns (Farwell et al. 1987:110), because the Quesnel run was clearly still undergoing recovery during the period of escapement summarized in Aro and Shepard; (3) adding from recent escapement figures for 1969-85 (Farwell et al. 1987:104) an average for the Seton and Bridge River systems, omitted in the Aro and Shepard summary.

It may well be the case that the Quesnel and other up-river runs should be increased even more. Other changes could also be made to meet various suggested possibilities. I have not shifted the dominance of the Chilcotin, the Nadina, or the Stellako runs of the Nechako system, which thus dampens the dominance of the 1901 line. Since we know that shifting of dominance occurs, it seemed more realistic in a model aimed at representing a long-term picture not to magnify the single year dominance – although once again we must note that it occurred. My model, then, does not show dominance in the sockeye cycles as extreme as it may well have been in the nineteenth century.

Percentages of the total annual Fraser River sockeye escapement for runs in each of the main tributaries were calculated and then slightly rounded. Some minor adjustments were necessary. For example, the /03 cycle year Bowron percentage was reduced, since with the much greater estimated run totals this small stream system would have received an unrealistically large portion well beyond the likely possible sustainable numbers.

Step 2: Estimates of total abundance are given in the four right-hand columns of Table F. These were selected after examination of the present and recommended optimum levels of escapement in the 1982 report of the Commission on Pacific Fisheries Policy (given in the four left-hand columns of Table F). In its view, 'optimum' level was a complex goal but, in general, one that would provide maximum sustained yield under well-managed fisheries and enhancement programs that would return streams to earlier, higher levels of production (Pearse 1982:4-6, 12-13, 283-8). These estimates were rejected, however, for they clearly underestimate substantially the sizes of runs in the pre-commercial era. Much larger estimated abundance for each species have been adopted.

Some explanations of the estimates are necessary. The figure of 60 million *sockeye* in the dominant 1801 year is arbitrary. It is several times larger than the proposed optimum but less than the 100 million for the dominant year which Ricker suggests to be 'not unreasonable' (Ricker 1987:8). In order to estimate the total sockeye for succeeding years in the four-year cycle, the total escapements calculated to obtain the percentage distribution of sockeye by tributaries were used to derive a ratio of the totals of the four years in a cycle, one to another. This was 18:3:3:4. The estimated totals for the three subsequent years (accepting 60 million for the 1801 year) following that ratio are: 1802 – 10 million, 1803 – 10 million, and 1804 – 13 million. These are the estimates used in calculating the sockeye figures for Tables 1, 2, and 3.

The *chinook* estimate is twice that of the optimum suggested by Pearse, a modest increase given the stream degradation we know to have occurred – especially the severe damage to such major systems as the Quesnel and Nechako. The number of *coho* has been increased to equate with that of chinook, for we know that substantial loss of spawning territory has occurred in the highly developed lower Fraser area. The *pink* abundance has been increased fourfold, again in recognition of the fact that the loss of runs resulting from the Hell's Gate slide has not yet been compensated for by recent regeneration of runs above the canyon.

TABLE F

Estimates of Fraser River salmon abundance (in 1000s of fish)

Species	Current		Optimum	
	Catch	Escapement	Catch	Escapement
Sockeye	4,460	1,370	8,000	4,00
Chinook	578	68	788	200
Coho	380	61	406	54
Pink	7,000	2,440	4,000	2,000
Chum	341	435	1,200	1,000

Late twentieth-century salmon abundance*

Estimated abundance (catch & escape)

Species	Cycle Years			
	1901	1902	1903	1904
Sockeye	60,000	10,000	10,000	13,000
Chinook	2,000	2,000	2,000	2,000
Coho	2,000	2,000	2,000	2,000
Pink	24,000	—	24,000	—
Chum	4,000	4,000	4,000	4,000

NOTE:* Current and optimum catches and escapements from Pearse (1982:283-7)

It may be argued that these estimated levels of abundance are not those which prevailed in the various sections of the river in 1800. That may well be the case. There is ethnographic evidence (see Chapters 5 and 6) suggesting that chinook were more abundant and more heavily used by Lillooet fishers in earlier times than in recent decades. This species has suffered heavily from stream degradation and from both sport and commercial fishing. It seems likely, as noted earlier, that this species, being largest of all, would be most heavily and adversely affected by the use of gill nets. The selective pressure of this factor is proposed as a major cause of the observed reduction in size of Fraser River pinks (see Ricker 1989:10-11). However, I have refrained from raising the estimates as high as one might be induced to do from such evidence. These are conservative estimates which leave no doubt of the direction in which any margin of error will lie.

Step 3: Presence of salmon by species in various portions of the watershed in numbers of fish were calculated from the assumed distribution and estimated totals and are shown as they distribute throughout the watershed over a four-year period. These are given in Table 1.

Step 4: Amounts of salmon in kilograms of all species combined, in different portions of the Fraser River, were calculated and are shown in Tables 2 and 3.

2: Indian Salmon Fishing Technology on the Fraser River: An Early Ethnographic Account

I am indebted to Elizabeth Furniss, Research Officer for the Cariboo Tribal Council, Williams Lake, for bringing to my attention a manuscript by Alexander Caulfield Anderson (1814-84), a trader with the Hudson's Bay Company in central British Columbia from 1832 to 1858. Anderson provides a summary of the natural history of the region and a sketch of the native Indians in the province. Of particular importance are his references to Carrier Indians, the people with whom he was most familiar. He also gives a succinct and clear account of indigenous salmon fishing devices used on the Fraser River, an account which is consistent with my own summary gleaned from extensive reading – reading which unfortunately missed this source. A transcription of the relevant passages is given here in recognition of their original contribution to an understanding of salmon on the Fraser. There is no date attached to the manuscript but references made within it suggest an approximate date of 1860.

It will thus be seen that the laws which govern the ascent of these fish [salmon] are fixed and undeviating. The knowledge of their habits, therefore, which by long experience has taught them, enables the Indians to prepare devices for their capture, in the full certainty that, when the fish do arrive, their preparation will not have been made in vain. In these various devices much ingenuity is displayed; but in different portions of the river, and by different tribes, various methods are practiced.

Before the Salmon enter the river they are readily caught in the adjacent straits and inlets with baited hooks, frequently affixed to long lines fastened to a [56] canoe, which is then paddled briskly through the water. The bait used in this system of trolling is a small fish, or some other substance, as even a piece of red cloth.

The lower Indians of the Fraser use small drift nets, which are plied from their canoes. Higher up they erect scaffolds on rocky projections, where the current is strong. From these scaffolds bag-nets distended by light frames, nearly similar to the drift-nets, are plied by the fishermen. This system continues as far as the borders of the Tacully tribe near Alexandria. The Tacully, who are peculiarly expert in preparing various devices for fishing and the snaring of the beasts of chase, construct weirs for catching the salmon. A close fence of light hurdles, supported by strong stakes driven into the bottom, is projected some forty or fifty feet into the stream, where the current is swift, and the bottom gradually shelving. Another fence is run downstream; then at a right angle six feet or so towards the bank, and again inwards nearly to the first transverse fence. The ascending fish thus intercepted in their progress by the upper fence seek in vain to round this obstacle, and after a while enter a large cylindrical basket which is sunk at the angle where the descending fence commences. The mouth of this basket is formed with slender rods converging inwards, like the entrance of a wire mouse- trap. Great numbers are thus caught. This is the plan adopted on the main stream, where, as before stated, the water is turbid. In the clear tributaries [57] the submerged basket is not found to answer, except where the stream can be fenced from side to side. Elsewhere the natives substitute an open basket, in the same position as the other, but sunk only a few inches below the surface, above which the top of the basket projects. An opening is left in the top of the fence opposite to the basket, through which the water rushes. The salmon leap this tiny fall, and drop unsuspectingly into the trap prepared for them. At the discharge of Fraser's and Stuart's Lakes the stream is fenced across, and the sunken basket is used; immense numbers are thus caught in ordinary years. The fence, however, is rarely so secure but that the main portion of the shoal contrives to force a passage; and even admitting it were perfectly close, the natives have a conventional understanding that the fish shall be allowed to pass towards their neighbours further inland, who in turn do not seek to intercept the main body from their spawning grounds.

The spear cannot be used save in the tributaries where the water is clear. (Anderson, n.d.:55-7)

NOTES

1 Many people have helped in the course of developing this paper. Special thanks are due to Patricia Berringer and other members of the graduate seminar: Len Ham, Franz Lamers, David Pokotylo, Rob Tyhurst, and Daphne von Hopfgarten. Data on salmon and sound advice were generously given by Stan Killick of the International Pacific Salmon Fisheries Commission and Murray Farwell of the Department of Fisheries and Oceans. Brian Hayden, Dorothy Kennedy, R.G. Matson, Tom Northcote, and Randall Peterman provided helpful comments.

2 I am indebted to Dr. Tom Northcote, Animal Resource Ecology, UBC, for pointing out the importance of changing effects of glaciation upon salmon resources.

3 In the early decades of the nineteenth century, fur traders in the Carrier territory of the upper Fraser depended heavily upon dried salmon to provision local trading posts and out-going canoe brigades (see, for example, Anderson n.d.:46; Harmon 1957:146; Jackson 1953; MacLean 1932:151-2). This must have placed additional pressure on the sockeye runs and, while it may not have initiated a dominance pattern, would have augmented any such tendency already present.

REFERENCES

Anderson, Alexander Caulfield. n.d. 'British Columbia.' Ms. M 304. Archives of British Columbia, Victoria, BC

Aro, K.V. and M.P. Shepard, 1967. 'Pacific salmon in Canada.' In *Salmon of the North Pacific Ocean – Part IV: Spawning Populations of North Pacific Salmon*, Bulletin 23, International North Pacific Fisheries Commission, Vancouver

Beacham, T.D. 1984. 'Catch, escapement, and exploitation of pink salmon in BC, 1961-1981.' In *Canadian Technical Report of Fisheries and Aquatic Sciences*, No. 1276, Department of Fisheries and Oceans, Nanaimo, BC

Berringer, P. 1976. 'Notes on salmon abundance in the Fraser River System.' Unpublished ms.

–. 1982. 'Northwest Coast Traditional Salmon Fisheries Systems of Resource Utilization.' MA thesis, Department of Anthropology and Sociology, UBC

Berry, Kevin. 1991. 'Salmonid vertebral analysis in archaeology, with reference to the Keatley Creek site.' Paper presented at the 1991 Northwest Anthropological Meetings, Missoula, Montana

Brett, J.R. 1965. 'The swimming energetics of salmon.' *Scientific American* 213(2):80-5

Carl, G.C., W.A. Clemens, and C.C. Lindsey. 1967. *The Freshwater Fishes of British Columbia*. Handbook No. 5, BC Provincial Museum, Victoria

Chisholm, B.S., D.E. Nelson, and H.P. Schwarzc. 1983. 'Marine and terrestrial protein in prehistoric diets on the British Columbia Coast.' *Current Anthropology* 24(3):396-8

Clark, Annette McFadyen. 1974. *Koyukuk River Culture*. National Museum of Man Mercury Series, Paper 16

Cooper, A.C. and K.A. Henry. 1962. *The History Of The Early Stuart Sockeye Run*. Progress Report No. 10, International Pacific Salmon Fisheries Commission, New Westminster, BC

Donald, L. and D.H. Mitchell. 1975. 'Some correlates of local group rank among the Southern Kwakiutl.' *Ethnology* 14:325-46

Duff, W. 1952. *The Upper Stalo Indians*. Anthropology in BC, Memoir No. 1, BC Provincial Museum, Victoria, BC

–. 1964. *The Indian History of British Columbia, The Impact of the Whiteman*. BC Provincial Museum, Victoria, BC

Farwell, M.K., N.D. Schubert, K.H. Wilson, and Harrison. 1987. *Salmon Escapements to Streams Entering Statistical Areas 28 and 29, 1951 to 1985*. Canadian Data Report of Fisheries and Aquatic Sciences 601, Department of Fisheries and Oceans, New Westminster, BC

Foerster, R.E. 1968. *The Sockeye Salmon*. Fisheries Research Board of Canada, Bulletin 162, Ottawa

Gilhousen, P. 1962. 'Marine factors affecting the survival of Fraser River pink salmon.' *Symposium on Pink Salmon*, Institute of Fisheries, UBC, Vancouver

Harmon, Daniel Williams. 1957. *Sixteen Years in the Indian Country: The Journal of Daniel Williams Harmon, 1800-1816.* W. Kaye Lamb (ed.). Toronto: Macmillan

Hart, J.L. 1973. *Pacific Fishes of Canada.* Bulletin 180, Fisheries Research Board of Canada, Ottawa

Hayden, B. 1981. 'Research and development in the stone age: Technological transitions among hunter gatherers.' *Current Anthropology* 22(5):519-48

Henry, K.A. 1961. *Racial Identification of Fraser River Sockeye Salmon By Means of Scales and Its Application to Salmon Management.* International Pacific Salmon Fisheries Commission, Bulletin 12, New Westminster, BC

Hewes, Gordon W. 1947. 'Aboriginal Use of Fishery Resources in Northwestern North America.' PhD thesis, Anthropology, University of California

–. 1973. 'Indian fisheries productivity in pre-contact times in the Pacific salmon area.' In *Northwest Anthropological Research Notes* 7(2):133-55 (reprint of part of Hewes, 1947)

Hourston, A.S., E.H. Vernon, G.A. Holland. 1965. *The Migration, Composition, Exploitation, and Abundance of Odd Year Pink Salmon Runs in and Adjacent to the Fraser River Convention Area.* Bulletin 17, International Pacific Salmon Fisheries Commission, New Westminster, BC

Hudson's Bay Company. Various dates. Fort Alexandra Journal, 1824-5, 1827, typed extracts in Library of International Pacific Salmon Fisheries Commission, New Westminster, BC

Idler, D.R. and W.A. Clemens. 1959. 'The energy expenditures of Fraser River sockeye during the spawning migration.' *International Pacific Salmon Fisheries Commission Progress Report,* No. 6, New Westminster, BC

Jackson, Roy I. 1953. 'Sockeye from the Fraser.' *The Beaver,* Mar. 1953:18-25

Killick, S.R. 1955. *The Chronological Order of Fraser River Sockeye Salmon During Migration, Spawning, and Death.* International Pacific Salmon Fisheries Commission, Bulletin 7, New Westminster, BC

– and W.A. Clemens. 1963. *The Age, Sex Ratio, and Size of Fraser River Sockeye Salmon, 1915-1956.* International Pacific Salmon Fisheries Commission, Bulletin 14, New Westminster, BC

Langdon, Steve. 1979. 'Comparative Tlingit and Haida adaptation to the west coast of the Prince of Wales Archipelago.' *Ethnology* 18(2):101-19

Lovell, N.C., B.S. Chisholm, D.E. Nelson, and H.P. Schwarzc. 1986. 'Prehistoric salmon consumption in interior British Columbia.' *Canadian Journal of Archaeology* 10:99-106

Maclean, John. 1932. *John Maclean's Notes of A Twenty-five Year's Service in the Hudson's Bay Territory.* W.S. Wallace (ed.). Toronto: Champlain Society

Manzer, J.I. and M.P. Shepard. 1962. 'Marine factors affecting the survival of Fraser River pink salmon.' In N.J. Wilimovsky (ed.), *Symposium on Pink Salmon.* Institute of Fisheries, UBC, Vancouver

Matson, R. G. 1983. 'Intensification and the development of cultural complexity: The Northwest versus the Northeast Coast.' In R.J. Nash (ed.), *The Evolution of Maritime Cultures on the Northeast and the Northwest Coasts of America.* Department of Archaeology, Simon Fraser University, Burnaby, BC

–. 1985. 'The relationship between sedentism and status inequalities among hunters and gatherers.' In M. Thompson, M.T. Garcia, and F.J. Kense (eds.), *Status, Structure, and Stratification: Current Archaeological Reconstructions.* University of Calgary, Calgary

Monks, G. 1987. 'Prey as bait: The Deep Bay example.' *Canadian Journal of Archaeology* 11:119-42

Neave, F. 1962. 'The observed fluctuations of pink salmon in British Columbia.' In N.J. Wilimovsky (ed.), *Symposium on Pink Salmon.* Institute of Fisheries, UBC, Vancouver

–. 1966a. 'Pink Salmon in British Columbia.' In *Salmon of the North Pacific Ocean, Part III: A Review of the Life History of North Pacific Salmon,* Bulletin 18. International North Pacific Fisheries Commission, Vancouver

–. 1966b. 'Chum salmon in British Columbia.' In *Salmon of the North Pacific Ocean, Part III: A Review of the Life History of North Pacific Salmon,* Bulletin 18. International North Pacific Fisheries Commission, Vancouver

Nelson, R.K. 1973. *Hunters of the Northern Forest: Designs for Survival Among the Alaskan Kutchin.* University of Chicago, Chicago

Northcote, T.G. 1974. *Biology of the Lower Fraser River.* Technical Report No. 3, Westwater Research Centre, UBC, Vancouver

– and P.A. Larkin. 'The Fraser River: A major salmonine production system.' In D.P. Dodge (ed.), *Proceedings of the International Large Rivers Symposium.* Canadian Special Publications in Fisheries and Aquatic Sciences No. 106. Fisheries and Oceans Canada

Pearse, P.H. 1982. *Turning the Tide: A New Policy for Canada's Pacific Fisheries.* The Commission on Pacific Fisheries Policy, Final Report, Vancouver

Ricker, W.E. 1962. 'Regulation of the abundance of pink salmon populations.' In *Symposium on Pink Salmon.* Institute of Fisheries, UBC, Vancouver

–. 1966. 'Sockeye salmon in British Columbia.' In *Salmon of the North Pacific Ocean, Part III: A Review of the Life History of North Pacific Salmon,* Bulletin 18. International North Pacific Fisheries Commission, Vancouver

–. 1987. 'Effects of the fishery and of obstacles to migration on the abundance of Fraser River sockeye salmon (*Oncorhynchus nerka*).' In *Canadian Technical Report of Fisheries and Aquatic Sciences,* No. 1522. Fisheries and Oceans Canada

–. 1989. 'History and present state of the odd-year pink salmon runs of the Fraser River region.' In *Canadian Technical Report of Fisheries and Aquatic Sciences,* No. 1702. Fisheries and Oceans, Canada

Romanoff, Steven. 1985. 'Fraser Lillooet salmon fishing.' *Northwest Anthropo-*

logical Research Notes 19(2):119-60

Ryder, J.M. and M. Church. 1986. 'The Lillooet terraces of Fraser River: Paleo-environmental enquiry.' *Canadian Journal of Earth Sciences* 23:869-84

Sanger, David. 1973. 'Development of the Pacific Northwest Plateau cultural area. 'In R. Cox (ed.), *Cultural Ecology.* Toronto: McClelland and Stewart

Schubert, N.D. 1986. 'The Indian food fishery of the Fraser River: 1985 Summary.' In *Canadian Data Report of Fisheries and Aquatic Services,* No. 560

Scott, W.B. and E.J. Crossman. 1973. *Freshwater Fishes of Canada.* Fisheries Research Board of Canada, Bulletin 184, Ottawa

Sneed, Paul G. 1971. 'Of Salmon and men: An investigation of ecological determinants and aboriginal man in the Canadian Plateau.' In A. Stryd and R. Smith (eds.), *Aboriginal Man and Environment on the Plateau of Northwest America.* Pp. 229-42. Calgary: University of Calgary Student's Press

Stewart, H. 1977. *Indian Fishing: Early Methods on the Northwest Coast.* Vancouver: J.J. Douglas

Suttles, Wayne. 1951. 'Economic Life of the Coast Salish of Haro and Rosario Straits.' PhD thesis, Department of Anthropology, University of Washington, Seattle

–. 1955. 'Katzie ethnographic notes.' In *Anthropology in B.C.* Memoir No. 2, BC Provincial Museum, Victoria

–. 1968. 'Coping With abundance: Subsistence on the Northwest Coast.' In R.B. Lee and I. Devore (eds.), *Man the Hunter.* Chicago: Aldine

–. n.d. 'Swinomish salmon fishing.' Ms. prepared for Swinomish people

Talbot, G.B. 1950. *A Biological Study of the Effectiveness of the Hell's Gate Fishways.* Bulletin 3, Part 1. International Pacific Salmon Fisheries Commission, New Westminster, BC

Teit, J. 1900. 'The Thompson Indians.' *Memoirs, American Museum of Natural History* 2:163-392

–. 1906. 'The Lillooet Indians.' *Memoirs, American Museum of Natural History* 5:193-300

–. 1909. 'The Shuswap.' *Memoirs, American Museum of Natural History* 7:443-814

Thompson, W.F. 1945. *Effect of the Obstruction at Hell's Gate on the Sockeye Salmon of the Fraser River.* International Pacific Salmon Fisheries Commission, Bulletin 1, New Westminster, BC

Verhoeven, L.A. and E.B. Davidoff. 1962. *Marine Tagging of Fraser River Sockeye.* Bulletin 13. International Pacific Salmon Fisheries Commission, New Westminster, BC

Vernon, E.H. 1962. 'Pink salmon populations of the Fraser River system.' In N.J. Wilimovsky (ed.), *Symposium on Pink Salmon.* Institute of Fisheries, UBC, Vancouver

Walters, Carl J. and Michael J. Staley. 1987. 'Evidence against the existence of cyclic dominance in Fraser River sockeye salmon (*Oncorhynchus nerka*)'. In H.D. Smith, L. Margolis, and C.C. Wood (eds.), *Sockeye Salmon (Oncorhynchus nerka) Population Biology and Future Management*. Canadian Special Publications in Fisheries and Aquatic Science, 96

Ward, F.J. and P.A. Larkin. 1964. 'Cyclic dominance in the Adams River sockeye salmon.' In *International Pacific Salmon Fisheries Commission Progress Report*, No. 11, New Westminster, BC

CHAPTER FIVE

Fraser Lillooet Salmon Fishing*

Steven Romanoff

INTRODUCTION

This chapter describes the general principles governing how the Lillooet Indians within the study area of this volume caught, processed, and distributed salmon, both historically and today. They continued in 1970-1, at the time of fieldwork, to capture and preserve salmon as a basic food, using traditional techniques at their fishery upstream from Lillooet. Salmon fishing is entirely confined to the River Valley resource use zone described in Chapter 2.

As Kew has pointed out in Chapter 4, the aboriginal inhabitants of the Northwest Coast and Plateau culture areas depended on salmon to such a degree that their population density depended in part on its availability. Complex social institutions, including feasting and trading (per Chapter 10) and potlatching (Suttles 1966), functioned to evenly distribute the supply of salmon – a critical and variable resource. However, fishing techniques were only part of the cultural repertoire needed to take advantage of salmon. Since each run was available for only a few weeks or months each year, and since there were months when few other major food resources were available, preserving the many fish caught in a short period was also a critical task.

Those interested in calculating the amount of food that was available to aboriginal peoples from salmon should take note that not all fish caught can be preserved using aboriginal techniques. On the Fraser River some fish are too fat to preserve and some days are too hot. Sometimes the fish come so fast that women cut them in a way

---

* This chapter is a modified version of an article that appeared under the same title in 1985 in *Northwest Anthropoligical Research Notes* 19(2):119-60.

that wastes some of the flesh and sometimes men stop fishing to help with the cutting. In short, the requirement that fish be preserved reduced the amount that people could eat. In the Interior, wastage or inability to dry was a relatively modest problem; it was a more serious one on the Coast.

The superior drying conditions in the Interior have been a reason for Coast people to trade with Interior people or move inland to fish. The large gatherings at Lillooet, like those at other seasonal Interior sites, have resulted from the quantity of salmon there and from the relative ease with which they can be preserved. Further, though fat salmon are generally tasty and a reason for people farther inland to come to Lillooet, they do not preserve as well as lean salmon. On the Coast, there was actually competition for low-quality, but very preservable, salmon. These and other modestly important adaptations will be described in this report.

The activities described here reflect the general pattern of economic organization in the 'Plateau' culture area, in that people from many ethnic or linguistic units had access to resources, and in that products were passed across social boundaries (Anastasio 1955; Walker 1967). Several aspects of aboriginal Lillooet culture were functionally linked to this general Plateau pattern – for example, the pattern of hostile relations with distant people while mutually sharing resources with nearby people described by Cannon in Chapter 10 and the pattern of using resources of affinal relatives.

Both the Lillooet fishery and Plateau-style social relations between Lillooet and non-Lillooet have continued. Though they have lost what was their major resource, spring salmon, to ocean or downstream fishermen, they continue with sockeye and a few springs, and in the hundred years since large numbers of whites came to the Lillooet area, the Lillooet and other Indians who fish at the Six Mile/Bridge River Rapids have provided themselves with food and have maintained a cultural tradition.

The fishing and drying techniques used today by the Fraser Lillooet are only modestly changed from those of their aboriginal counterparts. People dry fish in substantial amounts for their own consumption, and while I was visiting the Lillooet, home-produced salmon and deer, either fresh or preserved, were their main sources of protein.

Despite a gold rush, boarding schools, migrant labour in extractive industries, long trips to work as pickers, and other factors that might have disrupted the fishery, it has continued because its intensity and brief duration makes it compatible with other activities and because it supplies a real benefit. Government policy of recognizing Lillooet fishing rights, while banning commercial exploitation and net-fishing by Whites, has also contributed to the continuation of the fishery. Finally, fishing has become symbolically important as a marker of identity, with Lillooet people coming from as far away as Vancouver to fish and visit kin.

Background

Fishing was the base of aboriginal Lillooet diet. The Fraser Lillooet ate salmon in several forms (such as powdered salmon and oil), together with dried berries, roots, deer meat, and a wide variety of less important foods (Turner 1972). Deer meat and buckskin clothes were critically important secondary resources, though neither was plentiful. In fact, dried deer meat was a potlatch item, and several people often had to contribute to put together a full buckskin suit for someone going outside in winter. The special status of the hunter and his ecological significance are the subjects of Chapter 9.

In the nineteenth century (my earliest data), women and men worked at different, but co-ordinated, subsistence tasks, and there were some special statuses related to work. Boys could train spiritually and physically to be hunters, warriors, gamblers, or shamans, while chiefs and women had special forms of training, according to informants. Chiefs played an important role in scheduling subsistence activities, as Sam Mitchell, on whose accounts most of the following report is based, reported:

> In this particular reserve where I am now (Fountain), before the priests came, these people have clans like, families, but it seems to me that there's always more than one or two families in the clan. They always say, 'We have a chief. He's the head.' He tells them when to get ready to go and fish, when to get ready and go and hunt. He leads his people to everything they do to make their living. When it's early in the year, the women do the digging the roots, the picking the onions, and they barbecue them. Later around about June they start to pick the saskatoon berries, and they dry quite a bit of that. They bake some of it. From there on it's a continuous laboring for living. After that, when the fish start to run, then of course the men do the fishing. They have their nets ready, and they go fishing. Of course, the women do the butchering, drying the salmon, making the powdered salmon . . . In the fall of the year, around September, they cut lots of sp'áts'en7úl when it's dry ('milk weed,' for fiber). Then they also bundle it up; when they get good and dry, that's another work. They do that in winter time (make fiber for fishing nets, among other things).
>
> It's the chief's direction all this goes on. And them earlier days, them

earlier people, the son of a chief always becomes a chief again because the learning is supposed to be from the father. I know on this reserve . . . in later years they got on the white man's way, they vote. They nominate their chiefs now and vote for them.

'Potlatches' involved gifts of food and, later, manufactured objects. Aboriginally, they involved dried deer meat, and they continued after the formation of reserves. Sam Mitchell provided accounts of: (1) a week-long, deer meat give-away for 'Indian doctors' who helped a man find his lost son; (2) the general pattern of hunting to get dried meat to give away; (3) post-funeral meat give-aways to thank people for attending; (4) feasts/meat give-aways on becoming chief; (5) a sugar, flour, and candle give-away soon after contact with Whites; (6) a rum give-away in which the host told the guests, 'I'm the boss'; (7) a rum give-away around 1860 to make guests drunk and find a killer; and (8) Christmas feasting on the reserve after the priests came – 'the old potlatches sort of changed to Christmas.' (Potlatches are discussed more fully in Chapter 9.)

Aboriginal and nineteenth century Lillooet of the Fraser River maintained friendly relations with the people whom they might meet while out berrying, hunting, or fishing. In fact, they intermarried with neighbouring peoples, so that there were Lillooet-Shuswap marriages, Lillooet-Thompson marriages, and border settlements of mixed parentage (Kennedy and Bouchard 1978:34-5). Marriage outside immediate kin (and hence to people with somewhat different resources) was mandatory; Sam Mitchell estimated that the closest one could marry was third or fourth cousin. Hostile relations with distant people, on the other hand, are noted for the nineteenth century (Teit 1906:210, 236).

Today, Fountain is one of the main reserves of the Fraser River Lillooet and is located in the River Terrace zone of the study area of this volume. Sam Mitchell described some aspects of its history. Aboriginally, the village was on a flat place on the side of the canyon (a 'bench'). Two related families lived there in two pithouses. When the first miners came in 1858, the bench became a watering place on the trail to the gold fields. The chief of the Fountain residents told his people, 'Let's move on the top of the ridge.' Then they moved to the site of the present Fountain village. There was no reserve at that time, and the old village site was taken over by a farmer. Later the Canadian government bought the farm and restored it to the reserve.

Soon after, priests came and, under their influence, the chief called his friends and relatives to come to the new Fountain village. Depopulation due to smallpox probably promoted this aggregation of settlements as well. They came from the Bridge River area, Lillooet, and small sites down the Fraser River. Sam Mitchell's parents were among those who came. 'I should have been a Lillooet because my mother belonged to Lillooet and my father to Lakes.'

After the turn of the century, Fountain Reserve had forty or fifty families living in about twenty-five hewn-log houses. Like the Bridge River Reserve, Fountain is located several miles outside the town of Lillooet. The reserve had a school and church, and priests played a central role in its organization. With the arrival of large numbers of Whites and Chinese in the last half of the nineteenth century, Lillooet men took up work as miners, farmers, loggers, and carriers, either on their own account or as paid labour. For example, Jimmy Rodesket, chief of the Lillooet Band and son of the Lillooet chief who saw Simon Fraser drift down the river, was a guide for sports hunters and had several four-horse teams to carry freight from Lytton to Lillooet. Later, Lillooet people started working as migrant labour to harvest crops.

Contact history is reflected in population figures. Teit estimates aboriginal Lillooet population at 4,000 and an Upper Lillooet population of 1,200. At the time he wrote, he estimated a Lillooet population of 1,200, a Lakes Lillooet population of 200, and a Fraser Lillooet population of 500 (1906:199). The diseases that reduced the population were smallpox, tuberculosis, and venereal disease (Kennedy and Bouchard 1978:53) and – after Teit's estimates – influenza. In 1963, there were four Fraser Lillooet bands, whose populations were Bridge River (135), Fountain (385), Cayuse Creek (58), and Lillooet (88). The two Lake Lillooet bands were Anderson Lake (97) and Seton Lake (289) (Duff 1964). The Upper Lillooet thus suffered depopulation in the nineteenth and twentieth centuries; they are now recovering and are just reaching Teit's estimate of aboriginal population.

Sources of Data and Fieldwork

I base this report on fieldwork done in the summer of 1970. My goal was to discover what I could of the Plateau social system, Plateau ecological relations, and the place of salmon in social and ecological relations, having been introduced to these topics by David French. Wayne Suttles suggested that I concentrate on salmon preservation as a phenomenon which had social and ecological importance and which had not been adequately described for the Plateau or the Northwest Coast.

When I started my fieldwork, I knew only that Indians were drying salmon on the Fraser River, and I did not know that I would be working with the Lillooet. As I drove up the Fraser River Valley, I stopped for a day or two at various places to talk with people who were drying salmon. Each referred me to a new contact – someone else drying salmon, a council member, a librarian, or a shopkeeper. Where possible, I spoke with members of a Band Council before proceeding. On the whole I was well received, but some told me that I was not welcome. Finally, people told me that the place for me was Lillooet. After settling in there, I made one side trip to the North Thompson area.

I stayed in Lillooet for several weeks. William Adolph allowed me to use a cabin that he had built; I often ate with him and he loaned me a horse. Sam Mitchell invited me 'for tea' (a generous dinner) on several occasions. Except in a few cases, I did not pay informants, having no outside financing. I did give rides, provisions, and copies of photographs. Later, I typed my field notes and sent back some of the texts.

I spent several days at the Six Mile fishing camp, watching people fish and dry their salmon. Most of my data, however, are from tape recorded interviews. As I reflect on this experience, I see too many leading questions and not enough precision in dating informants' stories. I relied too heavily on my camera to record fishing routines that I should have described in writing, and I lost two of my best interviews when my tape recorder broke down.

My major Lillooet informants were Sam Mitchell, Tommy Napoleon, Mrs. A. Zabatel, and William Adolph. Sam Mitchell is a member of the Fountain Band born in 1894. He did not attend mission school. Mr. Mitchell has been very generous with many people seeking information on Lillooet culture. A man who taught himself to read, by his willingness to take on students Mr. Mitchell has put some of his knowledge into the historical record. Tommy Napoleon is a member of the Lillooet Band and is about sixty-five years old. He learned about aboriginal Lillooet culture from his uncle, who grew up in a semi-subterranean house. Mrs. Zabatel is Sam Mitchell's step-daughter. She lives near Cache Creek and is in her forties. Although she attended the mission boarding school at Kamloops, she listened at meetings of chiefs in her childhood. William Adolph was one of the first to attend mission school, and he spent a long time away from Lillooet as a logger. He is a member of the Fountain Band. All of these people catch and dry salmon. Among the others with whom I talked about salmon drying and who dry their salmon are Mrs. James of the Lillooet Band, Francis Bill Edwards of the Pavilion Band, Irene McKay of Pavilion, and Ernie Jacobs of Fountain. In the summer of 1972, I again visited Lillooet; the results of that trip are presented in my paper on Lillooet hunting (Chapter 9). In the winter of 1978 I was again in Lillooet briefly.

FISHING AND PRESERVATION TECHNIQUES

This description is of Lillooet salmon fishing which I saw upstream from the town of Lillooet at the Six Mile/Bridge River Rapids (Fountain Reserve). At the rapids there are several good places to fish with a dip net, and there are twenty-one drying racks. Every summer, Lillooet people from all their reserves come to camp and fish there, along with Indian visitors from other groups.

Salmon Taken

Starting in June, according to Sam Mitchell, there is a salmon run every lunar month. The first are spring salmon runs, while the later ones are sockeye salmon. Today, sockeye salmon (*Oncorhynchus nerka*), also called red or blueback salmon, comprise the bulk of the Fraser Lillooet catch. These fish run from late July to early September. The salmon of the early part of the run are the fattest, while those that come later are leaner and have red skins. Sockeye are relatively easy to catch because they run in pulses near the surface; they may be abundant at one time of day and scarce at another. Adult sockeye weigh between 3.5 and 8 lbs (Carl and Clemens 1948:50).

Families that regularly fish take an average of two to three hundred sockeye each year. In 1970, the run was poor, so few families reached the two hundred mark and others refused to fish at all. The quantity of sockeye declined precipitously in the early part of this century. Sam Mitchell said that before that decline a man with a large family would dry about four hundred sockeye, but at that time spring salmon were the main catch.

Spring salmon (*O. tshawytscha*), also called king, tyee, or chinook, are much larger and fatter than sockeye. Their run in June and July is more individualistic than are sockeye migrations, and each fish averages over 20 lbs (Kelez 1938:795). Though spring are still important, they formerly were the bulk of the Fraser Lillooet catch, and a man with a large family might take five or six hundred (Sam Mitchell). Humpback or pink salmon (*O. gorbuscha*) are caught in small quantities by a few people. Some informants say that they did not run as far as Lillooet until some fish ladders were installed downstream. They weigh between three and ten pounds and enter the Fraser in September and October (Carl and Clemens 1948:45). Informants also said that coho or silver salmon (*O. kisutch*) do not run by Lillooet. Others, however, said that they run in September, but not every year. The names 'dog' and 'chum' salmon (*O. keta*) elicited no reply, and informants mentioned no other kind of salmon. Steelheads (*Salmo gaird-*

nerii) are anadromous trout that run in fall and winter, but they and Dolly Varden trout are not currently important. Francis Bill Edwards said that they throw back Dolly Vardens if the salmon are running. Aboriginally, trout fisheries at some of the smaller rivers or lakes were seasonally very important.

Fishing Gear and Techniques

Current Techniques

The techniques currently used by the Lillooet for salmon fishing on the Fraser River are gill netting, set netting, and dip netting (some informants used 'set-net' for what I call 'gill net' here). Gill nets are large-mesh, nylon nets set across an eddy where the current moves upstream. Usually, the owner suspends the net from a steel wire running between two spikes driven into rock; I saw one case of a net suspended from a pole slung over the river. Salmon enter a gill net as they follow the current of the eddy. Usually they cannot see the net in the muddy water, but if the sun casts a shadow toward them, they leap over the net. Larger salmon can only get their heads through the mesh, and their gills prevent them from backing out. Gill nets may be set at any time. Often the fisherman (or woman) leaves the net out all night. People tend the nets about twice each day, or more often if the fish are plentiful or if the user of the net is staying at a fishing camp. If they are not tended enough, the struggles of several fish tangle the net.

A 'set-net' is the larger of two kinds of hand-held nets and has a sliding net attached by rings to the frame. Kennedy and Bouchard provide a detailed description of this net in Chapter 6. The dip net is a smaller, simpler version of the set-net. The net does not close and there is no anchor line. The fisherman puts the net in the water, swings it downstream against the eddy current, and withdraws the net. I saw dip nets used only when and where there was an abundance of salmon; in such a situation a single sweep with a dip net could catch two or three fish. People make unusually small nets (1.5 x 3 ft.) for very swift places where the salmon hug the walls of the river bed.

Men use set-nets in small, swift eddies. The fisherman holds the pole steady against the current, aided by the long anchor wire attached downstream (the current in the eddy is running upstream). When he feels a salmon strike the net, he releases the string that holds the net open and jerks the whole net upward and out of the water. Then, if his wife is present, he hands her the pole and grips the net, trying to hold the salmon still and get it to stick its snout through the mesh.

When the fish co-operates, he clubs it with a stick (undecorated) and hands it to his wife.

The woman now takes the fish to a crevice in the rock while her husband returns the net to the water. She breaks the head off the backbone (but the head remains attached to the body by the tissue over the backbone), and she holds the fish vertical while the blood pumps out. Then she lodges the fish in the crevice, where it continues to drain, and she returns to her husband. In the fishing that I saw at Six Mile site, there was a rope hanging down to the narrow rock ledge (a seasonally exposed part of the river's bed) where people stood to fish. When a couple down on that ledge had accumulated three or four fish, the helper strung them on a coat hanger attached to that rope. Then children hauled them up the rock wall to the camp.

Co-operation among family members was very important at the Six Mile site because there was no room to manoeuvre on the fishing rock. In fact, fishermen tied themselves to a safety line. Where footing is more ample, people often fish alone. I did not see any Lillooet fisherman use either hook-and-line or wire traps, though Whites do use the former at Bridge River and one non-Indian poacher used the latter at an eddy.

Historic Changes

The set-net and dip net are aboriginal and were observed by Whites in the nineteenth century. Teit (1906:228) mentions a 'bag net' and Milton and Cheadle (1865:339) saw Thompson Indians who 'grope untiringly.' The coat-hanger hook that children now use to pull salmon up from the fishing rock is the new version of a large, wooden hook. Netting was made from 'milk weed' (*Apocynum cannabinum*, more commonly known as Indian hemp; it is unrelated to eastern milkweed) which was dried and rolled on the thigh to obtain fibres (Tommy Napoleon). Sam Mitchell described the cords used for fishing:

> They sew reeds together with the only string they can get. In my language we call it *sp'áts'en*. That's the same weed they use to make fish twine. It's along the river. In English, I'm pretty sure they call it milkweed. There's some higher up on the higher benches. When these weeds get dry, around in the fall, maybe in September or October . . . they make lots of them, and they pound it up (to get the bark off). I've seen my grandmother making them. They pound it up on wood to get the bark out of it . . . then they weave it. They weave it and make string out of it . . . That's mostly for thread and its also used for fishnet. There was no such thing as wire or cable or rope or anything. No nylon ropes then.

But there are certain kinds of willows they call *nexwtín*. They make ropes out of it. They use that on the fishing racks they have . . . They tie the cross pieces with this . . . Certain places you can get this kind of willow they call *nexwtín*. They just twist it and make a rope out of it. The full length of a bush may be 10 or 12 feet long . . . There are four or five kinds of willow, but there's just this one kind of willow that'll make *nexwtín*. That's a rope . . . They can also use it to anchor a net.

See also Turner (1972:18) and Chapter 8, who refers to *nexwtínaź* (from *nexwtín* 'rope') as sandbar willow (*Salix exigua*). These changes in material are relatively minor. However, they may have been more important than they seem. Old women who used to make a very important tool, no longer do so and may have lost prestige.

More significantly, the Lillooet used to make small platforms to fish for spring salmon, but they no longer do so (Sam Mitchell and others). Gosnell (1903:281) shows a picture of such a Thompson platform. A second major change is adoption of gill nets, which substitute for spring salmon fishing platforms. It appears that fish traps were not an aboriginal alternative to gill nets. Though James Teit's discussion of fish traps is not sufficient to rule out the possibility that they were used on the Fraser River, it appears that they were confined to smaller streams (Teit 1900:250-4, 1906:228, 1909:524). Perhaps they were used on the Cayuse River near Lillooet, where Indians fished in the nineteenth century (Canada Department of Indian Affairs 1902:88).

The change from spring to sockeye salmon, the increasing use of gill nets, and the declining use of fishing platforms are related to each other and to another major change: a decline in the number of fishing sites. In the early part of this century, according to Sam Mitchell, there were family fishing sites along the Fraser; a fisherman could build a platform at any place where the swift current forced spring salmon to hug the river's shore. These sites were not as productive as the ones at the major rapids, and they were good only when the water was at the right level. However, a family might take six springs per day. With the decline in spring salmon, set-netting for springs became unrewarding, and people shifted to gill nets. Accordingly, they shifted to large, slow eddies, and there are few such sites near the town of Lillooet. (Thompson Indian fishermen south of Lytton have no major site like the Six Mile Rapids, but they have more minor sites than do the Lillooet.) Further, those are the same sites where sockeye are easily captured.

Consequently, the only fishing sites used at present near the town of Lillooet are 'Six Mile' and 'Bridge River' on opposite sides of the river at the rapids about five miles above Lillooet, 'Linktown' or 'the

falls' just outside Lillooet, and 'Three Mile,' a minor site. Informants
can recall a number of other sites that formerly yielded springs. These
and sites farther upstream that are still used are documented by
Kennedy, Bouchard, and Tyhurst in Chapters 6 and 7.

The following account provided by Sam Mitchell refers to several
of the technical changes so far described:

[In those days] they don't dry them sockeye. Its just got to be spring
salmon. The spring salmon run deep in this part of the river. So [bikol
Tom] makes a platform way out from the rock; that's a big platform.
That's where he sets his net. His net is four or five feet wide and it's
about six feet deep in length. He'll push it down so the top end of the
net is about five feet below surface. That will put the net all of ten feet
down. And he's got his platform way out.

The net was made out of this milkweed or *sp'áts'en7úl*. They weave
the net for one purpose, just for spring salmon. If there's any sockeye
that go in, they'll go right through because the mesh on the net was
wide enough for the sockeye to go right through. Only a spring salmon
will be caught there . . .

The bow was always made out of fir. They don't make it and put it
in the water [the same day] like we do now. Them days they have it
ready. They make these bows so it will dry out and harden before the
fishing season starts. I've seen them. That way when you get your bows
real dry and hard, it will stand lots of pressure.

. . . That trip on the net – there's a trip that goes to the finger on the
pole when he's sitting up there. That net is way down there ten feet.
If a spring salmon hits, he knows it's a spring salmon, he lets that trip
go. He pulls his pole up, and that net falls down to the bottom of the
bows. That holds whatever fish is in that net . . .

These platforms that the old Indians used to fish – them days they
don't dry sockeye, which we do now. Mostly spring salmon they dry.
They always go deep. They build platforms out. They put the net down
maybe six of seven feet from the surface [below the surface eddies to
where the current is steady] . . . They learn the current down there is
going in the right direction . . . It doesn't matter how much sockeye is
on the surface. The sockeye go on the surface. Deep down, when they
get one they'll get a spring salmon. That's the ones they dry . . . They
dry a few sockeye, maybe.

. . . now there's no such thing as spring salmon. They were all caught
before they get this far. So that way the people now have to dry the
sockeye, which is a good fish if you do it the right way.

Beyond the technical changes in salmon fishing, there have been changes in its role in an over-all subsistence strategy. Soon after the turn of the century, when Teit's Lillooet ethnography was published, the Fountain Band lived in about twenty-five hewn-log houses. Though the people of Fountain purchased some staples, having income from packing and extractive industries, they produced much of their own food. They cultivated potatoes in their gardens and continued to gather roots, berries, and other wild plant foods. Sam Mitchell, a boy at that time, fished at the Six Mile site for his mother to get a substantial supply of salmon.

He said that people fished harder then, going from daylight to dusk; and they did not go home after five or six days but, rather, stayed until they had enough food. Also, spring salmon were plentiful enough that you could get them at the falls with a dip net. Other things that he mentioned – the tents at the site, taking turns on a productive rock, children carrying fresh-caught salmon to their mothers, keeping the camp clean, and the drying techniques – are much the same now as they were then.

There is also a new governmental aspect to salmon fishing. The fish that reach Lillooet are there because a government agency limits downstream fishing, effectively allocating fish between ocean fishermen and river fishermen. The Cayuse Band of Lillooet lost its fishing spot on the creek when the hatchery was constructed. Agents check to make sure that fish are not being sold, and they are reasonably effective. Indians, however, can still fish at the falls, as Sam Mitchell explained:

[The visitors] are Indians. When the people from Vernon come over, they have to go to the fish warden here and they get a permit. As long as they prove that they're Indians, they can take any amount of fish back home, whether it's dried or not. They can dry some themselves. The check station, I'll say at Cache Creek, they check them. They show their permit, and that's theirs. They're gone . . . This is legal to any Indian, if he proves he's an Indian.

Salmon Preservation and Storage

There are only a few basic principles for food preservation, and the variegated salmon preservation techniques of the Coast and Plateau correspond to their permutations in particular environments. The first essential element of all of them is to reduce the amount of water available to bacteria, yeast, and moulds. Though there is probably nothing dangerous about eating 'rotten' food per se (Tanner and Tanner 1953), decomposing food may contain disease-causing bacteria, and microorganisms may consume the food before humans do. If salmon flesh has less than 12 per cent available moisture, it is stable and safe to eat (Krumperman 1971: personal communication). This is approximately the level of moisture in some Indian-dried salmon (Rivera 1949:31; Sinnhuber 1971: personal communication). The Lillooet use all the standard ways of reducing available moisture: dehydration, freezing, and salting (Frazier 1967:109, 122; Lee, J. E. 1971: personal communication). Modern Lillooet also 'can' salmon in jars, which involves sealing the meat in a container and killing its micro-organisms (Frazier 1967:101).

The second general principle of preservation is to reduce rancidity or oxidation of fats. Rancid salmon oil is not acceptable to Lillooet consumers and there is some evidence from laboratory trials that rancid fish oil can cause health problems (Matsuo 1962; Sinnhuber 1971: personal communication). Indian Lillooet fish processors select less-fatty fish to preserve, reduce the fat in some fish before drying, use techniques other than air-drying for fat fish, keep drying fish in the shade, and store fish in cool places.

The third principle for effective storage is to protect the salmon from animals such as flies, bears, and mice, and from thieves or (aboriginally) raiders.

Drying Racks

Drying salmon filets hang from the poles of a drying rack. The drying racks that I saw commonly had eight parallel poles resting on two beams, with the beams in turn supported by four posts or tripods. The largest ones were 15 x 25 feet. Fir is the usual wood for the rack's frame, and plywood or planks make a roof. In the past, fir boughs served for a roof. Rocks stabilize the posts or tripods, and occasionally people use wire or nails. Though crudely built, racks are sturdy: families use the same one each year.

Since the wind always blows along the river, the rack is built so that its poles are perpendicular to the river (or the supporting beams are parallel to the river). That way, the filets hang parallel to the river, allowing free air movement over the drying flesh.

The most important function of the rack's roof is to protect the salmon flesh from the sun. Sam Mitchell explained that if the fish is exposed to the sun, the oil runs out and becomes rancid. Of course, roofs also keep off the rain, but rain is infrequent. Further, the roofs provide shelter for the families that come to fish. If a family does not have a tent, its members sleep and cook at their rack; and they store their nets, utensils, clothes, bedding, and other articles there. Once it has a dry surface, the salmon has no unpleasant odour, nor does it attract flies.

Air-Dried Salmon

There are two kinds of fileting techniques for air-dried sockeye salmon. The more common technique (described in detail in Chapter 6 and in Romanoff 1971, 1985) yields a single filet of the whole fish; the filet remains attached (at the tail) to the backbone and ribs. In the second technique, the backbone is discarded; it results in two filets (the left and right sides of the fish) attached at the tail. I will call the first a 'single filet' and the second 'side filets.' Women cut and dry the fish; a man helps if the run is heavy. In both techniques, the first step is to cut off the head and gills. Then the slime is scraped off with a knife. The refuse is carried to fissures in the rock by the river, presumably to be washed away each year when the river rises. Alternatively, some heads and refuse were dumped in places well away from the river and living areas. Sam Mitchell recalled that, as a child, 'We just helped [my mother]. Packed the salmon up [from the river to the camp] and break the heads and she cuts it, and we dumped the garbage over the bluff. We put the head and the insides in a pot or a can and take it over the hill and dump it. So there was nothing rotten around.'

The side filet method is quick, but the meat of the backbone is lost. People use it when the run is heavy and the cutter cannot keep up with the fishermen. Others use this method all the time because they do not like the bony backbone section and because it is easier than the single filet method.

Mrs. James said that a woman could cut fifty or sixty salmon per day, but, from my count of last year's catches and from informant statements, it seems that a fisherman could easily catch more sockeye than this limit while the run was at its peak – if he worked steadily.

Either kind of filet is dry after four days, but they stay on the rack for six or seven days. The person taking them down removes the stick and the fins and separates the backbone from the filets. Then he or she piles them up and puts them in burlap bags for transport. If several families have used a rack, they can tell their fish by distinctive cuts on the filets. At Six Mile, people use horses to pack them home or up the steep, long path to the road; on the other side of the river, people bring a car to the site.

Air-dried salmon is tasty and may be eaten raw, boiled, or roasted. The backbone sections are for soup.

Insects and Drying

Flies are dangerous because the fish may develop maggots. Freshly cut salmon are susceptible, but salmon which have dried for a few minutes (Sam Mitchell) or for a day (William Adolph) are in less danger. Salmon which have not been cut are not in danger unless they are left lying about for a long time, as they were when people used to make salmon skin bottles or pulverized salmon. The danger from flies is greater after 20 August, when a large gray fly appears. There are dangers in places along the river that are too moist and in places away from the river that do not get enough breeze.

The most common measures taken against flies consist of sprinkling salt on the filets, keeping the camp clean, and discarding infested parts of the fish. Tommy Napoleon said that cedar and juniper kept flies away before there was salt. To avoid the flies, Mrs. James tries to dry her fish before 20 August. William Adolph said that the only way to avoid yellow jackets, which eat fish, is to dry at a very arid place along the river; Sam Mitchell said that to make salmon skin bottles or pulverized salmon (described below) you had to find a spot where flies would not get the fish. Perhaps the most interesting aspect of the fly problem is that it provided one motivation for the fine slicing that costs women so much work. If the filets are not scored finely enough, they dry slowly and attract flies.

Preservation of Fat versus Lean Salmon

Fat fish present several special problems. They can go rancid; they dry slowly and, hence, attract flies; and, finally, in the heat the filet may fall apart. Tommy Napoleon said that in the past the fattest fish of each run, and particularly springs, were dried with the aid of a fire. He did this himself. First, the fish were cut into single filets and then put by a fire to broil slightly. He turned them occasionally so that the flesh would not cook and fall off the stick. After an hour or so, they were placed on a rack above the fire to dry.

Currently, Tommy Napoleon air dries some springs. He cuts out the fattest part (the belly) lest it become rancid, and his wife salts it. Then he scores the flesh with slanted cuts (versus straight cuts for sockeye – the slanted cuts make the flesh hang open and exposed) and scores the backbone many times. The flesh adhering to the skin has to be cut thin. If these things are not done, the springs dry slowly and flies lay their eggs on them. Even if dried properly, the springs become rancid if they are not stored in a very cool place or if the weather becomes very hot.

Sam Mitchell, however, generalized that spring salmon were dried the same way as sockeye, though he also told stories about people bringing him springs to cut. The first sockeyes of a run are also fat. No informant said that he or she dried the first sockeyes; instead, they canned them, salted them, froze them, or kept them for immediate consumption. Some people just kept the fattest parts for such uses and threw away the rest, according to Ernie Jacobs. Tommy Napoleon said that in the past such fish were broiled before drying. Francis Bill Edwards said that they would become rancid.

While he does not dry the fattest sockeye, William Adolph does dry some moderately fat ones. He scores these filets on a slant, makes more cuts than usual, and slashes the belly to let the grease come out. Sam Mitchell said that the early fish (before August) are too fat – they rot and get mouldy. He said that they have too much oil, but if one knows how to cut them, it is possible to dry them. At the end of the run, said Tommy Napoleon, the lean sockeye can be dried without scoring the filets. However, several informants said that they did not dry lean fish, which dry like a board and do not taste as good as the fatter fish. Thus there is a contrast between fat species and lean species, between the fat part of the run and the lean part of the run, and between fat versus lean parts of the same fish.

Special Parts and Products

Salmon heads, according to Tommy Napoleon, are as fat as bellies, even when the rest of the fish is lean. The 'old timers' split the heads, roasted them on a stick stuck in the ground by the fire, and then put the heads on a rack to dry. He said that they were not smoked, however. If the heads were not broiled, then the oil would run out of them in storage and they would go rancid. If broiled and stored in a cool place, they would keep as well as any salmon.

Sam Mitchell differed on this point; he said that heads used to be dried, but that there was no special technique (note, however, his description of making salmon oil given below). They were soaked before being boiled to eat. Three informants kept heads for immediate use, not for storage; only William Adolph had tried to dry heads recently, and they went bad.

Salmon skin bottles were tight enough to hold salmon oil. Their manufacture is described by Kennedy and Bouchard in Chapter 6. Tommy Napoleon noted that when glass bottles became available, they replaced salmon skin as a container for salmon oil. Other special salmon products, such as salmon skin shoes, are described in Chapter 6.

Powdered salmon (*tupál*) was one of the foods that Sam Mitchell ate as a child, and it, rather than dried fillets, was the main food. Sam Mitchell is still enthusiastic about the traditional meal of salmon powder and saskatoon (service) berries, topped with salmon oil:

The best feed I used to have was the powdered salmon. I never forgot that yet. The powdered salmon my grandmother used to have and mixed with saskatoon berries and salmon oil – boy, that's the stuff. I get a handful of that – we never use a spoon, we just grab it by the handful. Couple of handfuls of that and you can run all day; it will never bother you . . . I still think that's the best grub I ever ate in my life, maybe because in them days that's the only thing I ever eat.

It took several days to make the powder: two days by the fire to soften the fish and another day in the sun to dry it. Women processed the fish like those for salmon bottles, but they cut the skin to get out all the flesh. Then they pounded it with a stone hammer and put it in the sun to dry; and, when it was dry, they pounded it again to get the bones out. The meal, with the consistency of sawdust, was stored in bags. Tommy Napoleon added that the meal was dried on either grass mats or rocks. The grass is a long variety that grows in swamps, and the mats are the same kind that people used for a 'table cloth' or seat. Sam Mitchell described the mats:

> Them days there was no such thing as rice sacks, burlap, or anything. My people used to get what they use for a sort of table – well, even on the ground. I've seen this and I have ate off it. It's made out of reeds – I'm pretty sure they call it that in English. If you go along close to a lake there's a long . . . sort of straw, sort of coarse, one quarter inch or one half inch thick. My people used to cut them. They'll sew it close together. Not all one end that way; they'll change ends and they'll sew it. I've seen it maybe three feet wide and five or six feet long. And that's where they used to make the powdered salmon.

Salmon eggs sometimes dry on a string hung from a drying rack or, less often, on the end of a pole. The ones I saw were almost always in the sun, as were some strips from over the backbone. I could elicit no reason for this practice.

In the past, according to both Sam Mitchell and Tommy Napoleon, salmon eggs might be put in a birch basket and buried for the winter. The next spring, their odour was very strong. After being washed, they were made into soup with tiger lily roots, wild potatoes, and dried saskatoon berries. A Thompson Indian man, William Samson, described his experience:

> Salmon eggs can taste kind of strong, but once you get the taste you'd like to have it to eat. You can't use it through the winter, because it's frozen in the ground. When the ground thaws out, that's the time you

can get to it. You dig it out in the spring. After they get it out an hour, they invite their friends to come and get some. They come and help themselves to it. Then try some of the saskatoons. There are a lot of different saskatoons. There is a special one that they dry. It is large and smooth. When it gets dry, it tastes really sweet. When they start digging the salmon eggs out, they'd have flour too. They boil the flour, put the saskatoons in with it, put the salmon eggs in with it. When you eat that, you never go hungry. They do that every winter. Now my wife and I put it in a jar, gallon jugs. If there's a hole in the bottom it would be all right, drain off. It's got to drain off. This way it doesn't drain off because it's in a jar. We tried it. One time people there in town said, 'Can you bring me some of that [eggs].' I said sure. I went in the beer parlor and this person opened it right in the parlor.

Sam Mitchell said that people once made salmon oil near the falls at Lillooet. There, the river had worn depressions into bedrock. People dumped in 'everything that is the fattest part of the salmon' (heads, eggs, innards) along with water and fire-heated rocks. This boiled until the next morning, when people skimmed and discarded the foam and then skimmed the oil to put into salmon skin bottles. An elder directed the work, and everyone got a share of the oil. Sam Mitchell said that this occurred in September (the last salmon):

The men make the oil because it's a big hole in this rock. On one end of the rock, it's kind of low, so he went and mudded it and made it even. That's where he built a fire and heated the rocks. He heated the rocks there. When the rocks got hot, that's where he dumped everything, mostly salmon heads and guts and everything that's got oil in it. Mostly salmon heads. They save them. Then he poured water in it and it boiled there for one afternoon to the next afternoon before the whole thing kind of settle down and cooled down.

I seen it because I was curious when I was a kid. I used to always hang around. After this big hole – I'll say six foot diameter – cooled down, I noticed a kind of yellowish layer on top. It looked like a sort of a cream on a milk pan. When it did cool down, this particular man that I watched work on this had a pretty good size spoon. In my language we call it *pelókw'*. It's big, sort of a ladle. This ladle is either made out of driftwood roots (polished down) or it could be made out of sheep horn. That holds damn near a cup in this big ladle. It's a wooden ladle. He skims this yellow stuff off, then he starts on the oil itself. That oil on top of the water is maybe two or three inches thick, and it's kind of a real brownish color. He skims from there and that's what he fills . . . I don't think there was such a thing as a funnel. But these salmon skin

bottles, you can open it pretty wide. It will open out, stretch out. So
the ladles that they use, they'll just skim the oil out and pour it in the
bottle . . . Whatever bones there are in there it just cooked like canned
fish. It's cooked. You can just chew the bones. There's nothing to it . . . We
used to eat that when we were kids. A whole bunch of us go down
and just grab them by the handful from that big hole. We ate until we
couldn't eat anymore.

Tommy Napoleon described a different technique for early, fat
salmon by which they cooked salmon in baskets and then skimmed
the oil, making powdered salmon from the leftover flesh. Teit (1906:215)
provided a picture of the type of basket used. '[This picture] represents
an oval basket with spout and a wide rim, which gives a firm hold.
This kind of basket was used in making fish-oil. The fish were boiled
in a boiling-basket, the oil skimmed off with spoons and poured into
the basket here described, from which it was finally poured into skins
or bladders.'

Finally, two minor practices end the catalogue of drying. Salmon
eyes were dried after the pupil was cut out. Fat strips from over the
backbone were then put out in the sun to dry with eggs.

Modern Lillooet people have added several ways of preserving
salmon; they salt, 'can' (bottle), and freeze the fish. These techniques
work best on fat fish. One day I watched Sam Mitchell salt some sockeye salmon. He put them in a large plastic garbage can, an innovation introduced by Baptiste Richie of Mount Currie in 1970. He laid
the fish in layers, each at a right angle to the ones below, and on each
layer he threw rock salt. He said that when the container was full he
would cover it with burlap and put a weight on top. This weight would
squeeze the liquid out of the fish and create a brine. Already, he had
several wooden barrels of salmon in his storage shed.

Ernie Jacobs said that the fat fish were the best for salting, and
William Adolph put spring salmon up in mason jars using a pressure
cooker. Those people who had freezers put salmon in them, mostly
springs. Fortuitously, the fat fish most appropriate for nontraditional
preservation are the ones most difficult to preserve by air drying.

Storage

Preserved salmon are stored today in sheds and cellars where they
will be dry and cool, usually in wooden or cardboard boxes. When
Sam Mitchell and Tommy Napoleon were young, people usually
stored salmon in 'little houses' on four posts, of which a few (built
differently) may still be seen. Sam Mitchell described these box-caches.

They were made of criss-crossed fir poles of about one inch diameter. Fir was used because it was the most available. The caches stood about five feet off the ground and were 4-6 x 6-8 feet. The salmon were stacked inside in piles 3-4 feet high. The houses were not locked.

Before Sam Mitchell was born, the box-caches were by the river. When people needed salmon, they got a weeks' or two weeks' supply from the cache. Usually, this was not difficult, since there was little snow by the river. Tommy Napoleon said that there was always a wind by the river, so keeping the salmon there helped to keep them dry. Mrs. Zabatel said that there were two ways of storing salmon: the little houses and in 'pine boughs.' Teit (1900:215) mentions both methods: 'The caches of the Upper Lillooet were mostly cellars, like those of the Upper Thompson; while the Lower Lillooet used the elevated box-cache made of boards or cedar-bark. Some of the Upper Lillooet also used elevated box-caches made of poles.' When Tommy Napoleon's uncle was a child, he lived in a semi-subterranean house and used cache pits for storage.

The dangers to stored salmon were stealing, insects, animals, mould, and rancidity. Both Sam Mitchell and Tommy Napoleon said that local people did not steal while the box-caches were in use. Outsiders did steal salmon, though raiders might be repulsed or they might fail to find the cache. William Adolph said that if you put the fish away before it is completely dry 'black bugs,' which look like centipedes, will breed in it. You can shake these off and store the salmon somewhere else. In July, some of Sam Mitchell's salmon from the previous year were filled with such bugs. Tommy Napoleon thought that white pepper would keep bugs away, though black pepper would do. Juniper berries had the same effect before pepper. Most animals could not get into the box-caches. Pits were lined with grass and pine needles to keep the mice out, according to William Adolph. Tommy Napoleon said that they were lined with grass and pine needles just to keep the fish clean. The box caches were built in a way meant to reduce mould. Sam Mitchell said that they needed a good roof to keep most water out. The sides of criss-crossed fir boughs were intended to let the air blow through; otherwise the fish would get mouldy in a wet fall. Rancidity could not be avoided once the fish were in storage. Storage in cold retards oxidation, but it does not prevent it entirely.

ACCESS TO FISHING SITES AND SALMON DISTRIBUTION

There were different degrees of social restriction to the access of fishing sites. Access was most restricted to *individually* (or family) owned sites and least restricted to *public* sites. Aboriginally, individuals owned rocks that one or a few people at a time used to catch spring salmon. Stretches of the river were associated with particular semi-sub-terranean villages, but my data on the nature of this association are not detailed. The most productive sites – the falls of Six Mile and Bridge River – were open to all the Fraser Lillooet and to outsiders. These were the sites for large fishing congregations and for selling or trading dried salmon.

Internal to the Fraser Lillooet of that period, differential access to salmon sites was the basis for a system of distribution and prestige. For people who were not Fraser Lillooet, access to dried fish and fish-ing sites varied with their distance from the Fraser Lillooet and the degree to which their home resources differed from those of the Lillooet. Today, both Fraser Lillooet and others continue to use salmon taken from the Fraser Lillooet area. Because the sockeye season is short, people are able to combine participation in the fishery with other work.

Historic Access to Fishing Sites

Individually Owned Rocks

According to Sam Mitchell and Tommy Napoleon, access to spring salmon was important because it was the preferred species and it was a major article of trade. The sockeye runs did not begin until late July, and there were no other important exploitable resources in the earlier part of the summer.

Men fished for springs from platforms built on 'rocks' beside swift-flowing, small eddies (Plate 5.1). According to Sam Mitchell, who provided the information for the rest of this section, the rocks had names; 'an anchor' (because one had to brace the platform), 'boiling water rising,' 'shallow,' and 'something that hangs' (because the plat-form hung well over the water). Each rock was owned and inherited and ownership was well-known. Even today, some older people might say, for example, 'that's Tom's rock.'

The rock's owner built its platform and supplied the net that he and visitors used there. It took a full day to make the platform. The owner camped and had his drying rack there. When he was done fishing he dismantled the platform because the materials were reusable and otherwise the river would wash them away. The owner of the rock had preference in its use and he caught most of the fish there, but other people could use it with no payment to the owner. When some-one went, for example, to Tom's rock to fish for springs, he was said to be 'going to wait for Tom.' The norm of sharing access to a rock

PLATE 5.1
Fishing for salmon from a traditional-style platform in the Lillooet area,
probably at Six Mile Rapids

appears to have been very strong.

When a person was old or dying, he would tell his heir to 'look after the rock.' Sam Mitchell said that the heir was usually a son, but could be any 'relative.' Teit (1906:255) writes that when a man died 'his fishing station was the property of all his sons.' Thus, the ownership of the rock would remain in the group which lived together because that group usually included the extended patrilocal family. The following account summarizes ownership/stewardship:

> A fishing rock can't be sold from way back. It can be handed down to relations like son, nephew, or anybody else, whoever the older guy that owns the rock, that fixes the platform, whoever he thinks will be capable to keep doing it, keep fixing it. But it doesn't mean for just himself. When he fixes that platform or that rock where he fishes, it's not only him that fishes. Everybody. When he sees anybody come and set, they wait for him, and he just calls them over. He tells them, 'Come on and fish.' They don't hog one rock. If he gets what he needs, the other fellow gets a share, and everybody else gets a share. (Sam Mitchell).

Of three rocks that today are used by individuals, one was passed from a man to his son and then to his son's son; the second was passed from a man to his daughter and then to her son ('He had a grandson . . . by his daughter'); and a third was passed from a man to his son and then to his son's daughter. In all three cases the third user is alive, but detailed questions about current usage simply elicited the response that today anyone can use a rock. In any case, people are not building platforms anymore. Certain people do use the same gill net site every year, but, for these also, questions elicited the answer that anyone could use the site.

The following anecdote does not identify the old man as a rock owner, though he owned the net:

> There's one particular rock they call *ts'iwt* [Chapter 6, site 21]. These fellow knew where to fish in June, so they went there. They seen this one old guy fishing there. He didn't come from this side of the river; he came from across the river. He knows this rock was pretty good. They seen he had three or four spring salmon already, laying out on the rock. So they sat down and waited for him.
>
> He got another one, he clubbed it, and he brought it out. He goes back on his net. This particular guy was sort of a joker, too. Billy Diablo and him and another guy. They were young guys then. He says, 'We just watch him. If he brings out another one and he wouldn't let us have his net, we'll fix him.'
>
> This old guy brings out another one, pulls out another salmon, clubs it, packs it out. He wouldn't ask these guys to go and use the net. So Billy Diablo says, 'OK, we'll fix him. Come on.' He told his partner, 'Go and get your sack. We'll take two apiece. We got the horses. He hasn't

got a horse here himself. He'll have to pack it to town if he's going to
sell it.'

So Billy and his partner went over there. They had those sacks and
they shove it in. Two apiece, the biggest ones, and they tie it on his
horse. And this old guy looked around. These fellow were loading the
horses with his salmon and everything. Boy, he jumped up and he started to holler. They told him to go to hell. 'Go ahead,' they told him, 'keep
fishing. It's alright. We're going. We have our share.'

Residence-Group-Associated Sites

Each aboriginal-style village of semi-subterranean houses was associated with a stretch of the river, according to Sam Mitchell. A man
could get access to the village's sites by marrying in, as I later discuss.
My data on this type of ownership are scanty and I cannot distinguish
the rights of a settlement's individuals from the collective rights of
a settlement.

By 1870, the Canadian government was gathering data to codify the
relation between bands and stretches of the river. Canada Department
of Indian Affairs (1902) sets out these data on 'privileges.' Anderson
Lake Band was fishing on that lake and on Mosquito River; Seton Lake
Band at the juncture of Seton and Anderson lakes; Lillooet Band on
a stretch of both Cayuse Creek and Fraser River; Cayuse Creek Band
on lower Cayuse Creek and the west bank of the Fraser; Bridge River
Band on both sides of the Fraser at the mouth of the Bridge River;
and upstream from there, in order, Fountain Band, Pavilion Band, Clin-
ton Band (Shuswap), and High Bar Band (Shuswap). Governor
Douglas's policy was to 'leave the extent and selection of lands entirely optional with the Indians who were most immediately interested in the reserves' (LaViolette 1961:105), but it is not certain that
Lillooet social organization in 1870 reflected aboriginal organization.
By that time, missionaries were trying to make them sedentary farmers
(Sam Mitchell) and they did sell salmon in the nineteenth century
(Teit 1906:259). Walker (1967:15) has noted for the southern Plateau that
a money market for salmon (plus the policies of government and mis-
sions trying to restrict people on reservations) influenced 'tribes' to
claim fishing grounds, in contrast to fairly unrestricted aboriginal
access.

Public Sites

The falls at Six Mile and Bridge River were never owned, according
to Sam Mitchell, though some individuals had rocks there. He and

Tommy Napoleon agree that this site has always produced most of the Fraser Lillooet's sockeye salmon and much of the spring salmon as well. When the river's level falls quite low there are between six and a dozen productive rocks at the Six Mile/Bridge River site.

This site has been a point of congregation. Sam Mitchell said that it seemed that the only time when all the residence groups got together was during the sockeye run at Six Mile. Moreover, as we shall see, many outsiders came to fish or trade here. His tradition is confirmed by Simon Fraser's journal.

On 15 June 1808, Fraser found what seems to have been a fortified fishing camp opposite the present site of Lillooet town (Fraser 1960:82). This would have been before the start of the sockeye run, while springs were still in the river. Returning to the spot on 17 July he found the camp, but the 'Chief' and many of the residents had gone up the river to what must have been Six Mile. There, Fraser rested in the Chief's 'shade,' which I presume to have been his drying rack. At that date – just before the sockeye run – there were upward of a thousand people in the camp (Fraser 1960:120-1). As we see in later sections on salmon distribution, the people who came to Six Mile during the nineteenth century included Lower Lillooets, Shuswaps, and non-Indians and they came to trade as well as to fish.

Historic Salmon Distribution and Stratification Within Settlements

Access to Sites and Stratification

The 'old timer' Lillooet society that Sam Mitchell and other informants describe was stratified (see also Teit 1906:255). This stratification included differential access to food. Thus, Sam Mitchell said that a rich man was one who had a lot to eat. In some years – when the runs were largest – public sites produced a great deal of salmon. Rounsefell (1938:760) estimated that at the turn of the century, the Indian catch in 'big' years at Bridge River averaged 40,000 fish. Hewes (1947) estimated that the Lillooet consumed an average of 600 pounds of salmon per person per year. If outsiders did not take a large portion of the catch, then the average 'big' year catch at public sites could have supported a large portion of the approximately 500 Fraser Lillooet of the turn of the century. However, that catch would not have supported a presumably much larger aboriginal population.

Further, the runs were not always plentiful (Teit 1906:199). As told to Tommy Napoleon by his uncle (who lived in a semi-subterranean house), it was often hard to keep the families going in aboriginal times. Sam Mitchell put the problem into a comparative perspective: the

Lower Lillooet could get food anytime they wanted it, but in the Interior things were rougher because people had to preserve food for the winter.

I think that occasional food scarcity was important for the late nineteenth century Lillooet. However, having privileged access to a spring salmon rock and the labour to dry fish, some individuals could produce much more than they could eat. Sam Mitchell estimated that in this century some people took as many as 600 spring salmon and 400 sockeye, which (using a 23 lb. average for the spring salmon and the Hewes consumption estimate) would feed twenty-four individuals or allow for trade. The number of such 'rich' people was limited by the scarcity of productive fishing rocks (Sam Mitchell, Mrs. Zabatel). On the other hand, there were 'moochers' or 'lazy buggers' – poor people who did not have enough to eat.

Distribution of Salmon within Settlements

Those people who had the spring salmon rocks had the best, though variable, supply of salmon. They also had access to the village residence and public sockeye sites. Those people who fished at the village residence-group-associated sites were fishing from inferior rocks. If they fished at the public rocks, they were in competition with many others, including many non-Lillooet and at least some of the owners of the spring salmon rocks. Based on Rounsefell's early century estimate of the catch of sockeye at the Six Mile fishery and the regional population estimate (about 500), it is apparent that the take of eighty sockeye per person was not adequate to feed the Lillooet population of the area even without considering visitors.

Therefore, the spring salmon catch was necessary. It was precisely the spring salmon sites that required platforms to exploit and which were owned by individuals or families.

Further, there was a need for a distribution system to get salmon from one segment of the population to another. In addition, because the productivity of salmon sites varied, there was a need to distribute salmon in a way which evened out the production from various rocks. Sam Mitchell gave one example of a spring fishing site which was usually very good, but which was not used at all in 1970 'because the river dropped too fast.'

The residents of semi-subterranaen houses shared their dried salmon (Tommy Napoleon), though it was dried and owned by kinship units smaller than the extended family that used the house (Sam Mitchell). Those who produced little or no salmon were called lazy or moochers, but they could beg at many different houses. In times of shortage they went hungry (Sam Mitchell, Mrs. Zabatel). Certain families always produced large quantities of spring salmon and they ensured that people who lived nearby had enough (Sam Mitchell).

Dried salmon was only rarely distributed at a potlatch feast 'because every family had their own' (Sam Mitchell). The usual potlatch good in aboriginal times was deer skin or meat; later, goods from white traders became important.

An extended family short of salmon could borrow from neighbours (Tommy Napoleon), with consistent giving rewarded with prestige and consistent borrowing castigated with the moocher title. The relation between such unbalanced giving or getting and prestige is illustrated in the following myth. One of the notable features of the myth is that the chief could not expropriate salmon but, rather, would have to send a child to ask for it.

In the myth of the deserted boy, recorded by Charles Hill-Tout (1905:201-4) among the Seton Lake Lillooet, the son of a chief goes to several houses where 'he told the inmates that his father had sent him to borrow some cured salmon' and other food. In fact, the boy is gluttonous and eats the food himself. After he did this for several days, 'the people begin to talk about the chief begging food each day, and the boy's aunt, hearing the gossip, suspects what has happened, and comes to the boy's parents and tells them, asking if their son is borrowing food with their knowledge and consent.' The chief is angered and contrives to have the boy abandoned on the opposite side of Seton Lake. When he is deserted, a few people leave some scraps of dried salmon in storage pits, and his grandmother slips away from the deserting party and lives with the boy. In a short time, the boy learns to be a man and acquires magic to attract trout to his camp. Meanwhile, there are hard times back at the village. People hear of the youth's prosperity and come to his camp:

> Those who had felt sorry at the desertion of the boy, and had left him some scraps of food in their [storage cellars] now reaped their reward. They found their cellars stocked with quantities of dried fish, but the cellars of the boy's father and uncles, and of those who had not been friendly disposed to him, contained nothing, and they had to go to bed hungry that night.
>
> The next morning the youth ... calls all the people and bids them help themselves. He now becomes a great man among them.

In this story, as in informants' reports, men gain prestige by producing and distributing fish, but those who receive fish lose prestige. Also, just as Sam Mitchell described it, recipients of food saved face when children brought it. Gifts of fish, as Tommy Napoleon said, were usual so long as they were not too unbalanced; getting fish too often became 'begging.' Finally, this myth illustrates how normal giving could escalate into potlatching.

Historic Inter-Group Relations and Access to Fraser Lillooet Salmon

The aboriginal Plateau peoples developed a remarkable regional system of access to each other's resources, trade, and seasonal congregations. Anastasio (1955) documented this system for the southern Plateau and showed that patterns of intergroup hostility and cooperation have survived until today, expressed now by group gambling games. The Fraser Lillooet were part of this system and Six Mile/Bridge River was a typical Plateau fishing/trade centre, though the Lillooet did not play *lahal* games at the fishing camp.

The special attraction of the Lillooet area resided in the quality of the dried salmon that could be obtained there. People came because they needed preserved food, not just because they needed fresh fish. Conversely, the labour requirements of preserving salmon were what made it impossible for the Lillooet to use all the salmon that they could catch at the height of the run. To the people living far upstream of the Lillooet, the Lillooet represented a source of relatively fat (and tasty) dried salmon. To the lower Lillooet, the Fraser Lillooet were a source of air-dried fish. Reciprocally, the Lillooet used the contrasting fish resources of some of their neighbours. The people who lived to either side of the Fraser were stewards of the trout runs that the Lillooet needed in their time of hunger. Social relations between the Lillooet and their neighbours varied depending on the neighbour's resources and their distance from the Lillooet. We shall now examine some of these relations in more detail, starting with people whose resources were like those of the Lillooet and proceeding to those with unlike resources (Table 1).

Some neighbouring groups had resources similar to those of the Fraser Lillooet; if they lived close by, they could use Fraser Lillooet fishing rocks on an occasional basis. According to Sam Mitchell, there were Shuswap residences to the north of the Lillooet on the east side of the river to a bit north of Clinton, and there were Thompson to the south on the west bank (the east bank to the south was unoccupied). These Thompson intermarried with Lillooet on the west bank and the Pavilion Band married with the Fountain Band (Boas 1906:292; Teit 1909:469; Sam Mitchell; Tommy Napoleon). Although they had their own fishing rocks, they could come to the Fraser Lillooet area at any time to fish and dry salmon, generally staying on their own

TABLE 1
Access to Lillooet salmon, by environmental differences and distance:
aboriginal to nineteenth century

Environment/distance	Group	Access to salmon
Similar environment		
Short distance	Shuswap to Clinton Thompson to south	Friendly, have access; marriage
Greater distance	Shuswap Thompson	Friendly, no fishing or trade
Different environment		
Short distance	Lakes Lillooet	Seasonal, cross- utilization (trout, fat salmon)
	Shuswap Bonaparte	Trade Marriage
Greater distance	Lower Lillooet Shuswap and Thompson in Thompson River Okanagan	Trade Some fishing Theft
Even greater distance	Shuswap Chilcotin	Raids

side of the river. Neither informant said that they had to be related
in a particular way; perhaps their attitude was like that of a modern
resident of Pavilion, who said, 'Well, sure, I'm related to everyone at
Fountain.' Teit (1906:536) reports that the Lillooet traded salmon to upriver Shuswaps, but my data generally indicate visits to fish.

For groups that lived at somewhat greater distances and still had
resources like those of the Lillooet, there was no motivation to use
Fraser Lillooet salmon. The Thompson and Shuswap who lived at
greater distances along the Fraser did not come to trade or to fish,
though relations were generally good (various informants). They had
access to resources similar to those of the Lillooet and they could get
trade goods elsewhere (Teit 1900, 1909).

The people who had dissimilar fish resources, but who lived at a
short distance from the Fraser, were the Lillooet of Seton and Anderson lakes to the west and the Bonaparte Shuswap to the east. The
Lillooet of the lakes had trout runs, and they could take spawning
salmon, while the Bonaparte Shuswap had access to Thompson River
salmon and to large numbers of trout. Mrs. Zabatel said that the

Thompson River salmon dried like boards, had no fat, and did not taste as good as the Fraser River salmon. These people used Fraser Lillooet resources and the Lillooet used their resources on a regular, seasonal basis. The Lakes Lillooet regularly came to fish and dry salmon with the Fraser Lillooet, according to Tommy Napoleon's uncle. They cached their salmon on the shores of Seton Lake before they went home. On the other hand, Fraser Lillooet (Lillooet Band) took trout from Seton and Anderson lakes.

The Shuswaps of Bonaparte River traded with the Lillooet for salmon and intermarried with the Lillooet, thus gaining access to salmon. Teit (1909:536) describes the trade: 'The Bonaparte and Lower Fraser River bands obtained from the Lillooet salmon, oil, woven blankets, goat hair robes, skins of small Columbia deer, a little *wáx-waz a'xaselp* (*Philadelphus Lewisii* Pursh.) and yew wood, giving in exchange dentalium-shells, skin robes, dressed buckskin, a little paint, and in later days horses.'

Mrs. Zabatel noted that in an early period there was quite a bit of marriage between the people of the Bonaparte River and the Fountain Band. Sam Mitchell commented on such marriages:

> If the head guy has daughters who marry out the sons-in-law live there because that's how they fish and gather. That's how they get grouped up. [The husband always comes to live with the wife?] If they like the country. That's how Shuswap came here. They came down and saw lots of fish and girls. Well sure they stay. I know that in the beginning our village [Fountain] had lots that spoke the Shuswap language. [If the husband doesn't like the wife's country?] Well they'll go home, and they got a better home somewhere else. But lots of them settle down here. That's the only thing I can answer.

For their part, some Fraser Lillooet went to the territory of the Bonaparte River Shuswap for the first trout runs of the year. The Loon Lake and Hiiume Lake runs lasted two weeks and were plentiful. The fishing was collective. Mrs. Zabatel said that the oldest person at the camp, who was usually a Bonaparte Shuswap, distributed the fish every morning. Every head of household got an equal share. So far as I know, the Lillooet did not travel to the more distant Green Lake trout fishery described by Teit (1909:450).

For people who had different fish resources than the Lillooet and who lived at a greater distance, the Fraser Lillooet fishing camps were a place to trade for dried fish that was fatter or better-preserved than their own or to trade for fish when their own runs failed. The main way that such people got Fraser River fish was through trade. They

included the Shuswap and Thompson to the east of the Lillooet in
the Thompson River drainage and the Okanagan at the north end of
Okanagan Lake: 'A noted resort for trading and fishing was at the
"Fountain," near the borders of the Shuswap and Lillooet territory,
where also the Lower Lillooet came. Here, on Fraser River, salmon
were caught in abundance. Later on, a pack-train from Hudson Bay
company came here once a year to buy salmon and to trade. When
fish were scarce in Thompson River, the Spences Bridge and Nicola
bands, Okanagon, and eastern Shuswap came here for salmon' (Teit
1900:259). The Lower Lillooet also came to trade: 'Large numbers of
the Lower Lillooet went with the Lake band right to the Fraser River,
where every August and September a great deal of trading was carried
on along the river between Lillooet and the Fountain, at the time when
the Upper Lillooet were congregated there for fishing salmon. Here
they also met Shuswap and sometimes Thompson Indians, and in
the later days traders from the Hudson Bay Company' (Teit 1906:232).

If they came in August and September, then they were there for
the sockeye run, including its lean end, and not for the spring salmon
run. Trade with the Lower Lillooet is described by Teit (1906:232):

> The large fat variety of Fraser River salmon, when cured in the dry
> climate of the region of the upper Fraser River and of Thompson River,
> was considered much superior to the same salmon cured in the damp
> countries of the Lower Fraser and Lower Lillooet, and brought a much
> higher price than any other kind of dried salmon. Although the Lower
> Lillooet put up in their own country more than enough salmon for
> winter use, still they always liked to obtain, besides, a quantity of the
> superior Fraser River cured salmon.

From far upstream, Shuswaps came to Lillooet: 'Frequently some
of the Kamloops people went over to The Fountain and traded with
the Lillooet directly' (Teit 1909:536). The trade relation also predomi-
nated with the Okanagan, but Sam Mitchell did not mention the
Thompson in our discussion of trade and fishing. The visitors to the
upper Lillooet did catch some fish for themselves, but this was mostly for food while at the camps. 'Anybody wants to go rustle something to eat, that's their business; lend them a net' (Sam Mitchell).

The benefits to the Lillooet from this trade were substantial.
According to Sam Mitchell and Tommy Napoleon, horses first came
to the Lillooet area in trade for dried salmon. This trade lasted into
the twentieth century, when the rate was fifteen to twenty dried spring
salmon for a horse. A major source of deer skins for the Fraser Lillooet
were the Shuswap who came to Six Mile, and the Lillooet suffered

in the winter from an inadequate supply of buckskin clothing. Speaking of his parents' generation, Sam Mitchell said: 'You don't have to be related to a trading partner. But once you trade with him, it can be a horse or anything, dried salmon or anything at all, in my language you call it *nák'elx*. Whenever he sees you, when you see him, or you go and see him, he knows you go there for some business of trading or something. If you want a horse, you'll get a horse from him.'

From even farther away, and also living in dissimilar environments, others came to get Fraser River salmon by raiding. Shuswap and Chilcotin raiders came in the fall when the fish were dried and many Lillooet were out hunting. They were different people than those who came to trade and appear to have been unfamiliar with some Lillooet practices: they 'didn't have the idea that the salmon would be stored down there' by the river (Sam Mitchell). There is a grave on a ridge near Fountain where two Shuswap raiders killed with arrows are buried (see Chapter 7). Teit (1906, 1909) records several stories of raiding. After 1850, friendly relations prevailed with the Chilcotin (Teit 1906:233; Sam Mitchell). Cannon explores the relationship of these hostile relationships to resource characteristics in greater detail in Chapter 10.

The more spectacular adaptations of the Coastal people to the variability of basic foods – particularly the regional potlatch/wealth object complex – are not replicated among the Lillooet. The Lillooet did have give-aways associated with some changes in status, but nothing so striking as those found on the Coast. Further, Lillooet potlatches were a direct part of their aboriginal food-getting system: they gave away dried deer meat, a critically important produce when salmon runs were poor.

Access to Salmon in the Twentieth Century

The current regional system of access to salmon retains similarities with that of the nineteenth century (Table 2). The annual fishery at the Fountain (or Six Mile/Bridge River) fishing site is still a major event and a multi-tribe gathering. The fishing and drying techniques in use are largely the same as those used aboriginally, and the Lillooet still depend on dried salmon for a substantial part of their diet.

Each Lillooet band that lives along the Fraser River is associated with a fishing and drying site. Fountain Band fishes and dries at Six Mile, Bridge River Band uses the area at the mouth or just south of the mouth of Bridge River, and Lillooet Band uses the west bank to the north of Bridge River's racks. The partially Lillooet people of Pavilion and Texas Creek also 'have their own rocks' to the north and south, respectively, of the Fraser Lillooet. The association of bands with sites is shown in the ownership of drying racks: eleven of the sixteen racks at Six Mile belong to Fountain people, and four of the five racks north of Bridge River belong to Lillooet Band people. Details of all site locations and use are presented in Chapters 6 and 7.

All informants said that any Indian could fish at any particular fishing site. When asked why they fished at a site, most informants mentioned co-operative aspects of fishing at a site (rides to and from the site by car or horse, for example), the quality of fishing at a site, or their ownership of a rack. Most of the sites are on reserves, and people normally use the site on their reserve.

TABLE 2

Access to Lillooet salmon, by environmental differences and distance: twentieth century

Environment/distance	Group	Access to salmon
Similar environment		
Short distance	Shuswap Pavilion	Friendly, have racks at Six Mile
Greater distance	Thompson	Friendly, no fishing or trade
Different environment		
Short distance	Shalalth	Have racks at Linktown
	Shuswap Bonaparte	Have access
Greater distance	Lower Lillooet	Have access
	Shuswap	Take home in ice
	Okanagan	Trade
Even greater distance	Vancouver	Purchase
	Fraser Valley	Have access
	Yakima (1 case)	

Today, some people fish only for sockeye and others fish for both spring and sockeye salmon. The spring run lasts for a long time, but the daily catch is not large. To fish for springs, one has to give up the alternative income available from migrant harvesting, and there is also the expense of a gill net. My impression is that those who fish for springs tend to be older, reluctant to go harvesting, or individuals who are more sedentary because they are involved in local farming. On the other hand, during the peak of the sockeye run the daily catch is large, so people forego other activities to fish.

Although rocks and eddies are not owned by individuals at present, certain people habitually set their gill nets at particular places. Further, the nets themselves are owned. The Bridge River people formerly would leave a gill net at their site for anyone's occasional use, but they stopped this practice after finding the net tangled and damaged. Sam Mitchell habitually uses a certain rock, but he lays no claim to it. Mrs. Zabatel said that it all depended on who got there first, yet there seems to be consensus about who uses which eddy.

Nuclear families, sometimes augmented by older relatives, catch, store, and consume salmon. I saw one case where the households of a woman and her unmarried brother shared a storage shed. Outside the nuclear family, people give salmon to relatives, old people who cannot fish, and visitors. Mrs. James, for example, gave salmon to her mother and her aunt. Sam Mitchell sent children with fish to members of the Fountain Band who were too old to fish, even though they were not related. People often visit for dinner, and reciprocity is expected.

The Shuswap of Pavilion Band still fish with the Fountain Band Lillooet, just as they did in the nineteenth century. Two of the sixteen racks at Six Mile are owned by Pavilion residents, and Pavilion people visit and eat salmon at Fountain. At least some of the residents of the settlements to the south of Lillooet come to fish at Bridge River. One of the five families that dry at Bridge River is from Texas Creek. Of the people living in a similar environment, but at a greater distance, almost none come to get fish at the Fraser Lillooet sites.

Of those who live nearby but who have dissimilar fish resources, the Shalalth (formerly designated Seton Lake) people have their own site by the town of Lillooet, Linktown, with two drying racks. The name derives from that of the Link family of Shalalth. In the 1902 schedule, the Seton Lake people used Seton Portage, but since then the Cayuse Canal has blocked the run to Seton Portage. Other people with dissimilar resources come to fish. The Lillooet of D'arcy were said to come frequently to fish along the Fraser. People from the Bonaparte Shuswap Band also come. Mrs. Zabatel, Sam Mitchell's step-daughter and now of the Bonaparte Band, stayed for a good part of the season and dried on his rack.

From a greater distance quite a few Lower Lillooet from Mount Currie come to fish and dry at both Bridge River and Six Mile. They usually stay with relatives and dry on relatives' racks. The salmon they have at home in the Lower Lillooet area comes later than that at Lillooet and it is lower in fat because it is nearer to spawning. Of non-Lillooet, very few Thompson Indians come to fish at Lillooet today, but large numbers of Shuswap from Kamloops, Chase, and Chu Chua as well as some Okanagan from Vernon fish at Bridge River or Six Mile. They use the nets provided by the Fraser Lillooet. Generally, they take their fish home packed in ice. In the recent past, those with dried salmon traded it for fruit, deer skins, or, less often, money. When they come only to fish, with no intention of trading, they may also bring gifts of fruit for their friends. When I was at Lillooet I saw no eastern Shuswap or Okanagan, because the runs those years were not plentiful.

When large numbers of people come from the east to fish the sites are crowded. Mrs. Zabatel said that there were sometimes six people waiting in line to fish from a particular rock. When this happens they set a limit of five or ten fish per turn. The total catch for the outsiders who pack fish home in ice may reach 50 or 100 fish.

Of the people from even greater distances, the ones whose ancestors raided the Lillooet; none come to Lillooet to fish, so far as I know. However, now there are some who come from Vancouver and the lower Fraser Valley and even one man who comes from Yakima. These people usually come to purchase dried salmon. Those of the Fraser River Valley, who have their own access to salmon, say that they cannot dry them the way the Lillooet do, instead having to smoke, salt, or freeze them.

In summary, I have shown that among themselves, the nineteenth century Lillooet had individually owned fishing sites, residence-group sites, and public sites. The Fraser Lillooet shared their sites but not to the extent that everyone had equal access to salmon. Stratification of access was the basis for a distribution system which, in turn, resulted in prestige differences.

The Fraser Lillooet were part of a typical Plateau system of trade, cross-utilization of resources, inter-marriage, and raiding. This regional system involved other divisions of the Lillooet as well as Shuswaps, Thompson, Chilcotins, Okanagans, and Whites. Their relations with other people varied depending on the fish resources that those other people had, including their ability to preserve their fish and their distance from Lillooet. The special place of the Fraser Lillooet in their Plateau social system resulted from the dry air, prevailing breeze, and modestly (but not excessively) fat salmon at the Six Mile/Bridge River fishing site near the Fountain village. There are few more striking examples of the impact of environment and resources on cultural and social adaptations.

The nineteenth-century patterns of access to Fraser Lillooet salmon – with functionally equivalent substitutions – have survived to a degree that would be astonishing were it not for two factors. First, we know from Anastasio (1955) that many patterns of Plateau social organization have survived. Second, the basic technology and goals of the fishery remain as they were in the nineteenth century. Salmon is still fatter downstream than upstream and people are still more willing to go short distances than long.

COMPARATIVE CULTURAL ECOLOGY AND SALMON PRESERVATION

For the Northwest Coast, 'The techniques for preserving food are certainly as important as those for getting food. Thousands of salmon swimming upstream in September would not make winter a time of ceremonial activity if people lacked the means of preserving them' (Suttles 1968:63). The data so far presented show that salmon preservation was no less important for the Plateau Lillooet. In fact, since their winters were more severe than the coastal winters, perhaps preservation was more critical. Comparison with coastal drying will highlight features of both areas.

Most of the techniques of salmon drying described in this report are the ones appropriate to the constellation of natural factors found in the Lillooet area, the most important of which are its summer abundance of modestly fat salmon and its hot, dry summer wind. The social environment (the demand for trade) probably promoted powdered fish production, as it did at Celilo Falls on the Columbia. Environmental differences resulted in other aboriginal techniques elsewhere. The environmental contrast between Coast and Interior was also the basis for trade and migration. The regional system described above is a consequence of such environmental factors.

The ways in which the Lillooet themselves respond to environmental variations suggest the factors that, writ large, explain differences between groups living in different environments. Lillooet techniques varied according to salmon species (principally, sockeye or spring), part of the salmon (head, eyes, eggs, dorsal strip, tail, backbone, ribs, skin, oil, guts, eggs, belly, flesh, and others), fat content of the part or species (or early/late in the run), condition of fish (e.g., spent), size of the fish, number of fish on hand, weather conditions (rain, temperature, clouds, wind), presence of pests (flies, yellow jackets, mice), other natural features (e.g., rock depressions for boiling), storage conditions, and human actions (trade, theft). Of these, I will deal with two general factors: drying conditions and fat content.

Drying Conditions

Sam Mitchell noted the exceptional features of the Lillooet area:

This is the only country that can dry that fish like that . . . You go fur-

ther south and it's too wet – they get moldy. The further you go down
the river the more moist the climate, well, they get moldy. Even down
here you have to make your poles toward the river so the wind goes
up and down and the wind will go through your fish. You can't make
it cross-wise . . . it would rot.

[What about upriver – can they make it this way?] Yes, but the further you go north from here there is no more rocks to fish. This is the
best country from here on down. Down the river there is lots of places
you can fish. But you go further north and the country levels out and
there is no more rocks. There may be one or two places like High Bar
– not too many, not like here. But up north, they fish differently. Like
around Quesnel – when the fish gets up there they drift down just like
down in the Fraser Valley. They drift down there too. You know, they
put down a gill net and they drift. That's the way they fish down there.

Even within their generally favourable environment, modern
Lillooet driers search out the places with constant wind. At the regional level, the Coast Salish put their fishing camps where the breeze
was best (Suttles 1951:165). The people of the lower Fraser River search
out wind, putting their racks on rocky outcrops below Yale (Stewart
1977), though only upriver from Hope is the wind good enough for
air drying (Duff 1952:17).

Where (or when) people did not have such good drying winds, they
had to smoke fish (fat content also contributed to the need to smoke,
a point to be discussed). Smoking is basically a form of drying, though
the smoke may also leave chemicals on the fish that inhibit bacteria
(Frazier 1967:140-1) or decrease rancidity (Sinnhuber 1971: personal
communication). Smoking might be restricted to a particular season
(Suttles 1968:63) but some recourse to it was general on the Coast, as
noted in Drucker's (1950) Northwest Coast culture trait lists (Drucker
1950). The more usually adequate drying conditions in the Interior required only an occasional smudge fire.

More strikingly, using residential houses for smoking (Suttles
1968:63), largely as a seasonal expedient, was also a widely distributed practice (Coast Salish (Suttles 1951:145); Sanpoil and Nespelem (Ray
1932:75); Sinkaietk or southern Okanagan (Spier 1938:14); Northwest
California generally (Driver 1939:315); Lower Chinook (Ray 1938:130,
plates 2, 3)). Storing dried fish in a residence, where a fire kept relative humidity down, was also common. Suttles (1966) notes that these
practices bind nuclear families to their extended family co-residents.

The most striking adaptations to the difference between Coast and
Interior drying conditions were trade and travel between the two
zones. This is a case of parallel cultural adaptations, because it occurred

on all three of the major rivers south of Alaska – the Columbia, the Fraser, and the Stikine. Deward Walker (1967:13) reports on the Columbia River: 'Gibbs ... early noted the substantial dried fish traffic between the coast peoples and those of The Dalles-Celilo region. Thus although fish are in their best condition at the mouth of the Columbia, they can be cured somewhat more easily somewhat further inland where the warm, dry winds of the interior dry them quickly. Both factors contributed to the substantial upriver and downriver travel and trade in salmon products.' I would agree that salmon are in their best condition at the mouth of the river in terms of fat content, taste, and appearance; but I would add that for long-term preservation, they were better when they had lost some fat.

For the Fraser River, we have Duff's report (1952:25-6, 67) that large numbers came up the river to fish for sockeye (which lose fat on the way upstream) and that downstream people stored their fish upstream. Teit (1900:259) also notes that the Lower Thompson sold dried 'Kwoi'a' salmon to the Coast. Since these sources of interior fish were located between the Fraser Lillooet and the Coast peoples, direct contact between the two was not significant, though the Lower Lillooet, living in a coast-like climate, did come to Lillooet. Going to the north, Emmons (1911:6-7) states that the Tlingit claimed a 15-mile stretch in the Interior for the advantageous drying conditions that prevailed there, as well as for certain berries. In all of these cases, the Interior sites had better drying conditions than the Coast sites. They also had lower-fat fish, which were more easily preserved. To hammer home the importance of the latter factor, we shall examine cases where coastal people showed their appreciation of low-fat fish.

Fat Content

The Lillooet treat the early, fat part of the sockeye run differently than they treat the later, low-fat fish. They also treat fatter spring salmon differently than they treat sockeye, which do not eat on their run and so lose their fat. Moreover, they use fatter parts differently than they use the rest of the fish. These differences result from two problems with fat fish: they are more difficult to dry (and so can rot or become fly-blown) and their oil goes rancid. The following list collects instances from the Coast and Plateau to show that lower fat species, parts, and individual fish were easier to dry for long periods. Use of roasting/smoking to get rid of excessive oil is notable.

Low-Fat Salmon Favoured for Preservation

(1) Lower fat species for longer or easier preservation

(a) Northwest California (Kroeber and Barrett 1960:101): steelhead
     fatter than salmon and moulds more easily; steelhead used first
     while salmon lasted the winter;
(b) Puyallup-Nisqually (Rivera 1949:36): dog salmon, the least rich
     and not appreciated fresh, kept over indefinite periods of time;
(c) Kwakiutl (Boas 1921:223): dog salmon important;
(d) Thompson (Romanoff: fieldnotes): sockeye dried, spring
     salmon canned;
(e) Tlingit (de Laguana: personal communication): dog salmon
     (skinny, less fat) last long time but not liked, 'like a board';
(f) Sanpoil, Nespelem (Ray 1932:75): spring salmon spoil more
     easily than other species, so kept well shaded;
(g) Nez Perce (Spinden 1908): sockeye salmon preferred for drying;
(h) Haida (Curtis 1911(4):131): dog salmon principal storage food
     on account of its keeping qualities;
(i) Tahltan (Emmons 1911): sockeye the major dried fish, 'being
     a dry fish it cures readily'; and
(j) Yukon (Warner: personal communication): fatter and larger
     springs cut into ten to twenty slices for smoking as human
     food; smaller, less fat chum air dried for dog food.

(2) Higher fat part treated specially

(a) Upper Stalo (Duff 1952): heads sometimes baked over open fire
     before drying;
(b) Chilkat Tlingit (Drucker 1950:240): spring salmon bellies cut off
     and dried separately when very fat;
(c) Thompson (Romanoff: field notes): backbone (fat) smoked,
     other parts air-dried; and
(d) other cases not so explicit – Kwakiutl consume backbone
     immediately (Boas 1921), Tlingit putrify heads (Niblack 1890),
     Bering Eskimo putrify heads (Nelson 1899).

(3) Lower fat part of run selected for preservation

(a) Lake Eyak (Kaydas, personal communication); old women col-
     lect spawned salmon that are said to last longer because of their
     lower fat content;
(b) Northwest California (Kroeber and Barrett 1960): less oily fall
     fish could be eaten by sick people;
(c) Thompson (Romanoff: fieldnotes): early sockeye too rich to dry,
     too greasy, tastes strong; early eggs not stored (tastes strong,
     too rich);

(d) Upper Stalo (Duff 1952): lean fish easier to dry;

(e) Kwakiutl (Boas-Hunt): 'old' sockeye and dog salmon (not fat) sun dried while others smoked or roasted.

The selection of lower fat fish is exemplified by the Puyallap-Nisqually. They dried their fat spring salmon and consumed them quickly because they would not keep. They smoked their dog salmon and these would keep indefinitely. The flesh of the dog salmon had deteriorated and had little fat when the fish were taken (Smith 1940:236, 238).

One of the most striking cases of selected low-fat fish is found in Boas's Kwakiutl texts (Boas 1921). The Kwakiutl obtained spawning (and hence very low fat) dog salmon on upstream spots that were hereditarily owned and jealously guarded. If anyone but the owner fished at a man's spot, the owner would attack the fisherman with a club. Hunt's texts, gathered for Boas, state that the fish taken at these sites were roasted and dried like other dog salmon, but they were not roasted as long. The text continues, 'even if it is kept a long time, it does not get moldy, and it does not get a bad taste [Lillooet: 'strong' taste-rancid], for it is not fat. Therefore it is liked by the Indians' (Boas 1921:223-35).

Fat fish are more tasty than lean ones. In the Lillooet case, people who had access only to low-fat fish which 'dry like boards' came to Fountain to get delicious food. However, low-fat fish are sure to last through the winter, so Coastal people needed an auxiliary supply of such fish. They selected low-fat fish in their own territories, went to Interior sites to fish, or traded for well-preserved salmon.

CONCLUSION

1. Salmon preservation, in addition to salmon fishing, was an essential part of the aboriginal Fraser Lillooet subsistence and it continues to be regionally important today.

2. Aboriginal Fraser Lillooet salmon fishing and preservation were typical of the cultural ecological basis for the Plateau system in the following points: (a) in each Plateau locality there were some rich resources that, at least in some years, surpassed the needs of the local population; (b) these resources were only seasonally available; (c) some resources could be preserved and populations relied on preserved foods; (d) the resources were variable from year to year; (e) the residents of each area suffered seasonal or occasional hunger – most areas could not be self-sufficient all the time; and (f) sometimes people could mitigate shortages by visiting a different area to get fish or preserved food.

3. Adaptations to the conditions for drying had social consequences. Their unusual, but not unique, conditions for salmon preservation made the Lillooet fishery a centre of trade and travel for other Plateau groups. The requirements for drying dictated that there be a Coast/Interior trade, as it did on all three major rivers of the Northwest Coast. Locally, the requirements of 'cross-utilization' of resources resulted in friendly relations with nearby people, with hostile relations limited to distant people. While salmon-fishing was related to local stratification, and while the local potlatch was related to subsistence, the system was different from that of the coastal potlatch system.
4. The requirements of preservation reduce the number of salmon that can be preserved, so that any estimate of the relation between available salmon and population density should take into account climate (need for warm, dry winds, but not excessive heat) and fat content (wastage of high fat fish and need for some lower-fat fish).
5. Drying conditions and fat content vary throughout the Northwest Coast and Plateau, with corresponding technological changes.
6. Salmon preservation has continued to be a vital part of Lillooet subsistence for one hundred years (1870 to 1971) of intense contact with Canadian society.

NOTE

The 1971 version of 'Fraser Lillooet Salmon Fishing' was a thesis prepared for the Division of History and Social Sciences of Reed College. I have rewritten some sections, inserted some comparative material, and added some of Mr. Mitchell's accounts; but most of the material remains as it was. Preparation of that thesis benefited from the advice of Dr. Wayne Suttles of Portland State University and the encouragement of Pat Honchar. My thesis committee comprised Claude Vaucher, David French, Gail Kelly, and Wayne Suttles. Thanks also to the Oregon State University Department of Food Science and Technology and to the U.S. Fish and Wildlife Service, individual members of which consented to be interviewed about fish preservation.

In 1970 and 1971, Sam Mitchell and William Adolph of Fountain Band taught me and showed me great hospitality. Tommy Napoleon of Lillooet Band spent considerable time with me and other informants mentioned in the text helped my investigation generously.

REFERENCES

Anastasio, Angelo. 1955. 'Intergroup Relations in the Southern Plateau.' PhD dissertation, University of Chicago, Chicago. Published in *Northwest Anthropological Research Notes* 6(2):109-229

Boas, Franz. 1906. 'Notes.' In 'The Lillooet Indians.' James A. Teit. Pp. 292-300. *Memoirs, American Museum of Natural History* 4(5):193-300

–. 1921. 'Ethnology of the Kwakiutl.' *Bureau of American Ethnology, Thirty-fourth Annual Report*, 43-1,481. Washington

Canada Department of Indian Affairs. 1902. *Schedule of Indian Reserves in the Dominion.* Annual Report of the Department of Indian Affairs, Supplement. Ottawa

Carl, G. Clifford and W.A. Clemens. 1948. *The Fresh-Water Fishes of British Columbia.* Victoria: British Columbia Provincial Museum

Curtis, Edward S. 1911. *The North American Indian.* Norwood: Plimton Press

Driver, Harold E. 1939. 'Culture element distribution: x, Northwest California.' *Anthropological Records* 1:297-434

Drucker, Philip. 1950. 'Culture element distributions: xxvi, Northwest Coast.' *Anthropological Records* 9(3):157-294

Duff, Wilson. 1952. 'The Upper Stalo Indians of the Fraser Valley, British Columbia.' *Anthropology in British Columbia, Memoir No. 1.* Victoria

–. 1964. 'The Indian history of British Columbia, Volume I, The impact of the Whiteman.' *Anthropology in British Columbia Memoir, No. 5.* Victoria

Emmons, G.T. 1911. 'The Tahltan Indians.' *University of Pennsylvania Museum Anthropology Publications* 4:1-120

Fraser, Simon. 1960. *The Letters and Journals of Simon Fraser, 1806-1808.* Edited with an introduction by W. Kaye Lamb. Toronto: Macmillan

Frazier, W.C. 1967. *Food Microbiology.* New York: McGraw-Hill

Gosnell, R.E. 1903. *The Yearbook of British Columbia and Manual of Provincial Information.* Victoria

Hewes, Gordon W. 1947. 'Aboriginal Use of Fishery Resources in Northwestern North America.' PhD dissertation, University of California, Berkeley. Ann Arbor: University Microfilms

Hill-Tout, Charles. 1905. 'Report on the ethnology of the StlatlumH of British Columbia.' *Journal of the Anthropological Institute of Great Britain and Ireland* 30:126-218

Kelez, George B. 1938. 'King salmon.' In *The Salmon and Salmon Fisheries of Swiftsure Bank, Puget Sound, and the Fraser River.* U.S. Department of Commerce, Bureau of Fisheries, Bulletin No. 27. Washington

Kennedy, Dorothy and Randy Bouchard. 1978. 'Fraser River Lillooet: An ethnographic summary.' In A. Stryd and S. Lawhead (eds.), *Reports of the Lillooet Archaeological Project, Number 1, Introduction and Setting.* Pp. 22-55. National Museum of Man, Mercury Series, Archaeological Survey of Canada Paper,

No. 73. Ottawa

Kroeber, A.L. and S.A. Barrett. 1960. *Fishing and the Indians of Northwestern California.* Berkeley: University of California

LaViolette, Forrest E. 1961. *The Struggle for Survival; Indian Cultures and the Protestant Ethic in British Columbia.* Toronto: University of Toronto Press

Matsuo, Noboru. 1962. 'Nutritional effects of oxidized and thermally polymerized fish oils.' In H.W. Schultz (ed.), *Symposium on Foods: Lipids and Their Oxidation.* Pp. 321-59. Westport, Connecticut: Avi

Milton, Viscount and W.B. Cheadle. 1865. *The North-west Passage by Land.* London: Cassel, Petter, Galpin & Co. Reprinted 1931 and 1971 as *Cheadle's Journal of a Trip Across Canada 1862-63*

Nelson, Edward William. 1899. 'The Eskimo About Bering Straight.' *Eighteenth Annual Report of the Bureau of American Ethnology* 18:3-518

Niblack, Albert. 1890. 'The Coast Indians of Southern Alaska and Northern British Columbia.' *United States National Museum Reports for 1888.* Pp. 225-386. Washington

Ray, Verne F. 1932. 'The Sanpoil and Nespelem.' *University of Washington Publications in Anthropology,* No. 5. Seattle

–. 1938. 'Lower Chinook ethnographic notes.' *University of Washington Publications in Anthropology* 7(2):29-165

–. 1939. 'Cultural relations in the Plateau of Northwestern America.' *Publications of the Frederick Webb Hodge Anniversary Fund,* No. 3. Los Angeles

Rivera, Trinita. 1949. 'Diet of a food-gathering people, with chemical analysis of salmon and saskatoons.' In Marian W. Smith (ed.), *Indians of the Urban Northwest.* Pp. 19-36. New York: Columbia University Press

Romanoff, Steven. 1971. 'Fraser Lillooet Salmon Fishing.' Bachelor's thesis, Reed College, Portland

–. 1972. 'The Lillooet Hunter.' Ms. on file at Cariboo College, Kamloops, BC, Indian Language Project, Victoria, and at Department of Anthropology, Columbia University, New York

–. 1985. 'Fraser Lillooet salmon fishing.' *Northwest Anthropological Research Notes* 19(2):119-60

Rounsefell, George A. 1938. 'Sockeye salmon.' In *The Salmon and Salmon Fisheries of Swiftsure Bank, Puget Sound, and the Fraser River.* Pp. 754-80. U.S. Department of Commerce, Bureau of Fisheries Bulletin No. 27. Washington

Smith, Marian W. 1940. *The Puyallup-Nisqually.* New York: Columbia University Press

Spier, Leslie (ed.). 1938. 'The Sinkaietk or Southern Okanagon of Washington.' *General Series in Anthropology,* No. 6. Menasha, Wisconsin

Spinden, Herbert J. 1908. 'The Nez Perce Indians.' *American Anthropological Association Memoir,* No. 9 (originally Vol. 2, Part 3). Lancaster

Stewart, Hilary. 1977. *Indian Fishing: Early Methods on the Northwest Coast.* Vancouver: J.J. Douglas

Stryd, Arnold and S. Lawhead (eds.). 1978. *Reports of the Lillooet Archaeological Project, Number 1, Introduction and Setting.* Ottawa: National Museum of Canada

Suttles, Wayne. 1951. 'Economic Life of the Coast Salish of Haro and Rosario Straights.' PhD dissertation, University of Washington, Seattle. Ann Arbor: University Microfilms

–. 1966. 'Private knowledge, morality, and social classes among the Coast Salish.' In *Indians of the North Pacific Coast,* Tom McFeat (ed.). Pp. 166-79. Seattle: University of Washington Press

–. 1968. 'Coping with abundance: Subsistence on the Northwest Coast.' In Richard B. Lee and Irven DeVore (eds.), *Man the Hunter* Pp. 56-68. Chicago: Aldine

Tanner, Fred W. and Louise B. Tanner. 1953. *Food-borne Infections and Intoxications.* Champaign, Illinois: Garrard Press

Teit, James A. 1900. 'The Thompson Indians of British Columbia.' *Memoir, American Museum of Natural History* 2(4):163-391

–. 1906. 'The Lillooet Indians.' *Memoir, American Museum of Natural History* 4(5):193-300

–. 1909. 'The Shuswap.' *Memoir, American Museum of Natural History* 4(7):443-789

–. 1930. 'The Salishan tribes of the Western Plateaus.' *Forty-fifth Annual Report of the Bureau of American Ethnology.* Pp. 23-396. Washington

Turner, Nancy. 1972. 'Lillooet Ethnobotany (Fountain Dialect).' Ms., BC Indian Language Project, Victoria

Walker, Deward E., Jr. 1967. 'Mutual cross-utilization of economic resources in the Plateau: An example from aboriginal Nez Perce fishing practices.' *Washington State University, Laboratory of Anthropology, Report of Investigations,* No. 41. Pullman

CHAPTER SIX

Stl'átl'imx (Fraser River Lillooet) Fishing

Dorothy I.D. Kennedy and Randy Bouchard

INTRODUCTION

This chapter examines the Fraser River Lillooet or *Stl'átl'imx* Indian people's knowledge and utilization of fish – the most important staple of the study area. In order to understand the specific potential of the prehistoric sites in the Lillooet study area and in order to understand the socioeconomic relationships that characterized both prehistoric and traditional historic communities in this area, it is necessary to document the fishing resources in the River Valley and Intermediate Lakes subsistence zones. While Kew (Chapter 4) has provided an overview of absolute salmon availability and accessibility for the entire Fraser drainage, including the Lillooet area, and while Romanoff (Chapter 5) has documented patterns of adaptations and access to fishing sites in general in the study area, we will focus on the detailed descriptions of fifty *Stl'átl'imx* fishing sites we have recorded along the Fraser between Della Creek and Pavilion Creek. Previous chapters have also alluded to the basic technology involved in capturing fish. We will provide a more in-depth review of all techniques used within the study area.

Stl'átl'imx Salmon Harvest

Every spring, when the sagebrush buttercup blooms in Lillooet, an event occurs along the banks of the Fraser River that has been happening here for several millennia – the first salmon run of the year appears. Nowadays, *Stl'átl'imx* Indian fishermen catch this first run of spring (chinook) salmon utilizing gill nets suspended from poles slung over back-eddies. This run provides a welcome change from a diet of store-bought commodities and dried, canned, and frozen salmon.

Following the decline in spring salmon stocks that began around the turn of this century, however, the *Stl'átl'imx* people's reliance on spring salmon has changed. Few spring salmon are caught today. Now these people depend on the sockeye runs for their winter supply of fish, so it is not until August that the majority of *Stl'átl'imx* fishermen make their way down to their fishing sites.

In early September of 1973 and again in August 1974 we accompanied eighty-year-old *Stl'átl'imx* Indian Sam Mitchell (Plate 6.1) down to the fishery at Six Mile, just north of where the Bridge River meets the Fraser. It was a long, steep drop of about 300 m (1,000 ft.) from the road down to the east side of the fishery, along a path that would challenge a sure-footed mountain goat. Yet this was the difficult hike

PLATE 6.1
The late Sam Mitchell (1894-1985) at Six Mile Rapids near Lillooet,
September 1974

that Sam had been making all his life during each fishing season.

'I used to pack twenty salmon and go up this hill just like that,' Sam Mitchell stated. 'I got so I could do it in twenty minutes, four to six times a day.' But when Sam suffered a mild heart attack and was found along this fish trail suspended by his feet from a bush, his family insisted that in future he should use a pack-horse.

The Fraser River is turbulent upstream from Lillooet. It rushes between steep canyon walls, reflects off rocky promontories, and nestles in small bays where back-eddies collect debris plucked from the riverbanks. At Six Mile, the entire flow of the Fraser River thunders through a gap no more than about 30 m (100 ft.) wide (Plate 6.2). 'The heavy current, that's where the fish go up,' explained Sam Mitchell, while pointing out to us the choice fishing sites along the riverbank. 'The salmon can go fast, especially where the current is really heavy. That's where we get them.'

PLATE 6.2

Aerial view of Six Mile Rapids ('Lower Fountain') at the confluence of the Bridge River. Drying rocks are visible on the banks.

The *Stl'átl'imx* name for Six Mile is *sxetl'*, meaning 'drop-off,' so named because here the Fraser River drops about 3 m (10 ft). It is here at *sxetl'* that Sam Mitchell's family joins many others each year to catch and preserve sockeye salmon. Most of the fishermen return home at night, but a few remain camped near the river to tend their drying fish.

'Bears are troublesome,' Sam told us, 'especially the two-legged kind with their truck at the top of the hill.' He spoke longingly about the 'old days' when his ancestors built their elevated storage caches near the river and left them unlocked without fear of their winter salmon supply being stolen. But the labour-intensive dried salmon was too highly valued in the 1970s to feed bears of any description.

Ethnographer James Teit (1906:227), who worked among the *Stl'átl'imx* in the early 1900s, reported that 'salmon fishing was the most important industry' of the *Stl'átl'imx*, so important that it 'occupied a more prominent position than among the other interior tribes.' And Sam Mitchell agreed. 'That's the Indians' main food,' he often commented.

Traditionally, it was only the women who cut fish, but in recent times men have also participated in this task. Sam Mitchell often told us how his wife, Susan, who was originally from Leon Creek at the mostly northerly extent of *Stl'átl'imx* territory along the Fraser, had not known how to cut salmon correctly until he taught her after their marriage. Eventually, Susan Mitchell became renowned for her ability to prepare wind-dried salmon of a superior quality, identified by her precise scoring of the flesh, resulting in an evenly dried tasty filet with no insect infestation.

On both our visits to the Six Mile fishery (September 1973 and August 1974), Susan Mitchell had set up a bench underneath one end of the drying rack. This bench also served as a cutting board. Here Susan expertly cut the sockeye salmon as quickly as the fishermen pulled it from the river. Her dexterity with the fish knife attested to her many seasons' experience. In a rapid series of fluid movements, she split the fish along its backbone, scraped out the blood, opened the flank and made a series of cross cuts through the flesh (Plate 6.3). A good fish butcher, Susan Mitchell explained, knows the exact amount of pressure to use for cutting through the flesh without cutting the skin at the back.

At the Six Mile fishery in the 1970s, each family had its own drying rack on which they hung the scored flanks of sockeye to wind-dry. Apart from several tents pitched nearby to accommodate those who camped overnight, and the appearance of numerous other modern materials, the scene we observed at this fishery was likely as it had been for many generations. A very casual and cheery attitude prevailed among the Indian people at the fish camp. As they engaged in this co-operative task that required all members of the family and utilized skills learned over many years, it was clear that these people at the fish camp were maintaining a tradition from the past that was still an integral part of contemporary *Stl'átl'imx* life.

PLATE 6.3

Susan Mitchell scoring the flesh on the second opened flank of a sockeye. Note that the backbone is still connected at the salmon's tail end.

The Study

The term *Stl'átl'imx*, used throughout this study, refers to the 'Upper
Lillooet' Indians and encompasses all those Lillooet-speaking people
living along the Fraser River from the vicinity of Della Creek, about
40 km (25 m) north of Lytton, and upriver as far as Leon Creek, near
Pavilion. This designation, *Stl'átl'imx*, generally includes the Seton
Lake and Anderson Lake Indians, who, together, constitute the 'Lake'
subgroup of the Upper Lillooet. But the present report is concerned
primarily with the Fraser River subgroup.

In the following chapter we describe in detail the *Stl'átl'imx* people's knowledge of fish and fisheries, including their beliefs and practices. Federal Fisheries data have been compiled to examine the timing of the distinct runs, the availability of the fish, and the weekly and yearly peaks in the sockeye harvest. Additionally, we discuss those aspects of the technology involved in harvesting the fish and the methods used to preserve them that are not already covered by Romanoff in Chapter 5. We also describe the use of fish in technology.

A major component of this study is the description of *Stl'átl'imx* fisheries found in the Appendix. The fisheries discussed are those along the Fraser River, roughly between Pavilion Creek, approximately 24 km (15 m) north from Lillooet, and Della Creek, about the same distance south. These creeks represent the approximate northerly and southerly extent of *Stl'átl'imx* territory along the Fraser River in the twentieth century.

Most of the information in this report has been provided by the late Sam Mitchell (SM), a *Stl'átl'imx* Indian, during interviews we conducted with him in 1973, 1974, 1975, and 1977. Many days were spent with Sam Mitchell, exploring traditional Lillooet territory and recording his knowledge of native activities. Additional data included in this study were provided by the following *Stl'átl'imx* people: the late Susan Mitchell (SUM); the late Slim Jackson (SJ); the late Madeline Sampson (MS); the late William Adolph (WA); Bill Edwards (BE); and Desmond Peters (DP). Data have also been provided by the late Paul Hickson of Lillooet, who was interviewed by Bouchard in 1969. As well, some comparative 'Lower Lillooet' data, contributed by Charlie Mack and used in our preliminary study of Mount Currie fishing (Kennedy and Bouchard 1975c), have been included in the present study, as have data recorded by University of British Columbia linguist Jay Powell in 1988 from the late Solomon Peter of Seton Lake. As in other chapters in this volume, information obtained from specific individuals is indicated by the use of their initials in parentheses. Short biographies are provided in Chapter 1.

SPECIES OF FISH KNOWN TO THE *STL'ÁTL'IMX*

Salmon

Five species of Pacific salmon are known to the *Stl'átl'imx*: sockeye (*Oncorhynchus nerka*); spring or chinook (*O. tshawytscha*); coho (*O. kisutch*); humpback (*O. gorbuscha*); and steelhead (*O. mykiss*). Speakers of the *Stl'átl'imx* language also distinguish specific runs of spring and sockeye salmon.

When the sagebrush buttercup (*Ranunculus glaberrimus*) blooms in

Lillooet around April, it is an indication that the first run of spring salmon, called *skwéxem*, is ascending the Fraser River. The average weight of the salmon in this first run is between 7 and 9 kg (15-20 lb.) (SM). The *Stl'átl'imx* term for the sagebrush buttercup is derived from the name for this run of salmon. Consequently, this flower is called *skwexemálus*, which means 'first-spring-salmon eye.'

A second run of spring salmon arrives at Lillooet around late May to early June, during the time of high water on the Fraser when most fishing rocks are inundated. Because the wild rose (*Rosa* spp.) bushes are blooming at this time, these fish are called *kelkásulh* or 'rose-hip fish,' derived from the term *kelk* or 'rose hip.' These salmon have a red stripe on their sides, and are noted for their swiftness. Sam Mitchell observed that fishermen must be quick when dip-netting these fish or else the salmon swim away before the net is pulled out of the water.

Concentrated numbers of the largest spring salmon arrive in July and August. These fish are called *zúmak*, except for the white-fleshed spring salmon, which are called *pkas*. Although these large spring salmon run together with the sockeye, the springs are found at greater depths (SM). At certain times, apparently, they could also be found on different sides of the river – a Fisheries official reporting on the Six Mile fishery wrote on 9 October 1924 that while the Indians on the Bridge River side (west side) of the river had been making good catches that were 'principally springs,' the people on the Fountain side (east side) were catching 'quite a few sockeye' (Motherwell 1924).

Prior to construction of the Carpenter Dam on the Bridge River in 1948, spring salmon spawned much further up this river, near Gun Lake, at a place the older *Stl'átl'imx* people call *tl'ayáks* (SM). In 1919, Indians and settlers alike informed the local Fisheries officer that salmon of all species ascended the Bridge River about thirty miles to the site of a falls which impeded their progress (Motherwell 1924).

Sam Mitchell recalled that when he was young, in the late 1890s-early 1900s, his family dried between 500 and 600 spring salmon each year for their own consumption. But spring salmon runs declined radically in the early years of this century, and the *Stl'átl'imx* people then caught and dried mostly sockeye salmon for winter storage. Spring salmon, however, was still the fish of choice in the 1940s, despite its rarity, according to field studies undertaken by Fisheries officers at that time. One such report noted that spring salmon were especially desired by those Indians residing below Lillooet. Their stated reason for this preference was that they dry better than sockeye, which become 'hard like board' (Simmons 1940) and because they 'cure better' (Strang 1933). Statistics obtained by Fisheries officers observing drying racks and interviewing fishermen indicate that spring salmon comprised only 6 per cent of the large 1940 salmon catch in the Lillooet area (Tremper 1940). This catch of approximately 1,600 spring salmon was the second largest recorded harvest of this species by *Stl'átl'imx* people subsequent to the 1913 Hell's Gate slide, an event that had a serious impact on the spawning runs of all salmon species. In 1925, when the sockeye catch amounted to only 6,100 fish, the larger spring salmon catch of 1,700 comprised a more significant percentage of the annual catch, although the numbers of both species were severely depleted (Halladay 1925). Indian Agent H. Graham expressed his personal view that the 1925 run was one of the largest since the Hells Gate slide (Graham 1925).

Sockeye salmon, called sxwa7s in the *Stl'átl'imx* language, begin to appear in the Fraser River around Lillooet at the end of June and continue in a series of runs through to early October. Sam Mitchell provided another *Stl'átl'imx* term, *tsekwalúps*, which appears to distinguish a sockeye that has turned red during the later stages of spawning. The last run of sockeye, according to SM, goes up Seton River to Seton Lake and on through to Anderson Lake where they spawn. The young sockeye spend their first year in this lake.

Sockeye smolt (fingerlings) used to be captured in traps set in the Seton River between the outlet of Seton Lake and the Fraser. This was during May when schools of the young sockeye passed downstream (SM). Fisheries Commissioner J.P. Babcock observed Indian people in early May 1903, using one of these traps in 'Portage Creek' (now called the Seton River) connecting Seton Lake and Anderson Lake (Babcock 1904:9). Sockeye smolt were considered a choice food, although only enough to eat fresh were trapped and distributed among the people; they were never preserved. Sam Mitchell recalled how schools of smolt swimming together caused the water to look white, because they were so numerous, and Paul Hickson noted that when foam berries (*Shepherdia canadensis*) began to ripen (in June), the *Stl'átl'imx* people knew that the smolt were no longer good to eat.

These comments of Sam Mitchell and Paul Hickson concerning the Indian utilization of sockeye smolt in Seton River are consistent with information that J.P. Babcock obtained in 1901 from both Indians and non-Indians living in this area. On the basis of their statements, Babcock reported that the sockeye fingerlings left Seton Lake between May and July, and that the Indians caught great numbers of them in traps as they passed out of this lake (Babcock 1902:822).

Most of the sockeye salmon that is dried for storage around Lillooet today is caught during August, when the fish are less fat than they are at the beginning of the run. Traditionally, the *Stl'átl'imx* people knew when the correct time for drying salmon had arrived because they could hear the distinctive sound made by a certain type of grass-hopper, called *tl'ek'atl'ék'a*. This word approximates the sound made when people cut salmon for drying.

Land-locked sockeye, commonly called kokanee, are known in the *Stl'átl'imx* language as *gwunís* or 'floaters.' They are called this because at a certain time each year they rise to the surface of Seton and Anderson lakes, their abdomens so distended with gas that they remain on the surface, where they die (SM; CM).

Solomon Peter of Shalalth noted that these fish spawn near the surface, and the change in air pressure causes them to bloat, preventing them from descending (Powell 1988:personal communication). In Seton Lake this phenomenon occurs in November and December, and in Anderson Lake it occurs in January and February (SM). J.P. Babcock observed the presence of these fish in Seton Lake in 1902 and reported that the Indians 'gather them in great quantities by means of scoop nets when they first come to the surface' (Babcock 1903:G20). Sam Mitchell and Charlie Mack stated that a westerly wind blows these fish to the edge of Seton Lake, where they can be simply picked up, taken home, and either dried or eaten fresh.

In Anderson Lake, the chinook winds in early January blow the 'floaters' to the northeast end of the lake. The Indian people living there know when the 'floaters' are around because of the presence of eagles which come to feed on the dying fish. 'Floaters' are still gathered for food by the natives living near these lakes, and although these fish are usually eaten fresh, some families string them on sticks and dry them (Powell 1988: personal communication; SM).

Pink or humpback salmon (*O. gorbuscha*), called *háni7* by the *Stl'átl'imx,* spawn in Cayoosh Creek during September and October; none go further up the Fraser River than the falls at Six Mile. After the fish ladder was put in here at Six Mile, however, a pink salmon apparently was seen at Eleven Mile by a man named Charlie Bob (SM). Pink salmon stocks were seriously depleted after the Hell's Gate slide and, according to Fisheries reports, were not recorded again around Lillooet until 1923, when Indian fishermen observed them in the Fraser River and around the mouth of Cayoose Creek (Arthur 1923).

Sam Mitchell stated that pink salmon ascend the Fraser only once every two or four years and are always accompanied by rainy weather. Bill Edwards of Pavilion made this same observation (see Chapter 8). As pink salmon return to the spawning streams in the Fraser River system in predictable and highly segregated odd-year runs (Scott and Crossman 1973:150), it is possible that SM's and BE's statements reflect their confusing the behaviour of pink salmon with the quadrennial dominance in sockeye.

Pink salmon have always been an unpopular fish amongst the *Stl'átl'imx* people; Sam Mitchell recalled throwing them back into the river whenever enough of the other salmon had been caught. The Indian people's disregard for this species may account for Mitchell's and Edwards' mistaken assumption regarding pink salmon migration.

Coho salmon, called s*xáyak*s ('crooked nose') in *Stl'átl'imx*, are caught in the Fraser River around September. Few coho ascend this far up the river, so those caught are usually obtained while the people are fishing for sockeye, which run at the same depth as do coho salmon (SM). The *Stl'átl'imx* have no name for chum salmon (*Oncorhynchus keta*), as they do not ascend the Fraser River as far as Lillooet. Steelhead (*Oncorhynchus mykiss*), referred to in *Stl'átl'imx* as *tsúgwlha7*, go up the Fraser River beginning in September and stay all winter. But, unlike other salmon, steelhead can spawn several times during a lifetime. SM noted that, formerly, steelhead were dried to take on hunting trips, as they kept well. In the 1970s, steelhead were not often fished by the *Stl'átl'imx* people.

Regardless of species, male salmon are called *nwik7ám* and can be found in the roughest part of the river, whereas female salmon, called *nkw'únam* or 'having eggs,' are found generally in back-eddies. Because the majority of dip-netting is done in back eddies, mostly female salmon are caught while fishing in this manner (SM).

No *Stl'átl'imx* ceremony celebrating the arrival of the first salmon has been recorded in the literature nor was it known to the people we interviewed. Such a ceremony has been reported for the Lower Lillooet, whose villages are situated between Birken and the north end of Harrison Lake (Hill-Tout 1905:140; Teit 1906:280; Kennedy and Bouchard 1975c). Sam Mitchell did note that special care was taken not to throw salmon entrails back into the river after butchering the fish, as this was believed to cause the salmon to leave that part of the river.

Mythological Origin of Salmon

It is said that in the beginning, the people were without salmon. They heard that some women living at the mouth of the Fraser River had built a weir which prevented the salmon from swimming upstream. Coyote decided that since he was smarter than anyone else, he would go and get the salmon from these women. When he got to the weir, Coyote transformed himself into a wooden plate and washed up against the weir so that the women would find him when they went to get some fish. 'Oh, look at the plate,' called one of the women, 'let's take it home.'

The next day the women left to dig roots, so Coyote changed back into his original form and ate the remainder of the cooked salmon that the women had put aside. He soon noticed the many containers that were in the room and wondered what was in them. Coyote flung open the lid of one of them and out flew hundreds of flies. They circled about Coyote and then began to fly upstream. The women sensed that something was wrong, but when they returned home, all they found was their new plate. The following day, the women again went root-digging, and again Coyote changed back into his original form. He lifted the lid of a second container. This time, wasps swarmed about Coyote and stung him before they flew upstream.

Again the women returned home, but found only a plate. On the third day that the women went to dig roots, Coyote opened another container. This one contained salmon lice! They crawled all over Coyote and then headed upstream behind the flies and the wasps.

On the fourth day that the women went root-digging, Coyote transformed himself back into his original form. He went down to the river, broke the fish weir, and released the salmon. 'Follow me,' he called out to the salmon. Coyote ran along beside the river as the salmon swam upstream. He called out, speaking in the Thompson language, 'Make your fire! The salmon are coming! The salmon are coming up the river!'

Coyote then distributed salmon to the people all along the Fraser River.

This story, related to us by the late William Adolph in 1977, is probably the most commonly told account of how salmon was distributed to the people in this region. But other stories explaining the origin of salmon in this area have also been recorded. One such story was transcribed by the late William Elliott, a Lillooet Indian from D'Arcy, on Anderson Lake, and author of the 1931 publication entitled 'Lake Lillooet Tales.' This story is summarized as follows:

The daughter of a family living at Anderson Lake was taken by North Wind to be his wife. Her four brothers searched but couldn't find where their sister had been taken. One day, hoping to find their sister, they attended Crow's potlatch being held at the Coast. Among the guests at this potlatch were Spring Salmon, Sockeye, and Coho. They were gathered in Crow's house listening to his lame daughter singing a song about her father's wealth. Whale was standing outside the door. Suddenly a cry was heard. Whale told everyone to go outside and listen. Again they heard a cry. It was the lost sister crying out the names of her brothers, one by one.

Quickly the brothers left. Spring Salmon announced that he was going too. Sockeye followed him. But Coho was late because he wanted some warm clothing. 'Make me a warm hat, for I am going to a cold country. I shall be up there until everything is frozen over,' he told the people. That, according to William Elliott's version of this story, is why salmon run up the Fraser and into the lakes and streams today. The brothers eventually caught up with their sister and soon the weather became warmer (Elliott 1931:166-7).

Among James Teit's Shuswap field notes appears the following brief summary of a Coyote story explaining the origin of the Six Mile fishery:

> Place near Bridge River where a kind of fall on the Fraser River called shettl [*sxetl'*] 'taking out' or 'coming out,''landing' because this is a famous fishing place where salmon are taken out. Coyote when bringing the salmon up the river made this kind of ridge or bar across the river as it would be a good fishing place for the people of this region. When he was through he sat down on a rock near the edge of the river and the marks of his seat and feet are there yet. The marks of his feet are also at other places nearby on the rocks where he walked about. These are just like marks of human feet in mud but all is stone not mud (Teit n.d.).

Coyote's work may be evident at the Six Mile fishery, but, unfortunately, we never did ask Sam Mitchell if he knew the location of these footprints. Concerning Teit's etymology for the name of the Six Mile fishery, it should be noted that contemporary *Stl'átl'imx* people translate *sxetl'* only as 'drop off.'

The above-mentioned story about the origin of the Six Mile falls was not published with Teit's collections of Shuswap or Lillooet mythology. However, two variants of this story appear in the published works of ethnographer Charles Hill-Tout. Both of them were recorded among the Thompson Indians in the late 1890s. In one variant, Coyote created the falls in the Fraser River at the mouth of the Bridge River by 'stepping to and fro across the river three times' (Hill-Tout 1899a:560).

The second variant is part of a much longer story about the wanderings of the mythological Transformers:

> Ascending the Fraser once more, they [the Transformers] came to the region of the Lillooet. On Bridge River Benign-face [one of the Transformers] found the people very poor and miserable. They did not know how to catch the salmon which passed up the river. So Benign-face stretched his leg across the river here, and the rocks rose up and

numbers. He then taught the people to make and use three different types of salmon spear, which they use to this day in that region. The name of the fall in the native tongue is *Neqoi'stem* (Hill-Tout 1899b:215-16).

The term '*Neqoi'stem*' used by this Thompson story-teller is *nxwistn*, which does not refer to the Six Mile falls. Rather, it is the name of a *Stl'átl'imx* village on a bench above the Fraser River, directly west of these falls (Kennedy and Bouchard 1978:29,33).

Fish Other than Salmon

Fresh-water fish were much less important to the *Stl'átl'imx* than were salmon. Although large numbers of some fresh-water species were caught, few were preserved for winter subsistence. Sam Mitchell recalled that river-resident rainbow trout, called *sts'éts'kwaz-úl* ('real trout') in the *Stl'átl'imx* language, were caught at outlets to lakes during the trout's spring spawn, beginning in March. Another trout, identified by SM as *stl'ík'sulh* [likely the lake-resident Kamloops trout (*Salmo gairdneri*) which is rounder and more silver-coloured than the rainbow trout], was also caught in large numbers during its spawning season.

Trout were caught with basketry traps, nets, leisters (three-pronged spears), and gaff-hooks in streams at outlets to lakes. When spearing, gaffing, or netting the trout, the *Stl'átl'imx* placed peeled willow sticks (that were then white in colour) on the stream bed so that the fish could be more easily seen as they swam overtop. The *Stl'átl'imx* word meaning 'to go trout fishing' is *wáwlam*. Trout were also caught by means of ice fishing in Cinquefoil, Kwotlenemo (Fountain), Pavilion, and Loon lakes.

Cinquefoil Lake, according to Sam Mitchell, was the only lake in the valley that had a significant fresh-water fish population. SM further noted that rainbow trout (*Salmo gairdneri*) were transplanted successfully from Cinquefoil Lake to Kwotlenemo (Fountain) Lake, after which these transplanted fish grew to about 55 cm (20 in.) in length. Dolly Varden char (*Salvelinus malma*), called *sem7ásulh*, were fished year-round in Seton and Anderson lakes and also in the Fraser River.

Today, trout are fished with a hook and line either from a boat or by casting from the shore. The late Solomon Peter (Powell 1988: personal communication) described a particularly good trout fishing site he used at the mouth of a creek draining into the east end of Anderson Lake directly across from Shalalth. Grasshoppers, earth worms, and lumps of bread dough were among his choice of bait.

SM stated that *Stl'átl'imx* people also made the occasional trip to the Bonaparte and Thompson rivers during the spring to fish mountain whitefish (*Prosopium williamsoni*), called *mámelt*, during their spawning season. They were also fished in the Fraser River. According to Charlie Mack of Mount Currie, eating too many whitefish causes a skin rash.

Spring was also the time to catch squawfish (*Ptychocheilus oregonensis*), called *(s)kw'a7k*, that are found in the Fraser River. Squawfish were formerly eaten, despite being so bony. Yet Sam Mitchell told a story about a time when eating squawfish caused misfortune: some people were camped at the head of Fountain Creek at a small lake known as *skw'a7k* because there were a lot of squawfish there. The people caught a few to eat. But a few of the young girls didn't like eating the bony fish, so they left their people and took a nap while the others ate. When they woke up, the girls walked over to where the people had been eating and found them all dead. This lake is a very powerful and strange place, SM concluded.

Suckerfish (*Catostomus* spp.) are called *gwugwlh* by the *Stl'átl'imx*. They, too, are filled with bones, but they were caught in the Fraser River (SM) and in Anderson and Seton lakes (Powell 1988: personal communication) during the spring and were eaten fresh. A more popular fish among the *Stl'átl'imx* was the freshwater ling (*Lota lota*), called *smetsáź*. The flesh was eaten barbecued, as was the oil-rich liver, considered a delicacy.

Large white sturgeon (*Acipenser transmontanus*), called *xwu7tl'*, were accidentally caught in nets while the people were fishing for salmon. Sam Mitchell was of the opinion that sturgeon were not fished aboriginally, although this is unlikely as they were eaten by neighbouring Plateau groups. A few places on the Fraser River are known as good sturgeon fishing areas (see fishing site No. 11 in Appendix). In more recent times, sturgeon were caught using a set line and then sold to the Chinese community. The sturgeon's spinal cord was eaten raw (SM).

The *Stl'átl'imx* people call the lamprey (*Lamperta ayresi*) *kwútwen*, a term that is cognate in several languages throughout the Northern Plateau. Lamprey could be seen hanging from the rocks at the Six Mile fishery. Sam Mitchell recalled that when he was a boy, he and the other children used to catch lamprey and tease one another by getting the lamprey to suck onto someone's face. He stated that lamprey were not eaten by his people. While at the fisheries, children also spent their time fishing for sculpin (*Cottus* spp.), called *sts'enáź*, and peamouth chub (*Mylocheilus caurinus*), called *késk'ets*. They were fished solely for fun in SM's time.

A Lillooet story recorded by Teit (1898:118), however, notes that sculpin were formerly eaten. In this story, the son of Hog-Fennel Root was taunted and chased away by a young man because of his unusual parentage. To avenge this act, Hog-Fennel Boy turned the rude man into a sculpin and, hitting him over the head with a stick, caused it to be the flat-headed fish it is today. Son of Hog-Fennel then cursed the sculpin by saying, 'You will be a fish, and people will take you and eat you, and you shall not be able to help yourself.'

FISHING IMPLEMENTS AND TECHNIQUES

Stl'átl'imx salmon fishing technology was appropriate to the physical conditions of the Fraser River in their territory. Here the swiftly flowing Fraser has carved out a deep, steep-sided, rocky trench where tongues of bedrock jut out from the riverbank. Within this stretch of the Fraser River between Pavilion Creek and Della Creek, where the canyon is constricted, the *Stl'átl'imx* people used several shapes and sizes of 'dip nets.'

'Set-nets' (large dip nets) are still used today. They are held steady in the water by means of an anchor rope. Dip nets, which are smaller than 'set-nets,' are simply dipped through the water. They are used only occasionally (see discussion that follows). As well, gill nets are also used in the study area.

Harpoons, spears, and a cylindrical basketry trap were also employed in former times to catch trout and, once they had entered the spawning streams, salmon. Line fishing, using individual lines and set lines, was also practised by the *Stl'átl'imx*. Formerly, before being prohibited in 1944, gaff hooks described in 1917 by one Fisheries officer as the largest he had seen (Newcombe 1917), were used in the vicinity of the Six Mile fishery and perhaps elsewhere.

In his description of Lillooet fishing, Teit (1906:227-8) stated that the fishing methods used by the Lillooet were the same as those found among the Thompson Indians. To this we would add that although *Stl'átl'imx* may differentiate and use the same salmon fishing devices as their Thompson neighbours to the south, the terms used to refer to the implements are not necessarily cognate.

Set-Net

Both Teit (1906:228) and Dawson (1892:15) used the term 'bag-net' (see Plate 6.4) to refer to the large dip net widely used on the Fraser River by the Lillooet and Thompson Indian people, whereas Hill-Tout (1899a:14) described it as a 'meshed bag.' We refer to this same net as a 'set-net' because of the manner in which it is used – the net is

PLATE 6.4
Indian man removing a salmon from a set-net in the vicinity of Lillooet,
early 1900s

held steady in a swift back-eddy. This 'set-net' consists of a bag-like netting fastened with rings onto an oval hoop or bow that is fixed to a long pole, to which an anchor line is also attached.

Sam Mitchell referred to the set-net as *ntsekts* on several different occasions. Yet he also used the term *zawmn* to refer to 'any type of dip net,' including the 'set-net' (see also the dip net discussion that follows). On the other hand, BE did not recognize the word *ntsekts* – he used only the term *zawmn* to refer to the 'set-net.' Possibly this is an indication that the word *ntsekts* was used only by previous generations. Both SM and BE used the term *záwem* when referring to fishing by means of the 'set-net.'

The hoop or bow of the net is called *súts'wi7x*. It is made from two young Douglas-fir saplings (*Pseudotsuga menziesii*). Fir is used because it is strong, can be shaped easily, and retains its shape after the hoop is completed. Once the saplings' branches are removed, they are peeled and then cut to the same length. First the thin ends of the saplings are bound together. Then the saplings' thick ends are whittled to make a notch on either side where the bow will later be bound to the pole. The bow is hung to dry (SM).

Traditionally, the Indian hemp plant (*Apocynum cannabinum*) was used for the binding and also for making the netting (see Chapter 8). This plant was harvested during the autumn, just as the leaves were turning yellow. After the leaves and branches were removed, the stalks were split open, the outer bark was peeled off, and the inner fibrous parts were hung to dry. The women could then twist the fibres together by rolling them on their bare thigh. The pieces of twisted fibres were spliced together into a continuous length by rolling the two ends together until they intertwined. Nowadays, commercial twine is used for the netting.

There are various sizes of set-net bows. Sam Mitchell stated that the length of the roughly oval-shaped bow used for spring salmon fishing is about 1.5 m (4.8 ft.). Set-nets used in extremely rough water among rocky outcrops are very narrow, some only 30 cm (1 ft.) wide, to lessen the possibility of the turbid water twisting the bow out of shape. Bows on some sockeye nets are about a metre (39 in.) long and between 30 and 60 cm wide (14-24 in.). Longer bows are used in deep water. In recent years, *Stl'átl'imx* people have tried to make more durable bows from aluminum but have found that in places where gravel and rocks are being churned up by the force of the water, the aluminum bows create too much noise and scare the fish (SM).

Sam Mitchell made his own netting, using a net gauge called *k'ts'áka7* and, consequently, was familiar with the mesh size of various nets. He explained that spring salmon nets have a mesh of between 15 and 18 cm (6-7 in.), and are made by starting at the bottom of the net, with fifteen knots on the front and back, and seven knots on the sides. The mesh of a spring salmon net is called *sláxyin*. SM also explained that a mesh of about 12 cm (4.5 in.), which is called *xwa7séyn*, is used for sockeye and small spring salmon. These nets are woven either with twelve knots on the front and back and five knots on the sides, or nine knots on the front and back and four knots on the sides. The depths of the nets range from between 1 m (3.25 ft.) to 1.33 m (4.5 ft.). Sam Mitchell demonstrated the measurements used in making nets, the process of which is called *nzázek*, by using the standard of arm spans.

Once completed, the net is fastened to the bow by means of horn rings called *k'ek'xwtn*. Formerly, these rings were made from mountain sheep horn, but more recently cow horn and metal rings have been used. Set-nets generally have a total of eight rings around the hoop, four on each side. Smaller set-nets that have six rings around the bow, instead of the eight rings used for a spring salmon set-net, were sometimes used as dip nets and swung through the water. The netting from all sizes of set-nets is removed from the bow at the end of the fishing season and stored separately. The handle of the set-net is a Douglas-fir pole measuring anywhere from 3-6 m (9-18 ft.), depending on the depth of the site where the net is to be used. Sam Mitchell noted that at one particular place the fisherman holds the net about 3.5 m (11 ft.) below the surface, so the pole must be very long. One end of the pole is fastened between the ends of the bow that had earlier been whittled to provide a place for the two to be bound together.

The handle and the bow are reinforced by a small but sturdy piece of fir placed between the ends of the bow and at right angles to the end of the pole forming the handle of the set-net. The bow is whittled slightly to form a groove on which this reinforcement stick rests. Using a figure-eight motion, the bow, the handle and the reinforcement stick are all bound firmly in place. This reinforcement piece, called *ll'ek7ápa7*, helps to prevent the bow from twisting.

When using the net, the fisherman holds it by a hand-held line attached to the uppermost ring on either side of the bow. This line is called *tskwápa7*. From these rings it runs up to the end of the set-net handle and then doubles back down the handle, a distance equal to the bow's length, to where it is tied to the pole. The fisherman holds a buckskin strap that is fastened to this line. When a fish is felt, the fisherman releases this trip line from his hand, causing the rings to slide down to the lower end of the bow, closing the mouth of the net and thus forming a closed bag or purse. Then the net is jerked straight up and out of the water.

The set-net is held in place in the water with the aid of a long anchor line, called *gatsáwlh*. One end of this line is attached to the shore. The other end of this line is split, and each piece is tied onto the second ring on either side of the net. In particularly rough water this anchor line is tied to the third ring on either side of the bow. Romanoff (1985:127, 129-30) also provides a description of the set-net.

Dip Net

Dip nets are similar in shape to set-nets, but are distinguished from them by two features: they are smaller and they are not anchored. According to Bill Edwards, dip nets are seldom used today. When they are used, BE added, it is only if there are a lot of fish available. This is consistent with a Fisheries officer's observation that in 1943, still [set] nets were the usual means by which salmon were caught, but that dip nets 'come into extensive use during the blockage period at the [Six Mile] rapids at which time 12 to 15 fish may be taken in one sweep of the net' (Killick 1943b). The same observer noted that set-nets were awkward and usually too large for use in shallow water when the salmon were plentiful (Killick 1943a).

Sam Mitchell used the term zázew̓ to refer to the dip net on several different occasions, but he also referred to this same net as zawmn, which is the generic term used to refer to both dip nets and set-nets. Bill Edwards referred to the dip net only by the term zaźew̓éyn. According to sm, a particularly narrow type of dip net called nxiw̓kwatn was used at the fishing site called nxiw̓kwm (see site 33h in Appendix).

We did not see any dip nets, ourselves, at the Six Mile fishery on the Fraser River when we were there in 1973-4. Indeed, BE recalled that he had not used a dip net, himself, since about 1950. This was at the Seven Mile fishery; the dip net had been left there on the rocks for anyone to use, BE noted. The use of a special net at this site is confirmed by statements we recorded from sm, indicating that a type of 'small dip net' was used at a few specific sites, including one at Seven Mile, one below the ranch at Eleven Mile, and a few sites in the vicinity of Six Mile. At these sites, sm observed that sockeye swam close to the surface and followed the curvature of the rocks. The fisherman lowered the small dip net into the water and, following the current, made a full dip, bringing the net once again to the surface.

Fishing Scaffolds

Set-nets and dip nets were often used in conjunction with platforms or scaffolds, called stl'ak, projecting out over swift parts of the water (see Plate 5.1). In an 1872 article on the natural history of British Columbia, A.C. Anderson noted, with reference to the Fraser River Canyon, that 'scoop nets are chiefly used, which are wrought from stages [scaffolds] suspended from the rocks bordering on rapid currents' (Canada 1873:182). According to Teit (1900:250), these platforms were built at those spots where the fish 'hug the shore in their attempt to get up a rapid stretch of water.'

After the fishing season was over, the scaffolds were disassembled and left above the high water mark. Sam Mitchell stated that scaffolds were last used in the Lillooet area in the late 1960s. Since that time, most fishing has been for sockeye that can be caught in small back-eddies with set-nets used from fishing rocks and ledges, and with gill nets that are positioned across large back-eddies (sm).

Fishermen occasionally built breakwaters by driving a number of stakes into the riverbed several metres upstream from the fishing scaffold (Teit 1900:250). This would make the water rough and therefore obscure the fisherman's net. We were unable to confirm this practice among the Stl'átl'imx, although we did record it among the

Thompson (Kennedy 1974-6). Similarly, a Shuswap Indian consultant told us that in the Thompson River near Deadman's Creek, where the river is swift but not deep, Shuswap people would sometimes pile rocks about 6 m (20 ft.) out into the river to create a back-eddy. The sockeye would try to hide in these artificial back-eddies, where they would be caught using a dip net (Kennedy 1974). However, because the Fraser River in the vicinity of Lillooet is deep and contains numerous protruding rocks creating back-eddies, such human-made breakwaters were not required.

Gill Net

Today, much of the salmon caught on the Fraser River by the *Stl'átl'imx* is fished using a gill net, called *stlheyn*. Sam Mitchell maintained that gill nets came into use after European contact. In 1940, only five gill nets were observed in use between Fountain and Texas Creek. Permits for its use were issued solely to the elderly and the infirm (Tremper 1940).

Nowadays gill nets are used when the water is either too high or too low to use a set-net or dip net. Several of the fishing sites where the early run of spring salmon was formerly caught using a set-net and scaffold are now fished using a gill net. In this method of fishing, salmon become caught when they swim with the river currents into back-eddies across which gill nets are set. The nets are suspended from a pole or from a cable slung over the river. The larger salmon manage to push their heads through the net but then are unable to extract themselves once the net is around their gills. The salmon do not see the gill net, because it is obscured by the muddy Fraser River.

Scoop Net

According to Teit (1900:250), nets used for the capture of small fish had the mesh attached directly to the bow. This is consistent with data elicited from Thompson Indian consultants (Kennedy 1974-76). *Nts'ets'kwaz7éyn* and *nlhukwmn* are *Stl'átl'imx* terms that both refer to small scoop nets. In 1974, such nets were still being made and used to scoop out trout from small creeks when these fish went upstream to spawn (SM). Formerly, scoop nets were also used for scooping fish out of basketry traps (see the following section).

Harpoon and Gaff Hook

Teit (1906:228) reported that the single and double-pronged harpoons

PLATE 6.5
Indian man holding a gaff hook in the vicinity of Lillooet,
in the early 1900s. Note the abundant salmon in the water here.

used by the Lillooet were similar to those of the Thompson, and that they were used from shore (Plate 6.5). He also stated that 'very long-handled spears and gaff hooks' were used for catching fish in muddy pools or large eddies, but he did not specify whether these latter sites were on the Fraser. In his Thompson monograph, Teit (1900:252) stated that the Lower Thompson living along the Fraser River below Lytton seldom speared fish, owing to the muddy state of the river.

Presumably the situation was the same for the Lillooet, where the Fraser River is equally muddy, but we obtained very little information on this subject. Sam Mitchell confirmed that ideally the fish had to be seen before harpoons could be used, but he observed long-handled gaff hooks being used in the Fraser during his time.

Gaff hooks were not used traditionally by the *Stl'átl'imx*, according to SM, but became common after iron was available. A photograph taken in the early 1900s shows a fisherman using a long-handled gaff hook at the Six Mile Rapids. Sam Mitchell stated that one place where sockeye salmon were fished using a gaff hook was at *menmánalts* (site No. 33e), and that spring salmon could be gaffed at the place called *púlhmekw* (site No. 33f), which is also at the Six Mile Rapids. The use of gaff-hooks at the Six Mile fishery was prohibited in 1944 (Killick 1945) due to the high number of fish that were injured but not caught when gaffs were used.

Gaff hooks measuring about three metres (ten ft.) long and with a detachable head were used to fish in the Seton River between Anderson and Seton lakes, according to Solomon Peter. The head of the gaff used here had both a point and a hook. The gaff was held above the water, and then once the fish was seen it could be either speared or hooked (Powell 1988: personal communication).

Tsiḵtn and *tl'exwḵw* are the *Stl'átl'imx* terms referring to harpoons. Sam Mitchell described the harpoon as a single-pronged implement consisting of a detachable head that was connected by a length of twine to a long fir-pole handle, sometimes as much as 6 m (20 ft.) in length. The head of the harpoon was about 5 cm (2 in.) long and consisted of a bone point fitted between two thin valves, called *p'ústen,* whittled from either juniper (*Juniperus scopulorum*) or mock-orange (*Philadelphus lewisii*) wood (some archaeological examples of bone have also been recovered). The foreshaft of the harpoon, which was fastened securely to the handle, fit snugly between the two valves. When the fish was impaled, the harpoon head became detached. Then the fish was hauled to shore by means of the line connecting the harpoon head to the handle. The only specific place that Sam Mitchell identified as a harpoon site was the Bridge River, where *Stl'átl'imx* fishermen obtained spring salmon.

Leister (Three-pronged Spear)

Steelhead, trout, and whitefish were formerly fished using a leister or three-pronged spear called *wawtsk.* When the spear was thrust straight down, hitting the back of the fish, the outer prongs spread slightly apart and then settled in either side of the fish while the centre prong impaled the spine.

Such a spear was used in clear water, especially in creeks and streams among fallen trees where the fish rest. Sam Mitchell stated that trees were sometimes felled across the stream near the outlet of Loon Lake to stop the trout as they went downstream to spawn. Either a three-pronged spear (whose head in recent years was made from iron) or a gaff hook was then used to remove the trapped fish from the stream.

Teit (1906:228) noted that three-pronged spears could be used from rafts and canoes, and that fish were speared by torch light or by the aid of fires built on rafts. He added that the construction of the Lillooet three-pronged spears was similar to those he described for the Thompson Indians (Teit 1900:252).

sm was also familiar with the construction of three-pronged spears.

He described the head of the spear as about 30 cm (1 ft.) long and consisting of three juniper or Rocky Mountain maple (*Acer glabrum*) wood prongs. The outer two prongs were the same length, about 30 cm (1 ft.) long, and the centre prong was about 15 cm (6 in.) in length. Each of the outer prongs was fitted with a 5 cm (2 in.) bone barb fastened securely with sinew and glued using the sticky gum from the spring buds of the cottonwood tree (*Populus balsamifera*). The centre prong was fitted with a bone point. In more recent times, iron has been used for the prongs and point. A three-finger space was left between the centre point and the outer barbs. Usually, the head of the spear was attached firmly to a fir pole handle, but sometimes these spears were made with a detachable spear-head.

Basketry Traps

Basketry traps were used for catching spawning trout in streams near the outlets of lakes and for sockeye salmon smolt (fingerlings) during the time they passed downstream from the lakes on their way to the ocean. Lillooet basketry traps were apparently the same as those used among the Thompson and Shuswap people and consisted of a box-shaped trap constructed from split pieces of pine wood and a cylindrical trap made of willow saplings. Both were used in creeks near the outlets of lakes or near the mouths of creeks flowing into lakes. Basketry traps could also be used along the banks of rivers where the current was swift. The fish would pass out through the upper end of the trap and into a small corral made of sticks and brush, from which they were speared or scooped out with a small dip net (Teit 1906:228).

The use in some streams of double weirs with traps set into the lower weir was also recorded by Teit (1906:228). Once the fish entered the traps, they swam through to the area between the two weirs where the fishermen either scooped them up or speared them.

A cylindrical basketry trap observed by Fisheries Commissioner J.P. Babcock in May 1903 was being used in the creek connecting Anderson and Seton lakes. He described it as follows:

> It was an ingenious and most destructive contrivance, built in the form of a great funnel. Its wings were made of logs, green boughs, willow brush and rock. At its lower end there was a basket-trap into which the fish were swept by the swift waters, and from which they were removed by the Indians. While the water passed more or less freely through the wings of the dam, the brush prevented the fish from doing so. (Babcock 1904:f9)

The *Stl'átl'imx* call basketry traps sk'ezák. Sam Mitchell stated that they were often conical in shape, measured about 1.5 m (4.5 ft.) long, and were constructed from red willow (*Cornus stolonifera*) saplings. The mouth of the trap was fitted with an inwardly-radiating hoop of willow sticks that prevented the fish from swimming back out of the trap once they had entered it. These 'teeth' were called kwákwelxwa. Larger versions of this trap sometimes had an open top that allowed the fisherman to scoop out the trapped fish. Sam Mitchell and Paul Hickson both stated that anyone was free to take the salmon smolt and trout that were caught in such a trap.

Wing Weir

Sam Mitchell's grandmother described to him a special device used during spring for fishing in the Fraser River at the place called *npim* (site No. 12). We have called this device a 'wing weir'; the *Stl'átl'imx* call it *ts'akín*.

Apparently groups of people joined together in constructing such a weir. They gathered on the riverbank, upstream from the large back-eddy at *npim*. Each person took with them armloads of cottonwood saplings and branches which were then woven together into a long latticework weir, sometimes measuring 16 m (50 ft.) in length. The weir was tied with willow withes.

The end of the weir nearest the back-eddy was anchored to the shore. Then several strong men, holding the end of the weir furthest upstream from the back-eddy, carried the weir into the river current. Once it was caught by the river current, the weir swung downstream, herding the fish into the back-eddy and toward the shore. When the free-flowing end of the weir got near the shore, the fishermen hauled it in by pulling on a rope tied to the end of the weir. Then the people waded into the river and scooped up the trapped fish. Sam Mitchell was told that suckers and squawfish were most often caught when this wing weir was used.

Louis Phillips, a Thompson Indian from Lytton, recalled the old people telling him that Thompson Indians used to fish in a similar manner, but instead of utilizing a floating weir made of brush, his people used a long net. This net was operated by a man in a canoe or boat who guided one end of the net downstream and then circled back into shore (Kennedy 1974-6).

Line Fishing

Set lines, called kiytl', were left overnight in back-eddies. One end was tied to a stake or bush on the shore and the other end was anchored on the bottom of the lake or river. Each set line was about 8 m (25 ft.) in length and had a number of shorter lines, each with a baited hook, tied at regularly spaced intervals along the main line. Ling fish and Dolly Varden char were often fished using a set line (SM). Slim Jackson told us about a place called *kwzaĺtst* (site No. 11) on the Fraser River where sturgeon were caught using set lines. Teit (1906:228) noted that hooks were formerly made from bone, wood, and spines of the black hawthorn (*Crataegus douglasii*) bush. Some were made from copper and were similar in shape to the double-bone hook used among the Thompson (Teit 1900:253), that is, two barbs tied together. The *Stl'átl'imx* call the barb of a hook *ntl-lixtn*. Hooks were baited with fish eggs, fish eyes, maggots, or small fish. The term referring to a fish regurgitating a hook is *kw'elkw'úlhkw'eltm*, and fishing with a hook and line is called *íwas*.

Sam Mitchell recalled fishing with a pole and line when he was a young boy. His line was hemp and attached to it was a .5 m (1.5 ft.) leader line made from braided human hair and baited with a spring salmon egg. The fish was usually caught when the bait became lodged in its throat.

Ice-fishing engaged both *Stl'átl'imx* men and women. First a hole was cut through the ice (this hole is called *xetkálkam*). Then the fishing line was tied to the centre of a pole laid across this hole. A dome-shaped framework covered with fir boughs was built over the top of the hole to conceal it from the fish. Sometimes these shelters were large enough for a person to sit inside on a layer of boughs placed around the fishing hole (SM).

PRESERVATION TECHNIQUES

Sam Mitchell demonstrated how the blood is drained from freshly caught salmon after they are taken to an area of the riverbank designated for this task. The smaller salmon, such as sockeye and coho, are bled by pulling back the head until the spinal cord is severed. Pulling the fish's head back in this fashion is called *pétskwekw*. The fish is held vertically and, as the heart continues to pump for several minutes, spurts of dark blood drain from the salmon. Spring salmon are bled by inserting a 50 cm (20 in.) long, paddle-shaped fir or birch wood stick into the fish's mouth and using it as a lever to pull back the head and sever the spinal cord. A knife is then thrust into the area below the fish's gills. The heart continues to pump out the remaining blood while the fish is being held vertical by its tail. Sam Mitchell explained that a fish caught in a dip net and bled immediately after it is taken out of the water dries a lighter colour than a fish caught in a gill net and left in the river overnight.

In former times, the people sometimes constructed a rock corral, called *lúxwelts*, alongside the river or stream in which the fish were left to bleed overnight. One of these corrals was used at the fishing spot known as *xwusesús* (site No. 33b) (SM). After the fish are bled they are carried up to where the women will process them. The *Stl'átl'imx* term for carrying fish up from the river is *zúxweltn* – this was done either by means of a large basket or by threading the fish onto a willow withe. Today, an opened coat hanger is used for this purpose. Before the salmon is butchered, its slime is scraped off the skin with a knife. Then the skin is wiped off with a rag or grass. Traditionally, women butchered the fish and preserved it for winter. Yet in the 1970s, we observed both men and women performing this task.

Wind-Drying

In the past, spring and sockeye salmon caught from August onward, as well as steelhead, rainbow, silver trout, and kokanee, were preserved for winter storage by wind-drying. Wind-dried fish is called *sts'wan* in the *Stl'átl'imx* language. Today, sockeye salmon are still preserved in this manner, although increasingly large numbers of fish are being frozen.

It was estimated that, in 1940, 88 per cent of the sockeye caught were dried, with the remaining 12 per cent eaten fresh (8 per cent) or salted (4 per cent) (Tremper 1940). Correspondence between Fisheries and Indian Affairs officials in 1915-16 suggests that the practice of salting salmon before it was hung on the drying racks was introduced by the Fishery Guardian. He believed that few of the dried salmon being preserved by the Indians without the use of salt were of a suitable condition to store all winter (Cunningham 1915; Webster 1916).

Susan Mitchell demonstrated the steps in butchering sockeye salmon when we visited the Six Mile fishery in August 1974. She noted that small spring salmon could also be cut in this fashion. What follows is a description of her method of cutting salmon: The first step in preparing salmon for wind-drying, Susan Mitchell explained, was to remove the head. After doing this, she placed the salmon in front of her, with the tail end nearest to her body. The salmon was cut down its dorsal side and around one side of its rib cage, so that one half of the fish could be folded flat. At that point the sack of milt or eggs was removed. Next, the dark blood was scraped off the inside of the exposed backbone.

The flesh of the opened half of the salmon flank was then scored horizontally, at about 2 cm (.75 in.) intervals, right through to the skin (see Plate 6.3). Susan explained that scoring the flesh allowed a greater amount of it to be exposed to the air and, therefore, to dry more quickly. The process of scoring the flesh is called *nxils* in the *Stl'átl'imx* language.

Mrs. Mitchell then turned the salmon so that its head end was towards her, and she cut along the other side of the backbone. Additional small cuts had to be made so that the second half-flank would lie flat. She cut the white, fatty strip containing the dorsal fin away from the backbone and rib cage section. This piece was eaten fresh, as it was considered too oily to dry.

The backbone was left connected to the flank at the tail end. She placed it to one side while she scored the flesh on the second half of the opened flank (see Plate 6.3). Then the flesh on the backbone was also scored. A small handful of salt was sprinkled over the flesh.

The salmon flank was hung by straddling the fish over a pole on the drying rack, tail upward, with the backbone section on one side balancing the weight of the flank on the other side of the pole. The flank was kept from folding by a saskatoon wood (*Amelanchier alnifolia*) salmon stretcher, called *ts'ekw7íkw*, that pierced the backbone and the far side of the opposite flank.

Sam Mitchell remarked that the *sts'wan* could also be cut so that the backbone was separated from the flank. After this was done, two holes were made near the tail end of the fish, completely through the flank. It was through this hole that a stick was then inserted by which the flank could be hung between two poles on the drying rack. The flank was kept from folding by placing a salmon stretcher across the skin side of the fish. As for the backbone, it was simply laid across one of the poles on the drying rack. Both Sam and Susan Mitchell referred to the dried backbones as 'neckties' and stated that the old-timers considered these 'neckties' a real delicacy. In the 1970s, older *Stl'átl'imx* people, such as Sam and Susan Mitchell, were still drying the salmon backbones and using them for fish soup during the winter.

Formerly, women used a slightly different method when butchering large spring salmon for wind-drying, SM recalled. Once the flank was opened, as demonstrated by Susan in the previous cutting style, the centre section of the flank was then cut out and eaten fresh. This was done because the oil in the belly area would eventually become tainted and spoil the rest of the flesh if preserved for storage. The flesh on the large flank was scored in the same manner as it was for sockeye. One or two salmon stretchers were then placed across the large spring salmon flank and poked into the backbone opposite it.

Sam Mitchell observed that drying racks used by the *Stl'átl'imx* people at the Six Mile fisheries in the 1970s were constructed in the same manner as those which were used when he was young. Such racks are called *lhemlhímen*. They are constructed on the riverbanks where a constant wind blows and where the yellow-jackets are fewer than at higher elevations. The salmon are hung on the rack so that the flesh faces the river, allowing the wind (which blows parallel to the river) to blow across the scored flanks.

Numerous racks are maintained on both sides of the Fraser River at the Six Mile fishery and are used yearly by the same families. In recent times, some families have been taking their catch to dry in shelters built beside their home. These drying racks are two-storey structures, in which the salmon are dried on the screened racks of the upper storey and then stored below where the structure is fully enclosed.

Sam Mitchell noted that he knew of only one site along the Fraser where fish cannot be wind-dried – this is the area up the riverbank from the site known as *nlikw'kánm* (site No. 33d in Appendix). He explained that this is a treed area where there is not enough of a direct breeze to dry the fish. Only a few hundred metres away, the conditions are again favourable.

Sts'wan takes about five or six days to dry sufficiently for storage, Susan Mitchell said, but during these few days, the drying salmon is exposed to many hazards. 'Blow flies' are a particular problem because they lay eggs on the hanging fish and these develop into maggots, which are called *mags* in the *Stl'átl'imx* language. One of the ways to reduce the chances of this problem occurring is by keeping a smudge fire lit underneath the drying rack (in Chapter 5, Romanoff records that the danger from flies is greater after 20 August).

During the time that the fish wind-dries, the sun is not permitted to strike the flesh, for it will draw the oil to the surface, causing the flesh to separate from the skin and leaving a space in which insects can deposit their eggs. Susan Mitchell noted that the *Stl'átl'imx* term referring to fish that has been so affected is *kw'ástnam*. There is a greater chance of this happening when the weather is particularly hot. The hot sun draws out the oil, which can then become rancid and cause the flesh of the salmon to turn yellow (SM).

The eggs of spring and sockeye salmon removed from the fish during butchering are hung over a pole near the outside of the drying rack, where they can be dried by the sun. Sun-dried salmon eggs are called *k'axalhkw'úna*. Formerly, the milt was kept to one side to be barbecued and eaten; it was never dried.

Salmon heads cut off when the fish are being butchered for wind-drying are also dried for winter storage. For large spring salmon, the head must be cut almost in half to expose the inside of the head. Next, the brains are removed and a second cut is made down either half of the opened head. This is done to maximize the amount of the inside flesh being exposed to the wind and sun. Then a cut is made partly around the eyes so that they hang from their socket, as the eyes, too, are dried and eaten. (Sam Mitchell had not recalled this technique when interviewed by Romanoff [Chapter 5]). Another *Stl'átl'imx* Indian, the late Tommy Napolean, told Romanoff (Chapter 5) that salmon heads were not smoked, although in the past the heads were split, barbecued, and placed on a rack to dry. The sockeye heads can simply be cut in half, threaded on a piece of twine, and hung from a pole on the drying rack. In the winter, dried salmon heads are soaked in water and then boiled for soup (SM).

Once the *sts'wan* has dried sufficiently on the drying rack, the backbone is separated from the flank and the latter are stacked up and tied together in bundles. Sam Mitchell stated that the salmon is not fully dry at this stage, so it can become mouldy. To prevent this from occurring, *Stl'átl'imx* people store their *sts'wan* in wooden boxes with a layer of rock salt sprinkled lightly between the fish. In former times, the *sts'wan* was stored in raised caches constructed so that the wind could continue to blow through the bundles of dried fish stored within them. Such a cache was called *p'ákw'ulh*. Dry pine needles were sometimes placed between the layers of *sts'wan* to help prevent it from becoming mouldy.

In the past, when the *sts'wan* was removed from the cache it was either eaten as it was, boiled with a variety of dried roots and berries and made into a soup, or toasted over a fire. 'Toasting' the dried fish is called *zem̓*. On several occasions throughout the 1970s we observed older *Stl'átl'imx* people toasting either a piece of dried salmon or a piece of skin left after eating dried salmon. These were placed on the end of a small stick and held over the fire. The heat draws the oil to the surface of the dried flesh, causing it to become softer. The *Stl'átl'imx* term referring to eating dried salmon is k̲'a7. Dried fins cut from a piece of *sts'wan* and then soaked in water were formerly used to nurse a motherless infant (SM).

Sockeye caught late in the season, around September, could be dried using a much simpler method than was required to cut fish for wind-drying, Sam Mitchell recalled. He explained that the fish are very thin at this time of the year and are referred to as *lhék̲w'ela7*. To prepare these salmon, the head was removed. Then the fish was cut along the dorsal side and around each side of the rib cage, so that the backbone and rib section was separated from the flank. Any eggs or milt inside the fish were left in place. After a salmon stretcher was placed across the flank to keep it from folding over, the fish was hung from a tree limb or pole on the drying rack and left there until fully dried. Although these fish dried easily, their flesh became extremely hard, once dry. Sam Mitchell stated that such fish were actually freeze-dried, as it was too late in the year for the wind to be warm enough to wind-dry them. Sockeye dried at this time had to be soaked overnight before being eaten.

This method is similar to a process of freeze-drying whole fish used formerly by the Lower (Mount Currie) Lillooet and Chase Shuswap to cure coho caught in November and by the Colville-Okanagan to cure spawned spring salmon. Each method was slightly different. The Lower Lillooet did not clean the coho salmon, although they did make an incision in its neck to drain the blood. Two fish were tied together around the tail and were hung over a tree branch to dry (Kennedy and Bouchard 1975c).

The Chase Shuswap people removed the head and viscera from coho that they processed late in the year. The fish was cut along its dorsal line completely through to its ventral side so that the spine was left on one side. Then the fish was straddled over a pole on the drying rack and left to air-dry. The Chase Shuswap also used this method to preserve late-caught kokanee and spring-caught trout (Kennedy and Bouchard 1975a).

Spring (king) salmon preserved late in the year by the Colville-Okanagan were fish that had already spawned and were picked up by hand from the river shore. They were bled and eviscerated. Additional small cuts were made in the flesh around the spine. Then the fish was hung from a tree limb by means of a small hole pierced through its tail end (Kennedy and Bouchard 1975b).

Freeze-dried salmon produced using these three methods were used in the early spring for making soup (after the dried fish had been soaked overnight). Apparently such fish were considered tasty, despite their strong smell.

Smoke-Drying

Sockeye salmon and white spring salmon could be smoke-dried. First the fish was cut into two large filets and left in the sun to dry slightly. Then it was laid flesh-side down on a low smoke-drying rack, where it was left for about three days while it smoke-dried. Each day the filet was turned. The smoked fish, called *sts'kaz̓*, could be eaten immediately after being smoke-dried or stored for winter. Occasionally it was boiled with saskatoon berries for soup.

The latticework top of the smoke-drying rack, which was made from saskatoon wood saplings, was about a metre (39 in.) above a small alder (*Alnus rubra*) wood or driftwood fire. Sam Mitchell noted that bedsprings have been used for smoke-drying racks in recent times. In Chapter 5, Romanoff reports that Tommy Napoleon described a method of preparing the fattest fish of each run, particularly spring salmon, that appears to be similar to the method Sam Mitchell called 'smoke-drying.'

Powdered Salmon

Powdered salmon was called *tupál*. It was stored in a basket and eaten mixed with salmon oil (see section on oil) and saskatoon berries. Sam Mitchell remarked that it was a good food for hunters because 'one handful kept you going all day.' Solomon Peter (Powell 1988, personal communication) referred to powdered salmon as 'trail mix.' The preparation of powdered salmon as described by Romanoff in Chapter 5 is confirmed by information we recorded from Sam Mitchell and Paul Hickson. Today, dried salmon is simply pounded with a hammer or pestle to make powdered salmon. It is sometimes sprinkled on soup and pasta dishes (Powell 1988, personal communication).

Barbecuing

Barbecuing was likely the most common method of cooking fish for immediate consumption in former times. Whole fish, flanks of salmon, and large steaks of fish could all be barbecued. The *Stl'átl'imx* term used to refer to barbecuing several small fish is *tl'nának*. The fish were placed horizontally, head to tail, between the split of a forked iron-wood (*Holodiscus discolor*) or red cedar (*Thuja plicata*) barbecue stick, called *stl'áksatn*. Then, the top of the split stick was tied to hold the fish firmly in place while they barbecued in front of a fire.

A forked barbecuing stick was also used when cooking one opened flank of salmon. Three small sticks were inserted between the skin and the flesh of the salmon flank to keep it from folding. Then it was clamped in the forked barbecuing stick and set, flesh-side first, to cook in front of the fire. The *Stl'átl'imx* term for barbecuing one large piece of fish is *stl'áksa7*. Salmon heads were also barbecued in a forked stick. The heads of large spring salmon had to be split open along the jaw and spread apart before placing them, one above the other, in the stick. Barbecued salmon heads are called *nkw'élekw*. Pieces of fish, or whole fish, were pierced with a single barbecue stick, called *kw'élten*, and also barbecued before a fire for immediate consumption.

Boiling

The *Stl'átl'imx* term *ízus* refers to 'boiling.' This method of cooking could be used for any fish. Formerly, food was boiled in baskets of water heated with hot rocks. Once a rock had been heated in the fire, it was picked up with tongs and set down in the basket of water and fish. As the rocks cooled, they were removed and replaced with hot ones. The rocks were prevented from burning the basket by a rack of saskatoon sticks placed on the bottom. Boiled dried salmon is called *ntspus* and boiled fish heads are called *npúplhekw*.

Salmon Oil

In Chapter 5, Romanoff describes the essential features of salmon oil (*smík'il*) production. Here, we simply add several details. Sam Mitchell stated that salmon oil used to be made in a distinctive rock basin located on the east side of the Six Mile fishery, about 16 m back from the riverbank at the site known as *nlikw'kánm* (site No. 33d). We observed this rock basin, called *ntsepkwtn*, to be a little over a metre (39 in.) in diameter, although SM remembered it as being twice as large (see Chapter 5).

The process of rendering oil was conducted under the supervision of an old man (SM). The cracks in the rock were plastered with mud to prevent leaking. A fire piled high with rocks used for boiling was then built inside the basin and left until the fire burnt down. The ashes were swept out of the hole and the remaining hot rocks covered with saskatoon sticks and rye grass. Then water, along with salmon heads, salmon eggs, and all the fatty parts of the fish, was added to the basin and left to boil to extract the fish oil. The following morning, the saskatoon sticks and grass were removed and the yellow-coloured scum was skimmed from the top of the basin. Underneath this was the reddish-brown coloured salmon oil which floated on top of the water. Salmon oil could also be rendered by boiling it in baskets (see Chapter 5).

Buried Eggs

Eggs taken from spring and sockeye salmon caught during September could be preserved for winter after being prepared in a special manner. The eggs were placed inside a birch bark basket, covered, and buried several feet underground (SM). Bill Edwards noted that the eggs were sometimes buried directly in a hole dug in the ground and lined with the leaves of the poison ivy (*Rhus radicans*) plant. In the spring, the buried eggs, called *lep'alhkw'úna*, were dug up and boiled together with tiger lily (*Lilium columbianum*) bulbs and bitter-roots (*Lewisia rediviva*), the latter received through trade from the Thompson Indians of the Ashcroft area. The buried spring salmon eggs remained red in colour, whereas the sockeye eggs turned black or brown (SM).

USES OF SALMON IN TECHNOLOGY

The *Stl'átl'imx* people not only ate salmon but also used it in the manufacture of various items, including jars, shoes, paint, and soap. Sam Mitchell saw his grandmother and an old man demonstrate the process used to make salmon skin jars, called *nmík'iltn*, which were strong enough to hold fish oil: first, a whole salmon was placed on a roasting rack over the fire and turned occasionally until the inside of the fish swelled. Then the head and tail were cut off and the bones and flesh removed from the inside of the salmon. The skin was washed clean. After the tail end was tied tightly, the vent and any other holes in the skin were plugged and glued with the slime from the outside of salmon eggs. The salmon skin jar was then left to dry. Once the salmon oil was poured into this container, the top of it was tied. Salmon-skin jars were made from both spring and sockeye salmon. Slight variations in this procedure were recorded by Romanoff (1985:135).

Salmon oil was used as a condiment, a hair oil (SM; Teit 1906:221), and as a medicine for what Sam Mitchell described as 'sore tonsils.' The use of salmon oil as a hair tonic has a mythological origin: When Owl abducted a young girl, he wiped his mucus in the girl's hair instead of the fish oil that she requested. But finally Owl went to gather some oil and she rubbed it in her hair. This is why, Sam Mitchell concluded, past generations of *Stl'átl'imx* people used salmon oil in their hair. Salmon oil used as hair oil is called *smik'ilúliya*.

Teit (1906:221) recorded that water in which semi-decomposed salmon eggs had been soaked was used for washing the face. However, perhaps one of the most intriguing applications for salmon was the use of its skin by poorer people for making shoes (Teit 1906:219). One style of shoe made of salmon skin was the sandal. The skin was cut to the shape of the foot and then furnished with strings for attaching around the foot and ankle. The sole was created by thickly smearing the salmon-leather with pine or fir gum that had been mixed with earth or sand. After being worn for one day, the sole was again treated in the same manner, after which the sandals' thick sole was quite sturdy. An example of such a pair of sandals is now in the collections of the American Museum of Natural History in New York City (artifact No. 16/8128).

Moccasin-style shoes were also made from salmon skins. A photograph of a pair of salmon skin moccasins that is presently in the collections of the Field Museum of Natural History in Chicago (artifact No. 11774) is published in *Lillooet Stories* (Bouchard and Kennedy 1977:67).

Sam Mitchell noted that the slime from the skin of a salmon, and also that from around the outside of the salmon's eggs, was mixed with burnt and powdered red ochre and used to make pictographs (rock paintings). Dried salmon heads could be used instead of deer brains for tanning hides if animal brains were not available (SM).

DISCUSSION OF *STL'ÁTL'IMX* FISHERIES

Each salmon species is available for harvesting only several weeks of the year (see Chapter 4), at times known by former *Stl'átl'imx* fishermen to correspond with other natural phenomena, such as the flowering of certain plants. Knowledge of the seasonality of salmon runs had considerable impact upon the seasonal movements of aboriginal *Stl'átl'imx* people. But as Kew notes in Chapter 4, access to salmon (both physical and technological) is as important as their presence (availability) in an environment.

Limitations to the Salmon Catch

The Appendix to this report describes approximately fifty fishing sites along the Fraser River between Della Creek and Pavilion Creek that are known to have been used (and in many cases are still being used) by the *Stl'átl'imx*. Some of these sites were made unusable by fluctuating river levels, especially during times of extremely high or low water. High water throughout June severely restricted the number of available fishing sites. Fishing rocks were not accessible to the majority of fishermen until August. For example, detailed catchment records compiled by Fisheries officers during the 1943 fishing season indicate that only fishing stations on the west side of the old highway bridge were in use for the first two weeks of the July run, and that a single man fished here each day. By the first week of August, all fishing areas were used, although no more than sixteen fishermen were employed on any one day (Killick 1943c).

It appears these fluctuating river levels were the most important factor governing physical access to salmon runs by the *Stl'átl'imx*. An example of the effect that water level had on the availability of the salmon run is contained in a 1913 report to the Commissioner of Fisheries by an unnamed observer of the Lillooet fisheries. He stated that the Indians at no time during July or August caught more salmon than they consumed or disposed of locally, due to the high water flowing over many of the rocky outcrops where the people normally fished (Anon. 1913).

In 1916, high water prevented use of the Six Mile fishery in early August, generally a time when large numbers of *Stl'átl'imx* people camped there to fish. The local Fisheries Guardian for the federal government noted that the river level was higher than it had been for several years, and that all the fishing rocks at Six Mile were under water. But *Stl'átl'imx* fishermen had alternate strategies for such times; the fisheries officer noted that instead of fishing at Six Mile, the Indian people caught salmon at Leon Creek, and at 'a place about half way between Lillooet and Lytton [which may possibly have been the fishery at Seah I.R. 5]' as well as along both banks of the Fraser River several miles below the Six Mile rapids (Webster 1916).

Sam Mitchell confirmed that before the water had dropped sufficiently to fish from the majority of fishing rocks at Six Mile, the Fountain people caught salmon at other sites, among them the fishery known as *yegwúg̱wsntm* (site No. 40) near Gibbs Creek.

Our review of *Stl'átl'imx* fishing sites along the Fraser suggests that these alternative sites likely satisfied the immediate needs of the people who later fished at Six Mile. Possibly, these sites would not provide the sufficient quantities of salmon required for winter storage. Furthermore, these alternative sites were not used by Lillooet groups from beyond the immediate area or by non-Lillooet speaking peoples. It was only at the public Six Mile sites, by far the most productive fishery, that large numbers of Indian people, both *Stl'átl'imx* and their neighbours, converged each August and September to fish and trade (see Chapter 5).

Catches of several hundred salmon per day per fisherman were possible during the few peak days in a run. Our review of the available data indicates that even in the early 1940s, when the recorded sockeye harvest ranged from only 6,000 to 10,000 fish, Lillooet fishermen averaged 6.5 days at their fishery and obtained sufficient salmon to provide every registered Upper Lillooet Band member with between 10 and 15 sockeye, exclusive of the supplemental catches of spring, coho, and pink salmon.

Just as extreme high water caused problems for the fisherman, extreme low water created problems for the fish. According to a 1912 Fisheries report, the water during the last two weeks of September in that year was so severely low that no sockeye could pass through, and yet 'the number of Indians assembled there . . . was greater even than in the years of big runs.' Estimates of the number of fish dried on the Indians' racks at Six Mile at this time were in excess of 30,000 (Anon. 1912).

Assistant Provincial Fisheries Commissioner J.P. Babcock reflected on the conditions of the Bridge River fishery in 1912. At a conference on fishing held in 1914 during the investigations of the Royal Commission on Indian Affairs, Babcock said that thousands of fish were caught at Bridge River in 1912 but that 'the women could only clean and dry a limited number and they naturally took the freshest caught fish and let the others go to waste' (Babcock 1914b).

Babcock was commenting on another potential restriction concerning the availability of salmon to the *Stl'átl'imx* – the limits imposed by an insufficient female work force to butcher the catch. One of the *Stl'átl'imx* Indian consultants cited in Chapter 5 stated that a woman could cut fifty or sixty salmon per day. Our own observations fully support Romanoff's conclusion that a fisherman could easily catch much more than this limit while the run was at its peak.

It is not clear to what extent slave labour alleviated this labour shortage, if at all. Although Teit (1906:233, 236) reported that the *Stl'átl'imx* both bought and sold slaves and had a tradition of having taken many slaves from the Squamish, Mainland Comox, and Stalo, he also noted that the *Stl'átl'imx* seldom went on raiding expeditions and were not so 'warlike' as other Interior tribes.

Possibly the problem of surplus fish was resolved by, and partially explains, the polygynous practices of the wealthier families with greatest access to productive fishing sites. Perhaps surpluses could also be distributed for butchering to people from more distant villages, who then butchered and cured the salmon themselves.

The manner in which timing and water levels are limiting factors on the productivity of salmon fishing is evident in the following examination of *Stl'átl'imx* sockeye fishing. The data base consists of detailed catchment records kept by Fisheries Officers during the 1942, 1943, and 1944 fishing seasons. These data are summarized in Table 1. Data compiled for the 1941 season are incomplete but have been included for comparative purposes inasmuch as this year had a significantly larger sockeye harvest than did the three following. Included in Table 1 is the number of fishermen using each fishing area, each man's mean annual catch, the mean number of days spent fishing, and the mean catch per day per fisherman. Figure 1 illustrates the daily productivity during the 1943 season of the main four fishing areas: the west side of the Bridge River rapids; the east side of the Bridge River rapids, the west side of the old highway bridge, and the east side of the old

TABLE 1
Salmon yields at specific fishing sites near Lillooet, 1941-4

Name of Fishery	n^*	$\bar{x}$ total catch per man	$\bar{x}$ total days spent fishing	$\bar{x}$ catch per day per man
1941 fishing season				
West side of Bridge River rapids	20	214	n/a	n/a
East side of Bridge River rapids	35	125	n/a	n/a
Both sides of old highway bridge	20	175	n/a	n/a
Texas Creek	5	40	n/a	n/a
Miscellaneous sites	6	66	n/a	n/a
1942 fishing season				
West side of Bridge River rapids	19	195	5.5	35
East side of Bridge River rapids	26	135	5.5	25
East side of old highway bridge	6	155	9	26
West side of old highway bridge	11	133	12.5	11
Texas Creek	2	85	2	43†
Miscellaneous sites	7	80	3	27
1943 fishing season				
West side of Bridge River rapids	16	114	6.75	17
East side of Bridge River rapids	27	87	4.5	20
East side of old highway bridge	6	96	10.5	9
West side of old highway bridge	9	75	9.5	8
Texas Creek	4	135	11.5	12
Miscellaneous sites	11	83.5	6	14
1944 fishing season				
West side of Bridge River rapids	25	128	4	31
East side of Bridge River rapids	36	70	4	20
Both sides of old highway bridge	11	70	4	17

*n = number of fishermen
† gill-net fishing

highway bridge. Figures 2 & 3 provide additional data on the relative intensity of salmon catches over the summer months for 1926, 1944, 1948, and 1952.

In 1941, the heaviest fishing of the season occurred between 3 and 5 September. Only twelve men remained fishing this late in the season, as the majority of the workforce had already left for the Fraser Valley hopfields. Salmon were hauled to the surface at the rate of 105 fish per hour for all fishermen at all the fishing sites. The damp weather prevented the fish from being dried, but eight pack horses employed on the east side of the river transported the fresh sockeye back to the village for processing (Tremper 1941).

The 1942 fishing season saw a decrease in the number of *Stl'átl'imx* fishermen. The exile of the non-Indian labour force to military duty during the Second World War opened up local jobs to young Indian men as farmers, loggers, and general labourers. Additionally, some *Stl'átl'imx* men enlisted for military service. Children and older people were left to fish for themselves, apart from those men who fished during their off-hours.

The Fountain people comprised the largest number of individuals engaged in fishing in 1942, with twenty-eight families camped at one time or another on the east side of the Bridge River rapids for an average of 5.5 days. Although the water fluctuated greatly, the numerous rocks permitted these fishermen access to salmon for the duration of the season. Such was not the case for the Bridge River people, whose set-net fishing rocks on the west side of the Bridge River rapids were not visible until 10 August, at which time the water had dropped sufficiently to fish. Most of these people returned home each night to salt or dry their catch. Later in August, the Fraser had dropped to near blockage levels. The Fisheries officer reported that the Indians made a 'mass killing' and that fishing was so intense that no one bothered to fish when conditions were less than ideal. The use of a gill-net accounts for the seemingly large mean catch per day at the Texas Creek fishery, both in the 1941 and 1942 fishing seasons. In addition to the mean catch of 139 sockeye for each *Stl'átl'imx* fisherman during 1942, the Fisheries observer noted that 667 sockeye were caught by 'scattered fishermen not alloted to any particular reserve' (Killick 1943a).

Catches were poorer in the 1943 season. Nevertheless, those having access to fishing stations on the east bank of the Bridge River Rapids secured sockeye early in the season and moved from rock to rock as the water dropped. As many as seven tents were pitched on the flats above the river, according to the Fisheries officer, S.R. Killick. The west bank fishing stations were highly productive, with the mean seasonal catch of 114 sockeye (compared with 87 on the east bank) per fisher-

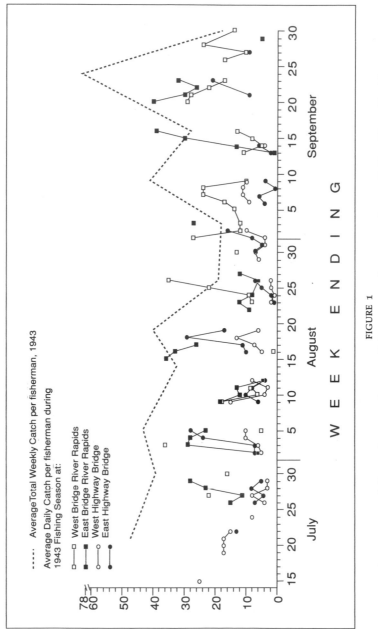

FIGURE 1

Average 1943 daily sockeye catches per fisherman at the east and west Bridge River Rapids, and the east and west Highway Bridge locations. The average total weekly sockeye catch per fisherman is also shown (data derived from Killick 1943c).

man taken from only a few sites that were usable for only a matter of days once the water had dropped. Few of the Bridge River people camped, choosing instead to return home after fishing each day (Killick 1943b).

The Shalalth fishermen camped near the old highway bridge, taking an average of only nine sockeye each. They spent twice as much time fishing as did those fishermen around the Bridge River rapids. Once the river had dropped to a level almost blocking the entire run, the Shalalth fishermen also moved to the Six Mile fishery where catches were plentiful and easily made (Killick 1943b).

During the 1944 fishing season, the federal Fisheries Department initiated a tag recovery program that provided independent calculation of the Indian sockeye catch based on the ratio of tagged to untagged fish caught during a specified period of time. This cross-check of catchment statistics suggested that approximately 30 per cent of the sockeye catch was unreported (Killick 1945). Statistics presented in Table 1 do not reflect this discrepancy. Such an adjustment to the mean total of sockeye taken by each fishermen would conform more closely to the estimated annual salmon requirement of forty fish per adult and twenty fish per child reported by a local Indian agent in 1933 (Strang 1933). Clearly, the salmon harvests for the 1942, 1943, and 1944 season barely met the personal consumption needs of the community, who at that time had increased their involvement in the wage economy and in tending their farms, at the expense of salmon fishing.

Access to Fishing Sites

Our *Stl'átl'imx* fishing data independently support the thesis presented by Romanoff in Chapter 5 that there were socially defined fishing sites within Fraser River Lillooet territory. Romanoff identifies three types of sites: (1) individually owned rocks suitable for catching spring salmon; (2) rocks along various sections of the river that were associated with residence groups; and (3) sites that were most productive, like some at the Six Mile fishery that were open to all the *Stl'átl'imx*, in addition to some outsiders. In the following section we review some of the evidence for stratified access to the fisheries that emerges from our detailed descriptions of the fifty *Stl'átl'imx* salmon fishing sites along the Fraser.

Because of the central importance of resource ownership to understanding other aspects of *Stl'átl'imx* life as well as other complex hunter/gatherer societies, we feel it is critical to establish a firm documentary foundation for ownership and to provide as many details as possible on all aspects of resource access. Our own presentation

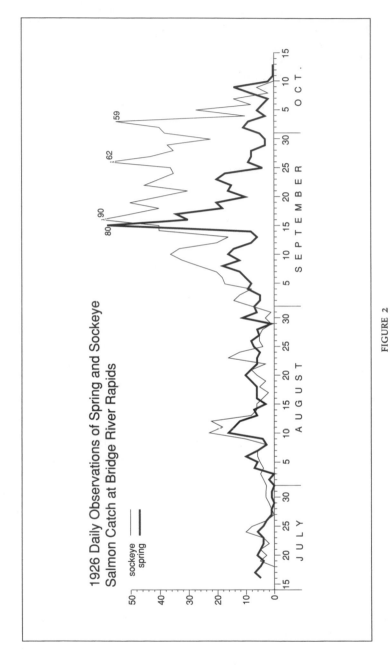

FIGURE 2

Daily observations on the number of spring and sockeye salmon caught at the
Bridge River Rapids in 1926 (data from Motherwell 1926a, b)

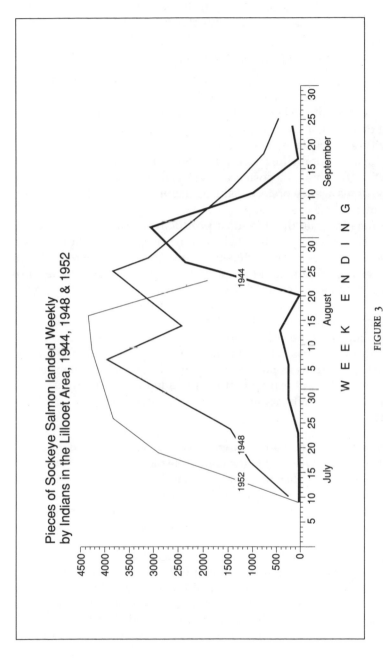

FIGURE 3

Pieces of sockeye salmon landed weekly by Indians in the Lillooet area in 1944, 1948, and 1952 (data from Killick 1945; Estabrook 1952; see also Argue et al. 1990)

may result in some duplication of data; however, given the theoretical importance of the topic, slight duplication is preferred to the risk of omitting details of potential importance.

Individually Owned Sites

Spring salmon was formerly the preferred species. These fish first arrived in April, when few other fresh foods were available. Furthermore, the flesh of the later spring salmon runs, according to SM, was less fat than that of sockeye and, consequently, could be stored longer and with less spoilage once the fish were wind-dried. This is confirmed in a questionnaire concerning native fishing practices completed by the Indian agent posted at Lytton in 1933. He noted that the Indians of his agency preferred spring salmon because they 'cure better' than the sockeye (Strang 1933).

Our data indicate that the most productive spring salmon fishing sites were owned by individuals. Sam Mitchell and Slim Jackson recalled the names of the owners for all but four sites where the April run of spring salmon could be caught. They noted that the level of the river resulted in few fishing rocks being accessible at this time of the year. Additionally, SM and SJ identified two named and individually owned fishing rocks where spring salmon could be caught late in the year. The type of salmon caught at three sites said to be individually owned was not specified, but according to Romanoff's thesis (Chapter 5), they were probably spring salmon procurement sites.

In a description of fishing that we included in *Lillooet Stories*, Sam Mitchell talked briefly about the individual ownership of *Stl'átl'imx* fisheries:

> Some dip-net fishing places . . . were owned by individuals, and the use of such spots was limited to the immediate members of that person's family. However, after that particular family had obtained enough salmon, then anybody could use that fishing rock. Nowadays, everyone is like a brother or sister; therefore it doesn't matter who uses any particular fishing rock. (Bouchard and Kennedy 1977:67)

SM stated further that the owner camped near his fishing rock, where he built a scaffold and fished using either a set-net or dip net which he supplied to visitors as well. Fishing spring salmon generally required this specialized equipment that the site owner maintained. After the owner had obtained as much as he needed or could process, he did not prevent others from using his equipment. Nor did the site owner receive payment in return for fishing privileges. Someone indicated his desire to fish at these owned sites simply by sitting down behind the fisherman-owner and waiting to be passed the net. The *Stl'átl'imx* term *alkwk* describes waiting for your turn to fish (sm).

As noted in Chapter 5, ownership of these early spring salmon rocks was hereditary. It would, therefore, remain the property of a group of individuals who lived and worked together. Sam Mitchell noted that if a man didn't have sons, his fishing rock could be passed down to his daughter, and, although she would not fish there herself, she was still acknowledged as the fishing rock owner. As with the male-owned sites, permission to use a fishing rock could be obtained after consulting with the woman who owned it. Two of the seven names of owners of individually owned sites recalled by Sam Mitchell were women, who each inherited the fishing rock from her father.

Several of the individually owned fishing rocks mentioned by Sam Mitchell in the 1970s were still being referred to by the name of the owner. On several occasions, Sam Mitchell referred to the rock at *xwusesús* (site No. 33b) as 'Vivian's *szaw* [fishing rock],' even though Vivian was old at that time and no longer lived in the community. In 1977 this site was being used by anyone, but Sam Mitchell quickly added that it still belonged to Vivian. Undoubtedly, there were formerly many more individually owned sites in this stretch of the Fraser River than we were able to record in the 1970s, but the decline in the spring salmon population in the early 1900s resulted in the abandonment of some such sites.

In a recent report containing data elicited from Pavilion Indian consultants, it is stated that all fishing sites were the inherited property of individuals and each 'tended to be used by one or two families' although 'anyone could use a given salmon fishing station.' Furthermore, the report states that 'old little-used fishing stations' are said to be named after 'the last long-term user' (Alexander 1987). These fragmentary data, which were obtained from native people a generation younger than Sam Mitchell, may reflect a diminished knowledge of fishing site ownership. The system of ownership of fisheries at Pavilion was more likely similar to that described by sm for the area further downriver.

Among the Thompson Indians on the Fraser River, we have recorded examples of the individual ownership of sites where set-nets and scaffolds were used to catch early spring salmon (Kennedy 1974-6). This form of ownership has also been recorded among the Upriver Halkomelem Coast Salish along the Fraser River in the vicinity of Yale and Hope, although it was not specified which species of salmon were caught at the individually owned sites (Duff 1950).

Residence-Group Fishing Sites

In our discussions of named fishing sites, Sam Mitchell often noted that certain sites along the river were 'the salmon fisheries of the people from x village.' When SM was asked where a certain village fished, he associated each village with a cluster of sites. Some sites were used by members of several villages, according to SM, and within these larger areas were situated individually owned fisheries. It is the groups utilizing these larger areas that Romanoff (Chapter 5) refers to as owners of 'residence-group-associated sites.'

Sam Mitchell stated to us on several occasions that the Fountain people fished on one side of the Fraser while the Bridge River people fished on the other side, but clearly he was referring to the contemporary use of the Six Mile fishery. Groups of Indians were also acknowledged to be the holders of fishing privileges defined by the Indian Reserve Commission in 1881. The groups of Indians larger than single villages were later identified as 'Bands' by the Department of Indian Affairs. We are aware of no equivalent *Stl'átl'imx* term denoting 'band'; traditionally, these native people generally recognized no social unit larger than the village. However, the term *'Stl'átl'imx'* is used to refer to all the 'Upper Lillooet' people (cf. Kennedy and Bouchard 1978:22-3).

Listed in Table 2 are the sites that are said to have been associated with particular groups in the late 1800s and early 1900s, as identified by our *Stl'átl'imx* consultants and as recorded by the Indian Reserve Commission (1881:Book 22:44-62). The name in the left-hand column is the name of the group to whom fishing privileges were assigned by the Indian Reserve Commissioner. The name in the next column is that used by Sam Mitchell to describe the users of a particular fishery. This is followed by the *Stl'átl'imx* name of the fishery and its site number as referred to in the Appendix of this report. The fisheries and Indian reserves in the southernmost area, that is, between Della Creek and Nesikep I.R. 6, have been included here because our native informants considered them to be used by villages comprised of both Thompson and Lillooet Indians. The Indian reserves and fisheries in this southernmost area, however, were assigned to the Lytton Indians (cf. Kennedy and Bouchard 1978:32, 34, 55).

As would be expected, the fisheries used by a particular residence group were most often situated in the vicinity of their village. The exception to this consists of the sites used by the Shalalth Indians, who came from Seton Lake to the fisheries located near the old Lillooet bridge crossing the Fraser (see site nos. 14, 16, 17, 18, 20). There has

TABLE 2

Fishing sites associated with specific residence groups

Band	Resident Group	Site Name	Site Number
Lytton Indians	Seah I.R. 5 (mixed *Stl'átl'imx* and Thompson people) (SM)	On both sides of the Fraser beginning 1/4 mile upriver from Seah I.R. 5 and extending downstream for 1 mile	1
	Nesikep I.R. 6	East side of Fraser downstream from mouth of Cinquefoil Cr.	
		West side of Fraser upstream from Village of *nsak'p*	2
		Both sides of Fraser between northern and southern boundaries of Nesikep I.R. 6	
Cayoosh Creek Indians	s̲k̲iká̲ytn	Name not remembered *púpelmt*	10 15
	Cayoosh Creek	West side of Fraser from mouth of Cayoosh Creek downstream for 2.5 miles	
		On Cayoosh Creek from mouth upstream one mile	
		káwkewe̲k	20
Lillooet Indians		East side of Fraser from mouth of Cayoosh Cr. downstream for 3 miles	
		Both banks of Seton River for a distance of 1/4 mile downstream from Seton Lake	13
		Both sides of Fraser from mouth of Cayoosh Creek upstream to 1/2 mile below Bridge River, a distance of about 4 miles	

(continued on next page)

TABLE 1 (continued)

Band	Resident Group	Site Name	Site Number
	McCartney's Flat	kílk̲w	6
		slhúk̲wxal	7
		púpeleḿt	15
		k̲wix̲wxn	8
		sax̲ám	9
	npim	npim	12
		púpeleḿt	15
	Lillooet Rancherie	zax̲k̲s	14
		tk̲wix̲w	16
		tsek̲wtsík̲walts	18
		tl'úg̲weg̲w	19
		káwkewek̲	20
Fountain Indians		Both banks of the Fraser from ¼ mile above 11 Mile Creek (Gibbs Cr.) downstream to the Bridge River Indians' fishery, a distance of about 4.5 miles	
	Fountain Indians	ts'iẃt	21
		ts'ex̲wamín	23
		lhúlhtsek̲	26
		nk'ák'mekstewal	30
		k'awáwk̲za7	31
		stsílek̲s	33a
		sex̲áx̲	33c
		púlhmek̲w	33f
		sx̲welp'ékstn	35
		yeg̲wúg̲wsntm	40
Bridge River Indians		Both sides of Fraser from 1/2 mile south of Bridge River upstream to Fountain Indians' fishery	
		About 3 miles up Fraser from mouth of Bridge River	
	Bridge River Indians	ts'miḿxw	24
		zenzánuts	27

TABLE 1 (continued)

Band	Resident Group	Site Name	Site Number
		zánwets	32
		kwútlex	33i
		names not remembered	33i
		smúmlek	39
	Seton Lake Indians	On the stream connecting Anderson and Seton Lakes	
	Shalalth	zaxks	14
		tkwixw	16
		menmán	17
		tsekwtsíkwalts	18
		káwkewek	20
Pavilion Indians		On both banks of Fraser from Leon Creek downstream to 1/4 mile above 11 Mile Cr. (Gibbs Cr.)	
	Pavilion	getgágta	41

been some suggestion that this practice is of recent origin – one of Turner's Shalalth consultants stated that her people started coming down to fish in the Fraser only when Cayoosh Creek was blocked off over fifty years ago (see Chapter 8). However, Sam Mitchell and Slim Jackson maintained that the Shalalth people had always come over to the Fraser River each year to fish at certain sites. The Bridge River people living farther up that river fished at the numerous sites located around its mouth. Most rocks identified within a specific residence-group's fishing area were named, just like the rocks owned by individuals.

Since the early 1900s, mostly sockeye salmon have been caught at these fisheries, although our native consultants mentioned several sites where runs of spring salmon beginning in June, as well as sockeye salmon, could be caught, providing the level of the Fraser permitted access to the fishing rocks. The number of sites used by each resident group indicates that alternative fishing sites were available when conditions were not favourable at any one particular site.

Set-nets were used more frequently than were dip nets at these sites. Among the named sites examined in this report, thirty-four of them required the use of a set-net, whereas it was specified in only nine instances that a dip net was used. Sixteen of these named set-net fisheries required the construction of a scaffold.

Public Sites

During the sockeye run, large groups of people gathered at public sites such as Six Mile and the mouth of the Bridge River. Although particular fishing rocks at these sites could only be used when the river was at a certain level, there were a great number of fishing rocks, and most of them did not require the construction of a scaffold. The fishing was easy, but the competition was great.

Many people camped at the Six Mile and Bridge River fisheries while the sockeye were running. In mid-July of 1808, when Simon Fraser returned up the Fraser River, he shook hands with upward of one thousand Indians camped at a site that appears to have been in the vicinity of the Six Mile Rapids (Lamb 1960:120-1).

We have no way of knowing how many Indians from outside of *Stl'átl'imx* territory were among those met by Simon Fraser. But Sam Mitchell maintained that in former times, Shuswap people from as far away as Kamloops, as well as Okanagan people from Vernon, visited the fisheries in the vicinity of Six Mile and participated in the fishing there. And on several occasions SM mentioned that anyone could fish at Six Mile. In a 1928 summary report on the Bridge River/ Six Mile fisheries, federal fisheries guardian, B. Cherry, wrote that the Indians fishing there were from Lillooet, Bridge River, Fountain, Cayoosh Creek, D'Arcy, Shalalth, Pavilion, 22 Mile, and Hat Creek (Cherry 1928).

Statements by Sam Mitchell suggest that some visitors – those who shared resources with the Fraser River Lillooet – had a right to full participation in the public fisheries. An example Sam Mitchell gave to illustrate this type of access was the reciprocity that existed between the Bonaparte Shuswap and his own people from the Fountain village. He explained that his people often travelled in the spring to Loon Lake in Shuswap territory, where they shared in the distribution of freshly caught trout, and that the Bonaparte Shuswap, in turn, went to the Six Mile fishery during August and September.

As described in Chapter 7, plant-collecting and hunting areas were also shared by some groups, and these may have also provided the basis for rights of neighbouring groups to fish at the *Stl'átl'imx* public sites, although there are no explicit statements to this effect. *St'átl'imx*-speaking people living not along the Fraser River but nearby, such as the Seton Lake and Anderson Lake Indians, also came to the Six

Mile/Bridge River fisheries. Fountain Indians, among others, gathered land-locked sockeye salmon from the shores of Anderson Lake and Seton Lake at specific times between November and February. In the 1970s, many of the Lower Lillooet, especially people from Mount Currie, were still coming to Six Mile to visit their relatives and to fish. They camped with them and dried their fish on their relatives' racks.

Anthropologist Michael Ames noted in a 1955 study concerning the Fountain Band that Shuswap people were then allowed to use both the fishing sites and the nets at the Six Mile fishery, though few people took advantage of this offer. Ames also described one occasion when an Okanagan man visited the fisheries with the intent of obtaining salmon, but instead of this Okanagan man having to fish for himself, his *Stl'átl'imx* host arranged for someone else to obtain the fish for him (Ames 1956).

Not all 'foreigners,' however, were permitted this type of access to the *Stl'átl'imx* salmon catch in earlier times. Slim Jackson recalled that the Chilcotin people used to come down the Bridge River during the fall to raid the *Stl'átl'imx* people's supply of dried salmon and, sometimes, to obtain slaves while the hunters were away in the hills. Stories of Chilcotin raiders in the Lillooet area have also been recorded by Teit (1906:237) and by Bouchard and Kennedy (1977:50-1). None of the *Stl'átl'imx* people we spoke to said that the Chilcotin people were ever permitted access to their fisheries.

What is clear from our discussions with native people throughout the Interior is the long-standing productivity of the Six Mile fisheries. On many occasions over the years we have heard Indian people speak with great envy about the quality and quantity of salmon that can be obtained there. Indeed, one of our Thompson consultants told us that many years ago a certain Thompson mother who, reluctant to see her daughter leave her home village and knowing the attraction that the salmon-rich *Stl'átl'imx* country held, advised the young woman against marrying a *Stl'átl'imx* man by saying that his seminal fluid was actually salmon oil (Kennedy 1974-6).

Yet the productivity of the Six Mile fisheries has varied greatly over the years. A review of Fisheries Department correspondence containing catchment figures at the Six Mile/Bridge River fisheries indicates that the sockeye catch has ranged from a documented low of only several hundred fish in the late 1930s to a high of over 56,000 in 1975 (see Figure 4). Interestingly, more than 30,000 sockeye were obtained in the 1912 fishing season; this was not a year of quadrennial dominance but it was prior to the Hell's Gate slide. Although a figure is not given for the 1909 catch, it was said that in this year both whites and Indian people remarked that 'every eddy in the Fraser River in this locality was "black with salmon"', as it had apparently been in former times (Webster 1915).

A view of the abundance said to have been similar to aboriginal times occurred in 1889. During the run, geologist George Dawson arrived at the Six Mile fishery and, fascinated with the scene before him, recorded in vivid prose the following account in his diary:

> The river still full of salmon. Watched them for a time today in eddys and behind rocky points, densely crowded. Now and then the water would change its course a little and sweep a mass of them out of eddy and down stream. Swirling in the current they resemble nothing so much as snow-flakes in a storm and appear to be equally numerous. They are actually and literally wearing out by friction in the eddys and whirlpools of the river. The small red sockeye (Quimax) salmon now red instead of silvery, only the head retaining a greenish silvery colour. The large white salmon, however, not such bad eating. Most of the salmon are practically stopped at the little fall of say 10' in river at present low stage of water. (Dawson 1889)

It was observed in 1941 that 14,200 sockeye and 750 spring salmon were taken from 27 fishing stations and dried on 18 racks (Cherry 1941). But only four fishing rocks on the Fountain side of the Six Mile fishery were said to be in use during Michael Ames's 1955 Fraser River Lillooet fieldwork. Ames (1956) implied that the other fishing sites had long since been abandoned.

In the 1970s, both we and Romanoff (1985:149) observed that the Pavilion people still fished with the Fountain people and constructed their drying racks at the Six Mile fishery, while the Texas Creek people still camped and fished at the mouth of Bridge River with the people from up that river, and the Shalalth people still camped and fished at 'Linktown' (on the west side of the Fraser near the old highway bridge).

The Salmon Trade

Clearly, the productivity of the fisheries in the Lillooet/Bridge River area placed the *Stl'átl'imx* in former times at the hub of an extensive trade network that reached far beyond their own territory to the coastal waters of the Klahoose, Sechelt, and Squamish and to the animal-rich forests of the Shuswap.

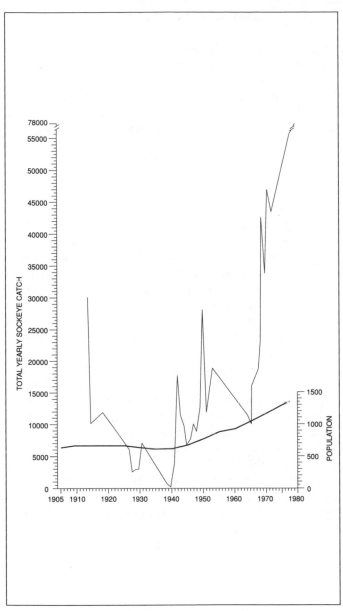

FIGURE 4

Total yearly sockeye catches in the Lillooet area from 1905 to
1978 (data from Anon. 1912, 1913, 1962, 1964, 1966, 1968, 1969,
1970; Babcock 1914a; Cherry 1941; Estabrook 1952; Graham
1925; Halladay 1925; Killick 1943a, b, c, 1945; Motherwell 1918,
1926a, b, 1927; Tremper 1940, 1941; see also Argue et al. 1990;
population data from Genealogical Unit, Indian and
Northern Affairs Headquarters, Hull, Quebec)

At the 'noted resort for trading and fishing' between Lillooet and Fountain, dried salmon and salmon oil were exchanged by the *Stl'átl'imx* for goods such as dentalium shells, dried seafoods, coastal woods, berries, and sometimes even slaves, who were brought by the coastal people. Dressed skins of deer, elk, and caribou as well as the occasional buffalo skin were traded from the east. Among those who came here to trade with the *Stl'átl'imx* were Thompson, Okanagan, Eastern Shuswap, Bonaparte Shuswap, and Lower Fraser River Indians (Teit 1900:259; 1906:231-2; 1909:536). Teit did not clarify whether salmon were obtained only through trade or whether these people fished here themselves.

Thompson people living along the Fraser south of Lytton, who enjoyed fisheries similar to those of the *Stl'átl'imx*, occasionally fished at Six Mile, according to one of our Thompson native consultants (Kennedy 1974-6). As well, Thompson Indians from Spences Bridge are said to have visited the Six Mile fishery when salmon were scarce in the Thompson River (Teit 1900:259).

From the very beginning of European exploration, travellers, traders, missionaries, and anthropologists wrote about the Fraser River Lillooet Indians' lifestyle amidst the apparent plenty allowed by salmon. Simon Fraser, the explorer who in June 1808 descended the river that now bears his name, had been told by his Shuswap guide that he 'could not suffer for want' among the *Stl'átl'imx*. This he found to be so when he camped along the Fraser near the present site of Lillooet. He was visited, Fraser wrote in his journal, by *Stl'átl'imx* people bearing dried salmon of excellent quality (Lamb 1960:77-9).

Included in the *Stl'átl'imx* Indians' lucrative salmon trading network in the early nineteenth century were the Hudson's Bay Company's Interior posts. It was noted in August 1822 at Fort Kamloops that the HBC employees had 'nothing else to depend on but dried Salmon' (MacMillan and McLeod 1822-3). In the spring of 1823, Company employee John McLeod wrote that 'the greatest part of the Salmon consumed at Kamloops is traded from . . . the Sta-lam-Cha [*Stl'átl'imx*] Indians' (McLeod 1812-18). Many years later, this was still so; A.C. Anderson reported in 1846 that in the vicinity of the Six Mile fisheries 'the greater part of the supply of salmon for Thompson's River district [of the HBC] is traded' (Anderson 1846).

Early HBC maps indicated the presence of the Lillooet/Bridge River fisheries; Archibald McDonald, in 1827, identified a 'Salmon Rock' at the confluence of the Bridge River and Fraser River (McDonald 1827). A 'Large Camp Inds' below the confluence of the Bridge River and Fraser was indicated on another map made several years later (Black 1833).

So plentiful were the salmon from the Lillooet/Bridge River area fisheries that the Fort Kamloops men could receive 6,000 fish at a time and then go back for more (McDonald 1826-7). Trader Archibald McDonald (Rich 1947:224) noted in 1827 at Fort Kamloops that 12,000 fish were required to sustain the employees of the Hudson's Bay Company's Thompson River District. Consequently, McDonald expressed disappointment when his men returned from one particular trip to the Bridge River fishery burdened with only four thousand salmon (McDonald 1826-7).

Amounts of dried salmon obtained in trade from the Lillooet/Bridge River area fisheries by the HBC post at Fort Kamloops included the following: 5,200 fish in early September 1822 (MacMillan and McLeod 1822-3); 8,400 fish in late September 1843 (Tod 1841-3); and 4,400 fish in early October 1851 (Fraser 1850-2).

Today, Lillooet is still renowned amongst Indian communities throughout British Columbia and Washington state as the source for exceptional wind-dried salmon. Indian people from as far away as the Colville Indian Reservation in Washington state still take their excess fruit to Lillooet and barter for the *Stl'átl'imx* people's fish.

Failure of the Salmon Runs

This chapter has reviewed some of the factors limiting the productivity of the *Stl'átl'imx* salmon fisheries. We have seen how the individual fisherman's mobility and access to fishing stations at different locations could compensate for fluctuating river levels that caused some sites to be unusable during peak runs. Such a strategy mitigated the effects of extreme high or low water. However, the salmon runs are reported to have failed occasionally; as a result, many people were said to have starved.

Examples of several salmon run failures in the general vicinity of Lillooet have been recorded. A Hudson's Bay Company employee at Fort Kamloops, Paul Fraser, wrote on 1 April 1852 that many deaths had taken place among the Indians 'from the almost total want of Salmon all over this district' (Fraser 1852). In April 1859, Judge Mathew Begbie was told while at Lillooet that many hundreds of Indians had died of starvation during the previous winter and that 'the salmon had failed them now for three years together' (Shaw 1861:243). Teit (1906:199) reported that 'some years before the smallpox' appeared, many Lillooet died from famine 'mainly caused by the failure of the salmon-run of the preceding season.' Presumably Teit was referring to the 1862 smallpox epidemic. Thus, both Begbie and Teit were likely referring to the same salmon run failures.

APPENDIX

Fishing Sites

In the section that follows, fishing sites within *Stl'átl'imx* territory on the Fraser River between Della Creek and Pavilion Creek are discussed. We provide the *Stl'átl'imx* name and translation for each site as well as information on when the site could be used, the species of salmon caught, the method of fishing utilized, and who fished there. Not all of these data were known for each site, and in some cases the lack of information is a reflection of our not pursuing the data rather than the limitations of the particular native consultant. In some instances, the information we wanted was simply not known. Locations of these sites are shown in Figures 5-10.

We have had the disadvantage of completing the descriptions of most of these fishing sites here in Victoria rather than in the field. Thus, in some cases there are details of site locations that remain unclarified. Wherever we are not sure of the information we have recorded, we indicate this uncertainty.

Named Fishing Sites within the Study Area

1. name(s) not remembered. According to Slim Jackson, there are a number of fishing rocks where set-nets can be used adjacent to the village of *nak̲'ák̲'tkwa7* on Seah I.R. 5 upriver from Della Creek on the west side of the Fraser. SJ did not recall the names of any of the specific fishing sites located here.

Undoubtedly, these are the same rocks identified as a fishery on the original Indian Reserve Commission sketch map of the Seah Indian Reserve. According to this sketch map, the fishery here was located in the back-eddy formed by the point at the north end of the reserve. A stretch of the Fraser River beginning 1/4 mile upriver from the north end of Seah reserve and extending downstream for one mile was reserved as a fishery for the people living here. They were given the exclusive right of fishing along both sides of the Fraser in this area (Indian Reserve Commission 1881: Book 22:44-46).

2. name(s) not remembered. None of our native consultants were able to provide any information concerning fishing sites in the vicinity of *np'agtsítsn*, the small settlement on the east side of the Fraser River north from the mouth of Cinquefoil Creek, within the boundaries of Nesikep I.R. 6. However, the original sketch map of this reserve identified a fishery on the east side of the Fraser, immediately downriver from the mouth of Cinquefoil Creek. The exclusive right of fishing along both banks of the Fraser between the northern and southern boundaries of the Nesikep Reserve, a distance of about 4 km (2.5 mi.), was allotted to the Indian people residing there (Indian Reserve Commission 1881:Book 22:44-6).

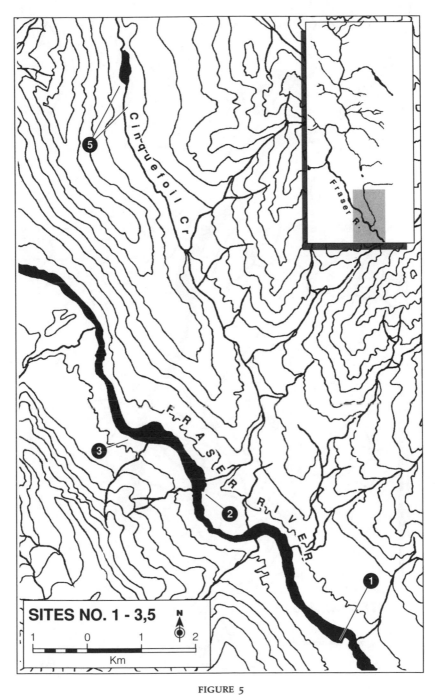

FIGURE 5

Map of a portion of the study area showing the location of fishing sites numbers 1-3 and 5

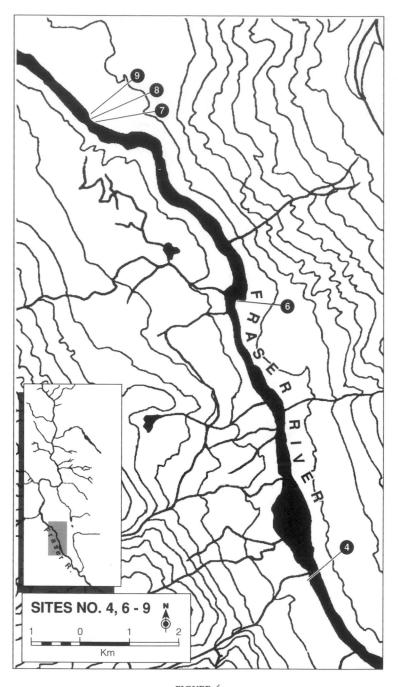

FIGURE 6
Map of a portion of the study area showing the location of fishing sites
numbers 4 and 6-9

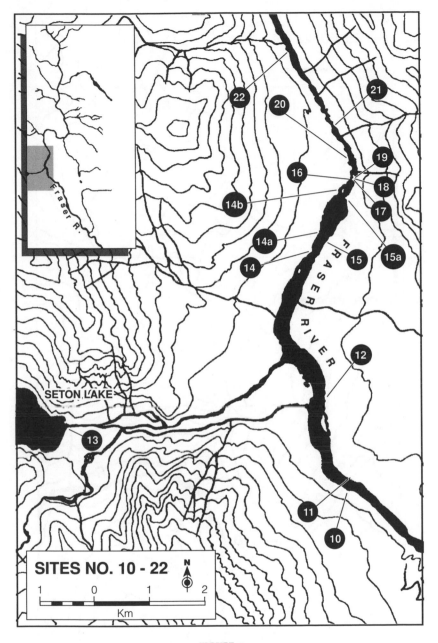

FIGURE 7
Map of a portion of the study area showing the location of fishing sites
numbers 10-22

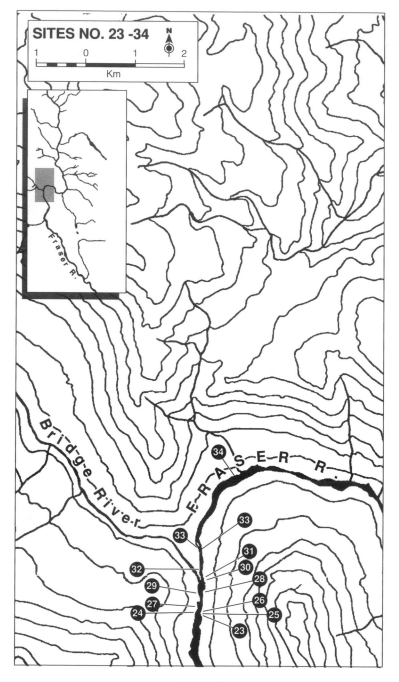

FIGURE 8
Map of a portion of the study area showing the location of fishing sites
numbers 23-34

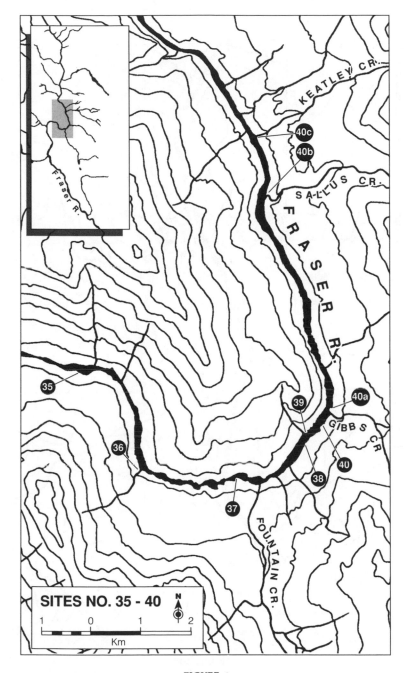

FIGURE 9
Map of a portion of the study area showing the location of fishing sites
numbers 35-40

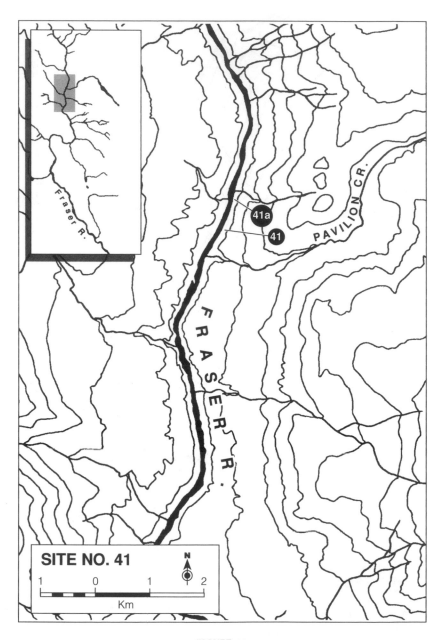

FIGURE 10
Map of a portion of the study area showing the location of fishing site
number 41

3. name(s) not remembered. The original sketch map of Nesikep I.R. 6 identified a fishery on the west side of the Fraser, upriver from the village of *nsak'p* and near the northwestern boundary of this reserve (Indian Reserve Commission 1881:Book 22:44-6). Although Slim Jackson knew that there were fishing rocks located on the west side of the Fraser in this vicinity, he did not know their precise locations or their Indian names. In January 1922 the Nesikep Band asked for 'exclusive rights of salmon fishing' from the lower end of Seah I.R. 5 up to the mouth of Texas Creek (Teit 1922), a distance of about 11 km (7 mi.).

4. name(s) not remembered. Slim Jackson stated that there are fishing rocks (whose Indian names he did not know) where set-nets can be used adjacent to the former village of *sezézell* at Towinock I.R. 2 on the west side of the Fraser River.

5. *ts'éts'kwaź* (SM) 'any trout.' This is the Indian name given to Fish Lake I.R. 7 located just south of the outlet of Cinquefoil Lake and established as a 'fishery reserve' for the Lytton (Thompson) Indians in August 1881. The Indian Reserve Commissioner identified Cinquefoil Lake as '*Stitz-quod*' [ts'éts'kwaź] (Indian Reserve Commission 1881:Book 22:44-6), reflecting the fact that locally Cinquefoil Lake is called 'Fish Lake.'

Fish Lake I.R. 7 was described in January 1922 by the Nesikep Band chief as 'much used by us when fishing.' Subsequently, this same man said his people and the Fountain Band wanted 'exclusive rights of fishing . . . at Fish Lake where reserve no. 7 is' (Teit 1922). *Ts'éts'kwaź*, the term applied to Cinquefoil Lake, is a *Stl'átl'imx* rather than a Thompson word.

According to Louis Phillips, a Thompson Indian from Lytton, it was the Thompson who used this fishery most often, although *Stl'átl'imx* Indians also used it occasionally. One such *Stl'átl'imx* man, LP recalled, was William Adolph of Fountain, who used a basketry trap in the stream at the south end of Cinquefoil Lake in the early 1940s. LP noted that Thompson Indians used to come to this lake every spring to catch trout and squawfish. Up until the early 1960s, LP himself often went fishing at this lake.

6. *kilkw* (SJ) 'on top.' This is the name of a fishing rock where a scaffold and set-net were used. The rock is located on the east side of the Fraser River about 3.2 km (2 mi.) downriver from the south end of McCartney's Flat I.R. 4. People from *kwixwxn* (site No. 8) used to fish here (SJ).

7. *slhúkwxal* (SM; SJ) 'dip net for fish.' This name is applied to a dip net fishing site on the east side of the Fraser River adjacent to the lower end of McCartney's Flat I.R. 4 and about 32 m (35 yd.) downstream from a distinctive bluff located alongside the river.

The *slhúkwxal* fishery was used when the level of the Fraser River was high, after which the fishermen moved to the fishery called *púpeleht* (site No. 15) several kilometres upstream. SM recalled that when he was a boy he was forbidden to fish at *slhúkwxal* because it was considered too dangerous for an inexperienced fisherman.

Although *slhúkwxal* was the furthest downriver named dip net site known to Sam Mitchell and Slim Jackson, there is little doubt there were named fishing rocks further dow n the Fraser River from here, within the area already discussed between sites No. 1 through No. 4. However, neither SM nor SJ were very familiar with this latter area. Yet it is reasonable to assume these rocks were named both in the *Stl'átl'imx* and Thompson languages because this area of the Fraser, at least in recent times, has been utilized by people of mixed *Stl'átl'imx* and Thompson ancestry. The known place names here reflect this mix (Kennedy and Bouchard 1978:25-6, 34).

8. *kwixwxn* (SM; SJ; BE; DP) 'bridge at base.' This name is applied to the area of McCartney's Flat I.R. 4 and the settlement here, but applies specifically to a rocky bluff on the shore of the Fraser River in the southern portion of this Indian reserve, which is located about 3.2 km (2 mi.) south from the mouth of the Seton River.

The name *kwixwxn* is derived from the fact that during the higher stages of the Fraser River, the people had to build a 'bridge' (called *ntkwixw* in the *Stl'átl'imx* language) to get across from the shore to the several small rock islands where they fished. In a previous publication (Kennedy and Bouchard 1978:26), we translated *kwixwxn* as 'rock at base.' But the translation 'bridge at base' is more accurate. During lower stages of the river, however, a bridge was not necessary as the area of the rock islands became dry (SM).

We did not record from SM or SJ whether a set-net or dip net was used at this site. However, Desmond Peters recalled his father fishing for sockeye here, using a set-net in a back-eddy on the upper side, around 1940. A gillnet was used between the shore and the rock islands. Among those who fished here, DP added, was a Cayoosh Creek man named *papxn*, also known as 'Michell Doctor' who was a relative of DP's father, Jacob Peters. *Stl'átl'imx* people also fished from *kwixwxn* bluff itself, using a set-net operated from a scaffold (SJ).

9. *saxám* (SM; SJ). *Saxám*, the ancestral name of Sam Mitchell's great-grandfather who died around 1900 (SM), is the term applied to a set-net fishing rock situated alongside a back-eddy about 40 m (45 yd.) upriver from *kwixwxn* bluff (site No. 8) (SJ).

10. name(s) not remembered. Slim Jackson noted that the people from the village of *skikáytn*, located on Pashilqua I.R. 2 on the west side of the Fraser, used to fish at several rocks located 'about a mile' upriver from the settlement. However, SJ's distance estimate was generous, as the sketch map accompanying the document establishing this reserve identified 'fishery rocks' only slightly upriver from s̲k̲ik̲áytn village. sj did not know any Indian names of these fishing rocks, which he noted were set-net fishing sites where scaffolds were used.

As well as fishing at these rocks, the s̲k̲ik̲áytn people also used to fish at púpelem̓t (site No. 15), sj added. The people living at s̲k̲ik̲áytn were considered part of the 'Cayoosh Creek Indians,' for whom the exclusive right of fishing was reserved along the west side of the Fraser, beginning at the mouth of Cayoosh Creek (in the area now known as the mouth of the Seton River) and extending downriver for a distance of two and one half miles (Indian Reserve Commission 1881:Book 22:52) (see also discussion of sites No. 12 and 13).

11. kwzaĺtst (sj) (translation not known). Slim Jackson identified *kwzaĺtst* as the name of a beach area on the east side of the Fraser River directly across from the fishing rocks (site No. 10) upriver from s̲k̲ik̲áytn. At *kwzaĺtst* the people used to catch sturgeon using a set line (sj).

12. npim (SM; sj) (translation not known). On the east side of the Fraser River and directly opposite the mouth of the artificial channel that today is called the mouth of Cayoosh Creek, was a former village, called *npim*. A special type of 'wing weir' was used here along the beach at *npim* (see Plate 6.6) (SM). Slim Jackson added that the people who fished at *npim* also fished at púpelem̓t (site No. 15) after the river level went down.

When the Indian Reserve Commissioner was in this area in 1881, he reserved exclusive fishing rights along the west side of the Fraser below Cayoosh Creek for the 'Cayoosh Creek Indians' (see site No. 10), but on the east side of the Fraser below Cayoosh Creek, he reserved fishing rights for the 'Lillooet Indians.' The area to which these latter fishing rights applied began at the mouth of Cayoosh Creek and extended downriver along the east side of the Fraser for a distance of three miles (Indian Reserve Commission 1881:Book 22:56).

13. sk'm̲kin (SM; sj; DP) 'top end.' This is the name of a former village at the easternmost end of Seton Lake, where the lake is drained by the Seton River. This area was set aside as Seton Lake I.R. 5 for the 'Lillooet Indians' (Indian Reserve Commission 1881:Book 22:55).

Speaking in the *Stl'átl'imx* language, Lillooet Indian Paul Hickson in 1969 told Randy Bouchard that k̲'pának (sockeye smolt) used to come down Seton River in schools and that the Indians used traps to catch them, although he did not say where in the Seton River these traps were utilized. Hickson added that these fish were eaten fresh and were not preserved (Hickson 1969).

A.C. Anderson of the Hudson's Bay Company described the Seton River on 19 May 1846. He commented that the Indians navigated it by canoe 'transporting their stores of salmon to & from the neighboring lake [Seton Lake] & the river [Fraser River]' (Anderson 1846).

PLATE 6.6

The long, low gradient beach at *npim* (site no. 12), where a special type of 'wing weir' was formerly used. Beach sands and cobbles are exposed in this photograph due to low water conditions.

On the sketch map accompanying the original document which established Seton Lake I.R. 5 on 31 August 1881, a fishery was identified that extended along both banks of the Seton River for a distance of one quarter mile downstream from the outlet of Seton Lake. This was a fishery for the 'Lillooet Indians' (Indian Reserve Commission 1881:Book 22:56).

The 'Cayoosh Creek Indians' living at the village of *sekw'elwás* (see also site No. 20) at the mouth of Cayoosh Creek had fishing rights reserved for them beginning at this creek's mouth (see also site No. 10) and extending up the creek one mile (Indian Reserve Commission 1881:Book 22:52).

The Shalalth people used to dry fish at *sk'mkin*, DP noted. Among the

Shalalth who went here were the Casper family, who stayed in a tent, and Joe Link, who had a cabin here (DP).

14. *zaxks* (SM; SJ; DP; BE) **'long point of land.'** According to DP and BE, we were wrong in a previous publication (Kennedy and Bouchard 1978:24, 27) and in earlier drafts of the present study, when we indicated that *zaxks* is located not far downriver from the west end of the old highway bridge. DP and BE both stated that *zaxks* is in fact located about 1,500 yards south from the old bridge. They said it is the distinctive rocky point jutting out from the west side of the Fraser near the north end of the town of Lillooet. A check of our original field notes with SM and SJ has confirmed this latter location (see also the discussion of site No. 15).

The term *zaxks*, Slim Jackson pointed out, applies to a set-net fishing site where scaffolds were used. It is also the name of a larger area where a village was formerly located (SM; SJ). We were led to believe, in 1977, that in a general sense the term *zaxks* is applied to an area along the west side of the Fraser, extending for a considerable distance northward from the actual fishing site.

SM stated that people fish at *zaxks* in June and July and catch springs and sockeye here. Shalalth people camped and fished at *zaxks*. Also, Lillooet I.R. 1 people fished here and dried their fish on the flats north from *zaxks*, toward the old highway bridge (SM) (see also site No. 16).

Gill nets as well as set-nets are used at *zaxks*, noted DP and BE, both of whom have fished here themselves. Among those who used to fish at *zaxks* was a man named *síkil* (Jack James, father of the late Gordon James) from Lillooet I.R. 1. Today (c. 1990) Marvin Tom from Shalalth fishes at *zaxks* and has a drying rack here (DP).

14a. *ts'iẃt* (DP) **(translation not known).** A point on the west side of the Fraser, about 400 yards upriver from *zaxks* (site No. 14), was identified by DP as *ts'iẃt*. SM, however, applied this same name, *ts'iẃt*, to a site about 1.5 miles further upstream and on the east side of the river (see site No. 21). According to DP, Benny Alexander from Shalalth fishes at *ts'iẃt* today (c. 1990).

14b. *k'ák'pa* (DP) **'sand.'** This name applies to a bay on the west side of the Fraser about 400 yards downriver from the old highway bridge. Here, on a sandbar, a set line was used to catch sturgeon, utilizing a squirrel for bait (DP) (be added that creek-spawning trout were also used for sturgeon bait).

15. *púpeleḿt* (SM; SJ) **(translation not known).** Initially, we concluded that *púpeleḿt*, which SJ said was directly across from *zaxks* (site No. 14), was on the east side of the Fraser, not far downriver from the old highway bridge (see site No. 15a). However, as discussed above, DP and BE stated that *zaxks* is much further downriver, and we have confirmed this by checking our original notes with SJ and SM. From these notes we have also confirmed that *púpeleḿt* is across from *zaxks*. Further confirmation is provided by DP's and

BE's statement that there is a fishing rock (DP and BE did not know the term *púpelemt*) across and just upriver from *zaxḵs*. BE said he had fished sockeye and spring salmon with a set-net at the site across from *zaxḵs*.

Formerly, the name *púpelemt* was applied only to a specific fishing rock, SJ noted, but in more recent times it was used to describe a larger area. Set-nets were used at *púpelemt* (SJ). Sam Mitchell pointed out that the people who used to live at *npim* village (site No. 12) would fish right at *npim* when the river level was high and then would dip net salmon at *púpelemt* when the river level dropped. Other people who fished at *púpelemt*, but who used a set-net, included those from Lillooet I.R. 1 and from the village known as Seven Mile (SM) as well as the people living at *sḵikáytn* (see site No. 10) (SJ).

Concerning the fisheries in this general area of the Fraser River, Indian Reserve Commissioner Peter O'Reilly reserved for the 'Lillooet Indians . . . the exclusive right of salmon fishing on both sides of the Fraser River . . . from the mouth of Cayoosh Creek upstream to 1/2 mile below Bridge River, a distance of about 4 miles' (Indian Reserve Commission 1881:Book 22:56).

There is a large bay located on the east side of the Fraser about 1/2 mile above *púpelemt* and about 1/2 mile below the old highway bridge. DP recalled that his father fished with a gill net in this bay. Where he fished was on the downriver side of the rocky point where a man named *lamxátsa* (the father of Willard Charlie – see the discussion of site No. 15a) from Lillooet I.R. 1 used to fish (DP).

15a. name not remembered. Initially, we estimated that this rocky point, located on the east side of the Fraser about 500 yards downriver from the old highway bridge, was the site called *púpelemt*. We have subsequently concluded that, in fact, *púpelemt* is further downriver (see the discussion of site No. 15). It is on this rocky point, whose name was not recalled by DP or BE, that Willard Charlie from Lillooet I.R. 1 fishes today (c. 1990) (DP). Upriver from this point, and on the downriver side of the first small rocky point south from the east end of the old highway bridge, is where the Link brothers from Shalalth fish today (c. 1990) with a gill net (DP).

16. *tḵwixw* (SM; SJ; DP) 'bridge' (?) This is the name of a fishing rock situated on the west side of the Fraser, directly below the footing of the old highway bridge (Plate 6.7). SM remarked in 1977 that gill nets were being used here in recent times and that this site could be used at any time of the year. We observed a small gill net in use to catch spring salmon on the downstream side of *tḵwixw* on 11 June 1991. In former times, set-nets were used at *tḵwixw*. DP noted that his uncle, Willie Casper from Shalalth, used a set-net and scaffold here in the 1950s.

Presumably, Paul Hickson was referring to *tḵwixw* or a site in its vicinity when he stated in 1969 that he used to fish with a gill net for spring salmon

PLATE 6.7

Tkwixw (site no. 16), on the west side of the Fraser River, directly below the old highway bridge footing. Note also the Indian fishing camp just downriver from the bridge.

and steelhead 'down at the Fraser River where the [old] highway bridge now crosses' (Hickson 1969).

Formerly, *tkwixw* was used by the Lillooet I.R. 1 people, SM and SJ noted, but in more recent years it has been utilized by the Shalalth Indians, who come from Seton Lake every summer and camp in the vicinity of the old highway bridge. SM and SJ said that as far as they knew, the Shalalth people have always come to the Fraser River to camp during the fishing season. One of their main campgrounds, located on the north side of the old highway just west of the bridge, became known locally as 'Linktown' (named after the Link family from Shalalth). Many shacks could still be seen at 'Linktown' throughout the 1970s.

In 1977, SM and SJ pointed out to us that gill nets were in use along the west bank of the Fraser extending from *tk̲wix̲w* to a considerable distance downriver, and that people had drying racks throughout this same area. In 1991, DP confirmed this, noting that as many as twelve or more gill nets are used between *tk̲wix̲w* and *k̲'ák̲'pa* (site No. 14b).

Right at *tk̲wix̲w*, and adjacent to the footing on the downriver side of the old bridge, Desmond Peters has a drying rack, which he built and has been using since 1984 (DP and his family fish with gill nets here). Other drying racks in this area were identified by DP as follows: about 100 feet south from DP's rack is one owned by Jimmy Saul of Lillooet I.R. 1; just south of this is the Leech family (from Lillooet I.R. 1) drying rack, although up until about 1970 this rack was used by the late Eddie Thevarge of D'Arcy; south of this is the Link family (from Shalalth) rack; south of this is the drying rack owned by Mike Pelgrin (from Texas Creek) and his family; and south of this is the rack owned by Margaret Purcell (of D'Arcy) and her family.

Just upstream from *tk̲wix̲w* is a large rocky point that is also a fishing site. DP did not recall the Indian name of this place, nor did we record it from SM or SJ who, we conclude, were referring to this site as a fishery utilized by the Cayoosh Creek and Shalalth Indians. On the downstream side of this point, Victor Adrian (from Seton Portage) uses a large-mesh gill net to fish for spring salmon. The Link brothers from Shalalth use a gill net on the downstream side of the next point upriver from this latter site (DP).

DP was told that Old Nancy Scotchman from Lillooet I.R. 1 used to fish from this point using a set-net and scaffold. Paul Leech and Jimmy Scotchman, both from Lillooet I.R. 1, used to assist her. She used to stay in a cabin just south of the west end of the old bridge during the fishing season. DP recalled that in the 1940s he used to see Nancy Scotchman (whose Indian name was *txwínak*) fishing with a gill net in the bay on the downriver side of this point. Just up river from this large point is a second point. Today (c. 1990) the Link brothers from Shalalth fish with a gill net on the downstream side of this point (DP).

17. *menmán* (SM; SJ; DP) 'shady area' (?) This name refers to a fishing rock located on the east side of the Fraser, immediately north from the upriver footing below the old highway bridge. This is a set-net fishing site where a small scaffold was used (SM; SJ). In the 1940s-50s, DP recalled, his father and a man named *lamx̲átsa* (from Lillooet I.R. 1) fished here with a set-net but no scaffold. DP added that he used a set-net here at *menmán*, himself, during the 1940s-50s. He noted that at this site it was necessary to use a set-net with a longer-than-normal handle.

18. *tsek̲wtsík̲walts* (SM; DP) 'red rock.' This is a fishing rock located about 30 m (100 ft.) north of the old highway bridge footing on the east side of the Fraser. *Tsek̲wtsík̲walts* is at the end of a distinctive, narrow rock peninsula that juts out into the Fraser here. When we visited this area on 11 June 1991, *tsekwtsíkwalts*, itself, was just underwater but the rock peninsula was above water.

Sam Mitchell stated that a fishing scaffold was used here when the level of the Fraser was low in July and August, but he did not specify whether the fishermen used a dip net or set-net at this site. Spring salmon and sockeye salmon were caught here. When the river is higher, access to this fishing site was made possible by constructing a bridge of boards between the shore and the rock peninsula (SM).

DP stated that his father and Patrick Oleman (from Shalalth) fished at *tsekwtsíkwalts* in the 1940s-50s utilizing a set-net but no scaffold. According to SM, people from Lillooet I.R. 1 also used to fish at this site. John Tom from Shalalth and Charlie Bob from Fountain used to camp near here. At one time there were drying racks on the shore near *tsekwtsíkwalts* (SM).

19. *tl'úgwegw* (SM; SJ; DP) **'hard' (?)** The fishing rock known as *tl'úgwegw* is on the east side of the Fraser about 45 m (150 ft.) north from *tsekwtsíkwalts* (site No. 18). It is a distinctive, narrow rock peninsula jutting out into the Fraser (Plate 6.8). SM and SJ said this site was used by the people from Lillooet I.R. 1, and DP added that the Leech brothers (from this latter reserve) in recent years have fished with set-nets here at *tl'úgwegw*. These same brothers have a drying rack on shore near the base of *tl'úgwegw* (DP).

Both Sam Mitchell and Slim Jackson mentioned another fishing rock in this area that is about 135 m (150 yd.) upriver from the east end of the old highway bridge, so presumably it is upriver from *tl'úgwegw*. But neither SM nor SJ remembered the name of this fishing rock. They stated that it is on a point and can only be fished at very low water. It is a set-net site where a scaffold was used (SM; SJ). Possibly this is the same site where today (c. 1990) the Leech brothers use a gill net late in the fishing season (DP).

20. *káwkewek* (SM; SJ; DP; BE) **'big sagebrush (*Artemesia tridentata*) at back end.'** This is a set-net fishing rock for springs and sockeye on the west side of the Fraser River about ¼-½ mile upriver from the west end of the old highway bridge (SM). It is a good place to fish from August through the fall, when the level of the river drops. The people from the village of *sekw'elwás* at the mouth of Cayoosh Creek fished here, as did people from Shalalth (SJ; SM). People from Lillooet I.R. 1 also fished here (SM).

DP was told that in former times a set-net and scaffold were used to catch fish at *káwkeweks*. Nowadays (c. 1990) people fish here with gill nets. Among those fishing here in recent times has been Johnny Frank of Cayoosh Creek (DP).

21. *ts'iwt* (SM) **(translation not known).** This is the name of a fishing rock on the east side of the Fraser just upriver from the east end of the BC Railway bridge. The rock is located directly below the late William Adolph's house;

PLATE 6.8
Tl'úgwegw (site no. 19), about 45 metres (150 feet) up river from site no. 18
(tsekwtsíkwalts)

the area of the reserve here, Fountain I.R. 11, takes its name, *ts'iwt*, from this
fishing rock. This rock, used only when the river level is high in June and
July, was a set-net fishing site where a scaffold was utilized to catch spring
and sockeye salmon (SM) (see also site No. 14a).

22. *nak'ák'tkwa7* **(MS) 'rotten water.'** Only Madeline Sampson identified this
fishing rock, which is a set-net fishing site on the west side of the Fraser several
hundred metres below where Dickey Creek enters the river. It was not
necessary to use a scaffold here, MS noted.

Sam Mitchell and Slim Jackson described another fishing rock located on
the west side of the Fraser about 180 m (200 yd.) upriver from the mouth of
Dickey Creek. This was a set-net fishing site where a scaffold was used, SM

and sj added, but neither of them recalled the Indian name of this place.

sm stated that in the early 1900s this fishing rock (the one just upriver from the mouth of Dickey Creek) was owned by an old woman named *xazíl* who was the daughter of Hunter Jack. *Xazíl* was the last person to live at the village of *skatl'* near the mouth of Dickey Creek. sj added that this was a particularly good fishing spot.

23. *ts'exwamín* (sm) (translation not known). This is a set-net fishing rock where scaffolds were used, located at the southern end of Dry Salmon i.r. 7. An old man named *xwuxwumíx* built his fishing scaffold where there is a dark ledge here at *ts'exwamín* and continued to move the scaffold down the rock as the river level dropped (sm).

We have also recorded the term *p'ákw'ulhk* ('raised storage cache at back end') as the name of a fishing rock located slightly north from *ts'exwamín*, but we have no further information about this site. Presumably *p'ákw'ulhk* is between *ts'exwamín* and *lhkw'úkw'lets* (site No. 25).

Ts'exwamín was clearly an important fishery – in response to a request made on 9 November 1914 by the chief of the Fountain Indians to members of the Royal Commission on Indian Affairs, an approximately five-acre fishing station 'for the use and benefit of the Indians of the Fountain Tribe or Band' was established in the vicinity of *ts'exwamín*. Indian Agent Graham remarked, on 3 February 1915, that 'a big number of Indians' fished here, and Mr. Shaw of the Royal Commission noted that Indian people had utilized this fishery 'for a great number of years' (Canada and British Columbia 1914: Lytton Agency, Part i:87-8; Part ii:447; 1916:ii:486).

24. *ts'mimxw* (ms) (translation not known). Only Madeline Sampson described this dip net fishing site, which she stated is named after a distinctive rock up on the riverbank, on the west side of the Fraser, across from and about 45 m (50 yd.) upriver from *ts'exwamín* (site No. 23). The fishing rock which takes its name from this distinctive rock *(ts'mimxw)* is also on the west side of the Fraser, almost directly across from *ts'exwamín*. ms also identified a set-net fishing site on the west side of the Fraser 'about 150-200 yards' upriver from the *ts'mimxw* fishing rock, but she did not recall its Indian name.

25. *lhkw'úkw'lets* (sm) (translation not known). This is a fishing rock about 90 m (100 yd.) upriver from *ts'exwamín* (site No. 23). There is a distinctive smooth rock bluff here that extends right down into the Fraser. Sam Mitchell noted that this was a place where the early run of spring salmon could be caught during April and May. We did not record what type of net was used at this site.

26. *lhúlhtsek* (sm) (translation not known). This is a set-net fishing rock located about 30 m (100 ft.) north from *lhkw'úkw'lets* (site No. 25). There is a distinctive light-coloured stripe in this rock. This fishing site, which did not re-

quire utilizing a scaffold, was used when the river was high, although in April
the Fountain people fished here for springs and steelhead (SM).

27. zenzánuts (SM; MS) 'lots of driftwood.' This is the name of an area along
the west side of the Fraser River that begins opposite from *lhúlhtsek* (site No.
26) and extends several hundred metres up to the mouth of the Bridge River.
The Bridge River Indians fish here. When the level of the Fraser River is high,
the area all along *zenzánuts* is good for gill net fishing, SM and MS stated. They
added that there is also a set-net fishing site within the larger area of *zenzánuts*
that was used when the level of the river dropped, but we did not record
the exact location of this site. There were several other fishing rocks within
the area of *zenzánuts* (see also site No. 29), whose use depended on the level
of the Fraser.

28. nlha7kánm (SM) 'lay on back.' This is a set-net fishing site located on a
distinctive rocky bluff that juts out into the Fraser River about 180 m (200 yd.)
north from *lhúlhtsek* (site No. 26). People from Fountain and from other
places caught spring salmon here from April to July. Sam Mitchell explained
that *nlha7kánm* is so named because the water boils up and pushes you back
against the rock.

29. s7ak' (SM) 'anchored with guy-lines.' Sam Mitchell identified this as a
set-net fishing site where a scaffold was used. It is located on the west side
of the Fraser, directly across from *nlha7kánm* (site No. 28) and is within the
larger area of *zenzánuts* (site No. 27).

30. nk'ák'mekstewal (SM) (translation not known). This is a set-net fishing
site on the east side of the Fraser, directly across from the rocky point on the
west side of the Fraser at the outlet of Bridge River. Sam Mitchell noted that
Fountain people fish here for spring and sockeye salmon but only when the
river is high. In our field notes of our discussion with SM concerning this site,
we have the following statement: 'At this place you use two nets, one behind
the other, one a little deeper than the other.' We did not record any further
details about fishing at *nk'ák'mekstewal*.

31. k'awáwkza7 (SM) 'net slants.' This name is applied to a set-net fishing
site on the east side of the Fraser about 45 m (150 ft.) upriver from
nk'ák'mekstewal (site No. 30), where there is a distinctive rock cut. SM stated
that this fishing rock is so named because you must stand back and push
your net out into the water rather than holding it straight up and down.
Fountain people go here during April to fish for spring salmon.

We also recorded a statement from SM about another set-net fishing rock,
also on the east side of the Fraser River, immediately upriver from *k'awáwkza7*,
but we did not record the exact location of this rock. SM referred to it as 'Tom's
szaw [fishing rock]'. We do not know who 'Tom' was. Apparently, spring

salmon were caught at this site (Romanoff 1985:139).

32. *zánwets* (MS) (no translation known). Only Madeline Sampson identified this fishing site, located on the west side of the Fraser River 'about 1/4 mile' north from the mouth of Bridge River. MS said this was both a set-net and a dip net fishing site. Scaffolds were not used at this site. From *zánwets* all the way along the west side of the Fraser River up to *sxetl'* (site No. 33) is a gill net fishing area.

33. *sxetl'* (SM; SJ) 'drop-off.' There are numerous named fishing rocks at the Six Mile Rapids which is well known by its *Stl'átl'imx* name, *sxetl'* (Plate 6.2). This term refers to the area just upriver from the confluence of the Bridge River with the Fraser, where the Fraser River is very constricted and there is a drop-off in the river. Although Teit (n.d.) translated *sxetl'* as 'taking out; coming out; landing,' Sam Mitchell consistently translated this term as 'drop-off'.

We obtained considerably more information about fishing rocks on the east side of *sxetl'* than on the west side, because Sam Mitchell was much more familiar with fishing on the east side. In general, SM noted, people fish at various rocks in the vicinity of *ts'exwamín* (site No. 23) between April and July, and then, toward the latter part of July when the river drops, the people fish at *sxetl'*.

On 1 September 1881, the 'Bridge River Indians' were allotted 'the exclusive right of salmon fishing on both sides of the Fraser River, from 1/2 mile south of Bridge River, upstream to the Fountain Indians' fishery' (Indian Reserve Commission 1881: Book 22:58). Thus, the entire *sxetl'* fishery was allotted to the Bridge River people. Several months later, Indian Reserve Commissioner Peter O'Reilly noted in a letter that the fishery of the Bridge River Indians was 'a valuable one' and that their fishery extended 'about 3 miles' up the Fraser from the mouth of the Bridge River (Indian Reserve Commission 1881:Book 4:169).

Our discussion of fishing rocks at *sxetl'* will progress from the furthest-south rock to the furthest-north rock on the east side of the rapids, followed by the same order for the west side of the rapids. The scale of the map in Figure 8 is such that it does not allow us to pinpoint the exact location of the fishing rocks on either side of *sxetl'*. These rocks can be seen, however, in the photographs accompanying this report.

33a. *stsíleks* (SM) 'pointing out.' Directly downriver from *sxetl'* rapids, on the east side of the rapids and immediately south from the rocky point where *xwusesús* (site No. 33b), *sexáx* (site No. 33c), and *nlikw'kánm* (site No. 33d) are located, there are two large back-eddies, each about 30 m (100 ft.) across. Between these two back-eddies there is a low, narrow rocky peninsula called *stsíleks*, which extends out from the beach. The Fountain people use this site as a set-net fishing station. Scaffolds were built here. This site can only be used to catch spring salmon around the end of August when the level of the river drops sufficiently.

33b. *xwusesús* (SM) '**foaming.**' The southernmost rocky point at the lower end of the *sxetl'* rapids is characterized by a relatively smooth, long rock outcropping that faces downstream. In the shelter of this point (see also site Nos. 33c and 33d) is a back-eddy in which the fishing site called *xwusesús* is located (Plate 6.9).

In our publication entitled *Lillooet Stories* (Bouchard and Kennedy 1977:67), *xwusesús* was translated as 'foamy place' – a better translation would be 'foaming.'

Sam Mitchell pointed out that when he was young, *xwusesús* was a spring salmon fishing rock that was used from July onward. When we visited this

PLATE 6.9
Xwusesús (No. 33b). Note the gill net being used here.

site in September 1974, gill nets were in use. We do not know if set-nets or dip nets were still being used here at this time. In our 1974 notes, we record-ed a comment from Sam Mitchell indicating that x̲wusesús was 'good anytime' as a place to fish.

X̲wusesús was, in the 1970s, one of the few fishing spots still recognized as being 'owned.' In 1977, SM told us that the owner of this site was 'Old Vivi-an,' who he said was living in a rest home in North Vancouver. Old Vivian had inherited the site from the previous owner, her father, 'Old Louie.' X̲wusesús was well known in the 1970s as 'Vivian's *szaw* [fishing rock].'

33c. se̲x̲áx̲ (SM) (translation not known). Se̲x̲áx̲ is on the upriver side of the rocky point on whose downriver side x̲wusesús (site No. 33b) is located. The distance between x̲wusesús and se̲x̲áx̲ is about 23 m (75 ft.), we estimated. This fishing rock was named after an old man named se̲x̲áx̲, who died a long time ago, according to Sam Mitchell. We did not record where se̲x̲áx̲ was from, but because SM identified this as one of the Fountain people's fisheries, we as-sume se̲x̲áx̲ must have been from Fountain.

Se̲x̲áx̲ is a spring salmon fishery utilized during low water beginning around the end of August. This is a dangerous place to fish; you have to use a short pole here, SM stated. We observed a set-net in use here when we visited this site in September 1974 (Plate 6.10).

In the course of our discussions with Sam Mitchell in March 1974, refer-ence was made to a fishing rock called *nkekáẃxn* that SM said was owned by a man named 'Old Saul.' We did not record precisely where this site is located, or the type of fishing done here, or which village Old Saul was from. But we conclude from the context of our notes that *nkekáẃxn* must be very close to se̲x̲áx̲ . In May 1977, however, Sam Mitchell stated that the fishing rock owned by Old Saul was *nli̲kw'kánm* (site No. 33d), which is only 'about 20 feet' upriver from se̲x̲áx̲ . From this we conclude that *nkekáẃxn* must be situated very close to *nli̲kw'kánm,* as well.

33d. *nli̲kw'kánm* (SM) 'splash on back.' This site is about 6.5 m (20 ft.) up-river from se̲x̲áx̲ (site No. 33c) and about 30 m (100 ft.) downriver from *men-mánalts* (site No. 33e). In fact, *nli̲kw'kánm,* x̲wusesús (site No. 33b), and se̲x̲áx̲ (site No. 33c) are all located on the same rocky point. SM told us in 1977 that *nli̲kw'kánm* was no longer used as a fishing site, although it was used as a spring salmon fishery when SM was a boy (c. 1900). According to Sam Mitch-ell, *nli̲kw'kánm* is so named because when you are out on the scaffold here, the rough water splashes on your back. Even though the water is rough on top and the fish run deep, SM explained, the water is calm underneath. This was primarily a spring salmon fishing site, where a scaffold was utilized. The people used to fish here from April onward. To fish here, you have to push your set-net down deep, said SM. As we have discussed (see site No. 33c), Sam Mitchell told us on one occasion that *nli̲kw'kánm* was formerly owned

PLATE 6.10
Sexáx (site no. 33c), a dangerous back-eddy to fish.
Note the set-net lying on the rocks here.

by a man named Old Saul.

33e. *menmánalts* (SM; BE) 'shady rock.' This fishing site is on a distinctive high point with a steep rock face that is about 30 m (100 ft.) upriver from *nlikw'kánm* (site No. 33d). This is a sockeye salmon fishing rock that is good anytime. SM noted that the sockeye run shallow here. Fish were gaff-hooked at *menmánalts* prior to the imposition of government regulations prohibiting this method of fishing. Subsequently, dip nets have been used here; no scaffolds were utilized at this site (SM). BE recalled seeing people fishing at *menmánalts* with gaff-hooks in the 1930s. They used to 'feel' around with the gaff-hook until a fish was encountered, then hook it (BE).

33f. *púlhmekw* (SM) 'boiling on bottom.' *Púlhmekw* is a low, blunt point of rock situated right at the narrowest part of the Fraser River at *sxetl'*. This point is separated from the point containing the *menmánalts* (site No. 33e) fishing rock by a back-eddy that is about 30 m (100 ft.) across. Sam Mitchell said that *púlhmekw* is one of the Fountain people's fishing places for spring and sockeye salmon. Scaffolds are not required here. Beginning in late August, when the river level is sufficiently low, the people in former times gaff-hooked spring salmon on the 'inner edge' of *púlhmekw*. It appears from our notes that what we meant by the 'inner edge' here was the area between the upriver side of *púlhmekw* and the downriver side of *tl'ek7úla7xw* (site No. 33g), but we are not certain of this. Dip nets were in use at *púlhmekw* when we visited this site in September 1974. We did not record on which side of the rocky point at *púlhmekw* these dip nets were being used at this time.

33g. *tl'ek7úla7xw* (SM) 'scaffold-land' (?) This is another rocky point situated about 8 m (25 ft.) upriver from *púlhmekw* (site No. 33g). The people fished from this site using a set-net that required two anchor ropes, one on either side of the net, to prevent it from being washed away. On several occasions, Sam Mitchell told us that the water is so rough and swift here at *tl'ek7úla7xw* that large rocks are swept into your net along with the salmon. 'You can see the top of the water; it just boils black with gravel,' SM added, 'and if you use a steel pipe [for a net bow] here, you can hear it just ringing [as the gravel and rocks hit it].'

In our notes, *tl'ek7úla7xw* was translated as 'anchored to the land'; in *Lillooet Stories* (Bouchard and Kennedy 1977:65) it was translated as 'a brace or prop in the land.' But the best translation would be 'scaffold-land.' This site is used when the river level is high. Mainly spring salmon are caught here, although occasionally sockeye are obtained. We did not record whether or not a scaffold was used at this site; certainly the name of the site, *tl'ek7úla7xw*, suggests that scaffolds were in fact utilized here. SM told us that one year, when the Fraser River level was high in September because of heavy rain at that time, about 250-300 spring salmon were caught in one day at *tl'ek7úla7xw*.

33h. *nxiwkwm* (SM) 'put something in water.' *Nxiwkwm* is the furthest-north fishing site on the east side of *sxetl'*. It is a V-shaped rock crevasse about 16.5 m (50 ft.) upriver from *tl'ek7úla7xw* (site No. 33g). This site is best when the river level is at its highest. SM told us in 1977 that a special type of dip net that was particularly narrow was used here at *nxiwkwm*. In fact, the name for this type of dip net, *nxíwkwatn*, is derived from the term *nxiwkwm*. In our notes we stated: 'The net is dipped from the river to the rock. One man holds the anchor rope and the other man holds the net.' Unfortunately, we did not clarify this information any further.

33i. Our field notes contain little data pertaining to fishing rocks along the

west side of *sxetl'* rapids, although we recorded Indian names for two sites
in this area. The furthest-south fishing rock that sm identified on the west
side of *sxetl'* is 'directly across from *stsíleks'* (site No. 33a). We recorded nothing about this site, other than its location. The next fishing rock above here
is about 138-184 m (150-200 yd.) downriver from the lower end of the present-
day lowermost fish ladder and directly across from *xwusesús* (site No. 33b),
according to both sj and sm. Slim Jackson identified this rock as *kwútlex*, 'water
boils up sharply,' and said it is a set-net fishing site. On another occasion,
sm said there is a fishing rock on the west side of *sxetl'* 'directly across from
nlikw'kánm' (site No. 33d). Given that the distance between *xwusesús* and
nlikw'kánm is only about 30 m (100 ft.), there is a possibility that the rock
directly across from *xwusesús* and the rock directly across from *nlikw'kánm*
may be, in fact, one and the same site. Proceeding upriver, the next fishing
rock we noted is 'across from *púlhmekw'* (site No. 33f) and 'at the lower end
of the fish ladder.' On another occasion, both sm and sj identified a set-net
fishing site which they called *tl'ugw,* 'hard,'(?) and which they both said is
located 'where the lower fish ladder is today.' Sam Mitchell said that this site
is directly across from *tl'ek7úla7xw* (site No. 33g). Given that the distance
between *tl'ek7úla7xw* and *púlhmekw* is only about 7.5 m (25 ft.), it is likely that
the rocks across from *púlhmekw* and across from *tl'ek7úla7xw* are, in fact, one
and the same site: *tl'ugw.*

We are uncertain about the translation of *tl'ugw* as 'hard.'
In the *Stl'átl'imx* language, *tl'ugw* means 'hard' only with respect to materials. Yet sm and sj stated this site was called *tl'ugw* because 'it was "hard" to
hold the net in the water here,' thereby implying that *tl'ugw,* in this context,
means 'difficult.' As far as we know, the *Stl'átl'imx* word meaning 'difficult'
is *xatl',* not *tl'ugw.* We have been unable to clarify this matter.

The furthest upriver fishing rock on the west side of *sxetl'* is directly across
from *nxiwkwm* (site No. 33h), according to sm, and about 92 m (100 yd.) north
of the upper end of the first fish ladder. We recorded nothing further about
this site. Undoubtedly, there are more named fishing sites along the west side
of *sxetl'.* We did not record any further information about this particular area
of the Fraser River, however.

34. *tsétskwalts* **(MS) (translation not known).** Only Madeline Sampson identified this site. She said it is a set-net fishing rock (no scaffolds were used
here) on the west side of the Fraser 'about one mile above *sxetl'.'* Thus, we
cannot pinpoint its location exactly on the accompanying map. Presumably,
the site referred to is across the river from the northern end of Fountain I.R.
10 and, possibly, in the vicinity of the stream entering the northwest side of
the Fraser at this point.

35. *sxwelp'ékstn* **(SM) (translation not known);** *nsástl'ank* **(SM) (translation
not known).** We are not certain whether these two names refer to the same

fishing site or to two different sites that are close together (BE recognized s*x̲welp'ékstn* as a place name but did not know which site it referred to; neither BE nor DP knew the term *nsástl'an̓k*). In any case, this is a dip net fishing area on the south side of the Fraser directly below the place called *s7ékwemkwem*, which is a village site near the eastern end of Fountain I.R. 2 on the bench of land along which the British Columbia Railway runs (SM). SM, BE, and DP referred to this area as 'Seven Mile'; the document which originally established Fountain I.R. 2 stated this reserve is 'near the 7 mile post' (Indian Reserve Commission 1881:Book 22:47).

BE recalled fishing for spring salmon at 'Seven Mile.' Where he fished is midway between two sets of rapids. It was here, BE noted, that he last used a dip net – this was around 1950 – and in fact this was the only time that BE ever fished at this site. It was during the month of June that he fished here at Seven Mile, BE noted, and it was almost two hours before he caught a fish – a large spring salmon. People fished at this place between June and September (BE). DP has used a set-net in July to catch sockeye here.

Indian Reserve Commissioner Peter O'Reilly, on 26 August 1881, reserved for the Fountain Indians 'the exclusive right of fishing on both banks of the Fraser River from 1/4 mile above the 11 mile creek [Gibbs Creek] ... downstream to the Bridge River Indians fishery, a distance of about 4½ miles' (Indian Reserve Commission 1881:Book 22:50).

In letters written to the Superintendent General of Indian Affairs in Ottawa in February 1882, O'Reilly referred to the Fountain Indians' fishery as a 'valuable one' and noted that this fishery began 'about 3 miles' upriver from an area that was 1/2 mile south from the mouth of Bridge River (Indian Reserve Commission 1881:Book 4:169,252). Given that s*x̲welp'ékstn* (*nsástl'an̓k*) is approximately three miles upriver from this latter area, we conclude that s*x̲welp'ékstn* marks the approximate boundary between the Bridge River Indians' and Fountain Indians' reserved fisheries as they were established by the Indian Reserve Commission.

36. *skatl'* **(SM) 'hanging; suspended.'** SM identified *skatl'* as a set-net fishing site which required the use of a scaffold during low water. BE and DP knew this site but not its Indian name. According to SM, *skatl'* is located on the south-west side of the Fraser below the upper end of *sxelílem* village. BE referred to the area of this village site as 'Fountain Station' and noted that the fishing site below here is on the downstream side of a creek that flows into the Fraser. People use set-nets here to fish for spring salmon (during June) and for sockeye (between July and September) (BE; DP). BE stated that he only fished once at Fountain Station. This was around 1960, during the month of June. He used a set-net and caught a spring salmon.

37. name not remembered. Along the south side of the Fraser and on the second rocky point downriver from the mouth of Fountain Creek is a set-net fishing site (SM; DP; BE). Formerly, a scaffold was used here (SM). This site has an Indian name, SM pointed out, but he did not recall it (nor did BE or DP know it).

SM identified this fishing site only as 'Mosquito Jim's *szaw* [fishing rock].' We assume, therefore, that this was an owned fishing rock. Mosquito Jim was from Fountain, noted BE, who added that Mosquito Jim's grandsons fish here today (c. 1990) with set-nets, as do other Fountain Indians. DP recalled fishing for sockeye here in the 1960s with a set-net.

38. *pepk̲* (SM; DP; BE) 'white bottom' (Stl'átl'imx term); *p̲k̲ak̲sxn* (SM) 'white foot;base' (Shuswap term). SM used both of these names, one in *Stl'átl'imx* and the other in Shuswap, on two different occasions to identify a dip-netting site located 'below *lagmímintn* village,' which is on the south side of the Fraser in the vicinity of the place known locally as '10-Mile Ranch.' According to BE, *pepk̲* is located not far downriver from the rapids at this location. SM said the people used to fish here for spring salmon in June and July, using a small dip net. BE recalled fishing here with a set-net himself, although he was last here around 1970. DP added that it was also around 1970 when he and Dave Harry from Pavilion fished at *pepk̲* using set-nets.

39. *smúmlek̲* (SM) 'sitting in water' (?) *Smúmlek̲* is a set-net fishing site on the north side of the Fraser, across and slightly upriver from *pepk̲* (site No. 38) and immediately downriver from the rapids. There is a sandbar at *smúmlek̲* (SM). According to SM, the Bridge River people used to fish here (using a scaffold) for spring salmon and the occasional sockeye salmon during July and August.

40. *yegwúg̲wsntm* (SM) (translation not known). Sam Mitchell stated that *yegwúg̲wsntm* is a Shuswap term – he did not provide a *Stl'átl'imx* equivalent. He said this name refers to a set-net fishing site on the southeast side of the Fraser upriver from the rapids (near *smúmlek̲*, site No. 39). From SM's description, we conclude that *yegwúg̲wsntm* is situated approximately midway between these rapids and the mouth of Gibbs Creek.

No scaffold is used here at *yegwúg̲wsntm*, SM stated. He added that the Fountain people fish here for sockeye and spring salmon around the beginning of July. They dry salmon at *yegwúg̲wsntm* but then move to *sxetl'* (Six Mile) when the river level drops (SM).

In the Indian Reserve Commission documents, Gibbs Creek was identified as '11-Mile Creek' (BE and DP confirmed that this term is still used locally). This creek was said to mark the boundary between the reserved fisheries of the Fountain and Pavilion Indians. The exclusive right of fishing for the Pavilion Indians was reserved 'on both banks of Fraser River from Leon Creek downstream to one-quarter mile above 11 mile creek' (Indian Reserve Commission 1881:Book 22:34-6).

40a. name not remembered. DP and BE identified a fishing site located on the east side of the Fraser just upriver from the mouth of Gibbs Creek and below the highway underpass. They did not know this site's Indian name (although SM had given k̲'ák'ezk̲n̓ as the name of a former village site along lower Gibbs Creek). Both DP and BE have used set-nets to fish for sockeye at this site. Among those who used to fish here was Charlie Narcisse from Fountain (BE; DP). Different rocks are used here, depending on the level of the Fraser. Today (c. 1990) this location has a drying rack (BE; DP).

40b. name not remembered. DP identified a gill net fishing site on the east side of the Fraser 'just above' the mouth of Sallus Creek, which is known locally as '14-Mile Creek.' The term *nkwast*, which SM had given as the name for the lower Sallus Creek village site, was not known to DP.

40c. name not remembered. There is a gill net fishing site around the mouth of Keatley Creek (known locally as '15-Mile Creek'), BE pointed out. The term *tl'atl'lh*, which SM had given for a village site along lower Keatley Creek, was not known to BE or DP. BE did not know exactly where the gill net site was located, but he noted that his brother, Rollie, and Dave Harry, both from Pavilion, fish here today (c. 1990) with gill nets.

41. getgág̲ta (SM) (translation not known); 'Johnny Edwards' *szaw*' (BE; DP). SM stated that g̲etgág̲ta is a Shuswap term referring to a fishing rock on the east side of the Fraser River, above the mouth of Pavilion Creek (we recorded nothing further from SM about this site). Undoubtedly, g̲etgág̲ta is the same site identified by BE and DP as 'Johnny Edwards' *szaw* [fishing spot],' located about 500 yards above the mouth of Pavilion Creek. But BE and DP did not know this site as g̲etgág̲ta. They pointed out that the fishing rock here was named after Johnny Edwards, whose Indian name was *sísa*. He was the older brother of BE's father, the late Francis Edwards (BE).

Set-nets were used at 'Johnny Edwards' *szaw*' (BE; DP). Mostly sockeye were caught at this fishing site, although some spring salmon were also obtained here (BE). There was one spot nearby where a gill net could be used (DP). According to DP, it has not been possible to use Johnny Edwards' *szaw* since the mid-1960s, when most of it was covered by a slide.

41a. 'Alec Louie's *szaw*' (BE; DP). This fishing site is located on the east side of the Fraser 'about half a mile' upriver from 'Johnny Edwards' *szaw*' (site No. 41) and just downriver from the mouth of a small creek (DP). BE and DP did not know any other name for this place. They stated it was named after Alec Louie from Pavilion, whose Indian name was *ts'yú7ma*.

There are actually two fishing rocks here, DP pointed out, although the two places together are known as 'Alec Louie's *szaw*.' One place is for spring salmon and the other is for sockeye – the spring salmon site is 'about 200 feet' downstream from the sockeye rock. Only set-nets are used at both portions of the site. Nowadays (c. 1990) Harriet MacDonald's family from Pavilion fishes here and has a drying rack here (DP).

ACKNOWLEDGMENTS

We are particularly indebted to the late Sam Mitchell of Fountain who provided much of the information in this report and generously shared with us his intimate understanding of the old ways. These data were elicited in a series of interviews we conducted in September 1973, March, May, July, August and September 1974, and May 1977. Also included is information recorded from Sam Mitchell by Randy Bouchard in August 1968 and July 1970. A field trip to the study area in June 1991 enabled us to clarify locations of several fishing sites and their uses and to cross-check some place names. We thank Desmond Peters and Bill Edwards for their assistance at this time.

The following *Stl'átl'imx* people also provided data incorporated into this study: the late Slim Jackson, the late Susan Mitchell, the late Madeline Sampson, the late William Adolph, and the late Paul Hickson. We gratefully acknowledge their contributions. As well, we are indebted to the late Charlie Mack of Mount Currie for the information he provided.

Information elicited in 1988 by Dr. J.V. Powell of the University of British Columbia from the late Solomon Peters of Shalalth has also been included and is gratefully acknowledged.

We are especially grateful to the Fountain Indian band for providing funding in 1986 which assisted us in preparing an earlier draft of this study. The special interest that Chief Roger Adoplh of Fountain has shown in this research is much appreciated. Franklin Ledoux (Economic Development Officer, Lillooet Tribal Council) also provided helpful assistance.

Financial support to the BC Indian Language Project in the 1970s that made our *Stl'átl'imx* fieldwork possible was provided by: the British Columbia Provincial Secretary's Ministry, the BC Ministry of Education, the Humanities and Social Studies research Division of the Canada Council, and the Canadian Ethnology Service of the National Museum of Man, Ottawa. Simon Fraser University research funds assisted with the completion of this study in June 1991.

We also wish to thank the archival staff at the following institutions: British Columbia Archives and Records Service, Victoria; Pacific Salmon Commission Library, Vancouver; National Archives of Canada, Ottawa; Treaties and Historical Research Branch and the Genealogical Unit of Indian and Northern Affairs Headquarters, Ottawa; Vancouver Regional Office of Fisheries and Oceans Canada; and Hudson's Bay Company Archives, Archives of Manitoba, Winnipeg.

REFERENCES

Alexander, Diana. 1987. *Ts'kw'aylaxw Ethnoarchaeology: A Preliminary Survey.* Report prepared for the Heritage Conservation Branch, the British Columbia Heritage Trust, and the *Ts'kw'aylaxw* Indian Band

Ames, Michael M. 1956. 'Fountain in a Modern Economy: A Study of Social Structure, Land Use and Business Enterprise in a British Columbia Indian Community.' BA essay, Economics, Political Science and Sociology. University of British Columbia, Vancouver

Anderson, A.C. 1846. *Journal of an Expedition Under Command of Alex C. Anderson of the Hudson's Bay Company, Undertaken with the View of Ascertaining the Practicability of a Communication with the Interior for the Import of the Annual Supplies.* Hudson's Bay Company Archives, Provincial Archives of Manitoba, Winnipeg. B.97/a/3

Anon. 1912. Letter to W.J. Bowser, Commissioner of Fisheries, 10 October 1912. British Columbia Archives and Records Service, Victoria. GR 435, Vol. 64, File 606

–. 1913. 'Conditions at the canyon in the Fraser above Lillooet.' British Columbia Archives and Records Service, Victoria. GR 435, Vol. 105, File 1,039

–. 1962. Indian permit fishery [1954-1962], Lillooet-Merritt sub-district. Fisheries and Oceans Canada, Regional Office, Vancouver. Records and Library Services, File 11-1-22, Vols. 2 and 3 (March 1958 - April 1968). Licences-District #1-Indian Permits-General

–. 1964. Summary of Salmon and Steelhead Taken by Indians of the Undernoted Bands [Bridge River, Fountain, Lillooet, Pavilion, Seton Lake] Under Free Permit During The Year 1964. Fisheries and Oceans Canada, Regional Office, Vancouver. Records and Library Services, File 11-1-22, Vol. 4 (April 1968 - March 1970). Licences-District #1-Indian Permits-General

–. 1966. 'An examination of the Fraser River Indian Fishery.' Report 8, June 1966. Fisheries and Oceans Canada, Regional Office, Vancouver. Records and Library Services, File 10-1-31, Vol. 4 (September 1962 - May 1968). Regulations-District #1-Indians.

–. 1968. Statement showing the approximate number of sockeye and pink salmon landed by Indians under free permit at various fishing stations [1968 season, Lillooet-Merritt sub-district]. Fisheries and Oceans Canada, Regional Office, Vancouver. Records and Library Services, File 11-1-22, Vol. 4 (April 1968 - March 1970). Licences-District #1-Indian Permits-General

–. 1969. Statement showing the approximate number of sockeye and pink salmon landed by Indians under free permit at various fishing stations [1969 season, Lillooet-Merritt sub-district]. Fisheries and Oceans Canada, Regional Office, Vancouver. Records and Library Services, File 11-1-22, Vol. 4 (April 1968 - March 1970). Licences-District #1-Indian Permits-General

–. 1970. Statement showing the approximate number of salmon by varieties landed by Indians under free permit at various fishing stations for the 1970 season, Lillooet-Merritt sub-district. Fisheries and Oceans Canada, Regional Office, Vancouver. Records and Library Services, File 11-1-22, Vol. 5 (March 1970 - October 1971). Licences-District #1-Indian Permits-General

Argue, A.W., Diana Campbell, P.A. Gee, and M.P. Shepard. 1990. 'Records of annual salmon harvest by British Columbia Indians prior to 1951.' *Canadian Data Report of Fisheries and Aquatic Sciences No. 782*. Department of Fisheries and Oceans, Pacific Region: Vancouver

Arthur, J.B. 1923. Letter from J.B. Arthur to J.P. Babcock, 22 October 1923. British Columbia Archives and Records Service, Victoria. GR 435, Box 112, File 1122

Babcock, J.P. 1902. *Report of the Fisheries Commissioner for British Columbia for the Year 1901*. Victoria: King's Printer

–. 1903. *Report of the Fisheries Commissioner for British Columbia for the Year 1902*. Victoria: King's Printer

–. 1904. *Report of the Fisheries Commissioner for British Columbia for the Year 1903*. Victoria: King's Printer

–. 1914a. 'Conditions in the Fraser River above the Scuzzy Rapids.' In *Report of the Fisheries Commissioner for British Columbia for the Year 1913*. Victoria: King's Printer

–. 1914b. Statement to the Royal Commission on Indian Affairs for British Columbia, at a conference with representatives of the Dominion and Provincial Fisheries Departments, 9 April 1914. In *Transcript of Cowichan Agency Evidence*. British Columbia Archives and Records Service, Victoria. Add Mss. 1056

[Black, Samuel]. [1833]. Unidentified ms. map of Thompson's River District, attributed to Samuel Black of the Hudson's Bay Company. Map Collection, British Columbia Archives and Records Service, Victoria. Accession No. 13,660

Bouchard, Randy, Sam Mitchell, and Bill Edwards. 1973. 'How to write the Lillooet language (Fraser River dialect)' (revised version). Unpublished manuscript, BC Indian Language Project, Victoria

Bouchard, Randy and Dorothy Kennedy (ed.). 1977. *Lillooet Stories* (Sound Heritage, Vol. 6, No. 1). Provincial Archives of British Columbia, Victoria.

Canada. 1873. *Sessional Papers* Vol. 4, No. 8., Appendix R, pp. 181-6. Ottawa

Canada and British Columbia. 1914. Evidence Presented to the Royal Commission on Indian Affairs for the Province of British Columbia. BC Archives and Records Service, Victoria. Add. Mss. 1056

–. 1916. *Report of the Royal Commission on Indian Affairs for the Province of British Columbia*. 4 vols. Victoria: Acme Press

Cherry, B. 1928. Letter from B. Cherry, Fishery Guardian, to Chief Inspector of Fisheries, 31 December 1928. British Columbia Archives and Records Service, Victoria. GR 435, Box 108, File 1073

–. 1941. Letter from B. Cherry, Fishery Guardian, to Supervisor of Fisheries,

31 October 1941. National Archives of Canada, Ottawa. RG 23, Vol. 690, File 713-2-141

Cunningham, F.H. 1915. Letter from F.H. Cunningham, Chief Inspector of Fisheries, Dominion Fisheries, British Columbia, to Superintendent of Fisheries, Department of Naval Service, 25 June 1915. National Archives of Canada, Ottawa. RG 23, Vol. 1,329, File 729-4-2(1)

Dawson, George. 1889. *Private Diaries*. Originals held by McGill University Archives and McGill University Special Collections, Montreal. Computer printout provided to the BC Indian Language Project by Professor Douglas Cole, History Department, Simon Fraser University, Burnaby, BC

–. 1892. 'Notes on the Shuswap people of British Columbia.' *Proceedings and Transactions of the Royal Society of Canada for the Year 1891*. 9(2):3-44

Duff, Wilson. 1950. *Stalo Field Notebooks*. Anthropology Collections, Royal British Columbia Museum, Victoria

Elliott, William. 1931. 'Lake Lillooet Tales.' *Journal of American Folk-lore* 44:166 181

Estabrook, O.G. 1952. Letter to Regional Supervisor of Fisheries, New Westminster, 28 August 1952. Fisheries and Oceans Canada, Regional Office, Vancouver. Records and Library Services. File No. 11-1-22, Vol. 1. (August 1949 - March 1958) Licences-District #1-Indian Permits-General

Fraser, Paul. 1850-2. Thompson's River Journal, 17 August 1850, 13 May 1852. British Columbia Archives and Records Service, Victoria. A/C/20/K12A/1850-1855, Vol. 1

–. 1852. Letter from Paul Fraser to George Simpson, 1 April 1852. Hudson's Bay Company Archives, Winnipeg. D5/33/f, 384-5

Graham, H. 1925. Letter from H. Graham, Indian Agent, Lytton, to Duncan C. Scott, Deputy Superintendent of Indian Affairs, Ottawa, 7 November 1925. National Archives of Canada, RG 23, Vol. 679, File 713-2-2 (8)

Halladay, A.P. 1925. Letter from A.P. Halladay, Inspector of Fisheries, to Major J.A. Motherwell, Chief Inspector of Fisheries, 10 November 1925. British Columbia Archives and Records Service, Victoria. GR 435, Box 107, File 1058

Hickson, Paul. 1969. Tape recording (in the *Stl'átl'imx* language) of Paul Hickson discussing early times in the Lillooet area. Taped by Randy Bouchard. British Columbia Indian Language Project, Victoria

Hill-Tout, Charles. 1899a. 'Notes on the *N'tlaka'pamuq* of British Columbia, a branch of the Great Salish Stock of North America.' *Report of the British Association for the Advancement of Science* 69:500-85

–. 1899b. ' "Sqaktktquaclt," or Benign-Faced, the Oannes of the *Ntlakapamuq*, British Columbia.' *Folklore* 10(2):195-216

–. 1905. 'Notes on the *Stlatlumн* of British Columbia.' *Journal of the Anthropological Institute of Great Britain and Ireland* 35:126-218

Indian Reserve Commission. 1881. Minutes of Decision, Book No. 1, Reg. No. 9211-310. Copy (Book No. 22) held by Reserves and Trusts, Indian and Northern Affairs, Regional Office, Vancouver

–. 1882. Minutes of Decision and Correspondence-P. O'Reilly, File 29858, No. 3. Copy (Book No. 4) held by Reserves and Trusts, Indian and Northern Affairs, Regional Office, Vancouver

Kennedy, Dorothy. 1974. Fieldnotes concerning Shuswap Indian fishing in the Deadman's Creek area. British Columbia Indian Language Project, Victoria

–. 1974-6. Fieldnotes concerning Thompson Indian fishing. British Columbia Indian Language Project, Victoria

Kennedy, Dorothy and Randy Bouchard. 1975a. 'Utilization of fish by the Chase Shuswap Indian People of British Columbia.' Unpublished working paper. BC Indian Language Project, Victoria

–. 1975b. 'Utilization of fish by the Colville Okanagan Indian People.' Unpublished working paper. BC Indian Language Project, Victoria

–. 1975c. 'Utilization of fish by the Mount Currie Lillooet Indian People of British Columbia.' Unpublished working paper. BC Indian Language Project, Victoria

–. 1978. 'Fraser River Lillooet: An ethnographic summary.' In A.H. Stryd, S. Lawhead (eds.), *Reports of the Lillooet Archaeological Project, Number 1, Introduction and Setting.* National Museum of Man, Mercury Series, Archaeological Survey of Canada, Paper No. 73, 22-55

Killick, S.R. 1943a. 'Report on the Indian fisheries at Bridge River Rapids during the 1942 season.' Pacific Salmon Commission Library, Vancouver. Item #2550.2-40

–. 1943b. 'Report on the Indian fisheries at Bridge River Rapids during the 1943 season.' Pacific Salmon Commission Library, Vancouver. Item #2550.2-48

–. 1943c. 'Indian fishery data, Bridge River Rapids, 1943.' Pacific Salmon Commission Library, Vancouver. Item #2550-2.50

–. 1945. 'Report on the Indian fisheries at Bridge River Rapids during the 1944 season.' Pacific Salmon Commission Library, Vancouver. Item #2550.2-57

Lamb, W. Kaye (ed.). 1960. *The Letters and Journals of Simon Fraser 1806-1808.* Toronto: Macmillan

MacMillan, James and John McLeod. 1822-3. *Thompsons River [Fort Kamloops] Journal.* Hudson's Bay Company Archives, Provincial Archives of Manitoba, Winnipeg. B.97/a/1

McDonald, Archibald. 1826-7. *Journal of Occurrences at Thompson's River 1826-1827.* Hudson's Bay Company Archives, Provincial Archives of Manitoba, Winnipeg. B.97/a/2

–. 1827. 'A sketch of Thompson's River District, 1827.' Original held by Hudson's Bay Company Archives, Provincial Archives of Manitoba, Winnipeg. B.97/a/2 (copy held by the British Columbia Archives and Records Service, Victoria, map collection CM/A354)

McLeod, John. 1812-18. Journals and Correspondence of John McLeod, Sr. British Columbia Archives and Records Service, Victoria. A/B/40/M22K

Motherwell, J.A. 1918. Letter from J.A. Motherwell, Chief Inspector of Fisheries to J.P. Babcock, Provincial Fisheries Department, 13 February 1918, with enclosures from Fisheries Guardians T.E. Scott and W.J. Smith. British Columbia Archives and Records Service, Victoria. GR 435, Box 42, File 380

–. 1924. Letter from J.A. Motherwell, Chief Inspector of Fisheries to J.P. Babcock, Assistant to the Commissioner, Provincial Fisheries Department, 9 October 1924. British Columbia Archives and Records Service, Victoria. GR 435, Vol. 107, File 1054

–. 1926a. Letter from J.A. Motherwell, Chief Inspector of Fisheries, to J.P. Babcock, Assistant to the Commissioner, Provincial Fisheries Department, 12 October 1926. British Columbia Archives and Records Service, Victoria. GR 435, Box 107, File 1061

–. 1926b. Letter from J.A. Motherwell, Chief Inspector of Fisheries, to J.P. Babcock, Assistant to the Commissioner, Provincial Fisheries Department, 22 November 1926. British Columbia Archives and Records Service, Victoria. GR 435, Box 107, File 1061

–. 1927. Letter from J.A. Motherwell to J.P. Babcock, 28 November 1927 with enclosed report dated 25 November 1927. British Columbia Archives and Records Service, Victoria. GR 435, Box 108, File 1066

–. 1941. Letter from J.A. Motherwell to R.W. MacLeod, 20 June 1941. Fisheries and Oceans Canada, Regional Office, Vancouver. Records and Library Services, File No. 10-1-31, Vol. 2 (April 1933-March 1942), Regulations-General-Indians-District No. 1

Newcombe, W.A. 1917. Letter/Report to J.P. Babcock, 5 October 1917. In history records from old Department of Fisheries files, 1913-18. Typescript held by the Pacific Salmon Commission Library, Vancouver. Accession 25.2, Vol. 1

Powell, J.V. 1988. Personal communication. Department of Anthropology, University of British Columbia, Vancouver

Rich, E.E. (ed.). 1947. *Part of Dispatch From George Simpson, Esqr., Governor of Ruperts Land to the Governor & Committee of the Hudson's Bay Company London.* Published by the Champlain Society for the Hudson's Bay Company Record Society

Romanoff, Steven. 1985. 'Fraser Lillooet salmon fishing.' *Northwest Anthropological Research Notes* 19(2):119-60

Scott, W.B. and E.J. Crossman. 1973. *Freshwater Fishes of Canada.* Fisheries Research Board of Canada, Ottawa

Shaw, Norton (ed.). 1861. Journey into the Interior of British Columbia, by Matthew Begbie. Part 18. In *The Journal of the Royal Geographical Society.* London

Simmons, Richard W. 1940. 'Notes on the Indian fishery of Lower Fraser and Canyon District, 1940.' Pacific Salmon Commission Library, Vancouver. Item #2550.2-24

Strang, A. 1933. Letter from A. Strang, Indian Agent, to C.C. Perry, Assistant Indian Commissioner, Victoria, 15 February 1933, with enclosed questionnaire. National Archives of Canada, RG 10, Vol. 11,298, Box 11

Teit, James. n.d. Salish Ethnographic Materials, Boas Collection 372 Roll 16, Item S.7 [1908-1920]. Originals held by the American Philosophical Society Library, Philadelphia, Pennsylvania (microfilm copy held by the British Columbia Archives and Records Service, Victoria)

–. 1898. 'Two traditions of the Lillooet.' *Traditions of the Thompson River Indians of British Columbia*. American Folklore Society

–. 1900. 'The Thompson Indians of British Columbia.' *Memoirs of the American Museum of Natural History* 2(4):163-392

–. 1906. 'The Lillooet Indians.' *Memoirs of the American Museum of Natural History* 2(5):193-300

–. 1909. 'The Shuswap Indians.' *Memoirs of the American Museum of Natural History* 4:443-758

–. 1922. 'Report on the Nesikep Band [based on interview with Chief James Antoine, 17 January 1922]. In Lytton Surveys-Reports Regarding Reserve Needs 1922. National Archives of Canada, Ottawa. RG 10, Vol. 11,302

Tod, John. 1841-3. Thompson River Journal, August 1841–December 1843. British Columbia Archives and Records Service, Victoria. A/B/20/K12A/1841-3

Tremper, S. 1940. 'Indian fishery of the Seton District, 1940.' Pacific Salmon Commission Library, Vancouver. Item #2550.2-27

–. 1941. 'Indian fishery, Seton-Anderson District, 1941.' Pacific Salmon Commission Library, Vancouver. Item #2550.2-41

Turner, Nancy J. 1987. 'Plant resources of the Fraser River Lillooet people: A window into the past.' Report prepared for Brian Hayden, Department of Archaeology, Simon Fraser University, Burnaby, BC

Webster, Ralph. 1915. Letter from Ralph Webster, Fishery Guardian, Lillooet, to F.H. Cunningham, Chief Inspector of Fisheries, 1 November 1915. British Columbia Archives and Records Service, Victoria. GR 435, Box 121, File 1205

–. 1916. Letter from Ralph Webster, Fishery Guardian, Lillooet, to F.H. Cunningham, Chief Inspector of Fisheries, 6 August 1916. National Archives of Canada, Ottawa. RG 23, Vol. 1,329, File 720-4-2(1)

CHAPTER SEVEN

Traditional and Contemporary Land and Resource Use by *Ts'kw'ayláxw* AND *Xáxli'p* Bands

Robert Tyhurst

INTRODUCTION

Hayden and others have written on, and continue to carry out research concerning, the questions of social group structure, indicators of social hierarchy, and differential access to and control of resources within the context of archaeological investigations of pithouse village sites in the Lillooet area (Hayden et al. 1985; Hayden et al. 1987; Hayden and Gargett 1987). The abundance, reliability, and control of resources have been implicated as important factors in understanding settlement sizes, settlement mobility, socioeconomic inequality, alliances, exchange systems, and warfare (e.g., Cannon, this volume). In order to evaluate such claims, it is essential to document resource use and ownership in relevant study areas. This analysis, based on two summers' fieldwork (1986 and 1987), is concerned with resource availability, use, and access in the area defined by the current knowledge of elders from the *Ts'kw'ayláxw* (Pavilion) and *Xáxli'p* (Fountain) bands, the names used by each band administration.

Methods used to obtain field data included ethnographic interviews (both at elders' homes and at sites in the field), judgmental archaeological surface surveys, and test excavations. An attempt was made to obtain as complete ethnographic and archaeological information as possible on: (1) riverside salmon fishing sites from the Ten Mile rapids area (below Fountain Reserve I.R. 1A) 22 km north to Moran Flats; (2) mountain hunting and plant-gathering sites from the Blustry Mountain area north to Pavilion Mountain; and (3) use of sites in the area between the river and the mountains, from the south end of Fountain Valley north to the east end of Marble Canyon and to the plateau area north of Pavilion.

Little information was obtained on resource use of the relatively unproductive River Terrace or Montane Forest zones. The Intermediate Lake zone near *Ts'kw'ayláxw* has been discussed by Alexander (Chapter 3). With respect to the Lake zone at Fountain, Kennedy and Bouchard (1986:14) indicate that there were no trout in *Kwotlenemo* (Fountain) Lake before they were recently introduced: the steepness of the lower portion of Fountain Creek made it impossible for trout to ascend Fountain Valley to the Lake. The Lake zone in Fountain Valley was cleared and settled by Fountain Band members in the late nineteenth and early twentieth centuries (LA; KB). Before that, it had served as part of one route to the Cariboo gold fields. Brief reference is made to the Lake zone in the following discussions of land use around Bald and Chipuin mountains and Moore Peak, but it is not of central importance in this chapter. Thus, I will primarily be concerned with describing resource use in the River Valley, Intermediate Grasslands, Montane Parkland, and Alpine zones. In the following presentations, I treat each mountain complex as an exploitation unit and describe resource use zones and sites separately within each montane complex. I conclude with a discussion of traditional rights of access to these sites. Fieldwork was conducted by myself and Diana Alexander. Although Alexander and I each carried out some interviews with elders alone, for the most part we carried out such interviews, and much of the archaeological survey, together. Throughout this report, elders are identified by initials, keyed to the short biographies presented in Chapter 1. Geological, climatological, and biogeoclimatic information is included in Chapter 2 of this volume. Prominent geographical features, place names, and sites are presented in Figures 1 and 2.

RIVER ZONE SALMON FISHING SITES

Introduction

Romanoff's analysis of fishing (Chapter 5) is concerned with both traditional and contemporary salmon fishing in the Fountain-Lillooet area. It is complemented by work by Kennedy and Bouchard (1978; Chapter 6), which includes a detailed list of Fraser River salmon fishing places between the Lochnore-Nesikep area (21 km south of Lillooet) and the mouth of Pavilion Creek. My purpose here is to extend the documentation of site use to the northern limit of the study area, consistent with the aims of the Keatley Creek archaeological investigations. I will discuss ethnographic and ethnoarchaeological results from interviews with *Ts'kw'ayláxw* and *Xáxli'p* band elders, and from a surface survey of the Fraser River's east bank from Eleven Mile (below

Fountain Reserve I.R.1) upstream to a point about 1 km north of the mouth of Pavilion Creek. Information obtained in this way includes: (1) notes and tape-recorded interviews on uses and names of salmon fishing sites; (2) notes and tape-recorded interviews on intra- and inter-band access to salmon fishing sites; (3) notes on the occurrence of river-side archaeological sites and of potential salmon fishing places between 11 Mile and Pavilion Creek.

Salmon and the River

As has been noted in Chapters 5 and 6, the Six Mile Rapids just north of Lillooet are a salmon fishing site of major importance. Nowhere else within *Xáxli'p* or *Ts'kw'ayláxw* band territory is such an important and productive fishing site found. Other fishing localities can be divided into five types (Figure 3).

There are places in the river within the study area where conditions make it possible to catch salmon without regard to the level of the water, except when the river level is either very high or very low (Type I). In some other locations, salmon can only be caught when the river is at a certain level (Type II). Type I and II sites are the most productive in this classification. In yet other locations, the river current is almost uniform and only small obstructions such as minor rock outcroppings or piles of boulders at creek mouths serve as resting places for salmon (Type III). In such places, dip nets or set-nets cannot be used either because the river is too shallow or because returns would be too low for the physical effort and vigilance required to operate the nets. In such places, gill nets are used.

Along most of the river between Ten Mile and Pavilion Creek, however, the shore consists of boulders which create no localized turbulence. Salmon fishing in such areas (Type IV) is of such low productivity, even in comparison to Type III areas, that no fishing is now carried out there. Some areas of steep rock bluffs which drop straight into the river may create localized areas of turbulence which would allow salmon fishing but either lack footholds for fishermen or are inaccessible (Type V locations). These may have been used in the past provided that substantial scaffolding could be erected over the water.

The Fraser River in the Lillooet area is geologically young: it has been cutting down through glacial sediments at a rate estimated to be up to 60 m per 5,000 years, that is, up to 12 m per 1,000 years (Chapter 3). Because of this, it is possible that the location of major fishing sites today bears little resemblance to the situation 3,000 or even 1,000 years ago (cf. Hayden et al. 1987:23). Nevertheless, it can be said that

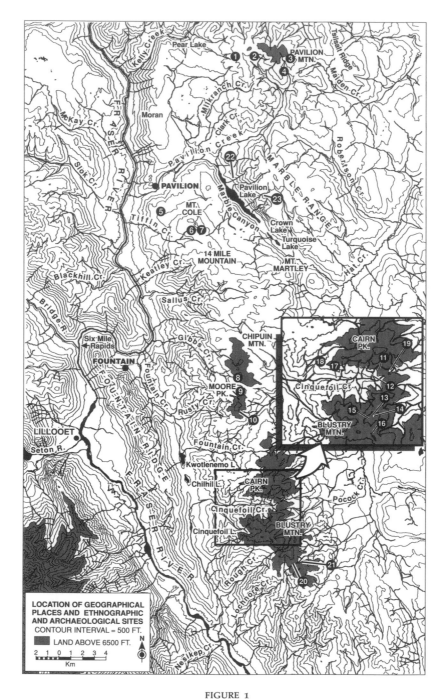

FIGURE 1

Location of geographical places and some ethnographic and
archaeological sites mentioned in the text:

(1) Area of greatest spring beauty occurrence, of ethnographic campsites, and of most numerous archaeological sites on Pavilion Mountain

(2) Area of rock spire and of associated deer-hunting drive

(3) Rock blind and cave shelter

(4) Campsite associated with rock blind

(5) 'Sagebrush Flats': spring beauty gathering area above *Ts'kw'áylaxw*

(6) Modern streamside campsite area and lithic scatter near the summit of Mount Cole

(7) Seasonal pond, contemporary campsite, lithic scatter

(8) Deer-hunting funnel location on Chipuin Mountain

(9) Contemporary campsite, and archaeological site including cultural depressions

(10) *Tswilx* (group hunting) locations on summit of Moore Peak

(11) Contemporary campsite and lithic scatter on south side of Cairn Peak

(12) Area of greatest spring beauty occurrence in the Bald Mountain area, of ethnographic campsites, and of most numerous archaeological sites

(13, 14, 15) Rock blinds for *tswilx* hunting near summit of Blustry Mountain

(16) Gravesite south of Blustry Mountain

(17) Ethnographic and archaeological site on the middle course of Cinquefoil Creek

(18) Ethnographic and archaeological site on the North Fork of Cinquefoil Creek

(19) Ethnographic and archaeological site on upper Pocock Creek

(20) Campsite at small lake south of Blustry Mountain

(21) Draw used for hunting near No. 20

(22) *Tswilx* (group hunting) location in Marble Canyon. Desmond Peters referred to the name of site as *k'lpálekw* '*coyote's penis.*' A prominent chimney rock formation constitutes part of the drive terrain

(23) *Tswilx* (group hunting) location above Marble Canyon

areas such as that between the mouth of Keatley Creek north to a point opposite Blackhill Creek, where the shores show little or no bedrock today and where the slopes above show only glacial till, were probably not very good fishing sites in the past: primarily Type IV

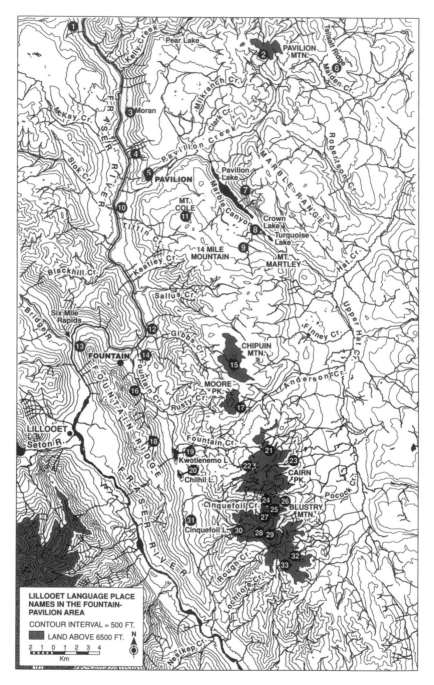

FIGURE 2

Lillooet language place names in the Fountain-Pavilion area (compiled by R. Tyhurst; all terms except 3, 9, 22, 30 and 32 were re-elicited by R. Bouchard from Desmond Peters and Bill Edwards):

(1) *tskwúkwsam:* Leon Creek; the creek and former reserve settlement
    (from *tskwúsem* 'tilt head backwards'); considered a *stl'átl'imx* term
    by BE and DP, although in Kennedy and Bouchard (1978:32, 35) the
    late Sam Mitchell identified this as a Shuswap term and gave the
    translation 'look upward'

(2) *texwláws:* top of Pavilion Mountain (from *stexw* 'straight; okay')
    (BE; DP); considered a *stl'átl'imx* term by BE and DP

(3) *tsetsxem:* Moran area; this term recorded by R. Tyhurst was not
    recognized by BE or DP; BE suggested the term *stek'7áks* (which he
    believes is a Shuswap term) for Moran Flats but was not certain of
    this; previously the term *tsxayl* (said to be a Shuswap term) was
    given as the name for a village site on the west side of Moran Flats
    (Kennedy and Bouchard 1978:32)

(4) *ts'yú7ma:* a salmon fishing site near Skwish Creek; this is the Indian
    name of Alec Louie, who was from Pavilion (BE;DP).

(5) *ts'kw'áylaxw:* the name of both the band and the location near Pavil-
    ion ('frosty ground' (BE; DP); or 'hoar frost in the trees'); considered
    a Shuswap term by BE and DP; the transcription '*tskw'áylaxw*'
    (Kennedy and Bouchard 1978:32, 34) should have *ts'* rather than *ts*

(6) *ts'elts'ál:* Tsilsalt Ridge ('piled-up rock slabs,' or columnar basalt);
    both BE and DP knew this term – DP provided this translation; consi-
    dered a Shuswap term by BE and DP

(7) *sxmeltám:* Marble Canyon; BE and DP both knew this word, and both
    considered this a Shuswap term but did not know its meaning (DP
    thought the meaning might possibly be related to Indian doctors
    testing each other's power)

(8) *getsgátsp:* Crown Lake-Turquoise Lake (BE; DP); considered a
    Shuswap term (meaning not known) by BE and DP; both No.8 and
    No.9 may be transcriptions of the same term; BE applies *getsgátsp*
    both to Crown Lake and to the nearby sidehill

(9) *getsgátsp:* applies to Crown Lake and to the nearby sidehill (BE)

(10) *tsekwtsíkwatkwa:* salmon fishing site below Diamond S River Ranch
    ('red water') (BE; DP); considered a *stl'átl'imx* term by BE and DP

(11) *k'exwtsítsen:* Mount Cole (BE only); BE believed this to be a *stl'átl'imx*
    term whose meaning might be related to 'surround'

(12) *tl'itl'k't:* white alkaline earth cliff on lower Gibbs Creek (DP only);
    Kennedy and Bouchard also provide this term (1978:31)

(13) *sxetl':* Six Mile rapids salmon fishing site

(14) *xáxelep* or *sxáxelep:* (name of the band and the location) (from *xal*
    'edge'; 'brow of the hill') (BE; DP); considered a *stl'átl'imx* term by
    BE and DP; the transcription '*sxáxelep,*' given in Kennedy and
    Bouchard (1978:31,34), should have had *x* rather than *x*

Note: the remaining place names are considered to be *stl'átl'imx* unless otherwise indicated:

(15) *tsípwen:* Chipuin Mountain ('underground cellar') (DP)
(16) *tl'ák'men:* crossing place on Fountain Creek near the main reserve ('crossing place') (BE; DP)
(17) *spolhḵemút:* Moore Peak; BE and DP noted this is the *stl'átl'imx* word meaning 'sloppy hat'
(18) *sxwená7am:* draw going southwestward from Fountain Valley to a hunting area ('Indian doctor'); this could also be transcribed as *sxwená7em* or *sxwená7m*
(19) *ḵwelh7inúymexw:* Kwotlenemo Lake (from *ḵwélh7in* 'birch') (BE; DP)
(20) *sxílxel:* Chilhil Lake ('silverweed roots' – *Potentilla anserina*)
(21) *kelhéxwa:* a hunting area on the north side of Cairn Peak at timberline; BE and DP noted this is the *stl'átl'imx* word meaning 'come into sight'
(22) *ntsxwimtn* (?) or *ntsúymtn:* a wide valley on the west side of Cairn Peak and a hunting area
(23) *tsekwtsíḵw:* a draw on upper Crater Creek on the northeast side of Cairn Peak; hunting area; refers to the 'red' earth there ('red') (BE; DP); Kennedy and Bouchard also recorded *tseḵwtsíḵw* as a place name here with Sam Mitchell
(24) *ts'ek'zánk:* southeast side of Cairn Peak (from *ts'ek'* 'whitebark pine edible cones')
(25) *sgaz7ús:* a hunting blind on the north side of Blustry Mountain ('piled up rocks'); Kennedy and Bouchard also recorded this place name with Sam Mitchell
(26) *tl'ekwekwíḵw:* draw on the northeast side of Blustry Mountain ('shooting fast like firecrackers')
(27) *ḵwiyuhánk* or *nḵwiyuhánk:* Blustry Mountain; Kennedy and Bouchard also recorded this place name with Sam Mitchell
(28) *xwlalhp:* grave site on Blustry Mountain ('grave; ghost')
(29) *p'xexáxnek:* upper area of a creek used for deer hunting just below the grave site on Blustry Mountain (a Shuswap term meaning 'thin ridge'); Kennedy and Bouchard also recorded this place name with Sam Mitchell
(30) *tloḵwist* (possibly the term is *tl'áḵwalts*); ridge on the southwest side of Blustry Mountain, a hunting area ('rock driven into the ground')
(31) *ts'éts'ḵwaz:* Cinquefoil Lake ('any trout') (BE; DP); Kennedy and Bouchard also recorded this place name with Sam Mitchell as the name for 'Fish Lake' Indian Reserve No. 7
(32) *tsimpelúlpa:* draw used for hunting deer near No.33
(33) *tsil'ílh:* a lake and camping area at the southeast end of the Blustry Mountain area (probably this is the term *tseléllh,* meaning 'little lake' – however, Kennedy and Bouchard recorded this place name with Sam Mitchell as *tseltsaléllh,* 'lots of little lakes')

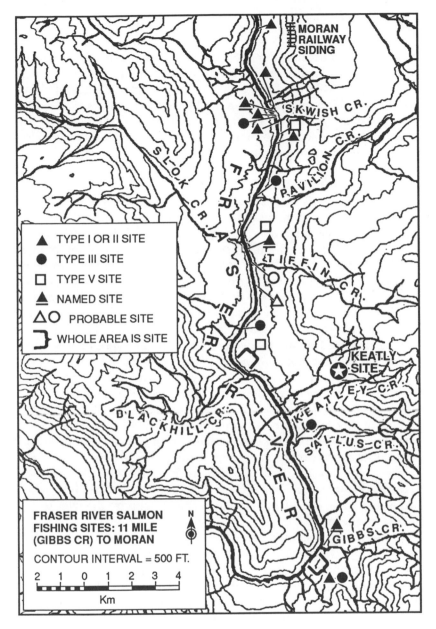

FIGURE 3

Fishing sites along the Fraser River, from Gibbs Creek (Eleven Mile Creek) to Moran Creek. For site names, see the text of Chapters 6 and 7

with some Type III sites at creek mouths. The mouth of Sallus Creek, where a steep rock bluff plunges straight into the river, may, however, have formerly been a very good fishing site. Because of the presence of bedrock, and because the river narrows there, Sallus Creek mouth may have been a highly productive Type I site (it may even have been as good as Six Mile). Today it provides only a Type III gill net fishing site at the creek mouth, where a boulder delta creates a back-eddy, and a possible Type II dip net site, unused for years, and useable only when the river is low. The present neglect of this locality may also be due to recent changes in fishing technology (e.g., greater reliance on gill nets), historic modification of fish runs, or the abandonment of platform constructions.

As noted below, *Ts'kw'ayláxw* and *Xáxli'p* people have remarked that different species of salmon (and even different geographical races within species) have different swimming capacities. Spring salmon (*Onchorhynchus tshawytscha*) are believed to be stronger swimmers than sockeye. Because of this, they will swim upstream in the middle of the river except where the current is strong, or where back-eddies produced by local turbulence encourage them to take advantage of favourable currents near the bank. Traditionally, this was the preferred species of salmon and was a valuable trading commodity but could only be procured in abundance at Type I, II, and, possibly, V sites.

Sockeye salmon (*Onchorhynchus nerka*) are believed to be weaker swimmers than Chinook and are known to swim closer to the bank. Even among the sockeye, the Stuart Lake race, which spawns north of Prince George, and which is in the river near Lillooet near the beginning of July, is believed to swim more weakly than the Chilko Lake race which passes through Lillooet later in July. Because of this, Stuart Lake sockeye can be caught at fishing sites where the current or the back-eddy are weaker, such as Type III sites. At one site, *tsekwtsíkwatkwa*, Stuart Lake sockeye can be caught in early July, while two weeks or so later, Chilko Lake sockeye swim by the site 'in the middle of the river' (DP).

Consequently, a salmon fishing site where spring salmon could be caught would also serve as a good or excellent fishing site for sockeye and other salmonids, such as pink salmon and limited numbers of steelhead, but the reverse is not necessarily true. At Pavilion Creek mouth, for example, the current and back-eddy are too weak to drive spring salmon into nets set there (DP). But both races of sockeye as well as steelhead may be caught. The assertion by Romanoff (Chapter 5) and by Kennedy and Bouchard (Chapter 6) that Chinook salmon sites were important because of the importance of spring salmon in the traditional diet should be considered in light of this fact: Sites at which spring salmon could be caught were often also the best fishing sites for any salmonid species, although some good spring fishing sites might not be used to catch sockeye because favourable water conditions at the sites do not occur during the sockeye runs.

Salmon Fishing Sites Between Eleven Mile and Moran

There are few good, easily accessible, and currently used salmon fishing sites on the Fraser River between Eleven Mile and the mouth of Pavilion Creek, and even fewer very good ones. About 2.5 km north of Pavilion Creek mouth, there are three or four Type I or Type II fishing sites clustered together. These are used by *Ts'kw'ayláxw* Band members and are productive, but access and egress are arduous and there is little space for camping (DP). South of Eleven Mile, the situation is quite different: there is an extensive Type I fishing site below Fountain Reserve at Ten Mile and, apparently, though we did not visit them, a number of possible dip net or set-net sites along the Fountain side of the Fraser between Ten Mile and the Six Mile rapids (see Kennedy and Bouchard, Chapter 6). We were not able to survey this area, but, as seen from the Lillooet-Big Bar ferry road on the opposite side of the river, the Fountain side between Ten Mile and Six Mile does have a large number of rocky bluffs which appear to produce optimal conditions for good salmon fishing. Two set-net sites are mentioned in this area by Kennedy and Bouchard (Chapter 6).

The Ten Mile and Eleven Mile (Gibbs Creek mouth) sites are discussed by Kennedy and Bouchard. To this information it is only necessary to add that both the Ten Mile and Eleven Mile sites are affected by water level. Set-net fishing is always possible there but is better when the water level is lower rather than higher. Toward the middle of July 1987, fishing had already begun but, we were told, would improve as the river level dropped.

For about 3 km above Gibbs Creek mouth, there are a few rocky outcroppings. These sites, some of which might be Type II or III, are not, apparently, used for salmon fishing at present. For the most part the shore in this area consists of boulders or sandy beaches and does not appear to provide any local turbulence at all (Type IV sites). It is worth noting that about 1 km above Gibbs Creek mouth, an archaeological site was discovered by survey on a small bench about 23 m above the river (Site # EeRl 196). Subsequent excavation at this site in 1987 and 1988 revealed a cultural deposit with a depth in excess of 70 cm and cache pits over 140 cm deep.

Sallus Creek mouth is about 4 km upstream of Gibbs Creek. As discussed above, there, is a very large rock bluff there, but this provides only a precarious dip net fishing site, and only when the water is low (Type II). Construction of fishing platforms may have increased the productivity of this and similar sites in the past. For the most part, salmon fishing at Sallus Creek mouth is carried out by gill nets set in the downstream eddy below the large boulder delta at the point where the creek joins the river (Type III). Despite the fact that Sallus Creek mouth is technically part of Fountain Reserve, only Ts'kw'ayláxw Band members fish there now using a gill net.

Sallus Creek is often mentioned by Xáxli'p Band members (RA; KB) as being the 'boundary' between the areas used by the two bands. 'Boundaries' are, in fact, areas of overlapping use rather than of mutually exclusive use. Although Teit (1906:461, 524) does not deal directly and unequivocally with the question of the location of the boundary zone between Ts'kw'ayláxw and Xáxli'p bands, he does give the impression that, before about the middle of the nineteenth century, the Ts'kw'ayláxw Band, which was then primarily Shuswap-speaking, had control and use of salmon fishing sites in the Sallus Creek area and perhaps even as far south as Eleven Mile.

For a distance of 2.5 km upstream above the mouth of Sallus Creek, the eastern shore of the Fraser River consists of boulders, with a few projecting boulder deltas at the mouths of seasonal creeks (including Keatley Creek) and a few small outcrops of bedrock which project only slightly into the river. This area appears to provide primarily Type IV sites with some possible Type III sites. No salmon fishing is done there now, but a survey of a small bench above a dry creek mouth did reveal some lithics indicating past use. Further survey and excavation of this site (Site # EeRl 195) was carried out in 1987 and 1988 (Alexander 1989).

The entire river shore between Sallus Creek and a point 2.5 km north has been heavily disturbed by road construction which, according to a Ts'kw'ayláxw Band member, was carried out by non-Indians in the 1960s or 1970s with the aim of examining possible placer deposits in the area of UTM EM797293. The greatest disturbance produced by the road building was in the area surrounding the end of the road at UTM EM797293. There, a large bench situated about 50 m above the river and measuring about 135 m (north-south) by about 75 m (east-west) has been criss-crossed by bulldozed roads. The uncontrolled excavation resulting from the road building has brought to the surface a large amount of cultural material, primarily lithic debitage. The extent of the archaeological site in this area is unknown, but a large Old Cordilleran bifacial point and the amount of debitage recorded in surface survey indicates that this may well be a large archaeological site (Site # EeRl-T-LIL-4) dating back to the early prehistoric period, earlier than 7,000 years ago.

Unlike the river shore between this area and Sallus Creek, the river shore here is rocky and the current is swift as the Fraser River goes through a major bend and a narrowing, with the greatest constriction occurring in the area of the mouth of Blackhill Creek (UTM EM792292). Because of steep rock bluffs along the river and because of the loose and steep nature of the gravel deposits in the areas between the rock bluffs, we were not able to survey the riverbank below this site directly. But the nature of the river here is such that several Type I, Type II, and especially Type V salmon fishing sites might be expected in this area, particularly if platforms were used to enhance access. Given knowledge of the terrain and time to plan a route to the river, access would be relatively straightforward.

The presence of such potentially good fishing sites and the presence of an extensive riverside archaeological site within 2.5 km (straight line distance) of the Keatley Creek site suggest that this site may well have been an important salmon fishing location for the residents of Keatley Creek (see Hayden et al. 1987:23). Indeed, it is possible that the past down-cutting action of the river and/or cliff face collapse (indicated by large fresh rock scars) have obscured a once prime salmon fishing location at this site. If so, this site might have provided a combination of excellent salmon fishing and a substantial flat area near the river – a combination that is now found only at Six Mile. If both Sallus Creek and this upstream site were at one time exploited together, they would have constituted a significant, dependable source of salmon within a relatively short distance of the pithouse village site at Keatley Creek.

Our 1987 riverside survey was interrupted at this point by the difficult nature of the terrain, but the survey was essentially continuous from a point about 4 km upstream of this area (i.e., 1 km downstream from the mouth of Tiffin Creek) to a point about 1 km above the mouth of Pavilion Creek. Tiffin Creek itself appears on Map 92-I/13 as a year-round stream, but in July 1987 it was dry. From the creek mouth, which provides a possible Type III site, the shore to the south consists of boulders (Type IV) with a few small rocky headlands (Type III or possibly Type II). About 1 km south of Tiffin Creek there is a rocky outcropping (possibly Type II). We did not go south past this point, but the shore as far south as we could see (i.e., to about UTM EM794313) consisted primarily of boulders with few projections into the river (i.e., on the basis of what we could see, Type IV sites).[1]

North of Tiffin Creek, the shore consists of boulders (Type IV sites) for about 500 m to the north. At this point, a large rock spire drops straight into the river (Type V). Beyond that there is a small beach (Type IV) and another Type V headland. None of this area appears to be particularly promising for salmon fishing sites. We also approached this northernmost headland (which we reached from Tiffin Creek) from the north by hiking down a very steep boulder-strewn arroyo to a named gill net fishing site at UTM EM 792337.

According to DP, this latter site is called *tsekwtsíkwatkwa* or 'red water' because of the prominent red rock bluffs of Slok Creek which face this site across the Fraser River. DP indicated that this site was usually approached by the route that we had followed, but, because of the steepness of the route, salmon were usually carried out via a path that went, about mid-level on the cliff face, 2.5 km north to Pavilion Creek, where the route is less steep. The fishing site itself consists of three rocky headlands separated by (Type IV) boulder or sand beaches. The northernmost headland appears to offer no foothold and is thus probably Type V. The middle headland is recessed from the river, produces no turbulence, and is thus a Type IV site, although it could have been a Type V site in the prehistoric past. The southernmost headland has a rocky sill, awash at the river level of July 10. It is a set-net site. The set-net is placed in the back-eddy below this sill and is best used in July when the water level is right (Type II).

DP indicated that *tsekwtsíkwatkwa* was a fairly productive site: it had been at least fifteen years since he had visited it, however. The steepness of the arroyo route and of the cliff face route to Pavilion Creek meant that not even horses could be used to pack salmon out. DP indicated that, to his knowledge, the site had not been used much since about 1972.

There is no place to camp at *tsekwtsíkwatkwa*, and there is room for only one set-net on the rocky sill. DP indicated that a gill net might also be used there but that 'nobody stays there that long' (i.e., long enough to set, check, and bring up the net repeatedly). DP has no recollection of drying racks or other camp furniture at the site. A healthy and fairly strong person can pack out 'about 12 sockeye' (i.e., about 30 kg gutted but not wind-dried) per trip. The site is most productive for the Stuart Lake run of sockeye, according to DP, because they are 'weaker' and hug the shore more than do later runs (such as the Chilko Lake run). In earlier times, this site may well have been an isolated salmon fishing site, with processing taking place at Pavilion Creek mouth or elsewhere.

To the north of this site, Pavilion Creek enters the Fraser River 2.5 km upstream. The route in to the Pavilion Creek mouth drops down over a series of benches to a valley containing Pavilion Creek. This valley, which varies in width from about 200 m to 100 m, extends inland 400 m to an abrupt headwall and waterfall. The valley bottom, which, unlike the surrounding area, is well watered, contains a number of creekside flat areas and numerous small surrounding benches, all suitable for camping or for the placement of drying racks, roasting pits, or cache pits. The creek, even with current irrigation and fresh water demands, runs year round, and there is abundant wood for camp furniture and for fuel.

There is a large boulder delta at the mouth of the creek, and it creates a large enough back-eddy for the placement of three gill nets (DP). If, as DP of Ts'kw'ayláxw and WN of Xáxli'p indicated, gill nets were not used traditionally for salmon fishing, there is some question as to what sort of salmon fishing technology was used there in the past. Set-nets or dip nets may have been used to fish in the upper edge of the back-eddy at the point of the delta. Whatever method was used, ten potential cache pits (2.5 to 4 m in rim diameter) were found near the creek mouth indicating that the site was productive in the past, since, according to oral history, dried salmon was stored here in stone caches in the historic period (DP).

DP related that, until twenty years ago or so, the N family would spend the middle of the summer at the mouth of Pavilion Creek. They would plant vegetable gardens, catch and dry salmon (probably both Stuart and Chilko runs plus whatever other sockeye runs and spring runs were available) and return to Ts'kw'ayláxw briefly before the fall hunt. According to DP, the N family some time ago built the two large square (4 x 4 m) caches made of piled river boulders which are located just southeast of the creek mouth. These caches are not traditional in form: the traditional cache pit for dried salmon consisted of a circular pit lined with dried grass (DP). Such pits were also used for the fermentation of salmon eggs (DP).

DP's family is the only group which still fishes at this site. They keep some camping supplies cached near the creek mouth and maintain a fish drying rack on a rocky and windy point of land just north of the creek mouth. The family uses one or two gill nets: the poles for these nets, which exceed 9 m in length, are made from long, thin Douglas-fir saplings and are kept at the site. The fishing site itself could be characterized as a good Type III site and, perhaps, though such technology has not been used there within living memory, as a possible Type II set-net or dip net site as well.

To the south of Pavilion Creek, the shore consists of boulders (Type IV) for about 1 km, at which point southward progress is stopped by a Type V headland. To the north, the shore also consists of boulders (Type IV). About 2 km north of Pavilion Creek there is a single Type I set-net site. This site is unnamed and, according to DP, provided enough space for only a single set-net. Further northward progress is halted by a Type V cliff. At this point it is just possible to see a drying rack beyond a bend in the river. This drying rack is located at the next currently used fishing site, about 700 m upstream, and is discussed below.

Access to Pavilion Creek mouth was easier in the recent past, when a vehicle road and bridge over Pavilion Creek led to a cable ferry landing about 250 m northwest of the creek mouth. This ferry, which was discontinued in the 1960s, was used by Leon Creek Band members and by ranchers who lived on the west side of the river (DP). The road is currently washed out, and access to the area of the creek mouth is now possible only by horseback or on foot.

Beginning about 2.7 km north of Pavilion Creek, an area of rocky shores and a swift river current combine to produce a series of important salmon fishing sites which were traditionally used, and are currently used, by Ts'kw'ayláxw Band members. Access to this area, just upstream of Skwish Creek, is by horse or by foot and involves a steep and unrelieved elevation change of 500 m from either Ts'kw'ayláxw I.R. 1, or from the BC Rail tracks directly above the area. In contrast, ascent from Pavilion Creek to the first large bench above it (at Diamond S River Ranch) requires an elevation change of only 120 m. We were not able to visit the area of the Skwish Creek salmon fishing sites but photographed it in its entirety from the opposite bank of the river and obtained a detailed description and sketch map of it from DP.

Because no archaeological site report exists for this site, a sketch map of the site is included with this report (Figure 4). This map is based on a sketch map by DP and on photos. It is not to scale but based on a perspective view, and the site numbers correspond to numbers in field notes and tape transcriptions ('Site 1' in this sequence is the set-net site 1.2 km upstream of Pavilion Creek mouth).

Site 2 (Figure 4) is a former set-net site, where one set-net could be used. This site was obliterated by a slide in about 1967. The slide destroyed a fishing rack at Site 2 and made it impossible to fish there. Site 2 was reached via a path from Site 3, which consists of a collapsed cabin and gill net site.

At Site 3, a small bay provides the site for up to two gill nets. The cabin, about 'eight by eight (feet)' (2.4 m by 2.4 m) was built and used by the E family of Ts'kw'ayláxw (DP). It was just large enough for two beds and was used as a sleeping place only. It collapsed some time ago and has not been rebuilt. Site 3 can be reached either by dropping down from the trail to Ts'kw'ayláxw, which runs above it, or via a lower path from Sites 4, 5, and 6. There was a drying rack there in the past.

Site 4 is a set-net site located just below small bay in the steep and rocky river bank. A single set-net was used there. The fishing spot provided little foothold for the person fishing, and that person had to be roped to the bank to prevent his being swept away by the river

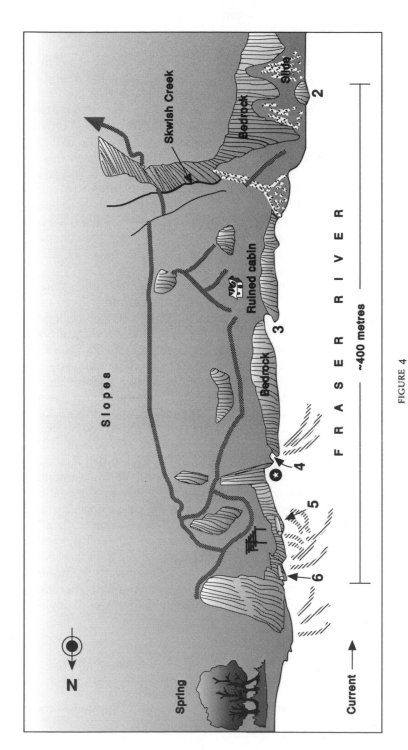

FIGURE 4

Sketch of salmon fishing sites above Skwish Creek as seen from the west bank of the Fraser River

should he fall or have trouble landing a large spring salmon. The bay just upstream of Site 4 is a resting place for spring salmon, and they can be seen there by people situated on or above that bay.

Site 5 is a narrow ledge '10 to 12 inches' (25-30 cm) wide situated directly below a drying rack. It provides enough room for only one set-net, and, like Site 4, requires the person fishing to be tied to the bank. Site 6, just upstream from Site 5, is the only site in this area for which DP knew the *Ts'kw'ayláxw* name: it is called *ts'yú7ma*, after a member of the L family who owned the site. It consists of a ledge above a large back-eddy and is about '10 feet' (3 m) long – long enough for two set-nets to be worked simultaneously. Because there is a ledge in the river below Site 6, the position of the net must be changed as the river level rises or falls, but the site is always productive, no matter what the river level.

Within this area, camping is possible only at Site 3 (the cabin site) and above sites 5 and 6, where a drying rack is located. Water can be obtained from the river or from a spring located upstream of Site 6, but wood for fuel must be brought in from the surrounding area. Although not as comfortable or as convenient as the Pavilion Creek mouth, the Skwish Creek fishing sites are more productive.

The river current here is strong enough to drive spring salmon in toward the riverbank. As discussed in the concluding remarks, spring salmon were traditionally the most important salmon species for the *Stl'átl'imx* people and the prime species used in trading. Being stronger swimmers than sockeye, they could be obtained only at better fishing sites. It is these sites that were owned by family groups. Among the Skwish Creek fishing sites, Sites 4, 5, and 6 were spring salmon fishing sites. DP, however, attributed ownership only to Site 6, though sites 4 and 5 were possibly also owned in the past. Sites 4, 5, and 6 are Type I sites, Site 3 is a Type III site, and Site 2 was probably a Type I site before the landslide obliterated it. Romanoff (Chapter 5), Kennedy and Bouchard (Chapter 6), and elders from *Ts'kw'ayláxw* and *Xáxli'p* bands all indicate that in the past spring salmon were the more important species. Reduction in spring salmon numbers because of modern non-native commercial fisheries practices has probably made sockeye salmon the more important species today.

INTERMEDIATE AND MONTANE ZONE SITES

Introduction

In a 1987 report on ethnoarchaeological work in Blustry Mountain-

Cairn Peak (Bald Mountain) (Tyhurst 1987) I discussed a number of factors which appeared to be important in determining the location of both ethnographically reported and archaeologically recorded camp-sites in the Montane Parkland zone (see Figures 1 and 2). These were: relatively flat, dry ground; wood for fuel; water; proximity to plant food collecting areas; good overview; and proximity to game trails and hunting trails (Table 1).

TABLE 1

Distance from water to cultural depressions in three subalpine areas near Lillooet

Approximate distance from water (m)*	Bald Mt. area	Chipuin area	Pavilion Mt. area
0-10	5	1	2
11-20	6	5	6
21-30	6	4	—
31-40	3	2	—
41-50	—	1	—
51-60	2	1	—
61-70	4	1	—
71-80	—	1	—
81-90	—	1	—
91-100	—	1	—
> 100	—	2	—
	26	20	8
Mean**	26.9	42.3	11.9
Median	17		12
Range	4-67		10-14

* Rounded to nearest whole number
** Using actual distances, rather than ranges, with >100 arbitrarily assigned 100

In 1986 and in 1987, Diana Alexander and I also carried out an ar-chaeological survey in a number of subalpine areas to the immediate north of the Bald Mountain area. From south to north these were, respectively, the Moore Peak-Chipuin area, the Mt. Cole area, and the Pavilion Mountain area – this last being located some 38 km north of the Bald Mountain (Cairn/Blustry Mountain) area (see Figure 1). This work has confirmed the criteria for campsite location mentioned above as well as their admittedly subjective ordering. I have also been able to add, however, an additional type of site to those discussed in the 1987 report (campsites, trails, hunting blinds, gravesite). This is the large mammal kill site without hunting blinds. Hunting blinds were not necessary at this site because thick and abundant willow brush provided excellent cover for hunters. This type of site was found only on Mount Chipuin, and its importance may be judged both by the fairly copious amounts of lithic materials found near the site as well as by the importance given to it in contemporary accounts by Xáxli'p people. The location of a site for large mammal (e.g., deer) drives is an accident of geography. What is required is a large declivity of some sort whose shape is such that deer can be driven in by hunters at the bottom and are funnelled toward a fairly narrow opening at the top. Such sites must be at least partially open so that the deer can be seen by the drivers as well as by the hunter waiting for them. On Bald Mountain, at the site named sgaʔ7ús (see Figure 2), the upper end of the 'funnel' is well above timber line. Thus, a rock hunting blind was placed at the top of the 'funnel' so that the deer would not see the hunter and shy away at the last moment.

These four Parkland areas associated with each mountain complex differed, often markedly, in terms of terrain, the availability of plant and animal foods, and ease of access (Table 2). Both the ethnographical and archaeological records varied accordingly. It is notable, however, that there was a remarkable correspondence between ethnographic information on the desirability of a given location and the abundance and variety of archaeological sites in that location. Mount Cole, for example, which was rated by Ts'kw'ayláxw elders (DP) as only moderately good for hunting and as mediocre for plant food gathering, provided only two very minor archaeological sites (both lithic scatters). Bald Mountain, on the other hand, which was rated by Xáxli'p elders as moderately good for plant food gathering and as excellent for hunting, provided both a large number and wide variety of site types and of features such as roasting or cache pits within sites. This correspondence between ethnographic information and the ability to predict the location and incidence of archaeological sites reinforces similar research results in the Chilcotin area (see Alexander et al., 1985).

The use of analogy in making inferences about the past has generated considerable controversy and discussion (see, for example, Freeman 1968; Gould and Watson 1982; Schiffer 1981). The types of analogical reasoning employed below are at a fairly low level of generality; they are site specific and thus resemble the direct historic approach (see e.g., Gould and Watson 1982). This level of analogy tends to be highly descriptive but is the most reliable of all types of analogies (Baerreis 1961) and is an indispensable field technique for locating and understanding the uses of archaeological sites where any sort of memory of traditional culture survives.

TABLE 2

Traditional resource availability and archaeological site types in four subalpine areas near Lillooet

	Bald Mt.	Chipuin	Mt. Cole	Pavilion Mt.
Mountain				
Spring beauty	+ +	+ +	+	+ +
Balsamroot sunflower	+		+ +	
Tiger lily			+	+
Wild onion	+		+	
Soapberry	+ +		+	
Dwarf blueberry	+	+		+
Whitebark pine	+ +	+ +	+	+ +
Flat areas near water	+ +	+ +	+	+ +
Cultural depressions	+ +	+ +		+ +
Deer	+ +	+ +	+	+ +
Tswilx sites	+ +	+ +		+ +
Funnel sites		+ +		
Extensive lithic scatters consistent with butchering	+	+		+

Symbols used: + present
+ + present and abundant
blank – not present or not known

Nevertheless, the acquisition of the horse has had a marked effect on how and where the animal and plant foods obtained in the mountain zone were processed. According to *Xáxli'p* elders (KB and WN), butchering was, traditionally, often carried out near a kill site. The liver might be roasted immediately while butchering was going on, or, if distance from camp and/or bad weather necessitated speed, the entire animal could be divided into five or six portions (two front legs and shoulders, two hind legs and haunches, the rib cage, and the rest of the carcass). If speed were required, the portions, and any edible internal organs could be wrapped in the skin and carried or dragged to a campsite.

The introduction of horses which was practically contempora-

neous with the acquisition of firearms in the west central interior of
BC (see, for example, Teit 1906:230), no doubt made it possible to carry
whole deer some distance before butchering. Some *Xáxli'p* elders, such
as KB, indicated that deer were occasionally carried on horseback,
whole or butchered, and processed into dry meat at winter dwelling
sites. During the time of KB's experience, these winter dwelling sites
were scattered among locations at a reserve on the opposite side of
the Fraser River from Lillooet, another on Sallus Creek (both about
400 m ASL), and in the Fountain Valley, at Fountain Flats (Fountain
Reserves IR1 and 1A: about 400 m ASL), and near Cinquefoil Lake (at
about 900 m ASL).

Contemporary accounts of the location and type of activities at hunting camps, both in the Chipuin area and elsewhere, may thus differ
considerably, in some respects, from the situation before the introduction of the horse. In the Chilcotin area, for example, introduction of
horses meant that dry meat preparation, skin processing, and even
butchering, could take place some distance from a kill site (Tyhurst
1985:21-2). Thus, not surprisingly, *Xáxli'p* elders indicate that, within
their experience, deer butchering took place near the sites where the
deer were killed, whereas dry-meat making and hide preparation often
took place at or near winter residence locations. Furthermore, few
could recall the use of cache pits or roasting pits at mountain locations near the area where the corms were obtained, even though they
were familiar with the methods for obtaining and cooking the corms.
All indicated that, within their lifetimes, spring beauty corms had been
cooked, or processed for storage, at lower elevations at or near winter
dwellings.

The following sections discuss the four Parkland areas surveyed,
from south to north, on Bald Mountain, Moore Peak-Chipuin Mountain, and Pavilion Mountain.

Bald Mountain

Bald Mountain includes two main peaks: Cairn Peak and Blustry
Mountain. According to elders from *Xáxli'p, Ts'kw'ayláxw,* Bonaparte,
and Lytton bands, the Bald Mountain area was traditionally used as
a hunting and plant gathering area by these (and perhaps other) native communities. The main traditional food resources of the area are
deer (*Odocoileus hemionus*) and spring beauty (often referred to as
'mountain potatoes' *Claytonia lanceolata*). Traditionally, hunting parties made up only of men might go deer hunting in the Bald Mountain area at any time when the weather and snow cover permitted
– usually from May to late October. Family groups travelled to the Bald

Mountain area at any time when spring beauty was available in the late spring and early summer. Women would primarily be involved in digging and processing spring beauty corms. Men would butcher deer at the kill site and then carry as much of the meat (wrapped in the skin) as they could back to the camp. Either men or women could process skins or prepare dry meat, but when active hunting occurred, these activities might more often be done by women.

As mentioned above, groups of men might hunt in the Bald Mountain area at any time when snow conditions permitted. Xáxli'p people as a whole would not generally hunt in large groups on Bald Mountain during the main salmon runs in July and August, since all available able-bodied people were required at fishing sites to catch and process salmon. Once the salmon runs were over, however, family groups might again go to the Bald Mountain area. From late August onward, deer were fat and whitebark pine (*Pinus albicaulis*) cones were available. These pine cones were a valued food source which required some on-site processing. As a food source, however, they were clearly secondary to spring beauty in quantity.

. Hunting groups today are made up of men who habitually hunt together, regardless of kinship. Unlike salmon fishing, where task groups are usually based on the nuclear or extended family, hunting groups are based on a group of three to six men who know each other and are comfortable hunting together. Within each hunting group, one man, selected by consensus, acts as hunting leader. This individual directs each day's hunting strategy and distributes meat among the hunters. One man, LA, who had acted as a hunting leader, told me that the distribution was based not upon a hunter's skill or contribution to a particular hunt but, rather, upon the needs of each hunter and his family.

In open and semi-open mountaintop areas such as Bald Mountain, hunting is often carried out by driving one or more deer up a mountainside toward a narrow passage at the top of a slope. One or two hunters, shooting from a concealed location, such as a natural depression, or from a blind made up of piled stones, shoot the game as it passes by. This type of hunting is known as *tswilx*. It requires careful co-ordination and planning. A hunting leader will also select the areas in which each day's hunting is to take place, whether *tswilx* hunting is used or simply the co-ordinated movement of hunters across an area in which game might be found. While deer are the most important game animal found in the Bald Mountain area, both black bear (*Ursus americanus*) and grizzly bear (*Ursus arctus*) are also found and were traditionally used as food sources.

Spring beauty is the single most important plant food species found in the Bald Mountain area, but its areas of occurrence are somewhat restricted. Spring beauty requires true subalpine meadow – an open and fairly moist grassy area. Such areas are found only along the course of upper Cinquefoil Creek and Pocock Creek in the immediate vicinity of Bald Mountain. Large hillside areas consisting entirely or primarily of subalpine meadow, such as are found in the Botanie Valley area near Lytton, do not occur in the immediate vicinity of Cairn Peak and Blustry Mountain (see Turner 1978:26).

Sites in the Parkland

Locations for possible campsites are restricted in the vicinity of Bald Mountain, especially for camps of more than one or two days' duration. As previously noted, the requirements for a campsite include: relatively flat dry ground, wood for fuel, water, proximity to plant-collecting areas, good overviews, and proximity to game trails and hunting trails. These criteria will be examined in detail in the context of Cairn Peak and Blustry Mountain.

Relatively flat dry ground. The need for this is intuitively obvious, yet flat dry ground in combination with the other requirements for a good campsite is not easy to find in the area. One notable campsite, the Cairn Peak Spur campsite (Figure 1, No. 11; site EdRk 42), where the Bald Mountain Project camped at the suggestion of Roger Adolph, provided ample room for more than a dozen tents on one large flat bench and several smaller ones. The campsite provided abundant fuel (lodgepole pine and alpine fir) and adequate water from a stream located about 150 m to the west. The overview was extremely good. The southernmost face of Cairn Peak, the entire north side of Blustry Peak, the headwaters of Pocock Creek, and almost the entire extent of Cinquefoil Creek could be seen easily and with little effort. Aside from a few whitebark pine (*Pinus albicaulis*), there were few plant foods in the immediate vicinity of the camp, but a good trail led to the divide between Cinquefoil and Pocock creeks, about 50 m to the southeast. There, the main areas of abundance of spring beauty (*Claytonia lanceolata*) followed the creek bottoms in both directions. A few cow-parsnip (*Heracleum lanatum*) and soapberry (*Shepherdia canadensis*) stands were also found along the creek bottoms in areas where several archaeological sites were recorded.

The Cairn Peak Spur site (Figure 1, No. 11) lay on the trail from northern Fountain Valley (via Fountain Creek) and was close to, but some 90 m above, the divide between Pocock and Cinquefoil creeks and the hunting trails that followed the courses of both creeks. Deer were sighted in close proximity to the camp several times during the four-day stay, and the camp was well situated for access to hunting areas on both Cairn Peak and Blustry Mountain.

There are considerably more flat areas suitable for camping along the courses of Cinquefoil and Pocock creeks. Areas that are both dry and flat along the upper courses of these creeks are relatively less common, however. As we only surveyed the headwaters of Pocock Creek (as opposed to the survey we conducted of the whole length of Cinquefoil Creek), these remarks are necessarily restricted to Cinquefoil (and upper Pocock) Creek, but, in general, wherever there was dry flat land near the creeks, we predictably found an archaeological site. The largest of these sites was situated near upper Cinquefoil Creek, about 750 m southwest of the Cairn Peak Spur site and about 275 m directly below it. The site (Figure 1, No. 12; site EdRk 37) was characterized by several large cultural depressions (probable roasting pits; possible cache pits) and satisfied all of the conditions mentioned above except for overview. It occupied a well-drained gentle slope dissected by a dry stream course. Wood for fuel (primarily lodgepole pine: *Pinus contorta*) was abundant. Although it was late in the season for spring beauty, test trowelling showed their presence at the site, and, from observation of a very similar site on Pavilion Mountain earlier in the summer, it would appear that the entire area surrounding the campsite would be productive of these plants.

Since the site is located near the bottom of a creekbed in a steep-sided valley, overview is poor. However, the site is directly below the Cairn Peak Spur: a lookout posted at the latter site would have, as mentioned above, an excellent overview of large areas of both Cairn Peak and Blustry Mountain and could easily signal individuals at the Cinquefoil Creek site should game movements be observed.

Because of time constraints, we were not able to survey the middle or upper course of a stream running north from a prominent cirque on the south face of Blustry Mountain (the area not surveyed runs approximately from UTM EM913090 to EM915077). I was told, however, that *Xáxli'p* people would camp along the upper course of this creek while hunting deer on Blustry Mountain. From aerial photographs and from direct observation from overview locations, it would appear that there is much flat dry ground near wood and water along this stream. Based on the ethnoarchaeological evidence, therefore, the probability of finding sites within this area is high.

Wood for fuel. The Cairn Peak-Blustry Mountain area ranges from about 1,500 m to about 2,300 m in elevation and is thus cold at night even in summer. Access to wood provides not only the means for cooking plant and animal foods but also a needed degree of protection from cold in an area where snow may fall in any month. Timberline, where the Alpine zone begins, on Cairn Peak and Blustry Mountain ranges from about 2,070 m to 2,160 m. Shrubby plants (primarily willow and stunted whitebark pine) do occur in the Alpine, but across large areas of both peaks the ground is either covered only by grass or is bare. We found no recognizable campsites above timberline. The only sites found above timberline were four circles or half circles of stone interpreted as game blinds (Figure 1, Nos. 13, 14, 15; sites EdRk 38, 40, 41) and the gravesite on Blustry Mountain (Figure 1, No. 16; site EdRk 39).

Proximity to water. All campsites – whether archaeological or mentioned by Xáxli'p people or both – were in close proximity to running water. Water is necessary for steam-cooking spring beauty corms in roasting pits, and drinking water would be of considerable importance to groups which, at least in the initial stages of a trip to the area, would probably be relying to a great extent on dried foods such as wind-dried salmon and deer meat.

Proximity to plant food collecting areas. Of the possible or definite ethnoarchaeological campsites recorded in the Cinquefoil Creek-Pocock Creek headwaters area, only the Cairn Creek Spur campsite was not located in very close proximity to (or amid) areas where spring beauty (*Claytonia lanceolata*) occurred. Ethnographically, plant food gathering was an integral part of the trips which Xáxli'p people made to the area in the early summer and in the fall (see Chapter 8). It is, therefore, not surprising that there should be a close correlation between the distribution of preferred campsites and the distribution of areas of abundance of such an important food as spring beauty.

Sites located further down Cinquefoil Creek in the Montane Forest zone (such as the clusters of cultural depressions at UTM EM903093 and EM886095; sites EdRk 45 and 46) are out of the expected range of *Claytonia lanceolata*. Given the probable absence of *Claytonia lanceolata* and the lack of investigations into the cultural depressions (aside from recording their location, depth, and diameter), any comments on factors governing these site locations must be speculative. If, as is expected, at least one of the cultural depressions at each site is in fact a roasting pit, the question arises as to what, if any, plant foods were roasted there. A primary observation is that both sites are very favourably located. The site at UTM EM903093 (the Cinquefoil Creek Canyon site; Figure 1, No. 17; site EdRk 45) is in a large, natural grassy opening with good access to both fuel and water. The site at UTM EM886095 (the 'North Fork Cinquefoil Creek' site; Figure 1, No. 18; site EdRk 46) is also well located with regard to fuel and water and, furthermore, is located at the junction of two important trails.

Assuming that both sites do, in fact, contain roasting pits, the food source processed or roasted there was most probably *Claytonia lanceolata* (brought about two kilometres down the Cinquefoil Creek trail) or some other plant food species more locally available, such as wild onions (*Allium* spp.). Roots and corms may have been brought to these sites to take advantage of more abundant wood or better shelter than was available in the Parkland zone (upper reaches of the creeks).

Good overview. Only the Cairn Peak Spur camp site has what might be described as excellent overview. All other possible recorded campsites are located in steep and deep valley bottoms (with the exception of a cultural depression and lithic scatter site on upper Pocock Creek at UTM EM931097; Figure 1, No. 19; site, EdRk 33), and overview is thus severely limited. With the exception of the Cairn Peak Spur site good overviews do not often co-occur with the other requirements for a campsite discussed here. However, overview was a clearly stated desirable quality of campsites, and access to the Cairn Peak Spur site and to locations on Blustry Mountain with good overviews is easily gained from sites on upper Pocock and Cinquefoil creeks.

Proximity to hunting trails and game trails. All recorded campsites and possible campsites are on, or very near, trails which are used by *Xáxli'p* hunters today. However, since the trails often pass through areas in which the necessary conditions for a campsite are found, this is hardly surprising. Moreover, game trails crisscross the entire area. Correlation between game trail location and campsite location is thus to be expected.

Access to the Cairn Peak-Blustry Mountain area can be gained by a number of routes, and several trails loop over and across the bare mountain top areas. Access trails are restricted by geography (e.g., steep hillsides, rockslides) only in the areas that lie between Hat Creek to the east and Fountain Valley to the west. The tops of both Cairn Peak and Blustry Mountain are rolling, open, grassy prairie. Travel in these areas, whether by horse or on foot, is unrestricted in any direction, and, aside from the necessity of avoiding areas of steep relief, mountaintop routes can be followed without regard to terrain.

The main routes to Cairn Peak and Blustry Mountain from Fountain Valley lie along Fountain Creek and Cinquefoil Creek (see Figure 5). The route along Fountain Creek begins at *Kwotlenemo* (Fountain) Lake and follows the course of the creek to a point at UTM EM888135, where the creek branches. Either branch may be followed. Both branches lead to an open area on the north side of Cairn Peak

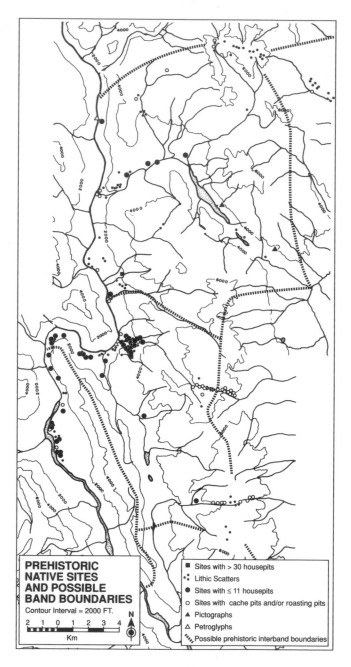

PREHISTORIC NATIVE SITES AND POSSIBLE BAND BOUNDARIES

Contour Interval = 2000 FT.

2 1 0 1 2 3 4
Km

N

■ Sites with > 30 housepits
•: Lithic Scatters
● Sites with ≤ 11 housepits
○ Sites with cache pits and/or roasting pits
▲ Pictographs
△ Petroglyphs
⋮⋮⋮ Possible prehistoric interband boundaries

FIGURE 5

Prehistoric village sites, salmon fishing sites, mountain hunting sites, with possible prehistoric interband boundaries (site data and map compiled by D. Alexander)

(*kelhéxwa*), which is a hunting area, and from which easy access can be gained to any other part of Cairn Peak.

The route along Cinquefoil Creek begins just east of Fountain Valley at UTM EM865097 and follows the north side of Cinquefoil Creek from the north. The northern branch follows the inflowing stream northward, climbing from an elevation of 1,370 m to 1,830 m in a distance of about 3.5 km as it follows the northern stream course north and then east. At UTM EM897107 this trail branches again, one branch following the stream bed east into a wide subalpine valley on the northwest side of Cairn Peak. The other branch of this trail follows a switchback route first south and then north along the west side of Cairn Peak, crossing timberline at about 1,980 m elevation. Both branches of the northern trail give quicker access to the alpine area of Cairn Peak than does the southern trail, which follows Cinquefoil Creek. After UTM EM897107, the southern trail follows Cinquefoil Creek, and Pocock Creek is reached at an elevation of 1,980 m. From this point, access can be quickly gained to Cairn Peak to the north or Blustry Mountain to the south.

As mentioned above, once in the Alpine, the gentle relief and open nature of the mountaintop areas makes defined routes unnecessary. From the point marked 'Blustry Mountain' on the 1:50,000 scale map, access can be easily gained to a number of important hunting areas. South of Blustry Mountain, a trail crosses a ridge where a named gravesite is located (see below). About 3 km southeast of this point are two named sites (Figure 1, Nos. 20, 21) on a high wooded ridge which is actually a southeastward extension of Blustry Mountain itself.

These two sites are, according to elders from *Xáxli'p* (KB, WN), Bonaparte (SN), and Lytton (LP) bands, the southeasternmost sites commonly recognized as being part of *Xáxli'p* Band territory. However, Lytton Band members coming from the south or Bonaparte Band members coming from the east might also camp at these two sites. According to an elder (LP) from Lytton Band, Lytton Band members would sometimes hunt on Blustry Mountain itself, though they recognize it as being within the commonly used hunting territory of the *Xáxli'p* Band. Access to these two sites from the south or east is via the ridge line leading north from Murray Peak (UTM EM019967) or from Upper Hat Creek. It is possible to gain access to Blustry Mountain via Rough Creek, but the elevation gain per unit distance (1,400 m in about 6 km) and the nature of the terrain makes this a much more difficult route than any other discussed above.

Sites in the Alpine

There are three definite, and one possible, hunting blinds located on
Blustry Mountain above timberline. All consist of circles or semi-circles
of piled stones and are located in areas with excellent overviews of
the surrounding terrain. No such sites were found on Cairn Peak: they
may exist but were not known to *Xáxli'p* people, and none were found
during our brief transit of the immediate vicinity of Cairn Peak, during which we, for the most part, followed hunting trails.

The two northernmost hunting blinds are located on the north side
of Blustry Mountain (at UTM EM921075; Figure 1, No. 13; site EdRk 38)
overlooking a deep bowl which drains into Cinquefoil Creek. Deer
were driven south from the bowl and up the steep hillside below the
blinds. Upon reaching the top of the incline, deer were killed by a
hunter who had concealed himself within one of the blinds. This type
of group hunting (or *tswilx*) was made easier by the fact that the site
is located on a small rocky bluff overlooking a declivity in the mountainside. If enough hunters were present below, deer could be driven
toward that point and would naturally follow it upward. No complete
artefacts were found at this site (EdRk 38), but a 50 cm by 50 cm test
excavation revealed several small pieces of lithic debitage within 5 cm
of the surface. For the dimensions of these hunting blinds and others
described below, see Alexander's report (1987) on the Bald Mountain
area.

Some 300 m to the southeast of this site, another circle of stones
is located on a small rise in the middle of an otherwise flat and gently
sloping area (at UTM EM023073; Figure 1, No. 14; site EdRk 41). According to *Xáxli'p* people, this site is probably a gravesite, but its size (3.8
m in diameter as opposed to 1 m for the definite cairn gravesite further south) indicates that it may have been a hunting blind instead.
Furthermore, there is no oral tradition connected with this site as there
is with the definite gravesite. If it were a hunting blind, it would be
well located to intercept deer being driven across the flat terrain near
the peak of Blustry Mountain. This site (EdRk 41) is the only one in
which there is some conflict between ethnographic and archaeological evidence; however, it is always possible that the site may have been
a hunting blind that was subsequently used as a gravesite. A black
basalt biface tip and a flake were located west near the stone circle
during a brief surface survey.

About 550 m to the west-southwest of this site, another semi-circle
of stones is located on a prominent knoll overlooking the headwaters
of a creek (at UTM EM918072; Figure 1, No. 15). According to *Xáxli'p* people, this blind is still used today. It provides a good overview of the

small valley directly below it, in an area where several deer were sighted during our survey. The knoll itself was grassy and no artefacts were found during a brief surface survey (EdRk 40).

To sum up, these sites indicate that hunting from concealed locations was practised in at least two and possibly three or more locations, all of which are located on or near the highest parts of Blustry Mountain.

To the south of the hunting blinds discussed above, a gravesite (EdR 39) is located on a saddle connecting Blustry Mountain to a peak southeast of it (at UTM EM920066; Figure 1, No. 16). Its physical dimensions are more fully discussed in the archaeological report by Alexander (1987), but, briefly, it is smaller than the hunting blinds discussed above, being less than one m at its greatest diameter. Furthermore, it has no central depression as do the hunting blinds discussed above.

According to an oral tradition shared by Bonaparte (JN), Lytton (LP), and Xáxli'p (KB; WN; RH) band members, a Shuswap hunter is buried there. He had been raiding a salmon fishing site on the Fraser River below, and was wounded in a fight with people whose descendants now belong to the Lytton Band. The Shuswap hunter, in attempting to get home, made it as far as Blustry Mountain, and died where he is now buried. It is a tradition shared by all three bands to leave remembrances such as food or money at the gravesite. Within the stone circle of the grave, a broken black basalt lanceolate projectile point was located and left in situ. The gravesite is an area of spiritual importance to all three bands, as, in a wider sense, is the entire Cairn Peak-Blustry Mountain area.

Moore Peak-Chipuin Mountain

Approaches to this area from Fountain Valley are steeper and, thus, more difficult than those to Bald Mountain. However, using horses, the time required to reach the main Montane Parkland camping areas on both mountains from Fountain Valley is about the same – in the order of four hours. Like Bald Mountain, the Moore Peak-Chipuin area (hereafter referred to as 'Chipuin' unless greater specificity is required) is fairly well supplied with adequate camping areas, moderately abundant plant foods, and locations suited to game hunting. It should be noted, however, that neither this site nor Pavilion Mountain (discussed below) provided the massive abundance of spring beauty encountered in the Potato Mountain sites in the Chilcotin or in Botanie Valley near Lytton. Correspondingly, and not surprisingly, the number of recorded cultural depressions which may have served as either roasting pits or cache pits was much higher in the Potato Mountain area (more than

900 depressions) than in any of the localities in the study area (less than 25 each). The Chipuin area may be characterized as a Montane and Parkland bowl, bounded on the north by the large, high mountain wall of Mount Chipuin (2,164 m) and on the south by the cone-shaped summit area of Moore Peak (2,222 m). Between these two peaks, this bowl is further bisected by a lower forested ridge at about 2,000 m, which divides the headwaters of Gibbs Creek to the west and the headwaters of a branch of Anderson Creek to the east. The bottom of the bowl is heavily forested with subalpine fir (*Abies lasiocarpa*) and lodgepole pine (*Pinus ponderosa*). True Parkland meadow, however, covers the entire south face of Chipuin Mountain for a distance of at least 6 km and is found intermittently in patches along the low forested ridge between the two peaks. Parkland meadow is more sporadic in the vicinity of Moore Peak. On the north side of the mountain, subalpine fir and willow brush grade quickly into alpine tundra, characterized by dry stony soil, lichens, and small flowering plants.

The bottom of the bowl between the two peaks is well watered, and though we came too late in the season to observe spring beauty in bloom, excavation at a semi-open campsite (EeRk-T-LIL12) revealed the presence of spring beauty corms in the soil, indicating that such would probably be abundant on the extensive moist areas along the southwest side of Mount Chipuin.

Parkland Sites

On Chipuin, the most important funnel for hunting drives is located in a transition zone between Montane Parkland forest and Montane Parkland meadow (Figure 1, No. 8). Willow brush, often as high as 2 m, fills wet areas in the bottom of the funnel. Deer were driven upward from the forest at the bottom of the funnel and were killed by hunters concealed behind trees or bushes at the top of the funnel. To the west of the funnel, the mountainside is steep, wet, and brushy. To the east, at higher elevation, it is more open, with mixed Montane Parkland meadow and forest. The ground is fairly dry and there are numerous small level areas or benches. All archaeological sites which might, by reasons of immediate proximity, be associated with the funnel and its use as a hunting area were located downslope on the benches in the more level and open terrain to the east of the funnel. These included a number of large lithic scatters and some bifaces and projectile points (e.g., site EeRk 17; EeRk-T-LIL14; see Pokotylo and Froese 1983; Stryd 1974). The absence of cultural depressions among the lithic scatters near this kill site indicates that the cooking and/or processing of spring beauty corms was not among the main activities carried out in this immediate area. Rather, given the proximity of the kill site itself and the presence of extensive lithic debitage, it might be predicted, in the absence of excavation, that the sites were used for butchering and possibly as temporary campsites during hunting excursions. The amount of lithic debitage is consistent with this interpretation in that it is probable that a high degree of resharpening or flaking would be required to provide effective cutting and chopping edges during butchering.

Alpine Sites

In addition to this funnel site, there were also some *tswilx* (cooperative group hunting) sites near the top of the Mt. Chipuin ridge (especially at the western end of the mountain). And there were at least two *tswilx* sites noted by *Xáxli'p* elders in the tundra area near the summit of Moore Peak. A broken biface was recovered near one of these (UTM EM892176; site EeRk-T-LIL11) during surface survey in 1987 (Alexander 1987).

Comments

In contemporary accounts by *Xáxli'p* people of resource use in the Chipuin area, the deer-hunting funnel was inevitably mentioned first, with plant food gathering usually mentioned as an afterthought. With Bald Mountain, on the other hand, contemporary accounts usually emphasized *both* hunting and plant-food gathering. Work elsewhere has shown that both roasting pits and cache pits can, with a great deal of confidence, be associated with plant food gathering and processing (Tyhurst 1985:21-2). Comparing numbers of cultural depressions from the Bald Mountain and Chipuin areas shows 26 from Bald Mountain and 24 from the Chipuin area despite more intensive surveys in the latter area. These numbers support the subjective impression given by *Xáxli'p* people regarding the relative importance of plant food gathering in the two areas.

On the other hand, there are many similarities between the Bald Mountain area and Chipuin, and though the above discussion has emphasized the differences between them, the two areas share many important characteristics, especially in comparison to such an area as Mt. Cole (or even Pavilion Mountain). Both Chipuin and Bald mountains are significant hunting areas easily accessible from the Fountain area. Both have extensive areas of well-watered Parkland meadow and have a fair abundance of two of the most important traditional plant foods: spring beauty and whitebark pine cones. Both have numerous areas in which it is possible to set up a traditional camp, that is, both have substantial areas of dry flat ground in proximity to water, wood for fuel, good overviews and proximity to plant food sources and game trails.

Mount Cole

Mount Cole (*k'exwtsítsen*), known locally as 'Tom Cole,' is a peak whose summit is 4 km southwest of *Ts'kw'ayláxw* Reserve (I.R. 1). The maximum elevation of Mt. Cole is approximately 1,700 m, and, unlike Chipuin or Bald mountains, the amount of open, treeless area is both limited and dry and thus unsuitable for spring beauty growth (though tiger lily does occur sporadically from about 1,000 m upward). Mt. Cole is too low to support many whitebark pine trees, and few were seen on our one-day survey of the summit area.

Mt. Cole is situated relatively near *Ts'kw'ayláxw* Reserve, and access is relatively easy. Several *Ts'kw'ayláxw* Band members said that hunters could travel on foot to the summit area and back in a day. The route is not particularly steep, and in July 1987 we travelled to the summit in a four-wheel-drive pickup truck across the Montane Parkland meadows.

The summit area itself is dry and open and is characterized by patches of meadow interspersed with areas of lodgepole pine (*Pinus contorta*) and trembling aspen (*Populus tremuloide*). There is little moisture on the summit itself aside from a small, probably seasonal, pond and a small stream which begins below the pond and runs southwest through an ethnographically important camping area at UTM EM840328 (site EfRk-T-Cole 2). Probably because of the dry conditions, we saw little spring beauty except in the campsite area. We were told by *Ts'kw'ayláxw* people that the Mt. Cole summit was unimportant as a source for spring beauty; the only significant concentrations known to occur in the vicinity of Mt. Cole were at 'Sagebrush Flats' (see Figure 1; UTM EM825345), some 3 km northwest of the summit and at considerably lower elevation in the Intermediate Grassland zone some 500 m below the summit (at about 1,200 m).

Time constraints did not permit us to survey the Sagebrush Flats area for cultural depressions such as cache pits or roasting pits. We were told by *Ts'kw'ayláxw* people that plant foods, such as spring beauty, obtained in the vicinity of Mt. Cole were brought back to *Ts'kw'ayláxw* for processing or cooking. The extremely short distance (about 1.5 km) between the two points suggests why this might have been so. Whether this practice would have been followed prehistorically, when neither pack animals nor automobiles were available, is unclear.

Parkland Use

No cultural depressions of any kind were found in the summit area. In fact, the only visible archaeological remains were very small amounts of lithic debitage at the streamside campsite mentioned above in the Parkland zone and at another campsite next to the pond (see Figure 1, No. 7; UTM EM855329; site EfRt-T-Cole 1). These findings are consistent with contemporary ethnographic accounts, which emphasize the importance of the Mt. Cole summit as a deer hunting area, and downplay or deny its importance as an area for gathering plant foods. The nature of the terrain (lacking any well-defined gullies) precludes any except the most simple forms of organized hunting. Certainly there were no sites such as the deer hunting funnel on Mt. Chipuin or the stone blinds on Bald Mountain or Pavilion Mountain.

Hunters from *Ts'kw'ayláxw* (DP and BN) told us that men would sometimes ride up to Mt. Cole and return in one day. Camping on the mountain has fallen off in recent times, but both DP and BN told us that, until recently, hunters might ride up Mt. Cole, camp at one of the campsites near the summit, and 'stay until they got a deer.' BN accompanied his grandfather on those hunting trips and, in fact, showed us a tree in which he had carved his initials while camped there with his uncle on 20 June 1964.

Due to the open terrain, there are no major game trails near the summit, except on the southeast side of Mt. Cole, where a game trail comes up from a series of lakes and a wooded pass between Mt. Cole and a ridge to the immediate south (DP). Hunting strategy on Mt. Cole is determined by deer behaviour and by the nature of the terrain. Deer hunting is best done at dawn, when, on first light, the deer emerge from thickets where they have spent the night and begin moving in search of browse. Deer can also be located during the day, because they move toward rocky, windy promontories to escape flies.

Hunters' behaviour in such circumstances is based on their knowledge of deer behaviour. Hunters on foot or on horseback may move single file or abreast toward places where deer are likely to be found. Organized driving of deer (*tswilx*, to use the Lillooet language term), however, conveys no particular advantage in these circumstances and is not used on Mt. Cole.

DP indicated that if family groups came to Mt. Cole at all, they would usually do so in early summer, 'following the berries' from the valley as they ripened, digging for spring beauty or wild onions (*Allium* spp.) as they became available, and hunting. In such a case, the groups would remain for 'about a week' on Mt. Cole. The only plant food processing that took place on the mountain was the roasting of white-bark pine corms in the fall. No roasting pits were made, according to DP. The only other food or material processing that took place on the mountain was the making of dry meat and some hide preparation (scraping and stretching but not tanning), if a stay on the mountain were extended due to good luck at hunting.

The camps used near the summit would be 'under the spruce trees' if no tents were brought (i.e., in the shelter of the thick clumps of subalpine fir) a pattern observed both on Bald Mountain and in the Potato Range in the Chilcotin (Alexander et al. 1985). Because of the proximity of Ts'kw'ayláxw, as noted above, it seems likely that 'camp furniture' such as meat drying racks, skin stretching frames, and so on, would only be constructed if too much game were killed to be brought down before spoilage became a problem.

Thus, there would be limited archaeological feature remains at any such camp (e.g., few post holes, few smudge fires). It would also be likely, given the fact that Ts'kw'ayláxw and Marble Canyon were close by and that stays were brief (in the order of a week or so versus two weeks or more at Pavilion Mountain), that lithic debitage would be relatively sparse. This was reflected in the extreme paucity of surface finds on Mt. Cole.

DP pointed out two main areas for camping in the Parkland, both already mentioned – the area of the seasonal pond and the area of the seasonal small stream. These sites would provide the only sources of water on the entire summit of Mt. Cole. What little debitage was found (one flake and one core) was found in those areas only. When compared to the complexity of remains found elsewhere in subalpine sites (cultural depressions, visible camp furniture, large amounts of debitage, and relatively large amounts of tools), these results suggest the comparative 'archaeological invisibility' – at least to surface collection – of hunting camps in close proximity to winter villages where there is little plant collecting and processing or extensive game butchering activities.

Although family groups, or small groups of hunters travelling without their families, were the norm in the more distant past, more recently Mt. Cole has been visited more often by 'three or four' hunters travelling on horseback (DP). This change is no doubt linked to a general decline in plant food utilization as well as to improved transportation (e.g., horses can now be easily trucked near to the summit of Mt. Cole). In the past, however, because Mt. Cole was so close to winter sites in Pavilion and in Marble Canyon, it was an important seasonal resource area. Despite its relative paucity of plant foods and its lack of *tswilx* sites, its proximity and ease of access gave it a contemporary importance far greater than the meagre archaeological remains which we were able to locate by surface survey would suggest.

Mt. Cole was also important to native people living in *Ts'kw'ayláxw* and Marble Canyon because of the plant and animal food resources available in the variety of Montane Forest ecological zones on its slopes (see Chapters 2 and 3). But it served, too, as an important travel corridor and spiritual training area. From the summit area of Mt. Cole, it was possible to travel south through a forested pass to Montane Parkland hunting areas on '14 mile mountain' (an unnamed peak on the 1:50,000 scale map 92-I/13; UTM EM872292) some 5 km to the south-southwest and thence south to Mt. Chipuin and the Bald Mountain area. The area to the west and northwest of Mt. Cole, including a series of small lakes at 1,200 to 1,300 m elevation, was also an important hunting area accessible from Pavilion or Marble Canyon or from Mt. Cole itself. Deer and berries such as soapberry were the primary resources found there.

Because the slopes of Mt. Cole are relatively easy to negotiate, there were numerous ways of getting to the summit. One of the more important of these led from Pavilion up a steep sidehill overlooking the site of the modern-day railway yard and thence up-slope to 'Sagebrush Flats' (Figure 1). Perhaps because travelling to '14 mile mountain' meant going through 3 or 4 km of dense upper Montane Forest to the south of Mt. Cole, perhaps because of the importance of Pavilion Mountain to *Ts'kw'ayláxw* people, both *Ts'kw'ayláxw* and *Xáxli'p* people indicated that '14 mile mountain,' at the head of Sallus Creek, was more often used by *Xáxli'p* than by *Ts'kw'ayláxw* people, although *Ts'kw'ayláxw* hunters did, and still do, go there to hunt occasionally.

As with sites on the north side of Marble Canyon, Mt. Cole was used for a type of spiritual training, which DP described as 'training for a special thing if you're a runner or a hunter or a fisherman.' Persons undergoing such training would stay in the vicinity of the seasonal pond near the summit of Mt. Cole. As indicated above, this area was also used as a campsite by hunters.

Mt. Cole was definitely within the commonly used hunting territory of people living in the *Ts'kw'ayláxw*-Marble Canyon area and was not usually used by hunters who lived in other areas. DP did indicate, however, that hunters from Bonaparte Band now occasionally use Mt. Cole for deer hunting 'in exchange' for *Ts'kw'ayláxw* Band hunters hunting for moose in the McLean's Lake area, west of Cache Creek. Although not on Mt. Cole itself, DP did mention an important *tswilx* site visible from Mt. Cole and located in Marble Canyon. This site was used by *Ts'kw'ayláxw* hunters and was located near the upper part of the canyon at a steep limestone cliff above and to the north of Pavilion Lake (Figure 1, No. 22).

Pavilion Mountain

Pavilion Mountain is located 16 km northwest of the *Ts'kw'ayláxw* Band office (near the village of Pavilion) in the divide between the Marble Canyon-Pavilion Creek and Kelly Creek watersheds. Like Bald Mountain, it was an important hunting and plant food gathering area. Like Bald Mountain, it marked the boundary between the commonly used hunting territories of different native groups and was used by people whose wintering sites were widely separated geographically. Unlike Bald Mountain, access to Pavilion Mountain is relatively easy from any direction, its slopes being gradual and the approaches uncomplicated by steep relief.

The area between the village of Pavilion and Pavilion Mountain rises steeply at first, from about 750 m to about 1,100 m in the first 0.75 km, and then becomes Intermediate Grassland, including rolling, semi-open terrain with trembling aspen, lodgepole pine, and large areas of natural grassland. This area is now used by the Diamond S Ranch as irrigated hayland and for cattle grazing but was previously of some importance as a hunting and plant food gathering area. It was also used as a travel corridor from the *Ts'kw'ayláxw*-Marble Canyon area to Pavilion Mountain.

DP related that, in the 1930s and 1940s, native people from *Ts'kw'ayláxw* Band worked on the Diamond S Ranch and lived at a site near the contemporary Pavilion-Kelly Lake road during the haying season. Previously, and to some extent today, the area between Pavilion village and Pavilion Mountain was of importance for deer hunting. The higher elevation parts of this area were also of importance for plant foods such as spring beauty, which, according to DP and ME, could be obtained earlier than at colder, higher elevation sites on Pavilion Mountain itself.

ME recalled that there was a concentration of cultural depressions (possible roasting pits or cache pits) 'near a small lake to the east of the road in the middle of the open rangeland' (UTM EM 862423). We were not able to locate this site, but the use of this area for obtaining *and* cooking or processing plant foods is consistent with the apparent abundance of plant foods such as spring beauty and with the distance (on the order of 8 km) from Pavilion village.

At UTM EM831433, a rough road leads from this plateau area down to Moran, on the Fraser River. DP and others told us that this road had been built by placer miners. The same route may have been followed by hunters going from *Ts'kw'ayláxw* to the Moran area to hunt for deer or for mountain sheep. Mountain sheep previously occurred naturally in this area and have since been re-established through restocking in the vicinity of Kelly Lake (DP). The slopes above Moran Flats were used by hunters from *Ts'kw'ayláxw* using *tswilx* or organized deer hunting drives. DP also indicated that, in the fall, deer would cross the Fraser River west to east at Moran at a narrow part of the river and could be hunted there. (There are several possible salmon fishing sites at Moran flats, but because of distance and difficult access, little is known of the area by people from the *Ts'kw'ayláxw* Band).

On Moran flats, two archaeological sites were found in a clearing beside the Kelly Lake road above the flats in the vicinity of UTM EM828433, but only one cultural depression was found in that area. This would indicate perhaps, that deer and mountain sheep killed between Moran and the upland were processed at this site, but that little thermal processing of plant foods (e.g., pit cooking of balsamroot, or spring beauty) took place there.

Pavilion Mountain itself takes the form of a high Montane Parkland ridge, trending east-west, lacking true Alpine terrain as the term is used in Chapter 2. Defined on the west by a pass leading north to Kelly Lake and on the east by a pass that leads northwest from the headwaters of Pavilion Creek, it exceeds an elevation of 1,800 m for a distance of at least 5 km in an east-west direction, with a maximum elevation of 2,089 m.

As with the other Parkland areas already discussed, the primary food resources of Pavilion Mountain were deer and spring beauty. Spring beauty was particularly abundant in one area west of the summit (see Figure 1; in the vicinity of UTM EM893482). This area was known to *Ts'kw'ayláxw* people as an area for gathering and processing spring beauty corms, and several archaeological sites were recorded in this area (see Alexander 1986), including several concentrations of roasting pits and cache pits.

Other plant food resources of the Pavilion Mountain area included abundant whitebark pine and sporadic occurrences of tiger lily and wild onion. Soapberry is found throughout the summit area and dwarf mountain blueberry (*Vaccinium caespitosum*) occurs whenever there are open, grassy spaces (i.e., sporadically, near the summit). Lodgepole pine, whose cambium was stripped and eaten as a sweet in the spring (cf. Turner, Chapter 8; 1987:72-3), is found on Pavilion Mountain (as in other mountainous areas discussed above) and over a wide elevation range, from Parkland near the summit to lower Montane Forests near Marble Canyon and Pavilion.

The most important animal species on Pavilion Mountain, according to *Ts'kw'ayláxw* people, was, and still is, deer. According to the season, deer could be found at different elevations on Pavilion Mountain, including the uplands to the south of it and along the course of Pavilion Creek, whose easternmost branch begins just below the summit of Pavilion Mountain. As with the other subalpine areas discussed above, spring beauty would blossom and, thus, would be visible among the other plants of the Parkland shortly after the snow melted. This season would also coincide with the first spring growth of other mountain plants and, thus, with the yearly arrival of deer in the Montane Parkland area.

It is no coincidence that from Bald Mountain to Pavilion Mountain, and in the Potato Ranges of the Chilcotin area as well, spring beauty and deer were the mainstays of subsistence in late spring for those native people who had access to Montane Parkland areas. These staples must have been of particular importance because of their relative abundance and because of the relative certainty of success in obtaining them wherever Parkland and Alpine habitats and geography were favourable. This importance must have been enhanced by the fact that they became available following the time of greatest scarcity (late winter, early spring) and at a time of year when few other food resources were at or near their peak availability (see Tyhurst n.d., Chapter 3).

The amounts of spring beauty on Pavilion Mountain were at least as great as those on Bald Mountain or Chipuin, based on our survey of both areas. Pavilion Parkland also had plentiful nearby dry, flat ground, water, and wood for fuel. Pavilion Mountain also has several sites for driving deer toward hunters (*tswilx*) which combine excellent overview with places in which hunters could conceal themselves. Originally, we were not able to survey an area south of the summit of Pavilion Mountain where DP told us hunters camped while hunting at *tswilx* sites just east of the summit. However, a later survey in 1987 by Alexander yielded only one small lithic scatter and revealed the area to be too steep, wet or forested for numerous good campsites.

Parkland Sites

We did find sites with roasting pits and cache pits concentrated within a relatively small area (Figure 1, No. 1 at UTM EM893482: see Alexander 1986) within a few hundred metres of (or within) a major concentration of spring beauty. Although no botanical analysis of excavated soil from this area has yet been carried out, the only reasonable conclusion that can be drawn from the proximity of these cultural depressions to a major concentration of spring beauty is that they were at least in part associated with the cooking and/or processing and storage of spring beauty corms. Ethnographic information from Ts'kw'aylāxw Band elders (ME; DP), supports this conclusion.

There were also at least two important *tswilx* sites in the Parkland zone on Pavilion Mountain. The westernmost, (Figure 1, No. 2; UTM EM904483), was located in a steep-walled valley dominated by a prominent rock spire. According to DP, deer would be driven up the valley, sighted by a hunter hidden near the top of the spire, and killed as they passed below, by hunters situated near the valley floor. Despite a fairly concentrated surface survey of this steep and brushy area, no artefacts were found, although excavation or shovel-testing might produce better results. On the other hand, lithic debris may be quite scarce at actual drive sites (Pokotylo and Hanks 1985) but more abundant at nearby gearing up, butchering, and/or camping locations. A small lithic scatter (EkRk-T-LIL 22) was found in the valley below the lookout.

The more easterly site is located on the easternmost spar of Pavilion Mountain (Figure 1, No. 3; UTM EM931475). The site consists of a series of limestone bluffs overlooking a long, grassy, south-facing slope. One bluff in particular was noted by DP as a *tswilx* site. There, a pile of stones had been used to conceal a hunter awaiting deer driven up-slope by his companions. A small lithic scatter (EfRk-T-PAV 2) was found above the blind and DP indicated that a rock shelter (EfRk-T-PAV 1) at its base had been used by hunters as shelter in inclement weather. Test excavation of the floor of this cave revealed one flake, charcoal, and three bone fragments amid a large number of limestone stones and boulders which had fallen from the shelter roof.

Three other lithic scatters were collected from the general area with 33 to 42 artefacts each. These sites (EfRk 37, EfRk-T-LIL 24 and 25) contained two Shuswap points and one Plateau point in all.

DP indicated that, in his experience, deer killed at the *tswilx* site were butchered at campsites located in the trees below (roughly: UTM EM930467). Because of limited time, distance to the campsite area, and uncertainty on DP's part as to the exact location of these campsites, we were not able to survey the area in which they were reported to be located. We do know, however, that they were located on a branch of the stream which also runs through the spring beauty processing area discussed above. Presumably, travel between these two areas would have taken place following the stream, a distance (following the stream) of about 6.5 km. Given the extensive meadows near this drive site, it is possible that the campsite area below the *tswilx* site also contains cultural depressions associated with spring beauty processing. Confirmation of this will have to await further survey.

To the east of the *tswilx* site, Pavilion Mountain drops away gradually toward the headwaters of Pavilion Creek, Maiden Creek, and Minch Creek. These three streams have a common area of origin near a low pass east of Pavilion Mountain. Together, the paths of these three watercourses form an important complex of hunting and travel routes between Marble Canyon, the upper part of Bonaparte River, and upper Kelly Creek, respectively. This fact alone must have contributed to Pavilion Mountain having been visited by hunters and plant collectors from a number of different bands.

Upper Maiden Creek is also an important source of fine-grained vitreous 'basalt' (DP). Excavations near the spring beauty processing site (site EfRk 38) on Pavilion Mountain in 1987 produced a large amount of early stage reduction debitage, which may eventually be identified as having come from Maiden Creek (Alexander: personal communication). Should that be so, it would indicate that groups using Pavilion Mountain in the pre-contact era had access to Maiden Creek basalt sources either directly or through trade.

A second excavation in the area also recovered a large amount of reduction debitage consisting of chalcedony (site EfRk-T-LIL 10). The amount (over 1,100 flakes) and the relatively large size of the debitage which was recovered by excavation (in one 1 square m test pit) would be most consistent either with the acquisition of the raw materials by those who carried out the reduction or with the acquisition of the raw materials by one group of individuals via trade or exchange (of the materials) while on the mountain and reduction of the raw material by the recipient. The second possibility is worth considering, because it would be consistent with what is known ethnographically about the designation of subalpine areas as boundaries between different groups or bands and with the fact that those utilizing Pavilion Mountain (and other subalpine areas) often came together at large summer mountaintop gatherings from groups whose winter settlements were widely separated geographically (see remarks on Bald Mountain, above; see also Tyhurst 1985; Alexander et al. 1985).

RESOURCES

Introduction

Romanoff (Chapters 5 and 9) has written on both salmon fishing and hunting and dealt with the question of access to these resources. Kennedy and Bouchard (Chapter 6) have discussed access to salmon fishing sites in light of their own ethnographic research and Romanoff's data. Teit generally indicates the boundaries of local groups, but is surprisingly silent on the question of access to resources within local groups. There is no point in reiterating Romanoff's and Kennedy's considerable information on the questions of both inter- and intra- group access to resources. Rather, I propose to briefly discuss the issue of economic conditions under which resource access may be restricted, using ethnographic and ethnoarchaeological information.

In the discussion below, I shall use 'band' to refer to local groups (such as Teit's 'Xa'xalp' village, the modern-day Xáxli'p or Fountain) which existed before the reserve system was instituted in the late nineteenth century (see Teit 1906:195-8). I shall use 'Band' to refer to the modern-day administrative entities, such as the Xáxli'p Band and Ts'kw'ayláxw Band, and to their precursors in the era since the institution of the reserve system.

Access to Salmon Fishing Sites

For salmon, it is interesting that the notion of salmon fishing sites of any kind being owned by families or by larger kin groups is not well remembered by older Lillooet members. This corresponds well with current social reality, in which access to salmon fishing sites is on a Band basis (in the sense of the contemporary administrative units such as Xáxli'p Band, the Ts'kw'ayláxw Band, etc.), but does not correspond at all well with older and highly reliable ethnographic information. Although 'Bands' are modern, I would suggest that the requirement of Band permission for non-Band members to fish at salmon fishing sites is a continuation of a much older pattern, with the exception that the older pattern also included kin-group ownership of some fishing sites.

The pattern today is that, almost without exception, salmon fishing sites are administered by Bands. Where a salmon fishing site is part of a Band's reserve (as is the case with the Ten Mile and part of the Six Mile fishing sites for Xáxli'p Band), that Band can and does require that non-Band members fish only with permission of the Band administration. We were told that, even before modern refrigeration and road transportation were available, native people in the recent past came from as far away as the Okanagan to fish at Xáxli'p sites. Today such people could, if not regulated, take considerable numbers of salmon and, without having to remain at the site to wind-dry them, return home with them. Given substantially reduced runs from nineteenth-century levels, especially of spring salmon, this could have a very significant impact on local fish procurement and consumption.

The current system of 'Band licensing' of salmon fishing can be viewed as an attempt to ensure that Xáxli'p and Ts'kw'ayláxw Band members can obtain enough salmon for their own needs without excessive outside competition at salmon fishing sites. Salmon as a food source, as a part of cultural identity, and as a symbol of the spiritual relationship between humans and nature, remains central to Lillooet life. Although a further discussion of this topic lies beyond the scope of this paper, it cannot be left without remarking that the strong defence which *Xáxli'p* people have mounted against governmental attempts to regulate salmon fishing is a strong, accurate, and very clear indicator of their recognition of that continuing importance.

Access to Hunting and Plant Gathering Sites

All *Xáxli'p* and *Ts'kw'ayláxw* elders indicated that, within bands, there was no ownership of hunting or plant food gathering sites and that access was free to all band members. One elder at *Ts'kw'ayláxw* gave what at first appeared to be an oblique answer to the question of ownership of hunting and plant food gathering sites. I believe, however, that this statement directly addresses the underlying reasons why such sites were *not* owned:

> The families went ... almost similar to seasonal, eh? Somebody went to camping place, everyone went to camping place. The population at that time wasn't that big, so everybody moved.
>
> Like nomads, you just follow whatever you require, like plants and that – fish, deer, every season they just kept moving but they always seem to come back to this place (*Ts'kw'ayláxw*) because it was their location.
>
> They didn't have calendars ... just based mostly on seasonal. Like now, (late July) is fishing season when everybody goes fishing. Then when you're finished fishing, then you get (food) plants, then when that's finished, fall hunting. (ME)

Unlike the situation at even the poorer salmon fishing sites, where a single resource occurs fairly predictably, resources on land (including the location of animals, and the timing of availability, and the yearly abundance of plant foods) were both diverse and relatively unpredictable. Furthermore, although the characterization of seasonal activities in the account above emphasizes the varying relative seasonal importance of animals and plants, unlike the situation at salmon fishing sites, there were almost no single-purpose resource activities on land. Summer trips to obtain spring beauty corms were accompanied by hunting. Late summer or early fall trips to hunt deer were accompanied by such activities as gathering edible whitebark pine corms.

The bands of the nineteenth century might defend their territory against unfriendly intrusion (and share boundary zones with bands with whom they maintained good relations reinforced by marriage or trade). Within those territories, however, access was unrestricted to band member. This pattern was not inconsistent with either prevailing social organization or the fact that within that territory, in any given year, any of the resources available might become crucial to survival (see Chapter 9). Within each band, band chiefs (rich men who maintained their status through giving feasts) acted as both ceremonial and diplomatic figureheads as well as being the stipulated owners of actual productive resources (Romanoff 1985; Grossman 1965). Within the band, however, it is unknown whether the chiefs exercised any other than consensual political control over other than their own immediate kin groups.

None of the above comments, however, should be taken to indicate that intra-band ownership of land sites would be impossible given slightly different circumstances. Given a pattern of widespread formalized exchange (including delayed reciprocity) and a slightly enhanced degree of social hierarchy and consolidation of sociopolitical power within the persons of lineage heads (chiefs), a system of intra-band land resource ownership might easily be compatible with the available resource base, especially if efforts had been expended to create resource facilities such as drive lines or hunting blinds. In fact Dawson (1892:4) and Mitchell (1925:3-4) report former ownership of hunting areas in Shuswap territory. This pattern may have existed in the Lillooet area as well.

Delayed reciprocity would make it possible to divide up the land base more finely: failure or diminution of resources within a sub-band's (or moiety's) territory in any given year could be 'balanced' by trading or by feasting and gifting by the recipients during a subsequent year (see Donald and Mitchell 1975). Such a system would allow for variation of land resource availability under conditions of intra-band land ownership by ensuring the presence of formal mechanisms for yearly redistribution of resources.

Traditional bands seem to have shared access in boundary zones with groups with whom they maintained friendly relations. One notable exception in the Lillooet area was *Xwalxástcin* ('many roots'), a plant gathering and hunting area located north of Bridge River on the boundary between the Upper Lillooet and the Chilcotin (Teit 1906:236-7). There was a long tradition of raiding and warfare between the Chilcotin and the Lillooet, and there was no inter-marriage or trade between them. Aside from such an isolated instance, the rule seems to have been that adjacent bands (whether belonging to the same or to different ethnic groups) maintained friendly relations, including trade, intermarriage, and shared access to both salmon fishing sites and land resources.

Band Boundaries

Within each band's territory, aside from boundary areas, permission to trespass for any sort of resource extraction was usually required and seems to have been given only where reciprocal resource use or kin ties existed. Specific examples of a band having access to resources in another band's territory include an instance, noted by DP, of Bonaparte Band members permitting Ts'kw'ayláxw Band members to fish for trout in Loon Lake in exchange for Bonaparte Band members receiving permission to fish for salmon within Ts'kw'ayláxw territory; or of Ts'kw'ayláxw Band members being permitted to fish at Xáxli'p or Bridge River Band salmon fishing sites because of kinship ties with those bands (DP; BE).

Where band boundaries met at a height of land, members of the two or more bands whose territory met in the boundary area would usually share use of that area amicably. Meetings in the mountains provided a chance to reaffirm cooperative relations, to trade, to play lehal, to exchange news, and to share oral traditions. The groups brought together under such conditions, as noted above (see intermediate and montane zone sites), would often come from a geographically widely dispersed area.

To summarize, the location of important salmon fishing sites along major rivers seems to have defined the limits of a band's territory in that zone in the Lillooet area. The location of hunting and plant collecting sites similarly defined the limits of a band's territory in the mountain zones. Information on intra- and inter-band access to sites in the terrace and lake zones is less complete, often simply because not much is remembered of traditional resource use in those specific areas. However, it is probable that lines drawn from a band's most widely separated fishing sites, up to the height of land at that band's most widely separated mountain hunting sites, and thence along the height of land, would contain most of a band's commonly used territory and *all* of its winter village site (see Figures 5 and 6).

If patterns of access to land resources included clearly defined intra-band kin group ownership of land in the past, the above-discussed pattern of shared use of boundary zones between bands probably still would have obtained for unrestricted resources available to the entire band. Indeed, it is difficult to imagine that a situation of continuing hostilities, such as that prevailing between the Chilcotin and the

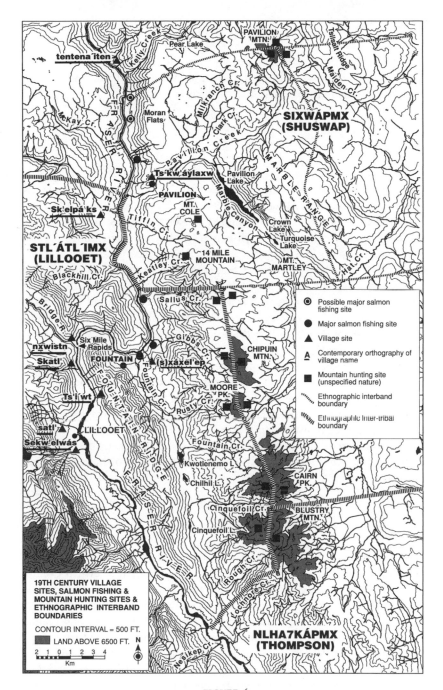

FIGURE 6

Nineteenth-century village sites, salmon fishing sites, mountain hunting sites, and ethnographic interband boundaries

Lillooet until about 1850 (see above and Teit 1906:236-7), could have been sustainable except between peoples who had little, aside from a mountain zone boundary, in common.

NOTE

Editor's note: In April 1991, the editor and Diana Alexander were able to examine the accessible part of the east bank of the Fraser River in the area not covered by Tyhurst and Alexander in 1986 and 1987 (i.e., 2.5 km north of Sallus Creek to 1 km south of Tiffin Creek). We observed just upstream from the steepest canyon stretch a small bench (2.6 km downstream from Tiffin Creek) with several earth platforms associated with small probable placer tailings as well as a cache pit near the edge of the bench. Possible fishing sites were precarious but bedrock based. Further upstream, 1.8 km south of Tiffin Creek, there was an extensive basin-shaped bench that could easily have provided camping for a thousand or more individuals. The river shore below this bench was predominantly bedrock without jetties, although at least one major jetty occurred a short distance upstream, after which the bedrock bank became precipitous. This could have been a Type II or III fishing site. Informants in the area provided no name or history of use of this site, however, we observed a small abandoned aluminum dip net at the jetty, and we believe that fishing was probably reasonably good there. The extensive bench area was disturbed in numerous places by placer mining tailings and materials (pickaxes, barrel parts, cans) and by earth slides of unknown age. No cultural lithic materials were observed in the area, although these may occur under the surface.

REFERENCES

Alexander, Diana. 1986. 'Ts'kw'ayláxw ethnoarchaeology: A preliminary survey.' Report prepared for the Heritage Conservation Branch of British Columbia (Permit No. 1986-26), the BC Heritage Trust, and the Pavilion Indian Band

-. 1989. 'Ethnoarchaeology of the Fountain and Pavilion Indian bands: Southwestern British Columbia.' Report prepared for the Heritage Conservation Branch of British Columbia, BC Government, and the BC Heritage Trust

Alexander, Diana, Robert Tyhurst, Linda Burnard, and R.G. Matson. 1985. 'A preliminary ethnoarchaeological investigation of the Potato Mountain Range and Eagle Lake Area.' Unpublished report on file with the Heritage Conservation Branch of BC

Baerreis, David A. 1961. 'The ethnohistoric approach and archaeology.' Ethnohistory 8:49-77

Dawson, George. 1892. 'Notes on the Shuswap people of British Columbia.' *Proceedings and Transactions of the Royal Society of Canada* 9(2):3-44

Donald, Leland and Donald Mitchell. 1975. 'Some correlates of local group rank among the southern Kwakiutl.' *Ethnology* 14:325-46

Freeman, L.G. 1968. 'A theoretical framework for interpreting archaeological materials.' In R. Lee and I. Devore (eds.), *Man the Hunter.* Pp. 262-7. Chicago: Aldine

Gould, Richard A. and Patty Jo Watson. 1982. 'A dialogue on the meaning and use of analogy in ethnoarchaeological reasoning.' *Journal of Anthropological Archaeology* 1:355-81

Grossman, Daniel. 1965. 'On the nature of descent groups of some tribes in the Interior of northwestern North America.' *Anthropologica* 2:249-62

Hayden, Brian. 1978. 'Snarks in archaeology: Or, inter-assemblage variability in lithics (a view from the antipodes).' In D. Davis (ed.), *Lithics and Subsistence: The Analysis of Stone Use in Prehistoric Economics.* Vanderbilt University Publications in Anthropology, No. 20. Pp. 179-98. Nashville, Tennessee

Hayden, Brian and Rob Gargett. 1987. 'Roofs, rims and resources: The anatomy of interior housepits.' Paper presented at the Annual Meeting of the Canadian Archaeological Association, Calgary

– et al. 1985. 'Complex hunter-gatherers in Interior British Columbia.' In T.D. Price and J. Brown (eds.), *Prehistoric Hunter-Gatherers.* Pp. 181-99. Orlando: Academic Press

–. et al. 1987. 'Report on the 1987 excavations at Keatley Creek.' Unpublished report of the Fraser River Investigations in Corporate Group Archaeology Project. On file with the British Columbia Heritage Conservation Branch

Kennedy, Dorothy and Randy Bouchard. 1978. 'Fraser River Lillooet: An ethnographic summary.' In A.H. Stryd and S. Lawhead (eds.), *Reports of the Lillooet Archaeological Project, Number 1, Introduction and Setting.* National Museum of Man, Mercury Series, Archaeological Survey of Canada, Paper No. 73, 22-55

–. 1986. 'Traditional Fraser River Lillooet fishing.' Report to Fountain Band, used with permission

Mitchell, D.S. 1925. 'A story of the Fraser River's great sockeye runs and their loss.' Unpublished ms. on file with the Pacific Salmon Commission and the BC Archives and Records Service

Pokotylo, David and Patricia Froese. 1983. 'Archaeological evidence for prehistoric root gathering in the southern Interior Plateau of British Columbia: A case study from Upper Hat Creek.' *Canadian Journal of Archaeology* 7:127-58

Pokotylo, David and Christopher Hanks. 1985. 'Mountain Dene ethnoarchaeology: Some preliminary perspectives.' Paper presented at Fiftieth Annual Meeting of the Society for American Archaeology, Denver

Romanoff, Steven. n.d. 'The Lillooet hunter.' Unpublished manuscript.

–. 1985. 'Fraser Lillooet salmon fishing.' *Northwest Anthropological Research Notes* 19(2):119-60

Schiffer, Michael B. 1981. 'Some issues in the philosophy of archaeology.' *American Antiquity* 46(4):899-908

Stryd, Arnoud. 1974. 'Lillooet Archaeological Project: 1974 Field Season.' Progress report to the Canada Council re research grant #S73-1760, and to the Archaeological Sites Advisory Board of BC re permit #74-12

Teit, James 1906. 'The Lillooet Indians.' *Memoirs, American Museum of Natural History* 2(5):193-300

–. 1909. 'The Shuswap Indians.' *Memoirs, American Museum of Natural History* 4:443-758

Turner, Nancy. 1978. *Food Plants of British Columbia Indians. Part II: Interior Peoples.* British Columbia Provincial Museum Handbook, No. 36. Victoria, BC

–. 1987. 'Ethnobotany of the Lillooet Indians of British Columbia.' Unpublished preliminary draft

Tyhurst, Robert. 1985. 'Chilcotin ethnoarchaeology: Culture and subsistence.' Paper read at 1985 Meetings of the Canadian Archaeological Association, Winnipeg

–. 1987. 'The Bald Mountain Project: Report to Fountain Band on ethnographic and ethnoarchaeological results.' Unpublished report

–. n.d. 'An Ethnographic History of the Chilcotin.' PhD dissertation draft, University of British Columbia

Plant Resources of the *Stl'átl'imx* (Fraser River Lillooet) People: A Window into the Past

Nancy J. Turner

INTRODUCTION

This chapter examines major traditional plant resources of the Lillooet-speaking peoples of the Fraser River dialect, including those of the communities of Shalalth, Lillooet, Fountain, and Pavilion. The ultimate goal of the research is to obtain, mostly through the knowledge, experience, and recollections of present-day Lillooet elders, some indication of past, particularly later prehistoric, plant use patterns of the indigenous peoples known to have occupied the region over the last several thousand years (cf. Stryd and Lawhead 1978; Hayden et al. 1986, 1987). It also attempts to determine how the use of plant resources influenced living and seasonal movement patterns of these peoples as well as their general lifestyles and group dynamics.

Information was collected on the present distribution and abundance of over ninety key resource plant species throughout all of the major resource use zones within the study area (described in Chapter 2). Discussion of specific plant species is restricted to those with moderate, high, or very high cultural importance to the Fraser River Lillooet per Turner (1988a). The utilization or cultural importance of these plants among the Fraser River Lillooet, and details of their harvesting, processing, and use or consumption are given. The data have been compiled from many sources. In particular, ethnobotanical interviews with several knowledgeable members of the Lillooet speech community have been undertaken over the past fifteen years in conjunction with previous research (cf. Turner 1974; Turner et al. 197). Major contributors are: the late Sam Mitchell (SM) of Fountain; the late Martina LaRochelle (MLR) of Lillooet; Edith O'Donaghey (EO), born and raised at Shalalth, now living in Lillooet; Desmond Peters (DP) (her brother), also born and raised at Shalalth, now at Pavilion

(*Ts'kwáylaxw*), and Bill Edwards (BE) of Pavilion. Biographical sketches
of these individuals are included in Chapter 1.

Published sources of information on traditional Lillooet plant use
are few. They include Teit (1906, 1912); articles by Kennedy and
Bouchard, and Mathewes in Stryd and Lawhead (1978); and Bouchard
and Kennedy (1977). For detailed information on identification features
of many culturally significant plants and general descriptions of plant
use by British Columbia Native peoples, the reader is referred to Turner (1975, 1978, 1979). Particular plant resource species are described in
Turner (1977, 1981, 1982, 1984). Plant use by neighbouring groups is
discussed for Thompson (*Nlaka'pamux*) by Steedman (1930) and Turner
et al. (1990), for Shuswap (*Secwepemc*) by Palmer (1975), and for
Okanagan-Colville by Turner, Kennedy and Bouchard (1980).

Many as yet unpublished sources of information were also consulted, including field notes of C.F. Newcombe (c. 1903) and a
manuscript on Lillooet ethnobotany (Turner et al. 1987). The formula
and the criteria used to obtain numerical values of cultural significance
of the plants (termed the 'Index of Cultural Significance') and, hence,
to make the selection of species discussed here, are described in Turner
(1988a). Emphasis in this report is on plant species and products of
higher cultural importance – those whose harvesting and processing
would have had a significant influence on prehistoric patterns of living
and seasonal movement.

FRASER RIVER LILLOOET PLANT RESOURCE USE

Archaeobotanical Research to Date

As indicated in the other chapters of this book, Interior Salish archaeological research and, in particular, ethnoarchaeology of the Lillooet
people was sparse until about two decades ago. However, there has
been increasing interest in the past lifeways of these traditionally
hunting-fishing-gathering people. The detailed history of this archaeological work and its reporting are described in other articles. However,
one recent paper, by Pokotylo and Froese (1983), is especially relevant
to plant harvesting and processing in an archaeological context. Based
on a study in the Upper Hat Creek Valley, an upland area in the Intermediate Grasslands zone between the Fraser and Thompson
plateaus and immediately east of our study area, the paper documents
the frequent occurrence of cooking pit depressions, including some
of unusually large dimensions, dating back to at least 2,250 years ago.
The study suggests that prehistoric Plateau populations relied heavily on roots and underground plant parts in their diet – even more

so than in the early historic period. The researchers found carbonized remains of fuel (mostly coniferous species), vegetable matting (including conifer boughs and needles and kinnikinnick), and plant food (including onions and other members of the lily family and unidentified composites – probably balsamroot). At least some of the cooking pits were found to have been reused. This evidence is consistent with the findings of large cooking pit depressions in the subalpine Montane parklands of Pavilion Mountain, Blustry Mountain, and Cairn Peak (D. Alexander, personal communication, 1987).

Another significant study directly relating to prehistoric plant use in the Lillooet area was carried out by Lepofsky (1986, 1987) at the Keatley Creek archaeological site, where over 100 pit-house depressions have been identified in an open sagebrush River Terrace zone about 600 m above sea level. In that study, pithouse remains (from samples taken at four house sites in 1986 and from one in 1987) were examined in order to distinguish roof and floor deposits and to determine any patterning of remains in these deposits. With minor exceptions, Lepofsky's study, done in conjunction with broader arachaeological investigations at Keatley creek (cf. Hayden et al. 1986), represents the first major archaeological project in British Columbia to incorporate paleoethnobotanical methods into the research design (Lepofsky 1987). Charring of plant materials within the pithouses and preservation through unusually dry conditions of plant remains deposited around the rims has resulted in the availability of a wide array of archaeobotanical samples to aid in reconstructing prehistoric plant use at the Keatley Creek site. Plant remains recovered by Lepofsky include: coniferous needles (of Douglas-fir[1] and ponderosa pine), mainly around the pithouse rim and especially on the southern edge; charcoal from a number of woody species – ponderosa pine, Douglas-fir, willow and/or poplar, birch, alder, maple, big sagebrush, and juniper; a variety of seeds – Douglas-fir, kinnikinnick, cactus, saskatoon berry, pine, juniper, seeds of two unidentified chenopods (one type small and charred, the other larger and uncharred – the latter is possibly of *Chenopodium album*, an introduced species); and other unidentified types, including an ericaceous species, stem of juniper, cone parts of pine, birch bark, and a leaf of big sagebrush. Virtually all of these species (except possibly the chenopods) are known to be culturally significant to the Lillooet people of historic times, and their probable prehistoric use as well as the significance of their distribution within the pithouse sites is discussed by Lepofsky (1987).

Ideally, valuable information from both prehistoric and ethnographic sources can be combined to provide the best possible reconstruction of past resource use. This suggestion is reinforced by Alexander (in

Chapter 3 and in 1986, 1987), who has used information from interviews with native consultants to indicate traditional land use patterns around Pavilion as well as around the Potato Mountain Range and Eagle Lake area of Chilcotin territory (cf. Alexander et al. 1985). This ethnoarchaeological approach has been very effective in guiding her archaeological survey work.

Continuity with the Past

The use of contemporary ethnographic data to determine past land-use patterns carries with it a number of tenuous assumptions. In the case of plant use, these assumptions include the premise of long-standing, similar use patterns for plants over many generations. Obviously, one cannot presume a completely unchanging status quo. Changes are particularly evident over the historic period, with the introduction of new food products and materials, new methods of food production, new means of transportation and landscape manipulation, and new language and cognitive systems – not to mention different lifestyles and religious and economic systems. Along with cultural changes, one must acknowledge the possibility that environmental alterations may influence the distribution and abundance of resource species (cf. Lepofsky 1986).

Nevertheless, there is every indication that use of native plants remained in many ways similar to prehistoric use patterns until approximately fifty to sixty years ago, within the living memories (and sometimes direct experiences) of contemporary native elders. In most cases, these recollections are the only data available on which to base perceptions of prehistoric plant use, because the archaeological record itself is very fragmented. Plant tissues, unless carbonized or maintained under frozen, desiccated, or anaerobic conditions, do not preserve well, and, hence, their occurrence in archaeological sites is sparse and probably unrepresentative of the full spectrum of activities in which plants were used (cf. Pokotylo and Froese 1983).

Some obvious differences and changes pertaining directly or indirectly to plant use that did occur between the last half century or so and the prehistoric and early historic periods include:

(1) more sedentary lifestyle, with longer time being spent in permanent winter homes and shorter times spent away from home on traditional subsistence-related activities;

(2) abandonment of traditional pithouses in favour of rectangular log and timber cabins;

(3) use of horses for transportation of people and resource materials from harvesting sites to processing and/or use sites;

(4) use of metal containers for cooking (sometimes harvesting) plant foods and of glass and crockery containers for preserving (making it possible to preserve many plant foods without having to dehydrate them);

(5) general abandonment of earth ovens or cooking pits for preparing plant foods;

(6) abandonment of traditional fire-making techniques (presently, the name for Pacific willow translates as 'match-plant,' the 'match' reference having entirely supplanted the earlier meaning of 'fire-drill' in the name);

(7) use of sugar in cooking and preserving, making some berry species, such as Oregon-grapes, more palatable and usable;

(8) increased use of other imported plant products, such as flour, rice, tea and raisins, to supplement or replace traditional plant foods (cf. Teit 1906:223);

(9) introduction of gardening as a major means of food production: widespread use of potatoes, corn, carrots, turnips, squash, cucumbers, onions, and apples to supplement or replace traditional plant foods (cf. Teit 1906:223) as well as the raising and use of domesticated animals, such as cattle, along with the production of hay and fodder;

(10) increased trading between the Lillooet and other indigenous groups, undoubtedly resulting in a wider availability of some plant resources;

(11) use of modern boats and general abandonment of bark and dugout canoes;

(12) use of modern implements and metal cutting tools (knives, iron root diggers, bark scrapers from tin cans, etc.) in preference to traditional tools;

(13) use of imported cotton, hemp and sisal cordage, and, later, nylon to replace Indian-hemp twine and netting;

(14) use of cotton, wool, and linen cloth for clothing and blankets in preference to hides and fabrics made from native plant fibres (e.g., Indian-hemp, sagebrush and willow bark, silverberry bark). Also, use of imported materials for bedding, instead of mattresses of tule or cattail, and of canvas for tents in place of bark and mats; and

(15) use of flour, rice, and potato sacking for storing dried foods.

Continuity with early plant use practices was maintained between prehistoric and contemporary times (up to within the past fifty years or so) in the following ways:

(1) knowledge of and continued – if possibly diminished – use of virtually all types of wild plant foods of the region, including fruits, 'roots' (roots, bulbs, corms, and all other underground parts), inner bark of trees, mushrooms,[2] green vegetables, black tree lichen, and pine seeds;

(2) knowledge of, and some use of, traditional plant materials used in manufacture of bows, digging sticks, dip nets, fishing weirs and traps, and baskets (particularly split cedar-root pack baskets and birch-bark containers for berry picking and transport of harvested products);

(3) continued, if somewhat altered, use of traditional fishing technologies, including the use of wooden implements, weirs and traps, fish-drying shelters, and salmon-spreaders;

(4) continued reliance on local woods as a source of fuel for heating and cooking;

(5) continued use of drying as a major method of preserving fruits and some root foods;

(6) continued use of many traditional plant medicines as tonics, laxatives, purgatives, poultices for wounds and skin infections, as remedies for colds and respiratory ailments, arthritis, rheumatism, eye troubles, heart and circulatory problems, ailments of the stomach and digestive tract, and for childbirth and infant care;

(7) continued employment of several species as protective agents against death and disease (e.g., Rocky Mountain juniper) and in other types of rituals;

(8) knowledge of traditional nomenclature for virtually all plant species important in Lillooet culture (cf. Turner et al. 1987; Turner 1987; 1989);

(9) knowledge of important harvesting locations, ripening or harvesting times, and processing requirements for key plant species; and

(10) continued, if somewhat diminished, seasonal travel to primary resource sites for harvesting, and sometimes processing, plant products.

Much of the continuity of knowledge and practice concerning plant use has been reflected in the vocabulary of the Lillooet language, which was still widely spoken in the childhood days of the contemporary grandparent generation. Names, references, and definitions do change, and languages evolve (cf. Turner 1987, 1989) but usually more slowly than cultural and lifestyle changes. Unfortunately, the Lillooet language today is scarcely spoken by members of the younger generations, and its use may further diminish within the next few decades (see Van Eijk 1986 for a detailed description of the language).

The changes in resource use within the last fifty years have followed the trends already established in the earlier historic period: further reduction in dependency on wild foods, with only a few berries (black-caps, saskatoons, soapberries, black huckleberries, and choke cherries) and mushrooms (e.g., cottonwood mushroom, described by Turner, Kuhnlein, and Egger 1987) being sought; food preservation by jamming, canning, and freezing rather than by drying; virtual disuse of pit-cooking for wild vegetables; almost total loss of knowledge of preparation techniques for Indian-hemp fibre and other types of fibrous materials and for manufacturing bows, arrows, pipes, dip nets and other traditional implements; and a low profile for traditional medicines and ritual uses of plants. Traditional animal resources are used to a greater extent than are plants. Salmon still forms a significant portion of the diet, and original techniques of cutting and drying are still used, however, freezing is common too (Chapters 5 and 6). Deer are still an important food source for many families, but they are hunted with thoroughly modern techniques.

Saskatoon berries are undoubtedly the most important plant food staple in traditional Lillooet society and, judging from existing evidence (including the existence of several varietal names in the Lillooet language for different types of saskatoon berries and their long-standing importance in many aspects of Lillooet culture), their use extends into the distant past. It is difficult to say what percentage of the overall caloric intake they provided in the early diet, but it must have been well over 5 per cent of all calories, including those from fish and meat. Other important plant foods, each of which may well have comprised at least 10 per cent of the total vegetable foods for early Plateau peoples, would have included choke cherries, blackcaps, black huckleberries, spring beauty corms, nodding onions, balsamroot (roots and budstems), and cow-parsnip. Many other plant foods, while not necessarily consumed in quantity, would have been significant in providing essential vitamins and minerals and in serving as emergency and famine foods. The technological material plants must also be regarded as vital to past Plateau cultures, since they allowed the successful use of fish and game resources. Indian-hemp, for example, would have been, as it was in recent times, a crucial material for making fishnets. Finally, the important role of medicinal plants in the maintenance of health and, hence, in the survival of early Plateau peoples can only be surmised, but in view of the broad spectrum of healing plants employed by Lillooet people within the historic period, their role in the past should not be underestimated.

The Environment, Past and Present

The study area – the area presumably encountered by prehistoric peoples of the major pithouse village sites from Pavilion to Lillooet[3] – as described in Chapters 1 and 2, encompasses a wide range of environmental features, ultimately leading to the availability of diverse floral and faunal resources.

Although Montane Forest or Parkland slopes of considerable steepness would have been traversed or even occupied temporarily for the purpose of hunting or harvesting berries or roots, the steepest valley sides consisting of rocky outcrops and talus slopes, such as those of Marble Canyon and Fountain Ridge, would have been generally avoided. Hunters sometimes used rocky chimneys or gulleys to drive animals so that they could more easily be shot from blinds (Chapter 7). However, it is doubtful whether any significant plant resources were obtained from such areas; almost all useful plants would have been available from other more easily accessible places. Nor would such slopes have been suitable for camping or processing activities such as pit-cooking. Similarly, the steep, rocky canyon walls of the 'inner gorge' of the Fraser River would probably not have been frequented for habitation or harvesting of plant resources.

Despite possible climatic changes that would have influenced the local distribution patterns of vegetation (Mathewes 1985, Lepofsky 1986, 1987), the very existence of Douglas-fir and ponderosa pine remains at the Keatley Creek site is an indication that these species and their associated vegetation were in the vicinity of the site at the time of occupation. One can extrapolate from this conclusion that the vegetation of other biogeoclimatic zones in the area was also in existence and available to the early occupants, even if there may have been some shifts in abundance and local distribution of species. In Chapters 3 and 7, Alexander and Tyhurst point out that archaeological evidence to date largely agrees with ethnographic data in the Pavilion region, and that the environment in the area over the last 4,500 years appears to have been relatively unchanging.

Even within a stable environmental regime, plant succession, due to both natural and human-caused fires, landslides, natural rerouting of creeks, and eutrophication of lakes, would have resulted in continually changing species composition in various locations. This can be observed even today, with sites that were burned ten, fifteen, or fifty years ago being gradually reforested and passing through a series of successional stages in which certain species predominate for a certain period of time. Lodgepole pine, for example, is well known as a successional species and occurs in large, often pure, even-aged stands in many parts of the study area above about 900 m. It is generally replaced gradually by climax species such as Douglas-fir and Engelmann spruce (cf. Turner 1988b). Saskatoon, too, thrives as a successional species after fires, and some of the best producing sites today are in areas that were burned over twenty to forty years ago (cf. Mathewes 1978). Indigenous Plateau peoples, undoubtedly including those of the study area, learned to enhance the growth of certain desirable plant resources, such as some berries and 'roots' and species suitable for game, through the use of controlled burning (cf. Turner et al. 1990 for Thompson examples; Turner 1991 for Lillooet and other examples).

Little is known about the effects of prolonged and continuous harvesting on populations of wild food plants. Although picking berries and harvesting wild greens might not be expected to have a major impact on a healthy plant population, one would think that intensive harvesting of edible roots and underground parts, such as those of spring beauty and yellow avalanche lily, would result in significant depletion of the plants. Yet, preliminary observations have not borne this out. Major root-digging areas I have seen, including Botanie Valley in Thompson territory and the slopes of Pavilion Mountain within Lillooet territory, are still rich in the root resource plants despite what has been many, many generations of intensive harvesting. Certain camas-digging meadows on southern Vancouver Island and traditional bitterroot digging grounds in Okanagan territory near Penticton are similarly lacking signs of depletion.

Possibly this seeming abundance of resource plants in tradiitonal harvesting areas is due to the fact that they have had about fifty years of relatively light use in which to recover, but I suspect that even during the time when these sites were being actively visited on an annual harvesting round, they maintained dense populations of plants, allowing a sustained yield harvesting regime. This may have been made possible by the 'cultivation' or encouragement of these plants that took place both actively and passively with the periodic controlled burning and tilling of the soil that accompanied harvesting. Selective removal of larger edible 'roots,' with the smaller ones being left to grow in successive years, was probably an effective means of sustaining the populations. Additionally, summertime harvesting, after the plants had had a chance to produce seed, and the inevitable, though not necessarily intentional, scattering of the seed into freshly dug soil during the harvesting activities, may have given the seeds a better chance to germinate and grow than they might have had if left undisturbed.

On the other hand, it would be unrealistic to maintain that harvesting had no deleterious effects on wild plants. It may be that yellow avalanche lily, which seems comparatively rare over much of the study area, was once more widespread and that its range and abundance were reduced in the past from over-harvesting. Analysis of pollen deposits and ancient packrat middens in the region may provide some clues about past abundance and frequency of such species. Experimental research on the relative effects of traditional harvesting practices and other human activities on wild plant populations would also be extremely helpful in providing answers to the question of susceptibility of various types of wild plants to overexploitation.

In summary, although there must have been some changes in the abundance and distribution of plant species over time in the study area, it seems likely that the general range of species existing in the region and their relative productivity and availability for use by people has remained fairly constant over the last two to three thousand years.

Seasonality of Plant Resources

Almost all of the plant resources encountered by the Lillooet were to some degree seasonal; either they were only available within a certain period of time each year or they were at their prime quality only within a given season (even though they might theoretically be available at other times). The seasonality of some resources is obvious. Most berries – saskatoons, huckleberries, blackcaps, strawberries, gooseberries, for example – have to be picked when fully ripe; quality will suffer if they are picked too green or when overripe. In any case, most drop from the bushes if left too long. Edible green shoots, such as fireweed, cow-parsnip, 'Indian celery,' balsamroot, and blackcap, must be harvested at an early growth stage in the spring or they soon become tough, woody, strong-tasting, and even toxic (cf. Kuhnlein and Turner 1987). Edible inner bark and cambial tissues of trees, too, are only available for harvest in spring; later, the tissues become dry and woody. Mushrooms grow only within a limited season, usually fall, and under particular environmental conditions (after heavy rains).

With other resources, seasonality may be more difficult to discern. Edible roots and other underground plant structures vary seasonally in nutrient content and texture, and most are best when dug at their dormant stage, before or after flowering (cf. Turner and Kuhnlein 1983). However, sometimes there can be difficulty in detecting them if their top growth is not well developed, and, hence, they were sometimes dug at flowering. Certain other plant foods, including cactus stems and black tree lichen, were apparently harvestable at almost any time, and this made them valuable as famine foods during periods of scarcity. For large-scale consumption, however, they, too, had their usual seasons of harvesting: cactus in the spring and black tree lichen in summer. Kinnikinnick leaves for tobacco could be obtained at any time, and kinnikinnick berries, though at their prime in late summer and early fall, could be obtained throughout the winter as well.

Plant technological materials are also often seasonal. Indian-hemp is an obvious example; it must be harvested in the fall, after its stems and fibres have reached full maturity but before they start to deteriorate from winter conditions. Tree barks, such as cottonwood bark (used for canoes and containers), were usually most easily peeled off in spring when the sap was running (cf. Teit 1906). Even woods vary in quality with seasons; Desmond Peters (personal communication 1987) explained that juniper wood for bows should be harvested, ideally, around February, because it is then dry enough to work without having to be cured.[4]

Many medicines, too, are available only at a certain time of year. Pacific anemone, for example, used medicinally as a counter-irritant for sores and aches, was only used when fresh and green; if it was dried, it would lose its effectiveness (cf. Turner 1984). Since many medicines are derived from the leafy stems of deciduous species, these would have to be harvested during the growing season and then dried for winter use.

Seasonality of plant resources, especially the most important resources, naturally had considerable influence on movement patterns of native peoples. By identifying, as far as possible, the times when key plant and animal resources were available for harvesting and processing, and by coupling this information with the known distribution of these resources and the times required for harvesting and processing the quantities that would have been used, a fairly accurate picture of seasonal movement patterns logically emerges. Realistically, there are still many gaps in the type of information required for a detailed version of such a reconstruction, particularly regarding relative quantities obtained and times required for harvesting and processing these quantities. However, with the known or implied details available for significant plant resources, many of the most important pieces of the spatial-temporal puzzle can be put in place.

Appendix 2 in its original form listed over ninety plant species known to have been used traditionally by Fraser River Lillooet people (or their close neighbours, such as the Shalalth people). Eleven of the most important plants are represented in the current appendix. Also provided for each species are: details of the major biogeoclimatic zones they inhabit, specific habitat preferences, and known and probable locations (in most cases these are shown on maps accompanying the data sheets); details of harvesting, processing, and consumption or use of the resources; and additional notations on trade or other relevant information. This information was compiled from all available sources, including interviews with native consultants, pertinent literature, unpublished materials (particularly Turner et al. 1987), British Columbia Forest Service forest cover maps, and field observations.

The traditional seasonal harvesting and resource use patterns as reported by Teit (1906) are provided in Chapter 3. In the following summary of the seasonal round, plant resource use is stressed. Teit's information is supplemented with details from Turner et al. (1987). Additionally, recollections of Edith O'Donaghey provide important insights into seasonal movement patterns, as they existed during her childhood, some fifty years ago (quoted from taped interviews made in July 1987).

In March and early April the subsistence round began with fishing and hunting and the harvesting of the young shoots and greens (cowparsnip, thimbleberry, blackcap, fireweed, Indian celery, and balsamroot). A number of roots and other underground parts were also dug at this time, namely, those of lower elevations (balsamroot, wild onions, and mariposa lily). Although the relative quantities of plant products harvested in early spring may have been low, their importance, as the first fresh foods after a winter of dried and stored products, would have been immense. In late April and May, the inner bark of lodgepole pine and cottonwood was harvested, and, as the snow cleared from the upland areas around mid to late May, other types of roots were sought (spring beauty and yellow avalanche lily corms – see Chapters 3 and 7). Edith O'Donaghey noted that, in April,

> there was that pine bark [inner bark of lodgepole pine]. My dad used to bring home many lard buckets full in the olden days [three, five, or ten pound sizes, with tight fitting lids on them]. [They ate it fresh.] . . . Even if the old man came home at midnight, we'd get up and eat some! . . . In April, May, we picked and ate the young flower bud stems of the spring sunflower. They also cooked the stems in soup. [Her granny used to dry them.] [And], early in the spring, they eat burdock roots raw, right there, or they boil them as a vegetable.[5]
>
> Then [in May] we used to go for that *'hákwa7'* [cow-parsnip shoots], just up on the mountain. [Her granny would go up for a day and bring lots of it down, and everyone would eat it fresh.] They got the cactus right at home [Shalalth]. They collected it and pit-cooked it, but usually only about a gallon at a time because it is hard to cook. [It has to be pit cooked, then squeezed to extract the edible inside part, which is then stewed.] We also got lots of Indian celery (*'s7ank'*) in the old days. Granny used to dry lots; we ate the green leaves fresh and dried the leaves and the seeds on their stalks [ripe in August].

Early to mid-June was known as the 'Seventh Moon,' translating as 'when strawberries are ripe.' At this time, the earliest ripening fruits (strawberries, saskatoons), at lower elevations, are ready for gathering. The first significant numbers of salmon were also caught then as well as various other smaller fish. Edith O'Donaghey recalled that in June and early July, 'We got lots of saskatoons [around Shalalth and elsewhere]. Of course there were several different kinds. They had special ones for cooking with fish soup ... There was only one place, in a hayfield at Queen Ranch near Shalalth, where there were great big wild strawberries; my auntie used to go and pick them there.'

From mid-June until about the 'Tenth Moon' (around September), a continuous succession of berries was harvested in the lower Montane Forest and River Terrace and River Valley zones by those not occupied in fishing. These included saskatoons, soapberries, gooseberries, blackcaps, thimbleberries, huckleberries, blueberries, and Oregon-grapes. By the end of the season, from mid-August through September, choke cherries, wild crabapples (around Shalalth only), and fruits of the uppermost elevations were picked. Choke cherries were picked in particularly large quantities. Also, at this time, whitebark pine cones were harvested. Black tree lichen was gathered when it was convenient, almost any time during the summer. Salmon fishing continued throughout the summer and early fall, primarily mid-July to mid-August for contemporary Pavilion and Fountain bands (see Chapters 3, 5, and 6). Edith O'Donaghey recalled the summer harvesting round as follows:

> We used to go [in mid July] up the Bridge River valley [from Shalalth] to get soapberries, or across Seton Lake [and camp for a night or two]. We used to dry them and store them in great big sacks. They had special buckets for soapberries and other kinds of berries, ones that won't leak ... woven of cedar roots. Nobody makes these baskets anymore. They use ice cream buckets now ...
>
> There used to be lots of gooseberries [at a place near Shalalth called White Slide]. We used to pick them when they were green and put them in flour sacks. We would go there to pick them for a whole day ... [Her granny stored them green, or dried them, or made jam from them]. They used to pick lots and lots of those Oregon-grapes [around Shalalth]. My dad used to make jam from them. We had six or eight large crocks of jam, covered with brown paper, which was sealed at the edges with flour paste ... [These berries are often available until late August. EO also noted that blackcaps were picked from mid to late July; she still picks them in large quantities (Plate 8.1).]
>
> [In July and early August] the Shalalth people came down to the

PLATE 8.1

Blackcaps *(Rubus leucodermis)* in a traditional coiled cedar-root basket, picked at Texas Creek by Edith O'Donaghey. On 13 July 1987, she picked about 6 litres of blackcaps in under three hours. She cans, freezes, and makes jam and jelly from them. On a good site, one can pick about one litre per hour of wild gooseberries *(Ribes inerme)*, 0.75 litres per hour of wild raspberries *(Rubus idaeus)*, and 2 litres per hour of soapberries *(Shepherdia canadensis)*.

mouth of Cayoosh Creek to fish for salmon. The Fountain and Bridge River people had their own fishing spots further upriver. Each family had its own fishing rocks. They would go down there in July and early August and camp there for about a month. This was the only time when people [from Shalalth] came down to fish for salmon. [They dried the fish on site and carried it home. Some of it they would take along to their huckleberry picking camp on Mission Mountain.] . . . [At Shalalth] they got the seeds of Indian celery [still on their stalks] in big bunches and tied them up with string to hang and dry. [These were used in flavouring soups and stews.]

[In mid August] a whole bunch of [many families, as described later] would go up . . . on top of the mountain, way up high, close to the snow line [to Mission Ridge, above Shalalth] by horseback every year . . . for a few days, three or four days or a week, mainly to pick [black] huckleberries. These berries are ripe in August, and that's when people would go up ... We got huckleberries, and dug roots while we were up there, wild potatoes [spring beauty corms], wild onions, whatever we could find up there on the mountain. They [the men] would hunt too ... I haven't been up there since I was young, but that used to be a tradition in the olden days ... They'd gather [avalanche lily corms], a whole bunch of tiger lily bulbs, ... that black moss [black tree lichen] ... We'd bring down six or eight [large coiled cedar root pack baskets] baskets with pack horses ..., baskets and sacks of mountain potatoes ... They also dried cow-parsnip roots (called *'sulí'*). They pick them after the plant has flowered and dry them [later they were boiled and eaten].

Well [in late August and September], there were the pine cones [white-bark pine with large, edible seeds] up there too. My dad used to bring home sacks full [three or four large gunnysacksful] from his hunting trips in the mountains [behind Mission Ridge] ... They were awfully messy [pitchy] ... Granny used to keep a special pan just for roasting them in the oven ... [or they would build a fire outside and throw them in and roast them until the cones opened and the seeds could be extracted.] They also dug balsamroots in August and the fall, after the leaves have all died down. They were dried, and later boiled as a vegetable ... My parents used to go up 'Tit Mountain' with pack horses to hunt. They cooked the deer right there ... My dad used to go hunting with about six or eight other men and boys ... Sometimes they were gone for a week, or ten days or more.

According to Teit (1906), the months of October and November – the 'Tenth' and 'Eleventh Moons' – were largely devoted to salmon fishing and salmon processing along the Fraser River and its major tributaries. Edible mushrooms were also gathered at this time, as noted by Edith O'Donaghey: 'Oh, yes! We got lots of mushrooms at Shalalth. The main ones were the "slippery tops" [*Hygrophorus* sp.]. There were lots among the pine trees in October and November, especially in the cemetery. They were only found in certain places, just like the other mushrooms. [During a previous session in 1985, we also collected many cottonwood mushrooms at Crown and Turquoise lakes in mid-October.]' The rest of the year, called 'late autumn' by Teit (1906), was generally devoted to hunting and trapping, probably including some digging of roots, where these could be located, and late season harvesting of upper elevation fruits. Cactus was usually harvested in spring but could be collected any time when necessity dictated, as could black tree lichen. Rose hips and kinnikinnick berries ripen in August but could be harvested, if necessary, in the winter and even into early spring.

Whereas many plants could be harvested in the Montane Parkland

and Forests in conjunction with hunting activities, this was not generally the case with salmon fishing (except for saskatoon berries and
choke cherries). Thus, fishing and plant gathering apparently created
scheduling conflicts. The nature of the individual fish runs could affect
the magnitude of these scheduling conflicts and choices of assigning
labour to specific food harvesting tasks. Bill Edwards and Desmond
Peters noted that the spring salmon start around May and continue
almost until the end of June, some of them even into mid-July. The
sockeyes start at the beginning of July and continue through to September. The Stuart Lake sockeye run is very fast, and, in 1987, for example, it started in mid-July (specifically, 13 July). This run would
demand concentrated labour and intense work in order to maximize
the catch. Desmond Peters noted: 'They're small, you know, four years
[old]. And they just shoot right through. It doesn't take very long.
You see them at Lytton, and then they'd be here, and then, just move
right along. The Chilco run is slower [and thus less concentrated effort is required to make the best use of this run]. The fish tend to stay
around, depending on the water conditions, but the Stuart Lake run,
they just move in one mass.' Every four years the humpback come
up, but Desmond Peters said that few people go after them, although
Edith O'Donaghey added, 'people like them!' They are more of a fall
fish, running mainly in late August and September. Steelhead run
year-round, and trout, too, can be caught at any time of the year
(BE; DP).

Another factor that must be noted in discussing scheduling and
seasonality of resource use is the year-to-year variation in the availability of certain foods. This is especially true of berries, mushrooms,
and, as already noted, fish. Sam Mitchell once commented that of
all the berries, saskatoons were the only ones which were available
in quantity every year. Even saskatoons, however, vary greatly in quality and abundance from one year to the next, according to Edith
O'Donaghey. She noted, for example, that in 1987 there were not very
many saskatoons, and many of them had dried up prematurely due
to the hot weather. Choke cherries, too, were not plentiful in 1987 because they were ripening and drying too soon. Soapberries seem particularly susceptible to yearly fluctuations in fruit production
(cf. Turner 1981). An 'off' year for saskatoons or for salmon could be
a serious matter and might cause severe hardship, especially in winter
and early spring. At these times, people had to rely on secondary
resources, such as the fruits of black hawthorn, kinnikinnick, wild
rose, and red-osier dogwood, which were not normally gathered in
quantity, as well as on foods such as cactus and black tree lichen whose
availability remained fairly constant. Roots and other underground

crops were more reliable and would have been available in a constant supply, but they would have required more energy to harvest than would saskatoons and other berries.

The seasonal harvesting of some major traditional plant resources (mostly foods) of the study area is summarized in Chapter 2. The species are grouped according to similarities in distribution, and harvesting times are based on the information provided in Appendix 2. Secondary plant resources would have been gathered on a more casual basis during slack times or, for those of areas more distant from winter dwellings, at the same time as the more important plant products or staples. Although the major impetus for an expedition would have been the need to harvest and process plant staples from a particular area, the duration of the trip was undoubtedly influenced by the concurrent harvesting and processing of secondary resources from the same general location or habitat as well as the need to move to other zones to harvest other major resources.[6] Some of the secondary resources were crucial to the processing of the staples. For example, the plant materials used as fuel and for surrounding roots and other foods being cooked in pits would have to have been harvested concurrently with the foods themselves, and the time required for gathering these auxiliary materials would have contributed significantly to the overall length of stay at a particular site.

From the seasonal use of plants graphed in Chapter 2 and described in Appendix 2, and from information provided previously in this chapter, the following general pattern emerges, which can, by extrapolation back in time, apply to some degree to the prehistoric peoples of the pithouse settlements between Lillooet and Pavilion:

(1)   The plant harvesting round started on the River Terrace near permanent village sites in late March and April. In the dry, treeless sagebrush clearings and open ponderosa woods, the season starts early; many flowers bloom in April and May and have completely died back by July. In these sites – in fact, right around the Keatley Creek site – some of the early available resources would have been: nodding onion, mariposa lily bulbs, desert parsley roots, Indian celery leaves, balsamroot shoots (and probably balsamroot roots as well), and prickly-pear cactus, which would have been available throughout the year. As the first fresh foods of the season, these resources were undoubtedly of prime importance.

Other, less intensively seasonal plant resources could also be harvested from the River Terraces starting in early spring. Technological materials, such as big sagebrush bark, kinnikinnick leaves, mock-orange, saskatoon, and oceanspray wood, and medicinal plants, such as yarrow, as well as kinnikinnick leaves, were all readily available from this time on in the growing season. Some of these resources, as well as ponderosa pine wood, needles, and pitch, were actually year-round commodities.

(2)   Some of these same resources – nodding onions, Indian celery, balsamroot, kinnikinnick, mock-orange, oceanspray – were also available from the lower Montane Forest zone at slightly higher elevations, and their harvesting season might have been slightly later, but only by a week or two. Douglas-fir wood, boughs, and pitch and Rocky Mountain juniper boughs and wood could be obtained in early spring as well as throughout the year.

(3)   From the moister areas of these two lower zones – along stream courses and around Intermediate Lakes and Marshes – another array of resource species was available for use in early spring: shoots of false Solomon's-seal, cow-parsnip, and fireweed; edible roots of water-parsnip and silverweed; birch and cottonwood bark sheets for making vessels of many kinds; bitter cherry bark for wrapping implement joints and basket decoration; red cedar roots (limited distribution) for basketry; and, for cordage, rope willow and Rocky Mountain maple bark.

(4)   By late April to mid-May, the snow had cleared from Intermediate Grassland areas (e.g., the plateau country below Pavilion Mountain, around Gillon Creek, where Diamond S Ranch and Fountain Valley are situated), and some of the Montane Forest and Parkland resources were ready to be harvested. These included, from forest areas: inner bark of lodgepole pine (whose availability is of relatively short duration); black tree lichen (also available throughout the growing season); young shoots of cow-parsnip and fireweed; and, from the meadowlands, nodding onions, cow-parsnip and fireweed shoots, Indian celery leaves, balsamroot shoots and roots (the latter also available later and at lower elevations), and the first spring beauty or 'mountain potato' corms (discussed next). Concurrently, harvesting of fuel and materials, such as Douglas-fir boughs (used to surround the roots of balsamroot and other foods in pit-cooking), would have been collected in the same vicinity.

(5)   'Mountain potatoes,' a prime resource and plentiful on the slopes of Pavilion, Tom Cole, and Mission mountains (Chapter 7), could be obtained anytime during the late spring and summer from early May (depending on elevation) to September. Ethnographic accounts of their harvesting refer to May and June (i.e., before the major salmon run) or August (after the salmon run, when deer are at their prime for hunting), depending on the source (SM; EO;

R. Bouchard, personal communication 1986).[7] Although access to these regions might have been feasible within a long day's hike, it is probable that a mountain harvesting trip of at least several days' duration would have been undertaken by prehistoric family groups sometime during the spring in May or early June, probably before the salmon run. In more recent times, horses have facilitated such trips. Men accompanying such an expedition would undoubtedly spend much of their time hunting. More recently, men on hunting trips at this season were often the ones to harvest and bring home spring Montane Forest resources such as lodgepole pine inner bark (SM; EO). In late May and June, other springtime resources of the Montane Forests and Parklands were coming into their prime: red cedar products, where available (mainly west of Lillooet, according to Lillooet consultants); Engelmann spruce roots; subalpine fir branches and pitch (availability of these continued until fall); and avalanche lily corms (mainly west of Lillooet in areas such as Mission Ridge).

(6) Meanwhile, in mid-June, at lower elevations saskatoon berries were starting to ripen. Because these were plant staples occurring in large numbers on the River Terraces and in lower Montane Forests, people must have spent considerable time in late June harvesting and processing saskatoons in the vicinity of, if not right at, their permanent village sites along the Fraser and its tributaries. In fact, there are depressions in the treed portions of the Keatley Creek site that may represent summer lodges (B. Hayden, personal communication, 1990). Fishing, too, would have required the presence of families in the river valleys at this time and over a major portion of the summer.

(7) In July, several other types of fruits were ripening in the woodlands and along the waterways of the River Terraces and lower Montane Forests. Notably, soapberries, gooseberries, blackcaps, and, of generally lesser importance, Oregon-grapes, wild raspberries, thimbleberries, and red-osier dogwood fruits were all ripening and requiring harvesting. Most of these fruits also occur at higher elevations, where they ripen up to two or three weeks later.

(8) A major fruit of at least some Fraser River Lillooet people, the black mountain huckleberry, occurs in the Montane Parkland zone on the west side of the Fraser and ripens in mid-August. This meant, for those who utilized this resource, a trip of several days' duration to the high country at this time. Other mountain resources could also be obtained: spring beauty and avalanche lily corms were still available; tiger lily and wild onion bulbs; some

of the fruits listed previously as well as oval-leaved blueberry (west of Lillooet) and dwarf mountain blueberry. Again, men would accompany women on the summer mountain harvest, spending their time hunting or even helping to pick berries (EO; SM). The 'root' foods were apparently cooked on site, and, hence, the gathering of fuel and vegetation, such as fir boughs to surround the cooking food, would have taken place concurrently, as would the gathering of fuel for fires to dry or partially dry the berries before transporting them.

(9)   During August, several River Terrace resources were also ready for harvest, including balsamroot roots (these could also be dug earlier) as well as cattail leaves and tule stems for mat-making. Choke cherries, too, were ripe and would have been gathered in large quantities.

(10)   In September, the main Montane Forest and Parkland resource was whitebark pine seeds. Recently, these were gathered by men during hunting expeditions (SM; EO), but, in earlier times, they were harvested by women and children camping in the uplands while men were hunting [cf. 'The Crippled Lady' by Charlie Mack in Bouchard and Kennedy (1977:51)]. Black tree lichen was still harvestable in the fall, but root resources, such as spring beauty, would be hard to locate (unless it was from the caches of marmots and other rodents).

(11)   Some of the edible roots mentioned earlier could also be dug in the fall in Intermediate Grassland and River Terrace Zones, notably silverweed and chocolate lily. However, the major River Terrace/River Valley resources of the fall included Indian-hemp fibre, which, along with willow for making fish traps, seems to have been available near at least some of the salmon fishing sites (DP). Mushrooms of several types, especially cottonwood mushrooms, were also harvested from the River Terrace and River Valley zones. Cottonwood mushrooms were concentrated under stands of cottonwood along waterways. Available mainly in late September and October, mushrooms were virtually the last type of plant food to be gathered and processed in any quantity before winter set in.

The preceding account concentrates on those important plant resources that are relatively seasonal and, hence, would have most influenced movement patterns. It shows that, in order to obtain the full range of plant, fish, and animal resources available within their territory, the early peoples of the study area would have had to move alternately between upland areas and regions of lower elevation. At least three plant harvesting sessions, one in spring (around May), one in summer (mid-August), and one in fall (around September), would have been necessary to acquire the various montane plant resources, and these sessions probably took place in conjunction with male hunting trips. These mountain trips would have been preceded by, alternated with, and succeeded by harvesting periods at lower elevations – at least some of which would have coincided with salmon fishing.

Group Dynamics and Plant Resource Use

All members of a family unit, except the very young and the old or infirm, participated in at least some types of plant resource gathering and processing. There was a general division of labour, in that women harvested and processed most of the plant foods, but, at least within Edith O'Donaghey's memory, men picked berries, too, when the families travelled up to Mission Ridge at huckleberry season. Her father also gathered inner bark of lodgepole pine and whitebark pine cones during his hunting expeditions and brought them back for his family. Hunting and fishing, on the other hand, were apparently almost always done by men, although women and even children might be taken along to help butcher and process the meat[8] and maintain a base camp (EO; BE; DP).

Most wood-cutting for fuel, construction, and implement manufacture was conducted by men, whereas the harvesting and processing of fibrous materials for making mats, baskets, and clothing was generally conducted by women. Even the harvesting of Indian-hemp fibre, so vital to fishing activities, was apparently undertaken mostly by women while the men were fishing (DP). There were, of course, exceptions. Men might collect bitter-cherry bark if it was to be used for wrapping an implement they were constructing, whereas women would harvest it for use in basketry. However, wood-working was apparently rarely done by women. Even knitting needles (post-contact), mat-making needles, and digging sticks were made by men, although they were to be used in women's activities (SM).

Medicines could be gathered, prepared, and administered by either men or women, but they were usually specialists whose knowledge was passed from one generation to another. Most of the shamans or 'Indian doctors,' who practised spiritual or magical forms of healing, were men. Only men – mostly old men and shamans – smoked tobacco in the old days (Teit 1906:250).

Very young children, at least in the case of Edith O'Donaghey's family, usually did not go along on harvesting expeditions such as the annual trip up to Mission Ridge. Desmond Peters, who is several years younger than his sister, Edith, stayed back at Shalalth with their grandfather while she went with the rest of the family. Only those children who were old enough to make a real contribution to resource acquisition were taken along. Edith accompanied adult harvesters, because, even as a pre-teenager, she was able to pick berries and make herself useful. She recalled: 'The girls would go out with the women to berry-pick. They were made to work very hard. There were no excuses in those days. My dad told me, "You are not going to marry a rich man. You've got to go and get it yourself!" ' Similarly, older boys were taken along on plant harvesting and hunting trips to gather firewood and look after the horses, even if they did not take an active part in the hunt or harvest (BE; DP). Young children and elders did accompany their families to the fishing grounds, according to Edith O'Donaghey and Desmond Peters. Undoubtedly, part of the reason that they were left behind on the mountain trips was that they were physically unable to withstand the arduous journey. Another reason may have been the relatively short duration of (some of) these trips. Elders and youngsters would have contributed to the family larder by harvesting easily accessible resources closer to their home base while the others were away in the uplands (D. Alexander, personal communication 1987).

Procuring and processing resources was regarded as a serious matter, and so it was, since obtaining enough food to last the family over the winter was essential to the survival of all. Thus, children were seen as learners 'in training' and were not just taken along for fun. Even an activity as seemingly straightforward as gathering boughs and materials for lining cooking pits was not necessarily entrusted to young children. As Edith O'Donaghey commented: 'Well, you have to know what kind to get . . . Sometimes they'd burn too fast. Men and women got them, certain kind of boughs . . . You can't just send children after them . . . But they learned!'

Sometimes harvesting of plant foods was carried out by one or two individuals alone, especially for trips of short duration. For example, Edith O'Donaghey's and Desmond Peter's grandmother sometimes went up Mission Ridge to dig roots all by herself in the Montane Parkland (or, occasionally, their grandfather accompanied her). She left very early in the morning with a great big basket on her back and stayed for the whole day, coming back down at dusk. For berry picking near the village, two or three women – sisters, mother and daughter, aunt and niece, grandmother and granddaughters – would go off together (EO). A similar situation existed in the Thompson area, according to Annie York of Spuzzum (personal communication 1984). As a young girl, some sixty years ago, she used to accompany her grandaunt on root-digging and berry-picking expeditions, and, as a young woman, she often went by herself to pick berries up in the mountains, occasionally camping overnight by herself but usually returning the same day (Turner et al. 1990).

However, for longer trips, such as the expedition by Edith O'Donaghey's family up to the Parkland on Mission Ridge in mid-summer, several families – women, men, and older children – would meet informally and go together. Although her family's trips, as recollected by her, may be unique, it seems more likely that this type of expedition was common throughout the Lillooet area, with families meeting and travelling to a camping spot near a resource base and staying several days to a week or more.

Edith O'Donaghey recalled that about a dozen families went with her and her grandmother on their annual huckleberry-picking and root-digging trip to the Parklands of Mission Ridge. These people included her aunt from Shalalth; her greataunt, Margaret Phillips, from Texas Creek; Adeline Gott and her mother from Texas Creek; several families from Fountain, including the Sauls, Charlie Bobs, and Chris Bobs; and several other families from Seton Portage and Shalalth. Each family brought its own horses, blankets, and food and maintained a separate campsite, with its own fire and, sometimes, cooking pit. Some brought tents; others used shelter frames and covered them with boughs each season. Tree boughs were used as mattresses. The camping area was up near the Alpine snow line but on a relatively flat, treed spot, with 'lots of creeks' in the vicinity. They brought dried salmon (from their fishing just previous to the trip) and some pre-cooked foods, such as potatoes, in order to minimize the amount of cooking. The men might hunt, and, if they shot a deer, it was roasted or pit-cooked. Although the campsites were separate, they were close together: 'Every family had their own, but they were all close together [within hearing distance]. I think they were all afraid of bears, banging their pots and pans, especially the old ladies, screaming their heads off!' (EO). There was enough grass nearby for all the horses to graze. Each family had two or three packhorses – special ones for carrying baskets and food, others for blankets and camping gear. At night at these camps, everyone would gather around a fire and the elders told stories – from Coyote tales to 'Peter Rabbit.' Edith O'Donaghey commented, 'if we heard them once, we heard them a thousand times!' Obviously, these times were happy and pleasant for everyone and are looked back on with nostalgia.

The fishing camps down on the Fraser River were similar.[9] Many families (including young children) congregated together, but each had its own fishing rock, drying shelters (in Edith O'Donaghey's time these were small screened houses on stilts, where the fish could be hung

to dry and stored below in layers interspersed with dried pine needles), and tent or camp shelters with pole frames (EO; DP; BE; see Chapters 5 and 6). Mattresses were of layers of ponderosa pine needles,
and horsehair blankets were used as covers (EO). Stories and other
social activities were an important aspect of the camps.

Annie York described similar multi-family trips in her parents' and
grandparents' time to various root-digging and berry-picking locations
in Thompson Indian territory. Group gatherings on a much larger scale
took place at Botanie Valley in Thompson territory (Turner 1978; Turner
et al. 1990) and in the Potato Mountain Range of Chilcotin territory
(Alexander and Matson 1986). These, too, had an important social element, with games, contests, races, and resource exchange taking place
throughout. At least in historic times, Botanie Valley served as a con-
vergence point for peoples from many communities, including various Thompson groups (from as far away as Spuzzum and the Nicola
Valley) and Lillooet and Shuswap peoples as well. Women spent their
time digging avalanche lily corms from the valley slopes, and, according to Thompson elder Louie Phillips (personal communication 1974),
they often bet their entire day's harvest on the horse races taking place
on the valley floor and easily visible from the root-digging grounds.
The traditions for such gatherings apparently go back for many generations and are probably prehistoric in their origins.

Trading of plant resources was itself an important means of extending the availability of plant species and products well beyond their
natural range. Teit (1906:231-2) reports that trade was well established
at the turn of the century. It undoubtedly took place, albeit at a somewhat reduced scale prior to the introduction of horses, in prehistoric
times. An important location for exchange of resources was right along
the Fraser River between Fountain and Lillooet when the Lillooet
people were congregated there for salmon fishing. Large numbers of
Lower Lillooet, Shuswap, and Thompson people (later, Hudson's Bay
traders as well) converged there for trading in August and September. Major plant resources that were imported into the Upper Lillooet
area include: dried bitterroots from the Thompson and Shuswap, and,
from the Lower Lillooet, hazelnuts, red cedar bark, yew wood, vine
maple and yellow cedar wood (for bow manufacture), and dried huckleberries. To their coastward Lillooet neighbours, the Fraser River
Lillooet traded Indian-hemp fibre and cordage, avalanche lily corms
and other types of roots, and dried soapberries, saskatoons, and choke
cherries (Teit 1906:231-2). To the Shuswap they traded cedar-bark and
cedar root baskets, Indian-hemp fibre, and dried roots and berries.
The full range of trading products, including many animal resources,
is given by Teit and by Turner et al. (1987).

It is also reasonable to assume that the Fraser River Lillooet people, like their Coast Salish counterparts, exchanged plant resources and manufactured items among themselves, within extended families, as gifts and favours to be reciprocated (at the same time or at a later date) with products of equivalent value. Such exchanges would have helped overcome the dilemma of scheduling conflicts between, for example, fishing at the river and berry picking on the mountain slopes. There would have been opportunities for those families who spent longer fishing to exchange any extra fish they accumulated for berries picked by those families who spent longer in the Montane Forests and Parklands.

Processing Plant Resources

Thus far, the discussion of plant resource use and group dynamics has concentrated on harvesting, but processing of plant resources must be recognized as a significant activity both in terms of time spent and in terms of determining seasonal movement patterns. Furthermore, some processing activities, such as pit-cooking foods, are more likely to leave evidence for the archaeological record than is the actual harvesting of those foods (cf. Pokotylo and Froese 1983). Waste materials – materials left behind after a resource is processed, used, or consumed – can themselves tell a story of resource use. For example, on observing the camp of a group of Thompson women out digging bitterroots in the Ashcroft area, botanist John Davidson made the following notation in 1916: 'From the examination of several Indian camping-places it was seen that the women evidently collect a supply of roots and return to camp to strip them. One can picture half a dozen Indian women, squatted before the campfire at the close of a day's digging, busy peeling the roots preparatory to packing them. The small heaps of skins left at most of the camps indicated that each party returned with many hundreds – perhaps thousands – of roots . . . (John Davidson, cited in Turner et al. 1990). Although the Lillooet people did not actually harvest bitterroots (because they were beyond their range), the processing of other foods – the pounding and de-barking of balsamroots (using heavy sticks or stone mauls), the cleaning of nodding onions before pit-cooking, or the cleaning and destemming of saskatoons, soapberries and other fruits, for example – was probably carried out in a similar way and would also have left some type of waste materials. These materials may occasionally be preserved in an archaeological context, such as in rim deposits of pithouses or as charred remains in hearths and roasting pits, and can give as much of an indication of resource use as can remains of the edible portions themselves.

Detailed processing of various types of plant resources of the Fraser River Lillooet is discussed in Turner et al. (1987) and, in a general way, by Turner (1979), Turner et al. (1987), and Lepofsky (1986). Tools required for harvesting and processing these resources as well as estimated processing times and suggested locations of processing of some of the more important plant resources are provided in Appendix 2 of this report.

It seems likely that, originally, berries and other products from upper Montane areas would have had to be processed (cleaned and dried, with or without being cooked) at a base camp near the harvest site before being transported home for storage. Fresh berries in the quantities gathered would have been too heavy and too bulky and probably would not have kept well enough to be transported long distances. Dehydrated (or even partially dehydrated) fruits would have been a fraction of the weight and volume and would have had a far longer 'shelf-life.' Even roots, although less subject to spoilage than soft fruits, can be significantly reduced in weight and volume by drying and, hence, more readily transported. The evidence of Pokotylo and Froese (1983) for the occurrence of cooking pit depressions dating back at least two millennia in Intermediate Grassland and Parkland areas adjacent to the study region confirms at least part of this conjecture, that is, that roots, at least, were cooked near harvest sites. The information provided by Edith O'Donaghey and Desmond Peters, that deer meat was cooked and often partially dried by hunters at base camps near the kill, also tends to support the argument that processing of foods, for practical reasons, was carried out near source areas.

Although cooking and dehydrating foods near the harvesting sites would have helped in the logistics of transporting these resources, it would have resulted in complications as well. Gathering fuel and materials for cooking, including the vegetation used to surround the food in cooking pits, would have taken time and energy. Extrapolating from my experiences with pit-cooking in coastal environments (cf. Turner and Kuhnlein 1982, 1983), I would suggest that the preparation time required for this process – for gathering sufficient fuel, accumulating cooking rocks, digging a pit, packing the necessary water, and gathering the vegetation for lining the pit – could take two people the better part of a day for an average pit, especially if one considers that implements such as saws and shovels would not have been available.[10]

There is at least one piece of linguistic and ethnogeographic evidence for the high elevation processing of plant foods in the region. Linguist and ethnographer Randy Bouchard recorded the name for

Askom Mountain in the Thompson language as *'nk'esk'estkíntn'* (liter-ally 'pit-cooking-on-top-place'). This mountain is located on the west side of the Fraser River, west from Seah I.R.5 and is the source of Nesikep Creek. It is known to contemporary Thompson speakers (notably Louie Phillips of Lytton) as a place where people pit-cooked roots (R. Bouchard, personal communication, 1986). Bouchard also recorded a place name pertaining to pit-cooking in the Lillooet lan-guage: *'nketktáshtn'* (literally 'pit-cooking place'). It is located on the southwest side of Bridge River but is only a short distance (about half a mile) up the hillside from the river. People from the village site called *'k'enk'ánaz'* (named after black hawthorn bushes – see Kennedy and Bouchard 1978:28) used to gather roots on the north slope of the hill there and pit-cook them at *'nketktáshtn'* in large quantities (R. Bouchard, personal communication 1986).

The introduction of the horse to the region may have profoundly influenced traditional processing patterns by allowing the relatively rapid transport of much larger quantities of harvested products than could be carried by individuals. Edith O'Donaghey recalled that, although some pit-cooking of meat and roots was done up at the mountain campsites, huckleberries that were harvested on Mission Mountain were carried home fresh in large pack baskets – six to eight large baskets[11] per household – by horseback and then dried. Although one might think the berries would become crushed and deteriorate in transit, EO and DP both repeated that they were transported fresh, and that they were not even partially dried at the campsite. Since air drying can be a lengthy process, requiring several days[12] of warm sun-ny weather, the use of horses made it possible to stay up at the har-vesting site for only the few days required for harvesting, then bring the berries back to the permanent home before they spoiled. Black tree lichen, too, could be carried back to the permanent home by horse-back in large gunnysacks, three or four per household (EO). Without horses, these would have been too bulky for a person to manage eas-ily, and the lichen would have had to be cleaned, leached in water, pit-cooked at base camps near the harvest site to reduce its volume, and probably also dried to reduce its weight and to prevent spoilage.[13] Similarly, with horses, large sacks of whitebark pine cones could be carried home for processing (EO) rather than having to be roasted (and the seeds extracted) at or near the mountain harvesting site.

Processing often involved several stages, and different facets of the total sequence might take place at different locations. Berries and roots might be cleaned and dried for storage, then, before being consumed, would be soaked to reconstitute them and then, possibly, cooked alone or mixed with other products (Laforet et al. 1991). For woods used in implement-making, the rough trimming of leaves and branches would take place at the harvesting site, then the finer work would be carried out back at a camp or permanent home. For fibrous materials, such as Indian-hemp, rough trimming of tops and cleaning of leaves might be carried out at the harvesting site; splitting and drying of the stems at a nearby campsite; pounding and stripping off of the fibrous materi-al at a different place and time; spinning into twine at another; and manufacture of nets, clothing, or bags at yet another. Undoubtedly, much of the final processing and manufacturing of plant products took place in and around the permanent winter dwellings, during the time of year when few fresh resources were available for harvesting and when there were few other pressing tasks to perform.

CONCLUSIONS

Plant resources of many types – edible fruits, roots, green vegetables, inner bark of some trees, black tree lichen, mushrooms, wood for fuel and construction, fibrous materials for cordage and weaving, dyes, glues and scents, medicines for injuries, sickness, childbirth, and the maintenance of physical and spiritual health – were used traditional-ly by the Fraser River Lillooet people and were extremely important for their survival. Most of these plants are seasonal to some extent, and many are confined distributionally to particular habitats and vege-tation zones within Fraser River Lillooet territory. Thus, to obtain these resources, people had to be present at particular locations within a given range of time on an annual basis, and this factor naturally has had a significant influence on seasonal movement patterns of both prehistoric and relatively contemporary Lillooet populations.

Specifically, there were at least three major periods of resource avail-ability for plant species of Intermediate and Montane areas: spring (lodgepole pine inner bark, edible green shoots such as cow-parsnip and fireweed, and early spring beauty and other 'root' resources); mid-summer (black huckleberry, spring beauty, and avalanche lily corms); and fall (whitebark pine seeds). The edible roots, as well as black tree lichen, were available over a wider time span, but the other plants were fairly specific in their required harvesting season. Since salmon fishing, combined with the necessity of harvesting important plant resources of lower elevations, such as saskatoon berries and choke cherries, required the frequent presence of at least major portions of the population in River Valley and Terrace areas throughout the spring, summer, and fall months, this meant that alternating trips to upland and lowland areas must have occurred annually throughout the growing season.

The time required for harvesting and processing plant resources as well as for harvesting and processing fish and game meant that people had to camp in given locations for definite periods of time (in some cases, as with the Fraser River salmon fishery, for up to a month, in other cases, for only a few days or a week). Generally, at least within the memory of contemporary Lillooet elders, most harvesting trips were undertaken by groups of people. For short trips, only two or three people might go together; for trips of longer duration several individuals, or even several families, might travel and camp in loosely organized groups, each unit self-sufficient and independent in terms of resource harvesting and use but with much interaction at a social level.

There was a definite, but not hard-and-fast, division of labour between women and men. Women generally undertook the harvesting and processing of plant foods, the processing of fish and meat, and the harvesting and processing of plant fibres for weaving, mat-making, and cordage. Men, almost exclusively, did the hunting and fishing and made the implements required for these activities. They did most other wood-working as well and usually harvested the wood and other plant resources required for implement-making and large-scale construction. In recent years, at least, men sometimes harvested plant resources, such as lodgepole pine inner bark and whitebark pine cones, in conjunction with hunting activities, and they even assisted women in berry picking and root digging if they were available during the harvest. Children were trained from an early age to undertake resource harvesting and processing, and, as soon as they were old enough to contribute to resource gathering or maintaining a support base for harvesters, they accompanied their parents and other relatives.

Trading and exchange of plant products with people of neighbouring areas increased the resource base of the Fraser River Lillooet, providing them with some foods and materials that would otherwise not have been available. Bitterroots, hazelnuts, cedar bark, and yellow cedar, yew, and vine maple wood (for implement manufacture) were among the imported plant resources, at least in the historic period.

The archaeological record for plant resource use in the Fraser River Lillooet area is expanding year by year. Use of contemporary knowledge of traditional activities is an important means of focusing on directions for future archaeological research and for interpreting available archaeological data. A complete and detailed reconstruction of prehistoric plant use by early Plateau peoples may be unrealistic, but by looking through the window of present-day knowledge concerning practices of traditional plant use and by superimposing this picture onto known archaeobotanical findings, we can obtain a fairly accurate understanding of the most significant inter-relationships between people and plants in prehistoric Plateau cultures.

APPENDICES

1. Index to Scientific Names of Plants Mentioned in Chapter 8

(Numbers refer to data numbers in original Appendix 2).

alder, Sitka (*Alnus sinuata*) (No. 46)
anemone, Pacific (*Anemone multifida*) (No. 73)
aspen, trembling (*Populus tremuloides*) (No. 88)
avalanche lily, yellow (see lily, yellow avalanche)
balsam poplar (see cottonwood)
balsamroot (*Balsamorhiza sagittata*) (No. 44)
baneberry (*Actaea rubra*) (No. 72)
birch, paper (*Betula papyrifera*) (No. 47)
bitterroot (*Lewisia rediviva*) (No. 71)
black tree lichen (*Bryoria fremontii*) (No. 1)
blackcap (*Rubus leucodermis*) (No. 85)
blueberry, dwarf mountain (*Vaccinium caespitosum*) (No. 60)
blueberry, oval-leaved (*Vaccinium ovalifolium*) (No. 62)
bluebunch wheat grass (see grass, bluebunch wheat)
bulrush, round-stem (see tule)
bunchgrass (see grass, bluebunch wheat)
cactus, prickly-pear (*Opuntia fragilis, O. polyacantha*) (No. 49)
cascara (*Rhamnus purshiana*) (No. 74)
cattail, common (*Typha latifolia*) (No. 32)
cedar, red (see cedar, western red)
cedar, yellow (*Chamaecyparis nootkatensis*) (No. 6)
cedar, western red (*Thuja plicata*) (No. 9)
cherry, bitter (*Prunus emarginata*) (No. 81)
cherry, choke (*Prunus virginiana*) (No. 82)
chocolate lily (see lily, chocolate)
chocolate-tips (*Lomatium dissectum*) (No. 35)
choke cherry (see cherry, choke)
cottonwood, or balsam poplar (*Populus balsamifera*) (No. 87)
cottonwood mushroom (*Tricholoma populinum*) (No. 2)
cow-parsnip (*Heracleum lanatum*) (No. 34)

crabapple, Pacific (*Malus fusca*) (No. 79)
desert parsley (*Lomatium macrocarpum*) (No. 36)
devil's-club (*Oplopanax horridus*) (No. 40)
Douglas-fir (see fir, Douglas-)
elderberry, red (*Sambucus racemosa*) (No. 51)
false box (*Paxistima myrsinites*) (No. 54)
false onion (*Triteleia grandiflora* ?) (No. 26)
false Solomon's seal (*Smilacina racemosa*) (No. 25)
field wormwood (see wormwood, field)
fir, balsam (see fir, subalpine)
fir, Douglas- (*Pseudotsuga menziesii*) (No. 16)
fir, subalpine (*Abies lasiocarpa*) (No. 10)
fireweed (*Epilobium angustifolium*) (No. 68)
gooseberry, white-stemmed (*Ribes inerme*) (No. 64)
gooseberry, swamp (*Ribes lacustre*) (No. 65)
grass, bluebunch wheat (*Agropyron spicatum*) (No. 28)
grass, bunch- (see grass, bluebunch wheat)
grass, giant wild rye (*Elymus cinereus*) (No. 30)
grass, reed canary (*Phalaris arundinacea*) (No. 31)
grass, pine (*Calamagrostis rubescens*) (No. 29)
hawthorn, black (*Crataegus douglasii*) (No. 76)
hazelnut (*Corylus cornuta*) (No. 48)
hellebore, Indian (see Indian hellebore)
hemlock, mountain (*Tsuga mertensiana*)
hemlock, western (*Tsuga heterophylla*) (No. 17)
highbush cranberry (*Viburnum edule*) (No. 53)
hog-fennel (see desert parsley)
horsetail, branchless (*Equisetum hyemale*) (No. 4)
horsetail, common (*Equisetum arvense*) (No. 5)
huckleberry, black mountain (*Vaccinium membranaceum*) (No. 61)
huckleberry, red (*Vaccinium parvifolium*) (No. 63)
Indian celery (*Lomatium nudicaule*) (No. 37)
Indian hellebore (*Veratrum viride*) (No. 27)
Indian potato (see spring beauty)
Indian rhubarb (see cow-parsnip)
Indian-hemp (*Apocynum cannabinum*) (No. 39)
'ironwood' (see oceanspray)
juniper, common (*Juniperus communis*) (No. 7)
juniper, Rocky Mountain (*Juniperus scopulorum*) (No. 8)
kinnikinnick (*Arctostaphylos uva-ursi*) (No. 58)
Labrador-tea (*Ledum groenlandicum*) (No. 59)
lichen, black tree (see black tree lichen)
lily, chocolate (*Fritillaria lanceolata*) (No. 23)

lily, desert (see lily, mariposa)
lily, mariposa (*Calochortus macrocarpus*) (No. 21)
lily, tiger (*Lilium columbianum*) (No. 24)
lily, yellow avalanche (*Erythronium grandiflorum*) (No. 22)
maple, Rocky Mountain (*Acer glabrum* var. *douglasii*) (No. 33)
mariposa lily (see lily, mariposa)
mint, wild (*Mentha arvensis*) (No. 67)
mock-orange (*Philadelphus lewisii*) (No. 66)
mosses, general (especially 'long' types) (Bryophytes) (No. 3)
mushroom, cottonwood (see cottonwood mushroom)
mushroom, slimy top (Unidentified)
nettle, stinging (see stinging nettle)
oceanspray (*Holodiscus discolor*) (No. 78)
onion, nodding wild (*Allium cernuum*) (No. 20)
Oregon-grape, tall (*Mahonia aquifolium*) (No. 45)
pine, lodgepole (*Pinus contorta*) (No. 13)
pine, ponderosa (*Pinus ponderosa*) (No. 15)
pine, white (*Pinus monticola*) (No. 14)
pine, whitebark (*Pinus albicaulis*) (No. 12)
pine, yellow (see pine, ponderosa)
pinegrass (see grass, pine-)
plantain, broad-leaved (*Plantago major*) (No. 69)
potato, Indian or mountain (see spring beauty)
raspberry, wild (*Rubus idaeus*) (No. 84)
red-osier dogwood (*Cornus sericea*) (No. 55)
'red willow' (see red-osier dogwood)
roses, wild (*Rosa nutkana, R. acicularis, R. woodsii*) (No. 83)
saskatoon berry (*Amelanchier alnifolia*) (No. 75)
sagebrush, big (*Artemisia tridentata*) (No. 43)
silverberry (*Elaeagnus commutata*) (No. 56)
silverweed (*Potentilla anserina* spp. *anserina*) (No. 80)
soapberry (*Shepherdia canadensis*) (No. 57)
spring beauty (*Claytonia lanceolata*) (No. 70)
spring sunflower (see balsamroot)
spruce, Engelmann (*Picea engelmannii*) (No. 11)
stinging nettle (*Urtica dioica*) (No. 93)
strawberries, wild (*Fragaria vesca, F. virginiana*) (No. 77)
thimbleberry (*Rubus parviflorus*) (No. 86)
'timbergrass' (see pinegrass)
tobacco, wild (*Nicotiana attenuata*) (No. 92)
twinberry, black (*Lonicera involucrata*) (No. 50)
tule (*Scirpus acutus*, syn. *S. lacustris*) (No. 19)
water-parsnip (*Sium suave*) (No. 38)

waxberry (*Symphoricarpos albus*) (No. 52)
willows, general (*Salix* spp.) (No. 89)
willow, Pacific (*Salix lasiandra*) (No. 90)
willow, 'rope' (see sandbar willow)
willow, sandbar (*Salix exigua*) (No. 91)
willow, Sitka (*Salix sitchensis*) (No. 89)
wormwood, field (*Artemisia campestris*) (No. 42)
wormwood, northern (*Artemisia frigida*) (under No. 42)
yarrow (*Achillea millefolium*) (No. 41)
yew, western (*Taxus brevifolia*) (No. 18)

2. Inventory of Major Plant Resources of the Fraser River Lillooet People

Note: Harvesting/processing times and quantities are approximations, based on experience or suggestions of native consultants or on information from Teit (1906). Information generally reflects uses and practices of 50-100 years ago that were general for Lillooet, or specific to Fraser River (Upper) Lillooet, as reported in Turner et al. (1987).

Index of Cultural Significance (ICS) is based on calculations described in Turner (1988a). In most cases, only those species having moderate (ICS: 20-49), high (ICS: 50-99), or very high (ICS: over 100) cultural significance were included in this inventory. There are some exceptions, however, for species such as giant wild rye grass and chocolate-tips, which, although apparently not particularly important, may occur in an archaeological context. Note that eleven representative resource plants have been listed here from over ninety plants that were originally inventoried.

Information on range within biogeoclimatic zones and scientific nomenclature is from Taylor and MacBryde (1977) and Krajina et al. (1982). Here, 'dry ponderosa pine' refers to Ponderosa Pine – Bunchgrass Zone; 'interior subalpine' refers to Engelmann Spruce – Subalpine Fir Zone; 'coastal subalpine' refers to Mountain Hemlock Zone; and 'interior Douglas-fir' refers to the Interior Douglas-fir Zone as per Krajina et al. (1982:11). Information on specific localities and accompanying species distribution maps is from native consultants, from personal observation (NT) and, in some cases, from British Columbia Forest Service Forest Cover maps (Figure 1).

Explanation of Data Sheet Notations

Species number (consecutive for order used – see Turner et al. 1987)
Plant: english common name, scientific name
Index of cultural significance: numeric value relating to overall significance
     of plant in traditional Lillooet life (see Turner 1988a)
Major use(s): including food, technological, and/or medicinal uses as well
     as importance in religion and/or mythology

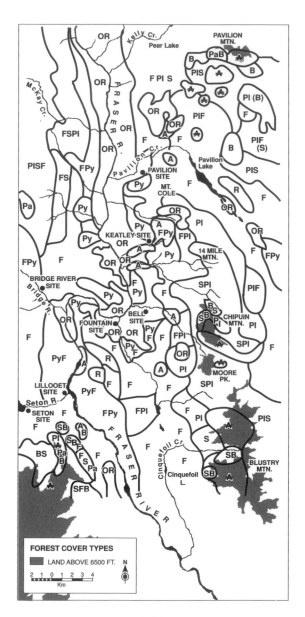

FIGURE 1

Forest cover types as designated on Forest Cover Map Series (BC Ministry of Forests, Inventory Branch Maps Nos. 921.071, 921.072, 921.081, 921.082). Symbols indicate species: *F* = Douglas-fir; *B* = balsam (true fir); *S* = spruce; *PA* = whitebark pine; *OR* = open range; *PL* = lodgepole pine; *PY* = yellow pine; *C* = cottonwood; *A* = aspen; ⋏ = alpine; *R* = rock

BGC zone(s) in study area: see Krajina (1969) for detailed description of biogeoclimatic zones named after dominant tree species (except Alpine Tundra); after Taylor and MacBryde (1977); only zones within the study area
are mentioned here

Habitat(s): general growing conditions for plant

Specific localities: place(s) where plant is known to occur, based on direct
observation or information provided by Native consultants

HARVESTING: means of gathering or collecting plant or plant product, including immediate activities associated with harvesting, such as removal of
tops (of 'roots' freshly dug)

Season(s): major time(s) of harvesting, given as accurately as possible, but
subject to variations in local weather patterns and usually dependent
on elevation (e.g., in mid-July, blackcaps in the vicinity of the Fraser River
were ripe whereas those around Cinquefoil Lake were still green)

People: Who were the major harvesters of the plant?

Time: Approximately how long (per family per year) was taken up in harvesting the plant?

Quantity (per family): Approximately how much, on average, was harvested
per family per year?

Rate: time taken to harvest specific quantities by one person (see Lefopsky
et al. 1985:238-9)

Tools used: What artefacts were required for harvesting?

Transport of product: How was plant or plant product carried to processing locality, or to where it would be consumed?

PROCESSING: What was done to the plant or plant product before it was used
or consumed? (sometimes several different processes were required)

Season(s): When did the processing take place?

Where: Where would the processing have taken place?

People: Who would have carried out the processing?

Time: How many days (per family per year) would processing have required?

Tools used: What artefacts were required for processing?

Fire?: Was fire required for some aspect of processing?

Water?: Was water required for some aspect of processing?

Waste produced: What would have been discarded by the processor during or after processing?

Other plant products used: What other plants or plant products might have
been involved in processing (e.g., pit-cooking materials for black tree
lichen)?

CONSUMPTION OR USE OF PRODUCT: How was the end product actually used
or consumed?

Season(s): When was the product used or consumed?

Where used: Where was the product used or consumed?

People: Who would have used or consumed the product?

Containers, implements: What vessels or tools would have been associated with the product's use or consumption?

Fire?: Was fire required or involved in the use or consumption of the product? (often this is coincident with previous question on fire needed for processing)

Water?: Was water required or involved in the use or consumption of the product? (often this is coincident with previous question on water needed for processing)

Waste produced: What would have been discarded during or after use or consumption of product?

Accompanying resources: What other resources were used or consumed together with plant or plant product in question? (e.g., sagebrush bark and willow bark were often woven together; red-osier dogwood berries were often mixed with saskatoons)

TRADE?: Was the plant, plant product, or processed product traded to or from regions outside of its natural area of distribution or high abundance, or area of manufacture?

COMMENTS: What other information about the plant is relevant to its use or possible occurrence in an archaeological context?

REFERENCES: sources of information provided in data sheet (see References below)

Geophytes

Spring beauty, or Indian potato (*Claytonia lanceolata*)

Index of cultural significance: 70 (high)

Major use(s): corms eaten

BGC zone(s) in study area: coastal subalpine; interior subalpine; dry ponderosa pine; (alpine tundra); Figure 2

Habitat(s): moist to relatively dry mountain slopes, meadows, and clearings

Specific localities: Pavilion Mt., Tom Cole Mt., Mission Mt.

HARVESTING: corms dug up (tops removed); sometimes obtained from caches of mice and other rodents

Season(s): May-Aug. (usually before, but also during or after flowering)

People: mostly women

Time: prob. 3-8 days

Quantity (per family): large quantities; prob. 10-25 kg (or more)

Tools used: digging sticks (some of mule deer antler)

Transport of product: large baskets

PROCESSING: 1. corms washed; 2. corms steamed over boughs or in baskets; 3. corms stored in underground caches (but most apparently eaten fresh

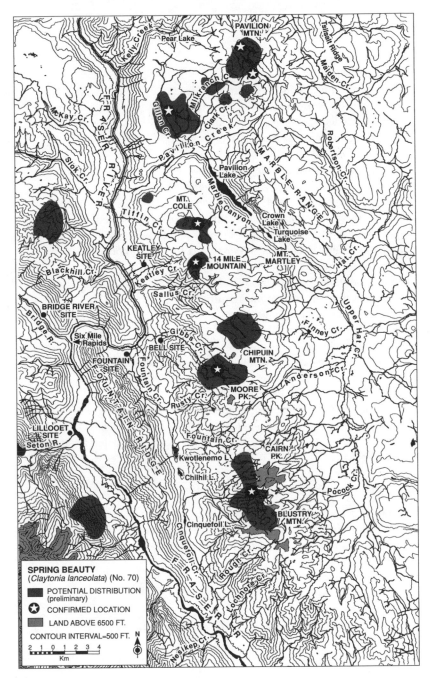

FIGURE 2

Distribution of spring beauty (*Claytonia lanceolata*) in the study area. Hatched zones indicate potential distribution (preliminary estimate); starred points indicate confirmed locations

after digging)

Season(s): May-Aug.

Where: prob. mountain base camps

People: mostly women

Time: as needed: prob. 1-2 days total

Tools used: steaming materials, baskets

Fire?: yes, for cooking

Water?: yes, for washing, steaming

Waste produced: cooking wastes, boughs, etc.

Other plant products used: (see above)

CONSUMPTION OR USE OF PRODUCT: corms eaten freshly cooked, or cooked after storage

Season(s): mainly May-Aug. (year-round for stored corms)

Where used: anywhere

People: everyone

Containers, implements: none required

Fire?: for cooking (see above)

Water?: for cooking (see above)

Waste produced: none

Accompanying resources: meat, fish, other foods eaten with corms

TRADE?: prob. to Lower Lillooet

COMMENTS: – common at Pavilion Mt.

– mentioned in mythology as stars of the sky-world

– often harvested and cooked with yellow avalanche lily corms

REFERENCES: Turner 1978; Turner et al. 1987; Teit 1906:222; Bouchard and Kennedy 1977:75

Balsamroot, or spring sunflower (*Balsamorhiza sagittata*)

Index of cultural significance: 76 (high)

Major use(s): young leaf- and bud-stalks eaten; large taproots cooked and eaten

BGC zone(s) in study area: dry ponderosa pine; interior Douglas-fir; interior subalpine; Figure 3

Habitat(s): dry, open slopes and meadows

Specific localities: Keatley Cr.; Fountain; Pavilion; lower elevations, Pavilion Mountain

HARVESTING: 1. stalks broken off (leaves/buds removed); 2. roots dug – v. large and deep; tops removed

Season(s): 1. Apr., May; 2. May-Jul., esp. Aug., Sept.

People: mostly women

Time: 1. casual; 2. prob. 2-5 days

Quantity (per family): 1. prob. 100-200 stems; 2. 'large quantities' – Teit 1906:222

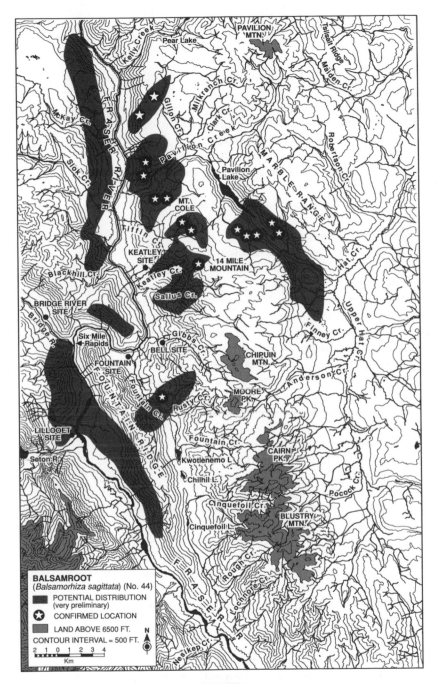

FIGURE 3

Distribution of balsamroot (*Balsamorhiza sagittata*) in the study area. Hatched zones indicate potential distribution (preliminary estimate); starred points indicate confirmed locations

Tools used: 1. knife; 2. digging stick

Transport of product: 1. eaten on site or carried in baskets, bags; 2. large pack-baskets

PROCESSING: 1. stalks peeled; 2. roots pounded, outer 'bark' removed, pit-cooked (or recently boiled); many dried on sticks

Season(s): 1. Apr., May; 2. Jun.-Sept.

Where: 1. on site or base camp; 2. base camp

People: 1. women, children; 2. mostly women

Time: 1. casual; 2. prob. 2-4 days

Tools used: 1. hands; 2. pounding tool to remove 'bark of root'; pit-cooking materials; sticks for drying

Fire?: 1. no; 2. yes, for pit-cooking

Water?: 1. no; 2. yes, for pit-cooking (?washing)

Waste produced: 1. discarded peelings; 2. discarded outer bark; pit-cooking wastes

Other plant products used: pit-cooking vegetation

CONSUMPTION OR USE OF PRODUCT: 1. (leaf- and) bud-stalks eaten fresh, raw, or cooked; roots eaten fresh/ or reconstituted; v. sweet, due to presence of inulin converted to fructose by cooking

Season(s): 1. Apr., May; 2. year-round

Where used: 1. on site, base camps; 2. anywhere

People: everyone

Containers, implements: not necessary

Fire?: yes, for cooking

Water?: yes, for soaking, cooking

Waste produced: discarded drying-sticks

Accompanying resources: prob. meat or fish

TRADE?: prob. yes, sticks of dried roots to Lower Lillooet

COMMENTS: – seeds apparently not eaten, as they were by Thompson and Okanagan-Colville

– dried upper root fibres sometimes used to make slow match

– inulin-containing plant; cooked roots extremely sweet, eaten as a 'kind of dessert'; juice from soaking roots also drunk as beverage

– barely used at all at present

REFERENCES: Turner 1978; Turner et al. 1987; Teit 1912:353, 1906:222

Yellow avalanche lily (*Erythronium grandiflorum*)

Index of cultural significance: 89 (high)

Major use(s): small, brittle corms steamed or pit-cooked and eaten; very important food; 'wild sweet potatoes'

BGC zone(s) in study area: (alpine tundra); coastal subalpine; interior subalpine

Habitat(s): moist montane meadows

Specific localities: Texas Creek (EO – ?); S. side of reserve at D'Arcy; mountains west of Lillooet; 'mountaintops'; Mission Mt.; prob. Pavilion Mt.

HARVESTING: corms dug (15-20 cm deep), removed from tops

Season(s): Jun.-Aug.

People: women

Time: prob. 5-10 days

Quantity (per family): prob. 5-20 kg

Rate: 2 l in 40 minutes

Tools used: digging stick, baskets, tumpline

Transport of product: pack baskets

PROCESSING: 1. corms cleaned, then steamed or pit-cooked; 2. corms dried loose or strung and dried, then reconstituted before being eaten

Season(s): Jun.-Aug.

Where: prob. upland base camps

People: women

Time: prob. 2-5 days

Tools used: 1. cooking container or pit-cooking materials; 2. awl, twine, or drying rack, mats, storage bags, baskets

Fire?: yes – for pit-cooking

Water?: yes – for pit-cooking

Waste produced: scraps of root, skin, leaves

Other plant products used: pit-cooking materials; saskatoon berries (sometimes dried with corms); tule or cattail mats for drying; Indian-hemp twine for stringing; sometimes prepared and cooked with tiger lily bulbs and spring beauty corms

CONSUMPTION OR USE OF PRODUCT: corms eaten, either freshly cooked or reconstituted and cooked (*not* raw)

Season(s): 1. summer; 2. year-round

Where used: 1. mountain base camps; 2. anywhere

People: everyone

Containers, implements: soaking and cooking containers (? birch bark)

Fire?: yes, for cooking

Water?: yes, for cooking

Waste produced: discarded strings

Accompanying resources: corms eaten with various other foods – saskatoons, spring beauty corms, tiger lily corms, black tree lichen, meat, fish in soups and stews

TRADE?: yes; mainly from Upper Lillooet to Lower Lillooet area

COMMENTS: – known to be important food for grizzlies; mentioned as 'wild vegetables' in several Lillooet myths

– apparently an inulin-containing food that tastes sweeter with storage and cooking; tastes 'really good'

REFERENCES: Turner 1978; Turner et al. 1987; Teit 1906:231

Wild nodding onion (*Allium cernum*)

Index of cultural significance: 58 (high)

Major use(s): bulbs pit-cooked and eaten in large quantities – 'barbecuing onions'

BGC zone(s) in study area: interior Douglas-fir; dry ponderosa pine; interior supalpine; Figure 4

Habitat(s): meadows, banks, open woods in sandy soil

Specific localities: open ponderosa woods east of Lillooet and across river; in hills all around Lillooet – v. common; Cayoosh Cr.; 'Onion Mountain' (?), Mission Mt., Pavilion Mt., Fountain Valley

HARVESTING: bulbs dug, with leaves intact

  Season(s): Apr., May (before flowering)

  People: women, children

  Time: prob. 2-5 days

  Quantity (per family): 'large quantities'; prob. 5-15 kg

  Tools used: digging stick, pack baskets, prob. with tumpline

  Transport of product: in large pack baskets

PROCESSING: 1. bulbs tied or braided together by leaves, in flat bundles, rubbed clean; sometimes tied with Rocky Mt. maple bark; 2. bulbs pit-cooked overnight; 3. bulbs dried and stored

  Season(s): Apr., May (later in montane areas)

  Where: base camps or near permanent dwellings – along river benchlands; also in upland areas

  People: mostly women

  Time: 2-4 days (?)

  Tools used: bundles of shrubby penstemon; pit-cooking materials; drying racks; storage bags, baskets

  Fire?: yes – for pit-cooking

  Water?: yes – for pit-cooking

  Waste produced: fragments of root, onion skins, etc.; pit-cooking wastes – charcoal, rye grass, saskatoon branches, etc.

  Other plant products used: cleaned with shrubby penstemon; tied with Rocky Mt. maple bark; often cooked with black tree lichen or with other roots (e.g., y. avalanche lily)

CONSUMPTION OR USE OF PRODUCT: bulbs eaten fresh cooked, or dried, reconstituted and cooked; highly favoured

  Season(s): spring (lower elev.), summer (high elev.); or year-round (dried)

  Where used: base camps, travelling, winter dwellings

  People: everyone

  Containers, implements: could be eaten with fingers; poss. dishes

  Fire?: yes, for cooking

  Water?: yes, if cooked in soups or stews

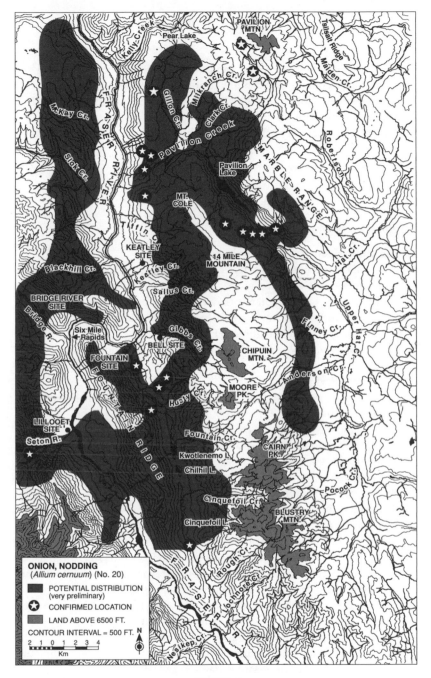

FIGURE 4

Distribution of nodding onion (*Allium cernuum*) in the study area.
Hatched zones indicate potential distribution (preliminary estimate);
starred points indicate confirmed locations

Waste produced: no

Accompanying resources: other foods – e.g., edible roots, meat, fish

TRADE?: possibly cooked, dried bulbs (but plant is quite widespread)

COMMENTS: – bulbs contain inulin; become extremely sweet after cooking
  through conversion to fructose
  – some contemporary Lillooet know the name only as one for garden
  onions

REFERENCES: Turner 1978; Turner et al. 1987; Teit 1906:222

Berries and Fruits

Saskatoon berry (*Amelanchier alnifolia*)

Index of cultural significance: 117 (very high)

Major use(s): berries eaten (five varieties recognized); most important of all
  fruits to Fraser River people; wood used for snowshoe frames, digging
  sticks, arrows, salmon spreaders, drying racks; branches in cooking pits

BGC zone(s) in study area: interior subalpine; interior Douglas-fir; dry ponderosa pine; coastal subalpine; Figure 5

Habitat(s): highly variable species; open woods, rocky slopes, along creeks

Specific localities: throughout region; Fountain, Lillooet, Cayoosh Creek, Keatley Creek, Pavilion, etc.

HARVESTING: 1. berries picked; 2. stem wood cut; 3. leafy branches cut

  Season(s): 1. Jun.-early Jul.; 2. prob. mostly Feb.-Nov.; 3. Apr.-Nov.

  People: 1. mostly women; 2. mostly men; 3. anyone

  Time: 1. prob. 5-10 days; 2. 1-3 days; 3. casual

  Quantity (per person): 1. large quantities (prob. 15-30 kg); 2. prob. 20-30 or
  more stems; 3. prob. 2-3 large bushes' worth, total

  Rate: 250 ml in 5 minutes (berries)

  Tools used: 1. none required; 2. knife, axe; 3. knife

  Transport of product: 1. baskets; 2., 3. bundles

PROCESSING: 1. berries cleaned, dried (sometimes smoke-dried in loaves or
  cooked first with hot rocks); or juice extracted 2. stems (for some uses)
  debarked, carved, sometimes fire-hardened (for arrows, chewed); 3. none

  Season(s): 1. Jun.-early July; 2. mainly Feb.-Nov.; 3. Apr.-Nov.

  Where: 1., 2., 3. base camp or permanent dwelling (note: fish-drying racks
  would be constructed on site at fishing camps)

  People: 1. women; 2. mostly men; 3. mostly women

  Time: 1. 2-4 days (total drying time – 7-10 days); 2. variable, depending on
  artefact or structure; at least 2-5 days; 3. casual

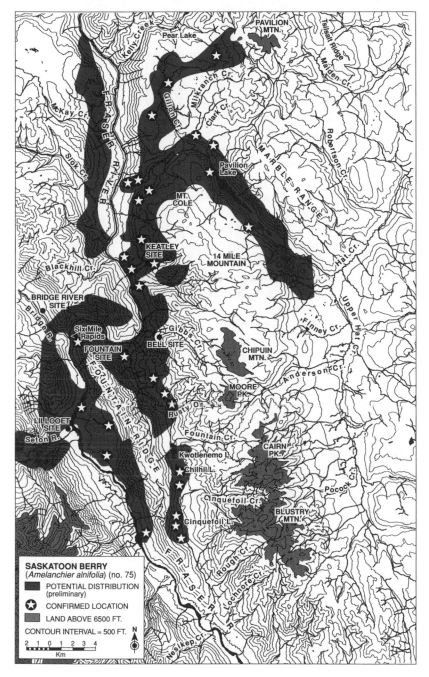

FIGURE 5
Distribution of saskatoon berry (*Amelanchier alnifolia*) in the study area. Hatched zones indicate potential distribution (preliminary estimate); starred points indicate confirmed locations

Tools used: 1. cooking vessels, rocks; drying mats, racks; 2. knife, adze, chisel, abrasive; 3. (?) knife

Fire?: 1. yes, if berries cooked, or for smoke-drying; 2. yes, for fire-hardening; 3. yes, in cooking pits and vessels

Water?: 1. not necessarily; 2. probably, for soaking materials; 3. cooking

Waste produced: 1. discarded stems, leaves; 2. bark shavings, wood chips;

Other plant products used: 2. other woods, cherry bark, Indian-hemp twine

CONSUMPTION OR USE OF PRODUCT: 1. berries eaten fresh, raw or cooked, or dried or reconstituted; 2. implements used in many activities; 3. branches in cooking pits and bottom of cooking vessels

Season(s) 1., 2. year-round; 3. mainly Apr.-Nov.

Where used: 1., 2., 3. anywhere required

People: 1., 2., everyone; 3. mostly women

Containers, implements: 1. soaking, eating vessels

Fire?: 1. yes, cooking; 2. sometimes (e.g., smoking fish); 3. yes, cooking

Water?: 1. for reconstituting, cooking soups, etc.; 2. often; 3. in cooking

Waste produced: 1. none; 2., old, discarded implements, drying racks; 3. discarded branches after cooking

Accompanying resources: 1. many other foods (e.g., dried salmon, salmon eggs, edible roots); 2. other implements (e.g., bows) and materials (e.g., bitter cherry bark); 3. other pit-cooking materials

TRADE?: Yes, in large quantities to Lower Lillooet from Fraser River

COMMENTS: – one of most important, versatile of all Lillooet plant resources

REFERENCES: Turner 1978; Turner et al. 1979, 1987; Teit 1906:222

Black mountain huckleberry (*Vaccinium membranaceum*)

Index of cultural significance: 56 (high)

Major use(s): berries eaten; extremely popular and important (apparently traded to Fraser River area, where they are not common)

BGC zone(s) in study area: coastal subalpine; interior subalpine; (alpine tundra); Figure 6

Habitat(s): mountain slopes; dry sites in coniferous forests

Specific localities: Mission Mt., Duffey Lake

HARVESTING: berries picked

Season(s): early Aug.

People: women (and sometimes men)

Time: 3-6 days

Quantity (per family): 10-20 kg (when available)

Tools used: none required

Transport of product: large baskets

PROCESSING: berries cleaned, dried (may have been cooked with hot rocks or smoke-dried)

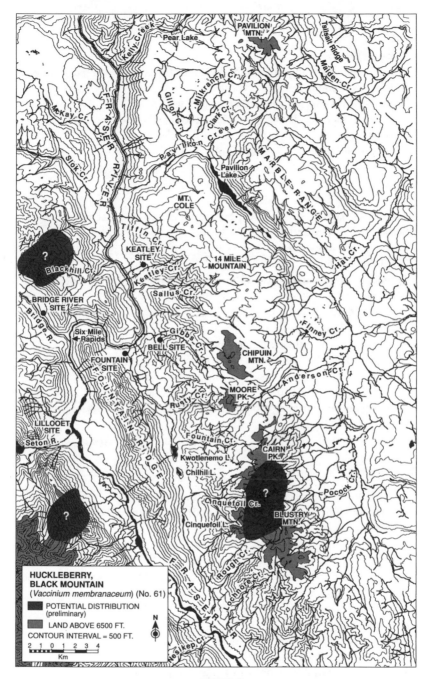

FIGURE 6

Distribution of black mountain huckleberry (*Vaccinium membranaceum*) in the study area. Hatched zones indicate potential distribution (preliminary estimate); starred points indicate confirmed locations

Season(s): early Aug.

Where: mountain camps or winter dwellings (might be carried down fresh)

People: women

Time: 1-2 days (drying time about 7-10 days)

Tools used: mats for drying (possibly hot rocks if berries cooked first); bags
  for storage

Fire?: yes, if berries cooked or smoke-dried

Water?: no

Waste produced: discarded twigs, leaves

Other plant products used: no

CONSUMPTION OR USE OF PRODUCT: berries eaten fresh or reconstituted

Season(s): year-round

Where used: anywhere

People: everyone

Containers, implements: vessel for soaking berries; dishes, spoon(?)

Fire?: no

Water?: yes, for soaking berries

Waste produced: none

Accompanying resources: other foods eaten with berries

TRADE?: yes, dried berries traded from Lower Lillooet (Teit 1906:22)

COMMENTS: – These were considered one of the most important fruits; people from Shalalth, Fountain, Texas Creek, Seton Portage all went camping up on Mission Ridge to pick these berries; they got 6-8 large baskets
  full per family (EO)

REFERENCES: Turner 1978; Turner et al. 1987; Teit 1906:22, 231-232

Choke cherry (*Prunus virginiana*)

Index of cultural significance: 62 (high)

Major use(s): cherries eaten, fresh or dried; (decoction of berries drunk for
  diarrhoea)

BGC zone(s) in study area: interior Douglas-fir; dry ponderosa pine; Figure 7

Habitat(s): rocky clearings, moist to dry gulleys, and along creeks

Specific localities: Fountain Valley, Cayoosh Creek, along hwy south of Lillooet
  toward Lytton and north toward Fountain; Sallus Creek gulley

HARVESTING: cherries picked in bunches

Season(s): Aug.-Sept. (Oct.)

People: women

Time: prob. 3-4 days

Quantity (per family): prob. 5-10 kg (about 30 l – EO)

Tools used: (?) long, hooked sticks

Transport of product: baskets

PROCESSING: 1. cherries de-stemmed; 2. cherries dried

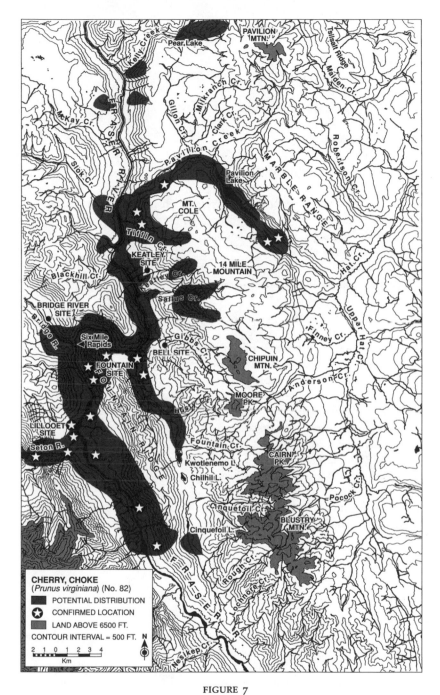

FIGURE 7

Distribution of choke cherry (*Prunus virginiana*) in the study area.
Hatched zones indicate potential distribution (preliminary estimate);
starred points indicate confirmed locations

Season(s): Aug.-Sep.

Where: base camps or permanent dwellings

People: women

Time: 1-2 days (total drying time: 7-10 days)

Tools used: drying mats

Fire?: not necessarily

Water?: no

Waste produced: discarded stems, leaves

Other plant products used: none

CONSUMPTION OR USE OF PRODUCT: cherries eaten fresh, raw or cooked, or
    reconstituted

Season(s): Aug-Sep.; year-round if stored

Where used: anywhere

People: everyone

Containers, implements: soaking vessels

Fire?: yes, if cooked

Water?: yes, for soaking

Waste produced: discarded seeds

Accompanying resources: (?) oil; other foods – meat, fish

TRADE?: yes, dried cherries to Lower Lillooet

COMMENTS: – nowadays, people can and freeze choke cherries and choke
    cherry juice and make syrup and jelly; two varieties recognized: red and
    black

    – eating too many said to cause constipation (prob. with seeds left in

    – potentially toxic)

    – Teit (1906:222) states that 'sap' was eaten; this seems doubtful

    – cherries a favourite food of bears

    – wood possibly used in carving or as fuel

    – decoction of cherries drunk as diarrhoea medicine

REFERENCES: Turner 1978; Turner et al. 1987; Teit 1906: 222, 231

Green Vegetables

Cow-parsnip, or Indian rhubarb (*Heracleum lanatum*)

Index of cultural significance: 77 (high)

Major use(s): young flower bud stalks and leaf stalks eaten in spring; roots
    eaten, used medicinally for colds or as purgative, or mashed as poultice

BGC zone(s) in study area: interior Douglas-fir; dry ponderosa pine; interior
    subalpine; coastal subalpine; Figure 8

Habitat(s): moist clearings and meadows

Specific localities: Fountain Valley; Mission Mt.; Pavilion Mt.

HARVESTING: 1. young stalks cut; 2. roots dug

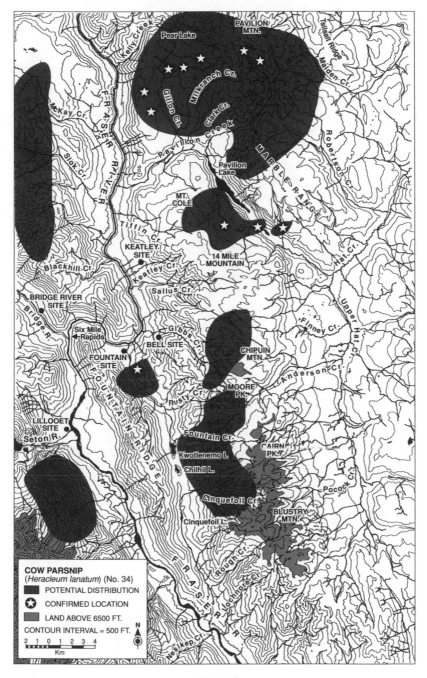

FIGURE 8

Distribution of cow-parsnip (*Heracleum lanatum*) in the study area. Hatched zones indicate potential distribution (preliminary estimate); starred points indicate confirmed locations

Season(s): 1. Apr.-early Jun., never after flowering; 2. year-round (?)
People: 1. mostly women, children, but also men; 2. anyone preparing medicine
Time: 1. 1-3 days; 2. casual
Quantity (per family): 1. prob. 10-20 kg shoots; 2. small amt; 100-200 gm
Tools used: 1. knife; 2. root-digger, knife
Transport of product: 1. bundles (?), baskets; 2. small bag or pouch
PROCESSING: 1. leaves, buds removed, stalks peeled; (leafstalks split first); 2. root cleaned, cut up, steeped or boiled, or mashed as poultice; could be dried; also drunk steeped as beverage
Season(s): 1. Apr.-early Jun.; 2. year-round
Where: 1. on site or base camp or permanent home; 2. camp or home
People: 1. mostly women; 2. anyone preparing medicine
Time: 1., 2. less than 1 day
Tools used: 1. knife; 2. knife, container, or maul
Fire?: 1. not necessarily; 2. for boiling water
Water?: 1. not necessarily; 2. yes
Waste produced: 1. leaves, peelings; 2. discarded root
Other plant products used: 2. purgative medicine sometimes made with Indian hellebore root
CONSUMPTION OR USE OF PRODUCT: 1. peeled stalks eaten; fresh/raw, fresh/cooked 2. root for medicine, beverage, food
Season(s): 1. Apr.-Jun.; 2. year-round
Where used: 1. base camps, on site, or permanent home; 2. anywhere
People: everyone
Containers, implements: 1. not required; 2. for infusion, decoction
Fire?: 1. only if cooked; 2. yes
Water?: 1. if cooked in soups, stews; 2. yes
Waste produced: 1. see above; 2. see above
Accompanying resources: 1. prob. meat, fish, fat, oil; 2. sometimes Indian-hellebore
TRADE?: prob. not
COMMENTS: – stalks known as grizzly bear food
– nowadays stalks frozen or canned
– whole plant, espec. leaves and skin, and contains phototoxic furanocoumarins that cause blistering and discolouration of skin; have to be peeled, handled carefully
– cold medicine may have been mistaken for angelica root
REFERENCES: Turner 1978; Turner et al. 1987; Kuhnlein and Turner 1987; Teit 1906:222

Indian celery (*Lomatium nudicaule*)

Index of cultural significance: 80 (high)

Major use(s): young leaves eaten raw or cooked; leaves, seeds used as flavouring; seeds used as fumigant, smudge against insects, and as protection against sickness; seeds chewed for cough

BGC zone(s) in study area: interior Douglas-fir; dry ponderosa pine; interior subalpine; Figure 9

Habitat(s): open meadows

Specific localities: around Pavilion; Shalalth; Texas Creek; particularly large plants around Chase (SM)

HARVESTING: 1. young leaves and stems picked; 2. seed heads picked

  Season(s): 1. Apr.-May; 2. Jun.-Aug.

  People: 1. women, children; 2. women, or anyone preparing medicine

  Time: 1-2 days

  Quantity (per family): prob. 3-10 kg

  Tools used: none

  Transport of product: bags or baskets

PROCESSING: 1. leaves used fresh or boiled, sometimes dried; 2. seeds removed from stalks, dried (if not already dry)

  Season(s): 1. Apr.-May; 2. Jun.-Aug.

  Where: base camps, winter homes

  People: 1. women, children; 2. anyone

  Time: 1 day or less

  Tools used: mats for drying; storage bags

  Fire?: yes, if leaves cooked

  Water?: yes, for cooking

  Waste produced: discarded seek stalks

  Other plant products used: none

CONSUMPTION OR USE OF PRODUCT: 1. leaves eaten fresh/raw, fresh/cooked, in soups, stews, or dried and reconstituted; 2. seeds used to flavour beverages, tobacco, stews, soups, or placed on fire as fumigant and smudge; chewed for colds

  Season(s): 1. mainly spring (also year-round); 2. year-round

  Where used: base camps, winter home

  People: everyone

  Containers, implements: for cooking soups, stews

  Fire?: yes (see above)

  Water?: yes (see above)

  Waste produced: no

  Accompanying resources: meat, fish, edible roots, etc., being cooked in soups

TRADE?: poss. dried seeds

COMMENTS: – roots said to have been eaten (Teit 1906:222), but this seems doubtful

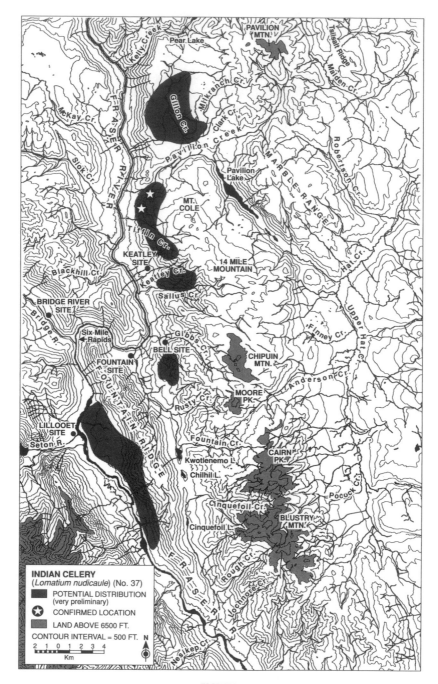

FIGURE 9

Distribution of Indian celery (*Lomatium nudicaule*) in the study area.
Hatched zones indicate potential distribution (preliminary estimate);
starred points indicate confirmed locations

– seeds were highly important medicine and trade item on the southern Coast, espec. Puget Sound and Vancouver Island

REFERENCES: Turner 1975; Turner et al. 1978, 1987; Bouchard and Kennedy 1977:72; Teit 1906:222

Nuts and Seeds

Whitebark pine (*Pinus albicaulis*)

Index of cultural significance: 58 (high)

Major use(s): seeds eaten

BGC zone(s) in study area: alpine tundra; coastal subalpine; interior subalpine; Figure 10

Habitat(s): open montane woods near timberline (1,200-1,500 m)

Specific localities: common in mountains above Lillooet; hillside above Cinquefoil Lake, south of Fountain Ridge, called 'whitebark-pine-on-the-sidehills, Pavilion Mt., Mission Mt., Mt. Brew

HARVESTING: branches cut, cones removed; seeds sought in rodent caches

Season(s): Sep.

People: mainly women, children

Time: 5-10 days

Quantity (per family): 'considerable quantities' – Teit (1906); prob. 5-15 kg per year; 3-4 gunnysacks full – EO

Tools used: axe, knife

Transport of product: packed in large sacks or bags

PROCESSING: cones roasted or pit-cooked, seeds removed, shells cracked open; for storage, seeds further dried

Season(s): Sep.

Where: mountain base camps, winter homes

People: women, children (while men were hunting)

Time: 2-5 days

Tools used: earth oven; hands for extracting seeds; stones for cracking

Fire?: yes, to cook cones (otherwise they will not open)

Water?: no

Waste produced: branches (at site); empty cones, shells of seeds

Other plant products used: none

CONSUMPTION OR USE OF PRODUCT: roasted seeds eaten as snack, ground into meal

Food: fresh/cooked, stored

Season(s): year-round

Where used: anywhere

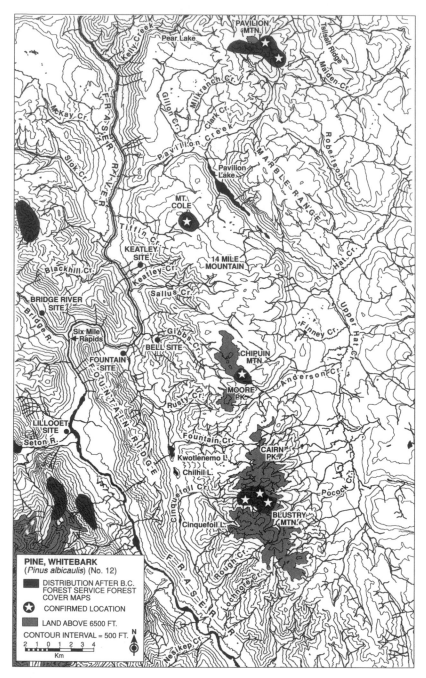

FIGURE 10

Distribution of whitebark pine (*Pinus albicaulis*) in the study area.
Hatched zones indicate potential distribution (preliminary estimate);
starred points indicate confirmed locations

People: everyone, esp. children
Containers, implements: baskets, dishes; stones for cracking shells
Fire?: no
Water?: no
Waste produced: seed shells
Accompanying resources: nuts sometimes mixed with mountain goat fat
TRADE?: prob. to Lower Lillooet area
COMMENTS: – seeds cached by squirrels and small rodents; also sought after
    by bears, who may climb or knock over trees to get them
    – wood prob. occasionally used as fuel
    – seeds hardly eaten at all at present time
REFERENCES: Turner 1978; Turner et al. 1987; Bouchard and Kennedy 1977:29
    – 'The Crippled Lady'; Teit 1906:222

Technological Plants

Indian-hemp (*Apocynum cannabinum*)

Index of cultural significance: 72 (high)
Major use(s): stem fibre used for twine, nets, binding, tying
BGC zone(s) in study area: interior Douglas-fir; dry ponderosa pine; Figure 11
Habitat(s): forms large patches along gravelly river banks and benches
Specific localities: nr. Lillooet airport; hwy. from Lillooet about 3-4 km along
    toward Fountain from bridge; roadside along hwy. between Lillooet and
    Lytton
HARVESTING: large plants selected; stems cut; leafy tops removed
    Season(s): Sep.-Oct. (when leaves turn yellow)
    People: mostly women? (while men fished)
    Time: 1-2 days
    Quantity (per family): many (100-500 stems?)
    Tools used: knife
    Transport of product: in bundles
PROCESSING: 1. stems dried, pounded and rubbed to remove fibre; 2. fibre
    spun on bare thigh and spliced into continuous length; 3. twine drawn
    through pine pitch and used as is for binding, tying, sewing; 4. made
    into fishing lines and nets
    Season(s): fall, winter
    Where: prob. around winter homes
    People: (?) men and women
    Time: 4-10 days (? more)
    Tools used:(?) spindle; netting measure
    Fire?: not necessarily (except for heating pine pitch)
    Water?: not necessarily

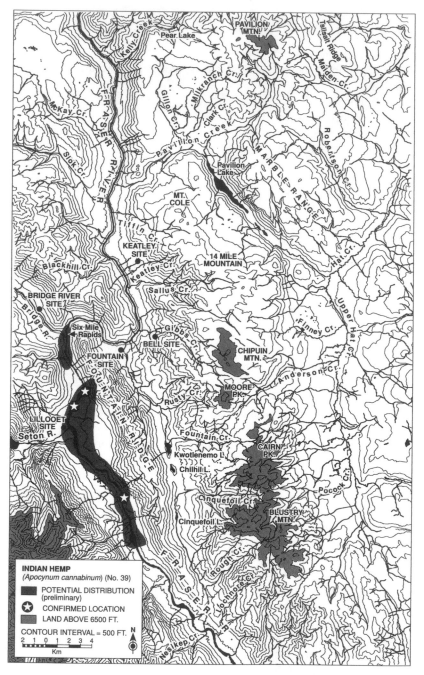

FIGURE 11

Distribution of Indian-hemp (*Apocynum cannabinum*) in the study area.
Hatched zones indicate potential distribution (preliminary estimate);
starred points indicate confirmed locations

Waste produced: discarded leaves, inner pith, skin, and brittle stem tissues

Other plant products used: Douglas-fir for dip net hoops, many materials – cattail, tule, sagebrush bark, silverberry bark, etc. – used with twine in manufacture

CONSUMPTION OR USES OF PRODUCT: twine for sewing, binding, tying, twining in making implements of many types: bows, arrows, fishing nets, mats, bags, clothing; also for threading roots, berries for drying

Season(s): year-round

Where used: everywhere, espec. around fishing camps

People: everyone

Fire?: not necessarily

Water?: fishing

Waste produced: old, broken discarded twine

Accompanying resources: fish and fishing implements, platforms; food stored in twine bags; other fibres used in clothing, bags; pine pitch

TRADE?: yes – twine and rope from Upper Lillooet to Lower Lillooet and from them to Coast Salish peoples (Teit 1906:231)

COMMENTS: – In Lillooet mythology, (Teit 1912:293), the Transformers crossed Lillooet Lake, where they pulled hairs from their legs and threw them on the ground to create Indian-hemp plants; they then showed man and wife how to harvest, prepare it, and make dip nets for fishing with it. In another myth, the tribal boundary between Upper and Lower Lillooet was the spot where one Transformer brother obtained Indian-hemp fibre (p. 296).

REFERENCES: Turner 1979; Turner et al. 1987; Teit 1906:231, 1912:293, 296; Kennedy and Bouchard 1986

ACKNOWLEDGMENTS AND NOTES

I am indebted to the knowledgeable Lillooet people from the Fraser River area for sharing their knowledge and experiences and for patiently answering hundreds of questions concerning traditional uses of plants. These include: the late Sam Mitchell, the late Martina LaRochelle, Edith O'Donaghey, Desmond Peters Sr., and Francis (Bill) Edwards as well as the late Annie York of Spuzzum and Louie Phillips of Lytton (both *Nlaka'pamux*, or Thompson). Randy Bouchard and Dorothy Kennedy of the British Columbia Indian Language Project have contributed significantly to research on Lillooet ethnobotany over the past eighteen or more years and kindly allowed me to cite some of their unpublished field data. Diana Alexander also shared her unpublished field observations, and she and Brian Hayden contributed valuable discussion and suggestions for improving the manuscript. My husband, Robert Turner, provided logistical support during field work and drew the base map for showing species distributions. This research was made possible by a grant to Dr. Brian Hayden by the Multiculturalism Directorate of Canada. Earlier research on Lillooet ethnobotany, on which much of the groundwork for the present report is based, was funded by a Social Sciences and Humanities Research Council of Canada grant to myself (No. 410-84-0146).

1 For the convenience of the reader, common names of plant species are used throughout this paper. Scientific names of all species mentioned can be found in Appendix 1.

2 As far as can be determined, only about four species of mushrooms were eaten traditionally by the Fraser River Lillooet. Certainly, there are many more edible species to be found in the region, but it seems doubtful, from linguistic evidence and from comparison with other groups, that more types were eaten by prehistoric peoples than by contemporary Lillooet.

3 These sites include Pavilion, Keatley, Bell, and Fountain (cf. Hayden et al. 1986). The Bridge River Lillooet and Seton sites are covered peripherally. Furthermore, since two of the major Lillooet consultants, Edith O'Donaghey and Desmond Peters, are originally from Shalalth, along Anderson Lake, some of the information in this report extends to this region, including Seton Portage and Texas Creek.

4 Desmond Peters also noted that the wood from the south side of the juniper sapling was better than that from the north side for bow-making, because 'the sap runs more on the north side,' and the south-facing wood was thus easier to work.

5 Burdock is actually an introduced species and, hence, would not have been used by early peoples, but Edith O'Donaghey was not aware that it was imported. She commented: 'It has always been there!' Notably, burdock is one of the most obvious plants near the stream at the Keatley Creek pithouse site.

6 The concurrent harvesting of primary and secondary resources and the suggestion that secondary resource harvesting may have influenced the length of stay in a location (and the overall importance of a resource area) was proposed by D. Alexander. She further suggested that the importance of a resource area is reflected by both the abundance of staple resource products and the diversity of resources – both primary and secondary. The overall importance of an area, and its distance from the permanent village, would thus have determined the length of stay at a resource site (D. Alexander, personal communication 1987).

7 Bouchard (personal communication 1986) reports that Louie Phillips of Lytton told him that Thompson women used to go up to Blustry Mountain and Cairn Peak (at the southern end of the study area) during June to dig roots while the ground was still soft.

8 Often, deer meat was barbecued or partially dried at a site near the kill,

both to help preserve it and to reduce its volume and weight. A whole hind quarter might be cooked at once or the meat might be cut up and roasted on sticks. Sometimes it was salted. EO recalled that her father used to bring home sacks and sacks of dried meat from the deer's belly from his hunting trips. The partially dried meat was transported home, where the women would finish drying it or smoke it to ensure that it would keep.

9 Edith O'Donaghey noted that, long ago, the Shalalth and Seton Portage people fished for salmon in Seton Lake, but Cayoosh Creek was blocked off over fifty years ago, and not enough salmon were able to enter the lake. At this time, the people started coming down to fish in the Fraser.

10 The vegetation for lining the pit and interspersing between the layers of food being cooked may have varied. Douglas-fir boughs and grasses are reported to have been used. Additionally, pine boughs, leafy stems of fireweed, and strawberry leaves, used in some parts of the interior Plateau, may have also been used by Lillooet people.

11 These measured about 0.5 m high and were tapered from top to bottom, with a base of about 10 x 15 cm and a mouth of about 30 x 40 cm. EO stressed that they were waterproof and, hence, could hold even very juicy berries without serious leakage.

12 In the summer of 1987, at Marble Canyon Provincial Park, I spread a large quantity of freshly picked soapberries out to dry in the sun, in the same manner for drying described by EO. I covered them at night to keep any dew off them. By the end of six days of sunny weather, they were still not fully dried, although significantly reduced in weight and volume. Mashing the berries prior to drying them would have reduced the drying time, but EO and DP maintained that they were usually spread out and dried whole.

13 Charlie Mack of Mount Currie recalled that the lichen was sometimes tied in large bales, then rolled down the hillside from the harvesting site to the processing site (Bouchard and Kennedy 1977:72). Nastich (1954:33) noted a camp, *kläktEkot*, which was used by women for processing and drying lichen in the summer.

REFERENCES

Alexander, D. 1986. 'Ts'kwáylaxw Ethnoarchaeology: A Preliminary Survey.' Unpublished report, Heritage Conservation Branch of British Columbia, British Columbia Heritage Trust and *Ts'kwáylaxw* Indian Band
–. 1987. 'Archaeological and Ethnographic Evidence for Traditional Native Use of Mount Cole, Southwestern British Columbia.' Unpublished report, Department of Archaeology, Simon Fraser University. Prepared for the Pavilion Indian Band

Alexander, D. and R.G. Matson. 1986. 'Preliminary Report on the Potato Mountain Archaeological Project (1985).' Unpublished report for Heritage Conservation Branch of British Columbia, Canadian Ethnic Studies Program,
and Nemiah Valley Indian Band Council. Laboratory of Archaeology,
University of British Columbia, Vancouver

Alexander, D., R. Tyhurst, L. Burnard-Hogarth, and R.G. Matson. 1985. 'A
Preliminary Ethnoarchaeological Investigation of the Potato Mountain Range
and the Eagle Lake Area.' Unpublished report for Heritage Conservation
Branch of British Columbia, Canadian Ethnic Studies Program, and Nemiah
Valley Indian Band Council

Bouchard, R. and D.I.D. Kennedy (eds.). 1977. 'Lillooet Stories.' *Sound Heritage*
4(1). Provincial Archives of BC, Aural History, Victoria

Hayden, B., D. Alexander, K. Kusmer, D. Lepofsky, D. Martin, M. Rousseau,
and P. Friele. 1986. 'Report on the 1986 Excavations at Keatley Creek.' Unpublished report of the Fraser River Investigations into Corporate Group
Archaeology Project, Department of Archaeology, Simon Fraser University, Burnaby, BC

Hayden, B., J. Breffitt, P. Friele, R. Gargett, M. Greene, W.K. Hutchings,
D. Jolly, I. Kuijt, K. Kusmer, D. Lepofsky, B. Muir, M. Rousseau, and
D. Martin. 1987. 'Report on the 1987 Excavations at Keatley Creek.' Unpub-
lished report of the Fraser River Investigations into Corporate Group Ar-
chaeology Project, Department of Archaeology, Simon Fraser University,
Burnaby, BC

Hill-Tout, C. 1905. 'Notes on the StlatlumH [Lillooet] of British Columbia.' *Journal of the Anthropological Institute of Great Britain* 35:126-218

Kennedy, D.I.D. and R. Bouchard. 1975. 'Utilization of Fish by the Mount Currie
Lillooet Indian People of British Columbia.' Unpublished manuscript. BC
Indian Language Project, Victoria

-. 1978. 'Fraser River Lillooet: An ethnographic summary.' In A.H. Stryd and
S. Lawhead (eds.), *Reports of the Lillooet Archaeological Project No. 1: Introduction and Setting.* Pp. 22-55

-. 1986. 'Stl'átl'imx (Fraser River Lillooet) Fishing.' Unpublished report to the
Fountain Indian Band, BC Indian Language Project, Victoria

Krajina, V.J. 1969. 'Ecology of forest trees in British Columbia.' *Ecology of Western
North America* 2(1):1-146

Krajina, V.J., K. Klinka, and J. Worrall. 1982. *Distribution and Ecological Characteristics of Trees and Shrubs of British Columbia.* Faculty of Forestry, University of British Columbia, Vancouver

Kuhnlein, H.V. and N.J. Turner. 1987. 'Cow-parsnip (*Heracleum lanatum* Michx.):
An indigenous vegetable of Native People of Northwestern North America.'
Journal of Ethnobiology 6(2):309-24

Laforet, A., N.J. Turner, and A. York. 1991. 'Traditional foods of the Fraser
Canyon *Nle7kepmx.*' In T. Montler and T. Mattina (eds.), *Laurence C. Thompson*

Festschrift. Missoula, MT: University of Montana Press

Lepofsky, D. 1986. 'An Analysis of Floral Remains from Keatley Creek House-pits.' Unpublished report prepared for B. Hayden, Department of Archaeology, Simon Fraser University, Burnaby, BC

–. 1987. 'Fraser River Investigations into Corporate Group Archaeology: Report on Floral Analysis.' Unpublished report prepared for B. Hayden, Department of Archaeology, Simon Fraser University, Burnaby, BC

Lepofsky, D., N. Turner, H. Kuhnlein. 1985. 'Determining the availability of traditional wild plant foods: An example of Nuxalk Foods, Bella Coola, British Columbia.' *Ecology of Food and Nutrition* 16:223-41

Mathewes, R.W. 1978. 'The environment and biotic resources of the Lillooet area.' In A.H. Stryd and S. Lawhead (eds.), *Reports of the Lillooet Archaeological Project, No. 1: Introduction and Setting*. Pp. 68-99

–. 1985. 'Paleobotanical evidence for climatic change in southern British Columbia during the late-glacial and holocene times.' In C.R. Harrington (ed.), 'Climatic Change in Canada 5: Critical Periods in the Quaternary Climatic History of Northern North America.' *Syllogeus* 55:344-96

Nastich, M. 1954. 'The Lillooet: An Account of the Basis of Individual Status.' Unpublished Master's Thesis, Department of Economics, Political Science and Sociology, University of British Columbia. (Ethnobotanical Extracts by R. Bouchard, BC Indian Language Project, Victoria. Unpublished notes, n.d.)

Newcombe, C.F. 1903. Unpublished notes on Lillooet plant names. Provincial Archives of BC, Victoria

Palmer, G. 1975. 'Shuswap Indian ethnobotany.' *Syesis* 8:25-81

Pokotylo, D.L. and P.D. Froese. 1983. 'Archaeological evidence for prehistoric root gathering on the Southern Interior Plateau of British Columbia: A case study from Upper Hat Creek Valley.' *Canadian Journal of Archaeology* 7(2):127-57

Romanoff, S. 1986. 'Fraser River salmon fishing.' *Northwest Anthropological Research Notes* 19(2):119-60

Ryder, J.M. 1978. 'Geomorphology and late Quaternary history of the Lillooet area.' In A.H. Stryd and S. Lawhead (eds.), *Reports of the Lillooet Archaeological Project, No. 1: Introduction and Setting*. Pp. 56-67

Steedman, E.V. (ed.). 1930. 'The ethnobotany of the Thompson Indians of British Columbia: Based on field notes of James A. Teit.' *Bureau of American Ethnology Thirtieth Annual Report: 1908-1909*. Pp. 33-102

Stryd, A.H. and S. Lawhead (eds.). 1978. *Reports of the Lillooet Archaeological Project. No. 1: Introduction and Setting*. Archaeological Survey of Canada Paper No. 73, Mercury Series, National Museum of Man, National Museums of Canada, Ottawa

Taylor, R.L. and B. MacBryde. 1977. *Vascular Plants of British Columbia: A Descriptive Resource Inventory*. Vancouver: UBC Press

Teit, J.A. 1906. 'The Lillooet Indians.' *Memoirs, American Museum of Natural History* 2(5):193-300

–. 1912. 'Traditions of the Lillooet Indians of British Columbia. *Journal of American Folk-Lore* 25(48):287-371

Turner, N.J. 1974. 'Plant taxonomies and ethnobotany of three contemporary Indian groups of the Pacific Northwest: Haida, Bella Coola and Lillooet.' *Syesis* 7, Supplement 1

–. 1975. *Food Plants of British Columbia Indians*. Part I: 'Coastal Peoples.' British Columbia Provincial Museum Handbook, No. 34, Victoria

–. 1977. 'Economic importance of black tree lichen (*Bryoria fremontii*) to the Indians of Western North America.' *Economic Botany* 31:461-70

–. 1978. *Food Plants of British Columbia Indians*. Part 2: 'Interior Peoples.' British Columbia Provincial Museum, Handbook No. 36, Victoria

–. 1979. *Plants in British Columbia Indian Technology*. British Columbia Provincial Museum, Handbook No. 38, Victoria

–. 1981. 'Indian use of *Shepherdia canadensis*, soapberry, in Western North America.' *Davidsonia* 12(1):1-14

–. 1982. 'Traditional use of devil's-club (*Oplopanax horridus; Araliaceae*) by Native peoples in Western North America.' *Journal of Ethnobiology* 2(1):17-38

–. 1984. 'Counter-irritant and other medicinal uses of plants in Ranunculaceae by Native peoples in British Columbia and neighbouring areas.' *Journal of Ethnopharmacology* 11:181-201

–. 1987. 'General plant categories in Thompson and Lillooet, two Interior Salish languages of British Columbia.' *Journal of Ethnobiology* 7(1):55-82

–. 1988a. 'The importance of a rose: Evaluating cultural significance of plants in Thompson and Lillooet Interior Salish.' *American Anthropologist* 9:272-90

–. 1988b. 'Ethnobotany of coniferous trees in Thompson and Lillooet Interior Salish of British Columbia.' *Economic Botany* 42(2):177-94

–. 1989. '"All berries have relations": Midlevel folk plant categories in Thompson and Lillooet Interior Salish.' *Journal of Ethnobiology* 9(1):60-110

–. 1991. '"Burning mountain sides for better crops": Aboriginal landscape burning in British Columbia.' Paper presented to the Society of Ethnobiology Annual Meetings, March 1991, St. Louis, MO. (Abstract in press, *Journal of Ethnobiology*, vol 2)

Turner, N.J., R. Bouchard, and D.I.D. Kennedy. 1981. *Ethnobotany of the Okanagan-Colville Indians of British Columbia and Washington*. BC Provincial Museum, Occasional Paper No. 21, Victoria

Turner, N.J., R. Bouchard, D. Kennedy, and J. Van Eijk. 1987. 'Ethnobotany of the Lillooet Indiana of British Columbia.' Unpublished ms., Royal British Columbia Museum, Victoria

Turner, N.J. and H.V. Kuhnlein. 1983. 'Camas (*Camassia* spp.) and riceroot (*Fritillaria* spp.): Two liliaceous "root" foods of the Northwest Coast Indians.' *Ecology of Food and Nutrition* 13:199-219

Turner, N.J., H.V. Kuhnlein and K.N. Egger. 1987. 'The cottonwood mushroom (*Tricholoma populinum* Lange): A food resource of the Interior Salish Indian

Peoples of British Columbia.' *Canadian Journal of Botany* 65:921-27

Turner, N.J., L.C. Thompson, M.T. Thompson and A. York. 1990. *Thompson Ethnobotany: Knowledge and Usage of Plants by the Thompson Indian People of British Columbia.* Royal British Columbia Museum, Memoir No. 3, Victoria

Van Eijk, J.P. 1985. 'The Lillooet Language.' Unpublished PhD dissertation, University of Amsterdam, the Netherlands

CHAPTER NINE

The Cultural Ecology of Hunting and Potlatches among the Lillooet Indians

Steven Romanoff

INTRODUCTION

Though salmon has been the staple of the Lillooet Indians of the Fraser River Valley, men trained as hunters had several wives, commanded a following, and were considered 'rich.' James A. Teit, writing about the Lillooet and neighbouring Thompson Indians at the turn of this century, used the term 'hunting chief' for such specialists, reporting that the occupation was surprisingly important to both groups: 'the Lower Thompson, although they had an abundance of fish, spent much time hunting' (1900, 1906:224). My principal goal is to document and place in an ecological perspective the high prestige of the hunting chief relative to other productive roles, particularly that of fishermen, among those Lillooet who lived near the Fraser River in the nineteenth and early twentieth centuries.

My first task will be to show that hunting in Lillooet society was more than just an individual activity. Hunting techniques favoured co-operation, and the men who led hunts were trained, acquired a spirit, acted as a kind of redistributor, and indirectly received rewards according to general norms of Lillooet society. This first ethnographic section presents a holistic description of the hunter's role, with reference to related cultural traits such as the potlatch. Dried, smoked meat was the principal item distributed at those feasts, and preparations involved special hunts for which village chiefs could call on related hunting chiefs from other villages.

The subsequent section argues that the hunter's prestige had several positive ecologically adaptive functions because the salmon runs that formed the resource base of the Lillooet were variable and not always easy to preserve. Hunting complemented fishing. Demonstrating that deer constituted a critical resource is a necessary precursor of the next argument: there was a ranking of occupations in Lillooet society based on characteristics of the tasks performed, including criticalness. Neither gross caloric production nor ownership of resources was correlated with occupational prestige.

Discussion of Lillooet occupations requires a term for specialists who control a resource and facilitate access to it without charging rent or fees, even while they may retain preferential access and, indirectly, receive other benefits. I will use the term 'steward.' Such men might be owners who inherit rights, yet their freedom to dispose of their property or its fruits was limited; in fact, in some situations their control over the resource may not look like ownership at all. Though Lillooet society has some traits of egalitarian, rank, and stratified types of societies, stewards are particularly appropriate to a redistributive or rank society. To differing degrees, the Lillooet hunter, fishing-rock owner, and chief were stewards, as they may still be. The term may correspond to a Lillooet term recorded among the lower Lillooet.

FIELDWORK

This chapter covers the period from the middle of the nineteenth century, when the effects of contact were still indirect, into the gold rush period, and through the first decades of the twentieth century, by which time the Lillooet were living on reserves. The major source of data presented here is Sam Mitchell of Fountain Band, interviewed in 1970 and 1971. For a few topics, my data on the Lillooet must be supplemented by reports on their immediate neighbours to the south along the Fraser River, the Thompson Indians. My main source there was Willy Samson, who lived near Lytton.[1]

ETHNOGRAPHIC DESCRIPTION OF THE LILLOOET HUNTER

Activity of Hunting

The aboriginal Lillooet hunted mule deer, white tail deer, bighorn sheep, hoary marmot, black bear, caribou, grizzly bear, rabbit, rock rabbit, porcupine, panther, and other species taken for their pelts, according to Teit (1906); Kennedy and Bouchard (1978:40) also sketch hunting practices. Mule deer were the most important species taken for meat, and I am concerned here with the deer hunter. Commercial trapping was not a major activity, though informants say that some Lillooet have taken coyotes for the bounty.

The Upper Lillooet used fences, snares, dogs, and bow and arrow to hunt deer, according to Teit, as well as hunting knives, clubs, canoes, and moccasins, the latter listed as a hunting tool because the hunter wore them out and took along extra pairs. Later, they used rifles. Deer were hunted primarily in the late fall when they were fat, slow, and accessible. Hunting was the main activity after salmon fishing, lasting from mid-September until the deer begin to rut around the first full moon in November. After hunting, people lived in winter villages until spring.

There were hunts of various distances; in the extreme case, the party stayed out most of the winter. More commonly, young men camped in the mountains for a few months in the fall. Dried or smoked meat was packed to the villages by women before the Lillooet obtained horses from the Shuswap. While an individual might hunt, groups were more effective at chasing a deer, and some of the techniques required combined effort, such as driving deer toward men known to be good shots. In some cases dogs pursued deer into corrals near lakes.

The main product of hunting was dried and smoked meat. Processors cut the deer into large sections, such as the front quarter or ribs, and hung them on sticks set upright in the ground around a fire. Then, they put the dry meat on a rack over the fire to smoke so that it would last for six months or more, to be chopped up for stew as needed. They kept the tallow apart, and they tanned the hide in a mixture of urine and deer brain, though buckskin clothing was scarce. The sinew was dried to be later soaked, pounded, slivered, and made into thread by women. Kennedy and Bouchard (1978:40) note that the bones were used for tools and the stomach contents were used as an ointment and condiment.

Role of Hunter

'Hunter,' in the sense used here, refers to a specialized role for men whose rights and duties went beyond the activity of hunting. Teit refers to such a person as a 'hunting chief,' in contrast to the general chiefs of the winter villages of semi-subterranean lodges; 'professional, trained hunter' is the gloss provided for the Lillooet *tewít* by Kennedy and Bouchard (1978; personal communication, 1989). Teit reports that each village had a hereditary chief. Chiefs scheduled subsistence activities and could call on hunters to hunt for them.

There were few hunting chiefs, according to informants. In aboriginal times, they were limited to those with speed, skill, training, and a spirit helper. Later, there were few hunting chiefs because not everyone had a gun. Other men did take part in hunts, following the hunter. The duties of the hunter were to organize the hunt, direct it, and kill the animal, sometimes bleeding and gutting it as well. The hunter did not pack the deer or process it, so long as others were present. The meat was divided while still fresh at the hunting camp, and each person was responsible for drying and smoking a portion.

Training of Hunter

To be a hunter, one had to have gone through spiritual, technical, and physical training. The role could not be filled by just anyone who might be able to kill a deer. 'Hunters ... first have to learn how to shoot an arrow and make an arrow. Then they had to have speed on top of that, and keep up with his game. That's what a hunter is: he has speed and can shoot an arrow. They practice a lot. Some of them can run game down' (SM).[2]

Older men supervised the early exercises that produced stamina and marksmanship, while games and mock hunts also taught skills. The physical training was very rigorous, including dawn runs of many miles over rough terrain with stops at every creek for bathing in icy water. The Lillooet environment allows a hunter to run relatively unimpeded by vegetation but forces him to go up and down steep slopes. As we shall see, hunters were trained as runners in the rough terrain.

Hunters knew where deer could be found in different seasons and where they would run when approached or wounded. Different informants told me that hunters could close their eyes, see where a wounded deer was fleeing, and tell others where to find it, an ability similar to that of shamans (also reported for Lillooet and Thompson people by Kennedy and Bouchard, personal communication). Similarly, hunters needed knowledge of a very large area; possibly the long training runs taught them some geography. Boys probably began this learning even earlier as they listened to myths, particularly the Coyote or Trickster cycle, in which the main character travels through the area creating geographic features. This became evident to me when an informant, after recounting a Coyote story, gave me instructions to someone's house by referring to places like 'Coyote's blood' and 'where the three brothers hit their heads on the rock.' Such landmarks are memorably named and arranged by the myth, so that a child hearing the myth acquired an internal map that he could follow on the ground.

The lad training to be a hunter also acquired a spirit helper. Teit said that the most powerful spirits for a hunter were wolf, lynx, wolverine, grizzly bear, deer, and beaver (1906:283), interestingly including both predators and the hunter's prey. Other specialist occupations that required spirits were warrior, foot racer, chief, and shaman. I asked

if a *sená7m* ('guardian spirit power') of a man was usually that of his
father: 'No. Maybe if it's handed down to him and he wants to be.
When a boy is growing up his father will ask him what he wants to
be and he'll have to practice certain things' (SM).

Distribution of Deer Meat and the Potlatch

Distribution of fresh meat on the hunt was obligatory and roughly
egalitarian. Teit reported that the catch was evenly divided among the
males of the hunting party (1906:256), and informants agree. While
Teit reports that it was the hunter who divided the products of the
hunt, my informants said that it was 'an elder' or the 'oldest person
there,' just as in the distribution of trout at a weir. The hunter might
even leave deer, bled and gutted, for others. As a child around the
turn of the century, an old man told Sam Mitchell the following story:
'One time he told me himself he killed a hundred game. Of course,
they're not all for himself. He just kills them. He describes the place,
they go pack it. They bring it home, skin it, pack it.'

After short hunts near the village, a hunter might send gifts of fresh
meat to other people of the village. Among the Lillooet, the act of giving confirmed status or gave prestige to the giver (see Chapter 5).
Giving and the consequent creation of inequality was mitigated by
face-saving devices, such as giving food through children or women,
or leaving scraps: 'Same with the meat in the fall time. The old people
crave for that and they know that . . . They don't have to ask. If you
got more than you can use, "Take some to so and so." Maybe after
I bring in some game and skin it I send the boy over' (SM). Once the
meat was dried, sharing was only occasionally obligatory. A hunter
would give some to his parents or parents-in-law if he had extra and
they needed it.

If the hunter had more than he needed, 'he might call a kind of
party or gathering or feed.' Sam Mitchell used the term x̱elítxal, 'a
gathering,' 'same as a potlatch.' Kennedy and Bouchard (1978) gloss
that term as 'calling the people together.' Though the Lillooet potlatches
were less spectacular than the coastal ones, some were characterized
by milder versions of similar features: validation of status and prestige, a marked distinction between the host group and guests, extraordinary and sometimes hostile giving, and inclusion of trade goods
among the gifts. While some accounts mention expectations of
reciprocity, this feature was not as evident as it was on the Coast.

Dried deer meat was the predominant gift at potlatches, though
Kennedy and Bouchard report the distribution of fresh meat and mention gifts of goat hair blankets. I have no references to giving away

wealth objects other than those blankets. Fresh meat was given in 'scrambles,' where a deer might be thrown into a house to be butchered there. On the other hand, dried salmon was not a potlatch good.

The hunter himself need not be the one to give a feast; rather, a chief could call on related hunters to help him, even from other residence groups, which my informant referred to as 'clans': 'This chief, he has relatives in different clans . . . so and so a good hunter over there, so and so a good hunter over there. So he went and see them and get a hand on this hunting deal' (SM).

The quantity of meat that was distributed was considerable. An informant said that it might take more than a season to accumulate enough deer meat for a funerary give-away. Tommy Napoleon of Lillooet said that three or four hunters would go out to prepare for a big gathering. When the guests received the meat, they were told, 'This is what they brought you here for': 'After the potlatch, when they get everything down and after the big feast, [there was still a lot of meat there], more than any of them can eat . . . Well, it's piled up. Whatever is left, the people that was there, they take it home for their own use, whether it's a big armful or if they got a sack, a sackful or more, they take it home. That's for their own use. That's why this potlatch goes on' (SM).

There were several kinds of feasts in which a host gave guests unusual quantities of objects. Such feasts sometimes marked changes of status or claims of superiority. Kennedy and Bouchard (1978) note occasions for potlatches: to honour the memory of the dead, to give ancestral names to children, merely to increase the status of the host, for the prepubescent eldest son of a deceased 'clan' chief, and for the same boy when he became a man. There were feasts when a man assumed a name or after a death:

My old man used to tell me [that they had potlatches] in the fall of the year . . . If there's a death in the family and lots of people help him, he and his family get together and go hunting deer [and] jerk it. If you want to give a potlatch to give thanks to whoever helped before. /Thanks for what?/ They give lots of grub for what help they done. 'This way we'll forget that's what happened.' Help [makes him think] he owes them. [A man potlatches if] he's chief and he wants to be recognized. 'So and so chief wants to be recognized.' Everybody gathered, not just certain parties.

[The funeral potlatch is] not right away – maybe next year. The best of the game – September and October – fattest. They go out and get enough of it. It will last quite a while . . . /If the chief dies will his son take the title at the potlatch?/ Yes, that's it . . . It will have to be announced. In them days, naturally the son would take the title. They give lots of grub . . . That's why they give a potlatch: to announce. That's why these potlatches are. They didn't have any newspapers. (SM)

Potlatching was a way of expressing appreciation for assistance. A man's son was caught in a snow slide while hunting in February, and shamans danced to 'see way out, where you can't see with the naked eye or anything' to help the man find the body:

> The following fall this same man with all that trouble, that hard luck with his son, he got his own people to go and hunt . . . They dried lots of deer meat, the best of the deer meat. They went way out where there's lots of game. They went for months. Get the meat and dry it. When they got home later in the fall, they called a potlatch. The ones that helped him when he had the hard luck about his son and the Indian doctors and also the ones that helped him to go and get all the meat he needed. So then they had a big potlatch over it, and all the outsiders – everybody neighboring, neighboring clans you call it then – they called them all to kind of smooth over his sorrow. Well, he was sort of a chief on this reserve, the Lillooet reserve now. (SM)

After initiation of substantial, first-hand contacts with whites and Chinese, the potlatch came to include distribution of manufactured trade goods. Kennedy and Bouchard (1978) note that long sticks imbedded with coins were tossed into the pithouse, where they were immediately broken apart by the eager participants.

The following accounts mention gaining prestige by giving, and the tenor of this giving is sometimes hostile. Though that element is muted in the next story (reference to ingenuously eating the candles), it is prominent in the following two, where the guests are mocked or put in jail. These accounts refer to the second half of the nineteenth century:

> When the White people first came into this country they brought rum and they brought everything, blankets. The Indians were curious at everything. One . . . chief guy, an Indian, he's kind of well-to-do. He got his tribe to make enough money to buy a hundred pounds of sugar and some candles . . . They called what they call a potlatch. He lit the candles in the [semi- subterranean house] . . . So he gave out his sugar to what people are in this big [house]. He gave a big potlatch of sugar. Maybe a couple of teaspoons each one, whoever was there, and some flour. That's the way he put up his potlatch . . . My dad said some of the people started to eat the candles. They light it and they eat it. They

chew it and they thought is was tallow. (SM)

Hostile giving was a way of asserting dominance. For example, soon after contact with whites, one man invited an upriver group to his village. He ladled out drinks from a keg of liquor, and with each ladle he proclaimed, 'I'm the boss.' His own people did not receive any liquor and laughed at the drunken guests, who vowed to return the hospitality. In general, people sometimes potlatched to 'be a big shot' or 'just to show off.' 'If you give, oh you're somebody' (SM).

In another story, said to have happened around 1865, the chief, Rodesket, offered to find a murderer if the local policeman looking for him would provide two bottles of rum. When he had the drink, 'The chief told his wives, "Make lots of grub. We'll give a potlatch. We'll call the strangers around." When all the grub was ready, the chief went and called everybody . . .' They ate and drank, giving the most to the strangers. 'Then the chief started to brag about himself. He said, "I never work for a living. Whenever I want money there's a lot of Chinamens washing gold down the river. I just throw them in and take their gold." At this one of the strangers said, "I never work for a living either. You see, I cut the shoemaker's throat, and I took his money" ' (SM).

By the early 1900s, week-long Christmas feasts had replaced potlatching. People went from house to house, sometimes masked and clowning. Reservation society was stratified, and this was reflected in the potlatches. People gave deer meat as well as pork and beef:

> The later years after the priests kind of put the Indians into reservations, they build villages. But the Indians still had that potlatch on their mind. Some they'll have pigs, some they'll have cattle. But when it comes to this particular feast days, like they call Christmas, everybody is supposed to eat . . . Out of 40 or 50 families, maybe 15 or 20 families can afford to give, well you can call it a potlatch, a feed. I've seen them. (SM)

In another text, he identifies the ones who gave food as, 'well-to-do people that get a lot of deer meat and good hunters and can afford to give a feast.' The order of eating was that of social rank: 'They usually choose the chief [to eat first], the head, like the bigger guys in the tribe, but mostly men. Then from there down, smaller people come in and then the kids, . . . the women first and then the children. They bring their family in and they have a feed' (SM).

In most of the reports of potlatches the giver obtains quantities of food to give away, and he includes people outside his residential group. The food is not salmon; it is usually dried deer meat, although cow, pig, liquor, sugar, flour, and trout are mentioned. The means of getting the food vary from story to story: hunting, purchase, request, and others. In the feasts of deer meat, the giver stimulated hunters to sustained and special productive efforts so that they either stayed out longer or went farther than usual. Food thus distributed went to all participants in the feast, including poor people who could not be expected to reciprocate.

Pre-feast hunting and food production is such a common trait that it sometimes escapes human ecologists looking for ecological functions of ceremonial occasions. Discussions of the potlatch on the Northwest Coast emphasize distribution of wealth objects, yet, for example, a Kwakiutl chief distributed food to 'all' the men of his tribe 'whenever he received a large supply of provision' (Sproat 1868, quoted in Ruyle 1973:615). Not enough is known about the distribution of food at feasts either on the Coast or in the Interior.

In the 1950s, widespread distribution of meat still happened; perhaps the importance of preservation was less in the fifties, though in 1970 I still saw a great deal of fish-drying and deer-canning: 'A man who brings home large quantities of fish or deer is respected because he will always distribute part of the catch; in the case of deer meat he will usually give away to relatives all what he cannot use fresh himself, for meat is not often preserved' (Ames 1956:111-12).

Hunter's Reward

Often the Lillooet hunter did not claim the animals he killed, leaving them for others. This generosity (though he could not have processed all the meat anyway) validated or secured his status, which was integrated into the larger structure of Lillooet society in such a way that his altruism ensured his reward. Of course, at the same time he had some of the products of the hunting group, such as meat and clothes.

The hunter had the power to determine when people would hunt, except when he was hunting for a chief, and he could go out with a group of his choosing. In the fall, his authority rivalled that of the chief. 'A good hunter – maybe two or three families follow him on a hunt . . . These fellows that follow the hunter – it's different than the chief. Maybe [the chief] goes along too' (SM).

Questions about being 'rich' elicited responses about people 'who tell them what to do,' notably, a hunter. 'That's the rich – gets lots of dried meat. It's not only [the hunter]; he's got lots of followers. In them days, a guy can hunt ahead of everybody else.' The hunter had a set of buckskin clothes, which was not usual:

My mother and father lived in a [semi-subterranean lodge] . . . Pretty lucky if you got something, a robe, something warm. I heard them say like, a young man 'Send him out for wood,' they say 'Someone lend him a pair of moccasins, somebody lend him . . .' No, not everybody has clothes. /They must have had lots of skins if they hunted so much./ Oh yes, those that could afford it. They used it for pants and bedding. Some, according to my old man, some had dog skin for pants and rabbit or whatever they could get a hold of. (SM)

Another reward was multiple wives, as Willy Samson, a Thompson from Lytton, reported for his group, also reiterating Mr. Mitchell's note about the scarcity of buckskin:

They say that the person that don't sleep, gets up early in the morning, goes around hunting, he always has a lot of wives. They say he'll have plenty of food all the time, plenty of meat. So he'll have plenty of wives too, in them days. Some of them have ten. That's the only guy who will have buckskin clothes, the guy who goes out and hunts. Never gets lazy, never stays at home. But the lazy guys have a little breech clout, nothing else. Kind of a buckskin here to hide his private parts. (WS)

In purely economic terms, a wife herself was a great reward for hunting, as women gathered and processed food. In fact, the amount of sockeye salmon that a family could store for the winter depended on the labour of women, since a man could catch more sockeye than the thirty or so that a woman could butcher in a day.

Hunting was a duty of a son-in-law. When I asked about living with the parents of one's wife, Mr. Mitchell said: 'Well, he lives there for a while. If he's a hunter. That's about the only way they live together . . . If the [wife's] parents are getting old, like in the fall of the year, they say, "You going to hunt for us." . . . /If a man wasn't a good hunter, would he go to the wife's people?/ It seems to me in the old days if you can't provide for a woman you got no business with one. Some of them got two or three – the good hunters.'

There was a one-time exchange of gifts several months after the marriage when the son-in-law or his parents gave dried meat to the parents of the woman. If the marriage was arranged at the summer fishing site, as was common, the husband would hunt that fall. In return for dried meat, the affines gave the tools of hunting: a gun, bow and arrow, hunting knife, moccasins, buckskin coat, or pants. They could also give dried berries or roots. 'They exchange gifts from both sides . . . That seems to bind the marriage.' (SM) Mr. Mitchell interpreted his description of affinal exchange: 'It seems to me that this doing (exchange) it's some sort of a meaning of accepting each other, accepting both sides.' His attitudes are appropriate to the upper stratum of Lillooet society; not all marriages were so proper, and Teit describes informal unions.

Thus, the hunter distributed meat to members of the hunting party, to members of his local group, to other groups if he himself potlatched or married out, and to a chief who, in turn, distributed widely. Without exact reciprocity, he acquired adequate reward: prestige, power to command labour, and wives.

The preceding ethnographic description of the hunting chief has shown him to be well integrated into his society. Co-operative hunting, socialization of boys, the meat distribution network, and the pattern of rewards for people 'who told them what to do' or gave food were aspects of his position. Yet, we are left with the question, 'Why the hunter?' To answer this question, we shall look at the role of deer meat in the diet and the characteristics of deer hunting relative to other activities.

ROLE OF DEER MEAT IN OVERALL SUBSISTENCE

We will now follow one of the ecological paradigms used to interpret the potlatch and related exchanges on the Northwest Coast in order to investigate the functional importance of hunting and the hunter's role. Salmon was the basis of Lillooet diet, being the main source of protein and, probably, calories. According to the method of analyzing human bone collagen from skeletal remains, two-thirds of the protein consumed by nine individuals living in what is now Lillooet territory was of marine origin, presumably salmon and anadromous trout (Lovell et al. 1986:102). We may suppose that deer supplied much of the 35 per cent of protein that did not come from the sea. Further, deer meat was available when the salmon runs were light and when other foods were rare or in bad condition. The Fraser Lillooet economy was developed and specialized relative to that of general hunters and gatherers not only because they had salmon but also because they depended on a 'storage strategy' even more than did the coastal lower Lillooet or the Coast Salish (Schalk 1977:231).

The Supply of Salmon

Despite their inland location, the amount of salmon practically available to the Lillooet was great relative to other groups, even including the coastal populations, because they had the rich Bridge River Falls site and because they could air-dry what they caught. However, informants confirmed what is generally known: the salmon runs are variable from year to year.

The normal cycles of plenitude and the destruction of salmon populations in the late nineteenth century are documented in fisheries statistics. In Chapter 4, Kew uses such data to model the variation in salmon available in tribal territories of the Fraser drainage in aboriginal times. He feels that his model understates fluctuations. Nevertheless, it is a useful simplification of complex variation into a somewhat unreal four-year cycle.[3] Sam Mitchell stated that only two kinds of salmon were caught around Lillooet – the spring and the sockeye. Of these, sockeye is now by far the most important. The model for the Fraser Lillooet shows an extremely good year for sockeye, two fair years, and a poor year (Table 1).

TABLE 1

Model fluctuations in salmon available to the Fraser Lillooet

Cycle by year	Salmon available model estimate (000,000 kilograms)
1	69,194
2	19,163
3	24,698
4	32,731

SOURCE: Chapter 4

Kew claims that tribal population density in the Fraser River drainage was closely correlated to the mean availability of salmon in the two middle years of his model cycle (Sneed 1972). If populations adapted to the two middle years of the cycle, then what did they do in the lean year? Comparing the lean year to the mean of the two middle years, the deficit was 30 per cent for the Fraser Lillooet, as it was for the Shuswap who lived upstream. It was 70 per cent for the Shuswap of the Thompson River and 48 per cent for the Thompson Indians. We should not put too much weight on these model figures, but the general pattern is clear and probably valid.

Moreover, other factors impinge on the suitability of salmon as a year-round food source. One is the timing of the run in relation to weather and fat content. As I note in Chapter 5, fat salmon are excellent as fresh food but are difficult to preserve for winter. When it is hot and windless, the flesh of filleted fat salmon can become soft; it falls off the skin, and the fish is ruined. For these reasons, the abundant sockeye are usually dried only after 25 July. But if the timing of the run were off, or if the weather were unusual, then most of

the sockeye run might be unpreservable. The result would be an insufficient supply for winter.

A second factor that might turn a numerically sufficient run into a
disaster is the level of the river. In Chapter 6, Kennedy and Bouchard
document some of the adverse effects of high water levels on fishing.
In addition to these effects, if the river does not fall sufficiently at the
Bridge River Rapids, the fish do not congregate below the roughest parts
for fishermen to take with dip nets. Along the main course to the river,
fishing also depends on the river falling so that salmon swim along
the shore where the current is slower or where there may be an eddy
going upstream. Men stationed on fishing rocks or platforms used dip
nets that were only a few feet wide; until the river falls, the fish swim
in a larger volume of water, with little chance of being caught by the
aboriginal techniques of the Interior Salish. The size of a run is unimportant if the fish are not landed.

A third factor that can adversely affect the procurement of fish is the
concentration of a run in too short a period so that food is lost for lack
of labour to preserve the fish. A woman currently filets, scores, and
hangs thirty fish per day. Sometimes men help, but if the run is concentrated this means loss of fishing opportunity. Some rapid cutting
methods waste flesh.

A fourth factor is the mix of species. The aboriginal Lillooet relied
on spring salmon for most of their food, and they needed some well-
preserved sockeye as well. If the springs failed and they had to depend
on sockeye, they would be competing in their own territory with the
many visitors who came to the rapids for the sockeye run. On the other
hand, a scarcity of sockeye would mean that they would have too few
of these less oily fish that were best preserved. Finally, even after salmon
had been stored, it could be lost to bears or raiders, or in the humid
conditions of a wet fall. Stored fish might also become rancid.

I do not know how serious the problem of steadily ingesting rancid
oil was among Indians. Modern Lillooet throw away fish that 'tastes
strong.' Informants described upset stomachs and excessive belching
as effects of eating rancid fish. Though animal experiments showing
that its effects can reach death are of doubtful applicability, Morice
(1905) did report that in 1845 at Fort Babine the servants shown 'the
deleterious effects of salmon on some constitutions.' In general, I
presume that there was a serious basis to the avoidance of rancid fat,
given the many techniques on the Coast and the Plateau for avoiding
rancid fish and the repugnance shown by people around the world
to eating rancid oil (but not many 'rotten' foods, such as stored salmon
eggs).

Thus, the amount of salmon that could be caught and preserved for winter varied from year to year. Though salmon was a rich resource, the runs sometimes failed; weather, timing of the runs, level of the river, concentration of the runs, species mix, predators, or rancidity could reduce its abundance or palatability.

Lillooet informants said that in the old days 'it was hard to keep the families going' and that the Interior Lillooet had a harder time than did the Lower Lillooet, because the former lived on preserved, stored food. Hunger varied with the seasons, late winter and spring being the most difficult times, and in winter people ate just one meal a day. As noted in Chapter 5, 'poor' people had less to eat than the 'rich.'

My best material on occasional hunger concerns the Thompson Indians. Willy Samson of Lytton provided detailed information on the area near the junction of the Fraser and Thompson rivers. Though more salmon passed through that area than through Lillooet, it is possible that the Thompson Indians found it harder to catch salmon for lack of rapids and harder to preserve it because of its higher fat content. Willy Samson reported: 'It's just that one year they say everything was on the famine. Everybody was hungry. Some of them were just falling dead. Just had to die. It's just that one time. The fish were in a famine. That's just like a story from the oldtimers . . . Everything was consumed by springtime.' The phrase 'it's just that one year' means that he is referring to a particular famine, probably in the nineteenth century, not that it was the only one. Storage was one way of surviving a shortage of salmon. At the time of the interview, we were discussing raised storage houses and then turned to storage pits: '/Did they ever keep dried salmon in the holes?/ Oh yes, they do that. That will stay for two years. When they get plenty this year then they thought next year might be a famine fish. So they bury that too. Way down . . . Stay for two years. Next year they don't have enough fish, dig that up. Live on it too. That's the way they store the fish' (ws).

Even in a normal year, spring was a season of hunger. The following description of the preparation for the first salmon ceremony among the Thompson makes very evident its ecological function for the hungry people conserving energy and awaiting news while a few men dip their nets for fish, using up a minimum of the group's scarce food:

Well, it will be the spring salmon at first, the first run on the fish. When the fish comes there will be a lot of them. Young guys go down to the river, start dipping away. They'll be hungry, and it's spring time. What they prepare last time will be consumed in the winter, and they will be hungry in the summer. Got nothing else to eat but fish and all the wild roots they make, all they had to eat. So that's finished, everything is finished, everyone is hungry, and they send four young guys down the river to dip away and try to get fish. Well, they'll be dipping away. 'Don't miss that fish.' Dipping away there. When they get that fish they come home. Be only one fish in a day. That's all they get. They come home. So that's the way . . . They have to invite everybody [to the first salmon ceremony]. (WS)

Deer as a Complement to Salmon

In a non-quantitative way, we have been searching for 'minimal occurrences in space, time, and quantity' of food sources (Suttles 1968:60). We shall now examine 'the availability of alternative resources' (Ames 1981:798). One strategy adopted by many of the Interior Salish during Kew's lean year was to hunt, with the unique adaptation of each individual settlement depending on its ecological situation: alternative resources, trade, storage possibilities, and surplus from prior years. For the Fraser Lillooet, perhaps the situation was not as critical as for other groups, because they usually produced an excess of salmon for trade and they had access to trout. Be that as it may, if we accept Lovell's cited estimate of the proportion of salmon protein in the Lillooet diet, and if we presume that most of the food shortfall was made up by deer meat, then hunters would have to double their efforts in the lean year compared to the two middle years of the cycle.

Deer meat and salmon were complements in several ways. Usually, deer were taken in the fall, after the salmon runs. Occasionally, hunting saved the day (when the salmon failed) by providing alternative stored food for the winter larder or by providing unseasonal spring hunts. The following quote concerns the Lytton Thompson Indians:

If there's some [salmon] left, we still eat it, it's consumed. There's some left in the springtime when these other fish come, but the fish don't run regular. The first run you see in March. That finishes off, and if that's finished off, we have to live on what's left over from last year's dry fish. Otherwise, it's sockeye, spring salmon, or the humpback. We have to live on that till we get the next fish again. But sometimes if that's all consumed we got nothing else to live on. Have to go out and hunt. Go out and hunt. (WS)

Suttles has pointed out that vegetable foods were not abundant on the Coast and formed a minor part of the diet. My impression is that berries were not rare in Lillooet territory, and the typical winter meal was described as a few handfuls of powdered salmon with dried berries. Thompson people had access to abundant root harvests. Still, I have no evidence that roots were stored in sufficient quantities to constitute a reserve or to last the winter (contra Ames and Marshall 1981). Sam Mitchell clearly stated that the main winter food was dried saskatoon and powdered fish: 'They dry fish and they powder it. They get the saskatoon berries and dry it. That's the biggest grub they have during the winter. Might be a few potatoes in the fall they dig.' He also mentioned that the Lillooet traded dried salmon for other kinds of dried berries. However, smoked deer, the early trout runs, and unseasonal hunting were the needed supplements to salmon.

That a Lillooet or Thompson father would marry his daughter to a hunter because the hunter 'always' had food for his wife, and presumably for his father-in-law as well, implies both that deer were available when salmon were not and that salmon was not always adequate. Deer meat complemented salmon in another way: deer fat is highly saturated, while salmon oil is unsaturated. Saturated deer fat or bear fat, put up in the late fall or winter, was unlikely to become rancid. The highly valued oulachen oil of the Coast was also resistant to rancidity. Different people had the necessary skills for hunting and fishing. Further, deer were taken when the salmon runs were almost over. Finally, when deer hunters went out they would take ten or fifteen dried salmon apiece to live on for a week or two while they were looking for deer.

In summary, meat compensated for failed salmon runs and for stored salmon in poor condition. Fishing and hunting were seasonally distinct, there were different experts, and deer meat and salmon were complementary in other ways. Deer meat was a partial solution to the problem of dense populations relying too much on fluctuating salmon supplies. A number of interpretations view the coastal potlatch as ecologically adaptive, and the above observations also indicate that there were positive functions of cultural traits that promoted the production and distribution of deer meat. These cultural traits included the potlatch gift-giving, kinship sharing obligations, food-for-prestige exchange, and other factors, such as wealth, winter clothes, and wives, that motivated boys to submit to rigorous training to become hunters and that motivated men to make special efforts to procure meat. In normal years, the demand was for a tasty food and for a potlatch good; occasionally, hunting was needed for survival.

WORK AND PRESTIGE IN LILLOOET SOCIETY

Discussion of status in relation to the organization of tasks follows the model of Julian Steward's analysis of Great Basin rabbit drives. Generally, he wrote that in the Basin-Plateau area: 'There was a multiple subsistence in that different categories of plant and animal foods entailed certain distinctive activities which affected the nature of complementarity between the sexes and cooperation between individuals, families and groups of families. Each subsistence activity was related to the characteristics of the species, its abundance, seasonality, distribution, and technology for obtaining it' (Steward 1977:371). These concepts are applicable to Lillooet productive roles.

Lillooet Occupational Structure

The three main resources captured by aboriginal Lillooet men were sockeye salmon, spring salmon, and deer. Social roles for producers corresponded to each resource. The least specialized role was that of sockeye fisherman; taking sockeye was simply part of the male role. On the other hand, the principal spring salmon fishermen were owners of fishing rocks, while the hunting chief had a well-developed role that has already been described. At the same time, ordinary men fished for springs and took part in hunts but in no special role.

A summary table (Table 2) presents the rather compartmentalized structure of Lillooet tasks and roles, which I will refer to as an occupational structure insofar as there were specialists. Some liberties have been taken for uniformity, such as naming the chief as steward of the village's labour. In earlier times, such as when Simon Fraser visited the area, Sam Mitchell recalled that 'Them days there's a lot of warriors, good runners.' Unfortunately, I lack further information on runners as specialists. I also lack knowledge of women's roles. The general pattern of discrete specialists and tools is notable.

Occupational Scale and its Correlates

The three male productive roles were ranked in terms of prestige and rewards: hunter, spring salmon fisherman, and sockeye salmon fisherman. We may also rank the roles in terms of several variables that, in a cultural-ecological framework, can explain prestige variation. The potential explanatory variables from an ecological standpoint are divided into two groups: (1) characteristics of the task that might enhance its prestige – danger or discipline of the task, complexity of the task, organization, tools required, and returns to scale; and (2) characteristics of the context of the work that might enhance the prestige of the work – the need for small amounts of the resource, the degree to which the producer affects supply, the scarcity of specialists, the brute contribution of the product to subsistence, and

TABLE 2
Partial occupational structure of the Lillooet

	Deer	Spring salmon	Sockeye salmon	Berries, roots	Trout*	Labour, external relations	Illness, health, and protection	Enemies, safety
Roles								
Steward/manager	hunter	rock owner	rack builder?	women	weir builder	chief	shaman	warrior
Others	men	men	men	pickers	fisher			
Processor	women	rock owner women	women	women				
Season of production	fall	summer	late summer	spring and summer	spring	all year		fall
Site of production	mountain valley	special rocks	falls	hills	lakes			

*Located in Shuswap territory

the perceived need for the product in high-prestige activities. Characteristics of the resource itself will be considered later.

With such an array of variables, it may seem that we are trying too many correlates to explain one dependent variable. Yet the goal here is exploratory, and perhaps such conceptual splitting is a reaction to the overly generalized discussion of resources and social structure on the Coast which seeks to explain responses such as stratification and kinship structure in terms of an amorphous cause such as abundance. Since we lack quantitative data on the different tasks, I shall make what I hope are reasonable judgements about the ranking of the roles and tasks on several variables, using a scale of 1 (highest of those considered) to 3 (lowest). I do not mean to claim precision for these judgements; they are an expedient for summarizing a discussion in a short table.

Characteristics of the Task

Let us consider the danger of the task, the discipline required, the skill or knowledge required, the number of people involved in joint effort, the kinds of tools required, and the benefits that derive from co-operation. Hunting deer was dangerous because it involved trips far from home, often alone and in adverse conditions. Going out on such trips required discipline. Neither spring nor sockeye salmon fishing was as dangerous, though both involved work beside the rushing waters of the Fraser River, where a fall could be fatal. The discipline of the spring salmon fisherman, who dipped his net from his platform for hours at a time, was substantial and was more than that of the sockeye fisherman, who took fish at the falls.

The hunter had the most complex task, having to make his tools, know a large area and the habits of his prey, and combine the skills of orientation, capturing an intelligent animal, and butchering it. The owner of a rock had to make his nets and platform, adjust the latter as the river rose and fell, capture the fish, and supervise butchering; while substantial skills were required, the deer hunter's were more complex. The sockeye fisherman had the least difficult tasks, and drying sockeye is easier than drying springs, because the fish are smaller and the fat content lower toward the end of the run (Chapter 5).

Hunting deer involved several men as well as women to filet, dry, and pack. Fishing for spring salmon involved fewer people: the owner and someone to help with building the platform as well as one or more women to help with the drying. Nor did fishing for sockeye involve many people in co-operation: an individual, perhaps someone to tie him to the rock or haul fish, and women to filet, dry, and pack. Of course, many people might be fishing in turn or at once, but here we are interested in the group needed for the task.

But why should people defer to a hunter? One reason is that they could have more meat by following a good hunter than by hunting themselves, a reasonable conjecture based on both the skills required to actually kill deer with a bow and the presumed efficiency of group hunting techniques. This is the 'return to scale' characteristic. In general, one presumes that management of elaborate tools and facilities operated by several people would be associated with high prestige, as in the case of fish weirs, large canoes, whaling kits, and so on. No such tools or facilities were found among the Fraser Lillooet; the trout weir that they visited was in Shuswap territory. Among tools used by the Lillooet, the platform, nets, and drying rack of the spring salmon fisherman might be considered the most substantial, particularly in light of the amount of fibre needed. Perhaps the weapons and winter buckskin clothes of the hunter were more difficult to produce. I have no knowledge of the fences mentioned by Teit. The sockeye fishery required several dip nets appropriate to different river conditions as well as a rack. Thus, this variable is difficult to code.

Characteristics of the Context of the Task

The second set of variables are those which show the relation of the roles to the overall adaptation of the group. Brute production does not vary as might have been expected: fish was the base of subsistence, but fishing had lower status than hunting. I have argued that dried deer meat was a 'critical' resource in that a relatively small increment was necessary for survival of the group, particularly when salmon failed and in the yearly hunger season. While all the resources considered were needed for survival, sockeye salmon was the least critical in that only large differences were significant; usually, there was enough to spare for outsiders.

The 'needed discipline' variable refers to the degree to which the producer in question can affect the supply of the resource. In the case of deer, the hunting chief's success, along with natural factors, determined the supply of dried deer meat; the hunter's activity was on the 'critical path' for producing an adequate supply of meat. The owner of the fishing rock was also needed to produce a supply of dried spring salmon; if he placed his platform in the wrong position, he would catch no fish. However, he was more easily replaced and there were alternative rocks. The efforts of the individual sockeye salmon fisherman had little effect on overall supplies for two reasons: first, the limiting factor for producing dried sockeye was either the capacity of women to filet or the size and preservability of the run; second, work-ing in a crowd of men who were taking turns, the individual producer could be replaced immediately.

There were few hunting chiefs, several owners of rocks, and many sockeye fishermen: 'It's not everybody can be a hunter. They got salmon, easier to get. All you need is a net. Them days used to be lots of salmon. Very few hunters. You got to have the speed. /Did every-body fish?/ Oh yeah. Everybody fished' (SM). Finally, to consider the demand for the products of prestige activities, the deer hunter con-tributed to the potlatch; the spring salmon fisherman produced the preferred food of the community and contributed to inter-tribal trade; and the sockeye fisherman produced a less-preferred food that was also used in inter-tribal trade.

The characteristics of the tasks and their contexts correlate with the degree of prestige granted to the productive roles (Table 3), showing that the hunter's situation was normal in the overall occupational struc-ture of the Lillooet. Some occupations fit on the scale in the expected way, but others do not. Women's tasks, like berry picking, root gather-ing, and fibre collecting, would rank fairly low on the task scales, but we know nothing about the prestige scale among women – a topic that is difficult to assess even in societies that we can observe first-hand. Certainly women's activities were necessary in that they processed all the deer, fish, berries, and fibre that the population used in the winter, but the contrast between the hunter and the fisherman shows that neither necessity nor brute contribution need confer prestige.

The chief had high prestige but not as a direct producer. He co-ordinated workers, scheduled activities, distributed some resources, and had extra-village relations (Chapter 5). The chief was a manager and redistributor whose actions were unlike those of the hunter or the fisherman. There is no evidence that the role was dangerous. Com-plexity, organization, and uniqueness would indicate high prestige, but criticalness and needed discipline are hard to judge. We may pre-sume that warriors, shamans, and runners had considerable prestige, but we lack data on their activities and the results thereof.

Rights to Resources and Prestige

Ownership of resources is a likely candidate to correlate with the pres-tige of a role. This is not easily checked. Among the Lillooet, un-processed animal resources were not owned in the sense that today one might own mineral rights or trees; but to the degree that some people had more access to resources than others, or were able to

TABLE 3
Characteristics of tasks and their contexts for three
major male productive roles

	Resource		
	Deer	Spring salmon	Sockeye salmon
Key producer	hunter	rock owner	fisher
Prestige	1	2	3
Characteristics of the task			
Danger	1	2	3
Discipline	1	2	3
Complexity/skill	1	2	3
Organization	1	2.5	2.5
Tools	2.5	1	2.5
Return to scale	1.5	1.5	3
Mean	1.3	1.8	2.8
Context:			
Relation of work to			
overall adaptation			
Criticalness	1	2	3
Needed discipline	1	2	3
Number of producers	1	2	3
Brute contribution	3	1?	2
Product use prestige	1.5	1.5	3
Mean	1.5	1.7	2.8

exclude others, they can be said to have been owned to different degrees and in different ways: by individual ownership of the site where they were taken, by ownership of tools, by ownership of spirit help, by investment of labour, by group control of territory, and so on; and, once preserved, fish and deer were clearly owned in that they could be traded or given with recognition. Other ethnographers document ownership of housing sites among other Interior groups.[4]

Ownership and Prestige

All men had some access to all three of the resources considered, the most widely distributed rights being to sockeye salmon at the public falls (though there were also non-public rocks) and the least access being to spring salmon (because of individually owned fishing rocks)

(Table 4). No rents or fees were charged for use of resource procurement sites. There is no clear relation between the degree to which a resource was owned and the degree to which the relevant producer had high prestige (Table 4).

TABLE 4
Degree of ownership of resources

| | Resource | | |
	Deer	Spring salmon	Sockeye salmon
Tools for capture owned?	yes (bow)	yes (net)	yes? (net)
Processing tools owned?	no (fire)	yes (rack)	yes (rack)
Site owned?	no individual, maybe group	yes (individual rocks)	some (residence +individual rocks possible)
Inherited?	no	yes	some
Rent charged?	no	no	no
Exclusion	maybe	yes, limited	less
Spirit owned?	yes	no?	no?
Uncaptured animal owned?	no	no	no
Processed food owned?	yes	yes	yes
Summary rank order	3?	1?	2?
Prestige	1	2	3

Ownership and Characteristics of Resources

The characteristics of each resource include its concentration (particularly the capacity of an individual or group owner to control who captures it), plenitude (particularly the amount that could be taken per unit of effort or time, given prevailing technology), and the preservability of that amount (which may be related to the degree that an individual or group would bother to try controlling a resource) (Schalk 1977, 1981; Suttles 1986). In fact, I find it hard to rank the resources according to their characteristics. Deer are clearly dispersed. Sockeye salmon runs are more concentrated than are the spring runs, but there are more sockeye fishing rocks. With regard to plenitude, informants say that the Lillooet used to take more springs than sock-eye, though many sockeye were taken for trade. All of the resources are preservable, especially the later part of the sockeye run (Table 5). Despite the problems in coding, the characteristics of the resources themselves appear to be related to the degree to which the resources are owned.

TABLE 5
Characteristics of the resources

	Deer	Spring salmon	Sockeye salmon
Concentration	3	1.5?	1.5?
Plenitude	3	1?	2?
Preservability	2?	3?	1
Summary	3?	1.5	1.5
Ownership rank (summary from Table 4)	3?	1?	2?

Resource Stewardship

Julian Steward noted that the term 'ownership' carries many inappropriate connotations when applied to Basin-Plateau groups, saying that informants' statements about ownership are 'almost invariably followed by the further statement that anyone was free to use the resources' (1977:375-7). The difference between the owners of Lillooet resources who may claim priority of access and owners in more stratified societies who can demand rent or fees seems important enough to warrant a different term – 'steward.' The term covers both Lillooet resource owners and other individuals who manage dangers and resources which they cannot be said to own in any sense.

Stewards are the resource owners appropriate to a society intermediate between Fried's categories of rank and stratified society (Fried 1960). Fried hypothesized evolution of societies classified as egalitarian, ranked, stratified, and state. The characteristic of a stratified society is the ownership of resources such that some people acquire access by paying dues, rent, or taxes in labour or in kind. Lillooet informants do talk of owning resources, of preferential access, and of inheritance of rights; moreover, specialists such as the village chief, hunting chief, and fishing rock owner were better off than others in part because of their privileged access to resources. On the other hand, some redistribution of food was a characteristic of Lillooet economy, a trait appropriate to rank, not stratified societies, and no fees were charged for others' use of resources (e.g., deer, where the issue was not hunting grounds). Thus, Lillooet society and its stewards appear to be intermediate between rank and stratified types.

When we refer to Lillooets that specialized in a particular resource as 'stewards,' we emphasize their management role over their capacity to exclude others from the resource, though the latter was sometimes manifested. The man who prepared a spring salmon fishing platform, the hunter, and the chief had preferential access to resources (spring salmon, deer, and labour, respectively), but they exercised their rights only in the company of others, and stewards benefited only if their privileged exploitation also benefited other people. Thus, the owner or steward of a rock built a fishing platform that others could use; and his privileged access would not be recognized if he did not let others use his tools and procurement site. In Chapter 5, informants approvingly tell a story about men who stole salmon from a rock owner who would not share.

Michael Ames (1956:21) reported something similar in the 1950s. In his graduating essay on the Fraser Lillooet, he wrote:

> In the past, fishing locations were inheritable but even then, most people were allowed to use them. Today, there are four main fishing rocks to which most of the men go to fish; none of them have recognized owners. A few men can still make the specific types of dip nets used at these rocks; once having made them, they leave them at the locations for everyone to use. Outsiders, usually Shuswap from the north, are allowed to use the fishing locations and the nets.

I found later that though people generally said that rocks are now unowned, they still referred to specific people's rocks.

The hunter, too, only had followers if he hunted with others and ensured that they benefited from the hunt. He only increased and secured his benefits by killing deer for his followers and by giving away deer meat to non-hunting supporters. The chief scheduled the activities of the whole group, and he, among other well-to-do people, validated his status by giving food in a potlatch. For this, he had to call on hunters in his and other villages, as previously described. The typical responsibility of an individual steward was to organize, schedule, and facilitate productive activities related to particular resources.

Among the Lillooet of the 1950s, even land rights were not decided by criteria of strict ownership, though the applicability of the concept of stewardship is not clear. The basis for land claims on the reserve were: need for land, intention to use, service to the previous owner during his lifetime, and kinship (Ames 1956:24).

The inheritance of stewardship was a matter of preference for a related child who showed predisposition and who accepted the work involved in training or assisting the current steward. There was a preference for sons to inherit fishing rocks and the chieftaincy. Inheritance was validated by spirit acquisition, by exercise of rights for the benefit of others, and by giving. It is difficult to imagine an incompetent heir exercising leadership among the Lillooet.

There was also group stewardship among the Lillooet in that they typically shared their resources with nearby groups and had access to the resources of those groups. This is the 'mutual cross-utilization' of resources that characterizes much of the Plateau (Walker 1967). Groups settled near resources but did not demand exclusive access to at least some of these. Sam Mitchell reported the following for trout lakes, where an individual steward supervised construction of a trap and distributed trout:

> In these lakes, any lakes up in this country, up in the Interior of British Columbia, any mouth of a lake, there's always an Indian reserve. Because that's where the Indians used to go around from April, May, when the fish [trout] starts to spawn, that's where they get the fresh fish. I'll say Fountain Lake, Cinquefoil Lake . . . Loon Lake, Hiiume Lake . . . Green Lake or [Watson?] Lake . . . They build a fish trap . . . I was there one time . . . So this fellow that was there . . . says 'O.K. You just go ahead and take what you want.' [He describes the trap]. So this fellow I was with says, 'you don't have to look at us. Just take what you want and go.' . . . You just go ahead and help yourself. What's left, the old ladies will split it [and dry it]. (SM)

Clearly, access to all resources was not unlimited for outsiders. The abundance of resources may have been one consideration, but there may have been other considerations as well, such as resource concentration and preservability. A comparative study of resource sites would be of great use in identifying the most important determinants of access, however, that is beyond the scope of this chapter.

COMPARATIVE PERSPECTIVES

Stewardship, occupational ranking with productive correlates, and distribution of food are found in the Plateau and on the Coast. For the Plateau, Bishop's discussion (1983) of the Carrier shows some striking resemblances to the Lillooet material on subsistence and distribution, though his main topic, commerce in luxury goods, has no parallel among the Lillooet. Among the Carrier, salmon was the staple, though it was not always sufficient. Hunting provided prestige food distribution at feasts (1983:151), and only food, principally beaver and bear meat, were given at feasts of men who gained prestige (1983:152). Bishop goes on to de-emphasize the chiefly nature of early Carrier leaders as a prelude to arguing for the necessity of trade in luxury goods to explain inheritable status differences. However, the Lillooet had inheritable status without major trade in luxury goods. One could discuss whether or not there were 'real' chiefs or potlatches among the Lillooet or whether the minor Lillooet trade in luxury goods (or salmon) could have caused inheritable status, but I think that such a discussion should wait for a systematic, regional ethnological review.

Suttles (1962, 1968) has argued for strong relations between natural resources and social structure on the Northwest Coast using Coast Salish data. Other anthropologists have investigated different hypothetical relationships between social and natural features. For example, one debate contrasted purely social explanations of slavery with economic explanations. The preponderance of evidence has confirmed that slaves were of economic importance, especially in northern latitudes (Ruyle 1973; Donald 1983; Mitchell and Donald 1985), others have reiterated the hypothetical relation between concentration of resources and unilineal inheritance (Riches 1979) or, reacting against that, have suggested a relation between abundance and development along preset social structural lines[5] (Rosman and Rubel 1986), still others have described natural resources and culture-resource correlations more quantitatively than did earlier investigators (Donald and Mitchell 1975; Schalk 1977, 1981; Sneed 1972; and Kew in Chapter 4).

The concepts developed so far in this paper – stewardship in contrast to more exclusive ownership as well as correlations among occupational structure, productive activities, and prestige – appear to be relevant to debates in this literature on the origins of ranking or exploitation, on the nature of exploitation, and on cultural evolution.

Stewards were also particularly appropriate to the Plateau culture area, where 'cross-utilization' of resources (Walker 1967) was more common than territorial exclusion. Both stewardship and ranked occupations are also found on the Northwest Coast, and the link between the spirit-quest and virtuous performance of useful work by upper class people is also found among the Coast Salish.

With regard to the correlates of prestige, in some cases Coastal occupations are ranked in the same manner as are the Lillooet ones, that is, by characteristics of the tasks performed. Eugene E. Ruyle (1973) argues for the importance of exploitation of lower classes by upper classes as the essence of Coastal stratification. However, other factors, related to the requirements of particular activities, were operating to promote stratification on the Coast as they were in Lillooet territory.

We may examine some of the sources used by Ruyle (1973) to demonstrate that upper class people did different work than did lower class people. Although fishing was the mainstay of Coastal subsistence,

> fishing was an occupation which was followed only by the inferior class of people ... the common business of fishing for ordinary sustenance is carried on by slaves, or the lower class of people – while the more noble occupation of killing the whale and hunting sea otter, is followed by none but the chiefs and warriors. [Meares 1790:145, 258, quoted in Ruyle 1973:611]

> A portion of them only attain the dignity of whalers, a second class devote themselves to halibut, and a third to salmon and inferior fish, the occupations being kept distinct, at least, in great measure. [Gibbs 1877, quoted by Nieboer 1910, quoted by Ruyle 1973:611]

> All the members of a household shared in the necessary labor involved in providing for themselves and for the household head and tribal chief. In this labor the slaves and even the chiefs took part. Slaves were often assigned to the more monotonous and menial tasks, but as often they and their masters worked side by side ... Even chiefs helped with the fishing and hunting which furnished the raw material for the various food products and also the horn for spoons, the mountain goat wool for weaving and furs and skins for clothing and trade. [Garfield 1939.2/1, 329, quoted in Ruyle 1973:611]

Since whaling, halibut fishing, and mountain goat hunting were critical, dangerous, and skilful in comparison to salmon fishing (Suttles 1968:59), the ranking of whaling+hunting, halibut fishing, and inferior-fishing+menial-tasks would seem to be the equivalent to the deer/spring salmon/sockeye salmon ranking among the Lillooet, both in terms of prestige and correlates. How much of Coast social ranking is due to occupational ranking as opposed to ownership and exploitation? How many Coast/Interior differences in stratification are due to differences in specific correlates of occupational ranking such as multi-person, elaborate tools? What specific activities would make it more profitable (in Ruyle's argument) or more functional (in the potlatch-style argument) to have a class of slaves doing menial labour? It is not simply a matter of abundance of salmon, since the Fraser Lillooet consumed as much salmon as did the Coastal peoples and had enough to trade out of the region.

Given strategies of occupational specialization, how did the occupations fit into overall social structure that also included classes, owners, and chiefs? Various arrangements were possible. For example, while Lillooet chiefs could call on hunters to provide game, the Kwakiutl chiefs 'owned' hunters and normally collected a substantial share of the game taken (Ruyle 1973:614).

There were also elements of stewardship and even cross-utilization on the Coast, at least among the Coast Salish. While the literature on the Coast emphasizes resource ownership, often with a note about 'flexibility,' the following description of the Coast Salish could as well apply to the Fraser Lillooet:

> Task groups were directed by the 'owners' of resources, such as fishing sites and clam beds; by owners of special gear, as the net for a deer drive; or simply by skilled specialists in the activity. Such subsistence activities and also ceremonial activities often brought together people from several villages over areas which crossed dialect or even language boundaries, but there were no structural principals that allowed for the definition of discrete social units. (Suttles 1968:65)

In his discussion of individual 'ownership' of resources among the Coast Salish, Riches (1979:151-2) describes a role like that of the Lillooet steward, though of course among the Lillooet the supposed link to ownership and control did not occur: 'One posits that the development of Coast Salish patterns of territorial ownership relates to the fact that, in the Coast Salish ecological situation, there is the facility for certain hunter/fishermen to evince a productive competence which fellow producers will recognize as importantly superior; these people attract a close stable following and thereby expand the territory which they, as individuals, control.'

The similarity between the Coast Salish and the Interior Lillooet is reflected in the ideological realm. Elmendorf (1977) has described the common elements in the Interior and Coast spirit quests. The ritual sequence he describes is training, seeking, vision, return, and suppression. The hunter, among other stewards, acquired his spirit in this way. The spirit quest has been noted as an essential part of the occupational structure of the Lillooet.

Elmendorf remarks that 'in both Plateau and southern Northwest Coast cultures it is guardian spirit conferred power which represents conceptually the principal means of establishment or enhancement of adult roles' (1977:68). This also characterizes the Lillooet hunter. Perhaps we should add another step to the common paradigm: adult assumption of a steward's role. Elmendorf writes that there was 'a Coast Salish emphasis on industry in high status families, for both men and women' (Ruyle 1973:619).

This spirit-steward complex is very distinct from the Central Coast.

There is a significant difference between a religion that expresses it-self in performance of work by privileged people and one that stress-es display of inherited rights to masks or resources. Putting aside the possible link between religion and style of resource control, the Coast Salish data are sufficient to warn that we should not 'treat notions of ownership as a given feature of Northwest Coast culture' if 'owner-ship connotes the exercise of exclusive rights in the disposal of resources or areas of territory' (Riches 1979:149).

CONCLUSIONS

Hunter's Prestige

The hunter had high prestige because he was a redistributor of a special sort – he received labour and tools and distributed (directly or through a chief) meat. His socialization through training, the spirit quest, and norms of adult upper class behaviour prepared him for his functionally important role. At the same time, he was rewarded with prestige, goods, and wives – a sort of 'enlightened self interest' in a redistributive society. The hunter's high prestige was part of the overall Lillooet ecological adaptation, which was based on salmon, but which included deer meat as a critical secondary stored resource in the absence of large quantities of alternative preserved foods or year-round fresh food. The hunter was also typical of the Lillooet occupa-tional organization.

Organization of Activities and Occupations

Each activity of the village had its resource, season, place, temporary settlement, specialist leader, tools, tasks, organization, processing methods, storage techniques, and products. The relative prestige of such productive roles as hunter, spring-salmon fisherman, and sockeye-salmon fisherman was correlated with characteristics of the task (such as danger, size of working group, and discipline) and the context of the task (such as contribution to the overall adaptation). Exclusive ownership of resource procurement sites was not recognized by the Lillooet. Occupational ranking was also found on the Coast along with other forms of ranking.

Resource Stewards

The resource steward was a specialist in dealing with a particular resource. He had tools that he used for the benefit of others, and he had training and competence. Obtaining spirit help was a requisite for stewardship, and inheritance was only relevant if the youth showed a predilection and aptitude for a specialized role. Though indirect, the rewards of stewardship could be substantial. In the case of the hunter, these included polygyny, labour, and gifts. Other roles that may have had similar requirements and rewards are fishing rock owner, warrior, shaman, and chief. Groups could act as stewards, and it was normal for a Plateau group to allow neighbouring groups access to certain resources although retaining some preferential access. Resource stewardship also occurred on the Coast, together with other ways of integrating occupational specialists into society.

Functions of the Fraser Lillooet Potlatch

Given seasonal and occasional fluctuations in food resources, plus the role of deer meat as an alternative resource, the cultural ecological functions of the Fraser Lillooet potlatch were: (1) distributing meat widely, even between villages, (2) sharing the hunter's scarce skills within and between villages, (3) keeping up the normal demand for dried deer meat that was occasionally of critical importance, (4) motivating special, long hunts, (5) promoting preservation of deer meat as opposed to immediate consumption, and (6) making the hunter's role more recognized and stable. Constant demand and yearly hunts (as opposed to hunts only when the salmon failed) allowed institutionalization of the role of hunter, made organizing hunts easier, maintained skills and physical ability, and protected against late fall loss of stores.

Cultural Continuity

In Chapter 5, I concluded that fishing has continued in a practical and significant way. Similarly, it is possible that today we can talk of the equivalent of hunting chiefs. While I was doing fieldwork, I met men who themselves hunt and who provide the stores and tools for others to hunt, just as Mr. Mitchell had a houseful of visiting salmon fishermen during that season. The Fraser Lillooet continue to put up deer meat for the winter, though they use jars now; moreover, there are still hunters who give meat to others. Thus, some of the patterns of work and organization described here may still occur among modern Lillooet hunters and are pertinent to discussions of modes of economic initiatives on modern reserves (Ames 1956:109, 113).

NOTES

This chapter is a modified version of an article with the same title that appeared in 1988 in *Northwest Anthropological Research Notes* 22(2):145-74.

1 I began fieldwork with members of the Lillooet tribe in 1970 to describe salmon preservation. Dr. Wayne Suttles, ethnographer of the Coast Salish, and Dr. David French advised me prior to that trip and another in 1971. In 1978, I again visited Lillooet, concentrating on early reservation life. I interviewed informants in their houses, at the Bridge River fishing site, and elsewhere, usually tape-recording the interviews. Mr. Sam Mitchell of the Fountain Band provided most of the information used here. Transcripts of many of the 1970 and 1971 interviews were sent to Mr. Mitchell; he transferred them to the files of the British Columbia Indian Language Project.

   Fieldwork in 1970 resulted in a Bachelor's thesis at Reed College on salmon fishing (an edited version of which appeared in 1985 and now appears as Chapter 5 of this volume). While investigating this topic, I discovered that potlatching involved gifts of deer meat rather than either preserved salmon or wealth objects, and this led to an interest in the high status of the hunter. The 1971 fieldwork was written up for a first-year qualifying paper at Columbia University under the direction of Dr. Alexander Alland. 'The Lillooet Hunter' manuscript (1972) was the predecessor of this article.

2 When I quote from notes, I make only minor changes, so the quotations sometimes read poorly.

3 Kew's model (Chapter 4) is an estimate of fish available multiplied by an index for loss of calories as the fish migrate. Since the Lillooet relied on spring salmon, which eat during migration, I have not used his caloric adjuster, which is based on data on sockeye, which stop eating.

   The model could be made as complex as one could wish. For example, a more complete model of the fish available to a human population consuming dried salmon could be straightforward but somewhat detailed. For each winter month, say February, the model would estimate the energy available for consumption in that month from a fish product made from a particular species. That figure would be the product of fish available in each summer month, multiplied by capture ratio (which itself becomes complex if there are several fishing techniques), by an adjuster that depends on river conditions, by allocation of the fish among different products, by a conversion ratio from fresh to preserved weight, by an adjuster that depends on weather and preservation conditions, by proportion traded away or otherwise lost to other populations, by post-processing loss ratio (taking into account rancidity, insects, etc.), and, finally, by caloric content of the product. Now the calculations would be repeated for each species that could be captured and some way found to model the allocation of time among the species. Of course, not all consumers had equal access to the stored products. This is a job for simulation.

4 For the Lillooet, Teit (1906) notes that deer fences were owned. Much later in the century, Kennedy and Bouchard (personal communication) recorded the term *skele7áwlh* (derived from *kéla*, 'first') among the Lower Lillooet. Their informant, Charlie Mack, translated *skele7áwlh* as 'leader; head man':

> Charlie said this term was used with reference to a leader or head man for hunting, fishing or horses. This is different than the term *kwúkwpi* which is usually translated as 'chief.' CM sometimes translated the term *skele7áwlh* as 'the resident.' And he noted that the man who built and managed the scaffolds from which salmon were harpooned and gaffed at a particular fishery up the Birkenhead River (near where the highway bridge crosses today), was called *skele7áwlh*. He also used this term to describe certain individuals who 'controlled the hunting' at specific locations. CM stated that if people wanted deer they went to the *skele7áwlh* and he 'showed them where to hunt.' They would not go on their own. A list of hunting areas that CM provided for us, along with several generations of 'owners' who he was able to identify, indicates to us that the position of *skele7áwlh* was hereditary. Spirit power was not involved, as far as we were able to determine. Perhaps this position would best be translated as 'steward.'
>
> The term for a 'professional, trained hunter' is *tewít* and is cognate in both Thompson and Lillooet. Several Lillooet people (and also Thompson) have described a *tewít* for us, and noted that this man would have exceptional abilities as a hunter because he was trained to the point that he was, as Baptiste Ritchie said, 'in contact with the animals.' Besides being able to forecast where the deer would be, the *tewít* was highly skilled in hunting techniques, whether it be shooting with a bow and arrow, or running the deer down in deep snow. The *tewít* showed special respect to the animals by handling the head of the animal in a proscribed manner after the kill. But the main difference between a *skele7áwlh* and a *tewít*, as we understand it, is that the *tewít* did not appear to be associated with a specific area. CM did point out, however, that a *skele7áwlh* could also be a *tewít*. (Kennedy and Bouchard, personal communication, 1989)

Their suggestion of ownership of hunting territory goes beyond my data, however. It is nevertheless interesting to note similar observations for the Shuswap area by Dawson (1892:14) and D.S. Mitchell (1925), who state that hunting territories were formerly owned by families.

5 Rosman and Rubel (1986) propose that Interior Salish social structure, including that of the Upper Lillooet, was a precursor to that of the central Northwest Coast. They discount that of the Coast Salish. The suggestion is that Interior social structure became more complex when it met Coastal abundance. They cite several similarities between the Interior Salish and the central Coast, as well as three differences that presumably constitute the elements that make the Interior groups less developed: absence of ranking, absence of enduring groups based on kinship, and resources not owned by individuals or descent groups. They exclude the Coast Salish on the grounds that they are predominantly patrilineal.

However, we have seen that the Fraser Lillooet have important resources owned by individuals (fishing rocks) and possibly by residence groups; I have used the term 'steward' for this kind of ownership. We have also seen that not everyone had an equal chance to be chief or fishing-rock owner and that there were 'rich' people and 'moochers.' We really know very little about the kinship composition of Lillooet residence groups, perhaps because interested observers visited the Coastal groups earlier than those of the Interior, and even after contact Coastal society elaborated complex social institutions. On the other hand, the patrilineality of the Coast Salish is not clear; their kin terms are bilateral, the incest rule was bilateral, there were no groups to which members belong by virtue of descent through one parent, and there were several rules of inheritance (Suttles, personal communication). On the other hand, fishing rocks and chiefdomship were passed to sons among the Lillooet. There seems to be little basis to choose between the Lillooet and the Coast Salish as a more likely origin of Central Coast institutions. Further, and again, the proposal that the Interior cultures developed on meeting abundant coastal salmon is not appropriate: the major fishing sites in the Interior, such as Bridge River and The Dalles on the Columbia River, were fishing and trading centres, and Hewes (1973) estimates Lillooet per capita consumption to be higher than that on the Coast.

REFERENCES

Ames, Kenneth M. 1981. 'The evolution of social ranking on the Northwest Coast of North America.' *American Antiquity* 46(4):789-805

Ames, Kenneth and Alan Marshall. 1981. 'Villages, demography and subsistence intensification on the southern Columbia Plateau.' *North American Archaeologist* 2:25-52

Ames, Michael M. 1956. 'Fountain in a modern economy: A study of social structure, land use and business enterprise in a British Columbia Indian community.' Graduating essay, University of British Columbia, Vancouver

Bishop, Charles A. 1983. 'Limiting access to limited goods: The origin of stratification in Interior British Columbia.' In Elisabeth Tooker (ed.), *The Development of Political Organization in Native North America.'* 1979 Proceedings of the American Ethnological Society

Dawson, George. 1982. 'Notes on the Shuswap people of British Columbia.' *Proceedings and Transactions of the Royal Society of Canada* 9(2):3-44

Donald, Leland. 1983. 'Was *Nuu-chah-nulth-aht* (Nootka) society based on slave labor?' In Elisabeth Tooker (ed.), *The Development of Political Organization in Native North America.* Pp. 108-19. 1979 Proceedings of the American Ethnological Society

Donald, Leland and Donald Mitchell. 1975. 'Some correlates of local group rank among the Southern Kwakiutl.' *Ethnography* 14:325-46

Fried, Morton H. 1960. 'On the evolution of social stratification and the state.' In S. Diamond (ed.), *Culture in History.* Pp. 713-31. New York: Columbia University Press

Hewes, Gordon. 1973. 'Indian fisheries productivity in pre-contact times in the Pacific salmon area.' *Northwest Anthropological Research Notes* 7(2):133-55

Hill-Tout, Charles. 1905. 'Report on the ethnology of the StlatlumH of British Columbia.' *Journal of the Royal Anthropological Institute* 30:126-218

Kennedy, Dorothy and Randy Bouchard. 1978. 'Fraser River Lillooet: An ethnographic summary.' In A. Stryd and S. Lawhead (eds.), *Reports of the Lillooet Archaeological Project, No. 1, Introduction and Setting.* Pp. 22-55. National Museum of Man, Mercury Series, Archaeological Survey of Canada, Paper No. 73, Ottawa

–. 1986. 'Stl'átl'imx (Fraser River Lillooet) fishing.' Victoria: British Columbia Indian Language Project

Lovell, N.C., B.S. Chisholm, D.E. Nelson, and H.P. Schwarzc. 1986. 'Prehistoric salmon consumption in Interior British Columbia.' *Canadian Journal of Archaeology* 10:99-106

Mitchell, D.S. 1925. 'A story of the Fraser River's great sockeye runs and their loss.' Unpublished ms. on file with the Pacific Salmon Commission and BC Provincial Archives

Mitchell, Donald and Leland Donald. 1985. 'Some economic aspects of Tlingit, Haida, and Tsimshian slavery.' *Research in Economic Anthropology* 7:19-35

Morice, A.G. 1905. *The History of the Northern Interior of British Columbia (Formerly New Caledonia), 1660-1880.* Toronto: William Briggs

Riches, David. 1979. 'Ecological variation on the Northwest Coast: Models for the generation of cognatic and matrilineal descent.' In P. Burnham and R.F. Ellen (eds.), *Social and Ecological Systems.* Pp. 45-66. New York: Academic Press

Rosman, Abraham and Paula Rubel. 1986. 'The evolution of central Northwest Coast societies.' *Journal of Anthropological Research* 42(4):557-72

Romanoff, Steven. 1972. 'The Lillooet hunter.' First year qualifying paper,

Department of Anthropology, Columbia University, New York. On file, Cariboo College, Kamloops, BC

–. 1986. 'Fraser Lillooet salmon fishing.' *Northwest Anthropological Research Notes* 19(2):119-60

Rowe, J.S. 1959. *Forest Regions of Canada*. Canada Department of Northern Affairs and Natural Resources, Forestry Branch Bulletin 123, Ottawa

Ruyle, Eugene E. 1973. 'Slavery, surplus, and stratification on the Northwest Coast: The ethnoenergetics of an incipient stratification system.' *Current Anthropology* 14(5):603-31

Schalk, Randall. 1977. 'The structure of an anadromous fish resource.' In L.R. Binford (ed.), *For Theory Building in Archaeology*. New York: Academic Press

–. 1981. 'Land use and organizational complexity among foragers of Northwestern North America.' *Senri Ethnological Studies* 9:53-75

Sneed, Paul G. 1972. 'Of salmon and men: An investigation of ecological determinants and aboriginal man in the Canadian Plateau.' In A. Stryd and R. Smith (eds.), *Aboriginal Man and Environments on the Plateau of Northwest America*. Pp. 229-42. Calgary: University of Calgary Student's Press

Steward, Julian. 1977. 'The foundations of Basin-Plateau Shoshonean society.' In J. Steward and R. Murphy (eds.), *Evolution and Ecology, Essays on Social Transformation*. Pp 366-406. Urbana: University of Illinois Press

Suttles, Wayne. 1962. 'Variation in habitat and culture on the Northwest Coast.' *Proceedings of the Thirty-fourth International Congress of Americanists, Vienna*. Pp. 522-37

–. 1968. 'Coping with abundance: Subsistence on the Northwest Coast.' In R. Lee and I. DeVore (eds.), *Man the Hunter*. Pp. 56-68. Chicago: Aldine

Teit, James A. 1900. 'The Thompson Indians of British Columbia.' *Memoirs of the American Museum of Natural History* 2(4):163-391

–. 1906. 'The Lillooet Indians.' *Memoirs of the American Museum of Natural History* 4(5):193-300

Walker, Deward E., Jr. 1967. 'Mutual cross-utilization of economic resources in the Plateau: An example from aboriginal Nez Perce fishing practices.' *Report of Investigations, No. 41*. Washington State University, Laboratory of Anthropology, Pullman

CHAPTER TEN

Conflict and Salmon on the Interior Plateau of British Columbia

Aubrey Cannon

This chapter uses a cultural ecological perspective to examine the role of salmon, the most important of Plateau resources, in structuring the pattern of hostile inter-group relationships. It specifically develops some of the insights provided by Romanoff in Chapter 5 concerning conflict and differential access to salmon.

The ethnographies of the Fraser Plateau Salish of British Columbia provide clear evidence of a causal relationship between the availability of salmon and patterns of regional conflict. This evidence contradicts regional analyses that have characterized Plateau peoples as pacifists who made extraordinary efforts to share or otherwise grant open access to resources (e.g., Jorgensen 1980:143; Ray 1939:35-8, 145). Such views have minimized the periodic intensity and long-term persistence of Fraser Plateau conflict, and they entirely overlook the private ownership of chinook salmon fishing sites documented in Chapters 5 and 6 as well as the basis of conflict in the unequal distribution of the vitally important salmon resource. To groups subject to salmon shortfalls, offensive raiding was an advantageous economic strategy for maintaining or improving access to salmon supplies. Raiding brought cultural and material advantages unmatched by other available strategies, and these advantages determined the pattern and intensity of conflict between groups. Material concerns, rather than personal motives of revenge or prestige, provided the underlying basis of Plateau conflict. Conflict was more a reasoned, chosen strategy than an inevitable response to resource deprivation.

In developing an ecological perspective on Interior Salish warfare, the present study focuses on the relationship between conflict and the practical problems of maintaining life and living standards (Ferguson 1984a:23), but it does not consider conflict a last resort in the face of extreme pressures of resource deprivation. The focus is on conflict as an economic strategy of choice, the advantages of which are defined and pursued within a context of cultural values that are structured but not determined by ecological circumstance. A similar perspective has been taken in a number of recent studies (e.g., papers in Ferguson 1984b), which view economic motives as the essential basis of human conflict, but which recognize that such motives are generated and tempered through systems of social and psychological values.

The Interior Salish of British Columbia provide a particularly good case study for the examination of the economic basis of conflict because the Lillooet, Thompson, and Shuswap groups of the Fraser Plateau: (1) shared a common linguistic and cultural background; (2) inhabited a well-defined and restricted area; (3) shared similar ecological adaptations; and (4) were the subject of the descriptive ethnographies of a single ethnographer. The ethnographies of James Teit (1900, 1906, 1909) were detailed, thorough, and consistent in their descriptions of Fraser Plateau conflict and resource exploitation. Although Teit recorded the intensity, form, and direction of Fraser Plateau conflict, he did not develop theoretical or ecological interpretations beyond the historical particularist perspective of his editor, Franz Boas. The relationship between environment and conflict that emerges from an ethnographic synthesis is therefore certainly not due to any materialist bias on the part of the ethnographer.

PEOPLE AND RESOURCES

In following Teit's ethnographies, this paper also makes use of his designations for tribal divisions and subdivisions. Lillooet, Thompson, and Shuswap tribal divisions are based on common territory as well as language and cultural affinities. Teit refers to these groups as tribes, and refers to some of their various subdivisions as bands. This usage is retained here as a matter of convenience, though it is important to emphasize that no unity of social or political organization is implied by the use of either term. The geographic location of these tribes (and their subdivisions) is presented in Figure 2 of Chapter 1.

Although the habitat of the Lillooet, Thompson, and Shuswap varies considerably, from the rugged hills of the eastern slope of the Coast Mountain range to the dry plateau and rolling hills of the regions further east, the territory is dominated throughout by the drainage system of the Fraser River. The availability of plant resources, deer, and other game also varies considerably throughout this region, but it is the availability of the anadromous salmon resource of the Fraser River system that is the key to understanding the pattern of conflict that prevailed among the Salish groups of the Fraser Plateau.

Salmon distribution controlled patterns of conflict because of the dominant importance of this resource in meeting the subsistence requirements of many Interior Salish groups. Teit's ethnographic descriptions are unfortunately brief, but from the data presented in Chapters 5 and 6, there can be no doubt that salmon fishing was the most important industry of the Lillooet. Salmon is also said to have been the principal food of the lower divisions of the Thompson, though of less importance to the upper divisions, who relied more on deer hunting (Teit 1900:230). Among the Shuswap, salmon was of greatest importance to the Fraser River and Canyon divisions, while game was most important to the rest of the tribe (Teit 1909:513). In comparison with the Thompson, the Shuswap were generally less dependent on salmon. A variety of game other than deer, and large numbers of plant foods, were also important to all groups living on the Fraser Plateau.

From early ethnographic descriptions it is difficult to discern the relative importance of salmon as a subsistence resource. In most cases relative importance is ascribed on the basis of the amount of time and energy invested in different subsistence activities. In other cases importance is discussed in terms of proportional contribution to diet, but it is not clear whether this proportion was constant or varied throughout the year. It is also not clear whether contribution to diet should be regarded as contribution to total caloric intake or some other nutritional requirement. This scope for different interpretations has left room for debate concerning Fraser Plateau Salish reliance on the salmon resource.

It has long been assumed that salmon was the critical resource on the Plateau, but recent work on the southern Plateau has demonstrated that a variety of alternative resources were potentially able to make a substantial contribution to the aboriginal diet (Hunn 1980, 1981; Hunn and French 1981; Ames and Marshall 1981; Norton et al. 1984). In the estimate of one study, plant resources supplied up to 70 per cent of the food energy needs of the people living in the southern half of the Columbia-Fraser Plateau (Hunn 1981:132). These studies lend support to the contention that salmon may have been considerably less important to the groups living in the Interior than it was to neighbouring groups on the Coast (Sanger 1969:17). Yet they stand in marked contrast to studies of the Fraser Plateau that have demonstrated a strong correlation between aboriginal population and the productivity of the local salmon resource (Sneed 1971; Kew, Chapter 4). Despite the real and potential contribution of other resources, the Fraser Plateau Salish were culturally oriented and adapted to the levels of the locally available salmon resource. It was culturally important to maintain that level of access to salmon even in the face of periodic local shortage, and an active strategy in this effort appears to have been offensive raiding to take advantage of the local resources of others.

RESOURCE AND CONFLICT

The Nature of Conflict

Understanding the nature of Plateau Salish conflict is essential to an appreciation of its patterns and causes. At issue are: (1) whether Plateau conflict is best characterized in terms of large-scale warfare or randomly directed and sporadic raids; (2) the motives for raids; and (3) whether conflict was ever of major significance in the region.

Analyses of Plateau ethnographies have often greatly exaggerated the extent and degree of pacifism in the region (e.g., Ray 1939:35-8, 145; Jorgensen 1980:143, 220). Recent analysis has been sharply critical of this view, particularly as it applies to the southern Plateau (Kent 1980), and it is clear that there is equally little evidence to suggest a pacifist ideal among the Fraser Plateau Salish. Ethnographic descriptions indicate extensive raiding activity on the Fraser Plateau, and it is only through acknowledgement of the significance, consistency, and scale of these raids that it becomes possible to establish the pattern and cause of conflict in the region.

The ethnographies of Teit and others are replete with general references to raiding activity, with detailed descriptions of specific raids. The size of raiding parties is described as varying from as few as two or three individuals to as many as several hundred, with numbers commonly averaging between twenty and seventy individuals (Teit 1900:267; 1909:542). One Thompson war-party was said to have been 500 strong (Teit 1900:246). Problems in provisioning and maintaining an element of surprise generally militated against the formation of very large raiding parties (Teit 1900:266-7), but large parties were necessary if booty or slaves were the object of a raid (Nastich 1954:37). Although it is difficult to characterize the normal size of raiding parties from the tales of informants, there is no doubt that the occasional major raid was a prominent component of conflict among the Fraser Plateau Salish.

Apart from the scale of raids, another indication of the intensity of conflict is the number of casualties that were incurred. There are few specific references, but there are stories of up to forty to sixty individuals being killed in a single attack, and as many as 400 Lillooet were reportedly killed during a week-long extended Thompson raid.

Even with the likelihood of informant exaggeration in these specific instances, the intensity of conflict was obviously severe and could be fairly characterized as more than simple raiding activity motivated by a spirit of adventure or personal revenge. Nevertheless, it is probable that such large-scale raids represented exceptions to the general pattern.

A better indication of the nature of Plateau conflict was its long-term persistence in some areas. Thompson attacks on the Lillooet, for example, lasted for seventy years or more (Teit 1900:245). The Lillooet also engaged in a long period of warfare with the Shuswap at one time (Teit 1906:235). A variety of indirect evidence also suggests that warfare, or at least persistent raiding activity, was a chronic concern among the various groups of the Fraser Plateau Salish. Teit (1900:263-6, 1906:234-5, 1909:538-9) provides detailed descriptions of a variety of offensive weapons and elaborate defensive armour. Substantial fortresses were built, and, in some cases, these were encircled by stockades. Stockaded fortresses were particularly common among the Lillooet. Lillooet bands were most subject to attack, and their fortresses were often substantial structures, built in addition to regular habitations. This investment indicates that the Lillooet were the object of more than occasional small-scale raids.

Teit's ethnographies give clear evidence of the prevalence of conflict among the Fraser Plateau Salish, but they are less clear in providing an explanation for the direction, scale, intensity, and persistence of raiding activity. The desire for plunder, revenge, adventure, and the use of fishing and hunting locations are all described as specific motives for raids (Teit 1900:267; Nastich 1954:36). Anthropological analyses of the Fraser Plateau Salish have tended to emphasize personal motives of revenge and prestige as the basis of conflict (Ray 1939:38-39; Jorgensen 1980:246). The attraction of plunder is never elevated beyond the acquisitive desires of individuals, thereby denying an economic or ecological cause for the overall pattern of regional conflict.

Revenge is most often cited as the proximate cause of conflict, but it is not sufficient to account for the prevailing pattern of regional conflict. Apart from the general deficiencies of the revenge motive as an explanation for pre-state warfare (Ferguson 1984a:8), there are specific objections to assigning revenge a causal role in Plateau conflict. The Lower Lillooet, for example, were subject to Thompson raids for seventy years, yet they never mounted a reprisal raiding expedition into Thompson territory. Clearly, it was not revenge that continued to motivate Thompson raids over this period of time nor was revenge sufficient motive for the Lillooet to mount raids in return.

To move beyond the proximate causes of specific raids and the motives of individuals it is necessary to view the pattern of conflict across the region. A regionally based approach is described by Ferguson (1984a) as a systematic method for separating the ultimate material causes of warfare from the personal motives involved in individual attacks. Using this approach,

> one could assess whether a regional war pattern, including changing intensities of conflict, who initiates attacks, and who is attacked, conforms to expectations based on the analysis of material needs. If material considerations do account for the observed patterns . . . the most parsimonious explanation would be that the participants themselves are acting on these considerations. Other motives offered by informants would be considered epiphenomenal, unless it could be shown that these other motives would, independent of material need, produce the actual pattern of fighting. (Ferguson 1984a:41)

On the Fraser Plateau, the long-term regional pattern of conflict conforms to expectations based on the temporal and spatial distribution of salmon, and a systematic effort to supplement supplies through an economic strategy of offensive raiding.

Salmon and Conflict

The role of salmon in structuring the regional pattern of conflict is apparent from an outline of the direction and intensity of offensive raiding activity. Teit (1900, 1906, 1909) gives a broad outline of the varying intensity of raiding activity among the different bands of the Lillooet, Thompson, and Shuswap. The Lillooet were generally less warlike than the other tribes of the Interior, and they seldom mounted offensive raids (Teit 1906:236). Among the Thompson, the Lytton, Spences Bridge, and Nicola bands were most warlike, while the Upper Fraser band and the Lower Thompson band were much less warlike (Teit 1900:269). Of the Shuswap, only the Fraser River, Bonaparte, and Kamloops divisions engaged in war to any significant degree. The other divisions seldom engaged in war except in defence. The Canyon division did not engage in any wars (Teit 1909:540-1).

Figure 1 is a graphic illustration of the origin and direction of offensive raids. The direction of the arrows shows that most raiding activity was directed downstream along the Fraser drainage system. In effect, raiding was from areas of lesser and less consistent salmon resources toward regions where salmon were more plentiful and more consistently available. The Lower Lillooet possessed some of the most consistently abundant salmon fisheries in the region, and they were

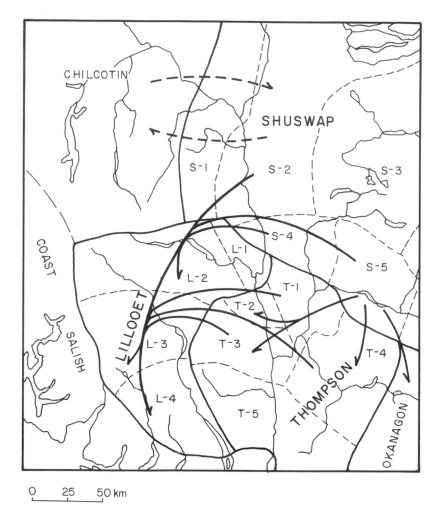

O   25   50 km

FIGURE 1
Location of Lillooet, Thompson, and Shuswap tribal divisions and subdivisions as well as neighbouring groups, showing the direction of consistent Thompson and Shuswap raiding activity

Lillooet:
L-1 Fraser River Band   } Upper Lillooet
L-2 Lake Band
L-3 Pemberton Band   } Lower Lillooet
L-4 Lillooet River Band

Figure 1 (continued)

Shuswap:
s-1 Cañon Division
s-2 Fraser River Division
s-3 Lake Division
s-4 Bonaparte Division
s-5 Kamloops Division

Thompson:
T-1 Spences Bridge Band
T-2 Upper Fraser Band
T-3 Lytton Band
T-4 Nicola Band
T-5 Lower Thompson

the frequent target of raids by many different groups living upstream.

Figure 1 also shows that although raids were generally directed downstream, it was rare for adjacent groups to be involved. Attacks were most often directed toward non-adjacent groups, even though adjacent groups were often in possession of rich salmon resources. The Fraser Lillooet and Canyon Shuswap had abundant salmon supplies, but they were rarely, if ever, the target of raids. These two groups were major trade suppliers of salmon to neighbouring groups (Teit 1900:259, 1909:535), and it is this role that helped to shelter them from attack. The role of trade in relation to conflict is discussed more fully below, but there were also other more immediate reasons for directing raids beyond adjacent groups. The attack of non-adjacent groups helped to discourage vengeance raids in return; the effectiveness of revenge as a motive for attack diminished with distance to the object of vengeance. Problems in the organization and provisioning of long-distance ventures, and the potential for interference from intermediary groups also acted to discourage the mounting of raids unless the potential returns were judged worthwhile.

Salmon acquisition was a worthwhile objective for upstream groups most liable to salmon shortage, and this motivation accounts well for the consistent downstream pattern of offensive raiding. In times of salmon shortage, groups with normally abundant resources could derive little gain by initiating raids against upstream groups subject to even more severe shortfalls in supply.

The correspondence between the spatial variability of salmon and the direction of raids is matched by a correspondence between the temporal variability of the salmon resource and the timing and periodicity of raids. The season of attack is not always described, and some raids took place at all seasons of the year, but the greatest number of attacks are described as having taken place in either the early spring or during the fishing season in the late summer and fall. Winter stores of dried salmon, if in short supply, would be nearing exhaustion in early spring, and it was at this time of year that the Lillooet became subject to attack by bands of the Thompson and Shuswap (Teit

1906:238, 243; 1909:556). The Lillooet stores of dried salmon were a principal object in these raids.

Attacks also took place during the end of the fishing season. The Fraser River Shuswap, for example, were subject to attack from Sekanai and Cree as they fished and prepared supplies of dried trout and salmon (Teit 1909:548, 551). During one period, the Sekanai made persistent attacks against the North Thompson Shuswap (Teit 1909:546-7) that eventually led to Sekanai occupation of Shuswap fisheries on the upper Fraser River. Later, the Sekanai mounted a major attack on the Shuswap who were gathered at the more productive fisheries of the North Thompson River. The Shuswap were forced to retaliate, and they finally drove the Sekanai from all of their occupied territory.

At least one other major incident of territorial occupation also centred around the fishing season. After a number of years of raids to steal fish, a large party of Shuswap occupied the principal salmon-fishing places of the Lower Pemberton band (Teit 1906:237-8). The Shuswap subsequently occupied the region every summer and fall and took away with them large supplies of dried salmon each winter. This pattern lasted for a number of years, though the Shuswap were eventually driven from the occupied territory after a period of progressively smaller incursions that may have signalled the return of full salmon productivity within their own territory.

Thus, on a seasonal scale, there is a definite correspondence between the timing of raids and seasons of maximum necessity or availability of salmon supplies. On a still larger scale, there is also indirect evidence of a relationship between the temporal cycles of salmon abundance and the periodicity of raiding activity. During a long period of Thompson raids on the Lower Lillooet, raids came at intervals of two, or sometimes four or five, years (Teit 1906:242). Shortfalls in the productivity of certain salmon species can occur at similar intervals. Pink salmon can show dramatic biannual variation in the size of spawning runs in the Fraser River system. At present, pink salmon are virtually absent in even numbered years (Aro and Shepard 1967:244). Fraser River sockeye salmon, one of the mainstays of the Native fishery, run in four-year cycles in which the size of the returning run is almost exclusively dependent on the spawning that occurred four years previously (Aro and Shepard 1967:232, 239). Sockeye runs eventually recover, but for some period a poor run will tend to repeat at four-year intervals. It is speculative, but not improbable, to suggest that raiding intervals in the above example were the direct result of cycles of salmon productivity.

The overall direction and timing of Fraser Plateau raids correlate well with variability in salmon productivity. Moreover, the descriptive accounts of raiding objectives support the view that salmon acquisition was the major factor in the motivation and structure of raiding activity. Salmon were obtained directly by stealing stored supplies or more dramatically by the occupation and control of fishing sites. Even the capture of slaves often provided an indirect means for gaining access to salmon.

The capture of 'booty' was a major incentive for launching raids, and stores of dried salmon were common booty. The Shuswap raided the Lillooet for the purpose of stealing salmon (Teit 1906:237; 1909:556), as did the Thompson (Teit 1900:268). Cree attacks on the Shuswap also had as their objective the capture of dried salmon supplies.

However, salmon was not the only gain to be derived from a successful raid. The capture of slaves was equally important and must be considered as a potentially integral factor in directing Fraser Plateau conflict. Interestingly, even the capture of slaves was at least partially related to ultimate efforts to acquire salmon.

Slavery

The taking of captives as slaves was an important component of raids on the Fraser Plateau, but the nature of slavery among the Interior Salish is not clear from ethnographic descriptions. Many captives were taken as slaves in raids (Teit 1900:269; 1906:238, 242-3, 246), and trade prices for slaves were high (Teit 1900:261; 1906:233), but the functional value of slaves is not clearly defined.

A number of recent studies have demonstrated that Northwest Coast slavery was of major economic importance (Mitchell 1984; Donald 1983, 1984), making the capture of slaves a prime motive for raids. Northwest Coast slaves served a direct economic role as captive labour (Mitchell 1984:39; Donald 1983) and objects of trade (Donald 1984), and the ownership of slaves was also of considerable prestige value. Therefore, to determine whether slave acquisition was of comparable importance as a motive for Plateau conflict, it is necessary to clarify whether slaves served similar economic and social roles among the Fraser Plateau Salish.

A major difference between Interior and Coast slavery was that there was no permanent class of slaves among the Fraser Plateau Salish as there was on the Northwest Coast. On the Plateau, many slaves, especially women, were kept to become a free and integral part of the owner's household, and children born to captive women assumed the social status of their fathers (Teit 1900:290; 1909:570, 582). The role of captive women as wives, child-bearers, and domestic workers was undoubtedly a major motive for their capture, but, unlike the situation on the Northwest Coast, the role of captive slaves as labour does not appear to have been of paramount importance.

On the Fraser Plateau, only a few slaves were ever kept in the households of their captors, though slaves did initially become the property of their captors (Nastich 1954:46) or other warriors who were proportionately awarded captives according to their bravery (Teit 1900:268). Western bands of the Shuswap were described as holding very few slaves (Teit 1909:576). Wealthy Lillooet households might maintain a number of slaves (Nastich 1954:23). But Teit (1900:269) notes that a Thompson warrior who took many slaves sold most of them when he reached home. This suggests that for many Plateau groups there was no economic advantage in holding and maintaining large numbers of slaves, and only the salmon-rich Lillooet were apparently able to do so. Certainly, ethnographies lack any description of an important labour role for captive slaves. Given this situation, it is difficult to understand the motive for taking large numbers of captives on major raids. This motive only becomes clear when the capture and distribution of slaves is seen in the context of the need to maintain a variety of strategies to obtain adequate salmon supplies in the face of periodic shortage.

Captive slaves played an important role in Plateau exchange relations, and most of the captives taken by the Shuswap, for example, were eventually sold back to their respective tribes (Teit 1909:469). An important focus for the return of captured slaves was the territory of the Fraser River Lillooet, where the Thompson and Shuswap frequently sold Lower Lillooet captives to the Upper Lillooet, who, in turn, received payment for their return to the Lower Lillooet (Teit 1906:233). The Fraser River Lillooet area was an ideal focus for the exchange of slaves because most captives taken by the Thompson and Shuswap were from Lower Lillooet bands, and all parties maintained good relations with the Fraser River Lillooet, who were important trade suppliers of salmon. In this area the institutions of trade, warfare, and slavery inter-related very closely in effecting the movement of salmon from areas of stable abundance to areas where the salmon resource was much less stable and abundant. Shuswap and Thompson bands that needed to supplement their locally available salmon supplies: (1) traded for salmon with the neighbouring Upper Lillooet, who had salmon in abundance; (2) raided nonadjacent Lower Lillooet bands for salmon and captives; and (3) traded some proportion of Lower Lillooet captives to the Upper Lillooet in exchange for salmon. Trading, raiding, and taking captives were all available strategies for obtaining salmon when supplies were needed.

Captives taken in raids also served more directly in the movement of salmon by carrying the heavy burdens of booty taken in raids (Teit 1906:244; 1909:547). In order to avoid immediate retribution, returning war-parties needed to move quickly and remain unencumbered so as to defend against possible attack while in unfriendly territory. Captive labour was therefore essential if war-parties were to carry home appreciable quantities of dried salmon.

As reconstructed here, the structure of raiding and slavery relationships on the Fraser Plateau was very much a function of salmon resource availability. With the exception of major salmon-suppliers, who were not subject to attack, the majority of large-scale raids were directed toward areas of greater salmon productivity. Although other motives for raids were no doubt important, the desire to obtain salmon as booty, hold and utilize salmon fisheries, and obtain captives to be used in subsequent exchange for salmon constituted a major part of the motives that directed and patterned Fraser Plateau raiding activity.

There was a definite economic basis to the pattern of Fraser Plateau conflict, but it is overly deterministic and simplistic to view conflict as the only viable economic alternative to resource deprivation and potential starvation. Conflict over salmon was not the only viable option in the face of salmon shortage. A variety of alternative solutions were available, and it is only by examining these and the extent to which they were utilized that the true nature of Plateau conflict as an economic strategy of choice becomes clear.

Alternatives to Conflict

Conflict was one of several options for maintaining living standards in the face of periodic salmon shortage. Alternatives included: (1) shared access to resources; (2) utilization of alternative resources such as plant foods; and (3) trade. Each of these alternatives was available and to some extent utilized, but their potential advantage fell far short of eliminating the strategic advantages provided by conflict.

Regional analyses of ethnographic data have exaggerated the extent and importance of resource sharing on the Fraser Plateau, while the potential dietary contribution of plant resources does not seem to have been capable of outweighing the returns provided by the critical cultural adaptations to the salmon resource. Trade was an important mechanism in the regional redistribution of salmon, but trade relations were complementary rather than alternatives to conflict. Groups that traded for salmon also raided, and groups geographically situated to act as salmon-suppliers in trade enhanced their economic advantage by acting as mediators in regional conflict. The options to share resources and trade for desired ends were pursued to mutual economic advantage, but a successful raid could be equally advantageous, and was culturally more acceptable and less costly than a radical refocus on alternative resources.

Shared Access

There has been an unwarranted tendency to overemphasize the importance and extent of shared access to Plateau resources (e.g., Ray 1939:16; Jorgensen 1980:130). There was some reciprocal access to extremely abundant local resources and resources at the perimeters of band ranges, especially among members of a particular tribal division or related individuals from adjacent tribal groups (e.g., Chapters 5 and 7; Teit 1900:293). Sites such as the Six Mile fishery could produce far more than local bands could process in short periods of time, and, therefore, these local groups could afford to share access to the site generously. In contrast, the more valuable chinook salmon fishing sites were individually owned and do not seem to have been shared with unrelated individuals (Chapter 5).

The recorded instances of local resource sharing are certainly insufficient basis for broad generalizations concerning the nature of regional inter-group relations. There is no justification for Jorgensen's (1980:130, 138-43) sweeping generalization that Plateau peoples emphasized communitarian principles and generally granted free and open access to resources whenever this was asked of them. Teit (1900:293) describes shared access to trout fishing and root digging locations, but, even in these instances, access was restricted to certain groups or related individuals, and outside intruders were liable to forfeit their lives.

Teit gives only two examples in which salmon was shared relatively freely. One example concerns the Nicola band of the Thompson, who had little salmon in their territory. In addition to bartering for salmon, some members of this group fished with their friends at Spences Bridge (Teit 1900:258). The other example concerns the Lake band of the Upper Lillooet, who fished with the neighbouring Fraser River Lillooet during the abundant salmon runs in the latter's territory. But this case appears to have been a special arrangement, since members of other tribes and Lower Lillooet bands generally had to trade for the salmon of the Fraser River Lillooet (Teit 1906:231-2). Free access to fish for salmon at the Six Mile fishery depended upon the distance between groups and the degree of intermarriage between them. Beyond the closest relations, access to salmon was either through trade or, at greater distances, raids (Chapter 5).

Teit's accounts of salmon trade are far more common than are his accounts of shared access to salmon, and the desire to obtain salmon as booty was a major motivation for raiding on the Fraser Plateau. Shared access was a localized phenomenon, based on kin and other immediate ties. To see it as the pattern for regional inter-relationships is a severe distortion of the recorded ethnographies. Conflict and economic trade were far more pervasive means for gaining access to salmon.

Trade

Trade was an important aspect of inter-group relations on the Fraser Plateau, and salmon was prominent among a wide range of commodities exchanged between groups. Salmon was an economic resource that was unevenly distributed but much in demand, and patterns of trade developed accordingly. Certain groups with particularly abundant salmon resources within their territories emerged as key players in trade relations, and they were able to turn their access to this important resource to their wider economic and political advantage. The Fraser River Lillooet and the Canyon Shuswap were particularly important salmon-suppliers to neighbouring groups. Not only did their favourable trade position allow these salmon-suppliers to accumulate wealth, it also provided them with virtual immunity from raids, despite the fact that other salmon-rich groups, such as the Lower Lillooet, were frequently the target of attack. The reason for this was the geographic relationships between groups and the complementary nature of trade and warfare as alternate means of salmon acquisition.

Figure 2 shows the direction of the salmon trade from three major suppliers. The general direction of trade was overwhelmingly upstream, as would be expected given the decreasing abundance and increasing variability of salmon in upstream localities. The one major exception was the Lower Lillooet trade for Fraser River Lillooet salmon, which they traded for in limited quantities because of the superior qualities salmon had when cured in a dryer climate (Teit 1906:232). The interesting point of the overall salmon trade pattern (Figure 2) is its contrast with the prevailing pattern of conflict in the region (Figure 1). Comparison of Figures 1 and 2 shows that groups that raided for salmon also traded for salmon. Access to salmon was through trade with adjacent suppliers and raids against nonadjacent salmon-rich groups. Salmon-rich trading partners, such as the Fraser River Lillooet and Canyon Shuswap, were not raided because of fear of easy reprisal and the greater advantage of trade over the less certain returns of conflict. A key trade position afforded salmon-suppliers protection from

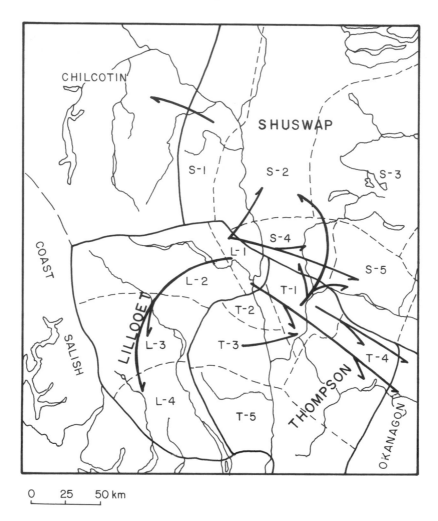

FIGURE 2

Location of tribal divisions and subdivisions showing the direction of
Upper Lillooet, Spences Bridge Thompson, and Canyon Shuswap
salmon trade (see legend in Figure 1)

attack, and they further enhanced their economic advantage by acting
as middlemen in the exchange of captives between hostile nonadjacent groups.

Although trade provided considerable access to salmon, it could
not supplant the advantages of raids in more adverse circumstances.

The ability to trade for salmon was restricted by the quantity of goods available for exchange. The available surplus of salmon was also limited by periodic shortfalls in the size of salmon runs and a ceiling on production determined by the availability of labour and points of access to salmon rivers.

Offensive raiding against nonadjacent salmon-rich groups was an advantageous complement to trade. The advantage of surprise and the low probability of reprisal made raiding a low risk enterprise, and any material yields were a clear gain over the returns of trade alone. Conflict and exchange were complementary strategies toward the same economic end, and neither was capable of serving as a complete alternative to the other.

Alternative Resources

Recent work has shown that the native populations of the southern Plateau depended on a variety of plant foods for a substantial portion of their subsistence needs (Hunn 1981; Hunn and French 1981). It is likely that such foods were also of equal importance to many of the peoples of the Fraser Plateau area (see Chapters 3 and 8). Therefore, it is possible to question whether or not there existed the potential for increasing the use of alternative resources in the face of salmon shortage or, in the face of consistent shortage, of reducing the critical dependence on salmon.

On a short-term basis, given a cultural adaptation to seasonal salmon fishing and preservation for winter use, it is unlikely that alternative resources could sufficiently compensate for salmon shortages. There was limited potential for increasing production of other resources, and little incentive to do so in the absence of any foreknowledge of specific shortfall in salmon runs. Over the long term, a refocus on alternative resources would likely be inadequate to replace salmon's critical extra-caloric dietary contribution (Hunn 1981:131), and major difficulties would result from the cultural restructuring attending subsistence reorientation.

The greatest potential for increasing yields of alternative resources was in the gathering of plant foods. To do this would require that men make a substantially greater contribution to what was predominantly women's work – and do so at the expense of time spent at traditionally male subsistence pursuits such as fishing and hunting. More importantly, placing greater emphasis on plant and other alternative resources would recognize the legitimate right of other groups to exercise exclusive control over the plentiful salmon resources in other regions. The costs and risks in seeking to exploit the salmon belonging to another group through raids were not prohibitive, and raiding provided an opportunity for individuals to enhance their prestige through acts of daring and skill. Such prestige could later be turned to social advantage, particularly when supported through distribution of the salmon, captives, and other booty acquired in raids. The group's subsistence needs and individual incentives, which were served by a strategy of conflict, probably could not be matched by a strategy of alternative resource utilization, which would require the labour-intensive harvesting and processing of plant resources only available for short periods during the year (see Chapters 3 and 8).

CONCLUSIONS

Fraser Plateau conflict and trade were complementary strategies in the maintenance of extra-territorial access to salmon. Relations of sharing (in limited circumstances), trade (with adjacent salmon-rich groups), and raids (against nonadjacent groups) were all part of an overall regional network that regulated the distribution of salmon to within generally tolerable limits for all groups. The ethnographically recorded pattern of conflict and trade was a direct function of variable salmon abundance and strategic efforts to maintain supply.

The emphasis here on a rational motivation for Fraser Plateau conflict is an important counterpoint to regional overviews that have over-emphasized the extent of pacifism and communitarian sharing among Plateau peoples. These studies present an idealized picture that is reminiscent of early views of the noble savage. They distort the ethnographic record in this case, and they further deny any possibility for an understanding of the causes of regional conflict.

Plateau conflict was neither an immediate emotional response nor an otherwise avoided last resort. It was, instead, the result of the choice of an acceptable threshold for war based on an assessment of its cultural and material advantages and disadvantages. Conflict was not the peripheral consequence of high spirits and individual aggressive tendencies nor was it the consequence of dire economic necessity. Conflict was a reasoned strategy for the resolution of unequal distribution of mutually desired resources, to the advantage of one group and the detriment of another. The potential for satisfying basic subsistence needs through shared access, trade, or alternative resources did not provide sufficient advantage to outweigh conflict as a successful and desirable strategy in this case. The wider implication of this study may be that because conflict has the potential to arise whenever a perceived advantage can be gained, its control must always involve far more than the simple provision of basic necessities.

REFERENCES

Ames, Kenneth and Alan Marshall. 1981. 'Villages, demography and subsistence intensification on the Southern Columbia Plateau.' *North American Archaeologist* 2:25-52

Aro, K.V. and M.P. Shepard. 1967. 'Pacific salmon in Canada.' Salmon of the North Pacific Ocean. Part IV. *International North Pacific Fisheries Commission Bulletin* 23:225-327

Donald, Leland. 1983. 'Was Nuu-chah-nulth-aht (Nootka) society based on slave labor?' In E. Tooker and M. Fried (eds.), *The Development of Political Organization in Native North America*. Pp. 108-19. 1979 Proceedings of the American Ethnological Society, Washington, DC: The American Ethnological Society

–. 1984. 'The slave trade on the Northwest Coast of North America.' In B. Isaac (ed.), *Research in Economic Anthropology*. Vol. 6. Pp. 121-58. Greenwich, Connecticut: JAI Press

Ferguson, R. Brian. 1984a. 'Introduction: Studying war.' In R. Ferguson (ed.), *Warfare, Culture, and Environment*. Pp. 1-81. Orlando: Academic Press

– (ed.). 1984b. *Warfare, Culture, and Environment*. Orlando: Academic Press

Hunn, Eugene. 1980. 'Sahaptin fish classification.' *Northwest Anthropological Research Notes* 14:1-19

–. 1981. 'On the relative contribution of men and women to subsistence among hunter-gatherers of the Columbia Plateau: A comparison with ethnographic atlas summaries.' *Journal of Ethnobiology* 1:124-34

Hunn, Eugene S. and David H. French. 1981. 'Lomatium: A key resource for Columbia Plateau native subsistence.' *Northwest Science* 55:87-94

Jorgensen, Joseph G. 1980. *Western Indians: Comparative Environments, Languages, and Cultures of 172 Western American Indian Tribes*. San Francisco: W.H. Freeman

Kent, Susan. 1980. 'Pacifism: A myth of the Plateau.' *Northwest Anthropological Research Notes* 14:125-34

Mitchell, Donald. 1984. 'Predatory warfare, social status, and the North Pacific slave trade.' *Ethnology* 23:39-48

Nastich, Milena. 1954. 'The Lillooet: An Account of the Basis of Individual Status.' Unpublished MA thesis, Department of Economics, Political Science, and Sociology, University of British Columbia, Vancouver

Norton, H.H., E.S. Hunn, C.S. Martinsen, and P.B. Keely. 1984. 'Vegetable food products of the foraging economies of the Pacific Northwest.' *Ecology of Food and Nutrition* 14:219-28

Ray, Verne F. 1939. *Cultural Relationships in the Plateau of North-Western America*. Publications of the Frederick Webb Hodge Anniversary Publication Fund, vol. 3. Los Angeles: Southwest Museum

Sanger, David. 1969. 'Development of the Pacific Northwest Plateau culture:

Historical and environmental considerations.' In D. Damas (ed.), *Contributions to Anthropology: Ecological Essays.* Pp. 15-23. National Museums of Canada, Bulletin No. 230, Ottawa

Sneed, Paul G. 1971. 'Of salmon and men: An investigation of ecological determinants and aboriginal man in the Canadian Plateau.' In A. Stryd and R. Smith (eds.), *Aboriginal Man and Environment on the Plateau of Northwest America.* Pp. 229-42. Calgary: University of Calgary Student's Press

Teit, James A. 1900. 'The Thompson Indians of British Columbia.' In F. Boas (ed.), *Memoirs, American Museum of Natural History* 2(4):163-392

–. 1906. 'The Lillooet Indians.' *Memoirs, American Museum of Natural History* 2(5):193-300

–. 1909. 'The Shuswap Indians.' *Memoirs, American Museum of Natural History,* 4(7):443-758

CHAPTER ELEVEN

Conclusions:
Ecology and Complex Hunter/Gatherers

Brian Hayden

The preceding chapters have presented abundant observations that will be useful for creating quantitative models of resource use (Reidhead 1979), settlement size and location (Croes and Hackenberger 1988), group mobility patterns and composition, archaeological settlement pattern models, and many other issues concerning traditional cultures in the study area. One basic aim of this volume is to provide as complete a descriptive base as possible for the generation and evaluation of such models. Another goal is to explore the relationship between ecology, resources, and technology on the one hand and fundamental social characteristics of traditional cultures on the other hand. In Chapter 9, Steven Romanoff documented the unusual status, privileged position, and the elaborate training of the specialized Lillooet hunter. He provided several suggestions as to ways in which this unusual complex of behaviour could be adaptive for the community.

Similarly, in Chapter 10, Aubrey Cannon examined one of the types of behaviour with clearest consequences for survival: warfare. Because of the considerable risks and costs involved, this type of social behaviour ought to be strongly influenced by ecological and adaptive considerations. The widespread cross-cultural occurrence of intergroup conflict and its considerable persistence over time also indicate that it has some fundamental ecological significance, although there is little consensus among anthropologists as to what that might be. Cannon's study of this phenomenon and the closely related occurrence of slavery in the Interior constitutes a major advance in our understanding of factors that determine the frequency and intensity of conflict in the Interior. Although it remains a provocative local model for the time being, awaiting broader comparative application, support for his general perspective on warfare does exist from other parts of the world.

In Australia, critical resource shortages were generally dealt with through alliance relationships but were also dealt with on some occasions by forceful displacement of groups from desired resource areas (Strehlow 1965). In the American Great Basin, Chagnon (1970) has documented almost identical behaviour and termed it the 'trade or raid' syndrome. Viewing warfare as one half of a double-barrelled adaptive strategy is obviously a topic for a much more extended analysis, but the outlines of a major advance in our understanding of conflict among hunter/gatherers may now be emerging.

In the remainder of this chapter, I would like to examine the implications of data presented in the preceding chapters for understanding the major social features that characterize the complex hunter/gatherers of the Lillooet study area: socioeconomic inequality, restricted access to resources, and corporate groups. I will not address models that deal with these phenomena from other perspectives (e.g., population pressure models) since those have been addressed in previous publications (Hayden 1981a, 1990) and since I intend to raise those issues in subsequent analyses.

In the introduction to this volume, I argued that there were strong reasons for viewing each of the above social features as strongly affected by ecological conditions. This provides the conceptual framework within which the following discussion is structured. This ecological conceptual framework has given rise to a number of relatively well established theories on the effects of resource characteristics on social characteristics of *generalized* hunter/gatherers, notably: obligatory sharing, alliance formation, mobile and fluid membership, general equality in access to resources within groups, and proscriptions on economically based competitive behaviour. From this theoretical foundation, a number of expectations, or hypotheses, can be developed to structure the inquiry into economic inequality, restricted access to resources, restricted sharing, and economically competitive behaviour. These can be evaluated in a preliminary, and at least qualitative, fashion at this point.

Specifically, one might expect that if egalitarianism, sharing, and open access to all resources or personal property are adaptive under conditions of limited, fluctuating, and vulnerable resources, then the occurrence of inequality, private property, and restricted access should reflect some fundamental change in the above resource characteristics. Are there any differences in resource characteristics that can be identified, even on a relative scale? I will examine these expectations. But since association of variables does not necessarily imply direct causality, I will also deal with the question of possible causal mechanisms responsible for changes. In the following discussion I will limit myself to evaluating the roles of only the most important staples in the study area: salmon, deer, saskatoon berries, and subalpine roots. Obviously, a full evaluation should also take into account less prominent food items; however, the preliminary nature of this synthesis does not permit such detailed analysis. The first step is to clearly set out the values of the resource variables in the study area.

RESOURCE CHARACTERISTICS IN THE STUDY AREA

Resource Abundance

The first variable of importance is abundance of resources. The authors have provided well-researched estimates of just how much food was potentially available for harvesting as well as how much was actually harvested with traditional technology. It is important to stress the role of technology and physical access in determining the amount of food actually procured. For example, it is clear from Kew's data in Chapter 4 that millions of salmon traversed the study area every year, however, aboriginal technology and limited points of access only permitted the harvesting of a small fraction of the total resource. Thus, it is also important to take into account observations on the actual quantities obtained, assuming that these represent the total amount that could be harvested by groups. Even if we consider the accounts recorded by Romanoff (Chapter 5) and Kennedy and Bouchard (Chapter 6) as 'best year' estimates and reduce them slightly, it appears that families with proper access could obtain at least 300-400 spring salmon and 200-300 sockeye per year (about 9,000 pounds total, or 1,800 pounds per person for a family of five, or 5 pounds per person per day). This most likely under-represents the amount of salmon procurable prior to Euro-Canadian impacts on resources; however, the absolute number of spring salmon may never have been great, and springs appear to have been available in quantity only to the owners of the twenty or so spring salmon fishing rocks (assuming sites with platforms would have been owned). Nevertheless, the above estimates still indicate surpluses for many families. Thus, some of these salmon may have been used for exchange, although, by the turn of the century, some traditional trading patterns were probably replaced by commercial transactions. At The Dalles, in Washington, a comparable fishery on the Columbia River produced even greater quantities of surplus (Hunn 1990:133).

Another technological factor to take into consideration is storage. Due to the rapid spoilage characteristics of fish resources, only a small portion of the amount harvestable could actually be consumed unless preservation technology was employed. While other resources certainly supplemented salmon staples, it is clear from density estimates that they did not compare to the enormous resource potential of salmon.

As Alexander notes in Chapter 2, the deer population of the core study area was limited to 100-600, depending on weather conditions, with a sustainable harvest of about 20 per cent; and probably considerably less than that was actually procured prior to the use of firearms, especially considering that, even today, wildlife researchers estimate that cougars cull two deer for every one that hunters take (Dave Low, personal communication 1990). Some replenishment, however, probably occurred from migration. There were many fewer mountain sheep in the area than deer, and sheep were considered less desirable than deer. Given their low population density and inferior eating status, it is not surprising that sheep bones are rare in archaeological assemblages.

Thus, the maximum average number of deer that might be expected from hunters competing with cougars (assuming a ratio of 1:2 for their respective kills) would be about ten to forty deer per year, although, under favourable conditions, much higher numbers might be achieved in specific years. Such culling rates are not enough to sustain a human population in the hundreds (and possibly as high as a thousand) for more than a few weeks in the year. Even though Sam Mitchell reported an oral account of a famous hunter having killed 100 deer in a single hunt (Chapter 9), this was undoubtedly during the major communal hunt of the year, and certainly by Indian standards was an extremely exceptional event. Even if this event was exaggerated, it still must have depleted the local deer population for a number of years. The recollection of such hunts is consistent with Dave Low's view (personal communication 1989) that traditional hunting was opportunistic to the extent that Indians killed as many deer as possible and could harvest large numbers if snow conditions were appropriate. The low estimates of average harvesting potential for ungulates are supported by Romanoff's documentation of the rarity of buckskin among the Lillooet (Chapter 9).

Similarly, the major geophyte staples, spring beauty and avalanche lily 'roots,' appear to have provided abundant food while groups were in the mountains during the spring, but stored supplies may have been relatively limited. In Chapter 8, Turner estimates that families harvested 8-33 kg of avalanche lily 'roots' and 10-25 kg of spring beauty 'roots.' Even in recent years, with packhorses, the bulk of these roots were consumed in the mountains and not stored (Chapter 6 & 9; Chapter 8, Appendix 2). Prior to the use of packhorses, the amount brought back to winter villages may have been limited by the weight that a family could carry out of the mountains in one or two trips. Certainly, the lack of any spring beauty plant remains in the intensive paleobotanical analysis of the Keatley Creek winter village site (Lepofsky, personal communication) is interesting and indicates that, prehistorically, stored spring beauty corms may have been largely consumed by late fall. On the other hand, these geophyte staples probably would have been processed high in the mountains and would not have left many remains when eaten at locations such as winter villages far from procurement and processing sites. Turner, Alexander, and Tyhurst all comment on the relatively restricted availability of spring beauty and avalanche lily 'roots' in the study area when compared to the much greater amounts obtainable in Botanie Valley and Potato Mountain. Only in the Intermediate Grassland around Pavilion Ranch does spring beauty occur in truly dense stands. Moreover, at least some of the subalpine plant resources are vulnerable to overharvesting (see below). The fact that salmon and berries are mentioned as winter food by Sam Mitchell and others, but that spring beauty and other plants are not, also indicates that these foods were more limited in abundance on the BC Plateau than some ethnographers for other parts of the Plateau suggest (Ames and Marshall 1981; Thoms 1989). Turner (Chapter 8) considers saskatoon berries to have generally been abundant enough to constitute 10 per cent of the total calories consumed. At present, there is no way of independently assessing abundance or use, although it is worth noting that crops vary significantly from year to year, and that berry abundance is not generally affected by excessive exploitation.

Despite the best attempts to assess both the availability and access to resources, the intervening effects of technology and the difficulty of gaining access to productive sites and labour render absolute measures difficult to obtain, although the above data certainly provide a solid general sense of the resource potential and realizable harvests of the area. Given this situation, an indirect but closely related and quantifiable measure of resource abundance may be more useful than complex calculations of absolute abundance. One of the best proxy variables for resource abundance is population density. Population density does not appear to have been significantly above the carrying capacity of the area, since large portions of the population were not consistently starving every year, as in the case of the Ik described by Turnbull (1972). On the other hand, factors such as disease and warfare do not seem to have been holding the early populations much below their maximum potential density, since there are reports of at least two pre-gold rush and pre-cannery food shortages (Chapters 5, 6, and 9). Thus, the early population seems to have been in a reasonable semblance of balance with resource abundance in the area. On this basis, the 1,000 people at the Bridge River and Six Mile fishery that Simon Fraser observed in 1808 (most of whom probably lived in the *expanded* study area) constituted a population density approaching one person per square kilometre. If the census figures at the end of the century are used instead, this still constitutes a population density of about 0.3 people per square kilometre. Prehistorically, the population of the core study area appears to have been considerably higher than either of these two estimates (Chapter 1). Whatever measure one wishes to use, population levels were far above those that characterize generalized hunter/gatherers. Resource levels must have been correspondingly greater than the resource abundances typical of generalized hunter/gatherers, and the absolute observations that we have obtained of extractable resources in the Lillooet region certainly support this conclusion.

For instance, if the availability of all salmon is averaged over the four-year sockeye cycle (Chapter 4), about 7.80 million salmon would be available on average per year. Ricker (1987) argues that the sockeye figures should be increased by 50 per cent for most of the nineteenth century and indicates that many more million pink salmon should have been available in the Lillooet area before the Hell's Gate slide (Ricker 1989). It is clear that Kew's estimates, as he himself indicates, are minima, and that the unusually low yields of the 1940s documented in Chapter 6 are atypical. The low catches of the 1940s were undoubtedly affected by increased emphasis on wage labour (Chapter 5), the unusual labour demands during the war years, and the continuing adverse effects of the Hell's Gate slide, which were not ameliorated until after 1945 when fish ladders were built. A population of 500 (100 families) that obtained 60,000 salmon per year (a culling rate of less than 0.8 per cent of Kew's estimated availability) could supply most of it's caloric needs for the year as well as use a considerable amount for trade. Hudson's Bay Company journals for Fort Kamloops, for instance indicate that fur traders expected to be able to obtain 6,000 salmon from trade along the Fraser River in 1826, and that they did obtain 8,400 salmon in 1843 (McDonald, 27 November 1826; Tod, 4 October 1843). The 'Fountain' fishery neighbourhood is specifically identified as the location 'where we trade our salmon' (McDonald, 30 September 1826; Anderson, 18 May 1846). Moreover, the Fort Kamloops traders sometimes had to compete with Natives who offered higher exchange rates than Fort Kamloops traders could afford (McDonald 3 January 1827). Thus, surpluses appear to have been of considerable proportions.

Fluctuations

All the authors dealing with salmon emphasize the variable nature of this resource. In Chapter 4, Kew documents the predictable cyclical fluctuations of the various salmon species, particularly the four-year peak-to-trough cycle of the sockeye. Unfortunately, no information is available on possible early cycles of the spring salmon. Kennedy and Bouchard (Chapter 6) and Romanoff (Chapter 9) document other local factors that have significant impacts on the salmon harvest in the study area. They also indicate that a number of pre-gold rush accounts of serious food shortages exist in unpublished oral histories and archival records (Chapters 6 and 9). Shortages in other regions are also reported for early years, for example, near Mount Curry in 1846 (Anderson 1846:21 May); Fort St. James in 1899 and 1900 (Cooper and Henry 1962:4-5); and a severely delayed run at Fort Kamloops in 1843 (Tod 1843: 12 August-7 September). Colvile reported that in 1851, not a single salmon was caught at Stuart Lake, Fraser Lake, Fort Alexandria, or Fort George due to the failure of the Fraser River salmon run (Bowsfield 1979:xxxi). Unusually high water temperatures or unusually high river levels appear capable of blocking salmon migrations up the Fraser River or of stressing salmon to the point where they fail to spawn after completing migrations (Cooper and Henry 1962; Gilhousen 1990). It is probably these factors that were largely responsible for prehistoric and early contact salmon failures and episodic famines.

For mammals, there are no quantified observations on fluctuations in the study area. However, natural deer populations in the Kamloops district have fluctuated between 12,000 and 55,000 according to cycles of severe winters that seem to occur about every eighteen years (Dave Low, personal communication 1990). Elsewhere, deer are also known to experience population cycles. These cycles, together with the periodic mass harvesting of deer under snow conditions restricting their mobility, must have severely depleted deer stocks in the study area from time to time and over a number of successive years. According to Low's estimates, deer in the core study area must have periodically dropped to very low levels, of about 125, and would have then provided little in the way of food for the resident human population.

Much less is known about plant staples. In an undisturbed situation, there is no reason to suppose that avalanche lily or spring beauty corms would fluctuate dramatically from year to year unless climatic conditions adversely affected their flowering, thereby greatly increasing the search time involved in their procurement, or unless they were heavily overexploited in patches where they only occurred in moderate densities. As for the other plant species, berries, especially saskatoon berries, are even today notable for their highly variable yearly production.

Thus, certainly with salmon, probably with deer, and possibly with spring beauty and avalanche lilies, there were major fluctuations in the availability and accessibility of staple resources. Some of this variability, such as the sockeye salmon cycles, was predictable while other periods of scarcity were not. One of the most fruitful questions that cultural ecologists can deal with is how communities cope with the prospect of both predictable and unpredictable (but expectable) food shortages. Given the seriousness of these occurrences for human survival, it is not surprising to find that most cultures have developed a variety of different strategies, a point to which I will return. Romanoff (Chapter 9) suggests that specialized hunting and feasting may be one such strategy. Clearly, storage of food, trading, and raiding are others; and I examine storage next.

Storage

A number of prehistorians have drawn attention to the fact that generalized hunter/gatherers do not tend to store significant amounts of food beyond a few days (except in Arctic or Subarctic winter conditions) whereas complex hunter/gatherers do (Testart 1982; Soffer 1989; Binford 1980:18). Storage enables a community to make much fuller use of extremely abundant resources that are only accessible for short periods of time, like salmon, spring beauty, and unusual numbers of deer trapped in deep snow. All of the staple foods of the study area are amenable to preservation and storage for varying lengths of time (up to two or more years for salmon). The major disadvantages of storing food are the high labour costs (drying, creating drying facilities, gathering fuel, smoking, and properly preparing foods), creating storage facilities, transporting food in bulk to storage or consumption locations, and becoming tethered for some length of time to locations where food is stored. Food species vary in many of these characteristics.

As documented by Romanoff (Chapter 5), Kennedy and Bouchard (Chapter 6), Turner (Chapter 8), and Alexander (Chapter 3), all three major staples (salmon, deer, and subalpine roots), require considerable labour investment in order to prevent them from rapidly spoiling. Salmon and deer require careful filleting, drying, and smoking, while elaborate earth ovens involve large amounts of fuel, rock, and protective plant material. Thoms (1989:226) records that 1,000 kg of rock was required for processing 500 kg of camas. Estimates for filleting sockeye salmon range from thirty to eighty per day using metal cutting tools (Chapters 5 and 9; Bouchard and Kennedy 1990:259). Presumably, this rate would have been lower when stone tools were used. Preparation of roasting pits would depend on quantities to be processed as well as desired cooking time. Alexander suggests that the whole cooking process could require a full day of preparation on the part of each person participating in the event and up to one day of actual cooking requiring only occasional monitoring. Turner (Chapter 8) provides an estimate of two people's labour for an entire day to fully prepare a single roasting pit. According to Thoms (1989:234), harvesting time must be more than doubled to properly process, transport, and store geophytes such as camas. His study is one of the few that includes transport costs involved in storage. He suggests that, beyond 10 km, transport costs become prohibitive in relation to returns (1989:228). All the above labour requirements logically entail possible important consequences for understanding social characteristics. These are discussed below.

Travel, Procurement, and Processing Requirements

Travel and procurement times to resources are dependent, among other things, on resource density and patch grain. Due to the high density of the most important staples and their coarse patch grain, these values are probably as low or lower than any values found among generalized hunter/gatherers. Absolute estimates for salmon procurement can be inferred from information provided by Romanoff (Chapter 5) and Kennedy and Bouchard (Chapter 6). These vary from a few fish per day at the beginning of the season to as much as 100 salmon per hour at the peak of the runs, according to Desmond Peters, who noted that he once obtained twenty-one sockeye and one spring salmon in a single sweep of a six-foot set-net. These last estimates are probably very exceptional; nevertheless, figures of similar orders of magnitude (200-300 salmon per night per fisherman) are recorded as early as 1822 for the Fort Kamloops area (MacMillan and McLeod, 22 August 1822) as well as several hundred per day per fisherman during peak runs near Lillooet and twelve to fifteen salmon per net sweep during peak runs (Chapter 6). The actual *usable* number of fish during peak runs, however, was limited by the number of women available to process the salmon (about thirty to sixty fish per day per woman). Both Romanoff (Chapter 5) and Kennedy and Bouchard (Chapter 6) record considerable waste of caught salmon because women could not butcher and dry them as fast as they could be caught.

Turner (Chapter 8) also provides procurement harvest yields per day for all staples, and these are on the order of 250 ml of saskatoon berries in five minutes, three kilograms per day for spring beauty 'roots,' and one to two kilograms per day for avalanche lily 'roots' (see also Hunn 1990:109). Unfortunately, we do not have good estimates of search times involved in deer hunting. Once at a hunting campsite, drives involved two to four men working for about half a day. They usually stopped when an agreed-to quota of deer kills was reached, usually about one per family. Desmond Peters also indicated that about one deer per hour could be obtained once hunters were in locations frequented by deer. It is unclear how many deer could be culled from specific localities before returns dropped to unproductive levels. The generally short travel and search times that characterize the study area enhance the overall effects of increased abundance on the social characteristics to be discussed shortly.

Processing times for the consumption of salmon, deer, and subalpine roots in their *fresh* state should not differ appreciably from processing values for generalized hunter/gatherers, although we lack direct information on this aspect. Processing time and effort necessary for the *storage* of all of these staples by groups in the study area (discussed in the previous section), on the other hand, are clearly much greater than are values for generalized hunter/gatherers. It is, in part, this added investment of labour in easily obtainable foods which may result in reduced obligatory sharing of these resources.

Vulnerability to Overexploitation

As noted by Kew (Chapter 4), salmon is one of the classic examples of an *r*-selected species that is difficult for humans to overexploit using pre-industrial technology. Female salmon lay an average of 4,500 eggs each. Prior to the arrival of Euro-Canadians, the Fraser River drainage was one of the richest spawning grounds in the world for salmon, and it is inconceivable that the Native fishery could have had any significant adverse impact on this resource (Chapter 4). As Kew states in Chapter 4, and as Bruce Winterhalder (personal communication) has also emphasized, salmon are among the few species that spend most of their life cycle in an environment that is immune to traditional human predation, where they accumulate and store energy from relatively vast areas. Salmon are only exposed to harvesting during their migration spawning phase when they enter streams in such a prolific pulse that it saturates the ability of traditional human predators to do much damage to the population.

Deer produce far fewer offspring but are sexually mature after their first year. Thus, while populations can be temporarily depleted, early sexual maturity and migrations from one area to another render these populations relatively resilient under moderate harvesting pressures and favourable weather conditions. Harvesting over 20 per cent of a herd per year on a regional basis should lead to lower deer densities, which would only stabilize at the point where increased search time diminished the caloric return value of the resource. Deer would still be pursued below this level on an encounter basis but such encounters would be infrequent. Given pre-industrial technology, it would probably have been difficult to overexploit deer populations under weather conditions favourable for their reproduction and survival (Chapter 2). However, in unfavourable weather conditions, with deep winter snow, herds could be severely depleted by groups using snowshoes and bows (Low, personal communication 1990). Mountain sheep populations appear to be less resilient, since they are more vulnerable in the winter and, in fact, were extirpated in the core study area at the beginning of this century.

Berries are not adversely affected by intensive harvesting. They are good examples of r-selected species. On the other hand, spring beauty and avalanche lilies may have been some of the most vulnerable resources to overexploitation where these occurred in only moderate amounts. Lilies, in particular, are K-selected types of species yielding few new plants and being easily overcropped. In fact, they are so vulnerable to overexploitation that picking flowers of some lily species is actively discouraged by conservation groups in British Columbia, who view these species as endangered in many regions.

Nutrition

Many hunter/gatherers experience difficulty in obtaining adequate lipids and starches for calories and for adequate metabolism of animal proteins. This is particularly problematical in late winter seasons or during dry seasons when animal fat levels are typically extremely low (Speth and Spielmann 1983). Staples in the study area provide a relatively balanced nutrition from this point of view, since avalanche lilies and spring beauty primarily provide carbohydrates, and the salmon that transited the Lillooet area were still relatively rich in fat and oil. However, the considerable effort expended by the Lillooet in extracting all possible oil from the salmon caught, and the manufacture of special salmon skin bottles to preserve and trade the oil, and the explicit desirability of fatter salmon and salmon parts (Chapters 5 and 6) attest to needs not completely fulfilled by the normal diet and underline the central role lipids played in Lillooet diets. Only a detailed nutritional study of a simulated traditional diet can determine if, in fact, there was an overabundance of protein and a still unsatisfied demand for carbohydrates and lipids. Surrounding groups, with less access to Fraser River salmon, would very likely have experienced periodic lipid deficiencies and would have been anxious to trade for any surplus oil that the Lillooet could produce.

Diversity and Evenness

The overall resource base of the study area can be characterized as having a moderate diversity, documented in Chapter 2. However, the diversity of *staples* was unusually low (spring and sockeye salmon, trout, deer, saskatoon berries, spring beauty, and avalanche lilies), with extremely skewed evenness values reflecting the overwhelming dependence on a few select staples. These, too, are values that tend to characterize complex hunter/gatherers (Chatters 1987:350; Grigson 1989; Zvelebil 1989).

CHANGES AND CONSEQUENCES

Almost all of these ecological variables had very different values during the Middle Prehistoric period, some 4,000-7,000 years ago. Population, and by implication resource accessibility and/or availability, was much lower; substantial fluctuations in resources must still have occurred, but there is no evidence for storage or seasonal semi-sedentism; therefore, processing and labour requirements would have been much lower; travel and procurement requirements may not have changed dramatically, but lipids and carbohydrates were probably less available seasonally; and staple diversity was probably higher, overall diversity lower, and evenness much more uniform across resources (Campbell 1985:489). In brief, the hunter/gatherers of the area underwent a transition sometime from the Middle to the Late Prehistoric Period from typical generalized hunter/gatherers to complex hunter/gatherers exhibiting characteristics found at the time of contact. Which, if any, of the variables mentioned above seem to play the most causal roles in changing the basic social behaviour of generalized hunter/gatherers? *How* were changes in resource characteristics translated into the major social consequences identified in Chapter 1?

In the following section, I will begin by examining the kinds of consequences that changes in those key variables discussed in Chapter 1 might have on basic social adaptations of generalized hunter/gatherers. The key resource variables tentatively identified in Chapter 1 are: resource abundance, fluctuations, and vulnerability. The key social variables that changed are: sharing, mobility, alliances, and proscribed competition.

Abundance

It can be argued that among generalized hunter/gatherers limited abundance of extractable resources placed important constraints on sedentism, group size, and consequent storage practicability (Chapter 1). By 'extractable resources,' I refer to those species and quantities that can actually be extracted with the technology used by a specific group at a specific time period, rather than all potentially recoverable edible resources. Limited extractable abundance probably also rendered sharing an important social trait, since the scarcer resources become in absolute terms, the greater the risk of failing to locate adequate amounts over any given period of time.

As extractable resource density increases, the range size needed to support a band or family constricts, thereby reducing the need for high residential mobility. In areas with rich extractable resources, seasonal or even full sedentism usually occurs together with logistical foraging and collecting strategies (defined by Binford 1980). These developments are frequently, but not inevitably, inter-related with large-scale storage. There is some question as to how critical the role of storage is in many of the developments of concern; this topic will be considered below. For now, it can simply be noted that sufficiently abundant resources render sedentism possible, and that sedentism facilitates the use of food storage as a strategy. On the other hand, in many cases storage makes sedentism possible.

Group size may also increase together with more resource abundance although this does not always occur. Certainly, significantly increased resource abundance makes larger groups more feasible than they were previously from an energy expenditure point of view, but there are other factors that can determine community size, such as levels of conflict, suitable sites, and extreme localization or dispersal of resources.

A common impression is that increases in extractable resource abundance also reduce food shortages for communities. This, however, is not necessarily the case. Simple increases in the amount of food extracted can be offset by natural increases in population until the pre-existing frequencies of resource stress are once again attained (Hayden 1972, 1990). On the other hand, if fundamental changes in the structure of the resource base (such as the use of a greater diversity of species or increased use of *r*-selected species) accompany increases in resource abundance levels, the frequency and severity of food shortages may in fact, be reduced. In these cases, the reduction in resource fluctuations would not technically be the result of increased abundance alone but of changes in other resource characteristics as well. Thus, simple increases in resource abundance may directly affect mobility, storage, sharing, and group size, although other factors also can exert influences on these parameters.

Fluctuations

One might expect that fluctuations of resources among complex hunter/gatherers, including those in the study area, would also contrast with those experienced by generalized hunter/gatherers. In 1981, I suggested that complex hunter/gatherers should experience significantly reduced periods of food shortages due to reduced fluctuations (Hayden 1981a). The reductions in fluctuations were thought to be due to greater reliance on species that were invulnerable to overexploitation as well as to the much greater overall diversity of resources that characterize complex hunter/gatherers. In the study area, these expectations clearly were not met. Romanoff (Chapters 5 and 9), and Kennedy and Bouchard (Chapter 6), and Teit (1906:199) record pre-gold rush accounts of famines largely due to the failure of fish. I mention famines in other regions earlier in this chapter. Chance and Chance (1982:418) record similar failures in early historical and probably prehistoric times for the Kettle Falls area. Deer populations also underwent cyclical lows during which very few would have been available (Chapter 2).

Impressionistically, there seems to be little difference between generalized versus complex hunter/gatherers of the Plateau in terms of the frequency or severity of long-term food shortages (compare Hayden 1981b). In both cases, famines seem likely to occur several times during the lifetime of an individual. Matson (1985:249) also notes periodic resource failures among complex hunter/gatherers. Thus, although data are very spotty on long-term food cycles, at this point it appears difficult to invoke changes in this variable as playing an integral role in the emergence of complex hunter/gatherers or the social features that are of main concern here.

There are several factors that are undoubtedly responsible for these severe long-term fluctuations. First, the fewer staples that communities rely upon, the more susceptible community resources will be to natural fluctuations in a particular species. Greater specialization entails greater risks. One of the characteristics of most complex hunter/gatherers (as well as of agriculturalists) is their specialization in a very narrow range of resources for the vast bulk of their food needs. This typifies the study area. Second, Kew (Chapter 4), Romanoff (Chapter 9), and Kennedy and Bouchard (Chapter 6) have documented the many local variables that can affect accessibility to salmon and their preservation, notably river levels, timing of runs, and climate. Third, with the emergence of differential access to resources and a 'poor' or disenfranchised sector in communities, even moderate drops in resource abundance could disproportionately affect the lower classes in communities, creating famine conditions among them.

Thus, the frequency and severity of long-term food shortages do not seem to have altered markedly from situations characterizing generalized hunter/gatherers. If anything, depending upon the extent of disenfranchisement, poorer families may have experienced more frequent privation. The fact that periodic famines continue to occur with about the same frequency among agricultural communities (Hayden and Gargett 1990) indicates that long-term severe fluctuations in resources characterize all levels of traditional societies. It is, therefore, difficult to invoke social complexity or other developments, such as domestication, as either solutions to, or results of, changes in resource stress. On the other hand, seasonal and short-term fluctuations characteristic of normal years do appear to be predictable and reliable and easily dealt with due to the recurrent abundance of fish runs combined with storage technology (see also Matson 1985).

Vulnerability to Overexploitation

There is a major change in values for this variable between general ized and complex hunter/gatherers. Although salmon have probably always been used by populations in the Fraser River and Columbia drainages (Matson 1976, Cressman 1960), they played only a limited role in the overall subsistence profile, presumably due to the lack of sophisticated storage technology, the limited portion of the year during which they were available, and, possibly, their lower availability during the first millennia after deglaciation. While Kew (Chapter 4) views the dip net as the basal fishing technology for the earliest groups, I would suggest that such nets may be Mesolithic/Archaic developments and that the first fishing equipment was more likely to have been a modified barbed hunting spear which later developed into the leister and harpoon. These fishing tools occur in the late European Upper Paleolithic before fish assume a significant role in the diet (Hayden et al. 1987) and are remarkably similar to archaeological examples from the Plateau and to the ethnographic equipment documented by Kennedy and Bouchard (Chapter 6). As salmon became increasingly important in diets due to improved procurement (e.g., nets) and storage techniques, it seems that their invulnerability to overexploitation may also have become an increasingly important characteristic. The unusual consequence of this situation was that all families could now harvest as much of their most important staple as they wanted without affecting the overall resource level and without jeopardizing anyone else's chances of obtaining as much salmon as they wanted. Thus, this factor may have played a critical role in some of the social changes that occurred in complex hunter/gatherers, and I will return to it shortly.

Storage

One additional resource variable has been promoted as playing a critical role in the transformation of generalized to complex hunter/gatherering societies: storage. Testart (1982), Binford (1980), and Soffer (1989) have argued that storage induces sedentism, private property, and inequality. There is a surfeit of evidence for storage in the study area in this volume as well as in the traditional ethnographies. On the Plateau, storage can certainly be viewed as playing an important role in the transformation from generalized to complex hunter/gatherers. However, large-scale storage is first of all dependent on being technologically capable of obtaining large enough amounts of resources to store. For this, mass harvesting technology is required. Second, large-scale storage is dependent upon the availability of abundant enough and invulnerable enough resources in the area. And third, storage is dependent upon the perfection of a storage technology that can reliably preserve resources in an edible state for months if not years. The development of such a storage technology may have taken several centuries or millennia to perfect once the capability of systematically obtaining resources in large enough quantities to warrant storage was attained. Thus, storage behaviour is dependent on other, more antecedent, causal factors such as resource and technological characteristics. As Matson (1985:250) has put it, storage is more appropriately viewed as a by-product rather than as an essential condition for rank society or sedentism. More recently, Binford (1990:144) has argued that storage is not unique to complex hunter/-gatherers.

Why is it that generalized hunter/gatherers do not store significant amounts of food? The most apparent answer is that resources are so sparsely distributed and vary so much in time and space that groups (1) only can harvest surpluses unpredictably, (2) cannot be certain of returning to specific locations where surpluses are stored before spoilage occurs, (3) might not be able to obtain other resources necessary for adequate health at surplus locations even if they could return to those locations before spoilage. The extra effort required to properly prepare most species for storage and the effort involved in the construction of storage facilities to protect foods from the elements and competitors must also have been viewed as undesirable. In addition, Bruce Winterhalder (personal communication) has pointed out that, given obligatory sharing, it makes little sense for anyone to obtain more than can be immediately consumed or to spend time and effort in preparing foods for storage because any extra will simply be appropriated by the other members of the community for their own consumption. Perhaps this is the most powerful deterrent of all to the accumulation of storable surpluses among generalized hunter/gatherers. Under these conditions, it makes little economic sense to invest extra labour in storing surpluses beyond amounts that can be carried. Thus, I would argue that storage is more appropriately viewed as an outcome of changes in basic resource conditions. Whenever harvests of seasonally fluctuating resources become abundant, regular, and invulnerable enough, communities will eventually find ways of preserving and storing those resources and of curtailing the obligatory sharing ethic. Examples include the Point Barrow whalers, the Northwest Coast Indians, the Upper Paleolithic reindeer hunters of the Perigord and Russian plain, the Natufians, and the Jomon.

Moreover, while storage in highly seasonal environments may be critical for a group's ability to become semi-sedentary or for groups to make full use of abundant resources, storage does not appear to be an absolute prerequisite for the emergence of complex hunter/gatherers with socially stratified communities. Widmer (1988:268) argues that the Calusa of Florida maintained one of the most complex hunter/gatherer societies anywhere in the world virtually without mass food storage. If this was so, it indicates that storage per se is not essential for the development of complexity but that abundant and invulnerable resources are. It may simply be that in highly seasonal environments with temporally restricted occurrences of abundant resources, year-around abundance can only be provided by means of storage. Similarly, while storage may logically lead to ownership claims at least of stored resources, as is the case in the study area (Chapter 5), the Calusa example again indicates that other, much more fundamental, underlying changes in resource relationships are at work favouring the development of ownership and socioeconomic complexity.

One other consequence of storage is that short-term fluctuations of resources are more easily accommodated within groups. This, together with the fungibility of wealth items, such as dentalium shells exchangeable for dried fish, appears to have reduced the importance of subsistence alliances among hunter/gatherers. Whereas these alli-

ances characterize generalized hunter/gatherers, there is very little in
the ethnographies of complex hunter/gatherers that can be interpreted
in such terms other than the continued use of marriage to gain access
to additional resources (Chapter 5). Rather, subsistence alliances
appear to have been largely supplanted by storage, trading, and raiding as strategies for dealing with short- and long-term severe food
shortages. This is an important shift in emphasis in hunter/gatherer
adaptations that has not been widely recognized but that certainly
deserves a great deal more attention.

Because of the essential nutritional balance required for any hunt-
ing/gathering community to survive, it seems dubious that this would
vary dramatically or be implicated as an important factor in models
of social change from generalized to complex hunter/gatherers. Thus,
this initial assessment of data from the study area and elsewhere in
the world indicates that the factors which seem to play the most important roles in social change are increased abundance and a much greater
reliance on resources invulnerable to overexploitation. Such a conclusion is consistent with Hunn's observation for the Columbia Plateau
that surpluses are correlated with population density, wealth, and political centralization (1990:214). Similar strong correlations between
these variables have also been demonstrated for coastal groups
(Donald and Mitchell 1975, 1990).

IMPLICATIONS

My own view is that the key to understanding the dramatic increases
in extractable resource abundance, population, and invulnerable types
of resources that occurred in favoured locations throughout the world
over the last 15,000 years is technological innovation (Hayden 1981a).
Nothing else seems adequate to explain the magnitude of changes that
took place in environments with high potentials, for these environments and resources have always existed in various parts of the globe.
Exactly why these technological innovations occurred at this time is
a matter I have dealt with previously (1981a) and which may still be
open to debate. However, it is clear that starting about this time, a
wide range of basic technological changes, including boiling, sophisticated basketry, grinding, effective fishing, transport, and more
sophisticated hunting, rapidly swept over most of the globe and
brought about a new, more complex and unequal social order in the
richest environments. The association between abundant and invulnerable resources on the one hand and socioeconomic inequality and
resource ownership on the other seems very pronounced, but the precise causality is still vague. In the following pages I will propose some

causal relationships between variables in order to advance the investigation of these phenomena.

One of the strongest cases for a causal relationship between resources and inequality seems to involve two factors: developments which allow differential access and control over resources and the ability to use surpluses for personal benefit. My treatment of these topics has been greatly influenced by Matson's stimulating discussion of ownership (1985) as well as Dyson-Hudson and Smith's work (1978).

Ownership

As noted in Chapter 1, 'ownership' is being used in a loose but convenient fashion to refer to any restriction of access to resources or items within a community. Precisely how and why restricted access to, or ownership of, resources comes about is perhaps the single most important issue in understanding changes that occur among complex hunter/gatherers. While answers at this stage of inquiry are far from definitive, I would suggest that there are at least two and possibly three conditions necessary for its initial development which are lacking among generalized hunter/gatherers. The first condition is that everyone in a community be guaranteed sufficient access to resources on an individual or family or lineage basis so as to ensure survival in normal times. Without this condition, the majority of any egalitarian community will simply refuse to recognize claims by any individuals to the privileged use of resources.

For such widespread self-sufficiency to occur, resources must occur in abundant, dense patches. There must be significant staples for everyone to obtain enough for their own needs in normal times. This, I would argue, is the critical importance of the Six Mile public fishery, probably the single most productive aboriginal fishery on the Middle and Upper Fraser River. Providing sufficient food for everyone in communities is also why the band-controlled fisheries are essential components in understanding cultural complexity in the study area (see Chapters 5 and 6). The public and band-owned root gathering areas in the Alpine, Parklands, and Intermediate Grasslands (Chapters 3 and 8) probably played similar roles.

Under these conditions of abundance, it becomes reasonable for each family to consider the products of their labour as their own, as was the case with stored produce in the study area (Chapter 5). Sharing as a strategy to compensate for the uncertainty of individual families failing to find resources due to short-term variations in resource occurrences is no longer as necessary as it once was. In fact, abundance invites abuse of sharing systems. Under sparse conditions, diligent individual efforts could easily fail to produce food. In contrast, under abundant conditions, the only excuse healthy individuals could have for not procuring their own food would be 'laziness' or general failure of the resource due to long-term fluctuations that would affect everyone equally. In normal years, those who performed all the work necessary to obtain food must have eventually resented those who did nothing but 'share' the products of the producers' labour. Why should a few individuals produce for other families without reciprocal benefits, especially if those people that were asking to receive a share of food were unrelated? Even among generalized hunter/gatherers, unrequited sharing has its limits. However, the references to 'moochers' and 'lazy' individuals (in Chapters 5 and 9 and in myths) are especially prominent in the study area and may constitute important preoccupations of elites and resource owners in all complex hunter/gatherers societies. I know of no such references to 'moochers' in ethnographies of generalized hunter/gatherers. Self-interest, therefore, seems to dictate that those who produced most of the food seem to begin to place restrictions on sharing and to claim more exclusive use for the products of their own labour.

A second condition that may be necessary for the emergence of private ownership of resource locations is a multiplicity of these locations. In addition to locations to which everyone has access, or which can be divided up among the general population, there must be alternate highly productive and probably desirable resource procurement locations, or even entire resources, the pre-emption of which will not dramatically affect the well-being of other community members under normal conditions of short-term resource fluctuations. In the Lillooet study area, these resource locations comprise the smaller, highly productive salmon fishing rocks requiring careful monitoring of water levels and often special knowledge of fish behaviour associated with the sites (Chapters 5 and 6).

A third factor which undoubtedly contributed to the recognition of claims over resource procurement sites in the study area (although it may not have been absolutely essential for ownership to develop) is improvement in the productivity of procurement sites by dint of labour investment in site facilities or special knowledge. Once the practice of ownership of resource produce became established, any special labour that enhanced the production at procurement sites could be claimed as grounds for privileged access to, and use of, those sites. Prime indications of improvement of such owned locations are deer fences, fish weirs, and fishing sites requiring the use of constructed wooden platforms for effective exploitation (Chapters 3, 5, 6, 7, and 9). In other regions of the Northwest, the construction of tidal fish traps, and the labour necessary to prepare land for cultivation (felling trees, clearing brush, spading, weeding – e.g., Turner and Kuhnlein 1982; Suttles 1951) provide further examples of this principle. The special knowledge of salmon behaviour at varying river levels, so necessary for the effective exploitation of specific locations in the study area, might also be viewed as a type of investment warranting claims of ownership.

Once resource ownership and élites had become established, they might be expected to extend control over other desirable resources using the same warranting principles, at least to the extent that others in the community would tolerate those claims. For instance, the principle of ownership by reason of special knowledge might have been extended to hunting areas by specialized élite hunters (Chapters 2, 6, 7, and 9) arguing that their special training enhanced the amount of deer captured by hunting parties. Among the more complex North American societies this special knowledge was typically acquired at great cost and effort and was only affordable by wealthy élite families; and it seems that the weaker the practical basis for such claims was, the greater the emphasis on the spiritual qualities and training supposedly necessary for competent exploitation of those resources (see Chapter 9). These claims may provide the justification for restricting general access, but it is the practical control of the élite in other domains, and the lack of major consequences for ordinary families, that must have provided the grounds for community acceptance of such élite claims of ownership. In contrast, it appears that wherever and whenever access to resources becomes critical for the survival of ordinary families in hunting/gathering communities, recognition of ownership claims are withdrawn.

This interpretation differs somewhat from Romanoff's analysis, but in the context of the following discussion, it is, I think, equally tenable. There are clear statements of ownership of hunting areas in very early contact times from a number of Interior sources (see Chapter 9; Dawson 1892:14; Teit 1909:582; Mitchell 1925:4; Kennedy and Bouchard, field notes). In the Subarctic, hunting area ownership has been attributed by some to the economic effects of the fur trade (Leacock 1954), although others contest this (Knight 1965). Bouchard (1968-91) and Kennedy (1971-91) indicate that ownership of hunting areas was probably not induced by the fur trade for the Lower Lillooet area, since ownership primarily pertained to specific types of animals, such as goats, whose skins had little value as fur trade items.

While the information presented in Chapters 5, 6, and 7 is sometimes ambiguous about precisely to what degree access was restricted at 'owned' fishing locations, the statements can be interpreted in a fashion consistent with the above view. Certainly, owners must have had priority of access to their sites, and since the wealth of a family depended largely on the number of salmon obtained, it must be assumed that wealthy families had some means of curtailing general access to the 'owned' sources of salmon. Requiring that those wishing to use the site had to ask permission of its owner (Chapter 5) was one barrier to indiscriminate use and also would have provided an opportunity for the owner to place further restrictions on the scheduling of site use by others so as to ensure that he obtained what he needed. Even if owners were obligated to grant use of their sites to others (which may not have been the case in all prehistoric periods), non-owner use would likely have been in terms that accommodated the owners' interests and schedules. It is clear from statements in Chapters 5 and 6 that at certain times many more fish could be caught than could be processed. I feel it is reasonable to interpret informants' statements on these matters to mean that the owned fishing sites could be used by other people only after the owner had caught as much fish as his task group could process for the day at the peaks of runs, or that the sites could be used at other times when owners were not actively using them. Explicit statements by Sam Mitchell (Chapter 6) verify that 'the use of such spots was limited to the immediate members' of an owner's family. 'After that particular family had obtained enough salmon, then anybody could use that fishing rock.' This technique of restricting access is very similar to the rules governing the use of owned resources on the Coast, where families that owned no resource locations 'were obliged to wait' until the owners had finished gathering and had given their consent for others to use the area (Swanton, cited in MacDonald 1983:6). Around Lillooet, it would make little sense for an owner to take the trouble and risk of constructing a wooden platform if he had to cede its use to everyone else indiscriminately, or if he could not obtain the use he wanted of the platform. This, in fact, may be why such facilities are so rare, or absent, among generalized hunter/gatherers.

In the final analysis, ownership of resource locations may not be an absolutely essential element for the development of initial socioeconomic inequality. It may be that simple ownership of harvested produce without obligatory sharing is sufficient to account for some of the inequality that is found in the study area. Certainly ownership of produce is all that is logically necessary for storage to occur and it is probably the only essential element in the subsequent use of surpluses to create inequalities. On the other hand, the ownership, or privileged access to, resource localities was a pronounced feature of cultures in the study area as well as of every other ethnographically documented group of complex hunter/gatherers with which I am familiar, such as groups on the Northwest Coast, the Calusa, and the Point Barrow Eskimo (where whaling boats were owned). Ownership of resource localities, therefore, probably at least played an important auxiliary role if not a more fundamental role in the initial establishment of socioeconomic inequalities.

Before addressing the use of surpluses, one further point needs to be made about resource ownership. Ownership, as a concept in industrial society, is an extreme form of restricted access. In comparative studies, there is a full spectrum of degrees of ownership, or restriction of access, extending from total indiscriminate use to the exclusive use by a single individual. Clearly, the ownership of resource locations, and even produce, in the study area was of a more contingent nature than ownership in state-level societies. Among complex hunter/gatherers, claims to privileged access during normal years were probably recognized by other community members only so long as the site was being used by the owner and only so long as exploitation of the site did not adversely affect other families. When periodic long-term fluctuations created severe food shortages, it appears that the interest of the majority of the community once again asserted itself by withdrawing recognition of claims to exclusive use of sites and produce (Semyonov 1990, citing Rink 1875:28-9; Jenness 1922:85, 90; Birket-Smith 1929:143, 162; Weyer 1962:184-6). Those who had food during famines were expected to share with those who had nothing (Chapters 5 and 9). This is another theme of some didactic myths of the Lillooet, undoubtedly most popular among disenfranchised families. In contrast, it would have been in the self-interest of those with stored supplies of food to share only as much as was absolutely necessary. Similar conditional ownership also characterizes agricultural communities with comparable levels of socioeconomic inequality (Hayden and Gargett 1990). There are probably few more dramatic demonstrations of how the practical and situationally dependent nature of human behaviour modifies or changes generally accepted or promoted social norms and values. Cultural norms and values are not generally the major determinants of behaviour, as structuralists and cognitivists have tended to argue. Cultural norms and values are far more frequently justifications or rationalizations of behaviour, attempts to promote the self-interest of subgroups, or simply means of avoiding constant protracted decisionmaking.

For the initial stages of developing socioeconomic inequality, when élites have not developed real coercive power or absolutely exclusive access to resources, the conditional nature of resource ownership implies that long-term fluctuations in resources cannot be directly related to the development of socioeconomic inequality since these conditions result in the reduction of resource ownership and hierarchical relations. Initial developments of socioeconomic inequality, and ownership, thus, must be predicated on the normal resource conditions that can be expected to occur in the vast majority of years. Among complex hunter/gatherers, alternative strategies, such as trading and raiding, seem to have been developed for dealing with long-term periodic shortages. However, this is a topic for more extended research. Once incipient élites consolidated their claims over resources to a certain point and developed their power within the community, it might be possible to use food crises to further enhance their control and power via debt servitude and acquisition of rights to more resource localities (Hayden and Gargett 1990). It does not seem that the historical Lillooet communities had developed to this extent.

Use of Surpluses

While the ownership of produce and resource locations is capable of creating some inequalities, these do not appear to be of a magnitude great enough to have resulted in slavery or some of the other more stratified features of Lillooet society. Recognition of claims to ownership were contingent upon others having enough food under normal conditions. The majority of the community held the balance of power in egalitarian communities and by the use of checks employed by generalized hunter/gatherers could revoke ownership claims to varying extents if inequalities became too exaggerated. In order to understand the elaborate development of inequality in the study area, further factors must be considered which account for the centralization of power, wealth, and resource control in the hands of minority elements within communities.

There are two basic approaches to understanding this centralization of power. The first has been termed the 'functionalist' approach (Earle 1977; Brumfiel and Earle 1987; Gilman 1981). This approach views élites as adaptive for communities in terms of providing important functions (e.g., storing food in case of famines, creating alliances in case of attack or famine, rendering production or information gathering more effective and efficient, or undertaking useful projects such as irrigation). According to the functionalist view, the community recognizes the benefits of these advantages and accords élites the power and trappings necessary to carry out their functions.

In contrast, the second, 'exploitative' approach views élites as opportunists that are primarily interested in their own self-interest and use every means to promote this end while making the minimum con-

Conclusions 549

cessions necessary to retain a sufficient support base in the community to achieve their goals (ibid.). Any benefits that are provided to the community are incidental to élite behaviour or are exacted by the community as a necessary price for their consent in allowing élites to operate.

These two views have fairly important consequences for models of conditions under which élites should develop. Under the functionalist model, researchers should look for conditions of stress that élites would alleviate. Élites are then viewed as adaptive. In contrast, under the exploitation model, no stress need be present. In fact, a better argument can be made for incipient élites emerging under conditions of resource abundance.

Since understanding important aspects of socioeconomic inequality in the study area seemed to hinge upon the resolution of the functionalist versus the exploitative issue, I spent considerable time examining ethnographies trying to determine whether élites in ranked and initially stratified societies provided any real help to ordinary families in times of crises, such as famines. I reasoned that if élites existed to help communities adapt to stresses, then they should use resources and alliances at their disposal to help their communities in times of crisis. Unfortunately, the available published observations on such matters were so rare and so vague that no clear conclusions could be drawn. I therefore set out to gather some information myself from an area with which I was already familiar: the Mayan communities of Central America. These communities exhibited considerable socioeconomic inequality consistent with ranked societies, but they were not internally stratified. I selected those that had been extremely isolated prior to 1950 in order to minimize effects of industrial economies on communities and to maximize the opportunities of dealing with relatively autonomous social adaptations. My informants were among the oldest individuals in the communities, and I asked them about élite and nonélite responses to famines that occurred in the early years of this century or before. Prior to beginning this project, I fully expected to find conclusive backing for the functionalist interpretations. I was perhaps more surprised than anyone to discover that the results were entirely contrary to this interpretation (Hayden and Gargett 1990). Incipient élites did not help their communities in times of crises but took advantage of every opportunity to advance their own self interest. While questions can be raised about the suitability of this comparison for the Lillooet study area, subsequent re-examination of most other accounts in the literature tends to confirm its applicability (ibid.), and I am confident that further comparative research along these lines will corroborate my conclusions. These results have considerably changed my perspective on the emergence of élites. Using them as a foundation, I would now make the following suggestions.

In all communities, at least a few individuals can be found who are motivated primarily by their own self-interest. This is part of the genetic and psychological variation of the human race, possibly having its roots in primate dominance hierarchies. Such individuals seek to gain advantages for themselves by influencing community affairs (i.e., acquiring power) and through material gains. Elsewhere, I refer to these individuals as 'accumulators'; Clark and Blake (in press) refer to them as aggrandizers.

Among generalized hunter/gatherers overt and economically based accumulator behaviour is not tolerated, although it can be redirected through ritual and age dominance hierarchies. However, once resources become abundant and ownership over individual produce is established, it becomes possible for accumulators to own and to use surpluses in attempts to further their own interests. An essential element in accounting for the centralized power and wealth of élites is understanding how surpluses can be converted to power and wealth, particularly if everyone in the community already has salmon and élites can only produce surplus salmon.

Solutions to this problem must be found that operate under normal conditions. Periodic famines occurred too infrequently and, especially given pre-existing egalitarian behaviour, famines appear to have reduced rather than increased socioeconomic inequality as well as recognition of élite claims on resources. Potential solutions to the problem of how to use and transform surpluses into power and advantages must also maintain a sufficient support base in the community to avoid reprisals from envious individuals who do not hesitate to employ underhanded means if they feel threatened.

One solution that many ambitious accumulators seem to have hit upon was the competitive feast. I have elaborated details concerning this mechanism elsewhere (Hayden 1990; Hayden and Gargett 1990), but, briefly, it entails the giving away of desired items or valued foods to someone else within the community or to someone from another community, with the understanding that the gifts will be returned in kind (or better) together with a sizable supplement (viewed as 'interest') to compensate for the loss of the use of those materials until their return. The key to understanding these transactions is the supplemental labour involved in the production of foods and items intended to make them desirable. This, in turn, creates debts that are used to acquire power, material gain, and recognition of ownership claims. The generation and careful structuring of debts is the key to understanding competitive feasts and complex hunter/gatherers

(Gosden 1989). I suggest that accumulators use the prospect of the desirability of gifts as well as the supplement to be gained on such gift/loans to attract other participants or supporters into the feasting and debt system. Ideally, everyone should benefit. However, in reality, it is evident that the system is inherently inflationary and that someone must eventually default under conditions of finite resources. Like defaults in modern commerce, this must have created problems and resulted in attempts by creditors to recoup losses. But for the present, the system of loans and repayments requires further explanation.

The key to making competitive feasting systems work is the ability to give or obtain items that are difficult to obtain or that require unusual amounts of labour to produce. Thus, delicacy foods are typically given away, particularly those with appealing taste or nutritional value. Why would anyone within the study area give or accept items that everyone had or could easily obtain under normal conditions? If fish were ever used within the study area as part of such a system, they must have been the most choice fish and the most labour-intensive fish products (such as oil). Oil certainly featured prominently in all accounts of trading for the area. In the Lillooet region, deer meat was the primary potlatching food. Spring salmon, which are the most oily of all the salmon, and which require the greatest care and labour to procure and prepare for proper drying, may well have been especially valued feasting and exchange items as well (see the preceding discussion on nutrition). The importance of oils and lipids for winter calories, nutrition, and trade may be the principal reason why many owned fishing sites were so important and why they ceased to be important once improved housing and commercial foods became widely available. These developments may also explain, in part, why the oil-rich spring salmon are considered of little importance at present in contrast to their former greater importance. On the Coast, fish oil was a standard potlatch item, as were tender starchy roots and tobacco, a non-native plant. The potlatch is one of the archetypal examples of the competitive feast. In New Guinea, specially fattened pigs were the major gifts.

In the context of the competitive feast not only special foods but also valued prestige items were given away and expected to be returned with some supplement. These items required either intensive labour to produce locally or they required the acquisition of exotica from distant areas, which also involved substantial labour costs. Most importantly, prestige items, such as copper, constituted a major means by which ordinary surpluses could be converted to more desirable goods for local consumption. Surpluses could be used to help local labour to produce valuable items such as nephrite adzes or carefully carved bone combs; surpluses could be exchanged with distant communities for items like dentalium shells. By all accounts (Chapters 5-7 and 10), Lillooet dried salmon were highly desired by all surrounding groups and even by peoples on the Lower Fraser River.

The information in this volume provides important support for parts of this scenario. Romanoff (Chapter 9) records early historic feasts that were called 'potlatches' and which were competitive in nature. On the basis of comparative studies, it is difficult to imagine competitive feasts that did not provide tangible benefits to all participants, such as the promised return of gifts plus supplements. As Romanoff notes, guests 'vowed' to return feasts. Moreover, given the rarity of ungulates in the study area (Chapters 2 and 3) and their desirability as food, Romanoff's observations on the central role of deer meat in Lillooet potlatches certainly fits the general pattern of competitive feasts elsewhere. And, as elsewhere, élites seem to have attempted to monopolize control over the desirable food resources critical for successful competitive feasts, in part via the creation of specialized hunter roles which excluded non-élites and, perhaps, in part via the private ownership of fishing locations/facilities where spring salmon could be obtained in greatest abundance. It seems inconceivable that the specialized training provided for historic Lillooet hunters would have been required during the period when the area was occupied by generalized hunter/gatherers; nor is such specialized training found among any ethnographic generalized hunter/gatherers that I know of. Thus, it is difficult to interpret the specialized hunting role among the Lillooet as either necessary or adaptive for effective hunting. It may have had some beneficial effects on communal hunting effectiveness, but the benefits seem outweighed by the tendency to exclude ordinary families from ungulate access. Specialized hunting does, however, make a great deal of sense in terms of élite attempts to control valued exchange and feasting foods. It is also of interest to note that the amount of time required to arrange sufficient gifts for major feasts among the Lillooet is comparable to better documented competitive feasts elsewhere, that is, up to 10 years (Strathern 1971) versus three to four years for the Lillooet (Chapter 9). While Sam Mitchell stated that it took three to four years to accumulate enough deer meat for a validation potlatch, it does not seem likely that meat would have preserved well for such a length of time. What he may have meant, or what those who passed on this oral tradition to him may have meant, is that three to four years were necessary to arrange all the gifts necessary (through the use of deer meat in a series of preparatory feasts) to arrange the requisite loans for a large potlatch.

There are many incidental aspects of this model that merit exploration. However, the key point for the present discussion is that, by organizing such feasts, accumulators placed themselves in privileged positions with respect to providing benefits to others within the community, whether in terms of goods or services. Competitive feasts, by definition, create widespread debts among both supporters and rivals. People are always seeking ways of giving away unneeded surpluses so that they can recoup their value at later dates together with agreed upon supplements. Once one enters the system, to refuse to accept such gifts in a competitive feast is tantamount to declaring bankruptcy and opening oneself to hostile retaliations. But it is above all the manipulation of debts that provides the organizers with exceptional influence in the community (Gosden 1989). And it must be the manipulation of varying supplement payments for loans versus borrowings together with the labour available from their own families that provides accumulators with an unusual amount of wealth in the form of exotic items and food.

To some extent, these advantages can be achieved by indulging in direct, long-distance trade and subsequently distributing desired trade goods to individuals within the community in exchange for their support. However, competitive feasts actively create debts involving far wider networks of people, which, I suggest, are the primary source of centralized power and wealth. Thus, competitive feasts are extremely powerful mechanisms for furthering the self-interest of accumulators. It is undoubtedly for this reason that one of the most frequently cited characteristics of chiefs among the Lillooet (as well as in other chiefdoms throughout the world) is the liberal 'giving' away of great amounts of food and goods (Teit 1906:255). Although Teit claims that no reciprocal return was expected, either he was mistaken, or he was influenced by the anti-economic bias of his editor, Franz Boas, or his information only refers to display gift-giving events (such as typically occur at élite marriages and funerals). The costly, obsessive, competitive gift-giving that characterizes rank and low-level chiefdom societies everywhere simply is incomprehensible according to common sense and ecological principles unless some tangible benefit results from such behaviour. The key question for understanding the origins of socioeconomic inequality is what that benefit was. Careful, detailed ethnographic investigations of these cases, such as Strathern's work (1971), have documented the underlying economic benefits for participants in such systems. I suggest that appealing simply to desires for 'status,' devoid of any associated tangible benefits, is not a viable answer. There is simply too much time and effort invested in these competitive activities. There must be material benefits, such as increased wealth and power, for organizers and participants in the communities.

It is precisely because of these benefits that accumulators can be expected to do everything possible to concentrate access to trade goods in their own hands, just as they sought to control access to the culinary delicacies used in feasting systems. Given these expectations, it comes as little surprise to find that Teit (1909:577) recorded some Interior élites as having special trading privileges, although these would have been difficult to impose at public inter-tribal resource harvesting sites such as the Six Mile fishery and Botanie Valley.

The concessions made by élites to the community for being permitted to operate competitive feasts take the form of distributing some of the desired prestige items and delicacies to other community members. It is the general desirability of these items that motivate other community and family members to surrender their surpluses or even to go into debt to acquire desired items. Accumulators simply use whatever tactics necessary to engage other members of the community in a system that will motivate large numbers of people to produce and surrender surpluses and to surrender some claim on their labour. Competitive feasts constitute one such very effective tactic. Under this system, accumulators can be expected to distribute as much as necessary in order to retain support in the community; accumulators should also retain as much surplus and prestige paraphernalia as they can for themselves.

In any event, all supporters of such a system theoretically benefit in some fashion, since they use their surpluses to obtain things they desire and since they potentially have access to considerable surpluses and support from others in the feasting network when in need. Trade goods were essential components in making these competitive feasting and debt systems function. In contrast, nonparticipants became progressively disenfranchised and were regarded by participants with scorn as being poor or lazy 'moochers.' Accumulators could be expected to do everything possible to pressure as many families as possible into participating, for the more families that participated, the more benefit and power accrued to the accumulators. This explains the use of disparaging epithets for nonparticipants in all complex societies as well as the other economic, survival, and social pressures brought to bear on nonparticipants. Accumulators seek to place nonparticipants in increasingly disadvantaged and disenfranchised positions in order to force nonparticipating families into producing and surrendering surpluses.

One final aspect of the competitive feasting system bears mentioning. This is the competition between accumulators for others' labour that characterized such systems both within and between communities. In order to attract labour and to convince prospective supporters of the potential benefits of providing material for a particular accumulator's feast, I suggest that organizers and committed supporters engaged in ostentatious displays of power and wealth. This is probably the origin and meaning of the destruction of property in Coastal potlatches. This is probably also the origin of slavery, dog breeding, sumptuous marriages, lavish burials, and the spectacular ritual displays that characterized cultures in many parts of the Northwest. These are types of behaviour meant to impress non-supporters as well as to remind supporters and rivals of the economic power of their own group. Such displays are essential psychological components of maintaining the loyalty of followers. Power that is unseen is unfelt and soon forgotten by the general community.

Thus, there were a number of motives for individual families to produce as much surplus as they could. Foremost was the ability to increase one's standard of living through direct exchange or loans or through participation in competitive feasts. Also important were various pressures from ambitious accumulators who used all the economic, social, and psychological levers at their disposal to increase the production of their supporters. Competitive feasting systems are explicitly economically based, expansionist systems. Such systems cannot exist for long among generalized hunter/gatherers because competitive harvesting of their limited and vulnerable resources would destroy those resource bases, just as competition over beaver during the early fur trade nearly exterminated these animals from large areas and precipitated widespread starvation that lasted for decades. Thus, competitive feasting systems and their élites must be based on resources that are both abundant and invulnerable to overexploitation. In this respect, the present study area was remarkably endowed.

Corporate Groups

There appear to be two basic ways in which accumulators structure their support base. One is to form a loose and possibly changing alliance of independent households. This kind of structure might be expected to occur under conditions where each family was relatively independent economically and where all households had equal access to approximately the same types of resources, being able to procure and process them relatively independently. Moreover, in this type of arrangement, little co-operative labor among males is generally required to most effectively procure important staples. Garden and pig producers in New Guinea provide good examples of this type of structuring.

The other way that support systems can be structured is by the formation of more permanent and more closely co-operative corporate groups. These are expected where resources are very restricted in terms of physical access and/or where there are unusual labour requirements for the procurement or processing of resources (e.g., in reef net fishing – Kew, Chapter 4; Matson 1985:250; in weir fishing – Beckerman 1983; in traditional means of exploiting caribou – Smith 1978:77; in traditional means of capturing tortoises – D. Venkatesan, personal communication). Given the occurrence of both highly restricted access and unusual labor requirements for processing and drying fish in the study area, it may be difficult to determine which variable plays the more important role. It is clear from Chapters 5 and 6 that single individuals could make only limited use of owned fishing sites. Some individuals might make and sustain claims to privileged use of these sites on the basis of having improved production at the sites via the construction of platforms. However, in order to derive the maximum benefit from their investment and privileged access rights, they required a large pool of co-operative labour. Desmond Peters indicated that, during peak runs, fishermen tired quickly and might only be able to work thirty minutes at a time. Because the peaks of some very productive runs last only two days (e.g., the Stuart Lake run) to seven days (in the case of the Chilko Lake run – DP), it would be important to have as much help as possible during these extraordinarily productive periods. Similarly, manning productive spring salmon platforms for the long periods necessary to derive maximum advantage from owning these sites would have entailed co-operation between several males (see Chapters 5 and 9). Adequate winter subsistence and trade surpluses might largely depend on such labour. Ideally, the most productive sites might be exploited in shifts almost around the clock during the peak runs, just as people fished throughout the night at more public sites during the peaks of runs (DP). The Shuswap of the Squilax area also fished throughout the nights at the peaks of salmon runs (Bouchard and Kennedy 1990:253). By this means the maximum possible surplus could be obtained.

Controlling the surplus of privately owned fishing sites to the maximum extent possible would logically lead the owners of the procurement sites to form some sort of corporate arrangement in which the owners could exert disproportionate control. It would be natural to expect a consortium of such families to act as an economic and residential unit, at least during the period when the resource stocks that were co-operatively produced were actively being used (i.e., during the winter). Such groups could also be expected to form mutual support systems for competitive feasts using surpluses under an administrative head or 'house chief.' These house chiefs would generally be the inheritors of titular ownership rights to the major economic resources of the group and may well have constituted the original basis for the hereditary élites of the area. Cressman (1960:35) documents six to ten men co-operatively owning and exploiting similar sites at The Dalles in Washington State, with rights being inherited. This provides an almost exact environmental, technological, and social analog to the type of situation that I envisage for the Lillooet region (see also Hunn 1990), and is what I believe that the large housepits at the Keatley Creek prehistoric site represent. Romanoff (Chapter 5) documents the inheritable nature of these sites for the Lillooet area, while Kennedy and Bouchard (Chapter 6) indicate that the coherency of local corporate groups was formerly much stronger than seems to have been the case at the turn of the century. A good argument can probably be made for the adaptive value of unilineal descent systems under such conditions (e.g., Riches 1979; Collier 1975), but I will not explore this issue here.

Due to this situation, labour would have been a limiting factor with respect to maximizing the returns from fishing sites. Chapters 5 and 6 clearly indicate that, for some periods, many more fish could be caught in an hour than one person could butcher, fillet, or tend around a fire. Desmond Peters amply confirmed this assessment, indicating to me that, at peak times, one fisherman could keep five or six women fully occupied in processing fish. Given a sexual division of labour, it became important to obtain more women than men to fully benefit from exploiting productive fishing sites and to maximize surpluses. Given the wealth and power differentials that were inherent in early communities in the study area, women would naturally tend to be differentially acquired by the wealthier and more powerful owners of fishing sites. It is probably the need for women's labour, more than anything else, that explains the polygynous practices of the Lillooet documented in Chapters 6 and 9 as well as at The Dalles (Hunn 1990:205).

The emergence of powerful corporate groups would have several other important social consequences. Foremost would be the progressive disenfranchisement of poorer families lacking prime access to the richest salmon fishing sites. These poorer families would have fewer, and probably less industrious, women (given the value placed on work and productivity by the élites and the élite ability to procure more industrious mates); poorer families would have fewer food stores to fall back on in times of food shortages; poorer, isolated families would be less able to defend themselves against raiders and less able to defend their own interests within the community; and poorer families would have fewer valuables that might be exchanged for food in times of scarcity. Their access to other community resources, such as hunting areas, could be progressively undermined by the more powerful corporate groups. Finally, poorer families would have less access to warm winter clothing made of buckskin and, thus, they would have more difficulty foraging or even collecting wood in the winter (Chapter 9). The epithets of 'lazy' and 'moocher' may have been justified on occasion, but it seems likely that élites were also partly responsible for creating the conditions of the poor and simply used these terms to justify their own aggrandizing behaviour.

Nevertheless, the power of corporate groups and their élites must have been ultimately limited by the amount of surplus that could be produced and by the periodic food shortages which must have galvanized the disadvantaged to demand more equitable rights, including access to all resources. Thus, the nature of the resource base placed definite constraints on the elaboration of socioeconomic inequality and complexity. Elsewhere, these limits could be expanded by the use of agriculture, and, under favourable food production resource conditions, élites grew in power and wealth.

CONCLUSIONS

The observations documented in this volume are an invaluable source for understanding both traditional historic and prehistoric Indian cultures in the Lillooet region. These cultures were remarkable by standards usually applied to hunter/gatherers. They provide one of the finest examples of complex hunter/gatherers in the world. For all the reasons stated in the Introduction, they make an almost ideal case for attempting to understand this increasingly critical phase of human development. While our results may not be definitive in all respects at this juncture, we have provided a wealth of basic data which can be used by ourselves and future researchers to evaluate models and theories concerning this development. I feel that an important step forward has been taken with the completion of this volume. At the very least, we have clearly defined the next generation of problems and identified a number of issues which ought to be dealt with by subsequent in depth case studies and comprehensive comparative studies. One conclusion seems relatively clear from the present perspective and from the perspective of prehistoric research at the Keatley Creek site: ownership, inequality, and corporate groups were not recent introductions into the area, as Ray (1939) and others have argued. Even if some iconological elements or details of social structure did diffuse from the Coast in early historic times, diffusion, as Flannery

(1967) pointed out, does not take place in a vacuum. Wherever behaviour involves significant amounts of time and energy, adoption of traits by other groups can only be understood in terms of ecological underpinnings and appropriate adaptive conditions. The archaeology of the area demonstrates that more than just potential conditions were present. The complex social potential of the area had been realized many thousands of years prior to the historic period. In this respect, Tyhurst's evaluation of the fishing potential of sites in the vicinity of Keatley Creek (Chapter 7) is especially valuable. The next step in this inquiry is to construct a more sophisticated, quantitative model of resource use for the study area and to examine the prehistoric record at Keatley Creek in light of our findings in this volume.

REFERENCES

Ames, Kenneth and Alan Marshall. 1981. 'Villages, demography and subsistence intensification in the southern Columbia Plateau.' *North American Archaeologist* 2:25-52

Anderson, Alexander. 1846. 'Thompson River Journal.' Hudson's Bay Company Archives B.97/a/3

Beckerman, Stephen. 1983. 'Optimal foraging group size for a human population: The case of Bari fishing.' *American Zoologist* 23:283-90

Binford, Lewis. 1980. 'Willow smoke and dogs' tails: Hunter-gatherer settlement systems and archaeological site formation.' *American Antiquity* 45:4-20

–. 1990. 'Mobility, housing and environment: A comparative study.' *Journal of Anthopological Research* 46:119-52

Birket-Smith, K. 1929. 'The Caribou Eskimos.' *Report of the Fifth Thule Expedition 1921-24*. Vol. 5(1). Material and social life and their cultural position: I, descriptive part. Copenhagen

Bouchard, Randy. 1968-91. 'Lillooet ethnographic and linguistic field notes.' Originals held by the BC Indian Language Project. Victoria

Bouchard, Randy and Dorothy Kennedy. 1990. 'Shuswap Indian use of the Squilax area.' Report prepared for Arcas Consulting Archaeologists Ltd., Coquitlam, BC. Appendix 1 of: *Report on the Archaeological Excavations at Site EfQv 121, EfQv 123, and EfQv 133 near Squilax, BC.* Report prepared by Arcas for the Ministry of Transportation and Highways, and the Archaeology and Outdoor Recreation Branch of the Ministry of Municipal Affairs, Recreation and Culture

Bowsfield, Hartwell (ed.). 1979. 'Introduction.' *The Hudson's Bay Record Society* 32:i-xi. Winnipeg: Winnipeg Hudson's Bay Company Society

Brumfiel, Elizabeth and Timothy Earle. 1987. 'Specialization, exchange and complex societies: An introduction.' In E. Brumfiel and T. Earle (eds.),

Specialization, Exchange and Complex Societies. Pp. 1-9. Cambridge: Cambridge University Press

Campbell, Sarah. 1985. *Summary of Results, Chief Joseph Dam Cultural Resources Project, Washington.* Seattle: University of Washington, Office Of Public Archaeology

Chagnon, Napolean. 1970. 'Ecological and adaptive aspects of California shell money.' *University of California Archaeological Survey Annual Report* 12:1-25

Chance, David and Jennifer Chance. 1982. *Kettle Falls: 1971 and 1974.* Anthropological Research Manuscripts Series, No. 69, University of Idaho, Laboratory of Anthropology

Chatters, James. 1987. 'Hunter-gatherer adaptations and assemblage structure.' *Journal of Anthropological Archaeology* 6:336-75

Clark, John, and Michael Blake. In press. 'The power of prestige: Competitive generosity and the emergence of rank societies in lowland Mesoamerica.' In E. Brumfiel and J. Fox (eds.), *Factional Competition and Political Development in the New World.* Cambridge: Cambridge University Press

Collier, George. 1975. *Fields of the Tzotzil.* Austin: University of Texas Press

Cooper, A.C. and K.A. Henry. 1962. *The History of the Early Stuart Sockeye Run.* International Pacific Salmon Fisheries Commission, Progress Report No. 10. New Westminster, BC

Cressman, L.S. 1960. 'Cultural sequences at the Dalles, Oregon.' *Transactions, American Philosophical Society* 50(10):1-108

Croes, Dale and Steven Hackenberger. 1988. 'Hoko River archaeological complex: Modeling prehistoric Northwest Coast Economic evolution.' In Barry Isaac (ed.), *Research in Economic Anthropology: Prehistoric Economies of the Pacific Northwest Coast.* Pp 19-86. Greenwich, Conn.: JAI Press

Dawson, George. 1892. 'Notes on the Shuswap People of British Columbia.' *Proceedings and Transactions of the Royal Society of Canada for the Year 1891* 9(2):3-44

Donald, Leland and Donald Mitchell. 1975. 'Some correlates of local group rank among the southern Kwakiutl.' *Ethnology* 14:325-46

–. 1990. 'Nature and culture on the Northwest Coast of North America: The case of the Wakashan salmon resources.' Paper presented at the 6th Conference on Hunting and Gathering Societies. Fairbanks, Alaska

Dyson-Husdon, Rada and Eric Smith. 1978. 'Human territoriality: An ecological reassessment.' *American Anthropologist* 80:21-41

Earle, Timothy. 1977. 'A reappraisal of redistribution: Complex Hawaiian chiefdoms.' In T. Earle and J. Ericson (eds.), *Exchange Systems in Prehistory.* Pp. 213-9. New York: Academic Press

Flannery, Kent. 1967. 'Review: "An introduction to American archaeology, vol. I": North and Middle America, by Gordon Willey.' *Scientific American* 217(2):119-22

Gilhousen, Philip. 1990. *Prespawning Mortalities of Sockeye Salmon in the Fraser*

River System and Possible Causal Factors. International Pacific Salmon Fisheries Commission, Bulletin 26, Vancouver, BC

Gilman, Antonio. 1981. 'The development of social stratification in Bronze Age Europe.' *Current Anthropology* 22:1-24

Gosden, Chris. 1989. 'Debt, production, and prehistory.' *Journal of Anthropological Archaeology* 8:355-87

Grigson, Caroline. 1989. 'Bird-foraging patterns in the Mesolithic.' In Clive Bonsall (ed.), *The Mesolithic in Europe.* Pp. 60-72. Edinburgh: John Donald

Hayden, Brian. 1972. 'Population control among hunter/gatherers.' *World Archaeology* 4:205-21

–. 1981a. 'Research and development in the stone age: Technological transitions among hunter-gatherers.' *Current Anthropology* 22:519-48

–. 1981b. 'Subsistence and ecological adaptations of modern hunter/gatherers.' In G. Teleki and R. Harding (eds.), *Omnivorous Primates: Gathering and Hunting in Human Evolution.* Pp. 344-422. New York: Columbia University Press

–. 1990. 'Nimrods, piscators, pluckers and planters: The emergence of food production.' *Journal of Anthopological Archaeology* 9:31-69

Hayden, Brian and Rob Gargett. 1990. ' "Big man, big heart?" A Mesoamerican view of the emergence of complex society.' *Ancient Mesoamerica* 1:3-20

Hayden, Brian, Brian Chisholm, and Henry Schwarcz. 1987. 'Fishing and foraging: Marine resources in the Upper Paleolithic of France.' In O. Soffer (ed.), *The Pleistocene Old World: Regional Perspectives.* Pp. 279-91. New York: Plenum

Hunn, Eugene. 1990. *Nch'i-Wana, 'The Big River': Mid-Columbia Indians and Their Land.* Seattle: University of Washington Press

Jenness, Diamond. 1922. *The Life of the Copper Eskimos.* Report of the Canadian Arctic Expedition 1913-18, Vol. 12. Ottawa: King's Printer

Kennedy, Dorothy. 1971-91. 'Lillooet Ethnographic Field Notes.' Originals held by the BC Indian Language Project, Victoria

Knight, Rolf. 1965. 'A re-examination of hunting, trapping, and territoriality among the northeastern Algonkian Indians.' In Anthony Leeds and A. Vayda (eds.), *Man, Culture, and Animals.* American Association for the Advancement of Science, No. 78, Washington, DC

Leacock, Eleanor. 1954. *The Montagnais 'Hunting Territory' and Fur Trade.* American Anthropological Association Memoir, No. 78, Washington, DC

Low, David. 1990. Unpublished observations on ungulates of the Kamloops Wildlife District. BC Ministry of the Environment, Kamloops, BC

McDonald, Archibald. 1826-7. 'Thompson River Journal.' Hudson's Bay Company Archives B.97/a/1&2

MacDonald, George. 1983. *Ninstints, Haida World Heritage Site.* Vancouver: UBC Press

MacMillan, James and John MacLeod. 1822-3. 'Thompson River Journal.' Hudson's Bay Company Archives B.97/a/1

Matson, R.G. 1976. *The Glenrose Cannery Site*. National Museum of Man, Mercury Series, No. 52, Ottawa

–. 1985. 'The relationship between sedentism and status inequalities among hunters and gatherers.' In M. Thompson, M.T. Garcia, and F. Kense (eds.), *Status, Structure and Stratification*. Pp. 245-52. Archaeological Association of the University of Calgary, Calgary

Mitchell, D.S. 1925. 'A story of the Fraser River's great sockeye runs and their loss.' Unpublished ms. on file with the Pacific Salmon Commission and BC Provincial Archives and Record Service, ms. 1/B/M/69

Pokotylo, David and Praticia Froese. 1983. 'Archaeological evidence for prehistoric root gathering in the southern Interior Plateau of British Columbia: A case study from Upper Hat Creek.' *Canadian Journal of Archaeology* 7:127-58

Ray, Verne. 1939. 'Cultural relationships in the Plateau of North-western America.' Publications of the Frederick Webb Hodge Anniversary Publication Fund 3. Los Angeles: Southwest Museum

Reidhead, Van A. 1979. 'Linear programming models in archaeology.' *Annual Review of Anthropology* 8:543-78

Riches, David. 1979. 'Ecological variation on the Northwest Coast: Models for the generation of cognatic and matrilineal descent.' In P. Burnham and R. Ellen (eds.), *Social and Ecological Systems*. Pp. 45-66. New York: Academic Press

Ricker, W.E. 1987. 'Effects of the fishery and of obstacles to migration on the abundance of Fraser River sockeye salmon (*Oncorhynchus nerka*).' *Canadian Technical Report of Fisheries and Aquatic Sciences*, No. 1,522. Department of Fisheries and Oceans, Fisheries Research Branch, Pacific Biological Station, Nanaimo, BC

–. 1989. 'History and present state of the odd-year pink salmon runs of the Fraser River region.' *Canadian Technical Report of Fisheries and Aquatic Sciences*, No. 1702. Department of Fisheries and Oceans, Fisheries Research Branch, Pacific Biological Station, Nanaimo, BC

Rink, Hinrich. 1875. *Tales and Tradition of the Eskimos*. Edinburgh: Blackwood & Sons

Semyonov, Yu I. 1990. 'Socioeconomic relations in the societies of early hunters and gatherers.' Paper presented at the Sixth Conference on Hunting and Gathering Societies, Fairbanks, Alaska

Smith, James. 1978. 'Economic uncertainty in an "original affluent society": Caribou and caribou eater Chipewyan adaptive strategies.' *Arctic Anthropology* 15(1):68-88

Soffer, Olga. 1989. 'Storage, sedentism and the Eurasian Palaeolithic record.' *Antiquity* 63:719-32

Speth, John and Katherine Spielmann. 1983. 'Energy source, protein metabolism, and hunter-gatherer subsistence strategies.' *Journal of Anthropo-*

logical Archaeology 2:1-31

Strathern, Andrew. 1971. *The Rope of Moka.* Cambridge: Cambridge University Press

Strehlow, T.G.H. 1965. 'Culture, social structure, and environment in Aboriginal Central Australia.' In R. Berndt and C. Berndt (eds.), *Aboriginal Man in Australia.* Pp. 121-45. Sydney: Angus and Robertson

Suttles, Wayne. 1951. 'The early diffusion of the potato among the Coast Salish.' *Southwestern Journal of Anthropology* 7:272-88

Teit, James. 1906. 'The Lillooet Indians.' *Memoirs, American Museum of Natural History* 2(5):193-300

Testart, Alain. 1982. 'The significance of food storage among hunter-gatherers.' *Current Anthropology* 23:523-37

Thoms, Alston. 1989. 'The Northern Roots of Hunter-gatherer Intensification: Camas and the Pacific Northwest.' Unpublished ph.d dissertation, Anthropology Department, Washington State University, Pullman

Tod, John. 1841-3. 'Thompson River Journal.' bc Archives a/b/20/k12a

Turnbull, Colin. 1972. *The Mountain People.* New York: Simon and Schuster

Turner, Nancy and Harriet Kuhnlein. 1982. 'Two important "root" foods of the Northwest Coast Indians: Springbank clover *(Trifolium wormskioldii)* and Pacific silverweed *(Potentilla anserina* ssp. *pacifica)*.' *Economic Botany* 36:411-32

Weyer, Edward. 1962 (orig. 1932). *The Eskimos, Their Environment and Folkways.* Hamden, Conn.: Archon Books

Widmer, Randolph. 1988. *The Evolution of the Calusa: A Nonagricultural Chiefdom on the Southwest Florida Coast.* Tuscaloosa: University of Alabama Press

Zvelebil, Marek. 1989. 'Economic intensification and postglacial hunter/-gatherers in North Temperate Europe.' In C. Bonsall (ed.), *The Mesolithic in Europe.* Pp. 80-8. Edinburgh: John Donald

Index

Printed on acid-free paper ∞
Set in Palacio by CompuType
Vancouver, BC
Printed and bound in Canada by
Friesen Printers, Altona, Manitoba

Copy-editor: Joanne Richardson
Proofreader: Sheldon Goldfarb
Jacket Design: George Vaitkunas